Lecture Notes in Computer Science 1706
Edited by G. Goos, J. Hartmanis and J. van Leeuwen

T0241074

Springer
Berlin
Heidelberg
New York
Barcelona
Hong Kong
London
Milan
Paris
Singapore
Tokyo

John Hatcliff   Torben Æ. Mogensen
Peter Thiemann (Eds.)

Partial Evaluation

Practice and Theory

DIKU 1998 International Summer School
Copenhagen, Denmark, June 29 – July 10, 1998

Springer

Series Editors

Gerhard Goos, Karlsruhe University, Germany
Juris Hartmanis, Cornell University, NY, USA
Jan van Leeuwen, Utrecht University, The Netherlands

Volume Editors

John Hatcliff
Department of Computing and Information Sciences
Kansas State University
234 Nichols Hall, Manhattan, KS 66506, USA
E-mail: hatcliff@cis.ksu.edu

Torben Æ. Mogensen
DIKU, Københavns Universitet
Universitetsparken 1, DK-2100 København Ø, Denmark
E-mail: torbenm@diku.dk

Peter Thiemann
Institut für Informatik, Universität Freiburg
Universitätsgelände Flugplatz, D-79110 Freiburg i.Br., Germany
E-mail: thiemann@informatik.uni-freiburg.de

Cataloging-in-Publication data applied for

Die Deutsche Bibliothek - CIP-Einheitsaufnahme

Partial evaluation : practice and theory ; DIKU 1998 international summer
school, Copenhagen, Denmark, 1998 / John Hatcliff ... (ed.). - Berlin ;
Heidelberg ; New York ; Barcelona ; Hong Kong ; London ; Milan ; Paris ;
Singapore ; Tokyo : Springer, 1999
(Lecture notes in computer science ; Vol. 1706)
ISBN 3-540-66710-5

CR Subject Classification (1998): D.3.4, D.1.2, D.3.1, F.3, D.2

ISSN 0302-9743
ISBN 3-540-66710-5 Springer-Verlag Berlin Heidelberg New York

Typesetting: Camera-ready by author
SPIN 10704931   06/3142 – 5 4 3 2 1 0   Printed on acid-free paper

Preface

As the complexity of software increases, researchers and practitioners continue to seek better techniques for engineering the construction and evolution of software. Partial evaluation is an attractive technology for modern software construction for several reasons.

- It is an automatic tool for software specialization. Therefore, at a time when software requirements are evolving rapidly and when systems must operate in heterogeneous environments, it provides an avenue for easily adapting software components to particular requirements and to different environments.
- It is based on rigorous semantic foundations. Modern applications increasingly demand high-confidence software solutions. At the same time, traditional methods of validation and testing are failing to keep pace with the inherent complexity found in today's applications. Thus, partial evaluation and the mathematically justified principles that underly it are promising tools in the construction of robust software with high levels of assurance.
- It can be used to resolve the tension between the often conflicting goals of generality and efficiency. In most cases, software is best engineered by first constructing simple and general code rather than immediately implementing highly optimized programs that are organized into many special cases. It is much easier to check that the general code satisfies specifications, but the general code is usually much less efficient and may not be suitable as a final implementation. Partial evaluation can be used to automatically generate efficient specialized instances from general solutions. Moreover, since the transformation is performed automatically (based on rigorous semantic foundations), one can arrive at methods for more easily showing that the specialized code also satisfies the software specifications.

Partial evaluation technology continues to grow and mature. ACM SIGPLAN-sponsored conferences and workshops have provided a forum for researchers to share current results and directions of work. Partial evaluation techniques are being used in commercially available compilers (for example the *Chez Scheme* system). They are also being used in industrial scheduling systems (see Augustsson's article in this volume), they have been incorporated into popular commercial products (see Singh's article in this volume), and they are the basis of methodologies for implementing domain-specific languages.

Due to the growing interest (both inside and outside the programming languages community) in applying partial evaluation, the DIKU International Summer School on Partial Evaluation was organized to present lectures of leading researchers in the area to graduate students and researchers from other communities.

The objectives of the summer school were to

- present the foundations of partial evaluation in a clear and rigorous manner,
- offer a practical introduction to several existing partial evaluators, including the opportunity for guided hands-on experience,

– present more sophisticated theory, systems, and applications, and

– highlight open problems and challenges that remain.

The summer school had 45 participants (15 lecturers and 30 students) from 24 departments and industrial sites in Europe, the United States, and Japan.

This volume

All lecturers were invited to submit an article presenting the contents of their lectures for this collection. Each article was reviewed among the lecturers of the summer school.

Here is a brief summary of the articles appearing in this volume in order of presentation at the summer school.

Part I: Practice and experience using partial evaluators

– Torben Mogensen. *Partial Evaluation: Concepts and Applications.* Introduces the basic idea of partial evaluation: specialization of a program by exploiting partial knowledge of its input. Some small examples are shown and the basic theory, concepts, and applications of partial evaluation are described, including "the partial evaluation equation", generating extensions, and self-application.

– John Hatcliff. *An Introduction to Online and Offline Partial Evaluation Using a Simple Flowchart Language.* Presents basic principles of partial evaluation using the simple imperative language FCL (a language of flowcharts introduced by Jones and Gomard). Formal semantics and examples are given for online and offline partial evaluators.

– Jesper Jørgensen. *Similix: A Self-Applicable Partial Evaluator for Scheme.* Presents specialization of functional languages as it is performed by Similix. The architecture and basic algorithms of Similix are explained, and application of the system is illustrated with examples of specialization, self-application, and compiler generation.

– Jens Peter Secher (with Arne John Glenstrup and Henning Makholm). *C-Mix II: Specialization of C Programs.* Describes the internals of C-Mix – a generating extension generator for ANSI C. The role and functionality of the main components (pointer analysis, in-use analysis, binding-time analysis, code generation, etc.) are explained.

– Michael Leuschel. *Logic Program Specialization.* Presents the basic theory for specializing logic programs based upon partial deduction techniques. The fundamental correctness criteria are presented, and subtle differences with specialization of functional and imperative languages are highlighted.

Part II: More sophisticated theory, systems, and applications

- Torben Mogensen. *Inherited Limits.* Studies the evolution of partial evaluators from an insightful perspective: the attempt to prevent the structure of a source program from imposing limits on its residual programs. If the structure of a residual program is limited in this way, it can be seen as a weakness in the partial evaluator.
- Neil Jones (with Carsten K. Gomard and Peter Sestoft). *Partial Evaluation for the Lambda Calculus.* Presents a simple partial evaluator called *Lambdamix* for the untyped lambda-calculus. Compilation and compiler generation for a language from its denotational semantics are illustrated.
- Satnam Singh (with Nicholas McKay). *Partial Evaluation of Hardware.* Describes run-time specialization of circuits on Field Programmable Gate Arrays (FPGAs). This technique has been used to optimize several embedded systems including DES encoding, graphics systems, and postscript interpreters.
- Lennart Augustsson. *Partial Evaluation for Aircraft Crew Scheduling.* Presents a partial evaluator and program transformation system for a domain-specific language used in automatic scheduling of aircraft crews. The partial evaluator is used daily in production at Lufthansa.
- Robert Glück (with Jesper Jørgensen). *Multi-level Specialization.* Presents a specialization system that can divide programs into multiple stages (instead of just two stages as with conventional partial evaluators). Their approach creates multi-level generating extensions that guarantee fast successive specialization, and is thus far more practical than multiple self-application of specializers.
- Morten Heine Sørensen (with Robert Glück). *Introduction to Supercompilation.* Provides a gentle introduction to Turchin's supercompiler – a program transformer that sometimes achieves more dramatic speed-ups than those seen in partial evaluation. Recent techniques to prove termination and methods to incorporate negative information are also covered.
- Michael Leuschel. *Advanced Logic Program Specialization.* Summarizes some advanced control techniques for specializing logic programs based on characteristic trees and homeomorphic embedding. The article also describes various extensions to partial deduction including conjunctive partial deduction (which can accomplish tupling and deforestation), and a combination of program specialization and abstract interpretation techniques. Illustrations are given using the online specializer ECCE.
- John Hughes. *A Type Specialization Tutorial.* Presents a paradigm for partial evaluation, based not on syntax-driven transformation of terms, but on type reconstruction with unification. This is advantageous because residual programs need not involve the same types as source programs, and thus several desirable properties of specialization fall out naturally and elegantly.
- Julia Lawall. *Faster Fourier Transforms via Automatic Program Specialization.* Investigates the effect of machine architecture and compiler technology on the performance of specialized programs using an implementation of the

Fast Fourier Transform as an example. The article also illustrates the Tempo partial evaluator for C, which was used to carry out the experiments.

- Jens Palsberg. *Eta-Redexes in Partial Evaluation*. Illustrates how adding eta-redexes to functional programs can make a partial evaluator yield better results. The article presents a type-based explanation of what eta-expansion achieves, why it works, and how it can be automated.

- Olivier Danvy. *Type-Directed Specialization*. Presents the basics of type-directed partial evaluation: a specialization technique based on a concise and efficient normalization algorithm for the lambda-calculus, originating in proof theory. The progression from the normalization algorithm as it appears in the proof theory literature to an effective partial evaluator is motivated with some simple and telling examples.

- Peter Thiemann. *Aspects of the PGG System: Specialization for Standard Scheme*. Gives an overview of the PGG system: an offline partial evaluation system for the full Scheme language – including Scheme's reflective operations (eval, apply, and call/cc), and operations that manipulate state. Working from motivating examples (parser generation and programming with message passing), the article outlines the principles underlying the necessarily sophisticated binding-time analyses and their associated specializers.

Acknowledgements

The partial evaluation community owes a debt of gratitude to Morten Heine Sørensen, chair of the summer school organizing committee, and to the other committee members Neil D. Jones, Jesper Jørgensen, and Jens Peter Secher. The organizers worked long hours to ensure that the program ran smoothly and that all participants had a rewarding time.

The secretarial staff at DIKU and especially TOPPS group secretaries Karin Outzen and Karina Sønderholm labored behind the scenes and provided assistance on the myriad of administrative tasks that come with preparing for such an event.

Finally, a special thanks is due to Jens Ulrik Skakkebæk for the use of his laptop computer and for technical assistance with DIKU's digital projector.

John Hatcliff
Torben Mogensen
Peter Thiemann
July 1999

Table of Contents

Partial Evaluation:
Concepts and Applications

Torben Æ. Mogensen

DIKU
Universitetsparken 1
DK-2100 Copenhagen O
Denmark
torbenm@diku.dk

Abstract. This is an introduction to the idea of partial evaluation. It is meant to be fairly non-technical and focuses mostly on *what* and *why* rather than *how*.

1 Introduction: What is partial evaluation?

Partial evaluation is a technique to partially execute a program, when only some of its input data are available. Consider a program p requiring two inputs, x_1 and x_2. When specific values d_1 and d_2 are given for the two inputs, we can run the program, producing a result. When only one input value d_1 is given, we cannot run p, but can *partially evaluate* it, producing a version p_{d_1} of p specialized for the case where $x_1 = d_1$. Partial evaluation is an instance of *program specialization*, and the specialized version p_{d_1} of p is called a residual program.

For an example, consider the following C function power(n, x), which computes x raised to the n'th power.

```
double power(n, x)
int n;
double x;
{ double p;
  p = 1.0;
  while (n > 0) {
    if (n % 2 == 0) { x = x * x; n = n / 2; }
    else { p = p * x; n = n - 1; }
  }
  return(p);
}
```

Given values $n = 5$ and $x = 2.1$, we can compute power(5,2.1), obtaining the result $2.1^5 = 40.84201$. (The algorithm exploits that $x^n = (x^2)^{n/2}$ for even integers n).

Suppose we need to compute power(n, x) for $n = 5$ and many different values of x. We can then *partially evaluate* the power function for $n = 5$, obtaining the following residual function:

```
double power_5(x)
double x;
{ double p;
  p = 1.0*x;
  x = x * x;
  x = x * x;
  p = p * x;
  return(p);
}
```

We can now compute power_5(2.1) to obtain the result $2.1^5 = 40.84201$. In fact, for any input x, computing power_5(x) will produce the same result as computing power(5,x). Since the value of variable n is available for partial evaluation, we say that n is *static*; conversely, the variable x is *dynamic* because its value is unavailable at the time we perform the partial evaluation.

This example shows the strengths of partial evaluation: In the residual program power_5, all tests and all arithmetic operations involving n have been eliminated. The flow of control (that is, the conditions in the while and if statements) in the original program was completely determined by the static variable n. This is, however, not always the case.

Suppose we needed to compute power(n,2.1) for many different values of n. This is the dual problem of the above: Now n is dynamic (unknown) and x is static (known). There is little we can do in this case, since the flow of control is determined by the dynamic variable n. One could imagine creating a table of precomputed values of 2.1^n for some values of n, but how are we to know which values are relevant?

In many cases some of the control flow is determined by static variables, and in these cases substantial speed-ups can be achieved by partial evaluation. We can get some speed-up even if the control flow is dynamically controlled, as long as some other computations are fully static. The most dramatic speed-ups, however, occur when a substantial part of the control flow is static.

1.1 Notation

We can consider a program in two ways: Either as a function transforming inputs to outputs, or as a data object (i.e. the program text), being input to or output from other programs (e.g. used as input to a compiler). We need to distinguish the *function* computed by a program from the *program text* itself.

Writing p for the program text, we write $[\![p]\!]$ for the function computed by p, or $[\![p]\!]_L$ when we want to make explicit the language L in which p is written (or, more precisely, executed). Consequently, $[\![p]\!]_L\, d$ denotes the result of running program p with input d on an L-machine.

Now we can assert that power_5 is a correct residual program (in C) for power specialized w.r.t to the static input $n = 5$:

$$[\![\text{power}]\!]_C\,[5, x] = [\![\text{power\_5}]\!]_C\, x$$

1.2   Interpreters and compilers

An interpreter $Sint$ for language S, written in language L, satisfies for any S-program s and input data d:

$$[\![\, s \,]\!]_S\, d = [\![\, Sint \,]\!]_L [s, d]$$

In other words, running s with input d on an S-machine gives the same result as using the interpreter $Sint$ to run s with input d on an L-machine. This includes possible nontermination of both sides.

A compiler $STcomp$ for source language S, generating code in target language T, and written in language L, satisfies

$$[\![\, STcomp \,]\!]_L\, p = p' \quad \text{implies} \quad [\![\, p' \,]\!]_T\, d = [\![\, p \,]\!]_S\, d \quad \text{for all } d$$

That is, p can be compiled to a target program p' such that running p' on a T-machine with input d gives the same result as running p with input d on an S-machine. Though the equation doesn't actually require this, we normally expect a compiler to always produce a target program, assuming the input is a valid S program.

2   Partial evaluators

A *partial evaluator* is a program which performs *partial evaluation*. That is, it can produce a residual program by specializing a given program with respect to part of its input.

Let p be an L-program requiring two inputs x_1 and x_2. A *residual program* for p with respect to $x_1 = d_1$ is a program p_{d_1} such that for all values d_2 of the remaining input,

$$[\![\, p_{d_1} \,]\!]\, d_2 = [\![\, p \,]\!]\, [d_1, d_2]$$

A *partial evaluator* is a program *peval* which, given a program p and a part d_1 of its input, produces a residual program p_{d_1}. In other words, a partial evaluator *peval* must satisfy:

$$[\![\, peval \,]\!][p, d_1] = p_{d_1} \quad \text{implies} \quad [\![\, p_{d_1} \,]\!]\, d_2 = [\![\, p \,]\!]\, [d_1, d_2] \quad \text{for all } d_2$$

This is the so-called *partial evaluation equation*, which reads as follows: If partial evaluation of p with respect to d_1 produces a residual program p_{d_1}, then running p_{d_1} with input d_2 gives the same result as running program p with input $[d_1, d_2]$.

As was the case for compilers, the equation does not guarantee termination of the left-hand side of the implication. In contrast to compilers we will, however, not expect partial evaluation to always succeed. While it is certainly *desirable* for partial evaluation to always terminate, this is not guaranteed by a large number of existing partial evaluators. See section 2.1 for more about the termination issue.

Above we have not specified the language L in which the partial evaluator is written, the language S of the source programs it accepts, or the language T of the residual programs it produces. These languages may be all different, but for notational simplicity we assume they are the same, $L = S = T$. Note that $L = S$ opens the possibility of applying the partial evaluator to itself, which we will return to in section 4.

For an instance of the partial evaluation equation, consider $p = $ power and $d_1 = 5$, then from $[\![peval]\!][\text{power}, 5] = \text{power\_5}$ it must follow that power$(5,2.1)$ $= \text{power\_5}(2.1) = 40.84201$.

2.1   What is achieved by partial evaluation?

The definition of a partial evaluator by the partial evaluation equation does not stipulate that the specialized program must be any better than the original program. Indeed, it is easy to write a program *peval* which satisfies the partial evaluation equation in a trivial way, by appending a new 'specialized' function power_5 to the original program. The specialized function simply calls the original function with both the given argument and (as a constant) the argument to which it is specialized:

```
double power(n, x)
int n
double x;
{ double p;
  p = 1.0;
  while (n > 0) {
    if (n % 2 == 0) { x = x * x; n = n / 2; }
    else { p = p * x; n = n - 1; }
  }
  return(p);
}

double power_5(x)
double x;
{ return(power(5, x)); }
```

While this program is a correct residual program, it is no faster than the original program, and quite possibly slower. Even so, the construction above can be used to prove existence of partial evaluators. The proof is similar to Kleene's (1952) proof of the s-m-n theorem [23], a theorem that essentially stipulates the existence of partial evaluators in recursive function theory.

But, as the example in the introduction demonstrated, it is sometimes possible to obtain residual programs that are arguably faster than the original program. The amount of improvement depends both on the partial evaluator and the program being specialized. Some programs do not lend themselves very well to specialization, as no significant computation can be done before all input is known. Sometimes choosing a different algorithm may help, but in other cases the problem itself is ill-suited for specialization. An example is specializing the power function to a known value of x, as discussed in the introduction. Let us examine this case in more detail.

Looking at the definition of power, one would think that specialization with respect to a value of x would give a good result: The assignments, p = 1.0;, x = x * x; and p = p * x; do not involve n, and as such can be executed during specialization. The loop is, however, controlled by n. Since the termination condition is not known, we cannot fully eliminate the loop. Let us for the moment assume we keep the loop structure as it is. The static variables x and p will have different values in different iterations of the loop, so we cannot replace them by constants. Hence, we find that we cannot perform the computations on x and p anyway. Instead of keeping the loop structure, we could force unfolding of the loop to keep the values of x and p known (but different in each instance of the unrolled loop), but since there is no bound on the number of different values x and p can obtain, no finite amount of unfolding can eliminate x and p from the program.

This conflict between termination of specialization and quality of residual program is common. The partial evaluator must try to find a balance that ensures termination often enough to be interesting (preferably always) while yielding sufficient speed-up to be worthwhile. Due to the undecidability of the halting problem, no perfect strategy exists, so a suitable compromise must be found. This can either be to err on the safe side, guaranteeing termination but missing some opportunities for specialization or to err on the other side, letting variables and computations be static unless it is clear that this will definitely lead to nontermination.

3 Another approach to program specialization

A *generating extension* of a two-input program p is a program p_{gen} which, given a value d_1 for the first input of p, produces a residual program p_{d_1} for p with respect to d_1. In other words,

$$[\![p_{gen}]\!]\, d_1 = p_{d_1} \text{ implies } [\![p]\!]\,[d_1, d_2] = [\![p_{d_1}]\!]\, d_2$$

The generating extension takes a given value d_1 of the first input parameter x_1 and constructs a version of p specialized for $x_1 = d_1$.

As an example, we show below a generating extension of the power program from the introduction:

```
void power_gen(n)
int n;
{
  printf("{power_%d(x)\n",n);
  printf("double x;\n");
  printf("{ double p;\n");
```

```
printf("  p = 1.0;\n");
while (n > 0) {
  if (n % 2 == 0) { printf("  x = x * x;\n"); n = n / 2; }
  else { printf("  p = p * x;\n"); n = n - 1; }
}
printf("  return(p);\n");
printf("}\n");
}
```

Note that power_gen closely resembles power: Those parts of power that depend only on the static input n are copied directly into power_gen, and the parts that also depend on x are made into strings, which are printed as part of the residual program. Running power_gen with input $n = 5$ yields the following residual program:

```
power_5(x)
double x;
{ double p;
  p = 1.0;
  p = p * x;
  x = x * x;
  x = x * x;
  p = p * x;
  return(p);
}
```

This is almost the same as the one shown in the introduction. The difference is because we have now made an *a priori* distinction between static variables (n) and dynamic variables (x and p). Since p is dynamic, all assignments to it are made part of the residual program, even p = 1.0, which was executed at specialization time in the example shown in the introduction.

Later, in section 4, we shall see that a generating extension can be constructed by applying a sufficiently powerful partial evaluator to itself. One can even construct a generator of generating extensions that way.

4   Compilation and compiler generation by partial evaluation

In Section 1.2 we defined an interpreter as a program taking two inputs: a program to be interpreted and input to that program

$$[\![s]\!]_S \, d = [\![Sint]\!]_L [s, d]$$

We often expect to run the same program repeatedly on different inputs. Hence, it is natural to partially evaluate the interpreter with respect to a fixed, known program and unknown input to that program. Using the partial evaluation equation we get

$$[\![\,peval\,]\!][Sint, s] = Sint_s \quad \text{implies} \quad [\![\,Sint_s\,]\!]d = [\![\,Sint\,]\!]_L[s, d] \quad \text{for all } d$$

Using the definition of the interpreter we get

$$[\![\,Sint_s\,]\!]d = [\![\,s\,]\!]_S d \quad \text{for all } d$$

The residual program is thus equivalent to the source program. The difference is the language in which the residual program is written. If the input and output languages of the partial evaluator are identical, then the residual program is written in the same language L as the interpreter $Sint$. Hence, we have compiled s from S, the language that the interpreter interprets, to L, the language in which it is written.

4.1   Compiler generation using a self-applicable partial evaluator

We have seen that we can compile programs by partially evaluating an interpreter. Typically, we will want to compile many different programs. This amounts to partially evaluating the same interpreter repeatedly with respect to different programs. Such an instance of repeated use of a program (in this case the partial evaluator) with one unchanging input (the interpreter) calls for optimization by yet another application of partial evaluation. Hence, we use a partial evaluator to specialize the partial evaluator *peval* with respect to a program *Sint*, but without the argument s of $Sint$. Using the partial evaluation equation we get:

$$[\![\,peval\,]\!][peval, Sint] = peval_{Sint} \quad \text{implies}$$
$$[\![\,peval_{Sint}\,]\!]s = [\![\,peval\,]\!][Sint, s] \quad \text{for all } s$$

Using the results from above, we get

$$[\![\,peval_{Sint}\,]\!]s = Sint_s \quad \text{for all } s$$

for which we have

$$[\![\,Sint_s\,]\!]d = [\![\,s\,]\!]_S d \quad \text{for all } d$$

We recall the definition of a compiler from Section 1.2:

$$[\![\,STcomp\,]\!]_L\, p = p' \quad \text{implies} \quad [\![\,p'\,]\!]_T\, d = [\![\,p\,]\!]_S d \quad \text{for all } d$$

We see that $peval_{Sint}$ fulfills the requirements for being a compiler from S to T. In the case where the input and output languages of the partial evaluator are identical, the language in which the compiler is written and the target language of the compiler are both the same as the language L, in which the interpreter is written. Note that we have no guarantee that the partial evaluation process terminates, neither when producing the compiler nor when using it. Experience has shown that while this may be a problem, it is normally the case that if compilation by partial evaluation terminates for a few general programs, then it terminates for all.

Note that the compiler $peval_{Sint}$ is a generating extension of the interpreter $Sint$, according to the definition shown in section 3. This generalizes to any program, not just interpreters: Partially evaluating a partial evaluator $peval$ with respect to a program p yields a generating extension $p_{gen} = peval_p$ for this program.

4.2   Compiler generator generation

Having seen that it is interesting to partially evaluate a partial evaluator, we may want to do this repeatedly: To partially evaluate a partial evaluator with respect to a range of different programs (e.g., interpreters). Again, we may exploit partial evaluation:

$$[\![peval]\!][peval, peval] = peval_{peval} \quad \text{implies}$$
$$[\![peval_{peval}]\!]p = [\![peval]\!][peval, p] \quad \text{for all } p$$

Since $[\![peval]\!][peval, p] = peval_p$, which is a generating extension of p, we can see that $peval_{peval}$ is a *generator of generating extensions*. The program $peval_{peval}$ is itself a generating extension of the partial evaluator: $peval_{gen} = peval_{peval}$. In the case where p is an interpreter, the generating extension p_{gen} is a compiler. Hence, $peval_{gen}$ is a compiler generator, capable of producing a compiler from an interpreter.

4.3   Summary: The Futamura projections

Instances of the partial evaluation equation applied to interpreters, directly or through self-application of a partial evaluator, are collectively called the *Futamura projections*. The three Futamura projections are:

The first Futamura projection: compilation

$$[\![peval]\!][interpreter, source] = target$$

The second Futamura projection: compiler generation

$$[\![peval]\!][peval, interpreter] = compiler$$

$$[\![compiler]\!]source = target$$

The third Futamura projection: compiler generator generation

$$[\![peval]\!][peval, peval] = compiler generator$$

$$[\![compiler generator]\!]interpreter = compiler$$

The first and second equations were devised by Futamura in 1971 [14], and the latter independently by Beckman et al. [5] and Turchin et al. [32] around 1975.

5   Program specialization without a partial evaluator

So far, we have focused mainly on specialization using a partial evaluator. But the ideas and methods presented here can be applied without using a partial evaluator.

Specialization by hand

It is quite common for programmers to hand-tune code for particular cases. Often this amounts to doing partial evaluation by hand. As an example, here is a quote from an article [29] about the programming of a video-game:

> Basically there are two ways to write a routine:
> It can be one complex multi-purpose routine that does everything, but not quickly. For example, a sprite routine that can handle any size and flip the sprites horizontally and vertically in the same piece of code.
> Or you can have many simple routines each doing one thing. Using the sprite routine example, a routine to plot the sprite one way, another to plot it flipped vertically and so on.
> The second method means more code is required but the speed advantage is dramatic. Nevryon was written in this way and had about 20 separate sprite routines, each of which plotted sprites in slightly different ways.

Clearly, specialization is used. But a general purpose partial evaluator was almost certainly not used to do the specialization. Instead, the specialization has been performed by hand, possibly without ever explicitly writing down the general purpose routine that forms the basis for the specialized routines.

Using hand-written generating extensions

We saw in Section 3 how a generating extension for the power function was easily produced from the original code using knowledge about which variables contained values known at specialization time. While it is not always quite so simple as in this example, it is often not particularly difficult to write generating extensions of small-to-medium sized procedures or programs.

In situations where no partial evaluator is available, this is often a viable way to obtain specialized programs, especially if the approach is applied only to small time-critical portions of the program. Using a generating extension instead of writing the specialized versions by hand is useful when either a large number of variants must be generated, or when it is not known in advance what values the program will be specialized with respect to.

A common use of hand-written generating extensions is for run-time code generation, where a piece of specialized code is generated and executed, all at run-time. As in the sprite example above, one often generates specialized code for each plot operation when large bitmaps are involved. The typical situation is that a general purpose routine is used for plotting small bitmaps, but special code is generated for large bitmaps. The specialized routines can exploit knowledge about the alignment of the source bitmap and the destination area with respect to word boundaries, as well as clipping of the source bitmap. Other aspects such as scaling, differences in colour depth etc. have also been targets for run-time specialization of bitmap-plotting code.

Hand-written generating extensions have also been used for optimizing parsers by specializing with respect to particular tables [28], and for converting interpreters into compilers [27].

Handwritten generating extension generators

In recent years, it has become popular to write a generating extension generator instead of a partial evaluator [3, 8, 19], but the approach itself is quite old [5].

A generating extension generator can be used instead of a traditional partial evaluator as follows: To specialize a program p with respect to data d, first produce a generating extension p_{gen}, then apply p_{gen} to d to produce a specialized program p_d.

Conversely, a self-applicable partial evaluator can produce a generating extension generator (cf. the third Futamura projection), so the two approaches seem equally powerful. So why write a generating extension generator instead of a self-applicable partial evaluator? Some reasons are:

- The generating extension generator can be written in another (higher level) language than the language it handles, whereas a self-applicable partial evaluator must be able to handle its own text.
- For various reasons (including the above), it may be easier to write a generating extension generator than a self-applicable partial evaluator.
- A partial evaluator must contain an interpreter, which may be problematic for typed languages, as explained below. Neither the generating extension generator nor the generating extensions need to contain an interpreter, and can hence avoid the type issue.

In a strongly typed language, any single program has a finite number of different types for its variables but the language in itself allows an unbounded number of types. Hence, when writing an interpreter for a strongly typed language, one must use a single type (or a fixed number of types) in the interpreter to represent a potentially unbounded number of types used in the programs that are interpreted. The same is true for a partial evaluator: A single universal type (or a small number of types) must be used for the static input to the program that will be specialized. Since that program may have any type, the static input must be coded into the universal type(s). This means that the partial evaluation equation must be modified to take this coding into account:

$$[\![\,peval\,]\!][p, \overline{d_1}] = p_{d_1} \land [\![\,p\,]\!][d_1, d_2] = d' \text{ implies } [\![\,p_{d_1}\,]\!]\,d_2 = d'$$

where overlining means that a value is coded, e.g. $\overline{d_1}$ is the coding of the value of d_1 into the universal type(s).

When self-applying the partial evaluator, the static input is a program. The program is normally represented in a special data type that represents program text. This data type must now be coded in the universal type:

$$[\![\mathit{peval}]\!][\mathit{peval}, \overline{p}] = p_{gen} \text{ implies } [\![\mathit{peval}]\!] [p, \overline{d_1}][\![p_{gen}]\!] \overline{d_1} = p_{d_1}$$

This encoding is space- and time-consuming, and has been reported to make self-application intractable, unless special attention is paid to make the encoding compact [24]. A generating extension produced by self-application must also use the universal type(s) to represent static input, even though this input will always be of the same type, since the generating extension specializes only a single program (with fixed types).

This observation leads to the idea of making generating extensions that accept uncoded static input. To achieve this, the generating extension generator copies the type declarations of the original program into the generating extension. The generating extension generator takes a single input (a program), and need not deal with arbitrarily typed data. A generating extension handles values from a single program, the types of which are known when the generating extension is constructed and can hence be declared in this. Thus, neither the generator of generating extensions, nor the generating extensions themselves need to handle arbitrarily typed values. The equation for specialization using a generating extension generator is shown below. Note the absence of coding.

$$[\![\mathit{gengen}]\!][p] = p_{gen} \wedge [\![p_{gen}]\!] d_1 = p_{d_1} \text{ implies } [\![p]\!] [d_1, d_2] = [\![p_{d_1}]\!] d_2$$

We will usually expect generator generation to terminate but, as for normal partial evaluation, allow the construction of the residual program (performed by p_{gen}) to loop.

6   When is partial evaluation worthwhile?

In Section 2.1 we saw that we cannot always expect speed-up from partial evaluation. Sometimes no significant computations depend on the known input only, so virtually all the work is postponed until the residual program is executed. Even if computations appear to depend on the known input only, evaluating these during specialization may require infinite unfolding (as seen in Section 2.1) or, even if finite, so much unfolding that the residual programs become intractably large.

On the other hand, the example in Section 1 manages to perform a significant part of the computation at specialization time. Even so, partial evaluation will only pay off if the residual program is executed often enough to amortize the cost of specialization.

So, two conditions must be satisfied before we can expect any benefit from partial evaluation:

1) There are computations that depend only on static data.

2) These are executed repeatedly, either by repeated execution of the program as a whole, or by repetition (looping or recursion) within a single execution of the program.

The static (known) data can be obtained in several ways: It may be constants appearing in the program text or it can be part of the input.

It is quite common that library functions are called with some constant parameters, such as format strings, so in some cases partial evaluation may speed up programs even when no input is given. In such cases the partial evaluator works as a kind of optimizer, often achieving speed-up when most optimizing compilers would not. On the other hand, partial evaluators may loop or create an excessive amount of code while trying to optimize programs, and hence are ill-suited as default optimizers.

Specialization with respect to partial input is the most common situation. Here, there are often more opportunities for speed-up than just exploiting constant parameters. In some cases (e.g., when specializing interpreters), most of the computation can be done during partial evaluation, yielding speed-ups by an order of magnitude or more, similar to the speed difference between interpreted and compiled programs. When you have a choice between running a program interpreted or compiled, you will choose the former if the program is only executed a few times and contains no significant repetition, whereas you will want to compile it if it is run many times or involves much repetition. The same principle carries over to specialization.

Partial evaluation often gets most of its benefit from replication: Loops are unrolled and the index variables exploited in constant folding, or functions are specialized with respect to several different static parameters, yielding several different residual functions. In some cases, this replication can result in enormous residual programs, which may be undesirable even if much computation is saved. In the example in Section 1 the amount of unrolling and hence the size of the residual program is proportional to the logarithm of n, the static input. This expansion is small enough that it doesn't become a problem. If the expansion was linear in n, it would be acceptable for small values of n, but not for large values. Specialization of interpreters typically yield residual programs that are proportional to the size of the source program, which is reasonable (and to be expected). On the other hand, quadratic or exponential expansion is hardly ever acceptable.

It may be hard to predict the amount of replication caused by a partial evaluator. In fact, seemingly innocent changes to a program can dramatically change the expansion done by partial evaluation, or even make the difference between termination or nontermination of the specialization process. Similarly, small changes can make a large difference in the amount of computation that is performed during specialization and hence the speed-up obtained. This is similar to the way parallelizing compilers are sensitive to the way programs are written. Hence, specialization of off-the-shelf programs often require some (usually minor) modification to get optimal benefit from partial evaluation. To obtain the best possible specialization, the programmer should write his program with partial evaluation in mind, avoiding structures that can cause problems, just like programs for parallel machines are best written with the limitations of the compiler in mind.

7   Applications of partial evaluation

We saw in Section 4 that partial evaluation can be used to compile programs and to generate compilers. This has been one of the main practical uses of partial evaluation. Not for making compilers for C or similar languages, but for rapidly obtaining implementations of acceptable performance for experimental or special-purpose languages. Since the output of the partial evaluator typically is in a high-level language, a traditional compiler is used as a back-end for the compiler generated by partial evaluation [1, 6, 10–13, 22]. In some cases, the compilation is from a language to itself. In this case the purpose is not faster execution but to make certain computation strategies explicit (e.g., continuation passing style) or to add extra information (e.g., for debugging) to the program [9, 15, 30, 31].

Many types of programs (e.g. scanners and parsers) use a table or other data structure to control the program. It is often possible to achieve speed-up by partially evaluating the table-driven program with respect to a particular table [2, 28]. However, this may produce very large residual programs, as tables (unless sparse) often represent the information more compactly than does code.

These are examples of converting *structural knowledge representation* to *procedural knowledge representation*. The choice between these two types of representation has usually been determined by the idea that structural information is compact and easy to modify but slow to use, while procedural information is fast to use but hard to modify and less compact. Automatically converting structural knowledge to procedural knowledge can overcome the disadvantage of difficult modifiability of procedural knowledge, but retains the disadvantage of large space usage.

Partial evaluation has also been applied to numerical computation, in particular simulation programs. In such programs, part of the model will be constant during the simulation while other parts will change. By specializing with respect to the fixed parts of the model, some speed-up can be obtained. An example is the N-body problem, simulating the interaction of moving objects through gravitational forces. In this simulation, the masses of the objects are constant, whereas their position and velocity change. Specializing with respect to the mass of the objects can speed up the simulation. Berlin reports speed-ups of more than 30 for this problem [7]. However, the residual program is written in C whereas the original one was in Scheme, which may account for part of the speed-up. In another experiment, specialization of some standard numerical algorithms gave speed-ups ranging from none at all to about 5 [17].

When neural networks are trained, they are usually run several thousand times on a number of test cases. During this training, various parameters will be fixed, e.g. the topology of the net, the learning rate and the momentum.

By specializing the trainer to these parameters, speed-ups of 25 to 50% are reported [20].

7.1   Polygon sorting

Section 5 mentioned a few applications of specialization to computer graphics. This, like compilation, has been one of the areas that have seen most applications of partial evaluation. An early example is [18], where an extended form of partial evaluation is used to specialize a renderer used in a flight simulator:

The scene used in the flight simulator is composed of a large number of small polygons. When the scene is rendered, the polygons are sorted based on a partial order that defines occlusion: If one polygon may partly cover another when both are viewed from the current viewpoint, the first is deemed closer than the other. After sorting them, the polygons are plotted in reverse order of occlusion.

In a flight simulator the same landscape is viewed repeatedly from different angles. Though occlusion of surfaces depends on the angle of view, it is often the case that knowledge that a particular surface occludes another (or doesn't) can decide the occlusion question of other pairs of surfaces. Hence, the partial evaluator simulates the sorting of surfaces and when it cannot decide which of two surfaces must be plotted first, it leaves that test in the residual program. Furthermore, it uses the inequalities of the occlusion test as positive and negative constraints in the branches of the conditional it generates, constraining the view-angle. These constraints are then used to decide later occlusion tests (by attempting to solve the constraints by the Simplex method). Each time a test cannot be decided, more information is added to the constraint set, allowing more later tests to be decided. Goad reports that for a typical landscape with 1135 surfaces (forming a triangulation of the landscape), the typical depth of paths in the residual decision tree was 27, compared to the more than 10000 comparisons needed for a full sort [18]. This rather extreme speed-up is due to the nature of landscapes: Many surfaces are almost parallel, and hence can occlude each other only in a very narrow range of view angles.

7.2   Ray-tracing

Another graphics application has been ray-tracing. In ray-tracing, a scene is rendered by tracing rays (lines) from the viewpoint through each pixel on the screen into an imaginary world behind the screen, testing which objects these rays hit. The process is repeated for all rays using the same fixed scene. Figure 1 shows pseudo-code for a raytracer.

Since there may be millions of pixels (and hence rays) in a typical ray-tracing application, specialization with respect to a fixed scene but unknown rays can give speed-up even for rendering single pictures. If we assume that the scene an viewpoint are static but the points on the screen are dynamic (since we don't wan't to unroll the loop), we find that the ray becomes dynamic. The objects in the scene are static, so the intersect function can be specialized with respect to each object. Though the identity of the closest object (object1) is dynamic, we

```
for every point ∈ screen do
    plot(point,colour(scene,viewpoint,point));

colour(scene,p0,p1) =
    let ray = line(p0,p1) in
    let intersections = {intersect(object,ray) | object ∈ scene } in
    let (object1,p) = closest(intersections,p0) in
        shade(object1,p)
```

Fig. 1. Pseudo-code for a ray-tracer

```
for every point ∈ screen do
    plot(point,colour(scene,viewpoint,point));

colour(scene,p0,p1) =
    let ray = line(p0,p1) in
    let intersections = {intersect(object,ray) | object ∈ scene } in
    let (object1,p) = closest(intersections,p0) in
        for object ∈ scene do
            if object=object1 then shade(object,p)
```

Fig. 2. Ray-tracer modified for "The Trick"

can nevertheless specialize the shade function to each object in the scene and select one of these at run-time in the residual program. This, however, either requires a very smart partial evaluator or a rewrite of the program to make this selection explicit. Such rewrites are common if one wants to get the full benefit of partial evaluation. The idea of using a dynamic value to select from a set of specialized functions is often called "The Trick". A version of the ray-tracer rewritten for "The Trick" is shown in figure 2.

Speed-ups of more than 6 have been reported for a simple ray-tracer [25]. For a more realistic ray-tracer, speed-ups in the range 1.5 to 3 have been reported [4].

7.3   Othello

The applications above have all been cases where a program is specialized with respect to input or where a procedure is specialized to a large internal data structure, e.g. a parse table. However, a partial evaluator may also be used as an optimizer for programs that don't have these properties. For example, a partial evaluator will typically be much more aggressive in unrolling loops than a compiler and may exploit this to specialize the bodies of the loops. Furthermore, a partial evaluator can do interprocedural constant folding by specializing functions, which a compiler usually will not.

An example of this is seen in the procedure in figure 3, which is a legal move generator for the game Othello (also known as Reversi). The main part of the procedure find_moves is 5 nested loops: Two that scans each square of the

```
#define index(var0,var1,x,y) \
   ((x<4) ? ((var0>>(x*8+y))&1) : ((var1>>((x-4)*8+y))&1))

#define index2(var0,var1,x,y) \
   ((x>=3 && x<=4 && y>=3 && y<=4) || index(var0,var1,x,y))

int find_moves(unsigned long full0, unsigned long full1,
               unsigned long bw0, unsigned long bw1,
               unsigned char moves[])
{
  int i,j,di,dj,k,l,found, moved, nmoves;

  nmoves = 0;
  for (i=0; i<8; i++) {
    for (j=0; j<8; j++)
      if (!(index2(full0,full1,i,j))) {
        found = 0;
        for (di=-1; di<=1 && !found; di++)
          for (dj=-1; dj<=1 && !found; dj++) {
            if (di != 0 || dj!= 0) {
              k=0; l=0;
              if ((i>1 || di>=0) && (i<6 || di<=0)
                  && (j>1 || dj>=0) && (j<6 || dj<=0)) {
                k=i+di; l=j+dj; moved = 0;
                while ((k>0 || di>=0) && (k<7 || di<=0)
                       && (l>0 || dj>=0) && (l<7 || dj<=0)
                       && index(bw0,bw1,k,l))
                  {k+=di; l+=dj; moved=1;}
                if (moved) {
                  if (di<0 && k==0 || di>0 && k==7 ||
                      dj<0 && l==0 || dj>0 && l==7) {
                    if (index2(full0,full1,k,l) && !index(bw0,bw1,k,l))
                      found = 1;
                  }
                  else if (index2(full0,full1,k,l))
                    found = 1;
                }
              }
            }
          }
        if (found)
          moves[nmoves++] = 8*i+j;
      }
  }
  return(nmoves);
}
```

Fig. 3. Legal move generator for Othello

board, two that determine the direction which is searched and one that steps in this direction. At various points are tests that guard or terminate loops. Some of these tests (e.g. to see if the edge of the board is reached) depend only on the loop variables, while other tests depend also on the contents of the board. Even though the find_moves procedure is specialized with no static input, the loop variables will be static and hence specialization can be done. The result is a complete unrolling of all the loops and specialization of the loop bodies (including calls to the index macros) to the values of the loop variables.

The move generator is slightly unusual in two respects: It uses bitvectors to represent the board rather than arrays and it has some tests that would not normally be found in a such a procedure.

One example is the test (x>=3 && x<=4 && y>=3 && y<=4) in the index2 macro, which exploits the knowledge that the middle four squares of the Othello board can never be empty (since they are full at the start of the game and counters are never removed) and hence we can statically compute the contents of the full vector for these squares. It is only because the test is static and the actual lookup is dynamic that the test is worthwhile. The cost of these added tests are about 30% of the total running time. This must be taken into consideration when judging the results below. The use of bitvectors instead of a byte-array does not significantly affect the running time.

I will not show the text of the residual function, only note that it is completely unreadable and compiles to about 50K of code, where the original compiles to 29K. The main interest is what, if any, speed-up is gained by specialization. A test has been made where a board is tested 100000 times for legal moves. The original program used 4.67 seconds (averaged over 4 different boards) where the residual program used only 0.54 seconds for the same. This is a ratio of 8.7. If we consider that the original program was slowed approximately 30% by the extra static tests, a "fair" measure of speed-up is 6.7.

The measurements were made on a HP9000/C160 using gcc, which for both programs generated substantially faster and smaller code than HP's C compiler. The partial evaluator for C, C-mix [16] was used for specialization.

8   Acknowledgements

Some parts of this paper are based on extracts of an encyclopedia article on partial evaluation co-authored with Peter Sestoft [26], which again is partly based on extracts of Jones, Gomard and Sestofts book on partial evaluation [21].

9   Exercises

Exercise 1. Specialize by hand the power program from the introduction to n = 13.

Exercise 2. Think of a possible application of partial evaluation besides the examples discussed in the text. Explain which parts of the computation you expect to be static and how much speed up you expect to obtain from partial evaluation.

References

1. S.M. Abramov and N.V. Kondratjev. A compiler based on partial evaluation. In *Problems of Applied Mathematics and Software Systems*, pages 66–69. Moscow State University, Moscow, USSR, 1982. (In Russian).
2. L.O. Andersen. Self-applicable C program specialization. In *Partial Evaluation and Semantics-Based Program Manipulation, San Francisco, California, June 1992 (Technical Report YALEU/DCS/RR-909)*, pages 54–61. New Haven, CT: Yale University, June 1992.
3. L.O. Andersen. *Program Analysis and Specialization for the C Programming Language.* PhD thesis, DIKU, University of Copenhagen, Denmark, 1994. DIKU Research Report 94/19.
4. P.H. Andersen. Partial evaluation applied to ray tracing. DIKU Research Report 95/2, DIKU, University of Copenhagen, Denmark, 1995.
5. L. Beckman et al. A partial evaluator, and its use as a programming tool. *Artificial Intelligence*, 7(4):319–357, 1976.
6. A. Berlin and D. Weise. Compiling scientific code using partial evaluation. *IEEE Computer*, 23(12):25–37, December 1990.
7. A.A. Berlin. Partial evaluation applied to numerical computation. In *1990 ACM Conference on Lisp and Functional Programming, Nice, France*, pages 139–150. New York: ACM, 1990.
8. L. Birkedal and M. Welinder. Partial evaluation of Standard ML. Master's thesis, DIKU, University of Copenhagen, Denmark, 1993. DIKU Research Report 93/22.
9. A. Bondorf. *Self-Applicable Partial Evaluation.* PhD thesis, DIKU, University of Copenhagen, Denmark, 1990. Revised version: DIKU Report 90/17.
10. M.A. Bulyonkov and A.P. Ershov. How do ad-hoc compiler constructs appear in universal mixed computation processes? In D. Bjørner, A.P. Ershov, and N.D. Jones, editors, *Partial Evaluation and Mixed Computation*, pages 65–81. Amsterdam: North-Holland, 1988.
11. M. Codish and E. Shapiro. Compiling or-parallelism into and-parallelism. In E. Shapiro, editor, *Third International Conference on Logic Programming, London, United Kingdom (Lecture Notes in Computer Science, vol. 225)*, pages 283–297. Berlin: Springer-Verlag, 1986. Also in New Generation Computing 5 (1987) 45-61.
12. C. Consel and S.C. Khoo. Semantics-directed generation of a Prolog compiler. In J. Maluszyński and M. Wirsing, editors, *Programming Language Implementation and Logic Programming, 3rd International Symposium, PLILP '91, Passau, Germany, August 1991 (Lecture Notes in Computer Science, vol. 528)*, pages 135–146. Berlin: Springer-Verlag, 1991.
13. P. Emanuelson and A. Haraldsson. On compiling embedded languages in Lisp. In *1980 Lisp Conference, Stanford, California*, pages 208–215. New York: ACM, 1980.
14. Y. Futamura. Partial evaluation of computation process – an approach to a compiler-compiler. *Systems, Computers, Controls*, 2(5):45–50, 1971.

15. J. Gallagher. Transforming logic programs by specialising interpreters. In *ECAI-86. 7th European Conference on Artificial Intelligence, Brighton Centre, United Kingdom*, pages 109–122. Brighton: European Coordinating Committee for Artificial Intelligence, 1986.

16. A. Glenstrup, H. Makholm, and J.P. Secher. C-mix: Specialization of C programs. In *Partial Evaluation: Practice and Theory.* Springer-Verlag, 1998.

17. R. Glück, R. Nakashige, and R. Zöchling. Binding-time analysis applied to mathematical algorithms. In J. Doležal and J. Fidler, editors, *System Modelling and Optimization*, pages 137–146. Chapman and Hall, 1995.

18. C. Goad. Automatic construction of special purpose programs. In D.W. Loveland, editor, *6th Conference on Automated Deduction, New York, USA (Lecture Notes in Computer Science, vol. 138)*, pages 194–208. Berlin: Springer-Verlag, 1982.

19. C.K. Holst and J. Launchbury. Handwriting cogen to avoid problems with static typing. In *Draft Proceedings, Fourth Annual Glasgow Workshop on Functional Programming, Skye, Scotland*, pages 210–218. Glasgow University, 1991.

20. H.F. Jacobsen. Speeding up the back-propagation algorithm by partial evaluation. Student Project 90-10-13, DIKU, University of Copenhagen, Denmark. (In Danish), October 1990.

21. N.D. Jones, C.K. Gomard, and P. Sestoft. *Partial Evaluation and Automatic Program Generation.* Englewood Cliffs, NJ: Prentice Hall, 1993.

22. J. Jørgensen. Generating a compiler for a lazy language by partial evaluation. In *Nineteenth ACM Symposium on Principles of Programming Languages, Albuquerque, New Mexico, January 1992*, pages 258–268. New York: ACM, 1992.

23. S.C. Kleene. *Introduction to Metamathematics.* Princeton, NJ: D. van Nostrand, 1952.

24. J. Launchbury. A strongly-typed self-applicable partial evaluator. In J. Hughes, editor, *Functional Programming Languages and Computer Architecture, Cambridge, Massachusetts, August 1991 (Lecture Notes in Computer Science, vol. 523)*, pages 145–164. ACM, Berlin: Springer-Verlag, 1991.

25. T. Mogensen. The application of partial evaluation to ray-tracing. Master's thesis, DIKU, University of Copenhagen, Denmark, 1986.

26. T. Mogensen and P. Sestoft. Partial evaluation. In Allen Kent and James G. Williams, editors, *Encyclopedia of Computer Science and Technology*, volume 37, pages 247–279. Marcel Dekker, 270 Madison Avenue, New York, New York 10016, 1997.

27. F.G. Pagan. Converting interpreters into compilers. *Software — Practice and Experience*, 18(6):509–527, June 1988.

28. F.G. Pagan. Comparative efficiency of general and residual parsers. *Sigplan Notices*, 25(4):59–65, April 1990.

29. G. Richardson. The realm of Nevryon. *Micro User*, June 1991.

30. S. Safra and E. Shapiro. Meta interpreters for real. In H.-J. Kugler, editor, *Information Processing 86, Dublin, Ireland*, pages 271–278. Amsterdam: North-Holland, 1986.

31. A. Takeuchi and K. Furukawa. Partial evaluation of Prolog programs and its application to meta programming. In H.-J. Kugler, editor, *Information Processing 86, Dublin, Ireland*, pages 415–420. Amsterdam: North-Holland, 1986.

32. V.F. Turchin et al., *Bazisnyj Refal i ego realizacija na vychislitel'nykh mashinakh (Basic Refal and Its Implementation on Computers)*. Moscow: GOSSTROJ SSSR, CNIPIASS, 1977. (In Russian).

An Introduction to
Online and Offline Partial Evaluation
Using a Simple Flowchart Language

John Hatcliff *

Department of Computing and Information Sciences
Kansas State University
hatcliff@cis.ksu.edu **

Abstract. These notes present basic principles of partial evaluation using the simple imperative language FCL (a language of flowcharts introduced by Jones and Gomard). Topics include online partial evaluators, offline partial evaluators, and binding-time analysis. The goal of the lectures is to give a rigorous presentation of the semantics of partial evaluation systems, while also providing details of actual implementations. Each partial evaluation system is specified by an operational semantics, and each is implemented in Scheme and Java. Exercises include proving various properties about the systems using the operational semantics, and modifying and extending the implementations.

1 Introduction

These notes give a gentle introduction to partial evaluation concepts using a simple flowchart language called FCL. The idea of using FCL to explain partial evaluation is due to Gomard and Jones [11, 15], and much of the material presented here is simply a reworking of the ideas in their earlier tutorial for offline partial evaluation. I have added analogous material for online partial evaluation, presented the binding-time analysis for offline partial evaluation using a two-level language, and specified FCL evaluation and partial evaluation using a series of operational semantics definitions. The operational semantics definitions provide enough formalization so that one can prove the correctness of the given specializers with relative ease.

The goal of this tutorial is to present partial evaluators that

- are easy to understand (they have a very clean semantic foundation),
- are simple enough for students to code quickly, and that
- capture the most important properties that one encounters when specializing programs written in much richer languages.

* Supported in part by NSF under grant CCR-9701418, and NASA under award NAG 21209.

** 234 Nichols Hall, Manhattan KS, 66506, USA. Home page: http://www.cis.ksu.edu/~hatcliff

For each specializer presented, there is an accompanying Scheme and Java implementation. The Java implementations include web-based documentation and are generally more sophisticated than the Scheme implementations. On the other hand, the Scheme implementations are much shorter and can be understood more quickly. For programming exercises, students are given code templates for the specializers and are asked to fill in the holes. The more mundane portions of the implementation (code for parsing, stores, and other data structures) are provided. Other exercises involve using the operational semantics to study particular aspects of the specializers, and applying the specializers to various examples. The current version of these materials can be found on my home page (http://www.cis.ksu.edu/~hatcliff).

Each section of the notes ends with some references for further reading. The references are by no means exhaustive. Since the presentation here is for a simple imperative language, the given references are mostly for related work on imperative languages. Even though the references there are slightly out of date, the best place to look for pointers to work on partial evaluation in general is still the Jones-Gomard-Sestoft book on partial evaluation [15]. In addition, one should look at the various PEPM proceedings and the recent special issue of ACM Computing Surveys (1998 Symposium on Partial Evaluation [6]), and, of course, the other lecture material presented at this summer school.

This tutorial material is part of a larger set of course notes, lecture slides, and implementations that I have used in courses on partial evaluation at Oklahoma State University and Kansas State University. In addition to online and offline partial evaluation, the extended set of notes uses FCL to introduce other topics including constraint-based binding-time analysis, generating extension generators, slicing, and abstraction-based program specialization. Correctness proofs for many of the systems are also given. These materials can also be found on my home page (the URL is given above).

Acknowledgements

I'm grateful to Shawn Laubach for the many hours he spent on the implementations and on helping me organize these notes. Other students in my partial evaluation course at Oklahoma State including Mayumi Kato and Muhammad Nanda provided useful feedback. I'd like to thank Matt Dwyer, Hongjun Zheng and other members of the SANTOS Laboratory at Kansas State (http://www.cis.ksu.edu/~santos) for useful comments and support. Finally, Robert Glück and Neil Jones deserve special thanks for encouraging me to prepare this material, for enlightening discussions, and for their very helpful and detailed comments on earlier drafts of this article.

2 The Flowchart Language

The section presents the syntax and semantics of a simple *flowchart language* FCL. This will be our primary linguistic vehicle for presenting fundamental

```
(m n)
(init)

  init:  result := 1;
         goto test;

  test:  if <(n 1)
            then end
            else loop;

  loop:  result := *(result m);
         n := -(n 1);
         goto test;

  end:   return result;
```

Fig. 1. An FCL program to compute m^n

concepts of program analysis and specialization. FCL is a good language to use for introducing basic concepts because it is extremely simple. Yet as Gomard and Jones note [11], all the concepts required for partial evaluation of FCL reappear again when considering more realistic languages.

2.1 Syntax

We usually think of a flowchart as a diagram containing boxes of various shapes connected by some arrows. One way to formalize flowcharts is using the notion of a graph. For example, one might start by saying that a flowchart is a directed graph with various types of nodes. This method of representing computation is intuitively appealing, but it somewhat awkward to work with in practice since we have grown accustomed to programming using text-based languages instead of diagramatic languages.

We will give a linguistic formalization of flowcharts. That is, we define a programming language FCL, and programs in FCL will correspond to the pictures that usually pop into our minds when we think of flowcharts. We begin an example, and then move to a formal presentation of the syntax of FCL.

A FCL program Figure 1 presents an FCL program that computes the power function. The input parameters the program are m and n. These are simply variables that can referenced and assigned throughout the program. There are no other declarations in FCL. Other variables such as result can be introduced at any time. The initial value of a variable is 0.

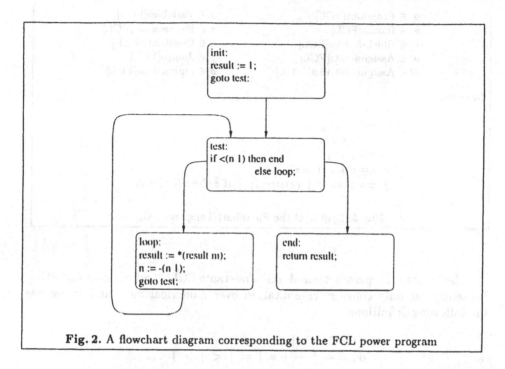

Fig. 2. A flowchart diagram corresponding to the FCL power program

FCL programs are essentially lists of *basic blocks*. The initial basic block to be executed is specified immediately after the parameter list. In the power program, the initial block is specified by the line (`init`).

Each basic block consists of a *label* followed a (possibly empty) list of *assignments*. Each block concludes with a *jump* that transfers control from that block to another one. For example, in the power program, the first block has label `init`, an assignment list of length one (`result := 1;`), and a jump `goto test;`.

FCL contains three kinds of jumps: an unconditional jump `goto` *label*, a conditional jump `if` *test* `goto` *label* `else` *label*, and a special jump `return` *exp* that terminates program execution and yields the value of *exp*. Instead of including boolean values, any non-zero value represents *true* and zero represents *false*.

Figure 2 displays the flowchart diagram corresponding to the FCL power program of Figure 1. Each node in the diagram corresponds to a basic block in the FCL program. The diagram helps illustrate that the basic aspects of computation in flowcharts are *transformations of computer memory* (computed by the assignments in each basic block) and *control transfers* (computed by the jumps).

Formal definition of FCL syntax Figure 3 presents the syntax of FCL. The intuition should be fairly clear given the example presented above. We will usually omit the dot · representing an empty list in assignment lists *al*.

Syntax Domains

$p \in$ Programs[FCL] $x \in$ Variables[FCL]
$b \in$ Blocks[FCL] $e \in$ Expressions[FCL]
$l \in$ Block-Labels[FCL] $c \in$ Constants[FCL]
$a \in$ Assignments[FCL] $j \in$ Jumps[FCL]
$al \in$ Assignment-Lists[FCL] $o \in$ Operations[FCL]

Grammar

$$p ::= (x^*) \, (l) \, b^+$$
$$b ::= l : al \, j$$
$$a ::= x := e;$$
$$al ::= a \, al \mid \cdot$$
$$e ::= c \mid x \mid o(e^*)$$
$$j ::= \textbf{goto } l; \mid \textbf{return } e; \mid \textbf{if } e \textbf{ then } l_1 \textbf{ else } l_2;$$

Fig. 3. Syntax of the Flowchart Language FCL

The syntax is parameterized on Constants[FCL] and Operations[FCL]. Presently, we only consider computation over numerical data and so we use the following definitions.

$$c ::= 0 \mid 1 \mid 2 \mid \cdots$$
$$o ::= + \mid - \mid * \mid = \mid < \mid > \mid \cdots$$

One can easily add additional data types such as lists.

The syntactic categories of FCL (*e.g.*, programs, basic blocks, *etc.*) are given in of Figure 3 (*e.g.*, Programs[FCL], Blocks[FCL], *etc.*). To denote the components of a syntactic category for a particular program p, we write Blocks[p], Expressions[p], *etc.* For example, Block-Labels[p] is the set of labels that label blocks in p. Specifically,

$$\text{Labels}[p] \stackrel{\text{def}}{=} \{l \in \text{Block-Labels[FCL]} \mid \exists b . b \in \text{Blocks}[p] \text{ and } b = l : a \, j\}.$$

We will assume that all FCL programs p that we consider are *well-formed* in that sense that every label used in a jump in p appears in Block-Labels[p].

Definition 1 (well-formed FCL programs). *A FCL program p is well-formed if*

- (**goto** $l;,\in$ Jumps[p] *imples* $l \in$ Block-Labels[p], *and*
- (**if** e **then** l_1 **else** $l_2;$) $\in$ Jumps[p] *imples* $l_1, l_2 \in$ Block-Labels[p].

2.2 Semantics

We now turn our attention toward formalizing the *behaviour* of FCL programs in terms of *execution traces*.

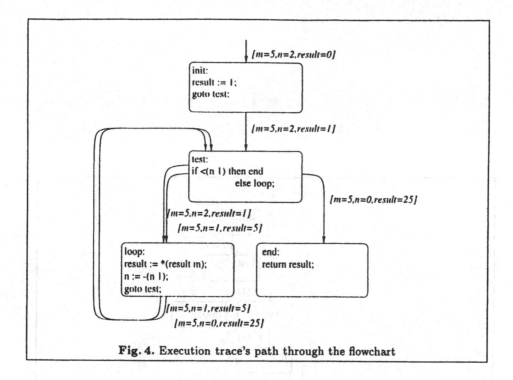

Fig. 4. Execution trace's path through the flowchart

Execution traces Intuitively, an execution trace shows the steps a program makes between *computational states* where a computational state consists of a label indicating the current basic block and the current value of the store. For example, the following is a trace of the power program computing 5^2.

$$(\text{init}, [\text{m} \mapsto 5, \text{n} \mapsto 2, \text{result} \mapsto 0])$$

step 1:	$\rightarrow (\text{test}, [\text{m} \mapsto 5, \text{n} \mapsto 2, \text{result} \mapsto 1])$
step 2:	$\rightarrow (\text{loop}, [\text{m} \mapsto 5, \text{n} \mapsto 2, \text{result} \mapsto 1])$
step 3:	$\rightarrow (\text{test}, [\text{m} \mapsto 5, \text{n} \mapsto 1, \text{result} \mapsto 5])$
step 4:	$\rightarrow (\text{loop}, [\text{m} \mapsto 5, \text{n} \mapsto 1, \text{result} \mapsto 5])$
step 5:	$\rightarrow (\text{test}, [\text{m} \mapsto 5, \text{n} \mapsto 0, \text{result} \mapsto 25])$
step 6:	$\rightarrow (\text{end}, [\text{m} \mapsto 5, \text{n} \mapsto 0, \text{result} \mapsto 25])$
step 7:	$\rightarrow (\langle \text{halt}, 25 \rangle, [\text{m} \mapsto 5, \text{n} \mapsto 0, \text{result} \mapsto 25])$

Here we have introduced an special label $\langle \text{halt}, 25 \rangle$ not found in the original program. In general, $\langle \text{halt}, v \rangle$ labels a final program state where the return value is v.

Computation tree An execution trace of program p gives a particular path through p's flowchart. For example, Figure 4 shows the path corresponding to the trace above. The trace steps are given as labels on the flowchart arcs.

Of course, a flowchart is just a finite representation of a (possibly infinite) tree obtained by unfolding all the cycles in the flowchart graph. We call such trees

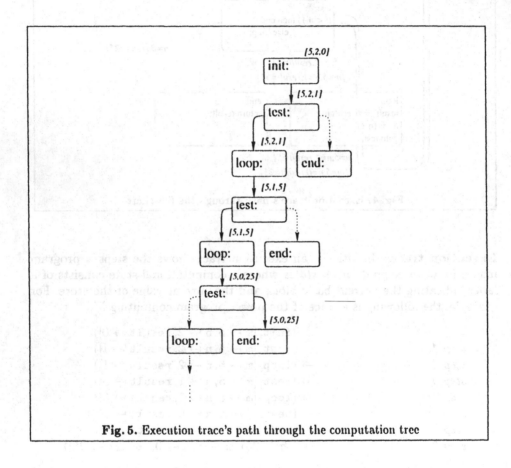

Fig. 5. Execution trace's path through the computation tree

computation trees. Instead of viewing as an execution trace as a path through a flowchart, it will be more convenient for us to view a trace as a path through an computation tree. For example, Figure 5 shows the tree path corresponding to the flowchart path of 4. When reasoning about program specialization in the following chapters, we prefer tree paths instead of flowchart paths since every node in the tree path has exactly one state associated with it.

Formal definition of FCL semantics We now formalize the notion of an execution trace using an *operational semantics*. Our main task will be to define the *transition relation* $\rightarrow$ between FCL computational states. Given this formal high-level specification of execution, it should be straightforward for the reader to build an actual implementation in the programming language of his or her choice.

Figure 6 presents the operational semantics for FCL. The semantics relies on the following definitions.

– **Values:** Each expression in the language will evaluate to some *value* $v \in$ Values[FCL]. The semantics is parameterized on the set Values[FCL], just like the syntax is parameterized on constants and operations. We previously decided to include constants and operations for numerical computation. Accordingly, we will define

$$v \in \text{Values[FCL]} = \{0, 1, 2, \ldots\}.$$

Another view of values is that they abstract the underlying implementation's representation of data objects. For example, it is important to distinguish between the numeral 2 (*i.e.*, syntax, source code – written in `teletype` font) and the corresponding value 2 (*i.e.*, semantics, abstraction of underlying representation – written in roman font) that is obtained when 2 is evaluated. We will use $[\![\cdot]\!]$ to denote an injective mapping from syntactic objects to their semantic counterparts. For example $[\![2]\!] = 2$.

The meanings of operations for numerical computation are as expected. For example,

$$[\![+]\!](n_1, n_2) = n_1 + n_2$$
$$[\![-]\!](n_1, n_2) = \begin{cases} 0 & \text{if } n_1 - n_2 < 0 \\ n_1 - n_2 & \text{otherwise} \end{cases}$$
$$\cdots$$
$$[\![=]\!](n_1, n_2) = \begin{cases} 1 & \text{if } n_1 = n_2 \\ 0 & \text{otherwise} \end{cases}$$
$$\cdots$$

Since we do not include boolean values, we define predicates is-true? and is-false? such that is-false?(0) and is-true?(v) for all $v > 0$.

– **Stores:** A *store* $\sigma \in$ Stores[FCL] holds the current values of the program variables. Thus, a store corresponds to the computer's memory. Formally, a store $\sigma \in$ Stores[FCL] is partial function from Variables[FCL]

Expressions

$$\overline{\sigma \vdash_{expr} c \Rightarrow [\![c]\!]} \qquad\qquad \overline{\sigma \vdash_{expr} x \Rightarrow \sigma(x)}$$

$$\frac{\sigma \vdash_{expr} e_i \Rightarrow v_i \qquad [\![o]\!](v_1 \ldots v_n) = v}{\sigma \vdash_{expr} o(e_1 \ldots e_n) \Rightarrow v}$$

Assignments

$$\frac{\sigma \vdash_{expr} e \Rightarrow v}{\sigma \vdash_{assign} x := e; \Rightarrow \sigma[x \mapsto v]} \qquad\qquad \overline{\sigma \vdash_{assigns} \cdot \Rightarrow \sigma}$$

$$\frac{\sigma \vdash_{assign} a \Rightarrow \sigma' \qquad \sigma' \vdash_{assigns} al \Rightarrow \sigma''}{\sigma \vdash_{assigns} a\ al \Rightarrow \sigma''}$$

Jumps

$$\overline{\sigma \vdash_{jump} \textbf{goto } l; \Rightarrow l} \qquad\qquad \frac{\sigma \vdash_{expr} e \Rightarrow v}{\sigma \vdash_{jump} \textbf{return } e; \Rightarrow \langle \textsf{halt}, v \rangle}$$

$$\frac{\sigma \vdash_{expr} e \Rightarrow v \quad \textsf{is-true?}(v)}{\sigma \vdash_{jump} \textbf{if } e \textbf{ then } l_1 \textbf{ else } l_2; \Rightarrow l_1} \qquad \frac{\sigma \vdash_{expr} e \Rightarrow v \quad \textsf{is-false?}(v)}{\sigma \vdash_{jump} \textbf{if } e \textbf{ then } l_1 \textbf{ else } l_2; \Rightarrow l_2}$$

Blocks

$$\frac{\sigma \vdash_{assigns} al \Rightarrow \sigma' \qquad \sigma' \vdash_{jump} j \Rightarrow l'}{\sigma \vdash_{block} l : al\ j \Rightarrow (l', \sigma')}$$

Transitions

$$\frac{\sigma \vdash_{block} \Gamma(l) \Rightarrow (l', \sigma')}{\vdash_\Gamma (l, \sigma) \to (l', \sigma')}$$

Semantic Values

$$
\begin{aligned}
l &\in \text{Labels[FCL]} &&= \text{Block-Labels[FCL]} \cup (\{\textsf{halt}\} \times \text{Values[FCL]}) \\
\sigma &\in \text{Stores[FCL]} &&= \text{Variables[FCL]} \rightharpoonup \text{Values[FCL]} \\
\Gamma &\in \text{Block-Maps[FCL]} &&= \text{Block-Labels[FCL]} \rightharpoonup \text{Blocks[FCL]} \\
s &\in \text{States[FCL]} &&= \text{Labels[FCL]} \times \text{Stores[FCL]}
\end{aligned}
$$

Fig. 6. Operational semantics of FCL programs

to Values[FCL]. If we are evaluating a program p, we want σ to be defined for all variables occuring in p and undefined otherwise. That is, $dom(\sigma) = $ Variables[p] where $dom(\sigma)$ denotes set of variables for which σ is defined. If a σ satisfies this property, we say that σ *is compatible with* p. Each assignment statement may change the contents of the store. We write $\sigma[x \mapsto v]$ denote the store that is just like σ except that variable x now maps to v. Specifically,

$$\forall x \in \text{Variables[FCL]} \ . \ (\sigma[x' \mapsto v])(x) \ \overset{\text{def}}{=} \ \begin{cases} v & \text{if } x = x' \\ \sigma(x') & \text{if } x \neq x'. \end{cases}$$

For the meantime, we will assume that execution of a program p begins with an initial store σ_{init} where all variables occurring in p have been initialized to the value 0. More precisely, the *initial store* σ_{init} *for program* p is defined as follows:

$$\forall x \in \text{Variables[FCL]} \ . \ \sigma_{init}(x) \ \overset{\text{def}}{=} \ \begin{cases} 0 & \text{if } x \in \text{Variables[}p\text{]} \\ undefined & \text{otherwise.} \end{cases}$$

- **Block maps:** In a typical implementation of FCL, one would use some sort of data structure to fetch a block b given b's label. We call such a data structure a *block map* because it maps labels to blocks. Formally, a block map $\Gamma \in$ Block-Maps[FCL] is a partial function from Block-Labels[FCL] to Blocks[FCL]. Thus, Γ is a lookup table for blocks using labels as keys. A block map Γ will be defined for all labels occurring in the program being described and undefined otherwise. For example, if Γ is a block map for the power program of Figure 1, then

$$\Gamma(\text{init}) \ = \ \texttt{init: result := 1;}$$
$$\texttt{goto test;.}$$

- **Computational states:** A *computational state* is a snap-shot picture of a point in a program's execution. It tells us (1) the current position of execution within the program (*i.e.*, the label of the current block), and (2) the current value of each of the program variables. Formally, a computational state $s \in$ States[FCL] is a pair (l, σ) where $l \in=$ Labels[FCL] and $\sigma \in$ Stores[FCL].

In Figure 6, a "big-step" semantics is used to define the evaluation of expressions, assignments, jumps, and blocks. The intuition behind the rules for these constructs is as follows.

- $\sigma \vdash_{expr} e \Rightarrow v$ means that under store σ, expression e evaluates to value v. Note that expression evaluation cannot change the value of the store.
- $\sigma \vdash_{assign} a \Rightarrow \sigma'$ means that that under store σ, the assignment a yields the updated store σ'.
- $\sigma \vdash_{assigns} al \Rightarrow \sigma'$ means that under the store σ, the list of assignments al yields the updated store σ'.
- $\sigma \vdash_{jump} j \Rightarrow l$ means that under the store σ, jump j will cause a transition to the block labelled l.

$\sigma \vdash_{block} b \Rightarrow (l', \sigma')$ means that under the store σ, block b will cause a transition to the block labelled l' with updated store σ'.

The final rule of Figure 6 defines the Γ-indexed transition relation

$$\rightarrow_\Gamma \subseteq (\text{Labels}[\text{FCL}] \times \text{Stores}[\text{FCL}]) \times (\text{Labels}[\text{FCL}] \times \text{Stores}[\text{FCL}]).$$

This gives a "small-step" semantics for program evaluation. We will write

$$\Vdash_\Gamma (l, \sigma) \rightarrow (l', \sigma')$$

when

$$((l, \sigma), (l', \sigma')) \in \rightarrow_\Gamma .$$

The intuition is that there is a transition from state (l, σ) to state (l', σ') in the program whose block map is Γ. We will drop the Γ it is clear from the context.

Example derivation We can obtain the power program trace in Section 2.2 simply by following the rules in Figure 6. As an example, we will build a derivation that justifies the third transition:

$$(\text{loop}, [\text{m} \mapsto 5, \text{n} \mapsto 2, \text{result} \mapsto 1])$$
$$\rightarrow (\text{test}, [\text{m} \mapsto 5, \text{n} \mapsto 1, \text{result} \mapsto 5]).$$

We begin with the derivations for evaluation of expressions in block loop (see Figure 1) taking

$$\sigma = [\text{m} \mapsto 5, \text{n} \mapsto 2, \text{result} \mapsto 1]$$
$$\sigma'' = [\text{m} \mapsto 5, \text{n} \mapsto 1, \text{result} \mapsto 5]$$

The following derivation ∇_1 specifies the evaluation of *(result n).

$$\nabla_1 = \frac{\sigma \vdash_{expr} \text{result} \Rightarrow \sigma(\text{result}) \qquad \sigma \vdash_{expr} \text{m} \Rightarrow \sigma(\text{m}) \qquad [*](1\ 5) = 5}{\sigma \vdash_{expr} *(\text{result m}) \Rightarrow 5}$$

The derivation is well-formed since $\sigma(\text{result}) = 1$ and $\sigma(\text{m}) = 5$. In the remainder of the derivations below, we omit application of the store to variables and simply give the resulting values (for example, we simply write 5 instead of $\sigma(\text{m})$).

Next, we give the derivation for the evaluation of the assignment statement result := *(result m); (we repeat the conclusion of derivation ∇_1 for clarity):

$$\nabla_2 = \frac{\dfrac{\nabla_1}{\sigma \vdash_{expr} *(\text{result m}) \Rightarrow 5}}{\sigma \vdash_{assign} \text{result} := *(\text{result m}); \Rightarrow \sigma[\text{result} \mapsto 5].}$$

Now let

$$\sigma' \stackrel{\text{def}}{=} \sigma[\text{result} \mapsto 5] = [\text{m} \mapsto 5, \text{n} \mapsto 2, \text{result} \mapsto 5].$$

Similarly, we can build a derivation showing the evaluation of -(n 1):

$$\nabla_3 = \frac{\overline{\sigma' \vdash_{expr} \mathbf{n} \Rightarrow 2} \quad \overline{\sigma' \vdash_{expr} \mathbf{1} \Rightarrow [1]} \quad \overline{[-](2\ 1) = 1}}{\sigma' \vdash_{expr} \text{-(n 1)} \Rightarrow 1}.$$

Next, we give the derivation for the evaluation of the assignment statement n := -(n 1);:

$$\nabla_4 = \frac{\begin{array}{c} \nabla_3 \\ \sigma' \vdash_{expr} \text{-(n 1)} \Rightarrow 1 \end{array}}{\sigma' \vdash_{assign} \mathbf{n} := \text{-(n 1);} \Rightarrow \sigma'[\mathbf{n} \mapsto 1]}$$

Note

$$\sigma'' = \sigma'[\mathbf{n} \mapsto 1] = [\mathbf{m} \mapsto 5, \mathbf{n} \mapsto 1, \mathbf{result} \mapsto 5].$$

Now we can build the following derivation showing the evaluation of the list of assignments containing exactly one assignment n := -(n 1);.

$$\nabla_5 = \frac{\begin{array}{cc} \nabla_4 & \\ \sigma' \vdash_{assign} \mathbf{n} := \text{-(n 1);} \Rightarrow \sigma'[\mathbf{n} \mapsto 1] & \overline{\sigma'' \vdash_{assign} \cdot \Rightarrow \sigma''} \end{array}}{\sigma' \vdash_{assigns} \mathbf{n} := \text{-(n 1);} \Rightarrow \sigma''}.$$

Piecing together the previous derivations gives the following derivation for the assignments of the loop block.

$$\nabla_6 = \frac{\begin{array}{cc} \nabla_2 & \nabla_5 \\ \sigma \vdash_{assign} \mathbf{result} := \text{*(result m);} \Rightarrow \sigma' & \sigma' \vdash_{assigns} \mathbf{n} := \text{-(n 1);} \Rightarrow \sigma'' \end{array}}{\sigma \vdash_{assigns} \mathbf{result} := \text{*(result m);n} := \text{-(n 1);} \Rightarrow \sigma''}$$

Now we can construct the derivation for the evaluation of the loop block. Here, we let $al = \mathbf{result} := \text{*(result m);n} := \text{-(n 1);}$.

$$\nabla_7 = \frac{\begin{array}{cc} \nabla_6 & \\ \sigma \vdash_{assigns} al \Rightarrow \sigma'' & \sigma'' \vdash_{jump} \text{goto test;} \Rightarrow \text{test} \end{array}}{\sigma \vdash_{block} \Gamma(\text{loop}) \Rightarrow (\text{test}, \sigma'')}$$

Now we can construct the derivation for the transition from the loop block to the test block.

$$\frac{\begin{array}{c} \nabla_7 \\ \sigma \vdash_{block} \Gamma(\text{loop}) \Rightarrow (\text{test}, \sigma'') \end{array}}{\vdash_\Gamma (\text{loop}, \sigma) \rightarrow (\text{test}, \sigma'')}$$

Execution properties Finally, we can formalize a notion of FCL program evaluation.

Definition 2. *Let $p = (x_1 \ldots x_n)\ (l)\ b^+$ be a well-formed program, let σ_{init} be an initial store for p, and let $v_1, \ldots, v_n \in \text{Values[FCL]}$. Define program evaluation $[\cdot]$ as follows:*

$$[p](v_1, \ldots, v_n) \stackrel{\text{def}}{=} \begin{cases} v & \text{if } (l, \sigma_{init}[x_1 \mapsto v_1, \ldots, x_n \mapsto v_n]) \rightarrow^* (\langle \text{halt}, v \rangle, \sigma) \\ \text{undefined} & \text{otherwise.} \end{cases}$$

Below are some possible properties of transitions and execution sequences (based on [14]).

Definition 3. *Let $p \in$ Programs[FCL] be a well-formed program, and let Γ be a block map for p.*

- *A block $l \in$ Block-Labels[p] is one-way if*

$$(l, \sigma_1) \to (l', \sigma') \text{ and } (l, \sigma_2) \to (l'', \sigma'')$$

implies $l' = l''$.
- *The state (l, σ) is terminal if there does not exit a l' and σ' such that*

$$(l, \sigma) \to (l', \sigma').$$

- *The program p is deterministic if for all states (l, σ),*

$$(l, \sigma) \to (l', \sigma') \text{ and } (l, \sigma) \to (l'', \sigma'')$$

implies $l' = l''$ and $\sigma' = \sigma''$.

Intuitively, a block is one-way if it does not end with an **if** jump.

2.3   Exercises

1. Write an FCL program to compute the factorial function.
2. Give the execution trace for the prime number generator of Figure 7 with input 3. In the generator program, % implements the *mod* operator, and / implements integer division.
3. Given the execution trace for the prime number generator of Figure 7 with input 3 constructed in the previous exercise, give the derivation justifying the first transition from block **prime** to block **next**.
4. Prove that all well-formed programs $p \in$ Programs[FCL] are deterministic.
5. Add lists and associated operations (car, cdr, cons, *etc.*) to FCL. You might also consider adding S-expressions as in Scheme or LISP (*i.e.*, include symbols and a quote construct for constructing literal data).
6. **Project:** Following the operational semantics definition, program the FCL interpreter in the language of your choice.

2.4   Further reading

As noted, the presentation of the FCL language syntax is based on that of Gomard and Jones [11, 15]. The operational semantics presentation is original, and it is designed to match closely the more abstract presentation of program points and transitions given by Jones in his work "The Essence of Program Transformation by Partial Evaluation and Driving" [14]. Winskel's textbook [28] on programming language semantics gives a nice introduction to operational semantics.

```
(n)
(start)
  start:  m := 0;
          s := 2;
          k := 2;
          goto loop;

  loop:   if <(k +(/(s 2) 1) then check else prime;

  check:  d := %(s k);
          k := +(k 1);
          if =(d 0) then next else loop;

  prime:  m := +(m 1);
          p := s;
          if =(m n) then done else next;

  next:   k := 2;
          s := +(s 1);
          goto loop;

  done:   return p;
```

Fig. 7. An FCL program to generate the nth prime

3 Online Partial Evaluation

In this chapter, we see our first form of program specialization: *online partial evaluation*. We begin by considering how the notion of an execution trace changes when we move from the situation where we have complete data to a situation where some data is unknown. We discuss how specialization might proceed for the power program. After this motivation, we systematically introduce the basic components of online partial evaluation.

3.1 A motivating example

A partial evaluator takes values for a portion $\vec{x_s}$ of a program p's input parameters $(\vec{x_s}, \vec{x_d})$ and tries to perform as much computation as possible. Code for computations that depend on the remaining parameters $\vec{x_d}$ is placed in a residual program. Thus, a partial evaluator blends *interpretion* and *compilation*: it interprets (*i.e.*, evaluates) constructs that depend on $\vec{x_s}$, and emits code for constructs that may depend on $\vec{x_d}$.

As an example, this section considers what would be involved in specializing the FCL power program of Figure 1. One may first consider how the execution trace of Section 2.2 would have to change when considering partial input data only. Intuitively, we expect a trace where some values in the store are unknown. Some of the expressions, assignments, and jumps in blocks may be computed because they depend only on known data. However, others cannot be computed because the depend on unknown data. Once we find all the states that could be reached with the partial data, we then consider how we could partially compute each block based on the partial data.

In summary, partial evaluation can be viewed as a three-step process [15, Chapter 4].

1. *Collect all reachable states:* Starting from an initial state (l, σ) where σ contains only partial data, collect all reachable states (l_i, σ_i) into a set $\mathcal{S}$
2. *Program point specialization:* For each reachable state $(l_i, \sigma_i) \in \mathcal{S}$, place a new version of block l that is specialized with respect to σ_i in the residual program.
3. *Transition compression:* Optimize the residual program by merging blocks connected by trivial **goto** jumps.

Although this three-step view is very enlightening, in practice, most partial evaluators carry out these steps in a single phase. After giving several examples using the three-step view, we will give a formalization of on-line partial evaluation that uses a single phase.

Abstract traces Section 2.2 showed the execution of trace of the power program computing 5^2. Let us consider what a trace might look like if we only know the exponent parameter n to be 2 but know nothing about the value m. We use the special tag D to represent an unknown value.

$$(\text{init}, [\text{m} \mapsto D, \text{n} \mapsto 2, \text{result} \mapsto 0]) \tag{1}$$

$$\rightarrow (\text{test}, [\text{m} \mapsto D, \text{n} \mapsto 2, \text{result} \mapsto 1]) \tag{2}$$

$$\rightarrow (\text{loop}, [\text{m} \mapsto D, \text{n} \mapsto 2, \text{result} \mapsto 1]) \tag{3}$$

$$\rightarrow (\text{test}, [\text{m} \mapsto D, \text{n} \mapsto 1, \text{result} \mapsto D]) \tag{4}$$

$$\rightarrow (\text{loop}, [\text{m} \mapsto D, \text{n} \mapsto 1, \text{result} \mapsto D]) \tag{5}$$

$$\rightarrow (\text{test}, [\text{m} \mapsto D, \text{n} \mapsto 0, \text{result} \mapsto D]) \tag{6}$$

$$\rightarrow (\text{end}, [\text{m} \mapsto D, \text{n} \mapsto 0, \text{result} \mapsto D]) \tag{7}$$

$$\rightarrow (\text{halt}, [\text{m} \mapsto D, \text{n} \mapsto 0, \text{result} \mapsto D]) \tag{8}$$

This trace is called an *abstract trace* because the data value for m has been abstracted by the symbol D.

Here is the intuition behind each step in the trace.

- **Line 1**: The trace begins at the init block with the value of m marked as unknown. In init, result is initialized to 1. This is reflected in the value of the store when test is reached for the first time.
- **Line 2**: The value of n is known, and so we can compute the test <(n 1) (it is false) and move to loop.
- **Line 3**: The expression *(result m) cannot be computed since m is unknown. Therefore, result must be assigned a value of unknown. Since n is known, the result of decrementing n is placed in the store. Thus we arrive at test with n $\mapsto$ 1 and result $\mapsto$ D.
- **Line 4**: The value of n is known, and so we can compute the test <(n 1) (it is false) and move to loop.
- **Line 5**: The expression *(result m) cannot be computed since m and result are unknown. Thus, result is assigned a value of unknown. The result of decrementing n is placed in the store. Thus we arrive at test with n $\mapsto$ 0 and result $\mapsto$ D.
- **Line 6**: The value of n is known, and so we can compute the test <(n 1) (it is true) and move to end.
- **Line 7**: The block end has no assignments and so we move to the terminal state with the store unchanged. We omit a value in the halt label since the value of the result variable is unknown.

Figure 8 shows the computation tree path corresponding to the trace above. It is important to note that for any value $v \in$ Values[FCL], the path of a trace with initial store

$$\sigma_{init} = [\text{m} \mapsto v, \text{n} \mapsto 2, \text{result} \mapsto 0]$$

must lie within the shaded area of the computation tree. This gives us insight about the structure of the residual program that the partial evaluator will produce.

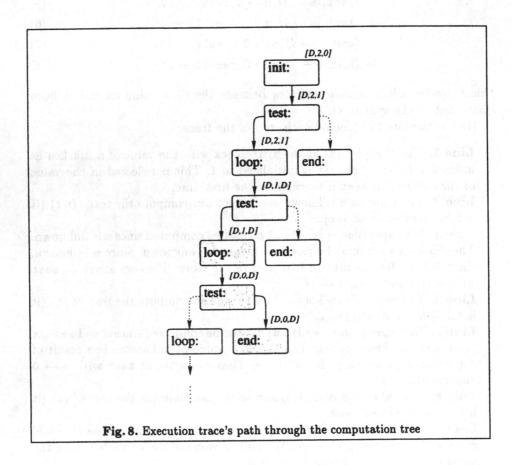

Fig. 8. Execution trace's path through the computation tree

The partial evaluator's task is to take the value 2 for n and produce an optimized residual program that is capable of handling any value v for m. In what sense is the residual program optimized?

- Since the trace using σ_{init} will always lie in the shaded area of the tree, the residual program can safely avoid having blocks corresponding to the unshaded nodes of the tree. It needs only to include blocks for the shaded portion of the tree. In fact, we will see that the next step in partial evaluation constructs a residual program that has exactly the same structure as the shaded portion of the computation tree.
- Notice that we will in general have several different reachable states $(l, \sigma), \ldots, (l, \sigma')$ for each block l. For example, in the trace above there are multiple states for blocks test and loop. Since the partial evaluator has collected all reachable states, it can customize each node in the shaded area of computation tree with the known information in the store that is flowing into that node. For example, we can create two versions of the loop block: one specialized to n $\mapsto$ 2 and result $\mapsto$ 1, and another specialized to n $\mapsto$ 1.

In other words, the partial evaluator uses the information that n has initial value of 2

- to prune unnecessary branches from the computation tree (those leading to unshaded area), and
- to specialize each reachable block (those in the shaded area) with respect to the different store values that are guaranteed to be flowing into that block.

Program point specialization For each reachable state (l, σ), we create a residual block labeled l' by specializing block l with respect to σ. For simplicity, we will simply use the pair (l, σ) as the value of label l'. For example, the residual block for state (init, $[m \mapsto D, n \mapsto 2, \text{result} \mapsto 0]$) will have label (init, [D,2,0]) (we drop the variables in the store for simplicity). In practice, a partial evaluator will generate a fresh label l' for each reachable state (l, σ) and maintain a table associating generated labels with reachable states.[1]

- State (init, $[m \mapsto D, n \mapsto 2, \text{result} \mapsto 0]$): In the init block, the assignment result := 1; does not depend on the dynamic data m so it can be completely executed as indicated in the construction of the trace. Customizing the init block involves computing the only assignment and customizing the **goto** so that we jump to the customized block for the next state in the trace.

  (init, [D,2,0]): goto (test, [D,2,1]);

- State (test, $[m \mapsto D, n \mapsto 2, \text{result} \mapsto 1]$): Since the value of n is known, the test expression of the if construct can be evaluated and the appropriate branch executed. Since in this state, n $\mapsto$ 2, the branch to be taken is the false branch.

---

[1] This is the case in our Scheme implementation.

```
(test, [D,2,1]): goto (loop, [D,2,1]);
```

- State $(\text{loop}, [m \mapsto D, n \mapsto 2, \text{result} \mapsto 1])$: The value of m is not known, and so the first assignment must be *residualized*.

```
result := *(1 m);
```

Note that the variable reference result on the right-hand side of the assignment can be replaced by its value (since it is known). The following assignment to n can be computed since n is known. Finally, we customize the jump as usual. The resulting block is as follows.

```
(loop, [D,2,1]): result := *(1 m);
                 goto (test, [D,1,D]);
```

- State $(\text{test}, [m \mapsto D, n \mapsto 1, \text{result} \mapsto D])$: Again, the test expression in the conditional jump can be computed. The resulting specialized block is given below.

```
(test, [D,1,D]): goto (loop, [D,1,D]);
```

- State $(\text{loop}, [m \mapsto D, n \mapsto 1, \text{result} \mapsto D])$:
Since the value of m is not known, the first assignment must be *residualized* as before.

```
result := *(result m);
```

However, in contrast to the previous entry to loop, result is not known this time and so the variable name is residualized on the right-hand side of the assignment. The following assignment to n can be computed since n is known. Finally, we customize the jump as usual. The result is as follows.

```
(loop, [D,1,D]): result := *(result m);
                 goto (test, [D,0,D]);
```

- State $(\text{test}, [m \mapsto D, n \mapsto 0, \text{result} \mapsto D])$: Again, the test expression in the conditional jump can be computed. However, this time the test expression is true, and so control is transferred to the appropriately specialized end block. The resulting specialized block is given below.

```
(test, [D,0,D]): goto (end, [D,0,D]);
```

- State $(\text{end}, [m \mapsto D, n \mapsto 0, \text{result} \mapsto D])$: The end block contains nothing but the return result; jump (which cannot be further specialized). The resulting block is as follows.

```
(end, [D,0,D]): return result;
```

Figure 9 gives the residual program that results from specializing the FCL power program with respect to $n \mapsto 2$. The residual program contains all the specialized blocks produced above, as well the declaration of the remaining parameter m and the label of the initial block $(\text{init}, [D, 2, 0])$.

Figure 10 presents the flowchart diagram for the specialized program of Figure 9. As promised, the structure of the residual program matches the structure of the shaded area of the computation tree in Figure 8.

```
(m)
((init,[D,2,0]))

  (init,[D,2,0]): goto (test,[D,2,1]);

  (test,[D,2,1]): goto (loop,[D,2,1]);

  (loop,[D,2,1]): result := *(1 m);
                  goto (test,[D,1,D]);

  (test,[D,1,D]): goto (loop,[D,1,D]);

  (loop,[D,1,D]): result := *(result m);
                  goto (test,[D,0,D]);

  (test,[D,0,D]): goto (end,[D,0,D]);

  (end,[D,0,D]):  return result;
```

Fig. 9. The FCL power program specialized to n = 2.

Transition compression There is a tight relationship between the original power program and the specialized version in Figure 9: there is a transition in the source program $(l, \sigma) \rightarrow (l', \sigma')$ iff there is a corresponding transition from block (l, σ) to block (l', σ') in the residual program. For example,

$$(\text{init}, [\text{m} \mapsto 5, \text{n} \mapsto 2, \text{result} \mapsto 0])$$
$$\rightarrow (\text{test}, [\text{m} \mapsto 5, \text{n} \mapsto 2, \text{result} \mapsto 1])$$

in the source program and

$$((\text{init}, [\text{D},2,0]), [\text{m} \mapsto 5, \text{result} \mapsto 0])$$
$$\rightarrow ((\text{test}, [\text{D},2,1]), [\text{m} \mapsto 5, \text{result} \mapsto 1])$$

in the residual program. However, the transition in the residual program isn't that interesting since it only involves chaining through a **goto**.

More generally, the control flow of the specialized program in Figure 9 is trivial in the sense that it does not contain any branches or loops. Thus, the **goto** jumps that exist are not necessary. Figure 11 shows a more natural specialized program where the transitions associated with the **goto** jumps have been eliminated.

Transition compression yields programs that are much more compact. However, one does not want to apply it indiscriminately — doing so may cause the partial evaluator to loop. For example, trying to eliminate all **goto**'s in the program below leads to infinite unfolding.

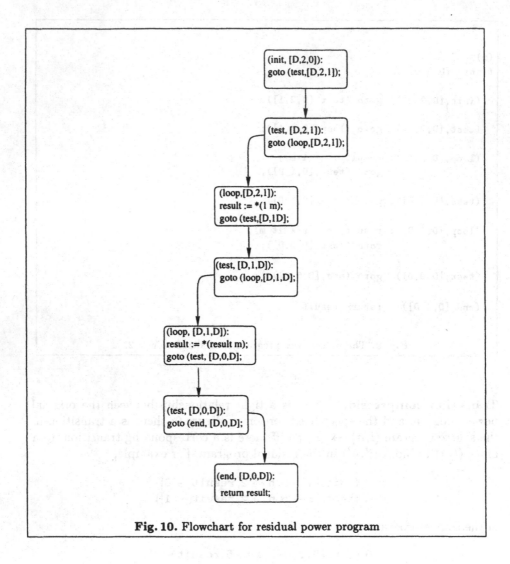

Fig. 10. Flowchart for residual power program

```
(m)
((init,[D,2,0]))

  (init,[D,2,0]): result := *(1 m);
                  result := *(result m);
                  return result;
```

Fig. 11. The specialized FCL power program after transition compression

```
11: a := b + 1;
    goto 12;

12: b := a + 1;
    goto 11;
```

Various heuristics are applied to obtain effective and non-overly-aggressive transition compression. We will discuss two strategies in Section 3.3.

Assessment We have seen the online partial evaluation can be viewed as a three step process: (1) collect all reachable states, (2) program point specialization, (3) transition compression.

There were some opportunities for specialization that we did not pursue.

– *Algebraic properties:* The multiplication operation in

```
    result := *(1 m);
```

could be further reduced to

```
    result := m;
```

using the knowledge that 1 is the identity element for multiplication. However, most partial evaluators do not incorporate such transformations since they will be taken care of by an optimizing compiler.
– *Unfolding variables:* In the following code,

```
    result := *(1 m);
    result := *(result m);
```

this first assignment could be unfolded into the second to obtain

```
    result := *(*(1 m) m);
```

This gives one less assignment operation. However, applying this transformation indiscriminately can cause code-size blowup and duplicate computation. For example, transforming the code below

```
    x := +(y 2);
    z := *(*(x x) x);
```

yields

```
    z := *(*(+(y 2) +(y 2)) +(y 2));
```

One can use a counting analysis to tell when unfolding will not cause code explosion. As with the use of algebraic identities above, it is generally best to leave these types of transformations to the compiler.

3.2 Handling branching and infinite abtract traces

The structure of the abstract trace of the power program in the preceding section had a particularly simple structure: it was finite and non-branching. In this section, we see how to handle more complicated traces.

Handling branching traces When specializing the power program in the preceding section, we were always able to decide which branch to execute in a conditional jump because the tests in the conditional jumps only depended on static data. Thus, the trace that we constructed when collecting all reachable configurations corresponded to a single non-branching path through the computation tree (see Figure 8).

In general, specializing a program may lead to a conditional whose test depends on dynamic data. In this case, we cannot decide which branch of the conditional to execute at specialization time — we have to consider the possibility that *either* branch of the conditional can be executed when the residual program is run. Thus, we need to residualize the conditional, and generate abstract traces for *both* branches of the condition. This leads to traces that are not just single non-branching paths, but instead to traces that branch at each dynamic conditional.

When generating an abstract trace for the program of Figure 12 using the initial store $[a \mapsto D, b \mapsto 2]$, the conditional in init cannot be decided. Therefore, we have two possible successor states $(\text{less}, [a \mapsto D, b \mapsto 2])$ and $(\text{more}, [a \mapsto D, b \mapsto 2])$, and we must continue building the trace from both of these.

In coding up an algorithm to generate branching abstract traces, we can handle branching traces using a *pending set* $\mathcal{P}$ of states that have yet to be processed. Managing the set in a LIFO manner gives a depth-first generation of the trace. For example, the steps in depth-first generation are as follows.

Processing	Pending Set $\mathcal{P}$
	$\{(\text{init}, [a \mapsto D, b \mapsto 2])\}$
$(\text{init}, [a \mapsto D, b \mapsto 2])$	$\{(\text{less}, [a \mapsto D, b \mapsto 2]), (\text{more}, [a \mapsto D, b \mapsto 2])\}$
$(\text{less}, [a \mapsto D, b \mapsto 2])$	$\{(\text{done}, [a \mapsto 2, b \mapsto 2]), (\text{more}, [a \mapsto D, b \mapsto 2])\}$
$(\text{done}, [a \mapsto 2, b \mapsto 2])$	$\{(\text{more}, [a \mapsto D, b \mapsto 2])\}$
$(\text{more}, [a \mapsto D, b \mapsto 2])$	$\{(\text{done}, [a \mapsto 0, b \mapsto 2])\}$
$(\text{done}, [a \mapsto 0, b \mapsto 2])$	$\emptyset$

Here, we begin with the initial state in $\mathcal{P}$ and continue until $\mathcal{P}$ is empty. Note, that we do not need to insert halt states into $\mathcal{P}$ since we know that they will have no successors. We have described $\mathcal{P}$ as a *set* because one can process the pending states in any order (*e.g.*, LIFO or FIFO).

Handling infinite traces with repeating states Figure 13 gives a flowchart program that will compute $m \times n \times term$. When this program is specialized wrt $n = 2$, the test at block test-n can be decided, but the test at block

```
(a b)
(init)

 init: if <(a 10)
          then less
          else greater;

 less: a := b;
       goto done;

 more: a := 0;
       goto done;

 done: return +(a b);
```

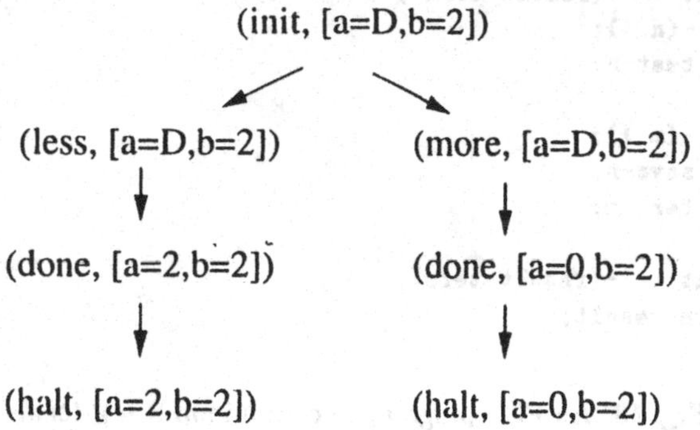

(init, [a=D,b=2])

(less, [a=D,b=2])   (more, [a=D,b=2])

(done, [a=2,b=2])   (done, [a=0,b=2])

(halt, [a=2,b=2])   (halt, [a=0,b=2])

Fig. 12. FCL program with branching abstract trace for $[a \mapsto D, b \mapsto 2]$

```
(m n term)
(init)

  init:   result := term;
          save-n := n;
          goto test-m;

  test-m: if <(0 m)
            then test-n
            else done-m;

  test-n: if <(0 n)
            then loop
            else done-n;

  loop:   result := +(result term);
          n := -(n 1);
          goto test-n;

  done-n: m := -(m 1);
          n := save-n;
          goto test-m;

  done-m: result := -(result term);
          return result;
```

Fig. 13. An FCL program to compute $m \times n \times term$

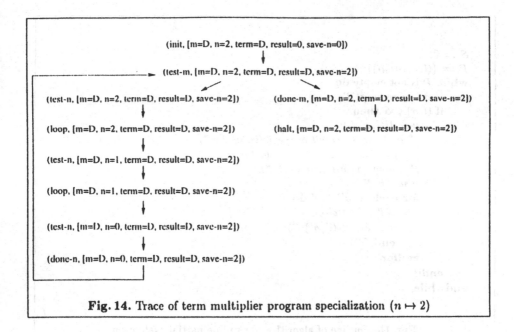

Fig. 14. Trace of term multiplier program specialization ($n \mapsto 2$)

test-m cannot. Thus, each time we process test-m we will generate two following configurations: one for test-n and one for done-m.

Figure 14 shows the trace that generates reachable configurations when specializing the program with respect to $n \mapsto 2$. Besides the branching path, there is another important difference from the power program specialization. In this example, if one always follows the true branch from the test-m node, a halt node will never be reached. Conceptually, a trace where only true branches are chosen from test-m is infinite, but in fact, a point will be reached where the configurations in the trace start to repeat themselves — that is, the trace contains a cycle. When we come to a configuration that we have already seen before, we can safely stop that branch of the trace because we know we have included all reachable configurations along that branch.

To deal with *branching traces* and *potentially infinite traces with repeating states*, partial evaluators include two data structures:

- a "seen before" set S containing the configurations that have already be processed, and
- a "pending" set P containing the configurations that are waiting to be processed.

Taking R to be a list of residual program blocks, and $(l_{init}, \sigma_{init})$ to be the initial configuration for specialization, the basic algorithm for online partial evaluation (without transition compression) is given in Figure 15.

Partial evaluation begins with an empty seen-before set S and the initial configuration in the pending set P. While the pending set is not empty, we repeatedly pull a configuration off the pending set, create a specialized block for

```
S := ∅;
P := {(l_init, σ_init)};
while P is not empty do
    (l, σ) := remove(P);
    if (l, σ) ∉ S then
        insert((l, σ), S);
        /* let b' be the result of specializing the */
        /* block labelled l and let N be the new */
        /* configurations generated. */
        insert(b', R);
        for each (l', σ') ∈ N do
            if l' ≠ halt then
                insert((l', σ'), P);
            endif
        endfor
    endif
endwhile
```

Fig. 15. Outline of algorithm for online partial evaluation

that configuration, get the new configurations N that result from processing the current block l, and we add these to the pending set. The function $remove(P)$ updates P by removing a state (l, σ) and returns the state as a result. Similarly, *insert* updates a set or list by adding the given element.

From an abstract view, the algorithm collects the reachable configurations from the computation tree and generates a specialized block for configuration. The pending set P holds a frontier of the tree of reachable nodes, and the S holds all the nodes in the tree above the frontier.

Notice that each iteration of the **while** loop transforms the pending set P, the seen before set S, and the residual program R. In the next section, we will give an abstract presentation of the algorithm of Figure 15, and each iteration of the **while** loop will correspond to a transition

$$\langle P, S, R \rangle \longmapsto \langle P', S', R' \rangle.$$

Using this notation, the transition sequence below shows the first few iterations of the online partial evaluation algorithm when specializing the term multiplier program with respect to n ↦ 2. Here, b_1, b_2, b_3, and b_4 represent the specialized versions of init, test-m, test-n, and loop, respectively (generating these specialized versions is left as an exercise for the reader).

$$\left\langle \begin{array}{l} \{(\text{init}, [\text{m} \mapsto D, \text{n} \mapsto 2, \text{term} \mapsto D, \text{result} \mapsto 0, \text{save-n} \mapsto 0])\}, \\ \emptyset, \\ . \end{array} \right\rangle$$

$$\longmapsto \left\langle \begin{array}{l} \{(\text{test-m}, [\text{m} \mapsto D, \text{n} \mapsto 2, \text{term} \mapsto D, \text{result} \mapsto D, \text{save-n} \mapsto 2])\}, \\ \{(\text{init}, [\text{m} \mapsto D, \text{n} \mapsto 2, \text{term} \mapsto D, \text{result} \mapsto 0, \text{save-n} \mapsto 0])\}, \\ b_1 \end{array} \right\rangle$$

$$\longmapsto \left\langle \begin{array}{l} \{(\text{test-n}, [\text{m} \mapsto D, \text{n} \mapsto 2, \text{term} \mapsto D, \text{result} \mapsto D, \text{save-n} \mapsto 2]), \\ (\text{done-m}, [\text{m} \mapsto D, \text{n} \mapsto 2, \text{term} \mapsto D, \text{result} \mapsto D, \text{save-n} \mapsto 2])\}, \\ \{(\text{init}, [\text{m} \mapsto D, \text{n} \mapsto 2, \text{term} \mapsto D, \text{result} \mapsto 0, \text{save-n} \mapsto 0]), \\ (\text{test-m}, [\text{m} \mapsto D, \text{n} \mapsto 2, \text{term} \mapsto D, \text{result} \mapsto D, \text{save-n} \mapsto 2])\}, \\ b_1 \, b_2 \end{array} \right\rangle$$

$$\longmapsto \left\langle \begin{array}{l} \{(\text{loop}, [\text{m} \mapsto D, \text{n} \mapsto 2, \text{term} \mapsto D, \text{result} \mapsto D, \text{save-n} \mapsto 2]), \\ (\text{done-m}, [\text{m} \mapsto D, \text{n} \mapsto 2, \text{term} \mapsto D, \text{result} \mapsto D, \text{save-n} \mapsto 2])\}, \\ \{(\text{init}, [\text{m} \mapsto D, \text{n} \mapsto 2, \text{term} \mapsto D, \text{result} \mapsto 0, \text{save-n} \mapsto 0]), \\ (\text{test-m}, [\text{m} \mapsto D, \text{n} \mapsto 2, \text{term} \mapsto D, \text{result} \mapsto D, \text{save-n} \mapsto 2]), \\ (\text{test-n}, [\text{m} \mapsto D, \text{n} \mapsto 2, \text{term} \mapsto D, \text{result} \mapsto D, \text{save-n} \mapsto 2])\}, \\ b_1 \, b_2 \, b_3 \end{array} \right\rangle$$

$$\longmapsto \left\langle \begin{array}{l} \{(\text{test-n}, [\text{m} \mapsto D, \text{n} \mapsto 1, \text{term} \mapsto D, \text{result} \mapsto D, \text{save-n} \mapsto 2]), \\ (\text{done-m}, [\text{m} \mapsto D, \text{n} \mapsto 2, \text{term} \mapsto D, \text{result} \mapsto D, \text{save-n} \mapsto 2])\}, \\ \{(\text{init}, [\text{m} \mapsto D, \text{n} \mapsto 2, \text{term} \mapsto D, \text{result} \mapsto 0, \text{save-n} \mapsto 0]), \\ (\text{test-m}, [\text{m} \mapsto D, \text{n} \mapsto 2, \text{term} \mapsto D, \text{result} \mapsto D, \text{save-n} \mapsto 2]), \\ (\text{test-n}, [\text{m} \mapsto D, \text{n} \mapsto 2, \text{term} \mapsto D, \text{result} \mapsto D, \text{save-n} \mapsto 2]), \\ (\text{loop}, [\text{m} \mapsto D, \text{n} \mapsto 2, \text{term} \mapsto D, \text{result} \mapsto D, \text{save-n} \mapsto 2]), \}, \\ b_1 \, b_2 \, b_3 \, b_4 \end{array} \right\rangle$$

$$\longmapsto \ldots$$

3.3 Semantics of online partial evaluation

We now formalize the online partial evaluation outlined in Figure 15. We do this using an operational semantics that follows the same structure as the interpreter for FCL given in Figure 6 of Chapter 2.

To understand how the semantics changes when moving from interpretation to partial evaluation, notice that processing each expression in Section 3.1 yielded either a value (if the expression depended on only static variables) or a chunk of code (if the expression depended on dynamic variables). For example, in the block

```
loop: result := *(result m);
      n := -(n 1);
      goto test;
```

processing the expression -(n 1) always produced a value, whereas processing the expression *(result m) always produced a chunk of code. To capture this, when our partial evaluator will always produce one of the following types of results (which we call *pe-values*) when processing expressions.

- Processing an expression that only depends on static variables returns a pair $\langle S, v \rangle$ where v is the resulting value.
- Processing an expression that depends on a dynamic variable returns a pair $\langle D, e \rangle$ where e is the resulting piece of code.

Semantic values Figure 16 presents the definition of partial evaluation for expressions and assignments. We first discuss the semantic values. As noted above, the essential difference between the semantic values used in interpretation and those used in partial evaluation is that partial evaluation manipulates pe-values: tagged objects $\langle S, v \rangle, \langle D, e \rangle \in$ PE-Values[FCL].

A store σ will hold pe-values as well.

- If a variable x has a known value v, then we will have $\sigma(x) = \langle S, v \rangle$.
- If a variable x has an unknown value, then we will have $\sigma(x) = \langle D, x \rangle$.

This ensures that whenever we look x up in σ, we will either get the appropriate value for x (v), or the appropriate piece of code for x (x). For example, we would use the store below as the initial store when specializing the power program to $n \mapsto 2$:

$$[\mathtt{m} \mapsto \langle D, \mathtt{m} \rangle, \mathtt{n} \mapsto \langle S, 2 \rangle, \mathtt{result} \mapsto \langle S, 0 \rangle].$$

The other semantic domains are the same as in FCL interpretation.

Expressions The judgement giving the partial evaluation of expressions has the form $\sigma \vdash_{expr} e \Rightarrow w$. The value of value of constant c is always known, and so $\langle S, [\![c]\!] \rangle$ is returned (recall that $[\![c]\!] \in$ Values[FCL] is the constant's semantic value). Given the above strategy of representing variable values in the store, $\sigma(x)$ always produces the correct result for partial evaluating a variable.

The rules for operations are the most interesting. The first operation rule covers the case where all the argument values are known. In this case, we can simply apply the operation to the argument values and return the resulting value (marked as static).

The second rule covers the case where at least one of the argument values is unknown (that is, at least one of the pe-values has the form $\langle D, e'' \rangle$). In this case, the operation cannot be evaluated, and so it must be reconstructed ($\langle D, o(e_1' \ldots e_n') \rangle$ is returned). However, there is still a subtle issue regarding what code to generate for the arguments e_i'. If specializing e_k yielded $\langle D, e_k'' \rangle$, then clearly e_k'' should be the code that is residualized for e_k. But if e_k yielded $\langle S, v_k'' \rangle$, we need to return the *code* corresponding to v_k''. That is, we need to return the constant that computes to v_k''

Expressions

$$\overline{\sigma \vdash_{expr} c \Rightarrow \langle S, [\![c]\!]\rangle} \qquad\qquad \overline{\sigma \vdash_{expr} x \Rightarrow \sigma(x)}$$

$$\frac{\sigma \vdash_{expr} e_i \Rightarrow \langle S, v_i\rangle \quad [\![o]\!](v_1 \dots v_n) = v}{\sigma \vdash_{expr} o(e_1 \dots e_n) \Rightarrow \langle S, v\rangle}$$

$$\frac{\sigma \vdash_{expr} e_i \Rightarrow w_i \quad w_i \Uparrow e_i' \quad \exists j \in \{1..n\} . w_j = \langle D, e\rangle}{\sigma \vdash_{expr} o(e_1 \dots e_n) \Rightarrow \langle D, o(e_1' \dots e_n')\rangle}$$

Lifting

$$\overline{\langle S, v\rangle \Uparrow [\![v]\!]^{-1}} \qquad\qquad \overline{\langle D, e\rangle \Uparrow e}$$

Assignments

$$\frac{\sigma \vdash_{expr} e \Rightarrow \langle S, v\rangle}{\sigma \vdash_{assign} x := e; \Rightarrow \langle \sigma[x \mapsto \langle S, v\rangle], [\,]\rangle}$$

$$\frac{\sigma \vdash_{expr} e \Rightarrow \langle D, e'\rangle}{\sigma \vdash_{assign} x := e; \Rightarrow \langle \sigma[x \mapsto \langle D, x\rangle], [x := e';]\rangle}$$

$$\overline{\sigma \vdash_{assigns} \cdot \Rightarrow \langle \sigma, [\,]\rangle}$$

$$\frac{\sigma \vdash_{assign} a \Rightarrow \langle \sigma', al'\rangle \quad \sigma' \vdash_{assigns} al \Rightarrow \langle \sigma'', al''\rangle}{\sigma \vdash_{assigns} a\ al \Rightarrow \langle \sigma'', al' +\!\!+ al''\rangle}$$

Semantic Values

$$
\begin{array}{ll}
v \in \text{Values[FCL]} & = \{0, 1, 2, \dots\} \\
w \in \text{PE-Values[FCL]} & = (\{S\} \times \text{Values[FCL]}) \cup (\{D\} \times \text{Expressions[FCL]}) \\
l \in \text{Labels[FCL]} & = \text{Block-Labels[FCL]} \cup \{\text{halt}\} \\
\sigma \in \text{Stores[FCL]} & = \text{Variables[FCL]} \rightharpoonup \text{PE-Values[FCL]} \\
\Gamma \in \text{Block-Maps[FCL]} & = \text{Block-Labels[FCL]} \rightharpoonup \text{Blocks[FCL]}
\end{array}
$$

Fig. 16. Online partial evaluation for FCL programs (part 1)

Jumps

$$\frac{}{\sigma \vdash_{jump} \textbf{goto } l; \Rightarrow \langle \{l\} , \textbf{goto } (l,\sigma); \rangle}$$

$$\frac{\sigma \vdash_{expr} e \Rightarrow w \qquad w \Uparrow e'}{\sigma \vdash_{jump} \textbf{return } e; \Rightarrow \langle \{\textbf{halt}\} , \textbf{return } e'; \rangle}$$

$$\frac{\sigma \vdash_{expr} e \Rightarrow \langle S , v \rangle \qquad \text{is-true?}(v)}{\sigma \vdash_{jump} \textbf{if } e \textbf{ then } l_1 \textbf{ else } l_2; \Rightarrow \langle \{l_1\} , \textbf{goto } (l_1,\sigma); \rangle}$$

$$\frac{\sigma \vdash_{expr} e \Rightarrow \langle S , v \rangle \qquad \text{is-false?}(v)}{\sigma \vdash_{jump} \textbf{if } e \textbf{ then } l_1 \textbf{ else } l_2; \Rightarrow \langle \{l_2\} , \textbf{goto } (l_2,\sigma); \rangle}$$

$$\frac{\sigma \vdash_{expr} e \Rightarrow \langle D , e' \rangle}{\sigma \vdash_{jump} \textbf{if } e \textbf{ then } l_1 \textbf{ else } l_2; \Rightarrow \langle \{l_1,l_2\} , \textbf{if } e' \textbf{ then } (l_1,\sigma) \textbf{ else } (l_2,\sigma); \rangle}$$

Blocks

$$\frac{\sigma \vdash_{assigns} al \Rightarrow \langle \sigma_1 , al_1 \rangle \qquad \sigma_1 \vdash_{jump} j \Rightarrow \langle \{l_{2_i} \mid i \in \{1, \dots n\}\} , j_2 \rangle}{\sigma \vdash_{block} l : al\ j \Rightarrow \langle \{(l_{2_i},\sigma_1) \mid i \in \{1, \dots n\}\} , (l,\sigma) : al_1\ j_2 \rangle} \quad \text{where } n \in \{1,2\}$$

Transitions

$$\frac{\sigma \vdash_{block} \Gamma(l) \Rightarrow \langle \{(l'_i,\sigma'_i) . \mid i \in \{1, \dots n\}\} , b' \rangle}{\begin{array}{l} \vdash_r \langle (l,\sigma) :: \mathcal{P} , \mathcal{S} , \mathcal{R} \rangle \longmapsto \langle \mathcal{P}_{new} +\!\!+ \mathcal{P} , \mathcal{S} \cup (l,\sigma) , b' :: \mathcal{R} \rangle \\ \text{where } \mathcal{P}_{new} = \text{remove-halts}([(l'_1,\sigma'_1), \dots , (l'_n,\sigma'_n)]) \end{array}} \quad \text{if } (l,\sigma) \notin \mathcal{S}$$

$$\vdash_r \langle (l,\sigma) :: \mathcal{P} , \mathcal{S} , \mathcal{R} \rangle \longmapsto \langle \mathcal{P} , \mathcal{S} , \mathcal{R} \rangle \qquad \text{if } (l,\sigma) \in \mathcal{S}$$

Fig. 17. Online partial evaluation for FCL programs (part 2)

The process of converting a semantic value to a piece of code for the purpose of residualization is called *lifting* (symbolized by $\Uparrow$). We use two lifting rules that will return a piece of code for any given pe-value. If the pe-value is static ($\langle S, v\rangle$), the constant corresponding to v is returned. The appropriate constant is given using the inverse of $[\![\cdot]\!]$ (which we write as $[\![\cdot]\!]^{-1}$). The inverse function exists since $[\![\cdot]\!]$ is required to be injective. If the pe-value is dynamic ($\langle D, e\rangle$), then the D tag is simply stripped off and the code e is returned.

As examples, the following derivations show the partial evaluation of power program expressions $*(\text{result m})$ and $-(\text{n } 1)$ using the store

$$\sigma = [\text{m} \mapsto \langle D, \text{m}\rangle, \text{n} \mapsto \langle S, 2\rangle, \text{result} \mapsto \langle S, 1\rangle].$$

$*(\text{result m})$:

$$\nabla_1 = \frac{\sigma \vdash_{expr} \text{result} \Rightarrow \langle S, 1\rangle \quad \sigma \vdash_{expr} \text{m} \Rightarrow \langle D, \text{m}\rangle \quad \langle S, 1\rangle \Uparrow 1 \quad \langle D, \text{m}\rangle \Uparrow \text{m}}{\sigma \vdash_{expr} *(\text{result m}) \Rightarrow \langle D, *(1\,\text{m})\rangle}$$

$-(\text{n } 1)$:

$$\nabla_2 = \frac{\sigma' \vdash_{expr} \text{n} \Rightarrow \langle S, 2\rangle \quad \sigma' \vdash_{expr} 1 \Rightarrow \langle S, 1\rangle \quad [\![-]\!](2\,1)}{\sigma' \vdash_{expr} -(\text{n } 1) \Rightarrow \langle S, 1\rangle}$$

where $\sigma' = \sigma[\text{result} \mapsto \langle D, \text{result}\rangle]$.

Assignments The strategy for handling an assignment is simple:

- if the right-hand side of an assignment $x := e$; is a static value v, then the assignment is computed (x is bound to $\langle S, v\rangle$ in the updated store), and
- if the right-hand side of the assignment is dynamic (returns $\langle D, e'\rangle$), then the residual assignment $x := e'$; is generated, and x is bound to $\langle D, x\rangle$ in the updated store.

Residual assignments are returned in lists so that they can easily be appended to the result of processing a list of assignments. Thus, in the former case, an empty list is returned. In the latter case, a singleton list is returned. There are two rules for processing assignment lists. The first simply returns the same store and an empty residual assignment list. The second appends the result of processing the first assignment to the result of processing the rest of the assignment list ($+\!\!\!+$ is the append operation).

Here are some example derivations. For $\text{result} := *(\text{result m})$; we have

$$\nabla_3 = \frac{\begin{array}{c}\nabla_1 \\ \sigma \vdash_{expr} *(\text{result m}) \Rightarrow \langle D, *(1\,\text{m})\rangle\end{array}}{\sigma \vdash_{expr} \text{result} := *(\text{result m}); \Rightarrow \langle \sigma', [\text{result} := *(1\,\text{m});]\rangle}$$

where $\sigma' = \sigma[\text{result} \mapsto \langle D, \text{result} \rangle]$. For n := -(n 1); we have

$$\nabla_4 = \frac{\nabla_2}{\sigma' \vdash_{expr} -(\text{n 1}) \Rightarrow \langle S, 1 \rangle}{\sigma' \vdash_{expr} \text{n := -(n 1);} \Rightarrow \langle \sigma'', [] \rangle}$$

where $\sigma'' = \sigma'[\text{n} \mapsto \langle S, 1 \rangle]$. Now, using the following abbreviations

$$a_1 = \text{result := *(result m);}$$
$$a_1' = \text{result := *(1 m);}$$
$$a_2 = \text{n := -(n 1);}$$

we have the following derivation ∇_5.

$$\frac{\nabla_3 \qquad \dfrac{\dfrac{\nabla_4}{\sigma' \vdash_{assign} a_2 \Rightarrow \langle \sigma'', [] \rangle} \quad \overline{\sigma'' \vdash_{assigns} \cdot \Rightarrow \langle \sigma'', [] \rangle}}{\sigma' \vdash_{assigns} a_2 \Rightarrow \langle \sigma'', [] \rangle}}{\sigma \vdash_{assign} a_1 \Rightarrow \langle \sigma', [a_1'] \rangle \qquad \sigma \vdash_{assigns} a_1 a_2 \Rightarrow \langle \sigma'', [a_1'] \rangle}$$

Jumps Figure 17 presents the rest of the definition of online partial evaluation. This figure defines partial evaluation *without* transition compression (excluding transition compression makes the definition easier to understand). Transition compression will be defined in the following section.

The specialization semantics of jumps is given by the following judgement form

$$\sigma \vdash_{jump} j \Rightarrow \langle S, j' \rangle$$

where $S \subseteq \text{Labels[FCL]} \times \text{Stores[FCL]}$ is a set of destination states, and j' is the jump to be placed in the residual program.

Specializing **goto** l; with store σ means that the residual program should **goto** the version of the block labeled l that is specialized with respect to σ (*i.e.*, the residual block labeled (l, σ). Specializing **return** x; simply copies that jump to the residual program. Note that it doesn't make sense to "execute" the **return** x; jump during partial evaluation even if x has a static value. Doing so would terminate the specialization process with a value. If we have passed through a dynamic conditional, there maybe more than one possible return value, and we cannot be sure that the current one is the correct one. More fundamentally, partial evaluation should produce a residual *program* that computes a value — not the value itself.

Proper treatment of conditional jumps is one of the most interesting aspects of partial evaluation. If the test expression of an **if** is static, then the **if** can be computed at specialization time. If the test result is true, then the label l_1 for the true branch is returned, and in the residual program we jump directly *via* **goto** (l_1, σ); to the version of block l_1 that is specialized with respect to σ (similarly, if the test result is false).

If the test expression is dynamic, then the **if** cannot be computed at specialization time — it must placed in the residual program. The residual **if** will cause a jump to the version of block l_1 and is specialized with respect to σ if the test is true, otherwise there will be a jump to the specialized block (l_2, σ). A set of labels $\{l_1, l_2\}$ is returned corresponding to branch in the computation tree of the residual program.

Below is the derivation for the jump in our example block from the power program.

$$\nabla_6 = \overline{\sigma'' \vdash_{jump} \textbf{goto test;} \Rightarrow \langle \{\textbf{test}\}, \textbf{goto (test}, \sigma''); \rangle}$$

Blocks For a block $l : al\ j$, we just

1. call the specializer on the assignment list al (obtaining a new store σ' and residual assignments al'
2. call the specializer on the jump j with store σ' and obtain a set of destination labels and a residual jump j.

The set of residual labels is going to contain one label if the jump is a **goto**, **return**, or a static **if**. It the jump is a dynamic **if**, it will contain two labels.

Using the abbreviations below (along with the ones previously introduced),

$$al = al_1\ al_2$$
$$al' = a_1'$$
$$j = \textbf{goto test;}$$
$$j' = \textbf{goto (test}, \sigma'');$$

we have the derivation

$$\nabla_7 = \frac{\overset{\nabla_5}{\sigma \vdash_{assigns} al \Rightarrow \langle \sigma'', al' \rangle} \quad \overset{\nabla_6}{\sigma'' \vdash_{jump} j \Rightarrow \langle \{\textbf{test}\}, j' \rangle}}{\sigma \vdash_{block} \textbf{test} : al\ j \Rightarrow \langle \{(\textbf{test}, \sigma'')\}, (\textbf{test}, \sigma'') : al'\ j' \rangle}$$

Transitions The transition rules formalize the **while** loop of Figure 15. Recall that this loop repeatedly transforms a pending set $\mathcal{P}$, a seen-before set $\mathcal{S}$, and a list of residual blocks $\mathcal{R}$. Figure 17 implements $\mathcal{P}$ with a stack used in a LIFO manner (*i.e.*, as a stack). This gives a depth-first generation of the trace that forms the structure of the residual program. In fact, one can safely processing the pending set in any order (*e.g.*, breadth-first), but it is typically done in a depth-first manner.

The first rule for transitions covers the case where the next item on the pending list has not been seen before. In this case, the state (l, σ) is removed from the pending list, and the specializer is called to process the block with label l. Given a list of states L, remove-halts(L) filters out states (l_j, σ_j) in L where $l_j = $ halt. Thus, non-halt destination states that result from specializing are added to the pending list. In addition, the processed state (l, σ) is added to the seen before set $\mathcal{S}$, and the residual block b' is added to the residual blocks $\mathcal{R}$.

Blocks

$$\frac{\sigma \vdash_{assigns} al \Rightarrow \langle \sigma_1, al_1 \rangle \quad \sigma_1 \vdash_{jump} j \Rightarrow \langle \{l_{2_i} \mid i \in \{1, \ldots n\}\}, j_2 \rangle}{\sigma \vdash_{block} l: al\ j \Rightarrow \langle \{(l_{2_i}, \sigma_1) \mid i \in \{1, \ldots n\}\}, (l, \sigma): al_1\ j_2 \rangle} \quad \text{where } j_2 \neq \textbf{goto } l';$$

$$\frac{\sigma \vdash_{assigns} al \Rightarrow \langle \sigma_1, al_1 \rangle \quad \sigma_1 \vdash_{jump} j \Rightarrow \langle \{l_2\}, \textbf{goto } (l_2, \sigma_2); \rangle \quad \sigma_2 \vdash_{block} \Gamma(l_2) \Rightarrow \langle \{(l_{3_i}, \sigma_{3_i}) \mid i \in \{1, \ldots n\}\}, l_2': al_2\ j_2 \rangle}{\sigma \vdash_{block} l: al\ j \Rightarrow \langle \{(l_{3_i}, \sigma_{3_i}) \mid i \in \{1, \ldots n\}\}, (l, \sigma): al_1 \mathbin{+\!\!+} al_2\ j_2 \rangle}$$

Fig. 18. Online partial evaluation with on-the-fly transition compression

---

The second rule for transitions covers the case where the next item on the pending list $\mathcal{P}$ has been seen before. In this case, the item is simply removed from $\mathcal{P}$ and processing continues. Notice that there will not be a transition when $\mathcal{P}$ is empty. Thus, the rules of Figure 17 exactly formalize the algorithm of Figure 15.

Definition 4 (online partial evaluation). Let $p = (x_1 \ldots x_n)\ (l)\ b^+$ be a well-formed program. Let the *static parameters* $(x_1^s \ldots x_m^s)$ be a subset (when the list is viewed as a set) of p's parameters. Let the *dynamic parameters* $(x_1^d \ldots x_o^d)$ be the remainder of p's parameters. Let $(x_1^i \ldots x_q^i)$ be p's internal variables (those not occuring as parameters). Let Γ be the blockmap for p.

Define online partial evaluation $[\![\cdot]\!]_{\text{onpe}}$ as follows:

$$[\![p]\!]_{\text{onpe}}(x_1^s, \ldots, x_m^s)(v_1, \ldots, v_m) \overset{\text{def}}{=}$$

$$\begin{cases} p_{res} & \text{if } \vdash_\Gamma \langle [(l, \sigma_{init})], \emptyset, [] \rangle \rightarrow^* \langle [], \mathcal{S}, \mathcal{R} \rangle \\ \text{undefined} & \text{otherwise.} \end{cases}$$

where

$$\sigma_{init} = \begin{bmatrix} x_1^s \mapsto \langle \mathcal{S}, v_1 \rangle, \ldots, x_m^s \mapsto \langle \mathcal{S}, v_m \rangle \\ x_1^d \mapsto \langle \mathcal{D}, x_1^d \rangle, \ldots, x_o^d \mapsto \langle \mathcal{D}, x_o^d \rangle \\ x_1^i \mapsto \langle \mathcal{S}, 0 \rangle, \ldots, x_q^i \mapsto \langle \mathcal{S}, 0 \rangle \end{bmatrix}$$

and $v_j \in \text{Values[FCL]}$, and

$$p_{res} = (x_1^d \ldots x_o^d)\ ((l, \sigma_{init}))\ \mathcal{R}.$$

Including transition compression A simple approach to transition compression is to compress transitions for all static **goto**'s and **if**'s on the fly during specialization [15, Chapter 4]. Incorporating this approach into our specialization semantics is straightforward: we only need to change the treatment of blocks. Figure 18 shows that we simply look to see if the generated residual jump is a

goto (which is what results when processing a **goto** or a static **if**). If it is, we immediately process the destination block and merge the results. This process is continued until a **return** or dynamic **if** is encountered.

For example, in the power program of Figure 1, the only block that does not end in a **goto** or static **if** is the final block **end** (it ends with a **return**. So using the formalization in Figures 16 and 17 with the definition of transition compression in Figure 18 yields the compressed residual power program in Figure 11. Intuitively, we will start with the **init** block and simply accumulate all dynamic assignments until we reach the **return result**; jump.

In Section 3.1 we noted that there are various subtleties involving transition compression. Naive transition compression can

1. cause the partial evaluator to go into an infinite loop on certain programs, or
2. lead to an increase in residual code size due to the loss of code sharing.

To illustrate the first problem, consider the program at the top of Figure 19. Although the program loops infinitely for any input value, specialization without transition compression (taking z to be dynamic, *i.e.*, no static information is supplied) terminates. The residual program is the second program in Figure 19. Termination is achieved because the state $(b2, [x \mapsto 1, y \mapsto D, z \mapsto D])$ which is reached upon exiting block **b3** will be found in the seen-before set.

In contrast, specialization with transition compression (as defined in Figure 18) will go into an infinite loop since compressing the **goto** at the end of block **b1** means that an entry for block **b2** will never be made in the seen-before set. If fact, the seen-before set is never consulted for this program since **goto**'s are the only form of jumps encountered.

In most of the partial evaluation literature, it is considered acceptable for the specializer to loop on some given static data if the source program always loops on the same static data. Taking this view, the problem of non-termination described above is acceptable, because the transition compression strategy will only lead to looping if the source program always loops on the given static data.

To illustrate the second problem (loss of code sharing) with the approach to transition compression of Figure 18, consider the program at the top of Figure 20. Now consider specializing x to 3 (with z dynamic) using specialization with the transition compression of Figure 18 (the residual program is given in Figure 20 along with the residual program for specialization without transition compression). On the first pass through the program, the **goto**'s in blocks **b1** and **b2** will be compressed. Thus, no entries will be made for **b2** and **b3** in the seen-before set. This means that when processing the true branch of the **if** in **b3**, that state $(b2, [x \mapsto 4, y \mapsto D, z \mapsto D])$ is inserted into the pending list even though we have already (in some sense) seen it before and generated code for it. However, this code lies in the middle of block of the residual block $(b1, [3,0,D])$ and there is no way to jump to it directly. Thus, we must duplicate the residual code for state $(b2, [x \mapsto 4, y \mapsto D, z \mapsto D])$. The residual code if <>(4 y) ... for state $(b3, [x \mapsto 4, y \mapsto D, z \mapsto D])$ is duplicated for similar reasons.

```
Source program

(z)
(b1)

   b1: x := 1;                       b3: x := 1;
       y := z;                           goto b2;
       goto b2;


   b2: x := +(x 1);
       y := +(y 1);
       goto b3;
```

Specialization without transition compression

```
(z)
((b1,[0,0,D])

   (b1,[0,0,D]): y := z;             (b3, [2,D,D]): goto (b2, [1,D,D]);
                 goto (b2,[1,D,D]);

   (b2, [1,D,D]: y := +(y 1);
                 goto (b3, [2,D,D]);
```

Post-processing transition compression as in Similix

```
(z)
((b1,[0,0,D])

   (b1,[0,0,D]): y := z;
                 goto (b2,[1,D,D]);

   (b2, [1,D,D]: y := +(y 1);
                 goto (b2, [1,D,D]);
```

Fig. 19. Illustrating possible non-termination of transition compression

Source program

```
(x z)
(b1)

 b1: x := +(x 1);              b3: if <>(x y) then b2 else b4;
     y := z;
     goto b2;

 b2: y := +(y 1);              b4: return y;
     goto b3;
```

Specialization without transition compression (x=3)

```
(z)
((b1,[3,0,D])

 (b1,[3,0,D]): y := z;                (b3,[4,D,D]):
               goto (b2,[4,D,D]);      if <>(4 y) then (b2,[4,D,D])
                                                 else (b4,[4,D,D]);

 (b2,[4,D,D]): y := +(y 1);           (b4,[4,D,D]):
               goto (b3, [4,D,D]);     return y;
```

Specialization with on-the-fly transition compression of Figure 18

```
(z)
((b1,[3,0,D])

 (b1,[3,0,D]): y := z;
               y := +(y 1);
               if <>(4 y) then (b2,[4,D,D])
                          else (b4,[4,D,D]);

 (b2,[4,D,D]): y := +(y 1);
               if <>(4 y) then (b2,[4,D,D])
                          else (b4,[4,D,D]);

 (b4,[4,D,D]): return y;
```

Post-processing transition compression as in Similix

```
(z)
((b1,[3,0,D])

 (b1,[3,0,D]): y := z;

 (b2,[4,D,D]): y := +(y 1);
               if <>(4 y) then (b2,[4,D,D])
                          else (b4,[4,D,D]);

 (b4,[4,D,D]): return y;
```

Fig. 20. Illustrating the loss of sharing due to transition compression

Instead of the on-the-fly transition compression given in Figure 18, one may adopt a post-processing strategy similar to the post-unfolding strategy used in Similix [2]. In this approach, one first generates a specialized block for each reachable state (as in the definition in Figures 16 and 17). Now, if a block l is the target of only one jump in the program, it is marked as unfoldable (meaning that a **goto** l; can be compressed). If a block l' is the target of two or blocks, it is marked as non-unfoldable (intuitively, compressing **goto** l'; would result in a loss of sharing). After this marking phase, the program is traversed and all **goto** transitions to unfoldable blocks are compressed. The last program of Figure 20 is the residual program that results from this approach.

This post-processing approach also avoids the problem of looping specialization induced purely by on-the-fly transition compression. All reachable cycles in the program must contain a block that is the target of at least two different blocks. This block would be non-unfoldable — thus, breaking the traversal of the cycle during transition compression. For example, post-processing the residual program (the second program) of Figure 19 yields the third program of Figure 19. Since (b2,[1,D,D]) is the target of blocks (b1,[0,0,D]) and (b3,[2,D,D]), **goto**'s to it are not compressed. However, the **goto** (b3,[2,D,D]); in block (b2,[1,D,D]) can be compressed since this is the only jump to (b3,[2,D,D]). It is important to note that even with this post-processing compression strategy, the specializer will still loop when there are an infinite number of reachable states.

Generalization When specializing, one usually wants as much static computation as possible — leading to the general view that "static is good, dynamic is bad". However, there are times when it is advantageous to have a particular construct be dynamic. Intentionally changing a construct's classification from static to dynamic is a form of *generalization*. Generalization is often used to avoid infinite specialization.

For example, consider specializing the power program to $m \mapsto 5$ instead of $n \mapsto 2$. Trying to accumulate all reachable configurations leads to the following infinite series of states.

$$(\text{init}, [m \mapsto 5, n \mapsto D, \text{result} \mapsto 0])$$
$$\rightarrow (\text{test}, [m \mapsto 5, n \mapsto D, \text{result} \mapsto 1])$$
$$\rightarrow (\text{loop}, [m \mapsto 5, n \mapsto D, \text{result} \mapsto 1])$$
$$\rightarrow (\text{test}, [m \mapsto 5, n \mapsto D, \text{result} \mapsto 5])$$
$$\rightarrow (\text{loop}, [m \mapsto 5, n \mapsto D, \text{result} \mapsto 5])$$
$$\rightarrow (\text{test}, [m \mapsto 5, n \mapsto D, \text{result} \mapsto 25])$$
$$\rightarrow (\text{loop}, [m \mapsto 5, n \mapsto D, \text{result} \mapsto 25])$$
$$\rightarrow (\text{test}, [m \mapsto 5, n \mapsto D, \text{result} \mapsto 125])$$
$$\rightarrow \ldots$$

The infinite trace situation is caused by a combination of two factors.

1. In the power program, the variable n is the *induction variable* — it controls the iteration. When n is known, the conditional controlling the loop in the power program is static, and the loop will be unfolded at specialization time. When n is unknown, we have a dynamic conditional and so we cannot tell how many times to unroll the loop.
2. The variable `result` is acting as an *accumulator*. Typically, the initial values of accumulators are given as constants in the program (so they are static). Here, the values used to update the accumulator (the values of variable m) are also known. Since `result`'s value is always known and always increasing, we have an infinite number of reachable configurations.

This is an instance of a general problem that occurs (in any language paradigm) when specializing code that uses an accumulator. Intuitively, we see that (a) knowing the value of `result` in this case is not dramatically increasing the amount of optimization, and (b) having `result` as static is leading to infinite specialization. Generalizing `result` from static to dynamic would solve the non-termination problem. One almost always wants to generalize an accumulating variable if the induction variable is unknown.

Tell handle situations like these, partial evaluators typically allow the user to force generalization by hand annotating the program. In FCL, we can incorporate this by adding an operator **gen** to expressions as follows.

$$e ::= \ldots \mid \mathbf{gen}\, e$$

gen is specialized using the following rule.

$$\frac{\sigma \vdash_{expr} e \Rightarrow w \qquad w \Uparrow e'}{\sigma \vdash_{expr} \mathbf{gen}\, e \Rightarrow \langle D, e' \rangle}$$

In essence, **gen** hard-codes a lifting operation. Of course, **gen** has meaning only when specializing, and it should be removed when executing the program (or the interpreter should be modified to ignore it).

Now we can changing the power program to use **gen** in the `init` block.

```
init: result := gen 1;
      goto test;
```

In this modified setting, generating reachable configurations when specializing to $m \mapsto 5$ would include the following transitions.

$$(\mathtt{init}, [\mathtt{m} \mapsto 5, \mathtt{n} \mapsto D, \mathtt{result} \mapsto 0])$$
$$\rightarrow (\mathtt{test}, [\mathtt{m} \mapsto 5, \mathtt{n} \mapsto D, \mathtt{result} \mapsto D])$$
$$\rightarrow (\mathtt{loop}, [\mathtt{m} \mapsto 5, \mathtt{n} \mapsto D, \mathtt{result} \mapsto D])$$
$$\rightarrow (\mathtt{test}, [\mathtt{m} \mapsto 5, \mathtt{n} \mapsto D, \mathtt{result} \mapsto D])$$

The state on the fourth line is identical to the one on the second line (we will find it in the seen-before set), and so the process terminates. Note that this sequence of states *is not* the complete trace of the power program. Since n is dynamic, the complete trace would be branching at each test node. The branches not shown above would include a state for block end.

3.4 Exercises

1. Show the values of the pending list $\mathcal{P}$, seen-before set $\mathcal{S}$, and the residual program for each partial evaluation transition (without on-the-fly transition compression) when specializing the power program to n = 2. Your solution should take the same form as the transitions for the term multiplier program at the end of Section 3.2.
2. Using the operational semantics specification of the online partial evaluator *with on-the-fly transition compression*, show the derivation for the specialization of the done-n block in the term multiplier program for the state shown at the bottom of the trace in Figure 14.
3. Extend the operational semantics specification of the partial evaluator to process lists and associated operations (car, cdr, cons, *etc.*).
4. **Project:** Following the operational semantics definition, program the FCL online partial evaluator in the language of your choice.
5. **Project:** Revise your implementation of the partial evaluator so that transition compression is performed as a post-processing step (by counting uses of blocks) as discussed at the end of Section 3.3.

3.5 Further reading

Some of the earliest work on online specialization of imperative languages is Ershov's work on "mixed computation" [8, 9] ([8] presents the now classic "power" example in an appendix). Meyer [21] gives techniques for online specialization of imperative programs. Marquard and Steensgaard [20] describe online partial evaluation of an imperative object-oriented language.

For functional languages, Glück and Klimov's work on supercompilation is a very clear and concise presentation of online specialization [10]. Consel and Khoo give a parameterized framework that incorporates both online and offline partial evaluation [4]. Ruf and Weise's work on Fuse [23, 24] is the most extensive work on online partial evaluation for functional languages.

4 Offline Partial Evaluation

This chapter introduces *offline partial evaluation* for FCL. There are several interesting trade-offs between online and offline partial evaluation. We will give a more detailed discussion of these trade-offs later. For now we will simply say that online partial evaluation is potentially more powerful but harder to control (*i.e.*, it is harder to ensure termination and compact residual code). There is anecdotal evidence that the offline strategy is better for handling the complex features of imperative languages such as pointers and side-effects.

4.1   Concepts

Online partial evaluation In FCL online partial evaluation, the task of distinguishing the constructs to be executed from those to be residualized was performed *online*, *i.e.*, as specialization was carried out. Partial evaluation of an expression e returned a tagged pe-value $\langle S, v \rangle$ or $\langle D, e' \rangle$. The tags S and D were checked to see if e could be executed, or if e had to be residualized.

For example, recall how the online FCL partial evaluator would have treated the following expression with the store $[a \mapsto \langle D, a \rangle, b \mapsto \langle S, 3 \rangle]$.

$$*(a + (b\ 2))$$

To handle the * operation, the partial evaluator would first process both arguments to see if the * operation should be executed or residualized. This would involve processing both arguments of the + operation. Processing b will return $\langle S, 3 \rangle$, and processing 2 will return $\langle S, 2 \rangle$. Since both the tags are static, we know the + operation can be executed — yielding $\langle S, 5 \rangle$. However, since processing a yields $\langle D, a \rangle$, the * operation must be residualized. This requires that the value 5 be lifted to the FCL constant 5.

Offline partial evaluation In offline partial evaluation, the task of distinguishing constructs to be executed from those to be residualized is performed *offline*, *i.e.*, in a separate phase *before* specialization is carried out. Thus, offline partial evaluation consists of two phases.

1. *Binding-time analysis (BTA):* In this first phase, the user does not supply the actual parameter values to be used in partial evaluation, but only a *specification* of which parameters will be known (static) and which will be unknown (dynamic). Based on this information, the partial evaluator will then classify each construct in the program as *eliminable* (*i.e.*, executable at specialization time) or *residual* (*i.e.*, the construct is to be placed in the residual program).[2] This classification is usually expressed by attaching an annotation to each construct in the source program.
2. *Specialization:* In this phase, the user gives the actual parameter values for the static parameters, and the partial evaluator processes the annotated program to produce the residual program. The interesting point is that the specializer does not need to manipulate tags to check to see if which constructs can or cannot be executed. It simply follows the classification annotations already made by the binding-time analysis.

Using the example expression above, we would supply a specification of $[a \mapsto D, b \mapsto S]$ to the binding-time analysis. Since both b and 2 represent values that will be known at specialization time, the BTA can determine that the + operation can be executed. However, since a is represents an unknown value,

---

[2] The *eliminable/residual* terminology is from Ershov [8].

the BTA can determine that the * operation cannot be executed. Based on this analysis, the BTA produces the annotated code below.

$$\underline{*}(\underline{a}\ \mathsf{lift}(+(\mathsf{b}\ 2)))$$

Residual constructs are underlined, eliminable constructs are not underlined. A special operator lift has been inserted to indicate that the result of +(b 2) needs to be lifted. Note that the lift operation is inserted in exactly the same place as where the online partial evaluator carried out lifting. Thus, the lifting operation is "compiled" into the annotated program.

Once the annotated program is produced, the partial evaluator takes in the values of the static parameters. In contrast to the online partial evaluator, the offline specializer only needs to hold the values of the static variables in the specialization store. Furthermore, there is no need to tag these static values with S since there are no dynamic values stored. We will see later on that the specializer will never attempt to update or fetch the value of a dynamic variable in a well-annotated program ("well-annotatedness" is a crucial property defined later).

Using the store $[b \mapsto 3]$, the specializer simply follows the annotations to produce the residual program. The + operation is executed to produce the value 5, the lifting directive is followed to produce the code 5, the * and both residual arguments yield the residual contruct *(a 5).

Assessment Moving from online to offline partial evaluation is a staging transformation: one factors the jobs of propagating tag information (S, D) and specializing into two phases. An analogy with type-checking gives a rough idea of the advantages and disadvantages of this approach. Online partial evaluation is analogous to run-time type-checking where values are tagged with types and type-checks are performed on the fly. Offline partial evaluation is analogous to static type-checking which checks types by computing a conservative approximation of the program's flow of values.

Just like dynamic type-checking, online partial evaluation has the advantage of being less conservative and more flexible. In this strategy, decisions about the execution or residualization of constructs can be based on the actual static values supplied for specialization. In the offline strategy, at binding-time analysis time one does not have the static values in hand — only the tags S and D. This becomes an important issue in stronger forms of program specialization such as supercompilation [10, 25, 27] where it seems difficult to construct an effective binding-time analysis.

Just like static type-checking, offline partial evaluation has the advantage of being more efficient and easier to reason about. Since the type-checking is done once-and-for-all, repeated executions of the program avoid the overhead associated with type-checking. Similarly, since binding-time analysis is done once-and-for-all, repeated specialization of the program (using the same parameter specification, but with different static values) avoids the overhead associated with inserting and inspecting binding-time tags. Finally, offline partial evaluation seems easier to reason about (easier to debug problematic specialization results) because the binding-time analysis computes a conservative classification of constructs before actually specializing the program. Thus, before specialization actually proceeds, the user can be presented with an annotated program, and the results of specialization can be predicted fairly well from this. For example, in the example annotated expression $\underline{*}(\underline{a}$ lift(+(b 2))), we can immediately see that the $*$ operation will appear in the residual program, whereas the + operation will not.

The first partial evaluators were online. The offline strategy was originally introduced to overcome problems associated with self-application of partial evaluators. But even as enthusiasm about self-application has waned, the offline strategy has proven to be very effective in handling complex language features.

4.2   Two-level FCL

The standard method of expressing annotated programs produced by binding-time analysis is to use a *two-level language* [22]. Using a two-level language is a general technique for expressing staged-computation [17]. In partial evaluation, the two stages are *specialization time* and residual program *run-time*. To connect with our previous terminology, eliminable constructs will be executed at specialization time; residual constructs will be executed at run-time.

Figure 21 presents a two-level version of FCL called FCL-2. In FCL-2, there are underlined and non-underlined versions of each computational construct To avoid confusion with regular FCL constructs, the FCL-2 syntax metavariables with a hat $\hat{\cdot}$.

In offline partial evaluation, we will encounter again the same three steps from online specialization (computing reachable configurations, program point specialization, transition compression). These will occur in the specialization phase that follows the binding-time analysis. In summary, the main components of offline partial evaluation are as follows.

1. binding-time analysis (inputs: source program and input parameter binding times)
   (a) propagating input parameter bindings to the whole program
   (b) annotating the source program (creating a two-level program)
2. specialization (inputs: two-level program and values of the static parameters)
   (a) computing reachable configurations
   (b) program-point specialization
   (c) transition compression

In partial evaluators for realistic languages with side-effects or higher-order functions, binding-time analysis is usually preceded by other analyses such as pointer analysis or closure analysis that compute other data and control flow properties.

Binding-time analysis is usually implemented using a iterative fixpoint algorithm or by constraint-solving methods. We will take a very simple approach and use two steps to construct an annotated program from the source program.

Syntax Domains

$\hat{p}$ ∈ Programs[FCL-2]	$\hat{x}$ ∈ Variables[FCL-2]
$\hat{b}$ ∈ Blocks[FCL-2]	$\hat{e}$ ∈ Expressions[FCL-2]
l ∈ Block-Labels[FCL-2]	$\hat{c}$ ∈ Constants[FCL-2]
$\hat{a}$ ∈ Assignments[FCL-2]	$\hat{j}$ ∈ Jumps[FCL-2]
$\hat{al}$ ∈ Assignment-Lists[FCL-2]	o ∈ Operations[FCL-2]

Grammar

$$\hat{p} ::= (x^*)\,(l)\,\hat{b}^+$$
$$\hat{b} ::= l : \hat{al}\,\hat{j}$$
$$\hat{a} ::= x := \hat{e};\ |\ \underline{x} := \hat{e};$$
$$\hat{al} ::= \hat{a}\,\hat{al}\ |\ \cdot$$
$$\hat{e} ::= \hat{c}\ |\ \hat{x}\ |\ o(\hat{e}^*)\ |\ \underline{o}(\hat{e}^*)\ |$$
$$\qquad \mathsf{lift}(\hat{e})$$
$$\hat{c} ::= 0\ |\ 1\ |\ 2\ |\ \ldots\ |$$
$$\qquad \underline{0}\ |\ \underline{1}\ |\ \underline{2}\ |\ \ldots$$
$$o ::= +\ |\ -\ |\ *\ |\ \ldots$$
$$\hat{j} ::= \mathbf{goto}\ l;\ |\ \underline{\mathbf{goto}}\ l;\ |$$
$$\qquad \mathbf{return}\ \hat{e};\ |\ \underline{\mathbf{return}}\ \hat{e};\ |$$
$$\qquad \mathbf{if}\ \hat{e}\ \mathbf{then}\ l_1\ \mathbf{else}\ l_2;\ |\ \underline{\mathbf{if}}\ \hat{e}\ \underline{\mathbf{then}}\ l_1\ \underline{\mathbf{else}}\ l_2;$$

Fig. 21. Syntax of the Two-Level Flowchart Language FCL-2

- First, we use an simple iterative fixpoint algorithm that will take as input the source program and a binding-time specification for its parameters, and will then classify *all* the variables in the program as either static or dynamic. The result will be what is called a *division* Δ — a splitting of the set of program variables into two categories (static or dynamic).
- Second, using the division as input data, we will make another pass through the source program and produce an annotation for each construct.

In practice (*e.g.*, in constraint-based algorithms), computing the division and computing the annotations are performed simultaneously (the annotations are repeatedly re-adjusted as data flow information becomes more precise). We use the two-step method above for pedagogical reasons, and also to connect with the division idea which was the original way of explaining the concept of binding-time analysis [16] — that is, binding-time analysis determines the *time* (*i.e.*, stage) at which each variable will *bind* to an actual value.

4.3   A motivating example

Binding-time analysis

Computing a congruent division As in the previous chapter, let's specialize the power program of Figure 1 to the exponent value of 2. As we begin with the binding-time analysis, in contrast to online specialization, we do not have the actual value for the exponent parameter n, but instead supply a specification $[\mathtt{m} \mapsto D, \mathtt{n} \mapsto S]$ that gives the binding-time of each parameter. From this specification we can construct an *initial division*

$$\Delta = [\mathtt{m} \mapsto D, \mathtt{n} \mapsto S, \mathtt{result} \mapsto S]$$

that matches the parameter specification and has all other program variables classified as static. Non-parameter variables such as `result` can be considered known since all FCL variables are initialized to 0.

To be usuable for specialization, a division must be *congruent*. A division is congruent if for any transition $(l, \sigma) \to (l', \sigma')$ the values of the static variables at block l' must be computable from the static variables at block l. As Gomard and Jones state, "any variable that depends on a dynamic variable must itself be dynamic". The notion of congruence can be made more precise (see *e.g.*, Jones [14]).

The initial division above is *not* congruent since the static variable `result` of block `loop` is not computable from the static variables at block `test`; specifically, the value to be assigned to `result` depends on the dynamic variable m.

To obtain a congruent division, we repeatedly traverse the program and keep updating the division until we make a traversal where nothing changes. The division must be *conservative* in that sense that if a variable is unknown at any point of the program, then it must be classified as dynamic — even if it is known at some other point. Thus, when updating the division, we are allowed to change a variable's classification from S to D but not vice versa. In essence the division will only change when a dynamic value is assigned to a variable previously classified as static. This strategy results in a congruent division called a *uniform division* since it holds for the entire program. Later, we will see how the constraints above can be relaxed to allow variables to have different classifications at different program points (*point-wise division*) or multiple classifications at the same program point (*polyvariant division*).

For now, we compute a uniform division as follows.

– *First traversal:*
  - `init` block: the division does not change here since `result` (which is static) is assigned the static value 1.
  - `test` block: the division does not change here since there are no assignments.
  - `loop` block: in this case, we cannot compute the $*(\mathtt{result}\ \mathtt{m})$ operation since m is dynamic. Therefore, `result` must be classified as dynamic. That is, we have the new division

$$\Delta' = [\mathtt{m} \mapsto D, \mathtt{n} \mapsto S, \mathtt{result} \mapsto D].$$

The assignment to n does not change the division, since $\mathtt{n} \mapsto S$ and the operation $-(\mathtt{n}\ 1)$ is static since both operations are static.

```
(m n)
(init)

init:   result := 1;
        goto test;

test:   if <(n 1) then end else loop;

loop:   result := *(result m);
        n := -(n 1);
        goto test;

end:    return result;
```

Fig. 22. Two-level version of the power program using the division $\Delta' = [\text{m} \mapsto D, \text{n} \mapsto S, \text{result} \mapsto D]$

- **end block:** there are no assignments here so the division does not change.
- *Second traversal:*
  - **init block:** the division does not change here since `result` (which is now dynamic) is assigned the static value 1 (remember, that we only change the a variable's classification from static to dynamic).
  - **test block:** the division does not change here since there are no assignments.
  - **loop block:** as before, the expression in the assignment to `result` is dynamic. Since `result` is already dynamic, nothing changes. The assignment to n proceeds as before, so the division does not change.
  - **end block:** there are no assignments here so the division does not change.

Since the second traversal does not cause any changes, the final division is Δ'.

We are guaranteed that computing a division in this manner will always terminate since (a) there are a finite number of variables, (b) there are only two possible values (S, D) that can be associated with each variable, and (c) the process is monotonic in the sense that we are only changing from S to D and not vice versa.

Producing a two-level program Given the division Δ' above, we can construct an annotated program in one traversal over the source program. Figure 22 shows the resulting program. We now explain how it was obtained.

- **init block:** since $\Delta'(\text{result}) = D$, the assignment to `result` must be residualized (underlined). This means that specializing the expression of the right-hand side of the assignment must also yield a residual piece of code. Therefore, we have the residual 1. Note that we could have also written lift(1) to obtain the same effect. For now, we will assume that transition compression is not performed. Therefore, all **goto**'s are underlined since they will all appear in the residual program.

- **test** block: all components of the test expression are static, and so the conditional jump itself can be performed at specialization time. Thus, nothing is underlined in this block.
- **loop** block: in the assignment to **result**, both **result** and m are dynamic, thus the * operation is residual, and the assignment itself is residual.
  In the assignment to n, $\Delta'(n) = S$ and so both the left- and right-hand sides of the assignment, as well as the assignment itself are not underlined.
- **end** block: the **return** is underlined since, as in online partial evaluation, we always want to residualize **return** jumps.

Specialization We now summarize how the three-step view of specialization changes when moving from online to offline partial evaluation.

Computing reachable configurations At this point, the partial evaluator accepts the actual values for the static parameters and computes the set of reachable configurations. In contrast to the online setting, the congruence property of divisions ensures that we can completely ignore the dynamic variables since no static variable will ever depend on a dynamic one. That is, we need only use the static portion $[n \mapsto \ldots]$ of a store $[m \mapsto \ldots, n \mapsto \ldots \text{result} \mapsto \ldots]$. Therefore, our initial state will be

$$(\text{init}, [n \mapsto 2]).$$

Here is the trace showing the reachable configurations.

$$(\text{init}, [n \mapsto 2])$$
$$\rightarrow (\text{test}, [n \mapsto 2])$$
$$\rightarrow (\text{loop}, [n \mapsto 2])$$
$$\rightarrow (\text{test}, [n \mapsto 1])$$
$$\rightarrow (\text{loop}, [n \mapsto 1])$$
$$\rightarrow (\text{test}, [n \mapsto 0])$$
$$\rightarrow (\text{end}, [n \mapsto 0])$$
$$\rightarrow (\text{halt}, [n \mapsto 0])$$

Again, when generating the trace we simply follow the program annotations. Presently, we ignore the the underlined constructs since they contribute nothing to the static store transformations. We only process the non-underlined constructs such as the conditional in the **test** block and the assignment to n in **loop**.

```
(m)
((init,[2]))

  (init,[2]): result := 1;
              goto (test,[2]);

  (test,[2]): goto (loop,[2]);

  (loop,[2]): result := *(result,m);
              goto (test,[1]);

  (test,[1]): goto (loop,[1]);

  (loop,[1]): result := *(result,m);
              goto (test,[0]);

  (test,[0]): goto (end,[0]);

  (end,[0]): return result;
```

Fig. 23. The FCL power program specialized to n = 2 using offline partial evaluation.

Program point specialization As with online partial evaluation, for each reachable state (l, σ_s), we create a version of block l that is specialized to σ_s. The difference is that in the offline case, we don't check S and D tags, we simply follow the annotations. For example, in the loop block

```
loop:   result := *(result m);
        n := -(n 1);
        goto test;
```

the components of the first assignment statement are all underlined, so they are copied to the residual program. All the components of the second component are non-underlined, so they are executed and n receives a new value in the static store. Finally, the **goto** is copied (minus the underline) to the residual program with the label changed to the appropriate specialized version of **test**. Figure 23 gives the residual program.

Transition compression Transition compression for FCL is orthogonal to the use of an online or offline strategy. We proceed the same as in the online case; the result is given in Figure 24.

Assessment Let's compare the results of offline partial evaluation in Figure 23 to the result of online partial evaluation in Figure 9. In both cases, there are

```
(m)
((init,[2]))

  (init,[2]): result := 1;
              result := *(result,m);
              result := *(result,m);
              return result;
```

Fig. 24. The compressed FCL power program specialized to m = 2.

seven reachable configurations, and thus seven residual blocks. The only real difference between the two (ignoring the irrelevant difference between labels) occurs in the init block and the first loop block. In the online case, we compute the assignment result := 1; since 1 is static. However, in our division Δ' for the offline case, we have result $\mapsto D$ because of the assignment that comes later in the loop block. Therefore, in contrast to the online case, the assignment to result in init is *not* executed, but is copied to the residual program.

The difference between the first version of the loop block is caused by the difference between the two init blocks. In the online case, in the loop block we have

$$result := *(1\ m);$$

but in the offline case we have

$$result := *(result\ m);.$$

In the online case, when we reach loop for the first time we have result $\mapsto 1$ because we computed the assignment in init. Therefore, the *value* of result gets lifted and residualized in the * operation. In the offline case, result is always dynamic, and so the *variable* result is residualized.

Even though these difference are small, they substantiate the claim that offline partial evaluation is more conservative than online. We performed one less assignment in the offline case than we did in the online case. In addition, even though in this example the number of reachable states was the same for both online and offline, online will generally have more. Since online variables do not receive a single S/D classification as in the offline case, more variations are possible.[3]

4.4 Binding-time analysis

Well-formedness of annotated programs The binding-time analysis phase must produce annotations that correctly instruct the specializer how to specialize

---

[3] Later we will see more general forms of binding-time analyses that allow multiple classifications.

a program. However, the two-level language in Figure 21 is so general that it is possible to produce annotations that incorrectly guide the specializer. For example, the two-level expression

$$*(\underline{\mathtt{a}} \underline{+}(\mathtt{b}\ 2))$$

is problematic because the $\underline{+}$ is marked as residual (and therefore will not produce a value) but the nonunderlined $*$ tells the specializer that $*$ can be evaluated. In short, when evaluating $*$, the specializer expects to receive values as arguments but gets a piece of code instead.

The opposite scenario is also problematic. In the expression,

$$\underline{*}(\underline{\mathtt{a}} +(\mathtt{b}\ 2))$$

the specializer expects to receive pieces of code as arguments when processing $\underline{*}$, but the result of $+(\mathtt{b}\ 2)$ will be a value since $+$ is non-underlined.

In summary, the binding-time analysis must produce an annotated program that is well-formed in the sense that it does not cause the specializer to "go wrong". Figure 25 gives a rule system that defines this notion of well-formedness.

The rules for expressions have the form

$$\Delta \vdash^{bt}_{expr} e\,[\hat{e} : t].$$

This judgment expresses that under division Δ, the two-level expression $\hat{e}$ is a well-annotated version of the source expression e with binding-time type $t \in \{S, D\}$. Having $t = S$ indicates that specializing $\hat{e}$ will produce a value; $t = D$ implies that specializing e will produce a piece of residual code.

We briefly summarize the intuition behind the expression rules.

- A constant c can be annotated as eliminable (with binding-time type S) or residual (with binding-time type D).
- The binding-time type for a variable x is found by in the division (*i.e.*, the type is $\Delta(x)$).
- For an operation to be eliminable, all its arguments must have type S (*i.e.*, they must also be eliminable an produce values at specialization time). When an operation is marked residual, all its arguments also be residual. That is, they must have type D.
- The lift construct is an explicit coercion from from a static to a dynamic binding-time type. In essence, this compiles into the program at binding-time analysis time the decision to lift or not to lift that was made at specialization time in the online partial evaluator of Section 3.3.

For example, using the division $\Delta = [\mathtt{a} \mapsto D, \mathtt{b} \mapsto S]$ we have the following derivations using the well-formedness rules.

$$\nabla_1 \quad = \quad \frac{\Delta \vdash^{bt}_{expr} \mathtt{b}\,[\mathtt{b} : S] \qquad \Delta \vdash^{bt}_{expr} 2\,[2 : S]}{\Delta \vdash^{bt}_{expr} +(\mathtt{b}\ 2)\,[+(\mathtt{b}\ 2) : S]}$$

Expressions

$$\overline{\Delta \vdash_{expr}^{bt} c\,[c:S]} \qquad\qquad \overline{\Delta \vdash_{expr}^{bt} c\,[\underline{c}:D]}$$

$$\overline{\Delta \vdash_{expr}^{bt} x\,[x:S]} \quad \text{if } \Delta(x) = S \qquad\qquad \overline{\Delta \vdash_{expr}^{bt} x\,[\underline{x}:D]} \quad \text{if } \Delta(x) = D$$

$$\frac{\Delta \vdash_{expr}^{bt} e_i\,[\hat{e}_i:S]}{\Delta \vdash_{expr}^{bt} o(e_1\ldots e_n)\,[o(\hat{e}_1\ldots\hat{e}_n):S]} \qquad \frac{\Delta \vdash_{expr}^{bt} e_i\,[\hat{e}_i:D]}{\Delta \vdash_{expr}^{bt} o(e_1\ldots e_n)\,[\underline{o}(\hat{e}_1\ldots\hat{e}_n):D]}$$

Lifting

$$\frac{\Delta \vdash_{expr}^{bt} e\,[\hat{e}:S]}{\Delta \vdash_{expr}^{bt} e\,[\text{lift}(\hat{e}):D]}$$

Assignments

$$\frac{\Delta \vdash_{expr}^{bt} e\,[\hat{e}:S] \quad \Delta(x) = S}{\Delta \vdash_{assign}^{bt} x := e;\,[x := \hat{e};]} \qquad \frac{\Delta \vdash_{expr}^{bt} e\,[\hat{e}:D] \quad \Delta(x) = D}{\Delta \vdash_{assign}^{bt} x := e;\,[\underline{x} := \hat{e};]}$$

$$\overline{\Delta \vdash_{assigns}^{bt} \cdot\,[\cdot]} \qquad \frac{\Delta \vdash_{assign}^{bt} a\,[\hat{a}] \quad \Delta \vdash_{assigns}^{bt} al\,[\hat{al}]}{\Delta \vdash_{assigns}^{bt} a\,al\,[\hat{a}\,\hat{al}]}$$

Jumps

$$\overline{\Delta \vdash_{jump}^{bt} \text{goto } l;\,[\text{goto } l;]} \qquad \frac{\Delta \vdash_{expr}^{bt} e\,[\hat{e}:D]}{\Delta \vdash_{jump}^{bt} \text{return } e;\,[\underline{\text{return }}\hat{e};]}$$

$$\frac{\Delta \vdash_{expr}^{bt} e\,[\hat{e}:S]}{\Delta \vdash_{jump}^{bt} \text{if } e \text{ then } l_1 \text{ else } l_2;\,[\text{if } \hat{e} \text{ then } l_1 \text{ else } l_2;]}$$

$$\frac{\Delta \vdash_{expr}^{bt} e\,[\hat{e}:D]}{\Delta \vdash_{jump}^{bt} \text{if } e \text{ then } l_1 \text{ else } l_2;\,[\underline{\text{if }} \hat{e} \underline{\text{ then }} l_1 \underline{\text{ else }} l_2;]}$$

Blocks

$$\frac{\Delta \vdash_{assigns}^{bt} al\,[\hat{al}] \quad \Delta \vdash_{jump}^{bt} j\,[\hat{j}]}{\Delta \vdash_{block}^{bt} l: al\,j\,[l: \hat{al}\,\hat{j}]}$$

Semantic Values

$$t \in \text{BT-Types[FCL]} = \{S, D\}$$
$$\Delta \in \text{Divisions[FCL]} = \text{Variables[FCL]} \rightharpoonup \text{BT-Types[FCL]}$$

Fig. 25. Well-formedness conditions for the two-level language FCL-2

$$\nabla_2 \;=\; \cfrac{\Delta \vdash^{bt}_{expr} \text{a } [\underline{\text{a}} : D] \quad \cfrac{\cfrac{\nabla_1}{\Delta \vdash^{bt}_{expr} +(\text{b } 2) \;[+(\text{b } 2) : S]}}{\Delta \vdash^{bt}_{expr} +(\text{b } 2) \;[\text{lift}(+(\text{b } 2)) : D]}}{\Delta \vdash^{bt}_{expr} *(\text{a} +(\text{b } 2)) \;[\underline{*}(\underline{\text{a}} \text{ lift}(+(\text{b } 2))) : D]}$$

Note that the well-formedness rules do not allow the problematic annotation $*(\underline{\text{a}} \underline{+}(\text{b } 2))$ to be derived, because the non-underlined $*$ requires the rule for eliminable operations, and this rule requires that all arguments have binding-time type S.

The other problematic annotation $\underline{*}(\underline{\text{a}} +(\text{b } 2))$ is disallowed because $\underline{*}$ requires the rule for residual operations, and this rule requires that all arguments have binding-time type D. However, the rules give $+(\text{b } 2)$ the type S. Before $+(\text{b } 2)$ can be used as an argument to $\underline{*}$, it must be coerced to type D using lift as in the derivation above.

The rules for assignments encode the strategy used for online partial evaluation. If the assignment expression has type D, then the assignment is residualized. If the expression has type S, then it is eliminated. Note that we require that the mode of the assignment match the variable's type in the division. That is, a residual assignment statement must assign to a dynamic variable, and an eliminable assignment must assign to a static variable.

For jumps: **goto**'s and **return**'s are always annotated as residual. We emphasized in the previous chapter that **return** must always be residualized so this rule is no surprise. However, the decision to always residualize **goto**'s is technical design decision. Including transition compression in specialization might prompt one to mark **goto**'s as eliminable (since they will always be removed in compression). However, in our presentation of transition compression, **goto**'s are removed not in jump specialization but afterwards in block specialization. Thus, we always residualize **goto**'s during jump specialization (but they may be removed later).

On the other hand, not *all* control transfers are residualized: an **if** is eliminable when its test expression is eliminable, otherwise it is residual.

An algorithm for attaching annotations The well-formedness rules yield constraints on annotated programs that a correct binding-time analysis algorithm must satisfy. Specifically, if Δ is a congruent division for program p, and if e is some expression in p, then a correct binding-time analysis must produce an annotated expression $\hat{e}$ such that $\Delta \vdash^{bt}_{expr} e \; [\hat{e} : t]$ for some t (similarly for assignments, jumps, and blocks).

The reader may have noticed that, for a given Δ and e, there may be more than one two-level term $\hat{e}$ such that $\Delta \vdash^{bt}_{expr} e \; [\hat{e} : t]$. For example, using the division and expression from the previous section, we have

(1) $\Delta \vdash^{bt}_{expr}$ *(a +(b 2)) [*(a̲ lift(+(b 2))) : D]

(2) $\Delta \vdash^{bt}_{expr}$ *(a +(b 2)) [*(a̲ ±(lift(b) lift(2))) : D]

(3) $\Delta \vdash^{bt}_{expr}$ *(a +(b 2)) [*(a̲ ±(lift(b) 2̲)) : D].

Clearly, (1) is better (allows more specialization) than (2) or (3) because it has
the + operation as eliminable whereas the others do not. The only difference
between (2) and (3) is that the 2 is residualized indirectly *via* lift in (2) but
directly in (3). In some sense, underlined constants such as 2̲ are redundant
since the same effect can be achieved using non-underlined constants and lift
only. One might argue that residual constants should be included since they
avoid the computing of lifting. In any case, whether or not to include residual
constants is largely a matter of taste. Most presentations in the literature do
include them, so we include them here.

The examples above illustrate that the binding-time analysis does have some
flexibility in producing correct output. In general, the annotation with as few
residual constructs as possible should be produced. In some cases, it may be
desirable to deliberately annotate some constructs as residual that could actually be marked as eliminable. This is sometimes done to avoid non-terminating
specialization (analogous to the discussion of generalization in Section 3.3.

Another motivation for increasing the number of residual constructs might
be to avoid code blow-up due to over-specialization. Just as we added the **gen**
construct for the online partial evaluator (Section 3.3), many offline partial evaluators include an analogous construct that lets the user force a particular fragment
of code to be residual.

For now, we will simply assume that we want annotations with as few residual
constructs as possible. Given a congruent division, it is relatively clear how to do
this, *i.e.*, how to map a program p to an annotated version $\hat{p}$. For completeness,
Figure 26 gives a rule-based system for attaching annotations given a congruent
division Δ. The rules describe a one-pass traversal of the program.

The rules for expressions have the form

$$\Delta \vdash^{ann}_{expr} e \vartriangleright \langle \hat{e}, t \rangle.$$

Given the division Δ, e should be annotated as $\hat{e}$ and its type is t.

Recall that one of the reasons that we can get multiple correct annotations
for a single expression is that lifting can occur in several different places (see
annotations (1) and (2) above). The purpose of lifting is to allow static computation in dynamic contexts, but in annotation (2), lifting is used in what is
intuitively a static context. The primary property of the annotating algorithm
of Figure 26 as opposed to the well-formedness rules of Figure 25 is that the annotating algorithm has a specific judgement for lifting $\cdot \uparrow \cdot$, and this judgement
is only used when there is a truly dynamic context. Note that the rules given
for lifting never insert a residual constant (*e.g.*, 1̲). Instead, a lift of the constant

Expressions

$$\Delta \vdash_{expr}^{ann} c \triangleright \langle c, S \rangle$$

$$\Delta \vdash_{expr}^{ann} x \triangleright \langle x, S \rangle \quad \text{if } \Delta(x) = S \qquad \Delta \vdash_{expr}^{ann} x \triangleright \langle \underline{x}, D \rangle \quad \text{if } \Delta(x) = D$$

$$\frac{\Delta \vdash_{expr}^{ann} e_i \triangleright \langle \hat{e}_i, S \rangle}{\Delta \vdash_{expr}^{ann} o(e_1 \ldots e_n) \triangleright \langle o(\hat{e}_1 \ldots \hat{e}_n), S \rangle}$$

$$\frac{\Delta \vdash_{expr}^{ann} e_i \triangleright \langle \hat{e}_i, t_i \rangle \quad \exists j \in \{1, \ldots, n\} . t_j = D \quad \langle \hat{e}_i, t_i \rangle \uparrow \hat{e}_i'}{\Delta \vdash_{expr}^{ann} o(e_1 \ldots e_n) \triangleright \langle \underline{o}(\hat{e}_1' \ldots \hat{e}_n'), D \rangle}$$

Lifting

$$\langle \hat{e}, S \rangle \uparrow \mathrm{lift}(\hat{e}) \qquad\qquad \langle \hat{e}, D \rangle \uparrow \hat{e}$$

Assignments

$$\frac{\Delta(x) = S \quad \Delta \vdash_{expr}^{ann} e \triangleright \langle \hat{e}, S \rangle}{\Delta \vdash_{assign}^{ann} x := e; \triangleright x := \hat{e};}$$

$$\frac{\Delta(x) = D \quad \Delta \vdash_{expr}^{ann} e \triangleright \langle \hat{e}, D \rangle \quad \langle \hat{e}, t \rangle \uparrow \hat{e}'}{\Delta \vdash_{assign}^{ann} x := e; \triangleright \underline{x} := \hat{e}';}$$

$$\Delta \vdash_{assigns}^{ann} \cdot \triangleright \cdot \qquad\qquad \frac{\Delta \vdash_{assigns}^{ann} a \triangleright \hat{a} \quad \Delta \vdash_{assigns}^{ann} al \triangleright \hat{al}}{\Delta \vdash_{assigns}^{ann} a\, al \triangleright \hat{a}\, \hat{al}}$$

Jumps

$$\Delta \vdash_{jump}^{ann} \mathbf{goto}\ l; \triangleright \underline{\mathbf{goto}}\ l; \qquad\qquad \frac{\Delta \vdash_{expr}^{ann} e \triangleright \langle \hat{e}, t \rangle \quad \langle \hat{e}, t \rangle \uparrow \hat{e}'}{\Delta \vdash_{jump}^{ann} \mathbf{return}\ e; \triangleright \underline{\mathbf{return}}\ \hat{e}';}$$

$$\frac{\Delta \vdash_{expr}^{ann} e \triangleright \langle \hat{e}, S \rangle}{\Delta \vdash_{jump}^{ann} \mathbf{if}\ e\ \mathbf{then}\ l_1\ \mathbf{else}\ l_2; \triangleright \mathbf{if}\ \hat{e}\ \mathbf{then}\ l_1\ \mathbf{else}\ l_2;}$$

$$\frac{\Delta \vdash_{expr}^{ann} e \triangleright \langle \hat{e}, D \rangle}{\Delta \vdash_{jump}^{ann} \mathbf{if}\ e\ \mathbf{then}\ l_1\ \mathbf{else}\ l_2; \triangleright \underline{\mathbf{if}}\ \hat{e}\ \underline{\mathbf{then}}\ l_1\ \underline{\mathbf{else}}\ l_2;}$$

Blocks

$$\frac{\Delta \vdash_{assigns}^{ann} al \triangleright \hat{al} \quad \Delta \vdash_{jump}^{ann} j \triangleright \hat{j}}{\Delta \vdash_{block}^{ann} l : al\ j \triangleright l : \hat{al}\ \hat{j}}$$

Fig. 26. Attaching annotations using the two-level language FCL-2

will be inserted (*e.g.*, lift(1)). To generate lifted constants, we can add the rule

$$\langle n, S \rangle \uparrow \underline{n}$$

and restrict n from occuring in existing rule for static expressions (which will force the added rule to be used).

Here are some example derivations using the division $\Delta = [a \mapsto D, b \mapsto S]$.

$$\nabla_1 \quad = \quad \frac{\Delta \vdash^{ann}_{expr} b \triangleright \langle b, S \rangle \qquad \Delta \vdash^{ann}_{expr} 2 \triangleright \langle 2, S \rangle}{\Delta \vdash^{ann}_{expr} +(b\,2) \triangleright \langle +(b\,2), S \rangle}$$

$$\frac{\Delta \vdash^{ann}_{expr} a \triangleright \langle \underline{a}, D \rangle \qquad \Delta \vdash^{ann}_{expr} +(b\,2) \triangleright +(b\,2)S \qquad \langle +(b\,2), S \rangle \uparrow \text{lift}(+(b\,2))}{\Delta \vdash^{ann}_{expr} *(a +(b\,2)) \triangleright \langle \underline{*}(\underline{a}\,\text{lift}(+(b\,2))), D \rangle}$$

with ∇_1 over the middle premise.

The annotating algorithm is correct in the sense that any annotation produced will be well-formed. That is, if Δ is a congruent division for p, then for any expression e in p, $\Delta \vdash^{ann}_{expr} e \triangleright \langle \hat{e}, t \rangle$ implies $\Delta \vdash^{bt}_{expr} e\,[\hat{e} : t]$ (similarly for the other syntactic categories).

4.5 Specialization

Figures 27 and 28 present the definition of offline specialization. Given the motivation for two-level terms in the previous sections, the intuition should be fairly clear. The rules are similar to the rules for online specialization (Figures 16 and 17), but instead of checking binding-time tags, the specializer simply follows the term annotations. Since the specializer does manipulate tagged values, the definition of PE-Values[FCL] is now a simple union of values and expressions instead of a tagged union with tags $\{S, D\}$.

4.6 Other notions of division

Up to this point we have only considered congruent divisions which give a single static/dynamic variable classification for the entire program. The notion of division can be generalized to allow a different classification for each block, or multiple classifications for the same block.

Pointwise divisions Often a variable can be static in one part of the program and dynamic in another. But using a uniform division forces the variable to be classified as dynamic throughout the entire program. A *pointwise* division allows a different classification for each block.

Consider the following program where **x** is static and **y** is dynamic.

Expressions

$$\overline{\sigma \vdash^{spec}_{expr} c \Rightarrow [c]} \qquad\qquad \overline{\sigma \vdash^{spec}_{expr} \underline{c} \Rightarrow c}$$

$$\overline{\sigma \vdash^{spec}_{expr} x \Rightarrow \sigma(x)} \qquad\qquad \overline{\sigma \vdash^{spec}_{expr} \underline{x} \Rightarrow x}$$

$$\frac{\sigma \vdash^{spec}_{expr} \hat{e}_i \Rightarrow v_i \qquad [o](v_1 \ldots v_n) = v}{\sigma \vdash^{spec}_{expr} o(\hat{e}_1 \ldots \hat{e}_n) \Rightarrow v}$$

$$\frac{\sigma \vdash^{spec}_{expr} \hat{e}_i \Rightarrow e_i}{\sigma \vdash^{spec}_{expr} \underline{o}(\hat{e}_1 \ldots \hat{e}_n) \Rightarrow o(e_1 \ldots e_n)}$$

Lifting

$$\frac{\sigma \vdash^{spec}_{expr} \hat{e} \Rightarrow v}{\sigma \vdash^{spec}_{expr} \text{lift}(\hat{e}) \Rightarrow [v]^{-1}}$$

Assignments

$$\frac{\sigma \vdash^{spec}_{expr} \hat{e} \Rightarrow v}{\sigma \vdash^{spec}_{assign} x := \hat{e}; \Rightarrow \langle \sigma[x \mapsto v], [] \rangle} \qquad\qquad \frac{\sigma \vdash^{spec}_{expr} \hat{e} \Rightarrow e}{\sigma \vdash^{spec}_{assign} \underline{x} := \hat{e}; \Rightarrow \langle \sigma, [x := e;] \rangle}$$

$$\overline{\sigma \vdash^{spec}_{assigns} \cdot \Rightarrow \langle \sigma, [] \rangle}$$

$$\frac{\sigma \vdash^{spec}_{assign} \hat{a} \Rightarrow \langle \sigma', al' \rangle \qquad \sigma' \vdash^{spec}_{assigns} \hat{al} \Rightarrow \langle \sigma'', al'' \rangle}{\sigma \vdash^{spec}_{assigns} \hat{a} \, \hat{al} \Rightarrow \langle \sigma'', al' \mathbin{+\!\!+} al'' \rangle}$$

Semantic Values

$$\begin{aligned}
v &\in \text{Values[FCL]} & &= \{0, 1, 2, \ldots\} \\
w &\in \text{PE-Values[FCL]} & &= \text{Values[FCL]} \cup \text{Expressions[FCL]} \\
l &\in \text{Labels[FCL]} & &= \text{Block-Labels[FCL]} \cup \{\text{halt}\} \\
\sigma &\in \text{Stores[FCL]} & &= \text{Variables[FCL]} \rightharpoonup \text{Values[FCL]} \\
\Gamma &\in \text{Block-Maps[FCL]} & &= \text{Block-Labels[FCL]} \rightharpoonup \text{Blocks[FCL]}
\end{aligned}$$

Fig. 27. Specialization for FCL-2 programs (part 1)

Jumps

$$\overline{\sigma \vdash_{jump}^{spec} \textbf{goto } l; \Rightarrow \langle \{l\}, \textbf{goto } (l, \sigma); \rangle} \qquad \overline{\sigma \vdash_{jump}^{spec} \underline{\textbf{goto } l}; \Rightarrow \langle \{l\}, \textbf{goto } (l, \sigma); \rangle}$$

$$\frac{\sigma \vdash_{expr}^{spec} \hat{e} \Rightarrow e}{\sigma \vdash_{jump}^{spec} \underline{\textbf{return}} \hat{e}; \Rightarrow \langle \{\textsf{halt}\}, \textbf{return } e; \rangle}$$

$$\frac{\sigma \vdash_{expr}^{spec} \hat{e} \Rightarrow v \qquad \textit{true-value}(v)}{\sigma \vdash_{jump}^{spec} \textbf{if } \hat{e} \textbf{ then } l_1 \textbf{ else } l_2; \Rightarrow \langle \{l_1\}, \textbf{goto } (l_1, \sigma); \rangle}$$

$$\frac{\sigma \vdash_{expr}^{spec} \hat{e} \Rightarrow v \qquad \textit{false-value}(v)}{\sigma \vdash_{jump}^{spec} \textbf{if } \hat{e} \textbf{ then } l_1 \textbf{ else } l_2; \Rightarrow \langle \{l_2\}, \textbf{goto } (l_2, \sigma); \rangle}$$

$$\frac{\sigma \vdash_{expr}^{spec} \hat{e} \Rightarrow e}{\sigma \vdash_{jump}^{spec} \underline{\textbf{if }} \hat{e} \underline{\textbf{ then }} l_1 \underline{\textbf{ else }} l_2; \Rightarrow \langle \{l_1, l_2\}, \textbf{if } e \textbf{ then } (l_1, \sigma) \textbf{ else } (l_2, \sigma); \rangle}$$

Blocks

$$\frac{\begin{array}{c} \sigma \vdash_{assigns} al \Rightarrow \langle \sigma_1, al_1 \rangle \\ \sigma_1 \vdash_{jump} j \Rightarrow \langle \{l_{2_i} \mid i \in \{1, \dots n\}\}, j_2 \rangle \end{array}}{\sigma \vdash_{block} l : al\ j \Rightarrow \langle \{(l_{2_i}, \sigma_1) \mid i \in \{1, \dots n\}\}, (l, \sigma) : al_1\ j_2 \rangle} \quad \text{where } j_2 \neq \textbf{goto } l';$$

$$\frac{\begin{array}{c} \sigma \vdash_{assigns} al \Rightarrow \langle \sigma_1, al_1 \rangle \\ \sigma_1 \vdash_{jump} j \Rightarrow \langle \{l_2\}, \textbf{goto } (l_2, \sigma_2); \rangle \\ \sigma_2 \vdash_{block} \Gamma(l_2) \Rightarrow \langle \{(l_{3_i}, \sigma_{3_i}) \mid i \in \{1, \dots n\}\}, l_2' : al_2\ j_2 \rangle \end{array}}{\sigma \vdash_{block} l : al\ j \Rightarrow \langle \{(l_{3_i}, \sigma_{3_i}) \mid i \in \{1, \dots n\}\}, (l, \sigma) : al_1 \mathbin{+\!\!+} al_2\ j_2 \rangle}$$

Transitions

$$\frac{\sigma \vdash_{block} \Gamma(l) \Rightarrow \langle \{(l_i', \sigma_i') \mid i \in \{1, \dots n\}\}, b' \rangle}{\vdash_r \langle (l, \sigma) :: \mathcal{P}, \mathcal{S}, \mathcal{R} \rangle \longmapsto \langle \mathcal{P}_{new} \mathbin{+\!\!+} \mathcal{P}, \mathcal{S} \cup (l, \sigma), b' :: \mathcal{R} \rangle} \quad \text{if } (l, \sigma) \notin \mathcal{S}$$
$$\text{where } \mathcal{P}_{new} = \textsf{remove-halts}([(l_1', \sigma_1'), \dots, (l_n', \sigma_n')])$$

$$\vdash_r \langle (l, \sigma) :: \mathcal{P}, \mathcal{S}, \mathcal{R} \rangle \longmapsto \langle \mathcal{P}, \mathcal{S}, \mathcal{R} \rangle \qquad \text{if } (l, \sigma) \in \mathcal{S}$$

Fig. 28. Specialization for FCL-2 programs (part 2)

```
(x y)
(b1)

b1: m := +(x 4);
    n := *(y m);
    goto b2;

b2: n := 2;
    m := *(3 y);
    n := +(n x);
    return n;
```

Using a uniform division, we would be forced to make both m and n dynamic because they both depend on y at some point. However, m only depends on x in block b1 and can be considered static for that block. The first assignment in b2 gives n a static value After that, n's value only depends on the static variable x.

Using a pointwise division, we can have $[m \mapsto S, n \mapsto D]$ in block b1 and $[m \mapsto D, n \mapsto S]$ in block b2. Formally, a pointwise division Δ^{pw} is a function from program labels to division tuples.

$$\Delta^{pw} \in \text{Point-Divisions[FCL]} = \text{Block-Labels[FCL]} \rightharpoonup \text{Divisions[FCL]}$$

A valid pointwise division for the program above would be

$$b1 \mapsto [x \mapsto S, y \mapsto D, m \mapsto S, n \mapsto D]$$
$$b2 \mapsto [x \mapsto S, y \mapsto D, m \mapsto D, n \mapsto S]$$

Polyvariant divisions There are also cases where it is useful to have multiple classifications for each block. Such divisions are called *polyvariant divisions*. Generally, this is desirable when there are multiple incoming paths to a particular block.

For example, consider the following program where x is static, y is dynamic, and there are multiple paths coming into block b4.

```
(x y)
(b1)

b1: if =(x y) then b2 else b3;

b2: m := 2;
    goto b4;

b3: m := y;
    goto b4;

b4: m := +(x m);
    return m;
```

Along the path from b2, m is static; along the path from b3, m is dynamic. Rather than forcing m to be dynamic throughout all the program (as with a uniform division), or forcing only one division for block b4 (as with a pointwise division), we may prefer to have two *variants* of a division for block b4 — one where m is static, and another where m is dynamic.

Formally, a polyvariant division maps each program label to a set of divisions.

$$\Delta^{pl} \in \text{Poly-Divisions[FCL]} = \text{Block-Labels[FCL]} \rightharpoonup \mathcal{P}(\text{Divisions[FCL]})$$

A valid polyvariant division for the program above would be

$$b1 \mapsto \{[x \mapsto S, y \mapsto D, m \mapsto S]\}$$
$$b2 \mapsto \{[x \mapsto S, y \mapsto D, m \mapsto S]\}$$
$$b3 \mapsto \{[x \mapsto S, y \mapsto D, m \mapsto D]\}$$
$$b4 \mapsto \{[x \mapsto S, y \mapsto D, m \mapsto S], [x \mapsto S, y \mapsto D, m \mapsto D]\}$$

Binding-time analyses that are not polyvariant are called *monovariant* (*e.g.*, those that compute uniform and pointwise divisions). Note that performing a pointwise or polyvariant binding-time analysis is significantly more complicated than performing computing a uniform division since one must take into account the control-flow of the program. For instance, in the program example for the polyvariant division above, we needed to know that blocks b2 and b3 have block b4 as a successor.

4.7   Exercises

1. Outline the steps involved in computing a uniform congruent division for the term multiplier program of Figure 13 where n is static and m and term are dynamic. Your solution should take the same form as the summary of computing the division for the power program in Section 4.3.
2. Using the division computed in the exercise above, give the annotated version of the term multiplier program that would result from using the annotation rules of Figure 26.
3. Continuing from the exercise above and using the rules of Figure 26, show the derivation for the annotation of the loop block of the term multiplier program.
4. Given the annotated program for the term multiplier program above, show the values of the pending list $\mathcal{P}$, seen-before set S and the residual program for each offline partial evaluation transition (without on-the-fly transition compression) when specializing the program to n = 2. Contrast your solution to the analogous transitions in the online specialization of the term multiplier program at the end of Section 3.2.
5. Extend the operational semantics specification of the offline partial evaluator (as well as the FCL-2 well-formedness rules of Figure 25 and annotation algorithm of Figure 26) to process lists and associated operations (car, cdr, cons, *etc.*).

6. Extend the operational semantics specification of the offline partial evaluator (as well as the FCL-2 well-formedness rules of Figure 25 and annotation algorithm of Figure 26) to handle a **gen** construct analogous to the one presented in Section 3.3.
7. **Project:** Implement the algorithm for computing a congruent uniform division, the annotation algorithm, and the offline specializer in the language of your choice.
8. **Project:** Modify the partial evaluator so that pointwise or polyvariant divisions are computed in the binding-time analysis (some subtle issues arise here).

4.8 Further reading

For additional perspective, the reader will find it worth returning to Gomard and Jones's original presentation of offline partial evaluation for FCL in [15]. The best documented work on offline partial evaluation for imperative languages is Andersen's work on C-Mix [1] (see also Andersen's chapter in [15]). Glück et al.[18] describe F-Spec — an offline partial evaluator for FORTRAN. Consel's group's Tempo system incorporates both compile-time and run-time specialization [3, 5] and many interesting applications have been made with it. There is a huge body of work on offline partial evaluation of functional languages (see [15]). For offline specialization of functional language with imperative features, see [7, 12, 13, 19, 26].

References

1. Lars Ole Andersen. *Program Analysis and Specialization for the C Programming Language*. PhD thesis, DIKU, Computer Science Department, University of Copenhagen, Copenhagen, Denmark, 1994. DIKU Report 94-19.
2. Anders Bondorf and Olivier Danvy. Automatic autoprojection of recursive equations with global variables and abstract data types. *Science of Computer Programming*, 16:151–195, 1991.
3. Charles Consel, Luke Hornof, François Noël, Jacques Noyé, and Nicolae Volanschi. A uniform approach for compile-time and run-time specialization. In *Proceedings of the 1996 International Seminar on Partial Evaluation*, number 1110 in Lecture Notes in Computer Science, pages 54–72, Dagstuhl Castle, Germany, February 1996.
4. Charles Consel and Siau Cheng Khoo. Parameterized partial evaluation. *ACM Transactions on Programming Languages and Systems*, 15(3):463–493, 1993.
5. Charles Consel and François Noël. A general approach for run-time specialization and its application to C. In *Proceedings of the Twenty-third Annual ACM Symposium on Principles of Programming Languages*, pages 145–156, St. Petersburg, FLA USA, January 1996. ACM Press.
6. Olivier Danvy, Robert Glück, and Peter Thiemann, editors. *1998 Symposium on Partial Evaluation*, 1998.

7. Dirk Dussart, John Hughes, and Peter Thiemann. Type specialisation for imperative languages. In *Proceedings of the 1997 ACM SIGPLAN International Conference on Functional Programming*, pages 204–216, Amsterdam, The Netherlands, June 1997. ACM Press.

8. Andrei P. Ershov. On the partial computation principle. *Information Processing Letters*, 6(2):41–67, 1977.

9. Andrei P. Ershov. Mixed computation: Potential applications and problems for study. *Theoretical Computer Science*, 18:41–67, 1982.

10. Robert Glück and Andrei Klimov. Occam's razor in metacomputation: the notion of a perfect process tree. In Patrick Cousot, Moreno Falaschi, Gilberto Filè, and Antoine Rauzy, editors, *Proceedings of the Third International Workshop on Static Analysis WSA'93*, volume 724 of *Lecture Notes in Computer Science*, pages 112–123, Padova, Italy, September 1993.

11. Carsten K. Gomard and Neil D. Jones. Compiler generation by partial evaluation. In G. X. Ritter, editor, *Information Processing '89. Proceedings of the IFIP 11th World Computer Congress*, pages 1139–1144. IFIP, North-Holland, 1989.

12. John Hatcliff. Foundations of partial evaluation of functional programs with computational effects. *ACM Computing Surveys*, 1998. (in press).

13. John Hatcliff and Olivier Danvy. A computational formalization for partial evaluation. *Mathematical Structures in Computer Science*, 7:507–541, 1997. Special issue devoted to selected papers from the *Workshop on Logic, Domains, and Programming Languages*. Darmstadt, Germany. May, 1995.

14. Neil D. Jones. The essence of program transformation by partial evaluation and driving. In Masahiko Sato Neil D. Jones, Masami Hagiya, editor, *Logic, Language and Computation, a Festschrift in honor of Satoru Takasu*, pages 206–224. Springer-Verlag, April 1994.

15. Neil D. Jones, Carsten K. Gomard, and Peter Sestoft. *Partial Evaluation and Automatic Program Generation*. Prentice-Hall International, 1993.

16. Neil D. Jones, Peter Sestoft, and Harald Søndergaard. MIX: A self-applicable partial evaluator for experiments in compiler generation. *LISP and Symbolic Computation*, 2(1):9–50, 1989.

17. Ulrik Jørring and William L. Scherlis. Compilers and staging transformations. In Mark Scott Johnson and Ravi Sethi, editors, *Proceedings of the Thirteenth Annual ACM Symposium on Principles of Programming Languages*, pages 86–96, St. Petersburg, Florida, January 1986.

18. Paul Kleinrubatscher, Albert Kriegshaber, Robert Zöchling, and Robert Glück. Fortran program specialization. *SIGPLAN Notices*, 30(4):61–70, 1995.

19. Julia L. Lawall and Peter Thiemann. Sound specialization in the presence of computational effects. In *Proceedings of Theoretical Aspects of Computer Software*, Lecture Notes in Computer Science, September 1997. (to appear).

20. M. Marquard and B. Steensgaard. Partial evaluation of an object-oriented imperative language. Master's thesis, University of Copenhagen, Copenhagen, Denmark, 1992.

21. U. Meyer. Techniques for partial evaluation of imperative languages. In Paul Hudak and Neil D. Jones, editors, *Proceedings of the ACM SIGPLAN Symposium on Partial Evaluation and Semantics-Based Program Manipulation*, SIGPLAN Notices, Vol. 26, No 9, pages 94–105, New Haven, Connecticut, June 1991. ACM Press.

22. Flemming Nielson and Hanne Riis Nielson. *Two-Level Functional Languages*, volume 34 of *Cambridge Tracts in Theoretical Computer Science*. Cambridge University Press, 1992.

23. Erik Ruf. *Topics in online partial evaluation*. PhD thesis, Stanford, Palo Alto, California, February 1993.
24. Erik Ruf and Daniel Weise. On the specialization of online program specializers. *Journal of Functional Programming*, 3, 1993.
25. Morten Heine Sørensen, Robert Glück, and Neil Jones. A positive supercompiler. *Journal of Functional Programming*, 6(6):811–838, 1996.
26. Peter Thiemann. A generic framework for partial evaluation of programs with computational effects. In *Proceedings of the Seventh European Symposium on Programming*, 1998.
27. Valentin F. Turchin. The concept of a supercompiler. *ACM Transactions on Programming Languages and Systems*, 8(3):292–325, 1986.
28. Glynn Winskel. *The Formal Semantics of Programming Languages: An Introduction*. MIT Press, 1993.

Similix: A Self-Applicable Partial Evaluator for Scheme

Jesper Jørgensen

Department of Mathematics and Physics
Royal Veterinary and Agricultural University
Denmark
jesper@dina.kvl.dk,

Abstract. Similix is an autoprojector (a self-applicable partial evaluator) for a large higher-order subset of the strict functional language Scheme. Similix handles source programs that use a limited class of side-effects, for instance input/output operations. Similix handles partially static data structures.

Similix is automatic: in general, no user annotations (such as unfolding information) are required. However, user assistance may in some cases be required to avoid looping. Similix gives certain guarantees concerning the residual programs it generates: computations are never discarded (partial evaluation thus preserves termination properties) and never duplicated. Similix is well-suited for partially evaluating interpreters that use environments represented as functions, and interpreters written in continuation passing style. Since Similix is self-applicable, stand-alone compilers can be generated from interpreters.

1 Introduction

In 1985 the first self-applicable partial evaluator Mix [30] saw the light of day at DIKU. This was a large step forward in the development of partial evaluation; now the Futamura projections could finally be realized in practice. The success of Mix was mainly obtained through the use of pre-processing based on program analyses which lead to a style now called *off-line* specialization. The tradition that started with Mix inspired the creation of many fully automatic and self-applicable partial evaluators. One of these was Similix [2,3], the first partial evaluator to handle imperative features, namely, global side-effects in Scheme. At the time the first version of Similix was written, the extension of partial evaluation to handle higher-order functions was the obvious next goal, so several system emerged more or less at the same time during 1989: Lambda-Mix [21,17], Schism [14] and a new version of Similix (version 2.0) [7,6,8] all handling higher order functions. Of these system only Schism[1] and Similix included memoization

---

[1] The specializer Schism by Consel is in many aspects similar to Similix and the two systems have more or less evolved in parallel. The interested reader is referred to [15].

and handled a realistic language: Scheme. Similix was rewritten in CPS style (from version 4.0) which enabled the addition of partially static data structures in a semantically safe way and later on (from version 5.1) a safe treatment of static errors under dynamic control (e.g. static division by zero). In 1993, most of Similix's pre-phase was rewritten such that the time and space complexity of this went down from cubic to almost linear time, making Similix (version 5.0) efficient and enabling it to handle big programs [4,5].

1.1 Outline and prerequisites

These notes contains, except for the description of static error under dynamic control, no new material on Similix.

The outline is the following. In Section 2 we give an introduction to Similix, describing its main features, its subject language and briefly how it is used. In Section 3 we give an overview of the system describing its different phases. In Section 4 we give a set of examples to illustrate how Similix specializes programs. Section 5 describes the specialization of an interpreter, compiler generation and the use of self-application to generate a compiler generator Cogen for Similix. In Section 6 we give a guide to the literature on Similix and in Section 7 we discuss some remaining problems.

We assume that the reader has some preliminary knowledge of partial evaluation, in particular of the *Mix-equation* and the *Futamura projections*. Readers not familiar with partial evaluation may either read Section 1 of the Similix manual [11] to get a short introduction or Chapter 1 of the book on partial evaluation by Jones, Gomard and Sestoft [24] for a longer one. We also assume that the reader has some familiarity with functional languages, preferably Scheme.

2   Similix

This section contains an introduction to Similix. We describes the main features of Similix, its subject languages and briefly describe how to use Similix.

2.1 The features of Similix

Similix is a fully automatic self-applicable partial evaluator for a large subset of Scheme. Some of the other important features of Similix are:

- it performs *polyvariant specialization*, i.e. it can produce many different specialized functions from the same function
- it is *off-line*, that is, it performs a range of program analyses on the subject program before the actual specialization
- it is *semantically safe*, e.g. preserves termination properties
- it specializes with respect to *higher order values* and *partially static data structures*
- it has an *extensible* set of basic functions and user defined data structures

– it handles *global side-effects*

Moreover, it is well documented [11] and comes with an elegant and simple command-line user interface and an on-line help facility.

2.2   The Similix subject language

The *Similix subject language* is a large subset of Scheme, extended with user defined data structures and pattern-matching facilities. Any Similix program not using the extensions is simply a Scheme program and can thus run directly in a Scheme environment. The extensions follow the syntax of Scheme so any program in the Similix subject language can therefore also be executed directly in a Scheme environment as long as the Similix system has been loaded. Furthermore, the Similix system contains a facility that can convert programs using the extensions into stand-alone Scheme programs.

Figure 1 shows the syntax of the Similix subject language. A number of standard Scheme syntax forms are not handled by Similix: lambda-expressions with variable arity (lambda V E), the set! operation, the case-expression, etc. The full list of the forms not handled can be found in [11]. We will not go further into detail with this syntax, but refer interested readers to the Similix manual [11].

User-defined primitives. The set of primitives such as cons, cdr, member, etc. can be extended arbitrarily. This is done by special definitions recognized by the keyword defprim. An example is:

```
(defprim (K x) (lambda (y) x))
```

These definitions may appear directly in the source files (from version 5.1) or in separate files, called adt-files, designated for this purpose. Most of the standard primitives of Scheme are define in a system file called "scheme.adt" which is always loaded by Similix.

The code of a primitive is never specialized by Similix. Similix divides primitives into different classes depending on their properties, and their specialization depends on this. The different classes are distinguished by various extensions to the defprim keyword:

defprim or defprim-transparent: This keyword defines a *transparent primitive*. Transparent primitives are guaranteed not to modify or access the global store, e.g. perform side-effects. If all the arguments of a call to a transparent primitive are static then the primitive is reduced at specialization time. Similix does this by letting the underlying Scheme system evaluate the call. However, if at least one of the arguments is dynamic, then the call is residualized, i.e. a call to the primitive is inserted into the residual program.

defprim-tin: This defines a variant of transparent primitives that is called *transparent if needed* (TIN). This implements a form of "poor mans generalization" [23], a way to improve termination of partial evaluation. A primitive

Pgm ∈ *Program*; D ∈ *Definition*; T ∈ *TopLevelExpression*; File ∈ *FileName*;
E ∈ *Expression*; B ∈ *Body*; K ∈ *Constant*; V ∈ *Variable*; O ∈ *PrimopName*;
C ∈ *ConstrName*; S ∈ *SelectorName*; P ∈ *ProcedureName*; MP ∈ *MatchPattern*;
CP ∈ *ConstrPattern*

```
Pgm ::= T* D T*
T    ::= D | (load File) | (loads File) | (loadt File)
```

D ::= (define (P V...V) B)	(procedure definition)
B ::= D* E⁺	(body)
E ::= K	(constant[a])
| V	(variable[a])
| (if E E E)	(conditional[a])
| (if E E)	(one-armed conditional)
| (cond (E E*)⁺)	(conditional)
| (cond (E E*)*(else E⁺))	(conditional)
| (and E*)	(logical and)
| (or E*)	(logical or)
| (let ((V E)*) B)	(parallel let[a][b])
| (let* ((V E)*) B)	(sequential let)
| (let P ((V E)*) B)	(named (recursive) let)
| (letrec((P (lambda(V*) B))*) B)	(letrec)
| (begin E*)	(sequence[a])
| O	(primitive operator (fixed arity))
| (O E*)	(primitive operator[a] (variable-arity))
| C	(constructor[a])
| S	(selector[a])
| C?	(constructor test predicate[a])
| P	(procedure name)
| (P E*)	(procedure call[a])
| (lambda (V*) E)	(lambda-abstraction[a])
| (E E*)	(application[a])
| (casematch E (MP E⁺)*)	(casematch)
| (caseconstr E (CP E⁺)*)	(caseconstr)

[a]Part of the core language (see Section 3.1)
[b]Only the simple form (let ((V E)) B) is part of the core language.

Fig. 1. Syntax of the Similix subject language.

is TIN, if it can be used inductively to produce an infinite set of values. For instance + can produce the set of values 1, 2, 3, ... by adding one to the previous number in the list. A TIN primitives will be generalized (made dynamic), if it is not used in determining the (static) control of the program. If a dynamically controled loop contains a static TIN primitive this may produce new static values for each iteration of the loop and this would course the generation of infinitely many residial functions. This is illustrated in Example 6 below. The primitives -, `cons`, `append` etc. are other examples of TIN primitives, while `car`, `cdr`, `null?`, and `max` are not.

defprim-dynamic: This defines transparent primitives that the specializer will never unfold. This can be useful in cases where one wants to postpone certain operations until (residual) run time, in order to ensure termination of specialization.

defprim-opaque: This defines *opaque primitives*. These are primitives that may modify or access the global store and are never reduced at specialization time. Similix will ensure that when the evaluation order of opaque primitives is well defined then this order is preserved by specialization. If the user places opaque primitives in arguments to function calls, in which case the evaluation order of these will not be defined by the Scheme standard, then Similix will not guarantee that the order is perserved.

defprim-abort: This defines primitives that abort execution. The simplest form are error handling as performed by _sim-error, Similix's version of Scheme's primitive **error** (defined in "scheme.adt").

defprim-abort-eoi: This define a variant of aborting primitives for which the specializer is allowed to ignore its evaluation order dependency. This can give better specialization and may for example be used in a interpreter to report syntax errors, if it does not matter in which order these are reported.

User-defined constructors. Constructors are used to create Similix's partially static data structures. Constructors and their corresponding selectors are defined analogously to primitives, e.g.

```
(defconstr (mycons mycar mycdr) (mynil))
```

defines constructors `mycons` and `mynil` and destructors `mycar` and `mycdr`. Instead of a selector name one may use a * in which case the system generates a default selector name C.*i* for this where *i* is the position of the field in the constructor (starting with 0). The following example illustrates this:

Example 1 (Default selector names). Consider the following subject program:

```
(defconstr (Mixed fst *))
(define (goal)
  (let ((con (Mixed 1 2)))
    (cons (fst con) (Mixed.1 con))))
```

since the second field of the constructor `Mixed` is declared with a * the program must use `Mixed.1` to access this.

We refer to the declarations of primitives and constructors as ADT declarations.

Pattern matching will not be described in these notes; see [11].

2.3   Input to programs being specialized

The static input to a program being specialized by Similix must be first-order, acyclic and it must not contain values constructed by user-defined constructors. The preprocessor of Similix assumes that these restriction hold when analyzing a program and may produce wrong results otherwise. If a lambda-abstraction is supplied as static argument to Similix and it has to be lifted (turned into code) then Similix will produce residual code that looks something like #<CLOSURE (x) x> instead of a real lambda-abstraction. Also dynamic input must be first-order since Similix assumes this during preprocessing. The restrictions are not checked by the Similix system.

2.4   Calling the specializer

For the sake of the examples shown in these notes we briefly describe how to specialize a program with Similix. When the Similix system is loaded into a Scheme session the specializer is called as follows:

> (similix 'goal arg-pat source-file)

where *goal* is the name of the goal function of the subject program, i.e. the program's entry point; *arg-pat*, the argument pattern, is a list of values describing the static and dynamic input to the specialization, where dynamic input is represented by ***; and *source-file* is the name of the file containing the subject program with or without the extension .sim.

Example 2 (Calling the specializer). Assume we want to specialize the program

```
(define (power x n)
  (if (= n 0)
      1
      (* x (power x (- n 1)))))
```

located in the file "power.sim". We specialize the function power with respect to a dynamic first argument and a static second argument with value 5 by using the call:

> (similix 'power '(*** 5) "power")

The result of this specialization will be:

```
(define (power-0 x_0) (* x_0 (* x_0 (* x_0 (* x_0 (* x_0 1))))))
```

3   A System Overview

Similix is an off-line specializer. This means that specialization is essentially divided into two phases. The first phase, called *preprocessing*, analyses the subject program and makes all the essential decisions regarding specialization of the program. The second phase is the specialization phase proper, which we will simply refer to as *specialization*. This process blindly follows the dictates of the preprocessor, much in the same way that evaluation for a strongly typed languages trusts the result of the type checker. The preprocessor communicates its decisions to the specializer by *annotations* on the subject program. Similix also contains a third phase, called *post-processing*, but in these notes we will consider it a part of the specialization phase.

In the following we describe the two phases in turn.

3.1   The preprocessing phase

The preprocessing phase consists of the following sub-phases:

1. front-end
2. flow analysis
3. binding-time analysis (bt-analysis)
4. specialization-point analysis (sp-analysis)
5. evaluation-order dependency analysis (eod-analysis)
6. abstract occurrence-counting analysis (aoc-analysis)
7. redundant let-elimination

The phases run in the order above and each phase will operate on an abstract syntax representation of the subject program annotating this for later phases, e.g. the result of the flow analysis is used by the bt-analysis and the eod-analysis.

The front-end. The front-end performs parsing of the subject program creating an internal representation (abstract syntax) of it on which the remaining phases and the specialization phase work. During parsing it will expand many of the syntactic forms into simpler core languages forms (see Figure 1), e.g. a procedure name P gets transformed into (lambda (V*) (P V*)).

The front-end also reads and parses the ADT declarations and checks if there are any unresolved references to names in the subject program. The front-end can be called by itself just to check a program, which may be useful even in cases where partial evaluation is not intended.

An extra goal function called _sim-goal is also inserted to ensure that the goal function is only called externally.

Finally, the front-end also inserts dummy let-expressions for all formal parameters of procedures and lambda-abstractions around the bodies in these expressions. This transformation ensures that unfolding a procedure call and applying a lambda-abstraction can be done without fear of duplicating or discarding code. The whole problem of avoiding duplicating and discarding code is moved to the unfolding of `let`-expressions. We will discuss this when we describe the abstract occurrence-counting analysis.

The following example illustrates a few of these aspects of the front-end. The program

```
(define (goal s d) (if s d))
```

is transformed into

```
(define (_sim-goal s d)
  (let ((s s)) (let ((d d)) (goal s d))))
(define (goal s d)
  (let ((s s))
    (let ((d d)) (if s d 'undefined)))))
```

Flow analysis. The flow analysis is a kind of type inference restricted to function types and user defined data types. It computes equivalence classes of program points and formal parameters that may be connected by value flow, and what kinds of values may occur in each equivalence class. For an example, consider the following contrived program:

```
(define (goal s d)
  (let ((fa (lambda (x) (mycar x)))
        (fd (lambda (y) (mycdr y)))
        (id (lambda (x) x)))
    (let ((f (if d fa fd))
          (g (if d fa id)))
      (g (f (mycons (mycons s d) d)))))))
```

For this program the flow analysis discovers that `fa`, `fb` and `id` are in the same equivalence class because they may flow to the variables `f` and `g`. This class also contains the occurrences of `f` and `g` in the body of the inner-most let-expression. This gives a safe approximation to the question of what possible values flow between lambda-abstraction and application point. Values (closures) created by a lambda-abstraction may flow to the application points in the equivalence class in which the lambda-abstraction occurs. In the example this means that only the three closures created and bound to `fa`, `fb` and `id` may flow to the application points where `f` and `g` are applied. This does not mean that all closures can actually occur at both application points, in fact this is not the case, and a more sophisticated and more expensive analysis might detect this. The reader is referred to [4, 5] for more details on the flow analysis. The result of the flow analysis is used by the bt-analysis and the eod-analysis.

Binding-Time Analysis. The job of the binding-time analysis is to work out the binding-time of expressions in the subject program and from this information annotate operations as reducible or non-reducible. The domain of binding-time values is shown in Figure 2. The value **S** describes a known base value, e.g. a number, a boolean, etc., **Cl$_n$** describes a known function value (closure) of arity n, and **Ps$_\xi$** describes a known partially static data structure of data type ξ. The value **D** describes an unknown values of any type.

An expression can only be assigned one of the binding-time values shown in Figure 2. This has the consequence that if function values of different arity or partially static data structure of different types or function values and partially static data structure are mixed, they get binding-time value dynamic (**D**). Similix will give a warning when this happens to help users debug their programs for binding-time errors.

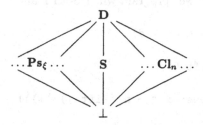

Fig. 2. Domain of binding-time values

The bt-analysis relies heavily on the result of the flow analysis. Consider the lambda-abstraction l of the form (lambda (x) e). To know what binding-time value to assign to the formal parameter x we need to know the binding-time values of all the actual parameters that l may be applied to. This is exactly the kind of information that the flow analysis supplies. The binding-time analysis simply forces x to have a binding-time value larger that all expressions that are possible actual parameters to l, and it can find this out by examining the flow equivalence class of l.

When binding-time analysis has worked out the binding-time values of all expressions in a program it will annotate all operations that cannot be reduced at specialization time as residual. Similix's utility, show can be used to display the result of preprocessing; residual operations will be prefixed with an underline character, e.g. _car and formal parameters are annotated with their binding-time values. If an expression with binding-time value **S**, e.g. 5, occurs in a dynamic context (where code is expected), the binding-time analysis will insert a lift operation, e.g. (lift 5) at the expression.

Example 3 (Annotation of the power program). Assuming that x is dynamic and n is static, we get the following annotation of the power program:

```
(define (power x:d n:s -> d)
  (_let ((x:d x))
    (if (= n 0) (lift 1) (_* x (power x (- n 1))))))
```

Specialization-point analysis. Insertion of specialization points is essential to make specialization terminate for a memoizing specializer like Similix. A specialization point is just an expression somewhere in the subject program. When Similix encounters (specializes) a specialization point for the first time it will remember it together with the static parts of the free variables, and generate a residual procedure call to a new function whose body is the residual code of the specialization point. If Similix encounters the specialization point again and the static parts of the free variables are the same as before, it will generate a call to the previously generated function. This prevents repeated specialization of the same configuration thus often preventing non-termination.

The example below shows the insertion of a specialization point (marked by memo-power-0) in the power program when both x and n are dynamic:

```
(define (power x:d n:d -> d)
  (memo-power-0
    (_if (_= n (lift 0))
         (lift 1)
         (_* x (power x (_- n (lift 1)))))))
```

Similix will insert specialization points at two places in programs: at dynamic conditionals (_if-expressions) and at dynamic lambda-abstractions (_lambda-expressions). These places have been chosen because partial evaluation is more strict than standard evaluation just at these places. Standard evaluation will never evaluate both branches of a conditional or the body of a lambda-abstraction, but partial evaluation will. This strategy will help prevent infinite loops that are controlled by these conditionals during standard evaluation, but not those that are controlled by the static ones. In other words, Similix will not prevent purely static infinite loops from making the specializer loop. There exists one other way in which Similix may loop infinitely, namely, if infinitely many residual functions are generated during specialization. This happens if the same specialization point is encountered again and again with some static part of the free variables increasing in size.

It is possible to switch off the automatic insertion of specialization points in Similix and manually insert one's own. This may in some case lead to better specialization; see [11].

Evaluation-order dependency analysis. The *evaluation-order dependency analysis* finds expressions that may possibly be evaluation order dependent, that is, might modify or access the global state. Since side-effects are introduced by opaque primitives, one might think that any expression that may call an opaque primitive during evaluation should be classified a *imperative* (**I**) meaning: may be evaluation order dependent, but this is not always the case. Consider the let-expression in the following piece of code:

```
(+ 3 (let ((dummy (display "Hello, world"))) 5))
```

If this were to be classified as imperative then the addition of 3 to 5 would be residualized. Actually, only the actual argument of the let-expression and possibly the whole piece of code will be classified as imperative.

The net effect of the analysis is the assignment of I to the eod-value of some expressions. In the eod-annotation phase, a let-expression is underlined (marked as non-reducible), if the actual parameter eod-value is I. Similar annotations are added to indicate where the specializer should insert let-expressions on-the-fly, such that all imperative expressions become bound in let-expressions; see [4].

Abstract occurrence-counting analysis. The purpose of this analysis is to ensure safe unfolding. Since the insertion of dummy let-expressions by the front-end ensures that all but let-expressions can be safely unfolded, this analysis only has to work out whether a let-expression can safely be unfolded. Unconditional unfolding may duplicate or discard residual code. For let-expressions where the actual argument is dynamic (if it is also imperative it is never unfolded) the analysis works out the number of occurrences of the formal parameter on any possible execution path. Only if the number of occurrences is 1 for all paths then the let-expression can safely be unfolded, otherwise it is residualized.

Example 4 (Occurrence counting). Consider the program

```
(define (goal x y)
  (let ((z (+ x y)))
    (let ((q (- x y)))
      (if (> x 0)
          (+ z q)
          (- z 1)))))
```

If x is static and y dynamic then the first let-expression can be unfolded, because no matter what branch of the conditional is taken, z will be referenced exactly once. If, however, x is dynamic and y static then it cannot be unfolded, because then the expression (+ x y) will be duplicated in the residual program. The second let-expression can never be unfolded, because there may be an execution path where q does not occur.

The post-processor also contains a (concrete) occurrence counting analysis to "clean up" residual let-expressions that, due to the conservatism of the abstract occurrence counting analysis, are left residual unnecessarily.

Redundant let-elimination. Some of the dummy let-expressions inserted by the front-end may turn out to be unfoldable and the purpose of the *redundant let-elimination* phase is simply to remove these.

3.2 The specialization phase

At the time when Similix was written it was considered essential that a partial evaluator was self-applicable in order to generate compilers. This is a consequence of the Futamura Equations which states how a compiler or a compiler generator may be produced by self-applying a specializer. Later it was discovered how compilers can be generated by specialization, without the used of self-application, using the so called cogen approach, by which one essentially writes the compiler generator by hand. A number of systems have been written based on the approach [1, 13, 20, 26]. Since Similix has been designed to be effectively self-applicable, it had to be written with care to ensure this. Also some elements of Scheme were left out, because it was not clear how to handle these elements together with self-application.

Similix's specializer is a CPS specializer, that is, it is written in *continuation passing style*. This has the advantage compared with a direct style specializer, as we shall demonstrate below, that certain improvements in specialization are possible, and that certain new features can be introduced safely, e.g. partially static data structures.

We will illustrate the difference between direct style specialization and CPS specialization by an example. Consider the program:

```
(define (goal d)
  (+ 1 (let ((x (car d))) 2)))
```

We will assume that d is dynamic and compare residual programs obtained by the two styles of specialization.

Direct style specialization. In direct style specialization the specializer is performing reductions that corresponds to the reductions that standard direct style evaluator performs, except that it only performs those marked by the pre-processor a reducible. The specializer will also sometimes perform reductions that the standard direct style evaluator would not. For example, the specializer will reduce both branches of an if-expression when the test is non-reducible. For our example that means that we will get the following trivial residual program:

```
(define (goal-0 d_0)
  (+ 1 (let ((x_0 (car d_0))) 2)))
```

This is unfortunate because the addition of 1 to 2 has not been performed. The specializer cannot perform this operation because it has to produce values for both arguments of the addition to reduce it, and the let-expression blocks the way. We would like to move the context in which the let-expression occurs into the body of the let, in essence performing a classic binding-time improvement on the subject program:

```
(define (goal d)
  (let ((x (car d))) (+ 1 2)))
```

This kind of improvement would be gained automatically by CPS style specialization. Let us take a detailed look at how a direct style specializer works. Let $\mathcal{D}$ be the function that specialize expressions. It takes an environment ρ, binding variables to values or code, as argument such that $\mathcal{D}_\rho$ transforms an annotated expression into a residual expression. In the above example, ρ maps d to d_0 and

ρ_1 is ρ extended with the binding of x to x_0. The full definition of $\mathcal{D}$ can be found in [10] along with a specification of the notation[2]. Function *bld-O* build residual code of kind O. The annotated version of our example program looks as follows:

```
(define (goal d)
  (_+ (lift 1) (_let ((x (_car d))) (lift 2))))
```

The specialization of this progresses as follows:

$$\mathcal{D}_\rho((\texttt{\_+ (lift 1) (\_let ((x (\_car d))) (lift 2))))}$$
$$= \textit{bld-+}(\mathcal{D}_\rho((\texttt{lift 1})), \mathcal{D}_\rho((\texttt{\_let ((x (\_car d))) (lift 2))))}$$
$$= \textit{bld-+}(1, \mathcal{D}_\rho((\texttt{\_let ((x (\_car d))) (lift 2))))}$$
$$= \textit{bld-+}(1, \textit{bld-let}(\texttt{x\_0}, \mathcal{D}_\rho((\texttt{\_car d})), \mathcal{D}_{\rho_1}((\texttt{lift 2))))}$$
$$= \textit{bld-+}(1, \textit{bld-let}(\texttt{x\_0}, \textit{bld-car}(d), \mathcal{D}_{\rho_1}((\texttt{lift 2))))}$$
$$= \textit{bld-+}(1, \textit{bld-let}(\texttt{x\_0}, (\texttt{car d\_0}), \mathcal{D}_{\rho_1}((\texttt{lift 2))))}$$
$$= \textit{bld-+}(1, \textit{bld-let}(\texttt{x\_0}, (\texttt{car d\_0}), 2))$$
$$= (\texttt{+ 1 (let ((x\_0 (car d\_0))) 2))}$$

CPS specialization. We will now look at how a CPS specializer will handle our example. The annotated version of our example program now looks a little different:

```
(define (goal d)
  (lift (+ 1 (_let ((x (_car d))) (lift 2)))))
```

This means that a different binding-time analysis is needed for CPS specialization than for direct style specialization. In a CPS-based specializer it would be a simple matter to move the context of a let-expression into its body, since the context is represented by a continuation. Let us see how this works in our example. We will introduce the abbreviation e_1 for the expression (_let ((x (_car d_0))) 2). A call to the CPS-specializer is represented by $\mathcal{C}$, ι is an identity continuation, and ρ and ρ_1 are defined as for the direct cases:

$$\mathcal{C}_\rho((\texttt{lift (+ 1 } e_1)))\iota$$
$$= \mathcal{C}_\rho((\texttt{+ 1 } e_1))\lambda v.\textit{bld-cst}(v)$$
$$= \mathcal{C}_\rho(1)\lambda v_1.\mathcal{C}_\rho(e_1)\lambda v_2.(\lambda v.\textit{bld-cst}(v))(v_1 + v_2)$$
$$= \mathcal{C}_\rho((\texttt{\_let ((x (\_car d\_0))) 2})\lambda v_2.(\lambda v.\textit{bld-cst}(v))(1 + v_2)$$
$$= \mathcal{C}_\rho((\texttt{\_car d\_0}))\lambda v_1.\textit{bld-let}(\texttt{x\_0}, v_1, \mathcal{C}_{\rho_1}(2)\lambda v_2.(\lambda v.\textit{bld-cst}(v))(1 + v_2))$$
$$= \textit{bld-let}(\texttt{x\_0}, (\texttt{car d\_0}), \mathcal{C}_{\rho_1}(2)\lambda v_2.(\lambda v.\textit{bld-cst}(v))(1 + v_2))$$
$$= \textit{bld-let}(\texttt{x\_0}, (\texttt{car d\_0}), (\lambda v.\textit{bld-cst}(v))(1 + 2))$$
$$= \textit{bld-let}(\texttt{x\_0}, (\texttt{car d\_0}), \textit{bld-cst}(1 + 2))$$
$$= \textit{bld-let}(\texttt{x\_0}, (\texttt{car d\_0}), \textit{bld-cst}(3))$$
$$= \textit{bld-let}(\texttt{x\_0}, (\texttt{car d\_0}), 3)$$
$$= (\texttt{let ((x\_0 (car d\_0))) 3})$$

So CPS specialization obtains a residual program in which the addition has been performed.

---

[2] We have here slightly simplified the notation for the sake of the presentation.

4   Specialization by Example

In this section we will go through a series of examples that illustrates how Similix specializes various parts of programs.

4.1   Conditionals

The many forms of conditional expression (see Figure 1) in the Similix subject language are all translated into a core form consisting only of simple two armed if-expressions, e.g. cond-expressions are expanded into a series of if-expressions. In this respect also the short-cut logical connectives and and or are treated as conditional expressions.

Let us see how Similix specializes a simple core if-expression:

$$(\text{if } E_1 \; E_2 \; E_3)$$

If the test E_1 is static, Similix just evaluates the test and then specializes the branch that standard evaluation would have chosen. If the test is dynamic things get a little more complicated, because Similix will insert a specialization point at the if-expression. However, often the user will not need to be concerned with this, because post-unfolding may remove the specialization point again and what is left is a residual if-expression. So how is the residual if-expression produced? Similix specializes the three subexpression of the if-expression and builds a new conditional expression from these. Let us consider an example:

Example 5 (Conditional).

Source program:
```
(define (goal s d)
  (if (= d 5)
      (+ d 1)
      (if (= s 7) 1 2)))
```
Similix call: (similix 'goal '(11 ***) "cond")
Residual program:
```
(define (goal-0 d_0)
  (if (= d_0 5)
      (+ d_0 1)
      2))
```

The program contains two if-expressions; the first one with a dynamic test and the second with a static test. The first one is residualized and becomes the if-expression in the residual program. The second one is reduced, and since the test evaluates to false (#f) the residual code of the second branch becomes the residual code of the if-expression, which is 2. Similix does not know that d is actually 5 in the first branch of the conditional and does not reduce (+ d 1) to 6. This kind of specialization is usually not performed by partial evaluators, but may be found in supercompilers [36] or generalized partial computation [16].

After specialization Similix will try to reintroduce cond-, and- and or-expressions into the residual program for readability. This is done by the post-processor.

4.2   Primitives

As described in Section 2.2 there are several kinds of primitives. The following
example illustrates some of these primitives:

Example 6 (Primitives).

Source program:
```
(define (goal s d)
  (display "I'm here")    ; opaque
  (car (g s d)))          ; transparent
(define (g s d)
  (if (> d 0)             ; transparent
      (cons s '())        ; transparent if needed
      (g
        (+ s 1)           ; transparent if needed
        (- d 1)))))       ; transparent if needed
```
Similix call: (similix 'goal '(3 ***) "prim")
Residual program:
```
(define (goal-0 d_0)
  (define (g-0-1 s_0 d_1)
    (if (> d_1 0)
        (list s_0)
        (g-0-1 (+ s_0 1) (- d_1 1))))
  (display "I'm here")
  (car (g-0-1 3 d_0)))
```

Notice that because the call to + in the function g is generalized, specialization
terminates. This would not have been the case had + not been classified as TIN;
see Section 2.2.

4.3   Side-effecting primitives

Primitives are generally not allowed to side-effect their arguments. The only
allowed side-effects are those performed on global entities such as top-level bound
variables or input/output, although there are cases where these restrictions may
be lifted; see [11]. Here is an example with side-effects:

Example 7 (Side-effects).

Source program:
```
(define (goal)
  (* (begin (display 1) 3)
     (begin (display 2) 14)))
```
Similix call: (similix 'goal '() "sf")
Residual program:
```
(define (goal-0) (display 1) (display 2) 42)
```

What is interesting about this example is that the side-effecting expressions are
lifted out of their context such that the call to * can be reduced. This is one of the
effects of CPS-specialization. In general one should not write programs in this

style in Scheme, since the order of evaluation of arguments is unspecified in the definition of Scheme. For Similix it was decided that for this situation specialization comes before preserving the order of evaluation for a given implementation of Scheme and the order of evaluation has been set to be left-to-right. It is therefore possible that the order of evaluation may be changed by specialization for programs that depend on the order in which arguments are evaluated.

4.4   Let-expressions

When specializing a let-expression

$$(\texttt{let } ((V\ E))\ B)$$

Similix might choose to unfold or residualize it. If the binding-time of the parameter V (and therefore also E) is static then Similix can safely unfold the let-expression, but if the binding-time of V is dynamic the situation is different. Unfolding a let-expression whose parameter is dynamic can lead to either code duplication or wrong residual programs. Code duplication could occur when it turns out that the parameter will be used more than once in the residual program. Depending on the context, code duplication could lead to a slowdown, if the duplicated code occurs on the same evaluation path in the residual program. A wrong residual program is one for which the Mix-equation does not hold. If, by unfolding a let-expression, a non-terminating computation is discarded, the residual program terminates more often than the original program, and can therefore not obey the Mix-equation[3]. The following is an example:

Example 8 (Let-expressions).

Source program:
```
(define (goal s d)
  (let ((x (+ s 5)))
    (let ((y (f d)))
      (if (= x 9)
          y
          x))))
(define (f x) (if (= x 0) 0 (f (- x 1))))
```
Similix call: (similix 'goal '(3 ***) "let")
Residual program:
```
(define (goal-0 d_0)
  (define (f-0-1 x_0)
    (if (= x_0 0) 0 (f-0-1 (- x_0 1))))
  (f-0-1 d_0)
  8)
```

If the residual program had not contained the call (f-0-1 d_0) then it would terminate for negative values of d_0 which would not be the case for the original

---

[3] The Mix-equation is here taken up to termination of specialization, but not up to termination of subject and residual program.

program when called as follows (goal 3 *d*) where *d* is a negative number. So in conclusion: a dynamic let-expression can only be unfolded when its actual argument is known to be executed exactly once in the specialized body of the let-expression.

When the expression E in the let-expression contains a side-effecting subexpression, unfolding the let-expression may change the order of side-effects, so in that case Similix never unfolds the let-expression. The next example illustrates this:

Example 9 (Lets and side-effects).

Source program:
```
(define (goal)
  (let* ((x (read))
         (y (read)))
    (if (> y 0) (+ x 1) (- x 1))))
```
Similix call: (similix 'goal '() "eod")
Residual program:
```
(define (goal-0)
  (let* ((x_0 (read))
         (y_1 (read)))
    (if (> y_1 0) (+ x_0 1) (- x_0 1))))
```

If the let-expressions in this example were unfolded then not only would the order in which input is read be changed, but also the number of values read. So Similix does not unfold the let-expressions in this case. Sequences, i.e. begin-expressions, are handled as if these were let-expressions with dummy formal parameters, not occurring free in the body of the let-expression. Note also that the order of evaluation is preserved.

4.5   Higher-order functions

As a simple example of how functions may be specialized w.r.t. higher-order values we consider the specialization of a version of the map function:

Example 10 (Higher-order functions).

Source program:
```
(define (goal xs)
  (my-map (lambda (y) (+ y 1)) xs))

(define (my-map f xs)
  (if (null? xs) '()
      (cons (f (car xs)) (my-map f (cdr xs)))))
```
Similix call: (similix 'goal '(***) "ho")
Residual program:
```
(define (goal-0 xs_0)
  (define (my-map-0-1 xs_0)
    (if (null? xs_0)
        '()
        (cons (+ (car xs_0) 1) (my-map-0-1 (cdr xs_0)))))
  (my-map-0-1 xs_0))
```

The residual function my-map-0 is a specialized version of my-map where the addition of 1 has been in-lined. Had map been defined as a primitive this would not have happened.

As can be seen from the example the higher order elements (the lambda-abstraction and the application) have been removed and the residual program is entirely first-order. In fact, if no lambda-abstraction is dynamic in a subject program, the residual program will be first-order. For interpreters using functions to represent environments this means that one may often get rid of the environment operations altogether when specializing the interpreter with respect to a program.

4.6 Partially static data structures

We give an example that illustrates the difference between constructors (mycons) and primitives (cons):

Example 11 (Partially static data-structures).

Source program:
```
(defconstr (mycons mycar mycdr) (mynil))

(define (goal d)
  (* 7 (cdr (cons (f d) 6)))
  (* 7 (mycdr (mycons (f d) 6))))

(define (f x)
  (if (= x 0) 0 (f (- x 1))))
```
Similix call: (similix 'goal '(***) "psds")
Residual program:
```
(defconstr (mycons mycar mycdr) (mynil))

(define (goal-0 d_0)
  (define (f-0-1 x_0)
    (if (= x_0 0) 0 (f-0-1 (- x_0 1))))
  (* 7 (cdr (cons (f-0-1 d_0) 6)))
  (f-0-1 d_0)
  42)
```

The example shows that even though the constructed value (mycons (f x) 6) contains a dynamic (unknown) component (f x), the static component of the value can still be accessed and used for further specialization. This is not the case for the value constructed by cons. Note also that although the value of (f x) is not used, it is still computed, since discarding the computation could be semantically unsound.

4.7 Static error under dynamic control

Using CPS specialization enables Similix to discard a strict context containing a static error. In the following example the context (+ 3 []) is strict and will be discarded. What is left is the code that would have produced the error had it been executed:

$$(/ \ 5 \ 0)$$

In this way Similix generates code that will produce the same error as the original code if it is ever executed, only slightly faster.

Example 12 (Static error).

Source program:
```
(define (goal s)
   (+ 3 (/ 5 s)))
```
Similix call: (similix 'goal '(0) "se")
Residual program:
```
(define (goal-0) (/ 5 0))
```

Similix even writes out a warning during specialization indicating that there is a potential error in the residual program. The error will only occur when the residual program is run.

5   Specializing Interpreters

In this section we will support the claim that Similix is well-suited for partially evaluating interpreters that use environments represented as functions. In the interpreter (Figure 3) for applicative (strict) lambda calculus, the environments are represented by functions. The initial environment, represented by (lambda (x) v) binds any variable to a value supplied as input to the interpreter (through its goal function run). The function upd updates an environment with a new binding. The syntax of the lambda calculus is

$$LExp ::= Var \mid (\backslash \ Var \ Lexp) \mid (LExp \ LExp)$$

where Var is any Scheme symbol except $\backslash$. The primitives isVar?, isLam?, etc. are defined in the file int.adt (Figure 4). Note also the use of the error function to report syntax errors. If we specialize the goal function run of the interpreter wrt. a static lambda term e and a dynamic input value v we get a Scheme representation of the lambda term. In other words we have compiled the lambda term into Scheme as described by the first Futamura projection. As an example let us take the following lambda term:

$$(\lambda x.(f(\lambda y.((xx)y))))(\lambda x.(f(\lambda y.((xx)y))))$$

which is a call-by-value fix-point operator. It computes the least fix-point for any expression we may substitute for f. In the interpreter the value of f is supplied through the input to the interpreter. We have the following Scheme representation of the lambda term:

```
((\ x (f (\ y ((x x) y)))) (\ x (f (\ y ((x x) y)))))
```

The call

```
(loadt "int.adt")

(define (run e v) (_eval e (lambda (x) v)))

(define (_eval e r)
  (cond
    ((isVar? e) (r e))
    ((isLam? e) (lambda (v) (_eval (Lam->B e) (upd (Lam->V e) v r))))
    ((isApp? e) ((_eval (App->E1 e) r) (_eval (App->E2 e) r)))
    (else (_sim-error "Unknown syntactic form ~s" e))))

(define (upd x v r)
  (lambda (y) (if (equal? x y) v (r y))))
```

Fig. 3. Lambda interpreter: int.sim

```
(defprim (isVar? e) (symbol? e))
(defprim (isLam? e)
  (and (list e) (= (length e) 3) (equal? (car e) '\)))
(defprim (isApp? e)
  (and (list e) (= (length e) 2)))
(defprim 1 Lam->V cadr)
(defprim 1 Lam->B caddr)
(defprim 1 App->E1 car)
(defprim 1 App->E2 cadr)
```

Fig. 4. Abstract data types for lambda interpreter: int.adt

```
(similix 'run
         '(((\ x (f (\ y ((x x) y)))) (\ x (f (\ y ((x x) y))))) ***)
         "int")
```
to Similix results in the following residual program:

```
(loadt "int.adt")
(define (run-0 v_0)
  (define (_eval-0-1 r_0)
    (lambda (v_1)
      (let ((g_4 (lambda (v_2) (let ((g_3 (v_1 v_1))) (g_3 v_2)))))
        (r_0 g_4))))
  (let* ((g_1 (_eval-0-1 v_0)) (g_2 (_eval-0-1 v_0)))
    (g_1 g_2)))
```

Similix's memoization has as an extra effect that (textually) identical source code will result in shared code in the target (residual) program.

Since the input value can be any Scheme value we can test the residual program with a functional value:

```
(define (fac f)
```

```
(lambda (x)
    (if (= x 0) 1 (* x (f (- x 1)))))))
```

With this (run-0 fac) becomes the factorial function, which we test by the following Scheme session:

```
> ((run-0 fac) 10)
3628800
```

5.1   Generating a compiler

We shall now show how to generate a compiler for the lambda calculus language with Similix. Theoretically this is done by applying the cogen of Similix to the code of interpreter. However, Cogen need to know a little more than this: the goal function and the binding-time of the input of the interpreter. Therefore the complete call to Similix's cogen (named cogen in the system) is:

```
> (cogen 'run '(s d) "int")
front-end flow bt sp eod oc rl
loading compiler generator
generating compiler
()
```

This produced a compiler that can be used immediately by calling the function comp (this always calls the most recently generated compiler). The call:

```
> (comp '(((\ x (f (\ y ((x x) y)))) (\ x (f (\ y ((x x) y))))) ***))
```

produces the same target program as above.

5.2   Generating Cogen

Generating the Cogen of Similix is usually not something the user of Similix has to be bothered with, as it comes with the system and can be called with the function cogen as seen above. Actually one can regenerate Cogen using Cogen itself by the call:

```
> (cogen '_sim-specialize '(s d s d) "spec")
```

Here _sim-specialize is the goal function of the Similix specializer. This takes four arguments: the goal function, the argument pattern (static values), the preprocessed program and the name of the residual goal function. The binding-time pattern of these are as shown: (s d s d).

Just to illustrate how Cogen can be generated using only the specialiser we present a session that does this. Recall the theoretical formula (the third Futamura projection) for generating Cogen:

$$Cogen = [Mix](Mix, Mix)$$

This hides a lot of details. For instance the first Mix needs to know the binding time pattern of the program it is going to specialize, i.e. the second Mix, but

more importantly it is not really the whole specializer Mix that we are specializing, only the specialization phase. Let us call this $Spec$. This means that the
computation that we are performing is:

$$Cogen = [Mix](Spec, [\text{spec}, ***, Spec^{ann}])$$

where spec is the goal function of $Spec$ and $Spec^{ann}$ is $Spec$ annotated by the
preprocessor of Mix. Recall that *** indicates a dynamic argument. It is actually
the annotation of the last specializer that makes the self-application effective.

Turning to our concrete specializer, Similix, the first thing we have to do is
to preprocess the specializer:

```
> (preprocess! '_sim-specialize '(s d s d) "spec")
```

This results in a preprocessed program in an internal representation (the form
expected by Similix's specializer). To get this data structure one has to use
the Similix system variable **Similix-preprocessed-program**. The call to
Similix that generates Cogen then has the form (using backquote notation):

```
> (similix '_sim-specialize
           `(_sim-specialize `(*** ,**Similix-preprocessed-program** ***)
           "spec")
```

6   Literature

In this section we will give a small guide to the literature on Similix. We will divide this literature into three groups. The first group contains books and papers
that one may read to learn more about the foundation of partial evaluation.
The second group contains papers concerned with theoretical aspects of Similix, or descriptions of Similix. The third group contains papers that describe
applications of Similix.

6.1   Foundation

The most comprehensive book on partial evaluation is [24]. This book contains a
theoretical description of partial evaluation as well as concrete examples of specialization of various programming languages. It contains a chapter on Similix.

6.2   Theory

The original first-order version of Similix is described by Bondorf and Danvy in
[2, 3] and the higher-order version by Bondorf in his thesis [7] or as an extended
abstract in [6, 8]. The CPS version is described in [10] where a compact formal
description of the specialization algorithm is presented. The efficient pre-analysis
of Similix 5.0 is presented in [4, 5]. The manual of Similix 5.0[11] also describes
some theoretical aspects, especially binding-time improvements.

Some papers that describes extensions of Similix are [32, 34, 31].

---
[4] There is at present no manual for Similix 5.1.

6.3 Applications

Many of the applications of Similix have to do with compiling, that is, using self-application to compile or generate compilers. Early examples are given by Bondorf [7, 6, 8]. Bondorf [9] also describes how to compile laziness by writing an interpreter for a lazy language and using self-application to compile lazy programs. Jørgensen [27] describes how to generate a pattern matching compiler by partial evaluation and how this technique can be used to produce an efficient compiler for a substantial part of a realistic lazy functional language [28, 29]. Similarly, Harnett and Montenyohl shows how to do efficient compilation of an object-oriented language [22] and Bondorf and Palsberg show how to compile Action Semantics [12]. A few compiler-related applications have been concerned with generating parser generators [33, 35].

Glück and Jørgensen have used Similix for generating optimizing specializers [18] and program transformers [19], by also using self-application on specially written interpreters.

7 Remaining Problems

The most important remaining problem with Similix is to ensure termination of specialization. Most of the theoretical background for this has been developed, but has to be adapted to the language treated by Similix.

Acknowledgement: Thanks to Peter Thiemann for many valuable comments and suggestions for improvements. Also thanks to Peter Sestoft and Robert Glück for giving comments on an ealier draft of the paper. Thanks to Anders Bondorf for introducing Similix me to and giving me a small part in its creation.

References

1. Lars Ole Andersen. *Program Analysis and Specialization for the C Programming Language.* PhD thesis, DIKU, University of Copenhagen, May 1994. (DIKU report 94/19).
2. Anders Bondorf and Olivier Danvy. Automatic autoprojection of recursive equations with global variables and abstract data types. Technical Report 90-4, DIKU, University of Copenhagen, Denmark, 1990.
3. Anders Bondorf and Olivier Danvy. Automatic autoprojection of recursive equations with global variables and abstract data types. *Science of Computer Programming*, 16:151–195, 1991.
4. Anders Bondorf and Jesper Jørgensen. Efficient analyses for realistic off-line partial evaluation: extended version. Technical Report 93/4, DIKU, University of Copenhagen, Denmark, 1993.
5. Anders Bondorf and Jesper Jørgensen. Efficient analyses for realistic off-line partial evaluation. *Journal of Functional Programming, special issue on partial evaluation*, 3(3):315–346, 1993.

6. Anders Bondorf. Automatic autoprojection of higher order recursive equations. In Neil D. Jones, editor, *ESOP'90, Copenhagen, Denmark. LNCS 432*, pages 70–87. Springer-Verlag, May 1990.
7. Anders Bondorf. *Self-Applicable Partial Evaluation*. PhD thesis, DIKU, University of Copenhagen, Denmark, 1990.
8. Anders Bondorf. Automatic autoprojection of higher order recursive equations. *Science of Computer Programming*, 17(1-3):3–34, December 1991. Revision of paper in ESOP'90, LNCS 432, May 1990.
9. Anders Bondorf. Compiling laziness by partial evaluation. In [25], pages 9–22, 1991.
10. Anders Bondorf. Improving binding times without explicit cps-conversion. In *1992 ACM Conference on Lisp and Functional Programming. San Francisco, California. LISP Pointers, vol. V, no. 1*, pages 1–10, June 1992.
11. Anders Bondorf. *Similix 5.0 Manual*. DIKU, University of Copenhagen, Denmark, May 1993. Included in Similix distribution, 82 pages.
12. Anders Bondorf and Jens Palsberg. Compiling actions by partial evaluation. In *FPCA'93, Conference on Functional Programming and Computer Architecture, Copenhagen, Denmark*, pages 308–317. ACM, June 1993.
13. Lars Birkedal and Morten Welinder. Hand-writing program generator generators. In M. Hermenegildo and J. Penjam, editors, *Programming Language Implementation and Logic Programming. Proceedings*, volume 844 of *LNCS*, pages 198–214, Madrid, Spain, 1994. Springer-Verlag.
14. Charles Consel. *Analyse de programmes, Evaluation partielle et Génération de compilateurs*. PhD thesis, LITP, University of Paris 6, France, June 1989. In French.
15. Charles Consel. A tour of Schism: a partial evaluation system for higher-order applicative languages. In *Proceedings of the Symposium on Partial Evaluation and Semantics-Based Program Manipulation*, pages 145–154. ACM Press, 1993.
16. Yoshihiko Futamura and Kenroku Nogi. Generalized partial computation. In Dines Bjørner, Andrei P. Ershov, and Neil D. Jones, editors, *Partial Evaluation and Mixed Computation*, pages 133–151. North-Holland, 1988.
17. Carsten K. Gomard and Neil D. Jones. A partial evaluator for the untyped lambda calculus. *Journal of Functional Programming*, 1(1):21–69, January 1991.
18. Robert Glück and Jesper Jørgensen. Generating optimizing specializers. In *IEEE International Conference on Computer Languages*, pages 183–194. IEEE Computer Society Press, 1994.
19. Robert Glück and Jesper Jørgensen. Generating transformers for deforestation and supercompilation. In B. Le Charlier, editor, *Static Analysis. Proceedings*, volume 864 of *LNCS*, pages 432–448, Namur, Belgium, 1994. Springer-Verlag.
20. Robert Glück and Jesper Jørgensen. An automatic program generator for multi-level specialization. *LISP and Symbolic Computation*, 10(2):113–158, 1997.
21. Carsten K. Gomard. Higher order partial evaluation – hope for the lambda calculus. Master's thesis, DIKU, University of Copenhagen, Denmark, student report 89-9-11, September 1989.
22. Sheila Harnett and Margaret Montenyohl. Towards effecient compilation of a dynamic object-oriented language. In Charles Consel, editor, *PEPM'92, ACM SIGPLAN Workshop on Partial Evaluation and Semantics-Based Program Manipulation*, pages 82–89, June 1992.
23. Carsten Kehler Holst. Language triplets: the Amix approach. In Dines Bjørner, Andrei P. Ershov, and Neil D. Jones, editors, *Partial Evaluation and Mixed Computation*, pages 167–185. North-Holland, 1988.

24. Neil D. Jones, Carsten K. Gomard, and Peter Sestoft. *Partial Evaluation and Automatic Program Generation*. Prentice-Hall, 1993.
25. Simon L. Peyton Jones, Graham Hutton, and Carsten Kehler Holst, editors. *Functional Programming, Glasgow 1990. Workshops in Computing*. Springer-Verlag, August 1991.
26. Jesper Jørgensen and Michael Leuschel. Efficiently generating efficient generating extensions in Prolog. In O. Danvy, R. Glück, and P. Thiemann, editors, *Proceedings Dagstuhl Seminar on Partial Evaluation*, pages 263–283, Schloss Dagstuhl, Germany, February 1996. Springer-Verlag.
27. Jesper Jørgensen. Generating a pattern matching compiler by partial evaluation. In [25], pages 177–195, 1991.
28. Jesper Jørgensen. Compiler generation by partial evaluation. Master's thesis, DIKU, University of Copenhagen, Denmark, University of Copenhagen, Denmark, Jan 1992.
29. Jesper Jørgensen. Generating a compiler for a lazy language by partial evaluation. In *Nineteenth Annual ACM SIGACT-SIGPLAN Symposium on Principles of Programming Languages. Albuquerque, New Mexico*, pages 258–268, January 1992.
30. Neil D. Jones, Peter Sestoft, and Harald Søndergaard. An experiment in partial evaluation: the generation of a compiler generator. In J.-P. Jouannaud, editor, *Rewriting Techniques and Applications, Dijon, France. LNCS 202*, pages 124–140. Springer-Verlag, 1985.
31. Karoline Malmkjær. Predicting properties of residual programs. In Charles Consel, editor, *PEPM'92, ACM SIGPLAN Workshop on Partial Evaluation and Semantics-Based Program Manipulation*, pages 8–13, June 1992. Available as Technical Report YALEU/DCS/RR-909 from Yale University.
32. Christian Mossin. Similix binding time debugger manual, system version 4.0. Included in Similix distribution, September 1991.
33. Christian Mossin. Partial evaluation of general parsers (extended abstract). In David Schmidt, editor, *ACM SIGPLAN Symposium on Partial Evaluation and Semantics-Based Program Manipulation, PEPM'93, Copenhagen, Denmark*, June 1993.
34. Bernhard Rytz and Marc Gengler. A polyvariant binding time analysis. In Charles Consel, editor, *PEPM'92, ACM SIGPLAN Workshop on Partial Evaluation and Semantics-Based Program Manipulation*, pages 21–28, June 1992. Available as Technical Report YALEU/DCS/RR-909 from Yale University.
35. Michael Sperber and Peter Thiemann. The essence of LR parsing. In *PEPM'95, ACM SIGPLAN Workshop on Partial Evaluation and Semantics-Based Program Manipulation*, pages 146–155. ACM, ACM Press, june 1995.
36. Valentin F. Turchin. The concept of a supercompiler. *Transactions on Programming Languages and Systems*, 8(3):292–325, 1986.

C-Mix
Specialization of C Programs

Arne John Glenstrup, Henning Makholm, and Jens Peter Secher*

DIKU
Universitetsparken 1
DK-2100 Copenhagen Ø
Denmark
fax: (+45) 35321401
email: cmix@diku.dk

Abstract. C-Mix is a partial evaluator that is able to specialize strictly conforming ISO C programs. C-Mix generates specialized versions of functions, unrolls loops and pre-computes expressions and control constructs that depend on known data only. These transformations are similar to what optimizing compilers do, but since C-Mix takes some of the program's input into account, it can potentially do better.

This article gives a bird's-eye view of several aspects of the C-Mix system: how it is used, a few examples of what it can do, and some information on how it works.

1 Introduction

One often has a class of similar problems which all must be solved efficiently. A solution is to write many small and efficient programs, one for each. This approach suffers from several disadvantages: much programming is needed, and maintenance is difficult, since a change in outside specifications can require every program to be modified.

Alternatively, one may write a single highly parameterized program able to solve any problem in the class. This has a different disadvantage: *inefficiency*. A highly parameterized program can spend most of its time testing and interpreting parameters, and relatively little in carrying out the computations it is intended to do.

Similar problems arise with highly modular programming. While excellent for documentation, modification, and human usage, inordinately much computation time can be spent passing data around and converting among various internal representations at module interfaces.

To get the best of both worlds: write only one highly parameterized and perhaps inefficient program; and *use a partial evaluator to specialize* it to each interesting setting of the parameters, automatically obtaining as many customized versions as desired. All are faithful to the general program, and the customized

*All authors are supported by DART (http://www.diku.dk/research-groups/topps/activities/dart.html).

versions are often much more efficient. Similarly, partial evaluation can remove most or all the interface code from modularly written programs.

1.1   The C Language

In this paper we will describe some aspects of specializing C programs. The fact that C is a "real" language, in the sense that it is in widespread commercial use and runs on virtually all platforms, makes it highly suitable as a vehicle for promoting advanced optimization techniques. The mere fact that millions of people know how to make C programs justifies an in-depth treatment of a language that, according to a lot of researchers, lacks the well-defined semantics and orthogonality that we are used to when dealing with programming language research.

The philosophy of the C language is to trust the programmer: the language itself should not restrict a programmer in achieving the goals of a certain project. The language is not strongly typed and it is possible to do all kinds of messy manipulation with the underlying representation of semantic objects. Luckily, in 1988 the International Standards Organization created a standard definition for the language which was later adopted by several national standards bodies, *e.g.*, ANSI [4]. Henceforth, we will denote this language ISO C. A strictly conforming program shall only use features described in the standard and may not rely on implementation defined behaviour, and we concern ourselves only with strictly conforming programs.

We require that programs are reasonably well-typed, which means that *e.g.*, unions can only be used to save space, not to type-cast data. Bit-fields in structs are accepted but may produce unexpected behaviour. In general, one cannot rely on implementation defined features when specializing programs.

We assume that the reader is familiar with the C language and able to read small C programs (cf. Kernighan and Ritchie [10]).

1.2   C-Mix

C-Mix is a partial evaluator that works together with existing C and C++ compilers. This article describes several aspects of the C-Mix system: how it is used (Sect. 2), a few examples of what it can do (Sect. 3), and some information on how it works (Sect. 4). These three components are compiled from notes handed out at the Partial Evaluation Summer School 1998, held at DIKU, Copenhagen, Denmark.

This article is *not* meant to be a general introduction to *off-line partial evaluation*; such articles are present elsewhere in this volume.

For the experienced and impassioned reader, we here present an overview of the limitations and features in C-Mix. On the positive side, we have the following capabilities.

- All analyses are inter-procedural.
- Polyvariant program-point specialization is supported.

- We allow non-local static side effects if they are under static control.
- Functions that contain dynamic actions can have static return values.
- Arrays can be split into individual variables.
- User annotations guiding the analyses and specialization can easily be made both in the subject program and in a separate directive file.

We have the following limitations:

- The pointer analysis is flow-insensitive and control-insensitive, and hence all other analyses are flow-insensitive.
- The binding-time analysis is monovariant for function parameters.
- Unions can only be used in a limited way.

2   The C-Mix Manual

Those of us who have been in the game long enough to have started programming in interpreted BASIC on a machine with an astronomical 48 kilobytes of RAM remember the shocking relevation that for Real Programming Languages running your program was a two-step process: one had to *compile* one's program before it could run. What an amazingly bizarre arrangement! We quickly learned, however, the clumsiness paid off: compiled programs are much faster than equivalent interpreted programs, typically by an order of magnitude or more. The difference between the two approaches is depicted in Fig. 1, where round boxes represent data and squares represent programs. The solid arrows represent production of output, while hollow arrows represent use of input.

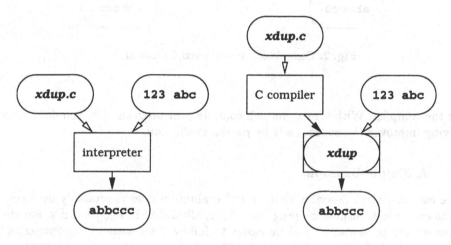

Fig. 1. Interpreting versus compiling

Partial evaluation does something similar to the process of running a program: what used to be a single process is split into two. Somewhat analogous to the compiler, we introduce a utility called a *specializer* (or, as it is also called: a *partial evaluator*, see *e.g.*, [9]) that transforms the program before we compile it.

The objective is the same as when compiling: the transformed program often runs much faster than when we run it directly. But the method is different: A compiler speeds up the program by expressing it in a language closer to the hardware of the machine. A specializer may be given the values of some of the program's input, and uses that knowledge to reduce the program's workload. This is illustrated in Fig. 2.

The similarities between compiling and partial evaluation are mentioned in an attempt to ease understanding, not to suggest the specializer as a replacement

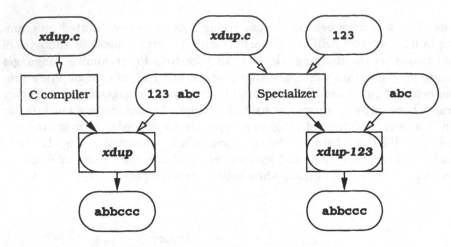

Fig. 2. Compilation versus partial evaluation.

for the compiler. With C-Mix you still compile your program, but you do it after having improved the source code by partial evaluation.

2.1 A Simple Example

The easiest way to describe what partial evaluation does is probably by a concrete example: Consider the program *xdup.c*, alluded to in Figs. 1 and 2. For the moment the presentation will be easier to follow if we assume the "program" is only a single function whose input 123 and abc come in two separate string parameters. Then the source *xdup.c* might look thus:

```
#include <stdio.h>
void xdupfun(char counts[], char data[]) {
    int i, t ;
    for( i=0; counts[i]; i++ ) {
        t = counts[i]-'0' ;
        while( t-- )
            putchar(data[i]) ;
    }
}
```

The specializer, presented with this *subject program*, and the information that counts is "123", sees that the values of the local variables i and t never depend on the values in the data parameter. Thus all of the i and t manipulation can be done as soon as "123" is available – that is, during the specialization process: we say that it is done *at specialization time*, or *at spectime* for short. Conversely the indexing of the data array cannot happen until the array is available.

The specializer produces a file *xdup-123.c* essentially containing

```
#include <stdio.h>
void xdupfun(char data[]) {
    putchar(data[0]);
    putchar(data[1]);
    putchar(data[1]);
    putchar(data[2]);
    putchar(data[2]);
    putchar(data[2]);
}
```

It is reasonable to expect this *residual program* to run faster than the original *xdup*, because it does not have to spend time parsing the counts parameter. It is called a residual program because it is what is left when the specializer has removed everything it can get away with.

If you had a program that called

> **xdupfun**(123, *something*);

thousands of times, the time needed to specialize *xdup.c* might pay back well in reduced execution times.

2.2 Some Advantages of Partial Evaluation

"This is all very well," the sceptical reader may object here, "but might I not just as well have written *xdup-123.c* by hand?" The answer is that yes, in some cases you might. But there are also reasons why you might benefit from the partial evaluation approach:

- You can easily change your mind about what you need. If you later find out that what you really want is not *xdup-123.c* but a *xdup-456.c* or *xdup-117.c*, you would be faced with the task of developing a new function from scratch. With C-Mix that would be as easy as rerunning an automatic utility with some revised parameters. You would save coding time as well as debugging time: even if you do not trust C-Mix so much as to completely skip testing the automatically generated *xdup-456.c*, C-Mix certainly makes fewer trivial typos and spelling errors than a human programmer.
- You may have *xdup.c* at hand already – perhaps because you're trying to speed up an existing program, or the code may just be lying around from an early prototype of the program you're developing. The advantage is the same as when you change your mind.
- It may actually be easier to develop *xdup.c* and specialize it than to develop *xdup-123.c*. This is hardly so in the example – because it was deliberately chosen to be simple enough that the residual program is easy to understand – but that is not always true; a residual program can easily have a more complex structure than the original subject program.

It might actually be worthwhile to think of the partial evaluator not as a tool for speeding up programs but as a tool that lets you develop efficient customized programs (*xdup-123* etc.) with little more development and maintenance effort than that of a single, general version (*xdup*). Analogously, a compiler can be viewed as either a program that speeds up other programs, or as a utility that saves you the time it would take to write your programs directly in assembler language for each machine type they have to run on.

2.3   How to Run C-Mix on the example

Now we describe what exactly must be typed to specialize the *xdup.c* shown on page 112 with C-Mix. It is a little more involved than it seems in Fig. 2, because the specialization which appears as a "black box" in Fig. 2 actually involves several steps when using C-Mix. It will later become apparent that this makes C-Mix much more flexible, just as enhancing a compiler with a separate linker step makes *that* more flexible. Figure 3 is closer to the full truth about C-Mix than Fig. 2 but a little more complex than we dared present to an unprepared reader.

Now, assume that you have C-Mix installed on your system and *xdup.c* is in the current directory. Now, give the command

```
cmix xdup.c -e 'goal: xdupfun($1,?)'
```

Let us have a closer look at that:

cmix is the name of C-Mix's main program.

xdup.c is the C source file that contains the subject program.

-e specifies that the next argument is a *specializer directive*. Specializer directives supply C-Mix with information that is not directly contained in the subject program alone. The full manual describes all of the possibilities; here we just use one.

goal is a keyword for this kind of specializer directive.

xdupfun is the name of the function that we want to specialize. The input to C-Mix may include several functions, so it needs to be told from which function we want to produce a specialized form.

$1 specifies that the first argument to xdupfun will be given at specialization time. Note that we do not yet specify what it is; its value will be given later, as the first (hence the 1 in $1) argument to the *generating extension*, see Sect. 4.4.

? specifies that the second argument to xdupfun will not be known at spectime.

If everything goes well, C-Mix will output two files: the generating extension in the file *xdup-gen.cc*, and an *annotated subject program* in the file *xdup.ann*.

The annotated subject program is an encoded version of the C input with annotations that aim at showing what will happen to the program as it gets specialized. The file is not human-readable; you need to use the cmixshow utility to read it. Give the command

```
cmixshow xdup.ann
```

and a window will pop up, showing a pretty-printed version of your program.

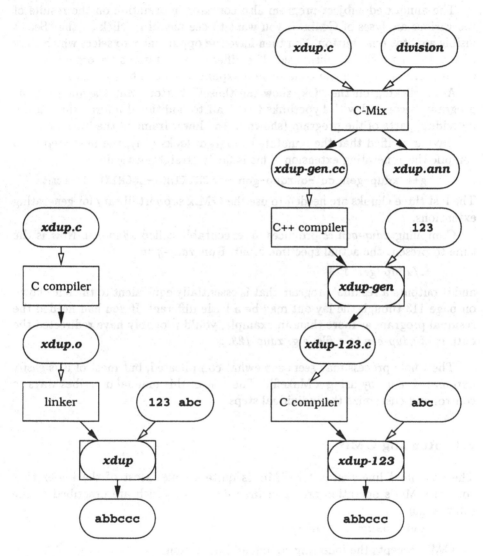

Fig. 3. Neither compilation nor specialization are really as simple as they seem in Fig. 2.

Some parts of the program will be shown in boldface in the annotation browser window. Those are the parts of the program that have been annotated *residual* (also called *dynamic*), meaning that they are not executed at spectime but will instead generate code to appear in the residual program.

The annotated subject program also contains information on the results of the various analyses of C-Mix. If you want to see any of it, click on the "Select visible annotations" button. You then have the opportunity to select which class of annotations you want displayed. The different annotations are organised in a tree-like structure; you can collapse and expand branches to your liking.

After clicking on the "Ok, show me those!" button, you'll again see your program, decorated with hyperlinks that lead to additional information on the individual parts of the program (shown in the lower frame of the browser).

Having verified that the annotated program looks okay, the next step is to compile the generating extension. This is fairly straightforward:

```
g++ xdup-gen.cc -o xdup-gen -I$CMIXINC -L$CMIXLIB -lcmix
```

The last three chunks are needed to use the C-Mix support library for generating extensions.

Compiling *xdup-gen.cc* produces an executable called *xdup-gen*. Now is the time to present the actual spectime input. Run *xdup-gen*:

```
./xdup-gen 123
```

and it outputs a residual program that is essentially equivalent to the one shown on page 113 though the lay-out may be a little different. If you had needed the residual program as more than an example, you'd probably have redirected the output of *xdup-gen* to a file, e.g. *xdup-123.c*.

The whole process may seem somewhat complicated, but most of it is easily automated, *e.g.,* by using a Makefile. The rest of this manual describes ways to control and customize the individual steps.

2.4   Running C-Mix

The command line syntax for C-Mix is quite simple. Most of the knobs that control C-Mix's operation are *specializer directives* which are described in the full manual.

> **cmix** *option ...   filename ...*

C-Mix accepts the following command line options:

- **-I** *path* – specifies where to look for #included files. Equivalent to the -I option usually found in C compilers.
- **-D** *symbol* or **-D** *symbol=expansion* – defines the given symbol as a preprocessor macro when reading in the C sources. Equivalent to the **define:** specializer directive and to the -D option usually found in C compilers.
- **-e** *directive* – give an arbitrary specializer directive. Note that the shell will probably need the directive text to be quoted except in very simple cases.

-o *basename* – controls the naming of the C-Mix output files, which will be called *basename-gen.cc* and *basname.ann*. Equivalent to the outputbase: specializer directive.

-q – suppresses routine messages about the progress of the analyses.

-s – output the .ann file in a format that resembles the data format used internally by C-Mix. The format is sufficiently close to C to be readable, but you may have trouble recognizing the structure of your program – or indeed to find your program amidst the definitions read from header files.

-b – make a generating extension that tries very hard to share code internally in each residual function. This slows down the specialization process very noticeably, usually with no great benefit.

-h – displays an option summary

Any command-line argument to C-Mix that is not an option is treated as a file name. If the argument ends with .c then it is assumed to be a C source file containing code to be specialized.

If a command line argument is not an option and does not look like a C source file name, it is interpreted as the name of a *script file*. The script file consists of specializer directives separated by semicolons or blank lines. Since most of C-Mix's actions can be controlled by specializer directives, once you have set up a script file, say myproject.cmx, a useful C-Mix command line can be as short as

        cmix myproject.cmx

C-Mix names its output files by appending -gen.cc and .ann to a basename obtained in the following way:

- An -o option, if it exists, always takes precedence
- If no -o option is found C-Mix looks for an outputbase: specializer directive.
- The name of the first script file named on the command line. By convention, script files have names ending in .cmx; this suffix is stripped from the file name before using it to derive output file names.
- If there is no script file, the name of the first C source file named on the command line is used.
- If everything else fails, the output files will be names cmix-gen.cc and cmix.ann.

2.5   The Annotated-Program Browser

The annotated-program browser accepts no command-line switches other than the name of its input file:

        cmixshow *filename.ann*

The program installs itself as a specialized HTTP server and automatically starts a browser subprocess to take care of the actual screen display.

While working on binding-time improvement of a program, it can be convenient to run cmixshow as a background job. When the .ann file has changed you just hit the browser's "reload" button which makes cmixshow reread its input file.

2.6   User annotations: telling C-Mix what it can't figure out itself

The core of the C-Mix system is a set of automatic analyses that decide which of the actions and values in the subject program should be spectime and which should be residual. Most of the time the analyses do a good job, but they don't perform miracles, nor do they read minds.

User annotations tell C-Mix that you know better than it which binding time a value or an action should have. Few programs need no user annotations, most programs need a few, and some programs need a lot of them to specialize satisfactorily. This section describes the types of user annotations you can attach to your program and how to do it.

The user may choose to place annotations either in the subject program itself or in a separate file. C-Mix supports both choices by expressing (most) user annotations as specializer directives, which can appear either in the subject program or in a script file.

User Annotations for Variables. You can attach these annotations to variable declarations in the subject program:

spectime – Use this for variables that you want to exist only at spectime. This doesn't actually change the binding-time analyses, but if C-Mix finds any reason to want the variable to be residual, it will not produce a generating extension, but instead give an error message and terminate.

This annotation cannot be used for variables that have extern declarations in the C-Mix input files. Such variables are always forced to be residual.

residual – Use this to tell C-Mix to assign binding-times so that the variable becomes residual. This normally forces other variables and values to be residual as well; that happens automatically and you need not provide user annotations for those. (Also, it might make it impossible to fulfill another spectime annotation).

This annotation is the primary tool for controlling a specialization that would otherwise proceed infinitely or produce unacceptably large residual programs.

On the other hand, if *all* variables are declared residual, then no speedup occurs.

visible spectime – This has the same effects as spectime and additionally specifies that the variable should have external linkage in the generating extension. Namely, the variable will be "visible" to other program modules. This annotation should be used for variables that you want to be shared between the generating extension and code that you (unbeknownst to C-Mix) link together with it. It might either be variables that are initialized by a user-supplied main function before the generator functions are called, or variables that are used by external functions annotated as spectime.

visible residual – The same as residual and additionally specifies that the variable should have external linkage in the residual program.

This annotation is useful for variables that should be shared among the residual program and program parts that have not been partially evaluated.

The two `visible` annotations can only be applied to variables that have

– external linkage, *and*
– a definition (*i.e.*, a file-level declaration without `extern`, but possibly with an initializer)

in the original program. These are the only variables where visibility is a question at all. If you wonder why one would want one of these variables to *not* have external linkage in *e.g.*, the residual program, the reason is that C-Mix can specialize several source files together to one, and that the variable might be used only by those files. The latter is actually what C-Mix assumes if you do not tell it otherwise – even if there is only one file: many C programmers are lazy and define their global variables as `int frob;` where `static int frob;` would have been more appropriate.

Note that the order of the words matter: there is no annotation called `residual visible`. The two concepts of "residual" and "visible" are not independent; it would be pointless to just declare a variable `visible` but leave it to C-Mix to decide if it should be visible in the generating extension or the residual program.

All other variables without user annotations will have a binding time selected by C-Mix and will be internal to the generated source files.

How to write user annotations for variables. For global variables – whether their linkage is internal or external – simply name them in the specializer directive, like in

> `visible spectime: global_name1 global_name2`

To identify local variables and function parameters, use a two-part syntax in C++ style

> `function_name::local_name`

It is also possible to write annotations directly in the source file. This is accomplished by using the `#pragma` preprocessor directive; if you write,

> `#pragma cmix residual: foo zugol::br`

in a C source file, it will force the global `foo` and the local or parameter `br` in function `zugol()` to be residual.

If you try to annotate a global which exists (with internal linkage) in several different files, or a local variable whose name is not unique within the function (because it is defined in several blocks inside it) you will have a warning thrown at you and every matching variable gets annotated. Please contact us if this is a real problem for you.

User Annotations for Functions. The specialization of functions defined in the subject program (*i.e.*, functions whose body is seen by C-Mix) can be controlled by adding annotations to their formal parameters or local variables. These functions (even those that have external linkage in the source files) are never "visible" outside either the generating extension or the residual program. (If you think you need to make a function visible in the generating extension, the **generator**: specializer directive described in the full manual is probably what you are really looking for).

However, when you call a function whose definition C-Mix cannot see, C-Mix has no way of deducing whether the call should be made at spectime or in the residual program, because C-Mix does not know what the function does. A number of annotations are available to tell it your preferences:

spectime – This annotation specifies that all calls to the function should be executed at spectime. If C-Mix cannot make sure that all parameters in a call are known at spectime, it aborts with an error message.

Additionally, C-Mix tries to make sure that the generating extension will perform calls to **spectime** functions in precisely the same sequence as if the source program was run unspecialized. Evidently, if the sequence and number of **spectime** calls depend on the program's dynamic input this is impossible, and an error message will result.

This annotation is intended to be placed on *e.g.*, functions that read in parts of the spectime input by means of side-effecting functions, *i.e.*, the spectime input is not given as arguments to the goal function.

pure – This annotation specifies that the function may be called either at spectime if all the arguments are known at spectime, or at residual time, otherwise. It is intended to be used for functions without side effects whose value depends solely on the arguments, like **sin()** and other mathematical functions.

pure spectime – This annotation specifies that all calls of the function should be executed at spectime. If C-Mix cannot make sure that all parameters in a call are known at spectime, it aborts with an error message.

Contrary to **spectime** it is not ensured that the number and ordering of the calls in the generating extension match the execution of the unspecialized program.

The intended use is for functions that provide pieces of spectime inputs but do not have any side effects and do not, for instance, depend on how many times they have already been called.

residual – This annotation specifies that the function may only be called in the residual program. This is the default for external functions; C-Mix dares not guess whether they might have any side effects, so this is the safest choice.

How to write user annotations for functions. This is even simpler than for variables:

```
pure spectime: gizmo() gadget()
```

You don't need the :: syntax, or worry about name clashes, since function annotations are only concerned with symbols with external linkage.

But this is not the whole story: you can also annotate an individual function call, thereby overriding the (perhaps default) annotation on the function *per se*.

This cannot be done as a specializer directive, primarily because the developers could not think of a good way to specify precisely which call the annotation is aimed at.

Overriding of single function calls is meant primarily for basic I/O functions such as fopen(), fgets(), etc. that are used to read spectime as well as residual input in the same program. Those calls that read the spectime input can be annotated spectime, leaving the reads of residual inputs residual.

You annotate a single function call by prefixing it with __CMIX(*annotation name*) right in the code. That is, to annotate the call to gor() in

        z = bul() + gor(42);

as spectime, you would write

        z = bul() + __CMIX(spectime)gor(42);

2.7   Further Information

This section is an excerpt from the C-Mix user manual. Up-to-date information can be found at

   http://www.diku.dk/research-groups/topps/activities/cmix.html .

3   Summer School Exercises

The following pages contain some exercises that introduce C-Mix and partial evaluation. They assume that you are on a UNIX-like system and that you use the GNU make utility. The exercises can be downloaded from

```
ftp://ftp.diku.dk/diku/semantics/partial-evaluation/system/cmix/
```

3.1   Getting Started

To try out your first example, change to the **pow** directory by typing **cd cmix/exercises/pow** and view the source file by typing **cat pow.c**:

```
double pow(double x, int n)
{
  double a = 1;
  while(n--) a *= x;
  return a;
}
```

The simplest way to process files with C-Mix is by using a makefile. Run your first C-Mix example by typing **gmake**, producing something like this:

```
gmake
gcc -c pow-time.c -o pow-time.o
gcc -c pow.c -o pow.o
cmix -s -q
    -e 'goal: pow(?,$1) producing ("pow_1")'
    pow.c                                             (run C-Mix)
g++ -I /usr/local/topps/cmix/cogen-include -L /usr/local/topps/mix/lib/cmix
    -o pow-gen pow-gen.cc -lcmix            (compile the generating extension)
./pow-gen 15 | gindent -br -ce > pow-res.c      (run generating extension to
gcc -c pow-res.c -o pow-res.o                       produce residual program)
gcc -o pow-time  pow-time.o pow.o pow-res.o   (link source & residual program
721 pow.o                                               for timing purposes)
1080 pow-res.o
pow-time 10000000 2 15 >> pow-time.txt
Timing source program...
Timing residual program...
Done.
cat pow-time.txt
============================================================
Program pow.c on host hermod, architecture hp700pa2ux10:
Input is '2 15'

Source   program size: 648 pow.o
Residual program size: 609 pow-res.o

Source   result: 32768.000000
Residual result: 32768.000000
```

	User time	(System time)
Source program	4.17 seconds	(0 seconds)
Residual program	1.47 seconds	(0.01 seconds)
Speedup factor	2.8	(0.0)

The makefile is set up as explained in the next section to call C-Mix for specializing the power function to static n=15, and then do some timing comparisons: The source program is run 10000000 times with x=2 and n=15, and the residual program is run 10000000 times with x=2.

Exercise: View the annotated source program that the C-Mix analyses produce by typing **cmixshow pow.ann**. This will start up a browser window, like the one shown in Fig. 4. Click on | Select visible annotations | and select which type

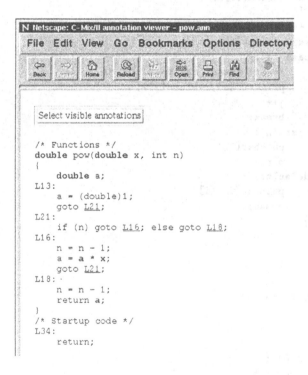

Fig. 4. The source code annotation browser

of annotations, e.g. dynamic program parts, you would like to see. If you re-specialize by invoking C-Mix again, you can update the browser window by clicking on the "Reload" button in your browser.

3.2   Text Formatting with printf

This exercise demonstrates partial evaluation in a nutshell: known constants are propagated and loops are unrolled.

Change to the printf directory and take a look at the source file printf.c; it contains three functions: a simple print formatting function mini_printf(fmt, values), the power function power(x, n) and a goal function goal(x, n) that acts as an entry point for C-Mix.

```c
#include <stdio.h>

void mini_printf(char *fmt, int *values)
{
    int i, j;
    /* Parse the format string */
    for (i = j = 0; fmt[i] != '\0'; i++) {
        if (fmt[i] != '%')
            putchar(fmt[i]);
        else {
            i++;
            switch (fmt[i]) {
            case 'd':
                /* %d: output the next int */
                printf("%d", values[j]);
                j++;
                break;
            case '%':
                putchar('%');
                break;
            default:
                putchar(fmt[i]);
                break;
            }
        }
    }
}

int power(int x, int n)
{
    int pow;
    pow = 1;
    while (n > 0) {
        pow = pow * x;
        n--;
    }
    return pow;
}

int goal(int x, int n)
{
```

```
    int v[2];
    v[0] = power(x, n);
    mini_printf("Power = %d\n", v);
    return 0;
}
```

The aim is to specialize away all operations on the formatting string "Power = %d\n" and the spectime variable n. If we fix n to 23, the following specialized program will be produced.

```
static char d[3] = "%d";

static void mini_printf(int *values)
{
  putchar('P');
  putchar('o');
  putchar('w');
  putchar('e');
  putchar('r');
  putchar(' ');
  putchar('=');
  putchar(' ');
  printf(d, values[0]);
  putchar('\n');
}

static int  power(int x)
{
  int pow = 1;
  pow = pow * x;   pow = pow * x;   pow = pow * x;
  pow = pow * x;   pow = pow * x;   pow = pow * x;
  pow = pow * x;   pow = pow * x;   pow = pow * x;
  pow = pow * x;   pow = pow * x;   pow = pow * x;
  pow = pow * x;   pow = pow * x;   pow = pow * x;
  pow = pow * x;   pow = pow * x;   pow = pow * x;
  pow = pow * x;   pow = pow * x;   pow = pow * x;
  pow = pow * x;   pow = pow * x;
  return pow;
}

static void goal(int x)
{
  int v[2];
  int *piTmp;
  int iTmp = power(x);
  piTmp = v + 0;
  *piTmp = iTmp;
  mini_printf(v);
  return;
}
```

3.3 Binary Search

This exercise demonstrates that there is a tradeoff between size and speed: partial evaluation can do too much specialization.

Given a sorted array of numbers, finding the index of some given number a can be done in logarithmic time by comparing a with an array element near the middle and continuing in this fashion with either the upper or lower half of the array. Looking for 42 in the list $17, 23, 42, 43, 67, 73, 79, 91$ can be done in 4 steps:

$$disp = 8 \quad \boxed{17 \quad 23 \quad 42 \quad \underline{43} \quad 67 \quad 73 \quad 79 \quad 91}$$
$$\uparrow$$
$$low = 0$$

$$disp = 4 \quad \boxed{17 \quad \underline{23} \quad 42 \quad 43} \quad 67 \quad 73 \quad 79 \quad 91$$
$$\uparrow$$
$$low = 0$$

$$disp = 2 \quad 17 \quad 23 \quad \boxed{\underline{42} \quad 43} \quad 67 \quad 73 \quad 79 \quad 91$$
$$\uparrow$$
$$low = 2$$

$$disp = 1 \quad 17 \quad 23 \quad \boxed{\underline{42}} \quad 43 \quad 67 \quad 73 \quad 79 \quad 91$$
$$\uparrow$$
$$low = 2$$

At each step, a is compared with the underlined element, the displacement $disp$ is halved, and the offset low is adjusted accordingly.

A function binsearch(x, size, a) that searches for a in an array x of length size initialized to $[0, 1, 2, \ldots, \text{size} - 1]$ can be found in the file binsearch1.c in the binsearch directory. Specializing and timing this function with spectime size = 512 yields

```
================================================================
Program binsearch1.c on host hermod, architecture hp700pa2ux10:
Compiler options were ''
Input is '42 512'

Source   program size: 1080 binsearch1.o
Residual program size: 34943 binsearch1-res.o

Source   result: 42
Residual result: 42

                 User time       (System time   )
Source   program  16.69 seconds  (  0.01 seconds)
Residual program   4.06 seconds  (  0.01 seconds)
Speedup factor      4.1          (  1.0         )
================================================================
```

As you can see, the specialization has produced a speedup of around 4, but at the cost of a residual program about 35 times the size of the source program! Take a look at the residual program: what makes it so huge?

```c
static int
binsearch (int x, int *a)
{
  if (a[255] < x) {
    if (a[384] < x) {
      if (a[448] < x) {
        if (a[480] < x) {
          if (a[496] < x) {
            if (a[504] < x) {
              if (a[508] < x) {
                if (a[510] < x) {
                  if (a[511] < x) {
                    return -1;
                  } else {
                    if (a[511] != x) {
                      return -1;
                    } else {
                      return 511;
                    }
                  }
                } else {
                  if (a[509] < x) {
                    if (a[510] != x) {
                      return -1;
                    } else {
                      return 510;
                    }
                  } else {
                    if (a[509] != x) {
                      return -1;
                    } else {
                      return 509;
                    }
                  }
                }
              } else {
                ...
              }
            }
          }
        }
      }
    }
  }
}
```

The problem is that the residual program contains one if statement for each element in the array – a total of 512 in this case! This kind of code explosion is often undesirable, and is a result of "too much" specialization. The residual program can be improved by instructing C-Mix to residualize some constructs that actually could be evaluated at spectime. This can be done by adding a directive like this: `residual: binsearch::low`. When the program is specialized with this directive, we obtain the following residual program:

```
static int
bsearch(int x, int *a)
{
    int low;
    low = -1;
    if (a[511] < x)      low  = 488;
    if (a[low + 256] < x) low += 256;
    if (a[low + 128] < x) low += 128;
    if (a[low + 64] < x)  low += 64;
    if (a[low + 32] < x)  low += 32;
    if (a[low + 16] < x)  low += 16;
    if (a[low + 8] < x)   low += 8;
    if (a[low + 4] < x)   low += 4;
    if (a[low + 2] < x)   low += 2;
    if (a[low + 1] < x)   low += 1;
    if (low + 1 >= 1000 || a[low + 1] != x) return -1;
    else                          return low + 1;
}
```

and a speedup of 3.5 at a code size blow-up cost of only 1.8.

3.4 Ackermann's Function

This exercise demonstrates that it can be necessary to duplicate code manually, due to limitations in the existing implementation.

In directory ack you will find a small program in ack1.c for computing Ackermann's function:

$$Ack(m,n) = \begin{cases} n+1, & \text{if } m = 0 \\ Ack(m-1,1), & \text{if } m > 0 \wedge n = 0 \\ Ack(m-1, Ack(m, n-1)), & \text{if } m > 0 \wedge n > 0 \end{cases}$$

```
int ack(int m, int n)
{
  int a;
  if (m == 0)
    a = n + 1;
  else
    if (n == 0)
      a = ack(m - 1, 1);
    else
```

```
    a = ack(m - 1, ack(m, n - 1));
  return a;
}
```

By specializing Ackermann's function for spectime $m = 3$, we obtain a residual program essentially like this:

```
static int  ack2(int n)
{
  return n + 1;
}

static int  ack1(int n)
{
  if (n == 0) {
    return ack2(1);
  } else {
    return ack2(ack1(n - 1));
  }
}

static int  ack0(int n)
{
  if (n == 0) {
    return ack1(1);
  } else {
    return ack1(ack0(n - 1));
  }
}

static int  ack(int n)
{
  if (n == 0) {
    return ack0(1);
  } else {
    return ack0(ack(n - 1));
  }
}
```

Note that there are three calls to functions where the arguments are the constant 1 that have not been reduced. The reason is that C-Mix makes a *monovariant* binding-time division: in all calls to ack, the second parameter must be residual (because it is so in *some* calls). If we make a copy of file ack1.c, call it ack2.c, then we can circumvent this problem by hand-rewriting the program duplicating the function definition and selecting one or the other at each call site, according to the binding time (spectime or residual) of the arguments:

```
int ackSS(int m, int n)
{
  int a;
```

```
  if (m == 0)
    a = n + 1;
  else
    if (n == 0)
      a = ackSS(m - 1, 1);
    else
      a = ackSS(m - 1, ackSS(m, n - 1));
  return a;
}

int ack(int m, int n) {
  int a;
  if (m == 0)
    a = n + 1;
  else
    if (n == 0)
      a = ackSS(m - 1, 1);
    else
      a = ack(m - 1, ack(m, n - 1));
  return a;
}
```

3.5   Turing Machine

This exercise demonstrates that infinite specialization can occur, and how to circumvent this. It is also shown how specialization can be used as compilation, and the concept of *bounded static variation* is introduced.

In the `turing` directory you will find a small Turing machine interpreter in file `turing.c`. The machine has an instruction pointer i, a tape pointer p and takes a list of instructions. Initially, p points to the first element of the tape, and the Turing machine handles these instructions:

Left	move p one step left on the tape, unless $p = 0$
Right	move p one step right on the tape, unless $p = tapemax$
Write a	write character a at the current tape position
Goto i	let next instruction be instruction i
If a goto i	if the character at the current tape position is equal to a, let the next instruction be i
Stop	stop and return the part of the tape that starts at the current tape position

The following Turing program that is hard-wired into the C program finds the first '0' on the tape changes it into a '1', and returns the rest of the tape, starting at this '1':

0 *If* '0' *goto* 3
1 *Right*
2 *Goto* 0
3 *Write* '1'
4 *Stop*

For instance, running this program on tape 110101 returns 1101. The source of the interpreter looks like this:

```
#include <stdio.h>

#pragma cmix pure spectime: printstatus()
extern printstatus(char*, int);

typedef int InstructionTag;
#define Left    0 /* Left        */
#define Right   1 /* Right       */
#define Write   2 /* Write a     */
#define Goto    3 /* Goto  i     */
#define IfGoto  4 /* If a Goto i */
#define Stop    5 /* Stop        */

typedef struct Instruction {
  InstructionTag tag;
  char a;
  int i;
} Instruction;

Instruction instruction[5];

void initTuringProgram() {
  instruction[0].tag = IfGoto; instruction[0].a = '0'; instruction[0].i = 3;
  instruction[1].tag = Right;
  instruction[2].tag = Goto;    instruction[2].i = 0;
  instruction[3].tag = Write;   instruction[3].a = '1';
  instruction[4].tag = Stop;
}

char* turing(char tape[], int tapelen) {
  int i;
  int p;
  initTuringProgram();
  i = 0; p = 0;
  while (instruction[i].tag != Stop) {
    printstatus("i=%d ", i);
    printstatus("p=%d\n", p);
    switch (instruction[i].tag) {
    case Left   : if (p > 0) p--; break;
    case Right  :
      if (p < tapelen - 2) {
        p++;
        if (tape[p] == '\0') {
          tape[p + 1] = '\0';
          tape[p] = ' ';
        }
      }
```

```
      break;
    case Write  : tape[p] = instruction[i].a; break;
    case Goto   : i = instruction[i].i; continue;
    case IfGoto :
      if (tape[p] == instruction[i].a) {
        i = instruction[i].i; continue;
      }
      break;
    case Stop   : printstatus("interpreter error\n", 0);
    }
    i++;
  }
  return tape + p;
}
```

The function turing(char tape[], int tapelen) implements the Turing machine. Specializing this function with only residual parameters may seem strange, but is quite useful: in this way we "compile" a Turing program into a C program. However, when specializing we run into problems.

The problem is *infinite specialization*: C-Mix does not know the length of the tape at specialization time, so it generates specialized code for all possible positions of the tape pointer – of which there are infinitely many. By forcing the tape pointer to become residual, this infinite specialization is avoided; so we add the directive residual: turing::p. Take a look at the residual program.

```
#include <stdio.h>
static void
initTuringProgram (void) { return; }

static char *
turing (char *tape, int tapelen)
{
  int p;
  char *pcTmp;
  char *pcTmp0;
  char *pcTmp1;
  initTuringProgram ();
  p = 0;
  if (tape[p] == '0') goto L; else goto L0;
L0:
  if (p < tapelen - 2) {
    p = p + 1;
    if (tape[p] == '\0') {
      pcTmp = tape + (p + 1);
      *pcTmp = '\0';
      pcTmp0 = tape + p;
      *pcTmp0 = ' ';
      if (tape[p] == '0') goto L; else goto L0;
    }
```

```
  }
L2:
  if (tape[p] == '0') goto L; else goto L0;
L:
  pcTmp1 = tape + p;
  *pcTmp1 = '1';
  return tape + p;
}
```

Note how well it resembles the Turing program! Only now it is in C code, so we have in effect obtained a compilation of Turing code into C code!

We can extend the Turing machine by adding a new instruction *ReadGoto* which reads a digit i off the tape and jumps to that instruction – a "computed goto", like this:

```
#define ReadGoto 6 /* ReadGoto     */
  ...
  switch (instruction[i].tag) {
  ...
  case ReadGoto : {
    int j, jmax;
    if (instrs < 10) jmax = instrs; else jmax = 10;
    for (j = 0; j < jmax; j++)
     if (j + '0' == tape[p]) { i = j; break; }
    continue;
  }
  ...
  }
```

We encounter a new problem: the instruction pointer i and consequently the instruction list becomes residual and cannot any longer be specialized away.

The present problem arises often in interpreters: the index of the next (spectime) instruction depends on some residual data, yet we *know* that it can only be one of finitely many different values. This *bounded static variation* can be exploited so that the instruction list can be specialized away.

The solution is so often seen in partial evaluation that it has been named *The Trick*: when an assignment s = d of a residual value d to a spectime variable s that can only evaluate to finitely many different values must be performed, a switch statement is inserted in the source program:

```
switch (d) {
  0 : s = 0; break;
  1 : s = 1; break;
  ⋮
  n : s = n; break;
}
```

In our case, we insert a for loop:

```
for (speci=0; speci<MAXINSTRS; speci++)
  if (computedi==speci) i=speci;
```

and the instruction list is once again specialized away.

3.6 Matrix Operations

This exercise demonstrates how certain mathematical properties can be exploited, and that tremendous speedups can be achieved.

In the `matrix` directory you will find a program `matrix1.c` that contains the following matrix and vector operations for $M = 25$:

`vector solve(matrix A, vector b);`	Solve $Ax = b$ and return x for $M \times M$ matrix A and $M \times 1$ vectors x and b
`vector mulMatVec(matrix A, vector b);`	return Ab for matrix A and vector b
`char* printMatrix(matrix A);`	return a text representation of matrix A
`char* printVector(vector b);`	return a text representation of vector b
`matrix makeMatrix(unsigned int seed);`	return a matrix with pseudorandom numbers deterministically generated from *seed*
`vector makeVector(unsigned int seed);`	return a vector of pseudorandom numbers deterministically generated from *seed*

At the bottom of the file you will find the goal function:

```
vector goal(unsigned int Aseed, int n) {
  int i;
  matrix A;
  vector x, b;
  i = 1;
  A = makeMatrix(Aseed);
  while (i < n) {
    x = makeVector(i * 523 % RANDMAX);
    b = mulMatVec(A, x);
    printstatus("/* solving A * x(i) = b for i = %d */\n", i);
    solve(A, b);
    i++;
  }
  x = makeVector(i * 523 % RANDMAX);
  b = mulMatVec(A, x);
  return solve(A, b);
}
```

This function takes a seed for generating a pseudorandom matrix `A`, and an integer n, and then it generates n different b vectors and solves `Ax = b`. If we specializing this goal function with residual n and spectime `Aseed = 17`, we encounter once again the problem of *infinite specialization:* the counter i in the while loop is spectime, but the loop is controlled by the *residual* limit n. As C-Mix doesn't know the value of n yet, it tries to specialize for i=1,2,3, ... , never terminating.

We solve the problem by inserting a directive residual: goal::i. The speedup and code blowup for the solver with matrix A as a spectime constant now becomes

```
===============================================================
Program matrix1.c on host hermod, architecture hp700pa2ux10:
Compiler options were ''
Input is '17 3'

Source   program size: 5039 matrix1.o
Residual program size: 131498 matrix1-res.o

                User time       (System time   )
Source    program   7.96 seconds  (      0 seconds)
Residual  program   0.37 seconds  (  0.01 seconds)
Speedup factor      21.5          (    0.0       )
===============================================================
```

If we extend the matrix operations *e.g.*, with dot product and matrix multiplication, it can be desirable to do algebraic reductions like $0A = 0$, $1A = A$, $0 \cdot b = 0$, $1 \cdot b = b$. This can be done by inserting tests like if (c == 1) return A; if c is a spectime constant, matrix A is not rebuilt by a lot of additions and multiplications, but simply returned unchanged, and the test disappears from the residual program! We call this technique *special casing*.

4   Overview of C-Mix

C-Mix consists of two separate parts. The first part analyses the subject program and produces a *generating extension*, based on the initial division of the input data, *i.e.*, its classification of input parameters into static and dynamic. The generating extension reads the static data and produces a *residual* program. This process utilises the second part of C-Mix, the specialisation library (speclib, for short), which takes care of memory management, memoization and code production during specialization.

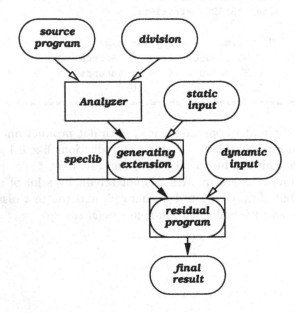

Fig. 5. Specialization with a generating-extension generator.

A *generating extension* [6] of a program p produces a specialized program p_s of p with respect to a portion s of the input. The generating extension generator (*gegen*) transforms a *binding-time* annotated program p_{ann} into its generating extension p_{gen}, *i.e.*, $[\![gegen]\!](p_{ann}) \Rightarrow p_{gen}$. The gegen phase essentially copies the static constructs to p_{gen} and transforms dynamic constructs into functions that produce residual code, such that $[\![p_{gen}]\!](s) \Rightarrow p_s$. This process is depicted in Fig. 6.

Many earlier partial evaluators were "monolithic" in the sense that they did not delegate any work to existing tools. In effect, they needed to contain an interpreter for the source language to be able to perform specialization-time actions.

Compared to this traditional `mix` approach based on symbolic evaluation of the subject program ($[\![mix]\!](p, s) \Rightarrow p_s$), the generating extension approach has several other advantages.

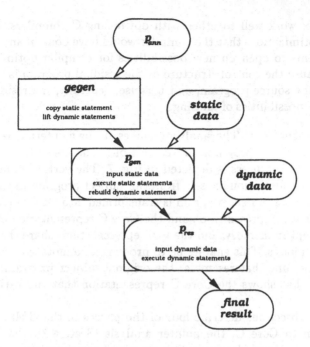

Fig. 6. The gegen and specialization phases

- During specialization, static constructs are evaluated directly by the underlying implementation, which often is an order of magnitude faster than symbolic evaluation.
- Static values can be represented directly so that potentially expensive encoding is avoided because there is no need for *tagged* representations.
- When a subject program has been assigned a satisfactory binding-time division and a generating extension has been produced, the generating extension will be a stand-alone program, completely detached from the original subject program. It can be made to produce any number of specialized programs (provided there is no need for a new binding-time division).
- The user of C-Mix can link the generating extension together with object code of his own. This means that the user can provide functions that can be called at specialization time, without C-Mix having to analyse and understand their source code. This is particularly convenient if the static input has a high-level format that has to be parsed (at spectime) before it can be used. C-Mix would, for example, perform rather badly when faced with the output of parser generators such as yacc. However this is irrelevant: since none of the parser code is supposed to be present in the residual program anyway, the parser can be compiled as-is and linked into the generating extension to achieve the same effect, without confusing C-Mix.

After having run the generating extension the residual program has to be compiled with a normal C compiler. Our experience is that the transformations done by C-Mix work well together with optimizing C compilers. Rather than performing optimizations that the compiler would have done in any case, partial evaluation seems to open up new possibilities for compiler optimization. This is mainly because the control structure of the residual program is often simpler than that of the source program, and because, generally, the residual program contains fewer possibilities of aliasing.

Phases of the Analyser. The analyzer makes its own internal representation of the original subject program and carries out a number of analyses on this representation; this process is depicted in Fig. 7. The vertical column of boxes depicts each transformation phase – from the subject program to the generating extension. After the subject program is transformed into Core C (see Sect. 4.1), both the original C representation and the Core C representation of the subject program are kept in memory, and the two representations share the annotations made by later phases. This enables us to produce an annotated program in two flavours: a short one that resembles the original subject program; and a more elaborate one that shows the Core C representation that the various analyses work on.

The next subsections describe four of the phases in the C-Mix system: The transformation to Core C, the pointer analysis (Sect. 4.2), the binding-time analysis (Sect. 4.3), and the generating extension generator (Sect. 4.4).

4.1   Core C

Even though C is a fairly small language, there is a lot of redundancy. For instance, a `for` statement is syntactic sugar for a special form of `while` statement – which again can be expressed by means of `if` and `goto` statements. All this redundancy is quite useful to the programmer. But if you want to reason about the control flow, data flow, etc., this freedom of expression is only an inconvenience.

C-Mix therefore transforms the subject program into a less vigorous language that we call Core C. In this subset of the original language, we can express exactly the same programs as before, but we have to be a bit more explicit.

Consider the well-known power function and its representation in Core C below.

```
int pow(int x, int n)
{
  int a = 1;
  while (n--) a *= x;      ⇒
  return a;
}
```

```
int pow(int x, int n)
{
    int a = {1 };
L23:
    if (n) goto L13; else goto L16;
L13:
    n = n - 1;
    a = a * x;
    goto L23;
L16:
    n = n - 1;
    return a;
}
```

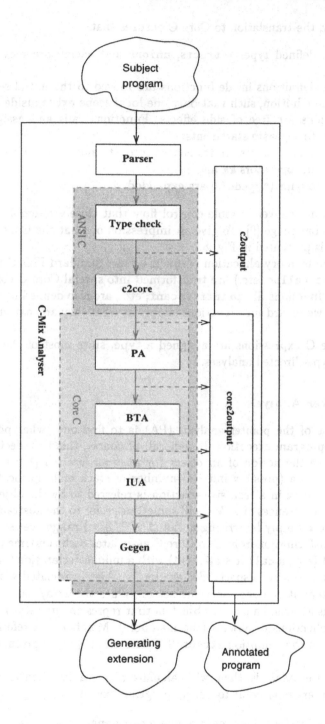

Fig. 7. C-Mix analyser phases. Each clear box is a transformation, and the shaded boxes show what representation a transformation processes.

In summary, the translation to Core C ensures that

- All user defined types (structs, unions and enums) are moved to global scope.
- Variable definitions inside functions are moved to the initial section of the function definition, such that only one local scope exists inside functions.
- Expressions are free of side effects. Functions calls and assignments are turned into separate statements.
- All control statements are translated into ifs and gotos. This includes the short-circuit operators && and | |.
- Type synonyms (typedefs) are expanded.

We thus have a very simple control flow that closely resembles that of the Flow Chart Language [9]. To give an impression of what the Core C language, a grammar is presented in Fig. 8.

Run-time memory allocation (defined by the Standard ISO C library functions malloc, calloc, etc.) are transformed into special Core C constructs. Input/output functions like printf, fscanf, etc., are also defined in the standard library, but we regard such functions simply as what they are: externally defined symbols.

All Core C expressions are assigned a type, since most of the analyses we apply are type-directed analyses.

4.2   Pointer Analysis

The purpose of the pointer analysis (PA) is to find out "what pointers point to" during program execution. In general, of course, this is undecidable, so we will introduce the notion of an *object* (or *abstract location* [1]): an object $\delta \in$ *Aloc* represents a (possibly infinite) number of stack or heap locations, *e.g.*, a declaration int x in a recursive function is referred to by the object δ_x, which represents all instances of x. We will sometimes refer to the abstract location δ_x of a variable x simply by writing x. Let $\Delta \in \mathcal{P}(Aloc)$ range over sets of objects.

The transformation from C to Core C associates each run-time memory allocation point (*e.g.*, a calloc statement) with a unique declaration that represents its contents. Likewise, a special declaration has been associated with each array object, so that it can represent the set of values the array can contain. Each function f is attached a unique object f_0 that represents its return value. Structures are collections of objects (the members). Members are referred to by an integer, *i.e.*, if the definition struct S { int x,y; } s; is given, s.2 refers to y.

The pointer analysis, then, will calculate a *safe* approximation of the set of objects pointers *may* point to during program execution [2].

Example 1. Consider this program where d is dynamic:

```
int f(int d)
{
```

$$
\begin{array}{lll}
\text{Types } t & ::= \text{int} \mid \text{double} \mid \ldots & \text{(simple)} \\
& \mid \text{struct } S & \text{(user type)} \\
& \mid t* & \text{(pointer)} \\
& \mid t[e] & \text{(array)} \\
& \mid t\,(t_1,\ldots,t_n) & \text{(function)} \\
\text{Expressions } e & ::= x & \text{(var)} \\
& \mid c & \text{(constant)} \\
& \mid \&\, e & \text{(address)} \\
& \mid *\, e & \text{(deref)} \\
& \mid uop\ e & \text{(unary)} \\
& \mid e_1\ bop\ e_2 & \text{(binary)} \\
& \mid (t)\ e & \text{(cast)} \\
& \mid e.i & \text{(member)} \\
& \mid \text{sizeof}(t) & \\
& \mid \text{sizeof}(e) & \\
\text{Jumps } j & ::= \text{if}(e) \text{ goto } l_1 \text{ else goto } l_2 & \text{(conditional)} \\
& \mid \text{goto } l & \text{(jump)} \\
& \mid \text{return } e & \text{(return)} \\
\text{Statements } s & ::= x = e & \text{(assign)} \\
& \mid *x = e & \text{(pointer assign)} \\
& \mid x.i = e & \text{(member assign)} \\
& \mid (*x).i = e & \text{(ptr/mem assign)} \\
& \mid x = f(e_1 \ldots e_n) & \text{(call)} \\
& \mid x = fp(e_1 \ldots e_n) & \text{(pointer call)} \\
& \mid x = \text{calloc}(e,t) & \text{(allocation)} \\
& \mid \text{free}(x) & \text{(deallocation)} \\
\text{Unary operator } uop & ::= + \mid - \mid \tilde{} \mid\, ! & \\
\text{Binary operator } bop & ::= * \mid / \mid \% \mid + \mid - \mid << \mid >> \mid < \mid > & \\
& \mid <= \mid => \mid == \mid != \mid \& \mid \mid \mid \hat{} &
\end{array}
$$

Fig. 8. Core C types, expressions and statements in a grammar-like form.

```
    int x = 1;
    int *p = &x;
    *p = d;
    ...
}
```

If no points-to information were present, the binding-time analysis would wrongly assume that x is static, which is not the case since a dynamic value is assigned to x through the pointer p.

Pointers in C. Compared to other imperative languages, C is rather difficult to analyze due to the presence of multi-level pointers, the address operator &, function pointers, and run-time memory allocation. Consider the program fragment

```
    int strcmp(char*,char*);
    int x, y, *p, **q, (*fp)(char*,char*);
    p = &x;
    q = &p;
    *q = &y;
    fp = strcmp;
```

where fp is a function pointer that is assigned the address of the library function strcmp. Close inspection of the program might tell you that p will point to y when the last statement is reached, but it is not immediately obvious.

We define two functions for determining which objects may be pointed to by other objects, and which objects may be read by expressions (let $\mathcal{E}$ denote the set of expression).

function	intuitive interpretation
$\mathcal{PT} : \mathcal{D} \to \Delta$	$\delta' \in \mathcal{PT}(\delta)$: δ may point to δ'
$\mathcal{L} : \mathcal{E} \to \Delta$	$\delta \in \mathcal{L}(e)$: e might reference δ

The pointer analysis will, from the above program fragment, infer that $\mathcal{PT}(p) = \{x, y\}, \mathcal{PT}(q) = \{p\}$, and $\mathcal{PT}(fp) = \{strcmp\}$, *i.e.*, it will *summarize* the set of objects a variable can point to, and thus not take into account that *e.g.*, p first points to x and then to y. This is why the analysis classified as flow-insensitive.

The analysis is also context-insensitive, which means that points-to information that flows to a function from several call-sites is summarized. Consider the program

```
    void f(int *p)
    {
      *p = *p + 1;
    }
```

```
int main()
{
  int x,y;
  f(&x);
  ...
  f(&y);
  ...
}
```

which would result in the points-to information $\mathcal{PT}(p) = \{x,y\}$. For a full description of the pointer analysis, see [2].

Information Derived from the Result of the Points-to Analysis. Based on the collected sets, the *transitive closures* $\mathcal{PT}^*$ can be calculated. Intuitively, $\mathcal{PT}^*(p)$ is the set of all objects reachable through pointer p by paths of length 0, 1, or more.

After the pointer analysis, various special sets of objects are collected because they will come in handy in other analyses. The set of global objects, including run-time allocated objects, are collected in the set *globals*. The set of objects that are definitely local to function f, is collected in the set *locals$_f$*. Also, Run-time memory allocation objects are marked to be either `freed` (if there exist a `free` statement that frees that object) or not `freed`.

External Objects. Pointers passed to external functions have to be treated with special care, since we have no way of knowing what such functions intend to do with the pointers. They could, say, assign a value to the object pointed to. In general, if a pointer p is passed to an external function, all objects in $\mathcal{PT}^*(p)$ can be reached through p. We collect a set *outside* of all such objects reachable by external functions.

When the above points-to information has been collected, it is possible to carry out the binding-time analysis.

4.3   Binding-Time Analysis

This section describes the binding-time analysis (BTA) of Core C in C-Mix. The analysis is based on the one described in [2] and extended with ideas from [3].

The aim of the binding-time analysis is to classify constructs in the subject program as either being known (static) or unknown (dynamic), given the initial division of the input. We would like as many constructs as possible to be classified static, thereby enabling as much specialization of the program as possible. This aim must, however, not break a simple and sane congruence principle: any construct that depends on dynamic data must also be classified dynamic.

The analysis is specified by means of a non-standard type system, such that every type is eventually assigned a binding time. In the first phase, the type system generates constraints that capture the dependencies between constructs in the subject program. In the second phase these constraints are solved, and the resulting binding times can be inspected.

Consider the expression

$$e \equiv \mathtt{p} + \mathtt{x}$$

where p is a pointer and x is an integer. A sensible constraint set for this expression would be

$$\{T_e \succeq T_p, T_e \trianglerighteq T_x\}$$

where T_e is the binding-time annotated type assigned to construct e. The first constraint says that the binding time of the whole expression has a type that must agree with the type of the pointer p. The last constraint says that if the variable x is dynamic, so is the pointer that results from the expression.

Types and Binding Times.

Definition 1. *A binding-time variable $\beta \in B$ ranges over the values S and D. The relation $\triangleright \subseteq B \times B$ is defined such that $D \triangleright S$, and its reflexive extension is denoted $\trianglerighteq$.*

Intuitively, $\beta \trianglerighteq \beta'$ means that β is at least as dynamic as β'.

Definition 2. *A binding-time type is a type annotated with binding times. It can be described by the following grammar.*

$$
\begin{array}{lll}
T ::= & \langle \mathrm{int} \rangle^\beta \mid \langle \mathrm{float} \rangle^\beta \mid \ldots & \text{(Simple)} \\
& \mid \langle \mathrm{struct}\, S \rangle^\beta & \text{(Structure)} \\
& \mid \langle \star \rangle^\beta T & \text{(Pointer to } T) \\
& \mid \langle [n] \rangle^\beta T & \text{(Array}[n] \text{ of } T) \\
& \mid \langle (T_1, \ldots, T_n) \rangle^\beta T & \text{(Function returning } T)
\end{array}
$$

where the last type schema represents a function with parameter types $T_1, \ldots, T_n$ returning type T. The binding time $bt(T)$ of a binding-time type T is the first (or outer-most) binding time.

Example 2. The declaration int *a[3] will result in variable a having binding-time type $T_\mathtt{a} = \langle [3] \rangle^{\beta_1} \langle \star \rangle^{\beta_2} \langle \mathrm{int} \rangle^{\beta_3}$. The binding time of this type is β_1, *i.e.*, $bt(T_\mathtt{a}) = \beta_1$.

Based on the observations in Sect. 4.4, we can define some constraints on annotated types: If we have a pointer to a type T, T must be at least as dynamic as the pointer; the same goes for arrays.

Definition 3. *A simple binding-time type $T = \langle \tau \rangle^\beta$ is trivially well-formed.*

A binding-time type $T = \langle \star \rangle^\beta T'$ is well-formed iff $bt(T') \trianglerighteq \beta$ and T' is well-formed. Likewise for array types.

A binding-time type $T = \langle (T_1, \ldots, T_n) \rangle^\beta T_0$ is well-formed iff for all T_i, T_i is well-formed and $\beta \trianglerighteq bt(T_i)$.

The relation $\succeq \subseteq \mathcal{T} \times \mathcal{T}$ is defined below. Intuitively, $T \succeq T'$ means that an object of type T can be constructed from an object of type T' at specialization time.

Definition 4. *For simple types T and T', $T \succeq T'$ iff $bt(T) \trianglerighteq bt(T')$. For all other types, $T \succeq T'$ iff $T = T'$.*

Example 3. The well-known power function

```
int pow(int base,int n)
{
        int a = 1;
  L1: if (n) goto L2; else goto L3;
  L2: n = n - 1;
      a = a * base;
      goto L1;
  L3: return a;
}
```

will generate the following constraints

$$\{bt(L2) \trianglerighteq bt(T_n), bt(L3) \trianglerighteq bt(T_n), bt(T_{pow_0}) \trianglerighteq bt(T_n)\}$$

$$\{T_1 \succeq T_n, T_n \succeq T_1, bt(pow) \trianglerighteq bt(T_n)\}$$

$$\{T_2 \succeq T_a, T_2 \succeq T_{base}, T_a \succeq T_2, bt(pow) \trianglerighteq bt(T_a)\}$$

$$\{T_{pow_0} \succeq T_a\}$$

For a treatment of the basics of binding-time analysis for imperative programming languages, see [9] and elsewhere in this volume. We will now investigate some of the situations that are of special interest when specializing C programs.

Static Pointers to Dynamic Data. Consider the following program, where d is dynamic.

```
int y,z;                        void swap(int* a, int *b)
                                {
int main(int d)                     int tmp = *a;
{                                   *a = *b, *b = tmp;
  int x = d+1;                  }
  swap(&d,&x); /* 1 */
  y = x;
  z = d;
  swap(&y,&z); /* 2 */
  return d;
}
```

The first call to swap contains static pointers to dynamic objects that are non-global and non-local (with regard to the swap procedure) – whereas the second contains static pointers to dynamic, global objects. If the former was allowed, the residual program would wrongly be

```
int y,z;                        void swap_1()
                                {
int main(int d)                   int tmp = d;      /* out of scope */
{                                 d = x, x = tmp;
  int x = d+1;                  }
  swap_1();
  y = x;                        void swap_2()
  z = d;                        {
  swap_2();                       int tmp = y;
  return d;                       y = z, z = tmp;
}                               }
```

The problem is that dynamic, non-local, non-global objects get out of scope during the first call. This can also happen with global pointers to non-local objects. To solve this problem, we generate constraints forcing dangerous pointers to be dynamic. To generate them, we define the function

$$\text{localglobal}(\Delta, \beta, \beta_*, f) = \text{if } \exists \delta \in \Delta \text{ s.t. } \delta \notin (\text{globals} \cup \text{locals}_f)$$
$$\text{then } \{\beta_* \unrhd \beta\}$$
$$\text{else } \{\}$$

and use it in the constraint generation to exploit the information produced by the pointer analysis for the $*e$ expression.

Non-Local Side-Effects. The binding-time analysis has to guarantee that static non-local side-effects do not occur under dynamic control to avoid having several end-configurations when a function is specialized. To avoid this, the side-effecting statement has be residualized. To ensure this, the BTA makes every non-local side-effecting statement[1] dependent on the binding time of the preceding basic block's control statement. Thus, if a basic block A ends in a conditional control statement of the form if(e) goto B else goto C, then both blocks B and C will be dependent on the expression e. To make this dependency transitive, every basic block is dependent on all immediately preceding blocks; and the first block in a function is dependent on all basic blocks from where the function is called.

Given a function f, a statement of the form x=e is locally side-effecting (and thus harmless) if x is a local variable in f. The same holds for statements of the form x.i=e. When assignments are done through pointers, however, we

---

[1] Recall that only statements can do side-effects in Core C.

cannot rely on syntactical scope anymore: we need to decide whether the objects reachable through a particular pointer are truly local objects[2].

Given the previously described points-to information (see Sect. 4.2), an approximation of the set of non-local variables in a function f can be calculated: the transitive closure of the pointer analysis information (denoted $\mathcal{PT}^*$) is calculated for all global variables and for each function f, such that $\mathcal{PT}^*(f)$ is $\mathcal{PT}^*$ of all formal parameters, and $\mathcal{PT}^*(globals)$ is $\mathcal{PT}^*$ of the globals. With these sets at hand, a side-effecting statement of the form *p=e is considered locally side-effecting if no object in $\mathcal{PT}(p)$ is contained in $\mathcal{PT}^*(globals)$ or $\mathcal{PT}^*(f)$. We can thus define a function that returns a set of constraints when given a declaration, the containing function, and the binding-time variable of the containing basic block.

$$\text{nonlocal}(d, f, bb) = \text{if } d \in \text{locals}_f \setminus (\mathcal{PT}^*(globals) \cup \mathcal{PT}^*(f))$$
$$\text{then } \{\}$$
$$\text{else } \{\text{bt}(T_d) \trianglerighteq \text{bt}(bb)\}$$

Constraint Solving. The binding-time constraints generated are solved by an efficient union-find-like algorithm, based on [7]. It takes advantage of the fact that all binding-time variables can be considered static if they not eventually assigned the value D. Further details can be found in [2].

4.4   The Generating Extension

In this section we describe a *generating extension generator* for the C language. Since the generating extension needs a binding-time separated program, we will in the following present *annotated* programs, where dynamic constructs are underlined and static constructs are represented as is. Consider now the power function with the following binding-time separation:

```
int pow(int base,int n)
{
        int a = 1;
   L1:  if (n) goto L2; else goto L3;
   L2:  n = n-1;
        a = a*base;
        goto L1;
   L3:  return a;
}
```

Notice that the function is in Core C representation (see section 4.1).

---

[2] A recursive function can have several instances of local variables at run-time, and thus a pointer can refer to a set of instances.

To be able to find out what gegen should do, let us first look at what the generating extension should do: it should output a version of the power function specialized with respect to base.

Intuitively this could be accomplished by executing the non-underlined parts of the program; when an underlined construct is met, the construct is *added* to the residual program, which is thus constructed incrementally. When this process finishes, the residual program will contain all the constructs that could not be executed statically. Observe that the statement a = a*base will appear (in some reduced form) a number of times, namely the number of times the loop has been executed under control of the static input.

To facilitate the generation of residual constructs we thus need a special data type Code in the generating extension that can represent variables that should appear in the residual program. In the generating extension, the variables base and a must be of type Code. We also need to be able to construct various residual expression and statement forms from residual components. In our case, we need a function cmixAssign(x,e) to produce a residual assignment statement, a function cmixBinary(e1,'*',e2) to produce a residual binary expression, and a function cmixReturn(e) that produces a residual return statement. At last we need a function cmixLift(e) that can produce a constant from a static value.

Using these operators, we can now describe what the gegen should produce on the basis of the annotated program:

```
Code pow(int n)
{
  Code base;
  Code a;
  cmixPushFun("pow", "int ");
  cmixParam("int %s", base);
  cmixLocal("int %s", a);
  cmixAssign(a,cmixLift(1));
L1:
  if (n) goto L2; else goto L3;
L2:
  n = n - 1;
  cmixAssign(a,cmixBinary(a,"*",base));
  goto L1;
L3:
  cmixReturn(a);
  return cmixPopFun();
}
```

The functions cmixPushFun, cmixParam and cmixLocal are used to produce the head of the specialized function in the obvious way, and the function cmixPopFun signals that the specialized function is completed and is ready to be written to the residual program.

Dynamic Branches. The above transformation is not sufficient when the annotated program contains branches that are controlled by a dynamic expression. Consider the annotated program

```
int sign(int x)
{
    int v = 0;
    if (x>=0) v = v+1; else v = v-1;
    return v;
}
```

Since we cannot decide which branch to take at specialization time, we must produce a residual if-statement and then produce specialized versions of both branches in turn. Therefore, we make use of a *pending list* in order to keep track of which branches we have yet to process. But then a problem arises. If we, say, specialize the then-branch first, the value of v will become 1, and the residual statement `return 1` is generated. If we then proceed by specializing the else-branch, the value of v will change from 1 to 0, and we wrongly produce the residual statement `return 0` instead of `return 1`.

The solution to this problem is to *memoize* at specialization time the static values whenever the specialization of a program point is suspended. This way we can *restore* the values of the static variables before we resume specialization of a suspended branch. (Above, v would be reset to 0 before specializing the `else` branch.) This effect can be achieved as illustrated by the following generating extension:

```
Code sign()
{
    int v = 0;
    void *cmix_sp;
    cmixPushFun("sign", "int ", statics);
    cmixParam("int %s", n);
    cmixPendinsert(&&cmix_lab1, statics);
cmix_loop:
    if (cmix_sp = cmixPending())
        goto *cmix_sp;
    else {
        return cmixPopFun(statics);
    }
cmix_lab1:
    cmixIf(n, &&cmix_lab2, &&cmix_lab3, statics);
    goto cmix_loop;
cmix_lab2:
    v = v + 1;
    cmixPendinsert(&&cmix_lab4, statics);
    goto cmix_loop;
cmix_lab3:
    v = v + 1;
    cmixPendinsert(&&cmix_lab4, statics);
```

```
  goto cmix_loop;
cmix_lab4:
  cmixReturn(cmixLift(v));
  goto cmix_loop;
}
```

Initially the the first program point `cmix_lab1` is inserted into the pending list to start up the *pending loop*. The pending loop causes a new program point to be specialized until the pending list is empty.[3] When this is the case, the specialized function is returned. The function `cmixPendInsert` inserts a program point into the pending list, provided it has not been seen before with the *same set of static values*. If the program point has already been specialized to the current configuration, this specialized program point can be reused and a jump to it is simply put into the residual program. This means, in general, that in constructs such as

$$\underline{\texttt{if}~(e)}~\{~s\_1;~\}~\underline{\texttt{else}}~\{~s\_2;~\}~s\_3$$

the control flow can either be *joined* in the residual program, as in

$$\texttt{if}~(e')~\{~s\_1';~\}~\texttt{else}~\{~s\_2';~\}~s\_3'$$

or s_3 can be *unfolded* into each branch and result in

$$\texttt{if}~(e')~\{~s\_1';~s\_3a';~\}~\texttt{else}~\{~s\_2';~s\_3b'~\}$$

if the values of the static data just before s_3 are different. In the latter case, we have employed what is called a *polyvariant* program-point specialization [9], because the statement s_3 has been used to generate two different residual statements, depending on the static values. C-Mix will always do the latter in case of different values for the static data.

Functions. Functions have to be specialized with respect both static parameters and static global objects[4], since it is possible to refer to global objects from inside a function.

If a generating function is called twice with the same arguments during the execution of the generating extension, it should be possible to only generate one specialized function, and then *share* this function between the two calls, like this:

```
Code fun(static parameters)
{
  ...
  CExpr *res_fun = cmixFunctionSeenBefore("fun", statics);
  if (res_fun) return *res_fun;
  /* Proceed with specialization */
  cmixPushFun("fun", "int ", statics);
  cmixParam( ... );
```

---

[3] Here we exploit that our compiler is able to use computed `goto`s, which is a non-standard feature. A switch statement could do the job, but it would be more clumsy.

[4] An object is a memory location or a set of memory location, see Sect. 4.2.

```
  cmixPendinsert(&&cmix_lab1, statics);
cmix_loop:
  ...

}
```

The function cmixFunctionSeenBefore will check whether the function already has been specialized with respect to the current set of static values. If it has, a representation of a residual call statement is returned via res_fun.

A generating function can call other generating functions (or itself). Because of this, we need to ensure that specialization is done depth-first to preserve execution order of side-effects. Consider the program

```
int x,y;

void swap()
{
  int tmp = x;
  x = y;
  y = tmp;
}

int main(int s)
{
  x = s;
  swap();
  x = y;
}
```

The side-effects caused by the call to swap must be executed before we proceed with the specialization of the statement x = y;. We thus need a residual-function stack to keep track of the functions being generated. Each function that produces a residual construct can then put this construct in the residual function that is currently being generated, i.e., the top of the residual-function stack.

In the above program, swap performs static side-effects on global variables. When static side-effects on global objects are *under dynamic control*, special care must be taken. We defer this subject until Sect. 4.3.

Pointers. During specialization, each dynamic variable will contain a piece of code indicating its residual location (variable name) – this allows for a simple handling of static pointers to dynamic data. Consider the following source code, where p is a static pointer to dynamic data:

<u>int</u> a, b, c, *p;   p = &b;   <u>a = *p;</u>   p = &c;   <u>*p = a;</u>

During specialization, dynamic variables a, b and c will contain code "a", "b" and "c". Variable p will be static and dereferenced (and assigned) at specialization time, so the residual code will be

```
int a, b, c;   a = b;   c = a;
```

In the same manner, we can split statically indexed arrays into separate variables. Consider the annotated program

```
int stack[10];    /* global stack */
int *sp = stack; /* stack pointer */

void push(int v)
{
  sp = sp + 1;
  *sp = v;
}

int pop()
{
  int v = *sp;
  sp = sp - 1;
  return v;
}

int main(int d)
{
  push(d);
  push(d);
  push(pop()+pop());
  return pop();
}
```

Because the array indexing only depends on static values, the array can be eliminated altogether, and the following residual program produced.

```
int stack_0;
int stack_1;
int stack_2;
...
int stack_9;

void push_0(int v) { stack_0 = v; }

void push_1(int v) { stack_1 = v; }

int pop_0()
{
  int v = stack_0;
  return v;
}

int pop_1()
{
  int v = stack_1;
  return v;
```

```
}

int main(int d)
{
  push_0(d);
  push_1(d);
  push_0(pop_1()+pop_0());
  return pop_0();
}
```

Of course, the small residual functions should be in-lined to give optimal results, but for now we leave this to the compiler.

Due to pointers, objects lexically out of scope may be accessible in a function, so if proper precautions are not taken, dereferencing a static pointer to a dynamic variable can result in residual code where an out-of-scope variable is being referenced! We defer the problem until Sect. 4.3, where a solution is presented.

Notice that it makes no sense to have a dynamic pointer to a static value, since the object pointed to must be present in the residual program.

4.5   Related Work

Most the material presented in this section is based on Andersen's "Program Analysis and Specialization for the C Programming Language" [2], in which the first generating extension generator for the C language was presented. Since then, the COMPOSE group has achieved to combine compile-time and *run-time* partial evaluation of C [5], which has led to the development of more fine grained analyses [8].

For a thorough treatment of partial evaluation and binding-time analysis in general, see [9].

References

[1] Alfred V. Aho, Ravi Sethi, and Jeffrey D. Ullman. *Compilers, Principles, Techniques, and Tools.* Addison-Wesley, 1986.

[2] Lars Ole Andersen. *Program Analysis and Specialization for the C Programming Language.* PhD thesis, Department of Computer Science, University of Copenhagen (DIKU, Copenhagen, Denmark, May 1994.

[3] Peter Holst Andersen. Partially static binding-time types in C-Mix. Unpublished, November 1997.

[4] ANSI. *American National Standard for Programming Languages — C.* New York, USA, 1990. ANSI/ISO 9899-1990.

[5] C. Consel, L. Hornof, F. Noel, and J. Noye. A uniform approach for compile-time and run-time specialization. *Lecture Notes in Computer Science,* 1110:54–??, 1996.

[6] A. P. Ershov. On the partial computation principle. *Information Processing Letters,* 6(2):38–41, April 1977.

[7] Fritz Henglein. Efficient type inference for higher-order binding-time analysis. In J. Hughes, editor, *FPCA,* pages 448–472. 5th ACM Conference, Cambridge, MA, USA, Berlin: Springer-Verlag, August 1991. Lecture Notes in Computer Science, Vol. 523.

[8] L. Hornof and Jacques Noyé. Accurate binding-time analysis for imperative languages: Flow, context and return sensitivity. In *Proceedings of the ACM SIGPLAN Symposium on Partial Evaluation and Semantics-Based Program Manipulation (PEPM-97),* volume 32, 12 of *ACM SIGPLAN Notices,* pages 63–73, New York, June12–13 1997. ACM Press.

[9] Neil D. Jones, Carsten K. Gomard, and Peter Sestoft. *Partial Evaluation and Automatic Program Generation.* Prentice-Hall, 1993.

[10] Brian W. Kernighan and Dennis M. Ritchie. *The C Programming Language.* Prentice-Hall, Englewood Cliffs, New Jersey 07632, 2 edition, 1988.

Logic Program Specialisation

Michael Leuschel

Department of Electronics and Computer Science
University of Southampton
Highfield, Southampton, SO17 1BJ, UK
mal@ecs.soton.ac.uk
www: http://www.ecs.soton.ac.uk/~mal

1 Introduction

Declarative programming languages, are high-level programming languages in which one only has to state *what* is to be computed and not necessarily *how* it is to be computed. *Logic programming* and *functional programming* are two prominent members of this class of programming languages. While functional programming is based on the λ-calculus, logic programming has its roots in first-order logic and automated theorem proving. Both approaches share the view that a program is a *theory* and execution consists in performing *deduction* from that theory.

Program specialisation, also called *partial evaluation* or *partial deduction*, is an automatic technique for program optimisation. The central idea is to specialise a given source program for a particular application domain. Program specialisation can be used to speed up existing programs for certain application domains, sometimes achieving speedups of several orders of magnitude. It, however, also allows the user to conceive more generally applicable programs using a more secure, readable and maintainable style. The program specialiser then takes care of transforming this general purpose, readable, but inefficient program into an efficient one.

Because of their clear (and often simple) semantical foundations, declarative languages offer significant advantages for the design of semantics based program analysers, transformers and optimisers. First, because there *exists* a *clear* and *simple* semantical foundation, techniques for program specialisation *can* be proven correct in a formal way. Furthermore, program specialisation does not have to preserve every execution aspect of the source program, as long as the declarative semantics is respected. This permits much more powerful optimisations, impossible to obtain when the specialiser has to preserve every operational aspect of the source program.

This course is situated within that context and is structured as follows. Section 2 starts out from the roots of logic programming in first-order logic and automated theorem proving and presents the syntax, semantics and proof theory of logic programs. In Section 3 the general idea of program specialisation, based on Kleene's S-M-N theorem, is introduced. A particular technique for specialising logic programs, called *partial deduction*, is then developed and illustrated.

The theoretical underpinnings of this approach, based on the correctness results by Lloyd and Shepherdson [69], are exhibited. We also elaborate on the control issues of partial deduction and define the *control of polyvariance problem*.

The advanced part of this course [60] (in this volume), builds upon these foundations and presents more refined techniques for controlling partial deduction, as well as several ways of extending its power, all situated within the larger objective of turning declarative languages and program specialisation into valuable tools for constructing reliable, maintainable *and* efficient programs.

2   Logic and Logic Programming

In this section we summarise some essential background in first-order logic and logic programming. Not every detail is required for the proper comprehension of this course and this section is mainly meant to be a kind of "reference manual" of logic programming.

The exposition is mainly inspired by [5] and [68] and in general adheres to the same terminology. The reader is referred to these works for a more detailed presentation, comprising motivations, examples and proofs. Some other good introductions to logic programming can also be found in [78] and [33, 6], while a good introduction to first-order logic and automated theorem proving can be found in [36].

2.1   First-order logic and syntax of logic programs

We start with a brief presentation of first-order logic.

Definition 1.   (alphabet) *An* alphabet *consists of the following classes of symbols:* variables; function symbols; predicate symbols; connectives, *which are* ¬ negation, ∧ conjunction, ∨ disjunction, ← implication, *and* ↔ equivalence; quantifiers, *which are the existential quantifier* ∃ *and the universal quantifier* ∀; punctuation symbols, *which are* "(", ")" *and* ",". *Function and predicate symbols have an associated* arity, *a natural number indicating how many arguments they take in the definitions following below.*
Constants *are function symbols of arity 0, while* propositions *are predicate symbols of arity 0.*

In the remainder of this course we suppose the set of variables is countably infinite. In addition, alphabets with a finite set of function and predicate symbols will simply be called *finite*. An *infinite* alphabet is one in which the number of function and/or predicate symbols is not finite but countably infinite.

We will try to adhere as much as possible to the following syntactical conventions throughout the course:
- Variables will be denoted by upper-case letters like X, Y, Z, usually taken from the later part of the (Latin) alphabet.
- Constants will be denoted by lower-case letters like a, b, c, usually taken from the beginning of the (Latin) alphabet.

- The other function symbols will be denoted by lower-case letters like f, g, h.
- Predicate symbols will be denoted by lower-case letters like p, q, r.

Definition 2. **(terms, atoms)** *The set of* terms *(over some given alphabet) is inductively defined as follows:*

- *a variable is a term*
- *a constant is a term and*
- *a function symbol f of arity $n > 0$ applied to a sequence $t_1, \ldots, t_n$ of n terms, denoted by $f(t_1, \ldots, t_n)$, is also a term.*

The set of atoms *(over some given alphabet) is defined in the following way:*

- *a proposition is an atom and*
- *a predicate symbol p of arity $n > 0$ applied to a sequence $t_1, \ldots, t_n$ of n terms, denoted by $p(t_1, \ldots, t_n)$, is an atom.*

We will also allow the notations $f(t_1, \ldots, t_n)$ and $p(t_1, \ldots, t_n)$ in case $n = 0$. $f(t_1, \ldots, t_n)$ then simply represents the term f and $p(t_1, \ldots, t_n)$ represents the atom p. For terms representing lists we will use the usual Prolog [28, 95, 23] notation: e.g., [] denotes the empty list, $[H|T]$ denotes a non-empty list with first element H and tail T and $[a, b]$ denotes a two-element list made up using a and b.

Definition 3. **(formula)** *A* (well-formed) formula *(over some given alphabet) is inductively defined as follows:*

- *An atom is a formula.*
- *If F and G are formulas then so are $(\neg F)$, $(F \vee G)$, $(F \wedge G)$, $(F \leftarrow G)$, $(F \leftrightarrow G)$.*
- *If X is a variable and F is a formula then $(\forall X F)$ and $(\exists X F)$ are also formulas.*

To avoid formulas cluttered with the punctuation symbols we give the connectives and quantifiers the following precedence, from highest to lowest:

$$1.\ \neg, \forall, \exists, \qquad 2.\ \vee, \qquad 3.\ \wedge, \qquad 4.\ \leftarrow, \leftrightarrow.$$

For instance, we will write $\forall X (p(X) \leftarrow \neg q(X) \wedge r(X))$ instead of the less readable $(\forall X (p(X) \leftarrow ((\neg q(X)) \wedge r(X))))$.

The set of all formulas constructed using a given alphabet A is called the *first-order language* given by A.

First-order logic assigns meanings to formulas in the form of *interpretations* over some domain D:

- Each function symbol of arity n is assigned an n-ary function $D^n \mapsto D$. This part, along with the choice of the domain D, is referred to as a *pre-interpretation*.
- Each predicate symbol of arity n is assigned an n-ary relation, i.e., a subset of D^n (or equivalently an n-ary function $D^n \mapsto \{\mathbf{true}, \mathbf{false}\}$).

– Each formula is given a truth value, **true** or **false**, depending on the truth values of the sub-formulas. (For more details see e.g., [36] or [68]).

A *model* of a formula is simply an interpretation in which the formula has the value **true** assigned to it. Similarly, a model of a set S of formulas is an interpretation which is a model for all $F \in S$.

For example, let I be an interpretation whose domain D is the set of natural numbers $I\!N$ and which maps the constant a to 1, the constant b to 2 and the unary predicate p to the unary relation $\{(1)\}$. Then the truth value of $p(a)$ under I is **true** and the truth value of $p(b)$ under I is **false**. So I is a model of $p(a)$ but not of $p(b)$. I is also a model of $\exists X p(X)$ but not of $\forall X p(X)$.

We say that two formulas are *logically equivalent* iff they have the same models. A formula F is said to be a *logical consequence* of a set of formulas S, denoted by $S \models F$, iff F is assigned the truth value **true** in all models of S. A set of formulas S is said to be *inconsistent* iff it has no model. It can be easily shown that $S \models F$ holds iff $S \cup \{\neg F\}$ is inconsistent. This observation lies at the basis of what is called a proof by *refutation*: to show that F is a logical consequence of S we show that $S \cup \{\neg F\}$ leads to inconsistency.

From now on we will also use **true** (resp. **false**) to denote some arbitrary formula which is assigned the truth value **true** (resp. **false**) in every interpretation. If there exists a proposition p in the underlying alphabet then **true** could, e.g., stand for $p \vee \neg p$ and **false** could stand for $p \wedge \neg p$.[1] We also introduce the following shorthands for formulas:

– if F is a formula, then $(F \leftarrow)$ denotes the formula $(F \leftarrow \textbf{true})$ and $(\leftarrow F)$ denotes the formula $(\textbf{false} \leftarrow F)$.
– $(\leftarrow)$ denotes the formula $(\textbf{false} \leftarrow \textbf{true})$.

In the following we define some other frequently occurring kinds of formulas.

Definition 4. (literal) *If A is an atom then the formulas A and $\neg A$ are called literals. Furthermore, A is called a* positive *literal and $\neg A$ a* negative *literal.*

Definition 5. (conjunction, disjunction) *Let $A_1, \ldots, A_n$ be literals, where $n > 0$. Then $A_1 \wedge \ldots \wedge A_n$ is a conjunction and $A_1 \vee \ldots \vee A_n$ is a disjunction.*

Usually we will assume $\wedge$ (respectively $\vee$) to be associative, in the sense that we do not distinguish between the logically equivalent, but syntactically different, formulas $p \wedge (q \wedge r)$ and $(p \wedge q) \wedge r$.

Definition 6. (scope) *Given a formula $(\forall X F)$ (resp. $(\exists X F)$) the scope of $\forall X$ (resp. $\exists X$) is F. A bound occurrence of a variable X inside a formula F is any occurrence immediately following a quantifier or an occurrence within the scope of a quantifier $\forall X$ or $\exists X$. Any other occurrence of X inside F is said to be free.*

---

[1] In some texts on logic (e.g., [36]) **true** and **false** are simply added to the alphabet and treated in a special manner by interpretations.

Definition 7. (closure) *Given a formula F, the universal closure of F, denoted by $\forall(F)$, is a formula of the form $(\forall X_1 \ldots (\forall X_m F) \ldots)$ where $X_1, \ldots, X_m$ are all the variables having a free occurrence inside F (in some arbitrary order). Similarly the existential closure of F, denoted by $\exists(F)$, is the formula $(\exists X_1 \ldots (\exists X_m F) \ldots)$.*

The following class of formulas plays a central role in logic programming.

Definition 8. (clause) *A clause is a formula of the form $\forall(H_1 \vee \ldots \vee H_m \leftarrow B_1 \wedge \ldots \wedge B_n)$, where $m \geq 0, n \geq 0$ and $H_1, \ldots, H_m, B_1, \ldots, B_n$ are all literals. $H_1 \vee \ldots \vee H_m$ is called the* head *of the clause and $B_1 \wedge \ldots \wedge B_n$ is called the* body.
A (normal) program clause *is a clause where $m = 1$ and H_1 is an atom. A* definite program clause *is a normal program clause in which $B_1, \ldots, B_n$ are atoms. A* fact *is a program clause with $n = 0$. A* query *or* goal *is a clause with $m = 0$ and $n > 0$. A* definite goal *is a goal in which $B_1, \ldots, B_n$ are atoms. The* empty clause *is a clause with $n = m = 0$. As we have seen earlier, this corresponds to the formula* false $\leftarrow$ true, *i.e., a contradiction. We also use $\square$ to denote the empty clause.*

In logic programming notation one usually omits the universal quantifiers encapsulating the clause and one also often uses the comma (',') instead of the conjunction in the body, e.g., one writes $p(s(X)) \leftarrow q(X), p(X)$ instead of $\forall X(p(f(X)) \leftarrow (q(X) \wedge p(X)))$. We will adhere to this convention.

Definition 9. (program) *A (normal) program is a set of program clauses. A definite program is a set of definite program clauses.*

In order to express a given program P in a first-order language L given by some alphabet A, the alphabet A must of course contain the function and predicate symbols occurring within P. The alphabet might however contain additional function and predicate symbols which do not occur inside the program. We therefore denote the underlying first-order language of a given program P by $\mathcal{L}_P$ and the underlying alphabet by $\mathcal{A}_P$. For technical reasons related to definitions below, we suppose that there is at least one constant symbol in $\mathcal{A}_P$.

2.2   Semantics of logic programs

Given that a program P is just a set of formulas, which happen to be clauses, the logical meaning of P might simply be seen as all the formulas F for which $P \models F$. For normal programs this approach will turn out to be insufficient, but for definite programs it provides a good starting point.

Definite programs To determine whether a formula F is a logical consequence of another formula G, we have to examine whether F is true in *all* models of G. One big advantage of clauses is that it is sufficient to look just at certain canonical models, called the Herbrand models.

In the following we will define these canonical models. Any term, atom, literal, clause will be called *ground* iff it contains no variables.

Definition 10. *Let P be a program written in the underlying first-order language $\mathcal{L}_P$ given by the alphabet $\mathcal{A}_P$. Then the* Herbrand universe $\mathcal{U}_P$ *is the set of all ground terms over $\mathcal{A}_P$.[2] The* Herbrand base $\mathcal{B}_P$ *is the set of all ground atoms in $\mathcal{L}_P$.*

A *Herbrand interpretation* is simply an interpretation whose domain is the Herbrand universe $\mathcal{U}_P$ and which maps every term to itself. A *Herbrand model* of a set of formulas S is an Herbrand interpretation which is a model of S.

The interest of Herbrand models for logic programs derives from the following proposition (the proposition does *not* hold for arbitrary formulas).

Proposition 1. *A set of clauses has a model iff it has a Herbrand model.*

This means that a formula F which is true in all Herbrand models of a set of clauses C is a logical consequence of C. Indeed if F is true in all Herbrand models then $\neg F$ is false in all Herbrand models and therefore, by Proposition 1, $C \cup \{\neg F\}$ is inconsistent and $C \models F$.

Note that a Herbrand interpretation or model can be identified with a subset H of the Herbrand base $\mathcal{B}_P$ (i.e., $H \in 2^{\mathcal{B}_P}$): the interpretation of $p(d_1, \ldots, d_n)$ is **true** iff $p(d_1, \ldots, d_n) \in H$ and the interpretation of $p(d_1, \ldots, d_n)$ is **false** iff $p(d_1, \ldots, d_n) \notin H$. This means that we can use the standard set order on Herbrand models and define minimal Herbrand models as follows.

Definition 11. *A Herbrand model $H \subseteq \mathcal{B}_P$ for a given program P is a minimal Herbrand model iff there exists no $H' \subset H$ which is also a Herbrand model of P.*

For definite programs there exists a *unique* minimal Herbrand model, called the *least Herbrand model*, denoted by $\mathcal{H}_P$. Indeed it can be easily shown that the intersection of two Herbrand models for a definite program P is still a Herbrand model of P. Furthermore, the entire Herbrand base $\mathcal{B}_P$ is always a model for a definite program and one can thus obtain the least Herbrand model by taking the intersection of all Herbrand models.

The least Herbrand model $\mathcal{H}_P$ can be seen as capturing the *intended meaning* of a given definite program P as it is sufficient to infer all the logical consequences of P. Indeed, a formula which is true in the least Herbrand model $\mathcal{H}_P$ is true in all Herbrand models and is therefore a logical consequence of the program.

Example 1. Take for instance the following program P:

$int(0) \leftarrow$
$int(s(X)) \leftarrow int(X)$

---

[2] It is here that the requirement that $\mathcal{A}_P$ contains at least one constant symbol comes into play. It ensures that the Herbrand universe is never empty.

Then the least Herbrand model of P is $\mathcal{H}_P = \{int(0), int(s(0)), \ldots\}$ and indeed $P \models int(0)$, $P \models int(s(0))$, ... But also note that for definite programs the entire Herbrand base $\mathcal{B}_P$ is also a model. Given a suitable alphabet $\mathcal{A}_P$, we might have $\mathcal{B}_P = \{int(a), int(0), int(s(a)), int(s(0)), \ldots\}$. This means that the atom $int(a)$ is consistent with the program P (i.e., $P \not\models \neg int(a)$), but is not implied either (i.e., $P \not\models int(a)$).

It is here that logic programming goes beyond "classical" first-order logic. In logic programming one (usually) assumes that the program gives a *complete* description of the intended interpretation, i.e., anything which cannot be inferred from the program is assumed to be false. For example, one would say that $\neg int(a)$ is a consequence of the above program P because $int(a) \notin \mathcal{H}_P$. This means that, from a logic programming perspective, the above program captures exactly the natural numbers, something which is impossible to accomplish within first-order logic (see e.g., Corollary 4.10.1 in [27] for a formal proof).

A possible inference scheme, capturing this aspect of logic programming, was introduced in [86] and is referred to as the *closed world assumption* (CWA). The CWA cannot be expressed in first-order logic (a second-order logic axiom has to be used to that effect). Note that using the CWA leads to *non-monotonic* inferences, because the addition of new information can remove certain, previously valid, consequences. For instance, by adding the clause $int(a) \leftarrow$ to the above program the literal $\neg int(a)$ is no longer a consequence of the logic program.

Normal programs We have already touched upon the CWA. Given a formula F, this rule amounts to inferring that $\neg F$ is a logical consequence of a program P if F is not a logical consequence of P. In the context of normal programs the situation is complicated by the fact that negations can occur in the bodies of clauses and therefore the truth of $\neg F$ can propagate further and may be used to infer positive formulas as well. This entails that a normal logic program does not necessarily have a unique minimal Herbrand model. To give a meaning to normal logic programs a multitude of semantics have been developed. We cannot delve into the details of these semantics and have to refer the interested reader to, e.g., [7].

2.3   Proof theory of logic programs

We first need the following definitions:

Definition 12.   (substitution) *A substitution θ is a finite set of the form $\theta = \{X_1/t_1, \ldots, X_n/t_n\}$ where $X_1, \ldots, X_n$ are distinct variables and $t_1, \ldots, t_n$ are terms such that $t_i \neq X_i$. Each element X_i/t_i of θ is called a* binding.

Alternate definitions of substitutions exist in the literature, but the above is the most common one in the logic programming context.

We also define an *expression* to be either a term, an atom, a literal, a conjunction, a disjunction or a program clause.

Definition 13.   (instance) *Let $\theta = \{X_1/t_1, \ldots, X_n/t_n\}$ be a substitution and E an expression. Then the* instance *of E by θ, denoted by $E\theta$, is the expression obtained by simultaneously replacing each occurrence of a variable X_i in E by the term t.*

We present some additional useful terminology related to substitutions. If $E\theta = F$ then E is said to be *more general* than F. If E is more general than F and F is more general than E then E and F are called *variants* (of each other). If $E\theta$ is a variant of E then θ is called a *renaming substitution for E*. Because a substitution is a *set* of bindings we will denote, in contrast to, e.g., [68], the *empty* or *identity substitution* by $\emptyset$ and not by the empty sequence ϵ. Substitutions can also be applied to sets of expressions by defining $\{E_1, \ldots, E_n\}\theta = \{E_1\theta, \ldots, E_n\theta\}$.

Substitutions can also be composed in the following way:

Definition 14.   (substitution composition) *Let $\theta = \{X_1/s_1, \ldots, X_n/s_n\}$ and $\sigma = \{Y_1/t_1, \ldots, Y_k/t_k\}$ be substitutions. Then the* composition of θ and σ, *denoted by $\theta\sigma$, is defined to be the substitution $\{X_i/s_i\sigma \mid 1 \leq i \leq n \wedge s_i\sigma \neq X_i\}$ $\cup \{Y_i/t_i \mid 1 \leq i \leq k \wedge Y_i \notin \{X_1, \ldots, X_n\}\}$.*

When viewing substitutions as functions from expressions to expressions, then the above definition behaves just like ordinary function composition, i.e., $E(\theta\sigma) = (E\theta)\sigma$. We also have that (for proofs see [68]) the identity substitution acts as a left and right identity for composition, i.e., $\theta\emptyset = \emptyset\theta = \theta$, and that composition is associative, i.e., $(\theta\sigma)\gamma = \theta(\sigma\gamma)$.

We call a substitution θ *idempotent* iff $\theta\theta = \theta$. We also define the following notations: the set of variables occurring inside an expression E is denoted by $vars(E)$, the *domain* of a substitution θ is defined as $dom(\theta) = \{X \mid X/t \in \theta\}$ and the *range* of θ is defined as $ran(\theta) = \{Y \mid X/t \in \theta \wedge Y \in vars(t)\}$. Finally, we also define $vars(\theta) = dom(\theta) \cup ran(\theta)$ as well as the restriction $\theta|_V$ of a substitution θ to a set of variables V by $\theta|_V = \{X/t \mid X/t \in \theta \wedge X \in V\}$.

The following concept will form the link between the model-theoretic semantics and the procedural semantics of logic programs.

Definition 15.   (answer) *Let P be a program and $G = \leftarrow L_1, \ldots, L_n$ a goal. An* answer *for $P \cup \{G\}$ is a substitution θ such that $dom(\theta) \subseteq vars(G)$.*

Definite programs We first define correct answers in the context of definite programs and goals.

Definition 16.   (correct answer) *Let P be a definite program and $G = \leftarrow A_1, \ldots, A_n$ a definite goal. An answer θ for $P \cup \{G\}$ is called a* correct answer *for $P \cup \{G\}$ iff $P \models \forall((A_1 \wedge \ldots \wedge A_n)\theta)$.*

Take for instance the program $P = \{p(a) \leftarrow\}$ and the goal $G = \leftarrow p(X)$. Then $\{X/a\}$ is a correct answer for $P \cup \{G\}$ while $\{X/c\}$ and $\emptyset$ are not.

We now present a way to calculate correct answers based on the concepts of resolution and unification.

Definition 17. **(mgu)** *Let S be a finite set of expressions. A substitution θ is called a unifier of S iff the set $S\theta$ is a singleton. θ is called relevant iff its variables $vars(\theta)$ all occur in S. θ is called a most general unifier or mgu iff for each unifier σ of S there exists a substitution γ such that $\sigma = \theta\gamma$.*

The concept of unification dates back to [45] and has been rediscovered in [87]. If a unifier for a finite set S of expressions exists then there exists an idempotent and relevant most general unifier which is unique modulo variable renaming (see [5, 68]). Unifiability of a set of expressions is decidable and there are efficient algorithms for calculating an idempotent and relevant *mgu*. See for instance the unification algorithms in [5, 68] or the more complicated but linear ones in [70, 80]. From now on we denote, for a unifiable set S of expressions, by $mgu(S)$ an idempotent and relevant unifier of S. If we just want to unify two terms t_1, t_2 then we will also sometimes write $mgu(t_1, t_2)$ instead of $mgu(\{t_1, t_2\})$.

We define the *most general instance*, of a finite set S to be the only element of $S\theta$ where $\theta = mgu(S)$. The opposite of the most general instance is the *most specific generalisation* of a finite set of expressions S, also denoted by $msg(S)$, which is the most specific expression M such that all expressions in S are instances of M. Algorithms for calculating the *msg* exist [59], and this process is also referred to as *anti-unification* or *least general generalisation*.

We can now define *SLD-resolution*, which is based on the resolution principle [87]. Its use for a programming language was first described in [56] and the name SLD (which stands for Selection rule-driven Linear resolution for Definite clauses), was coined in [9]. See e.g., [5, 68] for more details about the history.

Definition 18. **(SLD-derivation step)** *Let $G = \leftarrow L_1, \ldots, L_m, \ldots, L_k$ be a goal and $C = A \leftarrow B_1, \ldots, B_n$ a program clause such that $k \geq 1$ and $n \geq 0$. Then G' is derived from G and C using θ (and L_m) iff the following conditions hold:*

1. *L_m is an atom, called the selected atom (at position m), in G.*
2. *θ is a relevant and idempotent mgu of L_m and A.*
3. *G' is the goal $\leftarrow (L_1, \ldots, L_{m-1}, B_1, \ldots, B_n, L_{m+1}, \ldots, L_k)\theta$.*

G' is also called a resolvent of G and C.

In the following we define the concept of a complete SLD-derivation (we will define incomplete ones later on).

Definition 19. **(complete SLD-derivation)** *Let P be a definite program and G a definite goal. A complete SLD-derivation of $P \cup \{G\}$ is a tuple $(\mathcal{G}, \mathcal{L}, \mathcal{C}, \mathcal{S})$ consisting of a sequence of goals $\mathcal{G} = \langle G_0, G_1, \ldots \rangle$, a sequence $\mathcal{L} = \langle L_0, L_1 \ldots \rangle$ of selected literals,[3] a sequence $\mathcal{C} = \langle C_1, C_2, \ldots \rangle$ of variants of program clauses of P and a sequence $\mathcal{S} = \langle \theta_1, \theta_2, \ldots \rangle$ of mgu's such that:*
  – for $i > 0$, $vars(C_i) \cap vars(G_0) = \emptyset$;

---

[3] Again we slightly deviate from [5, 68]: the inclusion of $\mathcal{L}$ avoids some minor technical problems wrt the maximality condition.

– for $i > j$, $vars(C_i) \cap vars(C_j) = \emptyset$;
– for $i \geq 0$, L_i is a positive literal in G_i and G_{i+1} is derived from G_i and C_{i+1} using θ_{i+1} and L_i;
– the sequences $\mathcal{G}, \mathcal{C}, \mathcal{S}$ are maximal given $\mathcal{L}$.

The process of producing variants of program clauses of P which do not share any variable with the derivation sequence so far is called *standardising apart*. Some care has to be taken to avoid variable clashes and the ensuing technical problems; see the discussions in [53] or [32].

We now come back to the idea of a proof by refutation and its relation to SLD-resolution. In a proof by refutation one adds the negation of what is to be proven and then tries to arrive at inconsistency. The former corresponds to adding a goal $G = \leftarrow A_1, \ldots, A_n$ to a program P and the latter corresponds to searching for an SLD-derivation of $P \cup \{G\}$ which leads to $\square$. This justifies the following definition.

Definition 20. (SLD-refutation) *An* SLD-refutation *of* $P \cup \{G\}$ *is a finite complete SLD-derivation of* $P \cup \{G\}$ *which has the empty clause $\square$ as the last goal of the derivation.*

In addition to refutations there are (only) two other kinds of complete derivations:

– Finite derivations which do not have the empty clause as the last goal. These derivations will be called *(finitely) failed*.
– Infinite derivations. These will be called *infinitely failed*.

We can now define computed answers, which correspond to the output calculated by a logic program.

Definition 21. (computed answer) *Let P be a definite program, G a definite goal and D a SLD-refutation for $P \cup \{G\}$ with the sequence $\langle \theta_1, \ldots, \theta_n \rangle$ of mgu's. The substitution $(\theta_1 \ldots \theta_n)|_{vars(G)}$ is then called a computed answer for $P \cup \{G\}$ (via D).*

Theorem 1. (soundness of SLD) *Let P be a definite program and G a definite goal. Every computed answer for $P \cup \{G\}$ is a correct answer for $P \cup \{G\}$.*

Theorem 2. (completeness of SLD) *Let P be a definite program and G a definite goal. For every correct answer σ for $P \cup \{G\}$ there exists a computed answer θ for $P \cup \{G\}$ and a substitution γ such that $G\sigma = G\theta\gamma$.*

A proof of the previous theorem can be found in [5].
We will now examine systematic ways to search for SLD-refutations.

Definition 22. (complete SLD-tree) *A complete SLD-tree for $P \cup \{G\}$ is a labelled tree satisfying the following:*

1. *Each node of the tree is labelled with a definite goal along with an indication of the selected atom*

2. *The root node is labelled with G.*

3. *Let $\leftarrow A_1, \ldots, A_m, \ldots, A_k$ be the label of a node in the tree and suppose that A_m is the selected atom. Then for each clause $A \leftarrow B_1, \ldots, B_q$ in P such that A_m and A are unifiable the node has one child labelled with*

$$\leftarrow (A_1, \ldots, A_{m-1}, B_1, \ldots, B_q, A_{m+1}, \ldots, A_k)\theta,$$

   where θ is an idempotent and relevant mgu of A_m and A.

4. *Nodes labelled with the empty goal have no children.*

To every branch of a complete SLD-tree there corresponds a complete SLD-derivation. The choice of the selected atom is performed by what is called a *selection rule*. Maybe the most well known selection rule is the *left-to-right selection rule* of *Prolog* [28, 95, 23], which always selects the leftmost literal in a goal. The complete SLD-derivations and SLD-trees constructed via this selection rule are called *LD-derivations* and *LD-trees*.

Usually one confounds goals and nodes (e.g., in [5, 68, 78]) although this is strictly speaking not correct because the same goal can occur several times inside the same SLD-tree.

We will often use a graphical representation of SLD-trees in which the selected atoms are identified by underlining. For instance, Fig. 1 contains a graphical representation of a complete SLD-tree for $P \cup \{\leftarrow int(s(0))\}$, where P is the program of Ex. 1.

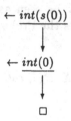

Fig. 1. Complete SLD-tree for Example 1

Normal programs Finding an efficient proof procedure for normal programs is much less obvious than in the definite case. The most commonly used procedure is the so called *SLDNF-procedure*. It is an extension of SLD-resolution which also allows the selection of ground negative literals. Basically a selected ground negative literal $\neg A$ succeeds (with the empty computed answer $\emptyset$) if $\leftarrow A$ fails *finitely*. Similarly a selected ground negative literal fails if there exists a refutation for $\leftarrow A$. This implements what is called the "negation as failure" (NAF) rule, a less powerful but more tractable inference mechanism than the CWA.

In this course we will mainly concentrate on definite logic programs. On the rare occasions we touch upon normal programs we use the definitions of

SLDNF-derivations presented in [68] based on ranks, where the rank indicates the maximal nesting of sub-derivations and sub-trees created by negative calls. Note that the definition of [68] exhibits some technical problems, in the sense that some problematic goals do not have an associated SLDNF-derivation (failed or otherwise, see [8, 7]). The definition is however sufficient for our purposes, especially since most correctness results for partial deduction (e.g., [68]), to be introduced in the next section, use this definition anyway.

Soundness of SLDNF-resolution (wrt the completion semantics) is due to Clark [22]. Unfortunately SLDNF-resolution is in general not complete, mainly (but not only) due to *floundering*, i.e., computation reaches a state in which only non-ground negative literals exist.

To remedy the incompleteness of SLDNF, several extensions have been proposed. Let us briefly mention the approach of *constructive negation* overcomes some of the incompleteness problems of SLDNF [20, 21, 34, 89, 97, 96] and can be useful inside partial deduction [44]. The main idea is to allow the selection of non-ground negative literals, replacing them by disequality constraints. For instance, given $P = \{p(a) \leftarrow\}$ the negative literal $\neg p(X)$ could be replaced by $\neg(X = a)$.

Programs with built-ins Most practical logic programs make (heavy) usage of built-ins. Although a lot of these built-ins, like e.g., `assert/1` and `retract/1`, are extra-logical and ruin the declarative nature of the underlying program, a reasonable number of them can actually be seen as syntactic sugar. Take for example the following program which uses the Prolog [28, 95, 23] built-ins $= ../2$ and $call/1$.

$$map(P, [], []) \leftarrow$$
$$map(P, [X|T], [P_X|P_T]) \leftarrow C = ..[P, X, P_X], call(C), map(P, T, P_T)$$
$$inv(0, 1) \leftarrow$$
$$inv(1, 0) \leftarrow$$

For this program the query $\leftarrow map(inv, [0, 1, 0], R)$ will succeed with the computed answer $\{R/[1, 0, 1]\}$. Given that query, the Prolog program can be seen as a pure definite logic program by simply adding the following definitions (where we use the prefix notation for the predicate $= ../2$):

$$= ..(inv(X, Y), [inv, X, Y]) \leftarrow$$
$$call(inv(X, Y)) \leftarrow inv(X, Y)$$

The so obtained pure logic program will succeed for $\leftarrow map(inv, [0, 1, 0], R)$ with the same computed answer $\{R/[1, 0, 1]\}$.

This means that some predicates like $map/3$, which are usually taken to be higher-order, can simply be mapped to pure definite (first-order) logic programs ([99, 77]). Some built-ins, like for instance $is/2$, have to be defined by infinite relations. Usually this poses no problems as long as, when selecting such a built-in, only a finite number of cases apply (Prolog will report a run-time error if more than one case applies while the programming language Gödel [47] will delay the selection until only one case applies).

In the remainder of this course we will usually restrict our attention to those built-ins that can be given a logical meaning by such a mapping.

3   Partial Evaluation and Partial Deduction

3.1   Partial evaluation

In contrast to ordinary (full) evaluation, a *partial evaluator* is given a program P along with only *part* of its input, called the *static input*. The remaining part of the input, called the *dynamic input*, will only be known at some later point in time. Given the static input S, the partial evaluator then produces a *specialised* version P_S of P which, when given the dynamic input D, produces the same output as the original program P. This process is illustrated in Fig. 2. The program P_S is also called the *residual program*.

The theoretical feasibility of this process, in the context of recursive functions, has already been established by Kleene [52] and is known as Kleene's S-M-N theorem. However, while Kleene was concerned with theoretical issues of computability and his construction yields specialised programs which are slower than the original, the goal of partial evaluation is to exploit the static input in order to derive more efficient programs.

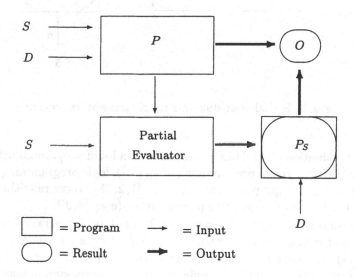

Fig. 2. Partial evaluation of programs with static and dynamic input

To obtain the specialised program P_S, a partial evaluator performs a mixture of evaluation, i.e., it executes those parts of P which only depend on the static input S, and of code generation for those parts of P which require the dynamic input D. This process has therefore also been called *mixed computation* in [35].

Also, it is precisely this mixture of full evaluation steps and code generation steps (and nothing else) which distinguishes partial evaluation from other program specialisation approaches.

Because part of the computation has already been performed beforehand by the partial evaluator, the hope that we obtain a more efficient program P_S seems justified. The simple example in Fig. 3 illustrates this point: the control of the loop in P is fully determined by the static input $e = 3$ and was executed beforehand by the partial evaluator, resulting in a more efficient specialised program P_e.

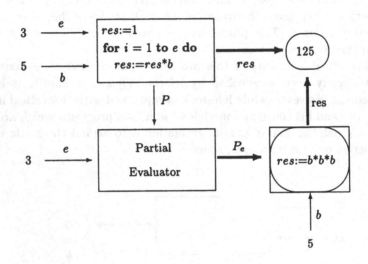

Fig. 3. Partial evaluation of a simple imperative program

Partial evaluation [24, 50] has been applied to a lot of programming languages and paradigms: functional programming (e.g., [51]), logic programming (e.g., [40, 55, 81]), functional logic programming (e.g., [1, 2, 58]) term rewriting systems (e.g., [13, 14], [75]) and imperative programming (e.g., [4, 3]).

In the context of logic programming, full input to a program P consists of a goal G and evaluation corresponds to constructing a complete SLDNF-tree for $P \cup \{G\}$. For partial evaluation, the static input then takes the form of a *partially instantiated* goal G'. In contrast to other programming languages and paradigms, one can still execute P for G' and (try to) construct a SLDNF-tree for $P \cup \{G'\}$. So, at first sight, it seems that partial evaluation for logic programs is almost trivial and just corresponds to ordinary evaluation.

However, because G' is not yet fully instantiated, the SLDNF-tree for $P \cup \{G'\}$ is usually infinite and ordinary evaluation will not terminate. A more refined approach to partial evaluation of logic programs is therefore required. A technique which solves this problem is known under the name of *partial deduction*. Its general idea is to construct a finite number of finite trees which "cover" the possibly infinite SLDNF-tree for $P \cup \{G'\}$. We will present the essentials of this technique in the next section.

The term "partial deduction" has been introduced by Komorowski (see [55]) to replace the term of partial evaluation in the context of pure logic programs. We will adhere to this terminology because the word "deduction" places emphasis on the purely logical nature of the source programs. Also, while partial evaluation of functional and imperative programs evaluates only those expressions which depend exclusively on the static input, in logic programming one can, as we have seen above, in principle also evaluate expressions which depend on the unknown dynamic input. This puts partial deduction much closer to techniques such as *supercompilation* [98, 43, 93, 90] and *unfold/fold* program transformations [19, 81], and therefore using a different denomination seems justified. We will briefly return to the relation of partial deduction to these and other techniques in the second part of this course [60] (see also [42, 49, 92]). Finally, note that program specialisation in general is not limited to just evaluating expressions, whether they depend on the static input or not. A striking illustration of this statement will be presented later in the course [60], where abstract interpretation is combined with partial deduction.

3.2   Partial deduction

In this section we present the technique of partial deduction, which originates from [54]. Other introductions to partial deduction can be found in [55, 40, 26].

In order to avoid constructing infinite SLDNF-trees for partially instantiated goals, the technique of *partial deduction* is based on constructing finite, but possibly *incomplete* SLDNF-trees. The derivation steps in these SLDNF-trees correspond to the computation steps which have already been performed by the *partial deducer* and the clauses of the specialised program are then extracted from these trees by constructing one specialised clause per branch.

In this section we will formalise this technique and present conditions which will ensure correctness of the so obtained specialised programs.

Definition 23.   (SLDNF-derivation) *A SLDNF-derivation is defined like a complete SLDNF-derivation but may, in addition to leading to success or failure, also lead to a last goal where no literal has been selected for a further derivation step. Derivations of the latter kind will be called* incomplete.

An SLDNF-derivation can thus be either failed, incomplete, successful or infinite. Now, an incomplete SLDNF-tree is obtained in much in the same way.

Definition 24. *An SLDNF-tree is defined like a complete SLDNF-tree but may, in addition to success and failure leaves, also contain leaves where no literal has been selected for a further derivation step. Leaves of the latter kind are called* dangling *([72]) and SLDNF-trees containing dangling leaves are called* incomplete. *Also, an SLDNF-tree is called* trivial *iff its root is a dangling leaf, and* non-trivial *otherwise.*

The process of selecting a literal inside a dangling leaf of an incomplete SLDNF-tree and adding all the resolvents as children is called *unfolding*. An SLDNF-tree for $P \cup \{G\}$ can thus be obtained from a trivial SLDNF-tree for $P \cup \{G\}$ by performing a sequence of unfolding steps. We will return to this issue in Sect. 3.3.

Note that every branch of an SLDNF-tree has an associated (possibly incomplete) SLDNF-derivation. We also extend the notion of a *computed answer substitution (c.a.s.)* to finite incomplete SLDNF-derivations (it is just the composition of the *mgu*'s restricted to the variables of the top-level goal). Also, a *resolvent* of a finite (possibly incomplete) SLDNF-derivation is just the last goal of the derivation. Finally, if $\langle G_0, \ldots, G_n \rangle$ is the sequence of goals of a finite SLDNF-derivation, we say D has *length n*.

We will now examine how specialised clauses can be extracted from SLDNF-derivations and trees. The following definition associates a first-order formula with a finite SLDNF-derivation.

Definition 25. *Let P be a program, $\leftarrow Q$ a goal and D a finite SLDNF-derivation of $P \cup \{\leftarrow Q\}$ with computed answer θ and resolvent $\leftarrow B$. Then the formula $Q\theta \leftarrow B$ is called the* resultant *of D.*

This concept can be extended to SLDNF-trees in the following way:

Definition 26. *Let P be a program, G a goal and let τ be a finite SLDNF-tree for $P \cup \{G\}$. Let $D_1, \ldots, D_n$ be the non-failing SLDNF-derivations associated with the branches of τ. Then the set of resultants resultants(τ) is the union of the resultants of the non-failing SLDNF-derivations $D_1, \ldots, D_n$ associated with the branches of τ. We also define the set of leaves, leaves(τ), to be the atoms occurring in the resolvents of $D_1, \ldots, D_n$.*

Example 2. Let P be the following program:
$$member(X, [X|T]) \leftarrow$$
$$member(X, [Y|T]) \leftarrow member(X, T)$$
$$inboth(X, L1, L2) \leftarrow member(X, L1), member(X, L2)$$
Figure 4 represents an incomplete SLD-tree τ for $P \cup \{\leftarrow inboth(X, [a], L)\}$. This tree has just one non-failing branch and the set of resultants *resultants*(τ) contains the single clause:

$$inboth(a, [a], L) \leftarrow member(a, L)$$

Note that the complete SLD-tree for $P \cup \{\leftarrow inboth(X, [a], L)\}$ is infinite.

If the goal in the root of a finite SLDNF-tree is atomic then the resultants associated with the tree are all clauses. We can thus formalise partial deduction in the following way.

Definition 27. (partial deduction) *Let P be a normal program and A an atom. Let τ be a finite non-trivial SLDNF-tree for $P \cup \{\leftarrow A\}$. Then the set of clauses resultants(τ) is called a* partial deduction *of A in P.*

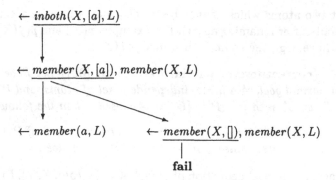

Fig. 4. Incomplete SLD-tree for Example 2

If $\mathcal{A}$ is a finite set of atoms, then a partial deduction of $\mathcal{A}$ in P is the union of one partial deduction for each element of $\mathcal{A}$.
A partial deduction of P wrt $\mathcal{A}$ is a normal program obtained from P by replacing the set of clauses in P, whose head contains one of the predicate symbols appearing in $\mathcal{A}$ (called the partially deduced predicates), with a partial deduction of $\mathcal{A}$ in P.

Example 3. Let us return to the program P of Ex. 2. Based on the incomplete SLDNF-tree in Fig. 4, we can construct the following partial deduction of P wrt $\mathcal{A} = \{inboth(X, [a], L)\}$:

$$member(X, [X|T]) \leftarrow$$
$$member(X, [Y|T]) \leftarrow member(X, T)$$
$$inboth(a, [a], L) \leftarrow member(a, L)$$

Note that if τ is a trivial SLDNF-tree for $P \cup \{\leftarrow A\}$ then $resultants(\tau)$ consists of the problematic clause $A \leftarrow A$ and the specialised program contains a loop. That is why trivial trees are not allowed in Definition 27. This is however not a sufficient condition for correctness of the specialised programs. In [69], Lloyd and Shepherdson presented and proved a fundamental correctness theorem for partial deduction. The two (additional) basic requirements for correctness of a partial deduction of P wrt $\mathcal{A}$ are the *independence* and *closedness* conditions. The independence condition guarantees that the specialised program does not produce additional answers and the closedness condition guarantees that all calls, which might occur during the execution of the specialised program, are covered by some definition. Below we summarise the correctness result of [69].

Definition 28. (closedness, independence) *Let S be a set of first order formulas and $\mathcal{A}$ a finite set of atoms. Then S is $\mathcal{A}$-closed iff each atom in S, containing a predicate symbol occurring in an atom in $\mathcal{A}$, is an instance of an atom in $\mathcal{A}$. Furthermore we say that $\mathcal{A}$ is independent iff no pair of atoms in $\mathcal{A}$ have a common instance.*

Note that two atoms which cannot be unified may still have a common instance (i.e., unify after renaming apart). For example, $p(X)$ and $p(f(X))$ are not unifiable but have, e.g., the common instance $p(f(X))$.

Theorem 3. (**correctness of partial deduction [69]**) *Let P be a normal program, G a normal goal, A a finite, independent set of atoms, and P' a partial deduction of P wrt A such that $P' \cup \{G\}$ is A-closed. Then the following hold:*

1. *$P' \cup \{G\}$ has an SLDNF-refutation with computed answer θ iff $P \cup \{G\}$ does.*
2. *$P' \cup \{G\}$ has a finitely failed SLDNF-tree iff $P \cup \{G\}$ does.*

For instance, the partial deduction of P wrt $A = \{inboth(X, [a], L)\}$ in Ex. 3 satisfies the conditions of Theorem 3 for the goals $\leftarrow inboth(X, [a], [b, a])$ and $\leftarrow inboth(X, [a], L)$ but not for the goal $\leftarrow inboth(X, [b], [b, a])$.

Note that the original unspecialised program P is also a partial deduction wrt $A = \{member(X, L), inboth(X, L1, L2)\}$ which furthermore satisfies the correctness conditions of Theorem 3 for any goal G. In other words, neither Definition 27 nor the conditions of Theorem 3 ensure that any specialisation has actually been performed. Nor do they give any indication on how to construct a suitable set A and a suitable partial deduction wrt A satisfying the correctness criteria for a given goal G of interest. These are all considerations generally delegated to the *control* of partial deduction, which we discuss in the next section.

[11] also proposes an extension of Theorem 3 which uses a notion of coveredness instead of closedness. The basic idea is to restrict the attention to those parts of the specialised program P' which can be reached from G. The formalisation is as follows:

Definition 29. *Let P be a set of clauses. The* predicate dependency graph of *P is a directed graph*

- *whose nodes are the predicate symbols in the alphabet A_P and*
- *which contains an arc from p to q iff there exists a clause in P in which p occurs as a predicate symbol in the head and q as a predicate symbol in the body.*

Definition 30. *Let P be a program and G a goal. We say that G depends upon a predicate p in A_P iff there exists a path from a predicate symbol occurring in G to p in the predicate dependency graph of P.*
We denote by $P \downarrow_G$ the definitions in P of those predicates in A_P upon which G depends.
Let A be a finite set of atoms. We say that $P \cup \{G\}$ is A-covered iff $P \downarrow_G \cup \{G\}$ is A-closed.

By replacing the condition in Theorem 3 that "$P' \cup \{G\}$ is A-closed" by the more general "$P' \cup \{G\}$ is A-covered", we still have a valid theorem (see [11]).

Example 4. Let us again return to the program P of Ex. 2. By building a complete SLD-tree for $P \cup \{\leftarrow member(X, [a])\}$, we get the following partial deduction P' of P wrt $A = \{member(X, [a])\}$:

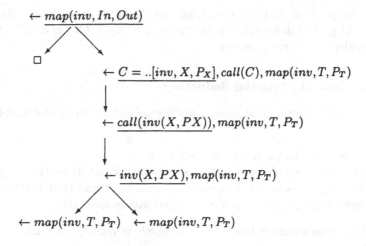

Fig. 5. Unfolding Example 5

$$member(a, [a]) \leftarrow$$
$$inboth(X, L1, L2) \leftarrow member(X, L1), member(X, L2)$$

Unfortunately, Theorem 3 cannot be applied for $G = \leftarrow member(X, [a])$ because $P' \cup \{G\}$ is not $\mathcal{A}$-closed (due to the body of the second clause of P'). However, $P' \cup \{G\}$ is $\mathcal{A}$-covered, because $P' \downarrow_G$ just consists of the first clause of P'. Therefore correctness of P' wrt G can be established by the above extension of Theorem 3.

The following example highlights one of the practical benefits of using partial deduction.

Example 5. Let us take the *map* program from Sect. 2.3.

$$map(P, [], []) \leftarrow$$
$$map(P, [X|T], [P_X|P_T]) \leftarrow C = ..[P, X, P_X], \; call(C), \; map(P, T, P_T)$$
$$inv(0, 1) \leftarrow$$
$$inv(1, 0) \leftarrow$$

If we now want to map the *inv* predicate on a list, then we can specialise the goal: $\leftarrow map(inv, In, Out)$. If we build the incomplete SLD-tree represented in Fig. 5 all the leaf atoms are covered and we can construct the following residual program:

$$map(inv, [], []) \leftarrow$$
$$map(inv, [0|T], [1|P_T]) \leftarrow map(inv, T, P_T)$$
$$map(inv, [1|T], [0|P_T]) \leftarrow map(inv, T, P_T)$$

All the higher-order overhead (i.e., the use of $= ..$ and *call*) has been removed and the function call has even been unfolded. When running the above programs (on SWI-Prolog) on a set of queries one notices that the specialised program runs about 2 times faster than the original one (and can be made even faster using filtering, as discussed in the next section).

The question that remains is, how do we come up with such (interesting and correct) partial deductions in an automatic way ? This is exactly the issue that is tackled in the next section.

3.3   Control of partial deduction

In partial deduction one usually distinguishes two levels of control [40, 74]:

- the *global control*, in which one chooses the set $\mathcal{A}$, i.e., one decides *which* atoms will be partially deduced, and
- the *local control*, in which one constructs the finite (possibly incomplete) SLDNF-trees for each individual atom in $\mathcal{A}$ and thus determines *what* the definitions for the partially deduced atoms look like.

Below we examine how these two levels of control interact.

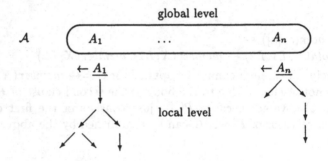

Fig. 6. Global and local level of control

Correctness, termination and precision When controlling partial deduction the three following, often conflicting, aspects have to be reconciled:

1. *Correctness*, i.e., ensuring that Theorem 3 or its extension can be applied. This can be divided into a local condition, requiring the construction of non-trivial trees, and into a global one related to the independence and coveredness (or closedness) conditions.
2. *Termination.* This aspect can also be divided into a local and a global one. First, the problem of keeping each SLDNF-tree finite is referred to as the *local* termination problem. Secondly keeping the set $\mathcal{A}$ finite is referred to as the *global* termination problem.
3. *Precision.* For precision of the specialisation we can again discern two aspects. One which we might call *local* precision and which is related to the unfolding rule and to the fact that (potential for) specialisation can be lost if we stop unfolding an atom in $\mathcal{A}$ prematurely. Indeed, when we stop the

unfolding process at a given goal Q, then all the atoms in Q are treated separately (partial deductions are defined for sets of *atoms* and not for sets of *goals*; see however "conjunctive" partial deduction which we will discuss later in this course). For instance, if we stop the unfolding process in Ex. 2 for $G = \leftarrow inboth(X, [a, b, c], [c, d, e])$ at the goal $G' = \leftarrow member(X, [a, b, c])$, $member(X, [c, d, e])$, partial deduction will not be able to infer that the only possible answer for G' and G is $\{X/c\}$.

The second aspect could be called the *global* precision and is related to the structure of $\mathcal{A}$. In general having a more precise and fine grained set $\mathcal{A}$ (with more *instantiated* atoms) will lead to better specialisation. For instance, given the set $\mathcal{A} = \{member(a, [a, b]), member(c, [d])\}$, partial deduction can perform much more specialisation (i.e., detecting that the goal $\leftarrow member(a, [a, b])$ always succeeds exactly once and that $\leftarrow member(c, [d])$ fails) than given the less instantiated set $\mathcal{A}' = \{member(X, [Y|T])\}$.

A good partial deduction algorithm will ensure correctness and termination while minimising the precision loss of point 3. Let us now examine more closely how those three conflicting aspects can be reconciled.

Independence and renaming On the side of correctness there are two ways to ensure the independence condition. One is to apply a generalisation operator like the *msg* on all the atoms which are not independent (first proposed in [11]). Applying this, e.g., on the dependent set $\mathcal{A} = \{member(a, L), member(X, [b])\}$ yields the independent set $\{member(X, L)\}$. This approach also alleviates to some extent the global termination problem. However, it also diminishes the global precision and, as can be guessed from the above example, can seriously diminish the potential for specialisation.

This loss of precision can be completely avoided by using a *renaming* transformation to ensure independence. Renaming will map dependent atoms to new predicate symbols and thus generate an independent set without precision loss. For instance, the dependent set $\mathcal{A}$ above can be transformed into the independent set $\mathcal{A}' = \{member(a, L), member'(X, [b])\}$. The renaming transformation then has to map the atoms inside the residual program P' and the partial deduction goal G to the correct versions of $\mathcal{A}'$ (e.g., it has to rename the goal $G = \leftarrow member(a, [a, c]), member(b, [b])$ into $\leftarrow member(a, [a, c]), member'(b, [b])$). Renaming can often be combined with argument filtering to improve the efficiency of the specialised program. The basic idea is to filter out constants and functors and only keep the variables as arguments. For instance, instead of renaming $\mathcal{A}$ into $\mathcal{A}'$, $\mathcal{A}$ can be directly renamed into $\{mem_a(L), mem_b(X)\}$ and G into $\leftarrow mem_a([a, c]), mem_b(b)$. Further details about filtering can be found in [41], [10] or [67]. See also [84], where filtering can be obtained automatically when using folding. Filtering has also been referred to as "pushing down metaarguments" in [94] or "PDMA" in [79]. In functional programming the term of "arity raising" has also been used (and it has been studied in an offline setting, where filtering is more complicated).

Renaming and filtering are used in a lot of practical approaches (e.g., [39–41, 62, 64, 65]) and adapted correctness results can be found in [10].

Local termination and unfolding rules The local control component is usually encapsulated in what is called an unfolding rule, defined as follows.

Definition 31. *An unfolding rule U is a function which, given a program P and a goal G, returns a finite and possibly incomplete SLDNF-tree for $P \cup \{G\}$.*

In addition to local correctness, termination and precision, the requirements on unfolding rules also include avoiding search space explosion as well as work duplication. Approaches to the local control have been based on one or more of the following elements:

- *determinacy* [41, 40, 39]
  Only (except once) select atoms that match a single clause head. The strategy can be refined with a so-called "look-ahead" to detect failure at a deeper level. Methods solely based on this heuristic, apart from not guaranteeing termination, tend not to worsen a program, but are often somewhat too conservative.
- *well-founded orders* [18, 73, 72, 71]
  Imposing some (essentially) well-founded order on selected atoms guarantees termination, but, on its own, can lead to overly eager unfolding.
- *homeomorphic embedding* [91, 65]
  Instead of well-founded ones, *well-quasi orders* can be used [12, 88]. Homeomorphic embedding on selected atoms has recently gained popularity as the basis for such an order. As shown in [61] the homeomorphic embedding relation is strictly more powerful than a large class of well-founded orders.

We will examine the above concepts in somewhat more detail. First the notion of determinate unfolding can be defined as follows.

Definition 32. **(determinate unfolding)** *A tree is* (purely) *determinate if each node of the tree has at most 1 child. An unfolding rule is purely determinate without lookahead if for every program P and every goal G it returns a determinate SLDNF-tree. An unfolding rule is purely determinate (with lookahead) if for every program P and every goal G it returns a SLDNF-tree τ such that the subtree τ^- of τ, obtained by removing the failed branches, is determinate.*

Usually the above definitions of determinate unfolding rules are extended to allow one non-determinate unfolding step, ensuring that non-trivial trees can be constructed. Depending on the definition, this non-determinate step may either occur only at the root (e.g., in [39]), anywhere in the tree or only at the bottom (i.e., its resolvents must be leaves, as in [41, 63]). These three additional forms of determinate trees, which we will call *shower*, *fork* and *beam* determinate trees respectively, are illustrated in Fig. 7.

Determinate unfolding has been proposed as a way to ensure that partial deduction will never duplicate computations in the residual program [41, 39, 40].

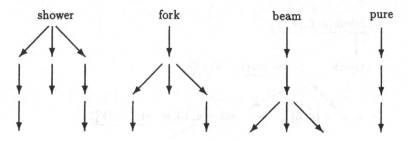

shower   fork   beam   pure

Fig. 7. Four forms of determinate trees

Indeed, in the context of the left-to-right selection rule of Prolog, the following fairly simple example shows that non-leftmost, non-determinate unfolding may duplicate (large amounts of) work in the transformation result. The one non-determinate unfolding step performed by a shower, fork or beam determinate unfolding rule, is therefore generally supposed to mimic the runtime selection rule.

Example 6. Let us return to the program P of Ex. 2:

   $member(X, [X|T]) \leftarrow$
   $member(X, [Y|T]) \leftarrow member(X, T)$
   $inboth(X, L1, L2) \leftarrow member(X, L1), member(X, L2)$

Let $\mathcal{A} = \{inboth(a, L1, [X, Y])\}$. By performing the non-leftmost non-determinate unfolding in Fig. 8, we obtain the following partial deduction P' of P wrt $\mathcal{A}$:

   $member(X, [X|T]) \leftarrow$
   $member(X, [Y|T]) \leftarrow member(X, T)$
   $inboth(a, L1, [a, Y]) \leftarrow member(a, L1)$
   $inboth(a, L1, [X, a]) \leftarrow member(a, L1)$

Let us examine the run-time goal $G =\leftarrow inboth(a, [z, y, \ldots, a], [X, Y])$, for which $P' \cup \{G\}$ is $\mathcal{A}$-covered. Using the Prolog left-to-right computation rule the expensive sub-goal $\leftarrow member(a, [z, y, \ldots, a])$ is only evaluated once in the original program P, while it is executed twice in the specialised program P'.

Restricting ourselves to determinate unfolding ensures that such bad cases of deterioration do not occur. It also ensures that the order of solutions, e.g., under Prolog execution, is not altered and that termination is preserved (termination might however be improved, as e.g., $\leftarrow loop, fail$ can be transformed into $\leftarrow fail$; for further details related to the preservation of termination we refer to [83, 15, 17, 66]). Leftmost, non-determinate unfolding, usually allowed to compensate for the all too cautious nature of purely determinate unfolding, avoids the more drastic deterioration pitfalls in the context of, e.g., Prolog, but can still lead to multiplying unifications.

Example 7. Let us adapt Example 6 by using $\mathcal{A} = \{inboth(X, [Y], [V, W])\}$. We can fully unfold $\leftarrow inboth(X, [Y], [V, W])$ and we then obtain the following partial deduction P' of P wrt $\mathcal{A}$:

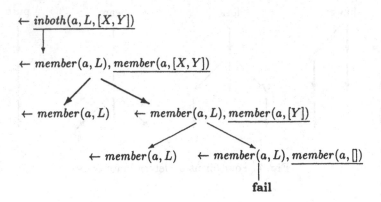

Fig. 8. Non-leftmost non-determinate unfolding for Example 6

$$member(X, [X|T]) \leftarrow$$
$$member(X, [Y|T]) \leftarrow member(X, T)$$
$$inboth(\underline{X}, [\underline{X}], [X, W]) \leftarrow$$
$$inboth(\underline{X}, [\underline{X}], [V, X]) \leftarrow$$

No goal has been duplicated by the leftmost non-determinate unfolding, but the unification $X = Y$ for $\leftarrow inboth(X, [Y], [V, W])$ has potentially been duplicated. E.g., when executing the runtime goal $\leftarrow inboth(t_x, [t_y], [t_v, t_w])$ in P' the terms t_x and t_y will be unified when resolving with the third clause of P' and then unified again when resolving with the fourth clause of P'.[4] In the original program P this unification will only be performed once, namely when resolving with the first clause defining $member$. For run-time goals where t_x and t_y are very complicated structures this might actually result in P' being slower than the original P. However, as unifications are generally much less expensive than executing entire goals, this problem is (usually) less of an issue.

In practical implementations one has also to take care of such issues as the clause indexing performed by the compiler as well as how terms are created (i.e., avoid duplication of term construction operations). Again for these issues, determinate unfolding has proven to be a generally safe, albeit sometimes too conservative, approach. Fully adequate solutions to these, more implementation oriented, aspects are still topics of ongoing research.

Let us return to the aspect of local termination. Restricting oneself to determinate unfolding in itself does not guarantee termination, as there can be infinitely failing determinate computations. In (strict) functional programs such a condition is equivalent to an error in the original program. In logic programming the situation is somewhat different: a goal can infinitely fail (in a deterministic way) at partial deduction time but still finitely fail at run time. In applications like theorem proving, even infinite failures at run-time do not necessarily in-

---

[4] A very smart compiler might detect this and produce more efficient code which does not re-execute unifications.

dicate an error: they might simply be due to unprovable statements. This is why, contrary to maybe functional programming, additional measures on top of determinacy should be adopted to ensure local termination.

One, albeit ad-hoc, way to solve this local termination problem is to simply impose an arbitrary depth bound. Such a depth bound is of course not motivated by any property, structural or otherwise, of the program or goal under consideration. The depth bound will therefore lead either to too little or too much unfolding in a lot of interesting cases.

As already mentioned, more refined approaches to ensure termination of unfolding exist. The methods in [18, 73, 72, 71] are based on well-founded orders, inspired by their usefulness in the context of static termination analysis (see e.g., [31, 25]). These techniques ensure termination, while at the same time allowing unfolding related to the structural aspect of the program and goal to be partially deduced, e.g., permitting the consumption of static input within the atoms of A. Formally, well-founded orders are defined as follows:

Definition 33. (wfo) *A (strict) partial order $>_S$ on a set S is an anti-reflexive, anti-symmetric and transitive binary relation on $S \times S$. A sequence of elements $s_1, s_2, \ldots$ in S is called admissible wrt $>_S$ iff $s_i > s_{i+1}$, for all $i \geq 1$. We call $>_S$ a well-founded order (wfo) iff there is no infinite admissible sequence wrt $>_S$*

To ensure local termination, one has to find a sensible well-founded order on atoms and then only allow SLDNF-trees in which the sequence of selected atoms is admissible (i.e., strictly decreasing wrt the well-founded order). If an atom that we want to select is not strictly smaller than its ancestors, we either have to select another atom or stop unfolding altogether.

Example 8. Let us return to the *member* program P of Ex. 2. A simple well-founded order on atoms of the form $member(t_1, t_2)$ might be based on comparing the list length of the second argument.
The list length $list\_length(t)$ of a term t is defined to be:
  - $1 + list\_length(t')$ if $t = [h|t']$ and
  - 0 otherwise.
We then define the wfo on atoms by stating $member(t_1, t_2) > member(s_1, s_2)$ iff $list\_length(t_2) > list\_length(s_2)$.

Based on that wfo, the goal $\leftarrow member(X, [a, b|T])$ can be unfolded into $\leftarrow member(X, [b|T])$ and further into $\leftarrow member(X, T)$ because the list length of the second argument strictly decreases at each step. However, $\leftarrow member(X, T)$ cannot be further unfolded into $\leftarrow member(X, T')$ because the list length does not strictly decrease.

Much more elaborate well-founded orders exist, e.g., continuously refining wfo's during the unfolding process. We refer the reader to [18, 73, 72, 71] for further details. These works also present a further refinement which, instead of requiring a decrease with every ancestor, only requires a decrease wrt the *covering ancestors*, i.e., one only compares with the ancestor atoms from which the current atom descends (via resolution).

Let us now turn our attention to approaches based on well-quasi orders, which are formally defined as follows.

Definition 34. **(quasi order)** *A quasi order $\geq_S$ on a set S is a reflexive and transitive binary relation on $S \times S$.*

Henceforth, we will use symbols like $<$, $>$ (possibly annotated by some subscript) to refer to strict partial orders and $\leq$, $\geq$ to refer to quasi orders. We will use either "directionality" as is convenient in the context.

Definition 35. **(wbr,wqo)** *Let $\leq_S$ be a binary relation on $S \times S$. A sequence of elements $s_1, s_2, \ldots$ in S is called admissible wrt $\leq_S$ iff there are no $i < j$ such that $s_i \leq_S s_j$. We say that $\leq_S$ is a well-binary relation (wbr) on S iff there are no infinite admissible sequences wrt $\leq_S$. If $\leq_S$ is a quasi order on S then we also say that $\leq_S$ is a well-quasi order (wqo) on S.*

Local termination is now ensured in a similar manner as for wfo's: we only allow SLDNF-trees in which the sequence of selected atoms is admissible. Observe that, while an approach based on wfo requires a strict decrease at every unfolding step, an approach based on wqo can allow incomparable steps as well. This, e.g., allows a wqo to have no a priori fixed weight or order attached to functors and arguments and means that well-quasi orders can be much more flexible and much better suited, e.g., to handle metainterpreters and metalevel encodings. See [61] for formal results substantiating that claim.

An interesting wqo is the homeomorphic embedding relation $\trianglelefteq$, which derives from results by Higman [46] and Kruskal [57]. It has been used in the context of term rewriting systems in [29, 30], and adapted for use in supercompilation [98] in [91].

The following is the definition from [91], which adapts the pure homeomorphic embedding from [30] by adding a rudimentary treatment of variables.

Definition 36. **($\trianglelefteq$)** *The (pure) homeomorphic embedding relation $\trianglelefteq$ on expressions is defined inductively as follows (i.e. $\trianglelefteq$ is the least relation satisfying the rules):*

1. *$X \trianglelefteq Y$ for all variables X, Y*
2. *$s \trianglelefteq f(t_1, \ldots, t_n)$ if $s \trianglelefteq t_i$ for some i*
3. *$f(s_1, \ldots, s_n) \trianglelefteq f(t_1, \ldots, t_n)$ if $\forall i \in \{1, \ldots, n\} : s_i \trianglelefteq t_i$.*

The second rule is sometimes called the *diving* rule, and the third rule is sometimes called the *coupling* rule. When $s \trianglelefteq t$ we also say that s is *embedded in* t or t is *embedding* s. By $s \triangleleft t$ we denote that $s \trianglelefteq t$ and $t \ntrianglelefteq s$.

Example 9. The intuition behind the above definition is that $A \trianglelefteq B$ iff A can be obtained from B by "striking out" certain parts, or said another way, the structure of A reappears within B. For instance we have $p(a) \trianglelefteq p(f(a))$ and indeed $p(a)$ can be obtained from $p(f(a))$ by "striking out" the f. Observe that

the "striking out" corresponds to the application of the diving rule 2 and that we even have $p(a) \lhd p(f(a))$. We also have, e.g., that:
$X \unlhd X$, $p(X) \lhd p(f(Y))$, $p(X,X) \unlhd p(X,Y)$ and $p(X,Y) \unlhd p(X,X)$.

The homeomorphic embedding relation is very generous and will for example allow to unfold from $p([], [a])$ to $p([a], [])$ but also the other way around. This illustrates the flexibility of using well-quasi orders compared to well-founded ones, as there exists *no* wfo which will allow both these unfoldings. It however also illustrates why, when using a wqo, one has to compare with every predecessor. Otherwise one will get infinite derivations of the form $p([a], []) \to p([], [a]) \to p([a], []) \to \dots$. When using a wfo one has to compare only to the closest predecessor [72], because of the transitivity of the order and the strict decrease enforced at each step. However, wfo are usually extended to incorporate variant checking (see e.g., [71,72]) and therefore require inspecting every predecessor anyway (though only when there is no strict weight decrease).

In order to adequately handle some built-ins, the embedding relation $\unlhd$ of Definition 36 has to be adapted. Indeed, some built-ins (like $= ../2$ or $is/2$) can be used to dynamically construct infinitely many new constants and functors and thus $\unlhd$ is no longer a wqo.

Example 10. Let P be the following Prolog program:

```
le(X,X).
le(X,Y) :- X1 is X + 1, le(X1,Y).
```

If we now unfold, e.g., the goal $\leftarrow$ le(1,0) we get the following sequence of selected atoms, where no atom is embedding an earlier one (i.e., the sequence is admissible wrt $\unlhd$): le(1,0) $\rightsquigarrow$ le(2,0) $\rightsquigarrow$ le(3,0) $\rightsquigarrow \infty$.

To remedy this [65], the constants and functors can be partitioned into the *static* ones, occurring in the original program and the partial deduction query, and the *dynamic* ones. (This approach is also used in [88].) The set of dynamic constants and functors is possibly infinite, and are therefore treated like the infinite set of variables in Definition 36 by adding the following rule:

$$f(s_1, \dots, s_m) \unlhd^+ g(t_1, \dots, t_n) \text{ if both } f \text{ and } g \text{ are dynamic}$$

Control of polyvariance If we use renaming to ensure independence and (for the moment) suppose that the local termination and precision problems have been solved by the approaches presented above, we are still left with the problem of ensuring *closedness* and *global termination* while minimising the *global precision loss*. We will call this combination of problems the *control of polyvariance problem* as it is very closely related to how many different specialised versions of some given predicate should be put into $\mathcal{A}$.[5] It is this important problem we address later in this course.

Let us examine how the 3 subproblems of the control of polyvariance problem interact.

---

[5] A method is called *monovariant* if it allows only one specialised version per predicate.

– *Coveredness vs. Global Termination*
  Coveredness (or respectively closedness) can be simply ensured by repeatedly adding the uncovered (i.e not satisfying Definition 30 or Definition 28
  respectively) atoms to $\mathcal{A}$ and unfolding them. Unfortunately this process
  generally leads to non-termination, even when using the *msg* to ensure independence. For instance, the "reverse with accumulating parameter" program
  (see e.g., [71,73] or Ex. 3 in [60]) exposes this non-terminating behaviour.
– *Global Termination vs. Global Precision*
  To ensure finiteness of $\mathcal{A}$ we can repeatedly apply an "abstraction" operator
  which generates a set of more general atoms. Unfortunately this induces a
  loss of global precision.

By using the two ideas above to (try to) ensure coveredness and global termination, we can formulate a generic partial deduction algorithm. First, the
concept of abstraction has to be formally defined.

Definition 37. (abstraction) *Let $\mathcal{A}$ and $\mathcal{A}'$ be sets of atoms. Then $\mathcal{A}'$ is
an* abstraction *of $\mathcal{A}$ iff every atom in $\mathcal{A}$ is an instance of an atom in $\mathcal{A}'$. An*
abstraction operator *is an operator which maps every finite set of atoms to a
finite abstraction of it.*

The above definition guarantees that any set of clauses covered by $\mathcal{A}$ is also
covered by $\mathcal{A}'$. Note that sometimes an abstraction operator is also referred to
as a *generalisation operator*.

The following generic scheme, based on a similar one in [39,40], describes the
basic layout of practically all algorithms for controlling partial deduction.

Algorithm 3.1 (standard partial deduction)
Input: A program P and a goal G
Output: A specialised program P'
Initialise: $i = 0$, $\mathcal{A}_0 = \{A \mid A$ is an atom in G $\}$
  repeat
    for each $A_k \in \mathcal{A}_i$ **do**
      compute a finite SLDNF-tree τ_k for $P \cup \{\leftarrow A_k\}$ by
        applying an unfolding rule U;
    let $\mathcal{A}'_i := \mathcal{A}_i \cup \{B_l \mid B_l \in leaves(\tau_k)$ for some tree τ_k, such that B_l is
        not an instance[6] of any $A_j \in \mathcal{A}_i\}$;
    let $\mathcal{A}_{i+1} := abstract(\mathcal{A}'_i)$; where *abstract* is an abstraction operator
    let $i := i + 1$;
  until $\mathcal{A}_{i+1} = \mathcal{A}_i$
Apply a renaming transformation to $\mathcal{A}_i$ to ensure independence;
Construct P' by taking resultants.

In itself the use of an abstraction operator does not yet guarantee global
termination. But, if the above algorithm terminates then coveredness is ensured,
i.e., $P' \cup \{G\}$ is $\mathcal{A}_i$-covered (modulo renaming). With this observation we can

---

[6] One can also use the variant test to make the algorithm more precise.

reformulate the *control of polyvariance problem* as one of finding an *abstraction operator which maximises specialisation while ensuring termination*.

A very simple abstraction operator which ensures termination can be obtained by imposing a finite maximum number of atoms in $\mathcal{A}_i$ and using the *msg* to stick to that maximum. For example, in [73] one atom per predicate is enforced by using the *msg*. However, using the *msg* in this way can induce an even bigger *loss of precision* (compared to using the *msg* to ensure independence), because it will now also be applied on *independent* atoms. For instance, calculating the *msg* for the set of atoms $\{solve(p(a)), solve(q(f(b)))\}$ yields the atom $solve(X)$ and all potential for specialisation is probably lost.

In [73] this problem has been remedied to some extent by using a static pre-processing renaming phase (as defined in [11]) which will generate one extra renamed version for the top-level atom to be specialised. However, this technique only works well if all relevant input can be consumed in one local unfolding of this top-most atom. Apart from the fact that this huge local unfolding is not always a good idea from a point of view of efficiency (e.g., it can slow down the program as illustrated by the Examples 6 and 7), in a lot of cases this simply cannot be accomplished (for instance if partial input is not consumed but carried along, like the representation of an object-program inside a metainterpreter).

One goal pursued in the advanced part of this course [60] is to define a flexible abstraction operator which does not exhibit this dramatic loss of precision and provides a fine-grained control of polyvariance, while still guaranteeing termination of the partial deduction process.

References

1. E. Albert, M. Alpuente, M. Falaschi, P. Julián and G. Vidal. Improving Control in Functional Logic Program Specialization. In G. Levi, editor, *Static Analysis. Proceedings of SAS'98*, LNCS 1503, pages 262–277, Pisa, Italy, September 1998. Springer-Verlag.
2. M. Alpuente, M. Falaschi, and G. Vidal. Narrowing-driven partial evaluation of functional logic programs. In H. Riis Nielson, editor, *Proceedings of the 6th European Symposium on Programming, ESOP'96*, LNCS 1058, pages 45–61. Springer-Verlag, 1996.
3. L. O. Andersen. Partial evaluation of C and automatic compiler generation. In U. Kastens and P. Pfahler, editors, *4th International Conference on Compiler Construction*, LNCS 641, pages 251–257, Paderborn, Germany, 1992. Springer-Verlag.
4. L. O. Andersen. *Program Analysis and Specialization for the C Programming Language*. PhD thesis, DIKU, University of Copenhagen, May 1994. (DIKU report 94/19).
5. K. R. Apt. Introduction to logic programming. In J. van Leeuwen, editor, *Handbook of Theoretical Computer Science*, chapter 10, pages 495–574. North-Holland Amsterdam, 1990.
6. K. R. Apt. *From Logic Programming to Prolog*. Prentice Hall, 1997.
7. K. R. Apt and R. N. Bol. Logic programming and negation: A survey. *The Journal of Logic Programming*, 19 & 20:9–72, May 1994.

8. K. R. Apt and H. Doets. A new definition of SLDNF-resolution. *The Journal of Logic Programming*, 8:177–190, 1994.
9. K. R. Apt and M. H. van Emden. Contributions to the theory of logic programming. *Journal of the ACM*, 29(3):841–862, 1982.
10. K. Benkerimi and P. M. Hill. Supporting transformations for the partial evaluation of logic programs. *Journal of Logic and Computation*, 3(5):469–486, October 1993.
11. K. Benkerimi and J. W. Lloyd. A partial evaluation procedure for logic programs. In S. Debray and M. Hermenegildo, editors, *Proceedings of the North American Conference on Logic Programming*, pages 343–358. MIT Press, 1990.
12. R. Bol. Loop checking in partial deduction. *The Journal of Logic Programming*, 16(1&2):25–46, 1993.
13. A. Bondorf. Towards a self-applicable partial evaluator for term rewriting systems. In D. Bjørner, A. P. Ershov, and N. D. Jones, editors, *Partial Evaluation and Mixed Computation*, pages 27–50. North-Holland, 1988.
14. A. Bondorf. A self-applicable partial evaluator for term rewriting systems. In J. Diaz and F. Orejas, editors, *TAPSOFT'89, Proceedings of the International Joint Conference on Theory and Practice of Software Development*, LNCS 352, pages 81–96, Barcelona, Spain, March 1989. Springer-Verlag.
15. A. Bossi and N. Cocco. Preserving universal termination through unfold/fold. In G. Levi and M. Rodriguez-Artalejo, editors, *Proceedings of the Fourth International Conference on Algebraic and Logic Programming*, LNCS 850, pages 269–286, Madrid, Spain, 1994. Springer-Verlag.
16. A. Bossi, N. Cocco, and S. Dulli. A method for specialising logic programs. *ACM Transactions on Programming Languages and Systems*, 12(2):253–302, 1990.
17. A. Bossi, N. Cocco, and S. Etalle. Transformation of left terminating programs: The reordering problem. In M. Proietti, editor, Logic Program Synthesis and Transformation. *Proceedings of LOPSTR'95*, LNCS 1048, pages 33–45, Utrecht, The Netherlands, September 1995. Springer-Verlag.
18. M. Bruynooghe, D. De Schreye, and B. Martens. A general criterion for avoiding infinite unfolding during partial deduction. *New Generation Computing*, 11(1):47–79, 1992.
19. R. M. Burstall and J. Darlington. A transformation system for developing recursive programs. *Journal of the ACM*, 24(1):44–67, 1977.
20. D. Chan. Constructive negation based on the completed database. In *Proceedings of the Joint International Conference and Symposium on Logic Programming*, pages 111–125, Seattle, 1988. IEEE, MIT Press.
21. D. Chan and M. Wallace. A treatment of negation during partial evaluation. In H. Abramson and M. Rogers, editors, *Meta-Programming in Logic Programming, Proceedings of the Meta88 Workshop, June 1988*, pages 299–318. MIT Press, 1989.
22. K. L. Clark. Negation as failure. In H. Gallaire and J. Minker, editors, *Logic and Data Bases*, pages 293–322. Plenum Press, 1978.
23. W. Clocksin and C. Mellish. *Programming in Prolog (Third Edition)*. Springer-Verlag, 1987.
24. C. Consel and O. Danvy. Tutorial notes on partial evaluation. In *Proceedings of ACM Symposium on Principles of Programming Languages (POPL'93)*, Charleston, South Carolina, January 1993. ACM Press.
25. D. De Schreye and S. Decorte. Termination of logic programs: The never ending story. *The Journal of Logic Programming*, 19 & 20:199–260, May 1994.
26. D. De Schreye, M. Leuschel, and B. Martens. Tutorial on program specialisation (abstract). In J. W. Lloyd, editor, *Proceedings of ILPS'95, the International Logic Programming Symposium*, Portland, USA, December 1995. MIT Press.

27. M. Denecker. *Knowledge Representation and Reasoning in Incomplete Logic Programming*. PhD thesis, Department of Computer Science, K.U.Leuven, 1993.
28. P. Derensart, A. Ed-Dbali, and L. Cervoni. *Prolog: The Standard, Reference Manual*. Springer-Verlag, 1996.
29. N. Dershowitz. Termination of rewriting. *Journal of Symbolic Computation*, 3:69–116, 1987.
30. N. Dershowitz and J.-P. Jouannaud. Rewrite systems. In J. van Leeuwen, editor, *Handbook of Theoretical Computer Science, Vol. B*, pages 243–320. Elsevier, MIT Press, 1990.
31. N. Dershowitz and Z. Manna. Proving termination with multiset orderings. *Communications of the ACM*, 22(8):465–476, 1979.
32. K. Doets. Levationis laus. *Journal of Logic and Computation*, 3(5):487–516, 1993.
33. K. Doets. *From Logic to Logic Programming*. MIT Press, 1994.
34. W. Drabent. What is failure ? An apporach to constructive negation. *Acta Informatica*, 32:27–59, 1995.
35. A. Ershov. Mixed computation: Potential applications and problems for study. *Theoretical Computer Science*, 18:41–67, 1982.
36. M. Fitting. *First-Order Logic and Automated Theorem Proving*. Springer-Verlag, 1990.
37. H. Fujita and K. Furukawa. A self-applicable partial evaluator and its use in incremental compilation. *New Generation Computing*, 6(2 & 3):91–118, 1988.
38. D. A. Fuller and S. Abramsky. Mixed computation of prolog programs. *New Generation Computing*, 6(2 & 3):119–141, June 1988.
39. J. Gallagher. A system for specialising logic programs. Technical Report TR-91-32, University of Bristol, November 1991.
40. J. Gallagher. Tutorial on specialisation of logic programs. In *Proceedings of PEPM'93, the ACM Sigplan Symposium on Partial Evaluation and Semantics-Based Program Manipulation*, pages 88–98. ACM Press, 1993.
41. J. Gallagher and M. Bruynooghe. The derivation of an algorithm for program specialisation. *New Generation Computing*, 9(3 & 4):305–333, 1991.
42. R. Glück and M. H. Sørensen. Partial deduction and driving are equivalent. In M. Hermenegildo and J. Penjam, editors, *Programming Language Implementation and Logic Programming. Proceedings, Proceedings of PLILP'94*, LNCS 844, pages 165–181, Madrid, Spain, 1994. Springer-Verlag.
43. R. Glück and M. H. Sørensen. A roadmap to supercompilation. In O. Danvy, R. Glück, and P. Thiemann, editors, *Proceedings of the 1996 Dagstuhl Seminar on Partial Evaluation*, LNCS 1110, pages 137–160, Schloß Dagstuhl, 1996. Springer-Verlag.
44. C. A. Gurr. *A Self-Applicable Partial Evaluator for the Logic Programming Language Gödel*. PhD thesis, Department of Computer Science, University of Bristol, January 1994.
45. J. Herbrand. Investigations in proof theory. In J. van Heijenoort, editor, *From Frege to Gödel: A Source Book in Mathematical Logic, 1879-1931*, pages 525–581. Harvard University Press, 1967.
46. G. Higman. Ordering by divisibility in abstract algebras. *Proceedings of the London Mathematical Society*, 2:326–336, 1952.
47. P. Hill and J. W. Lloyd. *The Gödel Programming Language*. MIT Press, 1994.
48. J.-M. Jacquet. *Constructing Logic Programs*. Wiley, Chichester, 1993.
49. N. D. Jones. The essence of program transformation by partial evaluation and driving. In M. S. Neil D. Jones, Masami Hagiya, editor, *Logic, Language and Computation*, LNCS 792, pages 206–224. Springer-Verlag, 1994.

50. N. D. Jones. An introduction to partial evaluation. *ACM Computing Surveys*, 28(3):480–503, September 1996.

51. N. D. Jones, C. K. Gomard, and P. Sestoft. *Partial Evaluation and Automatic Program Generation*. Prentice Hall, 1993.

52. S. Kleene. *Introduction to Metamathematics*. van Nostrand, Princeton, New Jersey, 1952.

53. H.-P. Ko and M. E. Nadel. Substitution and refutation revisited. In K. Furukawa, editor, *Logic Programming: Proceedings of the Eighth International Conference*, pages 679–692. MIT Press, 1991.

54. J. Komorowski. Partial evaluation as a means for inferencing data structures in an applicative language: a theory and implementation in the case of Prolog. In *Ninth Annual ACM SIGACT-SIGPLAN Symposium on Principles of Programming Languages. Albuquerque, New Mexico*, pages 255–267, 1982.

55. J. Komorowski. An introduction to partial deduction. In A. Pettorossi, editor, *Proceedings Meta'92*, LNCS 649, pages 49–69. Springer-Verlag, 1992.

56. R. Kowalski. Predicate logic as a programming language. In *Proceedings IFIP Congress*, pages 569–574. IEEE, 1974.

57. J. B. Kruskal. Well-quasi ordering, the tree theorem, and Vazsonyi's conjecture. *Transactions of the American Mathematical Society*, 95:210–225, 1960.

58. L. Lafave and J. Gallagher. Constraint-based partial evaluation of rewriting-based functional logic programs. In N. Fuchs, editor, *Proceedings of the International Workshop on Logic Program Synthesis and Transformation (LOPSTR'97)*, LNCS 1463, Leuven, Belgium, July 1998.

59. J.-L. Lassez, M. Maher, and K. Marriott. Unification revisited. In J. Minker, editor, *Foundations of Deductive Databases and Logic Programming*, pages 587–625. Morgan-Kaufmann, 1988.

60. M. Leuschel. *Advanced Logic Program Specialisation*. In J. Hatcliff, T. Mogensen, and P. Thiemann, editors, *DIKU 1998 International Summerschool on Partial Evaluation*, LNCS 1706, pages 271–292, Copenhagen, Denmark, July 1998. Springer-Verlag. In *this volume*.

61. M. Leuschel. On the power of homeomorphic embedding for online termination. In G. Levi, editor, Static Analysis. *Proceedings of SAS'98*, LNCS 1503, pages 230–245, Pisa, Italy, September 1998. Springer-Verlag.

62. M. Leuschel and D. De Schreye. Towards creating specialised integrity checks through partial evaluation of meta-interpreters. In *Proceedings of PEPM'95, the ACM Sigplan Symposium on Partial Evaluation and Semantics-Based Program Manipulation*, pages 253–263, La Jolla, California, June 1995. ACM Press.

63. M. Leuschel and D. De Schreye. Constrained partial deduction and the preservation of characteristic trees. *New Generation Computing*, 16(3):283–342, 1998.

64. M. Leuschel and D. De Schreye. Creating specialised integrity checks through partial evaluation of meta-interpreters. *The Journal of Logic Programming*, 36:149–193, 1998.

65. M. Leuschel, B. Martens, and D. De Schreye. Controlling generalisation and polyvariance in partial deduction of normal logic programs. *ACM Transactions on Programming Languages and Systems*, 20(1):208–258, January 1998.

66. M. Leuschel, B. Martens, and K. Sagonas. Preserving termination of tabled logic programs while unfolding. In N. Fuchs, editor, *Proceedings of the International Workshop on Logic Program Synthesis and Transformation (LOPSTR'97)*, LNCS 1463, Leuven, Belgium, July 1998.

67. M. Leuschel and M. H. Sørensen. Redundant argument filtering of logic programs. In J. Gallagher, editor, *Proceedings of the International Workshop on Logic Program Synthesis and Transformation (LOPSTR'96)*, LNCS 1207, pages 83–103, Stockholm, Sweden, August 1996. Springer-Verlag.

68. J. W. Lloyd. *Foundations of Logic Programming*. Springer-Verlag, 1987.

69. J. W. Lloyd and J. C. Shepherdson. Partial evaluation in logic programming. *The Journal of Logic Programming*, 11(3& 4):217–242, 1991.

70. A. Martelli and U. Montanari. An efficient unification algorithm. *ACM Transactions on Programming Languages and Systems*, 4(2):258–282, April 1982.

71. B. Martens. *On the Semantics of Meta-Programming and the Control of Partial Deduction in Logic Programming*. PhD thesis, K.U. Leuven, February 1994.

72. B. Martens and D. De Schreye. Automatic finite unfolding using well-founded measures. *The Journal of Logic Programming*, 28(2):89–146, August 1996.

73. B. Martens, D. De Schreye, and T. Horváth. Sound and complete partial deduction with unfolding based on well-founded measures. *Theoretical Computer Science*, 122(1–2):97–117, 1994.

74. B. Martens and J. Gallagher. Ensuring global termination of partial deduction while allowing flexible polyvariance. In L. Sterling, editor, *Proceedings ICLP'95*, pages 597–613, Kanagawa, Japan, June 1995. MIT Press.

75. A. Miniuissi and D. J. Sherman. Squeezing intermediate construction in equational programs. In O. Danvy, R. Glück, and P. Thiemann, editors, *Proceedings of the 1996 Dagstuhl Seminar on Partial Evaluation*, LNCS 1110, pages 284–302, Schloß Dagstuhl, 1996. Springer-Verlag.

76. T. Mogensen and A. Bondorf. Logimix: A self-applicable partial evaluator for Prolog. In K.-K. Lau and T. Clement, editors, Logic Program Synthesis and Transformation. *Proceedings of LOPSTR'92*, pages 214–227. Springer-Verlag, 1992.

77. L. Naish. Higher-order logic programming in Prolog. Technical Report 96/2, Department of Computer Science, University of Melbourne, 1995.

78. U. Nilsson and J. Małuszyński. *Logic, Programming and Prolog*. Wiley, Chichester, 1990.

79. S. Owen. Issues in the partial evaluation of meta-interpreters. In H. Abramson and M. Rogers, editors, *Meta-Programming in Logic Programming, Proceedings of the Meta88 Workshop, June 1988*, pages 319–339. MIT Press, 1989.

80. M. Paterson and M. Wegman. Linear unification. *Journal of Computer and System Sciences*, 16(2):158–167, 1978.

81. A. Pettorossi and M. Proietti. Transformation of logic programs: Foundations and techniques. *The Journal of Logic Programming*, 19& 20:261–320, May 1994.

82. S. Prestwich. An unfold rule for full Prolog. In K.-K. Lau and T. Clement, editors, Logic Program Synthesis and Transformation. *Proceedings of LOPSTR'92*, Workshops in Computing, pages 199–213, University of Manchester, 1992. Springer-Verlag.

83. M. Proietti and A. Pettorossi. Semantics preserving transformation rules for Prolog. In *Proceedings of the ACM Symposium on Partial Evaluation and Semantics based Program Manipulation, PEPM'91*, Sigplan Notices, Vol. 26, N. 9, pages 274–284, Yale University, New Haven, U.S.A., 1991.

84. M. Proietti and A. Pettorossi. The loop absorption and the generalization strategies for the development of logic programs and partial deduction. *The Journal of Logic Programming*, 16(1 & 2):123–162, May 1993.

85. T. C. Przymusinksi. On the declarative and procedural semantics of logic programs. *Journal of Automated Reasoning*, 5(2):167–205, 1989.

86. R. Reiter. On closed world data bases. In H. Gallaire and J. Minker, editors, *Logic and Data Bases*, pages 55–76. Plenum Press, 1978.

87. A. Robinson. A machine-oriented logic based on the resolution principle. *Journal of the ACM*, 12(1):23–41, 1965.

88. D. Sahlin. Mixtus: An automatic partial evaluator for full Prolog. *New Generation Computing*, 12(1):7–51, 1993.

89. J. C. Shepherdson. Language and equality theory in logic programming. Technical Report PM-91-02, University of Bristol, 1991.

90. M. H. Sørensen and R. Glück. *Introduction to Supercompilation*. In J. Hatcliff, T. Mogensen, and P. Thiemann, editors, *DIKU 1998 International Summerschool on Partial Evaluation*, LNCS 1706, pages 246–270, Copenhagen, Denmark, July 1998. Springer-Verlag. In *this volume*.

91. M. H. Sørensen and R. Glück. An algorithm of generalization in positive supercompilation. In J. W. Lloyd, editor, *Proceedings of ILPS'95, the International Logic Programming Symposium*, pages 465–479, Portland, USA, December 1995. MIT Press.

92. M. H. Sørensen, R. Glück, and N. D. Jones. Towards unifying partial evaluation, deforestation, supercompilation, and GPC. In D. Sannella, editor, *Programming Languages and Systems — ESOP '94. Proceedings*, LNCS 788, pages 485–500, Edinburgh, Scotland, 1994. Springer-Verlag.

93. M. H. Sørensen, R. Glück, and N. D. Jones. A positive supercompiler. *Journal of Functional Programming*, 6(6):811–838, 1996.

94. L. Sterling and R. D. Beer. Metainterpreters for expert system construction. *The Journal of Logic Programming*, 6(1 & 2):163–178, 1989.

95. L. Sterling and E. Shapiro. *The Art of Prolog*. MIT Press, 1986.

96. P. J. Stuckey. Constructive negation for constraint logic programming. In *Proceedings, Sixth Annual IEEE Symposium on Logic in Computer Science*, pages 328–339, Amsterdam, The Netherlands, July 1991. IEEE Computer Society Press.

97. P. J. Stuckey. Negation and constraint logic programming. *Information and Computation*, 118(1):12–33, April 1995.

98. V. F. Turchin. The concept of a supercompiler. *ACM Transactions on Programming Languages and Systems*, 8(3):292–325, 1986.

99. D. H. D. Warren. Higher-order extensions to Prolog: Are they needed? In J. E. Hayes, D. Michie, and Y.-H. Pao, editors, *Machine Intelligence 10*, pages 441–454. Ellis Horwood Ltd., Chicester, England, 1982.

Inherited Limits

Torben Æ. Mogensen

DIKU
Universitetsparken 1
DK-2100 Copenhagen O
Denmark
torbenm@diku.dk

Abstract. We study the evolution of partial evaluators over the past fifteen years from a particular perspective: The attempt to prevent structural bounds in the original programs from imposing limits on the structure of residual programs. It will often be the case that a language allows unbounded numbers or sizes of particular features, but each program (being finite) will only have a finite number or size of these features. If the residual programs cannot overcome the bounds given in the original program, that can be seen as a weakness in the partial evaluator, as it potentially limits the effectiveness of residual programs. We show how historical developments in partial evaluators have removed inherited limits, and suggest how this principle can be used as a guideline for further development.

1 Introduction

Much has happened in the field of partial evaluation in the past fifteen years. The evolution has taken many different paths, focusing on different problems. We will show below that many seemingly unrelated developments serve similar purposes: removal of *inherited limits*. More often than not, the developments have been introduced for solving immediate practical problems observed through experiments, without explicit awareness of the general underlying principle.

In this paper we first introduce the concept of inherited limits, and discuss why we think these may be a problem. We then investigate specific inherited limits and how these historically have been solved. We then round up by discussing how to use the principle of inherited limits to suggest further studies in partial evaluation methods, and noting some important developments in partial evaluation that can not be related to removal of inherited limits.

2 Inherited Limits

It has been stated (I forget by whom) that in computer science (as well as many other areas) there are only three reasonable limits: zero, one and infinity.

This principle has often been used in language design, such that there typically is no arbitrary bounds on nesting depth, size of program, number of variables etc, unless that bound is uniformly set to one, as e.g. the nesting depth of function definitions in C.

But while the language as a whole imposes no such bounds, each program (being finite) will normally be limited to a finite depth, size or number of these features. For example, any Pascal program will have a finite nesting depth of functions, a finite number of variables and a finite dimension of arrays, even though the language definition imposes no uniform bound on these features.

The fact that any single program uses only a bounded number or size of a feature does not usually cause any problem, and there really is no natural way to avoid it, even if it did.

It is when new programs are derived by specialization or other transformations from a single original program that we may encounter a problem: The derived programs may not be able to exceed the limits imposed by the original program.

Why is this a problem? Intuitively, we can argue that the derived programs can not use the full potential of the programming language: A better result may be obtained by using one more level of nesting, one more variable or one more dimension in an array. It is less clear to what extent this is a practical problem, though. I will argue that if partial evaluators are to be used for compiling by specializing interpreters, then it is indeed a problem.

When compiling by partial evaluation, each object program is a specialized version of the interpreter. The interpreter, being a single program, will have finite bounds on features that the language itself has no limitations for. If the residual programs can not exceed these bounds, only a subset of the target language is exploited. If the source language has uniform limits for these features, this is not a problem. But if not, in particular if the source language is an extended version of the target language, this is a problem.

In the "challenging problems" collection from the '87 PEMC workshop [13], Neil Jones suggested that a partial evaluator is "strong enough" (later the term *optimal* is used) if it is possible to completely remove the interpretation overhead of a self-interpreter by specialization. The case of self-interpretation is interesting, as it is easy to judge to what extent the interpretation overhead has been removed, simply by comparing the source and target programs. If the target program is identical to the source program (bar renaming and reordering and similar trivial differences) it is safe to conclude that all interpretation overhead has been removed.

Note that for the test above to be a test on the quality of the partial evaluator, not the self-interpreter, we must not insist on a particular self-interpreter. To conclude that a partial evaluator is sub-optimal, we must argue that no matter how a self-interpreter is written, we can not obtain optimal translation by specialization of the interpreter by that partial evaluator. This is where considering inherited limits becomes a useful yardstick: If the partial evaluator inherits a bound from the original program, relating to a feature that the language has no limit for, then we can conclude that optimality can not be achieved.

Inherited limits are only problematical for features where there is a cost involved in simulating an unbounded number or size with a bounded number or size. This is the usual case, but one can argue that one-dimensional arrays can simulate multi-dimensional arrays at no extra cost, since the code generated for explicit index calculation that simulate multi-dimensional arrays using one-dimensional arrays is the same as the index calculation code generated by a compiler for multi-dimensional arrays. Such arguments are, however, often implementation-specific and not always convincing. For example, it is common for strength reduction to be performed only on compiler-generated index calculation code.

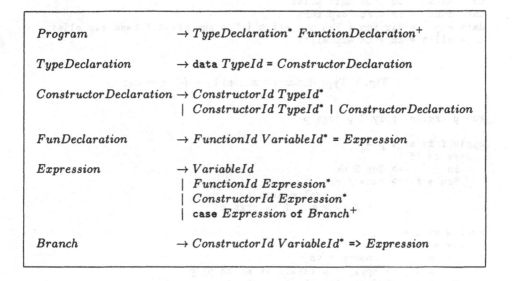

Fig. 1. Syntax of a small functional language

3 Language features and limits

We will in the following sections investigate some language features that in the past have caused problems with inherited limits and see how these have been overcome. Often, several quite different solutions have been used.

We illustrate this discussion by presenting a self-interpreter for a simple language and show the effects of the inherited limits (and their removal) on the residual programs obtained by specializing the interpreter using different specialization methods.

```
data int  = Zero | Succ int
data list = Nil | Cons int list

f a b = case a of
          Nil      => b
          Cons n l => Cons (g n) (f b l)

g n = case n of
        Zero   => Zero
        Succ m => m
```

Fig. 2. A small program.

```
data num   = Z | S num
data univ  = Con num ulist
data ulist = Un | Uc univ ulist
data funs  = Fn | Fun exp funs
data exp   = Var num | Fap num elist | Cap num elist | Case exp elist
data elist = En | Ec exp elist
```

Fig. 3. Type declarations used by self-interpreter.

```
run p args = apply Z p args p

apply f fs args p =
  case fs of
    Fn       => Con Z Un
    Fun e fs => case f of
                  Z   => eval e args p
                  S f => apply f fs args p

eval e vs p =
  case e of
    Var n    => lookup n vs
    Fap n es => apply n p (evallist es vs p) p
    Cap n es => Con n (evallist es vs p)
    Case e es => case (eval e vs p) of
                  Con n vs1 => eval (select n es) (append vs1 vs) p

evallist es vs p =
  case es of
    En      => Un
    Ec e es => Uc (eval e vs p) (evallist es vs p)

select n es =
  case es of
    En      => Cap Z En
    Ec e es => case n of
                 Z   => e
                 S n => select n es
```

Fig. 4. Self-interpreter for a small functional language.

Obviously, the choice of language features in the language we choose for our presentation will dictate the set of potentially inherited limits. The pure untypes lambda calculus has only one potential inherited limit: The size of a lambda term. This limit is removed by even simple partial evaluators, so the lambda calculus would be a poor choice for our discussion. The language shown in figure 1 is a compromise between a set of interesting feature and sufficient simplicity that we can show a complete self-interpreter and several residual version of it. The semantics of the language is as one would expect. The choice of call-by-value versus call-by-need isn't important for our discussion, so we leave this open. We will, however, assume that case-expressions are exhaustive. A small example program is shown in figure 2.

We also need a self-interpreter for our discussion. This needs data types for representing values and programs in the language. Declarations of these types are shown in figure 3. The program is represented by a list of un-names functions, which in function calls are referred to by position. Similarly, variables and constructors are represented by their positions in declarations. Type declarations are not explicitly represented in the interpreter. The self-interpreter is shown in figure 4. Missing from this are definitions of lookup, append, hd and tl, which we have omitted for reasons of space.

3.1   Program Size

The most obvious "feature" that a language usually puts no bound on is the size of programs. Yet, obviously, every program is of finite size.

Partial evaluation has often been compared to the constant folding that is done by optimizing compilers. Constant folding will replace some variables by constants and reduce some operations that depend solely on these constants. As such, the "specialized" program can be no larger than the original program (assuming constants are small).

It is thus no surprise that constant folding alone does very little to remove interpretation overhead: Basically, all we can hope is to remove the variable containing the program text and replace every instance of that variable by the program text. In most instances no operations can be performed during special-ization, as most operations on the program text will operate on different parts of the text at different times during execution.

The obvious (and traditional) way of removing the inherited limit on program size is by unfolding: Unrolling loops, inlining function calls or both. Indeed, inlining is enough to provide optimal specialization of a self-interpreter for the pure untyped lambda calculus, as shown in [18]. Typically, denotational-style interpreters can be specialized quite well using a combination of unfolding and constant folding: The recursion over the syntax tree is unfolded and operations on the program text are specialized with the particular text at each program point. If interpreters are not denotational in nature (in particular if a copying rule is used), finite unfolding may, however, be insufficient for obtaining good specialization.

Before:

```
... eval (select n es) (append vs1 vs) p
```

After:

```
... eselect n es (append vs1 vs) p

eselect n es vs p =
  case es of
    En      => Con Z Un
    Ec e es => case n of
                 Z   => eval e vs p
                 S n => eselect n es vs p
```

Fig. 5. Applying "The Trick" to selection of case-branches.

```
run args = apply Z args

apply f args =
 case f of
   Z   =>
    case (hd args) of
      Con n vs1 =>
       case n of
         Z   => hd (tl args)
         S n =>
          case n of
            Z   =>
             Con (S Z)
                 (Uc (apply (S Z)
                            (Uc (hd (append vs1 args)) Un))
                 (Uc (apply Z
                            (Uc (hd (tl (tl (tl (append vs1 args)))))) Un)
                            (Uc (hd (tl (append vs1 args))) Un)))
                      Un))
            S n => Con Z Un
   S f =>
    case f of
      Z   =>
       case (hd args) of
         Con n vs1 =>
          case n of
            Z   => Con Z
            S n =>
             case n of
               Z   => hd (append vs1 args)
               S n => Con Z Un
      S f => Con Z Un
```

Fig. 6. Residual program obtained by partial evaluator using unfolding.

In order to obtain good specialization of the self-interpreter by a partial evaluator that does unfolding, we need to modify the interpreter slightly, doing *binding time improvement*. We will feel free to do this as required, as inherited limits is supposed to be a test on the partial evaluator, not the interpreter. The problem with the original self-interpreter is that the expression returned by `select` is dynamic, as the constructor is not known. If we move the recursive call to `eval` into a modified version of `select`, we can safely unfold the recursive call to `eval`, as the controlling parameter (the expression) is now known. This is an instance of a well-known binding time improvement called "The Trick". The modification is shown in figure 5. We will not go into details about how we select calls for unfolding.

The result of applying specialization with unfolding to the self-interpreter and the example program is shown in figure resid2. Though this isn't actually larger than the original self-interpreter, a larger source program would yield a larger residual program. Hence, the inherited limit on size has been removed.

3.2   Number of Definitions

Since inlining a function call will never add a new function definition (under some reasonable assumptions), the number of function definitions in a program can not increase unboundedly if the partial evaluator only uses unfolding and constant folding.

This argument assumes that recursively inlined functions do not contain local definitions, which will then indeed be duplicated by the unfolding. This is basically what makes unfolding sufficient for the pure lambda calculus. But for languages without local definitions, e.g. C or Prolog, unfolding will never increase the number of function (or predicate) definitions. Even languages with local definitions will not increase the number of global function definitions by unfolding.

A similar argument can be applied to loop unrolling: Loop unrolling can not unboundedly increase the depth of nested loops in a program. Hence, when the partial evaluator uses unfolding and constant folding only, the inherited limit is certainly present in languages that do not have recursion.

Is this limit a problem? It can be, as a program that naturally uses 17 functions may have to combine many of these into one function and use a parameter to select the appropriate part of its body. Similarly, loop unrolling (even when combined with inlining) can not arbitrarily increase the complexity of the control-flow graph.

The usual solution for overcoming this inherited limit is to use *polyvariant specialization*, allowing each original function to be specialized in several different versions, depending on the known arguments. This idea was essential for the success of the MIX-project described in [14], but had earlier been applied to imperative languages e.g. by Itkin [12] and Bulyonkov [2]. In the latter case, it is not functions that are specialized with multiple sets of known arguments but program points that are specialized with respect to multiple sets of values of known variables. Polyvariant specialization is usually combined with unfolding and constant folding.

For reasons of space, we won't show the residual program obtained by poly-variant specialization. What happens is that the `apply` function is specialized to two versions, one for each of the functions in the program. Hence, the `f` parameter and the tests on this have been removed. The bodies of the two residual `apply` functions are the expressions that begin with `case (hd args)`. In this example, polyvariant specialization did not improve the residual program by very much. For some applications, though, polyvariant specialization is essential for obtaining good results.

3.3   Number of Parameters

The partial evaluator developed in the MIX-project [14] was able to remove most of the interpretation overhead when specializing an interpreter.

```
run args_0 args_1 = apply_0 args_0 args_1

apply_0 args_0 args_1 =
 case args_0 of
   Con n vs1 =>
     case n of
       Z   => args_1
       S n =>
         case n of
           Z   =>
             case vs1 of
               Un        => Con Z Un
               Uc v0 vs1 =>
                 case vs1 of
                   Un        => Con Z Un
                   Uc v1 vs1 =>
                     Con (S Z)
                       (Uc (apply_1 v0)
                       (Uc (apply_0 args_1 v1)
                       Un))
           S n => Con Z Un

apply_1 args_0 =
  case args_0 of
    Con n vs1 =>
      case n of
        Z   => Con Z
        S n =>
          case n of
            Z   => case vs1 of
                     Un        => Con Z Un
                     Uc v vs1 => v
            S n => Con Z Un
```

Fig. 7. Residual program obtained by partial evaluator using partially static structures.

However, every residual function in specialized interpreters had a single parameter. This parameter corresponded to the environment used in the interpreter for binding variables to values. Hence, the look-up in the environment was retained in the residual programs. To overcome this problem, a post-processing pass was added to the partial evaluator, which guided by user annotations would split a residual parameter into several. Hence, the list of variable names was used as a template for splitting the list of values into its components. This approach was automated by Romanenko [21], using type-inference on the residual program to find templates for the residual parameters.

An alternative approach was suggested in [16], where the partial evaluator can keep track of known parts of values that may contain unknown components. When specializing a function it is specialized with respect to the known parts of the partially known parameters, and each unknown part becomes a separate parameter. The number of parameters to a specialized function hence depends on the number of unknown components of a partially known value. In the self-interpreter, the environment has a known structure and only the values bound to the variables are unknown. The partial evaluator will detect this and let each value become a separate parameter.

The first of these approaches allows the partial evaluator to remain simple, at the cost of adding a complicated postprocess stage. The latter requires a somewhat more complex partial evaluator, but no postprocessing. This makes specialization potentially faster when using the latter approach. Furthermore, it allows more freedom in the representation of environments. Basically, the postprocess approach requires that the names and values of variables are kept in separate lists, whereas the environment can be represented using the traditional list-of-pairs structure if the partial evaluator can handle partially static structures.

We need a further binding time improvement to keep the environment (list of values) static in the self-interpreter. The problem is again the case expression. The point is that the completely unknown argument list to the constructor is appended to the environment, which means that the spine of the list isn't static, as we hoped. We don't show the details of the required binding time modification, which again uses "The Trick". We do, however, note that we need to change the representation of programs slightly so the modified `select` function knows the number of parameters to each constructor. The residual program is shown in figure 7. We note taht the `args` paramter to the residual `apply` functions have been split into several argument.

3.4 Complexity of Types

Even when using partially static structures or a variable-splitting post-pass, the types of variables in residual programs are always simpler than those in the original program. Basically, each residual variable will have a type that is a component of a type in the original program. If the original program is polymorphically typed, instantiation of type schemas may create types that are more complex than those explicitly written in the original program. However, in

Hindley-Milner typing, the number of instantiations is bounded by the program, so even this can not give an unbounded number or complexity of types in the residual program.

Additionally, the constructors from datatypes used in residual programs will be a subset of those used in the original program. The latter point is addressed in [19], which suggests specializing constructors with respect to the known parts of their arguments, similar to the way functions are specialized to the known parts of their parameters. In addition to allowing an unbounded number of constructors (with unbounded arity) in the residual program, static values can be propagated during specialization in non-local ways not possible using the previously described specialization methods.

The method sketched in [19] puts all specialized versions of a constructor in the same residual type (together with the specialized versions of the other constructors from the same original type). Hence, the number of datatype declarations is the residual program is still an inherited limit. This problem was addressed in [7]. An approach, that on the surface seems quite different, but has similar non-local data-flow, is the type specializer described in [11]. In this approach, each expression is specialized to a residual expression and a type. The type contains all static information that is known about the value of the result of the expression. A post-pass uses this information to find the type for the residual expression. Hughes' type specializer has explicit constructions for emulating polyvariant specialization and constructor specialization. Partially static values is an integral part of the approach.

```
data univ_0 = Con_0 | Con_1 univ_0
data univ_1 = Con_2 | Con_3 univ_0 univ_1

run args_0 args_1 = apply_0 args_0 args_1

apply_0 args_0 args_1 =
 case args_0 of
   Con_2       => args_1
   Con_3 v0 v1 => Con_2 (apply_1 v0) (apply_0 args_1 v1)

apply_1 args_0 =
  case args_0 of
    Con_0       => Con_0
    Con_1 v0    => v0
```

Fig. 8. Residual program obtained by type specialization.

In addition to allowing optimal specialization of self-interpreters for typed languages or languages with user-defined constructors (e.g. Prolog), type and constructor specialization allows a residual program to choose datastructures fit for the particular instance rather than coding the data using a general (universal) type. Very little practical experience has been obtained using these techniques on "real" programs, so it is not known how important this is.

The residual program obtained by type specialization is shown in figure 8.

We have two specialized versions of the univ type, each with its own specialized constructors. univ_0 corresponds to the int type of the source program, and univ_1 corresponds to list. Con_0 and Con_2 both correspond to Con Z Un, but are given different names because the residual types are different.

With the sole exception of the superfluous run function, the residual program is just a renaming of the source program. We can argue that (after removing run and with some simple assumptions about how residual constructors are grouped into residual types) the target program will *always* be a renaming of the source program. Hence, we can reasonably conclude that all inherited limits have been removed, and with that also all interpretation overhead.

4   Other Evolution and Natural Selection

Our focus on a single aspect of the evolution of partial evaluation is in some way similar to the way a palaeontologist may focus on the evolution of thigh bones from early salamanders to humans. While this shows an important aspect of adaptation to land-based life, it is not the whole story.

One may choose to focus on entirely different aspects to show how the field has developed. Indeed, Olivier Danvy [3] has suggested that reducing the need for manual binding time improvement (rewriting programs to get better results from a specific partial evaluator) is a driving force behind much of the developments of partial evaluators – something which is only incidental to this study.

There may also be different ways to remove inherited limits than those shown above. We noted that the limit on number of parameters has been handled in two ways: by a post-process, e.g. in [21] or by using partially static structures [16]. Similarly, it is possible that limits on types and constructors can be handled by post processing. When several methods exist, a form of "natural selection" may determine which method survives. By all appearances, the use of partially static structures has ousted post-processing as a means of removing the bound on parameters. It is too early yet to tell for the later developments. Also, some inherited limits may be considered unimportant (as they have little significance for effectivity), so no great effort is likely to be spent in removing them.

As we mentioned in relation to partially static structures, some methods for removing inherited limits may also reduce the need for binding time improvements. This was indeed one of the original motivations for introducing partially static structures. This may have been a major reason for the success of this approach over arity raising [21], which only solves the variable splitting problem, and bifurcation (Mogensen [17]), (De Neil *et al.* [6]), which solves the binding time improvement aspect, but does not remove the inherited limit.

5   Further Work

The methods described above can remove all inherited limits for a simple first-order functional language, as evidenced by achieving optimal specialization of a self-interpreter in [20]. Every time a new feature is added to a language, a new inherited limit may potentially be added. Below, we list a number of common programming language features that are not covered by the described methods, and discuss how to remove the inherited limits that these features may introduce.

Nesting of Scopes. It is common to have unbounded nesting of function or procedure declarations in programming languages (notable exceptions being C and Polog). It turns out to be simple to obtain arbitrary nesting in the residual program, just by unfolding calls to non-locally defined functions/procedures. This has been done in lambda-mix [9] and ML-mix [1]. Some non-trivial interactions between nested scoping and higher-order functions have been studied by Malmkjær and Ørbæk [15]. An important requirement is that functions with local definitions can be recursive, as the bound on unfolding otherwise may limit the depth of nesting. An alternative approach is to rearrange scopes in a post-process, as described in [5].

Array Dimensions. I doubt any existing partial evaluator can take a source program using (at most) two-dimensional arrays and produce a residual program using three-dimensional arrays. Nor is it easy to see how to do this in a natural fashion. A post-process may detect that access patterns to a one-dimensional array corresponds to using a higher-dimensional array, but it is hard to see how "dimension raising" may be done as an integral part of the specialization process.

Modules. When specializing a modular language, it should, by our principle, be desirable to create residual programs with more modules than the original program. The work by Heldal *et al.* [10, 8] presents a possible solution to this, where the modularization of the residual program reflects modularization of the static data.

Classes. In object oriented languages, it is natural to generate specialized instances of objects within a class. But the principle of removing inherited limits extends to creating entirely new class hierarchies in residual programs, which is less clear how to achieve.

Patterns. Languages with pattern matching usually allow arbitrarily complex patterns. If a partial evaluator can not generate patterns that are more complex than those found in the original program, this is an inherited limit. A solution to this problem is to combine several residual patterns into fewer, but larger patterns. It might be argued that a compiler will separate the pattern matching into nested tests anyway, so this inherited limit may have no significance for the speed of residual programs. This is, however, implementation dependent.

Other. Similar problems may occur for features like exceptions, constraints, processes, streams etc. It is not clear to the author if moving to a polymorphic language will introduce new potentially inherited limits.

6 Conclusion

What we have tried to impart to the reader is an awareness of the idea that a partial evaluator may cause residual programs to inherit limits from the original program, and that this may be a problem.

The intention is to inspire developers of partial evaluators to consider if their partial evaluators exhibit such inherited limits, and decide if they think these important enough to deal with. In other words, the awareness of the problem may be used as a guideline for refining specialization technology.

Identifying the problem is, however, only the first step. Knowing that a limit is inherited does not always suggest a solution. A good example of this is the array dimension limit, which has no obvious solution.

It may not be obvious which limits, if any, are inherited. A test for this may be done by attempting to write a self-interpreter and specialize this. If the residual programs are identical to the original (bar renaming and reordering), it is evidence that no inherited limits exist. Otherwise, the problem may be in either the interpreter or the specializer (or both), and the experiment may suggest which. In general, if a limitation in residual programs can be solved by rewriting the original program (no matter how extensively), then the limitation is not due to an inherited limit in the specializer.

Note that we have only required that a self-interpreter *exists* which allows the residual programs to be identical to the source programs, not that *all* self-interpreters do this. Hence, we have not out-ruled the possibility of writing self-interpreters where partial evaluation produces residual programs in some sub-language, e.g. CPS style. This ability is important, and we should aim to retain this.

Not all improvements of partial evaluators are instances of removing inherited limits. Important subjects such as improved binding time analysis, control of termination, automatic binding time improvements, speed of specialization, self-application, addition of language features etc. are all important developments that are not directly linked to the removal of inherited limits.

References

1. L. Birkedal and M. Welinder. Partial evaluation of Standard ML. Master's thesis, DIKU, University of Copenhagen, Denmark, 1993. DIKU Research Report 93/22.
2. M.A. Bulyonkov. A theoretical approach to polyvariant mixed computation. In D. Bjørner, A.P. Ershov, and N.D. Jones, editors, *Partial Evaluation and Mixed Computation*, pages 51–64. Amsterdam: North-Holland, 1988.
3. O. Danvy. On the evolution of partial evaluators. Technical report, DART Technical Report, University of Aarhus, 1993.
4. O. Danvy, R. Glück, and P. Thiemann, editors. *Partial Evaluation. Dagstuhl Castle, Germany, February 1996*, volume 1110 of *Lecture Notes in Computer Science*. Berlin: Springer-Verlag, 1996.
5. O. Danvy and U. P. Schultz. Lambda-dropping: Transforming recursive equations into programs with block structure. In *Partial Evaluation and Semantics-Based*

Program Manipulation, Amsterdam, The Netherlands, June 1997, pages 90–106. New York: ACM, 1997.

6. A. De Niel, E. Bevers, and K. De Vlaminck. Program bifurcation for a polymorphically typed functional language. In *Partial Evaluation and Semantics-Based Program Manipulation, New Haven, Connecticut (Sigplan Notices, vol. 26, no. 9, September 1991)*, pages 142–153. New York: ACM, 1991.

7. D. Dussart, E. Bevers, and K. De Vlaminck. Polyvariant constructor specialisation. In *Partial Evaluation and Semantics-Based Program Manipulation, La Jolla, California, June 1995*, pages 54–65. New York: ACM, 1995.

8. D. Dussart, R. Heldal, and J. Hughes. Module-sensitive program specialisation. In *SIGPLAN '97 Conference on Programming Language Design and Implementation, June 1997, Las Vegas*, pages 206–214. New York: ACM, 1997.

9. C.K. Gomard and N.D. Jones. A partial evaluator for the untyped lambda-calculus. *Journal of Functional Programming*, 1(1):21–69, January 1991.

10. R. Heldal and J. Hughes. Partial evaluation and separate compilation. In *Partial Evaluation and Semantics-Based Program Manipulation, Amsterdam, The Netherlands, June 1997*, pages 1–11. New York: ACM, 1997.

11. J. Hughes. Type specialisation for the λ-calculus; or, a new paradigm for partial evaluation based on type inference. In Danvy et al. [4], pages 183–215.

12. V.E. Itkin. On partial and mixed program execution. In *Program Optimization and Transformation*, pages 17–30. Novosibirsk: Computing Center, 1983. (In Russian).

13. N.D. Jones. Challenging problems in partial evaluation and mixed computation. In D. Bjørner, A.P. Ershov, and N.D. Jones, editors, *Partial Evaluation and Mixed Computation*, pages 1–14. Amsterdam: North-Holland, 1988.

14. N.D. Jones, P. Sestoft, and H. Søndergaard. An experiment in partial evaluation: The generation of a compiler generator. In J.-P. Jouannaud, editor, *Rewriting Techniques and Applications, Dijon, France. (Lecture Notes in Computer Science, vol. 202)*, pages 124–140. Berlin: Springer-Verlag, 1985.

15. K. Malmkjær and P. Ørbæk. Polyvariant specialisation for higher-order, block-structured languages. In *Partial Evaluation and Semantics-Based Program Manipulation, La Jolla, California, June 1995*, pages 66–76. New York: ACM, 1995.

16. T. Mogensen. Partially static structures in a self-applicable partial evaluator. In D. Bjørner, A.P. Ershov, and N.D. Jones, editors, *Partial Evaluation and Mixed Computation*, pages 325–347. Amsterdam: North-Holland, 1988.

17. T. Mogensen. Separating binding times in language specifications. In *Fourth International Conference on Functional Programming Languages and Computer Architecture, London, England, September 1989*, pages 14–25. Reading, MA: Addison-Wesley, 1989.

18. T. Mogensen. Self-applicable partial evaluation for pure lambda calculus. In *Partial Evaluation and Semantics-Based Program Manipulation, San Francisco, California, June 1992 (Technical Report YALEU/DCS/RR-909)*, pages 116–121. New Haven, CT: Yale University, 1992.

19. T. Mogensen. Constructor specialization. In *Partial Evaluation and Semantics-Based Program Manipulation, Copenhagen, Denmark, June 1993*, pages 22–32. New York: ACM, 1993.

20. T.Æ. Mogensen. Evolution of partial evaluators: Removing inherited limits. In Danvy et al. [4], pages 303–321.

21. S.A. Romanenko. Arity raiser and its use in program specialization. In N. Jones, editor, *ESOP '90. 3rd European Symposium on Programming, Copenhagen, Denmark, May 1990 (Lecture Notes in Computer Science, vol. 432)*, pages 341–360. Berlin: Springer-Verlag, 1990.

Partial Evaluation for the Lambda Calculus

Neil D. Jones, Carsten K. Gomard, Peter Sestoft*

DIKU, University of Copenhagen

1   Introduction

This paper (essentially [12, Chapter 8]) describes partial evaluation for the lambda calculus, augmented with an explicit fixed-point operator. The techniques used here diverge from those used in [12, Chapters 4, 5] and [11] in that they are not based on specialization of *named* program points. The algorithm essentially leaves some operators (applications, lambdas, etc.) untouched and reduces others as standard evaluation would do it. This simple scheme is able to handle programs that rely heavily on higher-order facilities. The requirements on binding-time analysis are formulated via a type system and an efficient binding-time analysis via constraint solving is outlined. The partial evaluator is proven correct.

History and recent developments Self-applicable partial evaluation was first achieved in 1984 for a simple first-order functional language. This promising result was not immediately extendable to a higher-order language, the reason being that a specializer, given incomplete input data, in effect traces all possible program control flow paths and computes as many static values as possible. This seemed hard to do, since flow analysis of programs that manipulate functions as data values is non–trivial.

Breakthroughs occurred independently in 1989 by Bondorf (then at Dortmund) and by Gomard and Jones (Copenhagen). The latter, called *Lambdamix* and the subject of this paper, is conceptually simpler, theoretically motivated, and has been proven correct. Bondorf's work is more pragmatically oriented, led to the now widely distributed system Similix, and is the subject of [12, Chapter 10].

In common with the partial evaluators of the earlier book chapters, Lambdamix represents the concrete syntax of programs as constants (in fact Lisp S-expressions are used, though this is not essential). The natural question of whether partial evaluation is meaningful and possible in the classical *pure* lambda calculus without constants has recently been answered affirmatively.

Briefly: Mogensen devised a quite efficient self-interpreter for the pure lambda calculus, using 'higher-order abstract syntax' to encode lambda expressions as normal form lambda expressions. These are not difficult to interpret and even to

---

* Chapter 8 from *Partial Evaluation and Automatic Program Generation*, Prentice-Hall International, 1993, ISBN 0-13-020249-5 (pbk). Reprinted with permission from Pentice-Hall International. All references to "book" in this article refers to this book.

specialize, although they are rather hard for humans to decipher. The ideas were later extended to give a self-applicable partial evaluator for the same language, using essentially the two level type system to be seen in this paper. The partial evaluator was implemented, self-application gave the usual speedups, and it has since been proven correct by Wand using the technique of 'logical relations' [17, 26].

2   The lambda calculus and self-interpretation

The classical lambda calculus (extended with constants, conditionals, and a fix-point operator) is used here for simplicity and to allow a more complete treatment than would be possible for a larger and more practical language.

A lambda calculus program is an *expression*, e, together with an initial *environment*, ρ, which is a function from identifiers to values. The program takes its input through its free variables. The expression syntax given below differs from that of [12, Section 3.2] in that we have introduced an explicit fixed-point operator.

$$\langle \text{Lam} \rangle ::= \langle \text{Constant} \rangle \qquad \qquad \text{Constants}$$

	| ⟨Var⟩	Variables
	| λ⟨Var⟩.⟨Lam⟩	Abstraction
	| ⟨Lam⟩ ⟨Lam⟩	Application
	| fix ⟨Lam⟩	Fixed point operator
	| if ⟨Lam⟩ then ⟨Lam⟩ else ⟨Lam⟩	Conditional
	| ⟨Op⟩ ⟨Lam⟩ ... ⟨Lam⟩	Base application

$$\langle \text{Var} \rangle ::= \text{any identifier}$$

Examples of relevant base functions include =, *, cons, etc. The fixed-point operator fix computes the least fixed point of its argument and is used to define recursive functions. For example, a program computing x^n can be defined by

```
(fix λp.λn'.λx'.
   if (= n' 0)
   then 1
   else (* x' (p (- n' 1) x'))) n x
```

Note that fix λf.e is equivalent to the Scheme constructs (rec f e) and (letrec ((f e)) f). Why introduce an explicit fixed-point operator instead of using the Y-combinator written as a lambda expression [12, Section 3.2] to express recursion? This is because an explicit fix allows a simpler binding-time analysis.

As a first step towards partial evaluation we show a self-interpreter for the lambda calculus in Figure 1. Below we explain the notation used in Figure 1 and the remainder of the paper.

Value domains

$v : Val \ = Const + Funval$
$Funval \ = Val \to Val$
$\rho : Env = Var \to Val$

$\mathcal{E}: Expression \to Env \to Val$
$\mathcal{E}[\![c]\!]\rho \qquad\qquad\quad\ = \mathcal{V}[\![c]\!]\!\uparrow Const$
$\mathcal{E}[\![var]\!]\rho \qquad\qquad\ = \rho(var)$
$\mathcal{E}[\![\lambda var.e]\!]\rho \qquad\quad = (\lambda value.(\mathcal{E}[\![e]\!]\rho[var \mapsto value]))\!\uparrow Funval$
$\mathcal{E}[\![e_1\ e_2]\!]\rho \qquad\quad = (\mathcal{E}[\![e_1]\!]\rho\!\downarrow Funval)\ (\mathcal{E}[\![e_2]\!]\rho)$
$\mathcal{E}[\![fix\ e]\!]\rho \qquad\qquad = fix\ (\mathcal{E}[\![e]\!]\rho\!\downarrow Funval)$
$\mathcal{E}[\![if\ e_1\ then\ e_2\ else\ e_3]\!]\rho = (\mathcal{E}[\![e_1]\!]\rho\!\downarrow Const) \to \mathcal{E}[\![e_2]\!]\rho, \mathcal{E}[\![e_3]\!]\rho$
$\mathcal{E}[\![op\ e_1 \ldots\ e_n]\!] \qquad = (\mathcal{O}[\![op]\!]\ (\mathcal{E}[\![e_1]\!]\rho\!\downarrow Const)$
$\qquad\qquad\qquad\qquad\qquad \ldots (\mathcal{E}[\![e_n]\!]\rho\!\downarrow Const))\!\uparrow Const$

Figure 1: Lambda calculus self-interpreter.

Notation *Const* is a 'flat' domain of constants large enough to include concrete syntax representations of lambda expressions (as input to and output from mix) and booleans for use in conditionals. As in earlier book chapters (and in our implementation) a suitable choice is the set of Lisp S-expressions. Further, we assume there are enough base functions to test equality, and to compose and decompose abstract syntax.

The separated sum of domains *Const* and *Funval* is written $Val = Const + Funval$. Given an element $b \in Const$, $v = b\!\uparrow Const \in Val$ is tagged as originating from *Const*. In SML or Miranda this would be written $v = Const\ b$. We have introduced the $\uparrow$ notation for symmetry with $v\!\downarrow Const$. This strips off the tag yielding an element in *Const* if v is tagged as originating from *Const*. If v has any other tag, then $v\!\downarrow Const$ produces an error.

We assume that all operations are strict in the error value but omit details. The domain $Funval = Val \to Val$ contains partial functions from *Val* to *Val*. Function $\mathcal{V}$ computes the value (in *Const*) of a constant expression (in *Exp*). Function $\mathcal{O}$ links names to base functions. The notation $\rho[var \mapsto value]$ is, as in [12, Section 2.1], a shorthand for $\lambda x.if\ (x{=}var)\ then\ value\ else\ (\rho\ x)$ and is used to update environments. Expression $v_1 \to v_2$, v_3 has the value v_2 if v_1 equals *true* and value v_3 if v_1 equals *false*, else the error value.

Since we use lambda calculus both as an object level programming language and as a meta-language, we distinguish notationally between the two for clarity. Object level lambda expressions are written in typewriter style: e e, λvar.e, fix e etc., and the meta-language is in *italics*: *e e*, $\lambda var.e$, *fix e* etc.

The self-interpreter The structure of the self-interpreter is not much different from that of the lambda calculus interpreter written in ML and presented in [12, Section 3.3.1]. First-order structures have been replaced by functions in two places:

⟨2Lam⟩ ::= ⟨Constant⟩	Constant
| ⟨Var⟩	Variable
| lift ⟨2Lam⟩	Lifting
| λ⟨Var⟩.⟨2Lam⟩	Abstraction
| ⟨2Lam⟩ ⟨2Lam⟩	Application
| fix ⟨2Lam⟩	Fixed point
| if ⟨2Lam⟩ then ⟨2Lam⟩ else ⟨2Lam⟩	Conditional
| ⟨Op⟩ ⟨2Lam⟩ ... ⟨2Lam⟩	Base application
| λ̲⟨Var⟩.⟨2Lam⟩	Dyn. abstraction
| ⟨2Lam⟩ @̲ ⟨2Lam⟩	Dyn. application
| fix̲ ⟨2Lam⟩	Dyn. fixed point
| if̲ ⟨2Lam⟩ then̲ ⟨2Lam⟩ else̲ ⟨2Lam⟩	Dyn. conditional
| ⟨Op̲⟩ ⟨2Lam⟩ ... ⟨2Lam⟩	Dyn. base appl.

Figure 2: Two-level lambda calculus syntax.

- The environment is implemented by a *function* from variables to values. Looking up the value of a variable var thus amounts to applying the environment ρ. This replaces the parallel lists of names and values seen in the interpreters from earlier book chapters.
- The value of an abstraction λvar.e is a *function* which, when applied to an argument value, evaluates e in an extended environment binding var to the value. The value of an application e_1 e_2 is found by applying the value of e_1, which must be a function, to the value of e_2. This mechanism replaces the use of explicit closures.

It should be clear that, despite the extensive use of syntactic sugar, Figure 1 does define a self-interpreter, as the function $\mathcal{E}$ can easily be transformed into a lambda expression: fix $\lambda\mathcal{E}.\lambda e.\lambda\rho.\text{if} \ldots$.

3   Partial evaluation using a two-level lambda calculus

As in the previous book chapters we divide the task of partial evaluation into two phases: *first* we apply binding-time analysis, which yields a suitably annotated program, *then* reduce the static parts, blindly obeying the annotations. An annotated program is a two-level lambda expression. The two-level lambda calculus has two different versions of each of the following constructions: application, abstraction, conditionals, fixed points, and base function applications. One version is *dynamic*, the other is *static*. The static operators are those of the standard lambda calculus: if, fix, λ, etc. and the dynamic operators are underlined: if̲, fix̲, $\underline{\lambda}$, @̲. (@̲ denotes a dynamic application.) The abstract syntax of two-level expressions is given in Figure 2.

Intuitively, all static operators λ, @, ... are treated by the partial evaluator as they were treated by the self-interpreter. The result of evaluating a dynamic operator ($\underline{\lambda}$, @̲, ...) is to produce a piece of *code* for execution at run-time —

a constant which is the concrete syntax representation of a residual one-level lambda expression, perhaps with free variables.

The lift operator also builds code — a constant expression with the same value as lift's argument. The operator lift is applied to static subexpressions of a dynamic expression.

A two-level *program* is a two-level expression te together with an initial environment ρ_s which maps the free variables of te to constants, functions, or code pieces. We shall assume that free dynamic variables are mapped to distinct, new variable names. The $\mathcal{T}$-rules (Figure 3) then ensure that these new variables become the free variables of the residual program.

Variables bound by $\underline{\lambda}$, will also (eventually) generate fresh variable names in the residual program, whereas variables bound by λ can be bound at specialization time to all kinds of values: constants, functions, or code pieces.

The $\mathcal{T}$-rule for a dynamic application is

$$\mathcal{T}[\![\text{te}_1 \ \underline{@} \ \text{te}_2]\!]\rho = \textit{build-@}(\mathcal{T}[\![\text{te}_1]\!]\rho{\downarrow}\textit{Code}, \mathcal{T}[\![\text{te}_2]\!]\rho{\downarrow}\textit{Code}){\uparrow}\textit{Code}$$

The recursive calls $\mathcal{T}[\![\text{te}_1]\!]\rho$ and $\mathcal{T}[\![\text{te}_2]\!]\rho$ produce the code for residual operator and operand expressions, and the function *build-@* 'glues' them together to form an application to appear in the residual program (concretely, an expression of the form (te$_1$' te$_2$')). All the *build*-functions are strict.

The projections ($\downarrow$*Code*) check that both operator and operand reduce to code pieces, to avoid applying specialization time operations (e.g. boolean tests) to residual program pieces. Finally, the newly composed expression is tagged ($\uparrow$*Code*) as being a piece of code.

The $\mathcal{T}$-rule for variables is

$$\mathcal{T}[\![\text{var}]\!]\rho = \rho(\text{var})$$

The environment ρ is expected to hold the values of all variables regardless of whether they are predefined constants, functions, or code pieces. The environment is updated in the usual way in the rule for static λ, and in the rule for $\underline{\lambda}$, the formal parameter is bound to an as yet unused variable name, which we assume available whenever needed:

$$\mathcal{T}[\![\underline{\lambda}\text{var}.\text{te}]\!]\rho = \text{let nvar} = \textit{newname}(\text{var})$$
$$\text{in } \textit{build-}\lambda(\text{nvar}, \mathcal{T}[\![\text{te}]\!]\rho[\text{var} \mapsto \text{nvar}]{\downarrow}\textit{Code}){\uparrow}\textit{Code}$$

Each occurrence of var in te will then be looked up in $\rho[\text{var} \mapsto \text{nvar}]$, causing var to be replaced by the fresh variable nvar. Since $\underline{\lambda}\text{var}.\text{te}$ might be duplicated, and thus become the 'father' of many λ-abstractions in the residual program, this renaming is necessary to avoid name confusion in residual programs. Any free dynamic variables must be bound to their new names in the initial static environment ρ_s. The generation of new variable names relies on a side effect on a global state (a name counter). In principle this could be avoided by adding an extra parameter to $\mathcal{T}$, but for the sake of notational simplicity we have used a less formal solution.

Two-level value domains

$$2Val \quad = Const + 2Funval + Code$$
$$2Funval = 2Val \to 2Val$$
$$Code \quad = Expression$$
$$2Env \quad = Var \to 2Val$$

$\mathcal{T}: 2Expression \to 2Env \to 2Val$

$\mathcal{T}[\![c]\!]\rho \qquad\qquad = \mathcal{V}[\![c]\!]\!\uparrow Const$

$\mathcal{T}[\![var]\!]\rho \qquad\qquad = \rho(var)$

$\mathcal{T}[\![lift\ te]\!]\rho \qquad = build\text{-}const(\mathcal{T}[\![te]\!]\rho\!\downarrow Const)\!\uparrow Code$

$\mathcal{T}[\![\lambda var.te]\!]\rho \qquad = (\lambda value.(\mathcal{T}[\![te]\!]\ \rho[var \mapsto value]))\!\uparrow 2Funval$

$\mathcal{T}[\![te_1\ te_2]\!]\rho \qquad = \mathcal{T}[\![te_1]\!]\rho\!\downarrow 2Funval\ (\mathcal{T}[\![te_2]\!]\rho)$

$\mathcal{T}[\![fix\ te]\!]\rho \qquad = fix\ (\mathcal{T}[\![te]\!]\rho\!\downarrow 2Funval)$

$\mathcal{T}[\![if\ te_1\ then\ te_2\ else\ te_3]\!]\rho$
$$\qquad\qquad = \mathcal{T}[\![te_1]\!]\rho\!\downarrow Const \to \mathcal{T}[\![te_2]\!]\rho,\ \mathcal{T}[\![te_3]\!]\rho$$

$\mathcal{T}[\![op\ e_1 \ldots\ e_n]\!]\rho = (\mathcal{O}[\![op]\!]\ (\mathcal{T}[\![e_1]\!]\rho\!\downarrow Const) \ldots (\mathcal{T}[\![e_n]\!]\rho\!\downarrow Const))\!\uparrow Const$

$\mathcal{T}[\![\underline{\lambda} var.te]\!]\rho \qquad = let\ nvar = newname(var)$
$\qquad\qquad\qquad\quad in\ build\text{-}\lambda(nvar,\ \mathcal{T}[\![te]\!]\ \rho[var \mapsto nvar]\!\downarrow Code)\!\uparrow Code$

$\mathcal{T}[\![te_1\ \underline{@}\ te_2]\!]\rho \quad = build\text{-}@(\mathcal{T}[\![te_1]\!]\rho\!\downarrow Code,\ \mathcal{T}[\![te_2]\!]\rho\!\downarrow Code)\!\uparrow Code$

$\mathcal{T}[\![\underline{fix}\ te]\!]\rho \qquad = build\text{-}fix(\mathcal{T}[\![te]\!]\rho\!\downarrow Code)\!\uparrow Code$

$\mathcal{T}[\![\underline{if}\ te_1\ \underline{then}\ te_2\ \underline{else}\ te_3]\!]\rho$
$$\qquad\qquad = build\text{-}if(\mathcal{T}[\![te_1]\!]\rho\!\downarrow Code,$$
$$\qquad\qquad\qquad \mathcal{T}[\![te_2]\!]\rho\!\downarrow Code,\ \mathcal{T}[\![te_3]\!]\rho\!\downarrow Code)\!\uparrow Code$$

$\mathcal{T}[\![\underline{op}\ e_1 \ldots\ e_n]\!] = build\text{-}op((\mathcal{T}[\![e_1]\!]\rho\!\downarrow Code) \ldots (\mathcal{T}[\![e_n]\!]\rho\!\downarrow Code))\!\uparrow Code$

Figure 3: Two-level lambda calculus interpreter.

The valuation functions for two-level lambda calculus programs are given in Figure 3. The rules contain explicit tagging and untagging with $\uparrow$ and $\downarrow$; Section 4 will discuss sufficient criteria for avoiding the need to perform them.

Example 1. Consider again the power program:

```
(fix λp.λn'.λx'.
    if (= n' 0)
    then 1
    else (* x' (p (- n' 1) x'))) n x
```

and suppose that n is known and x is not. A suitably annotated power program, power-ann, would be:

```
(fix λp.λn'.λx'.
    if (= n' 0)
    then (lift 1)
    else (* x' (p (- n' 1) x'))) n x
```

Partial evaluation of power (that is, two-level evaluation of power-ann) in environment $\rho_s = [\text{n} \mapsto 2\uparrow Const, \text{x} \mapsto \text{xnew}\uparrow Code]$ yields:

$$\mathcal{T}[\![\text{power-ann}]\!]\rho_s$$
$$= \mathcal{T}[\![(\text{fix } \lambda\text{p}.\lambda\text{n}'.\lambda\text{x}'.\text{if} \ldots) \text{ n } \text{x}]\!]\rho_s$$
$$= * \text{ xnew } (* \text{ xnew } 1)$$

In the power example it is quite clear that for all $d2$, $\rho = [\text{n} \mapsto 2, \text{x} \mapsto d2]$, $\rho_s = [\text{n} \mapsto 2, \text{x} \mapsto \text{xnew}]$, and $\rho_d = [\text{xnew} \mapsto d2]$ (omitting injections for brevity) it holds that

$$\mathcal{E}[\![\text{power}]\!]\rho = \mathcal{E}[\![\mathcal{T}[\![\text{power-ann}]\!]\rho_s]\!]\rho_d$$

This is the mix equation (see [12, Section 4.2.2]) for the lambda calculus. [12, Section 8] contains a general correctness theorem for two-level evaluation.

4   Congruence and consistency of annotations

The semantic rules of Figure 3 check explicitly that the values of subexpressions are in the appropriate summands of the value domain, in the same way that a type-checking interpreter for a dynamically typed language would. Type-checking on the fly is clearly necessary to prevent partial evaluation from committing type errors itself on a poorly annotated program.

Doing type checks on the fly is not very satisfactory for practical reasons. Mix is supposed to be a general and automatic program generation tool, and one wishes for obvious reasons for it to be impossible for an automatically generated compiler to go down with an error message.

Note that it is in principle possible — but unacceptably inefficient in practice — to avoid partial evaluation-time errors by annotating as dynamic all operators in the subject program. This would place all values in the code summand so all type checks would succeed; but the residual program would always be isomorphic to the source program, so it would not be optimized at all.

The aim of this section is to develop a more efficient strategy, ensuring before specialization starts that the partial evaluator *cannot* commit a type error. This strategy was seen in [12, Chapters 4, 5] and [11]. The main difference now is that in a higher-order language it is less obvious *what* congruence is and *how* to ensure it.

4.1   Well-annotated expressions

A simple and traditional way to preclude type check errors is to devise a type system. In typed functional languages, a type inference algorithm such as algorithm W checks that a program is well-typed prior to program execution [15]. If it is, then no run-time summand tags or checks are needed. Type checking is

$$(\text{Const}) \qquad \tau \vdash c : S$$

$$(\text{Var}) \qquad \tau[x \mapsto t] \vdash x : t$$

$$(\text{Lift}) \qquad \frac{\tau \vdash \text{te} : S}{\tau \vdash \text{lift te} : D}$$

$$(\text{Abstr}) \qquad \frac{\tau[x \mapsto t_2] \vdash \text{te} : t_1}{\tau \vdash \lambda x.\text{te} : t_2 \to t_1}$$

$$(\text{Apply}) \qquad \frac{\tau \vdash \text{te}_1 : t_2 \to t_1 \quad \tau \vdash \text{te}_2 : t_2}{\tau \vdash \text{te}_1 \ \text{te}_2 : t_1}$$

$$(\text{Fix}) \qquad \frac{\tau \vdash \text{te} : (t_1 \to t_2) \to (t_1 \to t_2)}{\tau \vdash \text{fix te} : t_1 \to t_2}$$

$$(\text{If}) \qquad \frac{\tau \vdash \text{te}_1 : S \quad \tau \vdash \text{te}_2 : t \quad \tau \vdash \text{te}_3 : t}{\tau \vdash \text{if te}_1 \text{ then te}_2 \text{ else te}_3 : t}$$

$$(\text{Op}) \qquad \frac{\tau \vdash \text{te}_1 : S \ \dots \ \tau \vdash \text{te}_n : S}{\tau \vdash \text{op te}_1 \ \dots \ \text{te}_n : S}$$

$$(\text{Abstr-dyn}) \qquad \frac{\tau[x \mapsto D] \vdash \text{te} : D}{\tau \vdash \underline{\lambda} x.\text{te} : D}$$

$$(\text{Apply-dyn}) \qquad \frac{\tau \vdash \text{te}_1 : D \quad \tau \vdash \text{te}_2 : D}{\tau \vdash \text{te}_1 \ \underline{@} \ \text{te}_2 : D}$$

$$(\text{Fix-dyn}) \qquad \frac{\tau \vdash \text{te} : D}{\tau \vdash \underline{\text{fix}} \ \text{te} : D}$$

$$(\text{If-dyn}) \qquad \frac{\tau \vdash \text{te}_1 : D \quad \tau \vdash \text{te}_2 : D \quad \tau \vdash \text{te}_3 : D}{\tau \vdash \underline{\text{if}} \ \text{te}_1 \ \underline{\text{then}} \ \text{te}_2 \ \underline{\text{else}} \ \text{te}_3 : D}$$

$$(\text{Op-dyn}) \qquad \frac{\tau \vdash \text{te}_1 : D \ \dots \ \tau \vdash \text{te}_n : D}{\tau \vdash \underline{\text{op}} \ \text{te}_1 \ \dots \ \text{te}_n : D}$$

Figure 4: Type rules checking well-annotatedness.

quite well understood and can be used to get a nice formulation of the problem to be solved by binding-time analysis [4, 22].

We saw in [12, Section 5.7] and [11] that type rules can be used to check well-annotatedness, and we now apply similar reasoning to the lambda calculus.

Definition 1. *The* two-level types *t are as follows, where α ranges over type variables:*

$t ::= \alpha \mid S \mid D \mid t \to t$

A type environment τ *is a mapping from program variables to types.*

Definition 2. *Let τ be a type environment mapping the free variables of a two-level expression* te *to their types. Then* te *is well-annotated if $\tau \vdash$* te $: t$ *can be deduced from the inference rules in Figure 4 for some type t.*

For example, the two-level expression power-ann of Example 1 is well-annotated in type environment $\tau = [\mathbf{n} \mapsto S, \mathbf{x} \mapsto D]$. The whole expression has type D, and the part (fix p ...) has type $S \to D \to D$.

Our lambda calculus is basically untyped, but the well-annotatedness ensures that all program parts evaluated at partial evaluation time will be well-typed, thus ensuring specialization against type errors. The well-annotatedness criterion is, however, completely permissive concerning the run-time part of a two-level expression. Thus a lambda expression without static operators is trivially well-typed — *at partial evaluation time.*

Two-level expressions of type S evaluate (completely) to *first-order* constants, and expressions of type $t_1 \to t_2$ evaluate to a function applicable *only at partial evaluation time.* The value by $\mathcal{T}$ of a two-level expression te of type D is a one-level expression e. For partial evaluation we are only interested in fully annotated programs p-ann that have type D. In that case, $\mathcal{T}[\![\text{p-ann}]\!]\rho_s$ (if defined) will be a piece of code, namely the residual program.

In our context, the result about error freedom of well-typed programs can be formulated as follows. Proof is omitted since the result is well-known.

Definition 3. *Let t be a two-level type and v be a two-level value. We say that t suits v iff one of the following holds:*

1. $t = S$ *and $v = ct{\uparrow}Const$ for some $ct \in Const$.*
2. $t = D$ *and $v = cd{\uparrow}Code$ for some $cd \in Code$.*
3. *(a) $t = t_1 \to t_2$, $v = f{\uparrow}2Funval$ for some $f \in 2Funval$, and*
   (b) $\forall\, v \in 2Val\colon t_1$ suits v implies t_2 suits $f(v)$.

A type environment τ suits an environment ρ if for all variables $\mathbf{x}$ bound by ρ, $\tau(\mathbf{x})$ suits $\rho(\mathbf{x})$.

The following is a non-standard application of a standard result [15].

Proposition 1. *('Well-annotated programs do not go wrong') If $\tau \vdash$* te $: t$, *and τ suits ρ_s, then $\mathcal{T}[\![\text{te}]\!]\rho_s$ does not yield a projection error.*

Of course $\mathcal{T}$ can 'go wrong' in other ways than by committing type errors. Reduction might proceed infinitely (so $\mathcal{T}[\![\text{p-ann}]\!]\rho_s$ is not defined) or residual code might be duplicated. We shall not discuss these problems here.

5   Binding-time analysis

Definition 4. *The* annotation-forgetting function ϕ: *2Exp* $\to$ *Exp, when applied to a two-level expression* te, *returns a one-level expression* e *which differs from* te *only in that all annotations (underlines) and* lift *operators are removed.*

Definition 5. *Given two-level expressions,* te *and* te_1, *define* te $\sqsubseteq te_1$ *by*

1. $\phi(\text{te}) = \phi(te_1)$
2. *All operators underlined in* te *are also underlined in* te_1

Thus $\sqsubseteq$ is a preorder on the set of two-level expressions. Given a λ-expression e, let a *binding-time assumption* for e be a type environment τ mapping each free variable of e to either S or D.

Definition 6. *Given an expression* e *and a binding-time assumption* τ, *a completion of* e *for* τ *is a two-level expression* te_1 *with* $\phi(te_1) = $ e *and* $\tau \vdash te_1 : t$ *for some type t. A* minimal completion *is an expression* te_2 *which is a completion of* te *fulfilling* $te_2 \sqsubseteq te_1$ *for all completions* te_1 *of* e.

Minimal completions are in general not unique. Assume $\tau = [y \mapsto D]$, and e $= (\lambda x.x+y)$ 4. There are two minimal completions, $te_1 = (\lambda x.x\underline{+}y)$ (lift 4) and $te_2 = (\lambda x.(\text{lift } x)\underline{+}y)$ 4 which yield identical residual programs when partially evaluated. The definition of $\sqsubseteq$ does not distinguish between (minimal) completions which differ only in the choice of lift-points. Residual programs are identical for completions te_1 and te_2 if $te_1 \sqsubseteq te_2$ and $te_2 \sqsubseteq te_1$, and the impact of different choices on efficiency of the partial evaluation process itself is of little importance.

The requirement that τ be a binding-time assumption implies that all free variables are first-order. This ensures the existence of a completion. Note that a λ-bound variable x can get any type in completions, in particular a functional type. Possible conflicts can be resolved by annotating the abstraction(s) and application(s) that force x to have a functional type.

The task of binding-time analysis in the λ-calculus is briefly stated: given an expression e and a binding-time assumption τ find a minimal completion of e for τ. [12, Section 7], shows by example that this can be done by type inference, and [12, Section 8] shows how to do it in a much more efficient way.

Proposition 2. *Given an expression* e *and a binding-time assumption* τ *there exist(s) minimal completion(s) of* e *for* τ.

Proof. Follows from the properties of the constraint-based binding-time analysis algorithm in [12, Section 8.7].

6 Simplicity versus power in Lambdamix

A value of type $t \neq D$ can only be bound to a variable by applying a function of type $t \to t'$. The partial evaluation time result of such a statically performed application is found by evaluating the function body, no matter what the type of the argument or the result is. This corresponds closely to unfolding on the fly of *all* static function calls (see [12, Section 5.5] and [11]).

Lambdamix does not perform specialization of *named* program points. Rather, generation of multiple variants of a source expression can be accomplished as an implicit result of unfolding a `fix` operator, since static variables may be bound to different values in the different unfoldings.

The only way to prevent a function call from being unfolded is to annotate the function as dynamic: $\underline{\lambda}$. All applications of that function must accordingly be annotated as dynamic. Dynamic functions $\underline{\lambda}\ldots$ can only have dynamic arguments (Figure 4). Note that this restriction does not exist in [12, Chapter 5] where named functions are specialized. As an example, consider the append function, app, written as a lambda expression:

```
(fix λapp.λxs.λys.
    if    (null? xs)
    then ys
    else (cons (car xs) (app (cdr xs) ys))) xs0 ys0
```

Partial evaluation with xs0 = '(a b) and dynamic ys0 yields (cons 'a (cons 'b ys0)), a result similar to that produced by the Scheme0 specializer from [12, Chapter 5] (with any reasonable unfolding strategy). Lambdamix handles this example well because the recursive calls to app should be unfolded to produce the optimal residual program. Unfolding the calls allows Lambdamix to exploit the static argument, (cdr xs).

Now assume that xs0 is dynamic and that ys0 is static with value '(c d). When applied to a corresponding problem, the techniques from [12, Chapter 5] would produce the residual Scheme0 program

```
(define (app-cd xs)
  (if (null? xs)
      '(c d)
      (cons (car xs) (app-cd (cdr xs))))))
```

where the recursive call to app-cd is not unfolded. Now consider this problem in the Lambdamix framework. With dynamic ys0, a minimal completion of the append program is:

```
(fix λapp.λxs.λys.
    if    (null? xs)
    then (lift ys)
    else (cons (car xs) (app (cdr xs) ys))) xs0 ys0
```

Note that even though xs0 and xs are dynamic the function λxs.λys.... is still static in the minimal completion. Lambdamix will loop infinitely by unfolding the recursive applications of app. To avoid infinite unfolding, the recursive application (app (cdr xs) ys) must be annotated as dynamic, which forces the whole expression fix λapp.... to be annotated as dynamic. This means that no computation can be done by terminating partial evaluation.

In this particular example, specialization of the named function app with respect to first-order data ys0 = '(c d) could be obtained by simple methods but to get a general solution to this class of problems we must also consider specialization with respect to higher-order values, i.e., functions. We shall return to this in [12, Chapter 10].

6.1 Optimality of Lambdamix

Lambdamix has been tested on several interpreters derived from denotational language definitions [5]. Such interpreters are compositional in the program argument, which means that recursive calls in the interpreter can be safely unfolded when the interpreter is specialized with respect to a concrete source program. Lambdamix often performs well on interpreters fulfilling compositionality, and is often able to specialize away interpretive overhead such as syntactic dispatch, environment lookups, etc.

A compelling example: when the self-interpreter from Figure 1 (after removing all tagging and untagging operations) is specialized with respect to a lambda expression e, the residual program is an expression e' which is *identical* to e modulo renaming of variables and insignificant coding of base function applications. Thus Lambdamix is nearly optimal as defined in [12, Chapter 6]. (A small difference: the call: (+ e₁ e₂) is transformed into (apply '+ e₁ e₂), etc. The problem can be fully eliminated by treating base functions as free variables, bound in the initial environment [5] or by a simple post processing like in [12, Chapter 10].)

7   Binding-time analysis by type inference

An intuitively natural approach to binding-time analysis for the lambda calculus uses a variant of the classical Algorithm W for polymorphic type inference [5, 16, 22]. The guiding principle is that the static parts of an annotated program must be well-typed. This naturally leads to an algorithm that tries to type a given program in its given type environment.

If this succeeds, all is well and specialization can proceed. If type inference fails, the application of a user-defined or base function that led to the type conflict is made dynamic (i.e. an underline is added), and the process is repeated. Eventually, enough underlines will be added to make the whole well-typed and so suitable for specialization.

We only give an example for brevity, since the next section contains a much more efficient algorithm. Recall the power program of Example 1:

```
(fix λp.λn'.λx'.
```

```
    if (= n' 0) then 1
    else (* x' (p (- n' 1) x'))) n x
```

with initial type environment $\tau = [n \mapsto S, x \mapsto D]$. At the if, Algorithm W works with the type environment:

$$[p \mapsto (S \to D \to \alpha), n' \mapsto S, x' \mapsto D, n \mapsto S, x \mapsto D]$$

where α is an as yet unbound type variable. Thus expression (p (- n' 1) x') has type α, which is no problem. This leads, however, to a type conflict in expression (* x' (p (- n' 1) x')) since static operator * has type $S \times S \to S$, in conflict with x', which has type D.

The problem is resolvable by changing * to *, with type $D \times D \to D$. This forces $\alpha = D$ so the else expression has type D. The single remaining conflict, that 1 has type $S \neq D$, is easily resolved by changing the 1 to lift 1, or by underlining it. The first solution leads to the annotation of Example 1.

8   BTA by solving constraints

Due to space constraints, the reader is referred to [12, Chapter 8] for this section.

9   Correctness of Lambdamix

Due to space constraints, the reader is referred to [12, Chapter 8] for this section.

10   Subsequent Work [thanks to John Hatcliff]

Due to its simplicity, aspects of lambda-mix have been widely used for exploring foundation issues such as correctness of binding-time analysis and specialization, binding-time improvements, and specialization of programs with computational effects.

10.1   Basic correctness issues

As noted in the introduction, Mogensen [17] presented a self-applicable offline partial evaluator for the pure lambda-calculus. His specification of binding-time analysis using a two-level language is essentially the same as the one used with lambda-mix. However, the specializer is more compact (and thus somewhat harder to decipher) since program terms are represented by higher-order abstract syntax. Wand [26] subsequently carried out a thorough investigation of the correctness issues for the partial evaluator and binding-time analysis of Mogensen. Mogensen has also defined an online self-applicable partial evaluator for the pure lambda calculus [18].

Palsberg [24] gives an alternative view of correctness of binding-time analysis for lambda-terms. In his presentation, correctness is not based on a single definition of specialization. Instead he gives conditions that an arbitrary specializer and binding-time analysis must satisfy if they are to avoid producing "confused redexes", i.e., situations where the specializer can "go wrong" (see Section 3).

Hatcliff [6] defines an alternate specification of the lambda-mix specializer using operational semantics and shows how this allows correctness to be mechanically checked using the Elf implementation of the logical framework LF [25]

10.2   Two-level languages

Two-level languages, as used in Flemming Nielson's work in abstract interpretation, were adapted by Gomard and Jones to define well-formedness of lambda-mix's annotated programs and to direct the actions of the specializer. The lambda-mix development was independent of Nielson and Nielson's [22].

Oddly, paper [22] has no references to Copenhagen's work in partial evaluation, which includes the invention of the term "binding-time analysis" and its first use in practice. The framework used in [22] has somewhat different assumptions about static-dynamic divisions and typing, making it unsuitable for lambda-mix in particular, or for self-applicable partial evaluation in general.

Since [22], the Nielsons have refined the theory of two-level languages [23], and extended it in several directions.

More recently, Moggi [21] has given a category-theoretic semantics for variants of the two-level language used in lambda-mix and in [22].

10.3   Binding-time analysis algorithms

The original binding-time analysis algorithm for lambda-mix was derived from the well-known type inference algorithm called "algorithm W" [16]. Henglein subsequently developed an constraint-solving algorithm that runs in almost-linear time [9]. Many partial evaluators (including the Similix system – See Chapter 12 of [12]) implement binding-time analysis using adaptations of Henglein's algorithm.

10.4   Binding-time improvements and continuation-based specialization

Many studies of binding-time improvements have used lambda-mix style specialization as a foundation. Danvy, Malmkjær, and Palsberg investigate dataflow binding-time improvements based on eta-redexes [3] (see also Palsberg's article in this volume). Lawall and Danvy show how control-flow binding-time improvements can be incorporated using control operators shift and reset [13]. Bondorf and Dussart present a hand-written continuation-based cogen for the lambda-calculus [1].

10.5   Dealing with computational effects

Naively incorporating language features that cause side-effects (such as I/O and update of mutable variables) into lambda-mix leads to unsound specialization. Hatcliff and Danvy [8, 7] give a formal presentation of offline partial evaluation for both the call-by-name and call-by-value lambda-calculus using Moggi's monadic metalanguage [20]. This provides a foundation for specializing programs with computational effects and provides a category-theoretic explanation of previous work on control-based binding-time improvements.

Lawall and Thiemann [14] give an alternate presentation for call-by-value lambda-terms using Moggi's computational lambda-calculus [19]. Their approach has the effect of extending lambda-mix with a **let**-construct an introducing extra reduction rules (based on the laws of monads) that ensure sound specialization in the presence of any computational effect that can be described using a monad.

10.6   Other approaches to specializing the lambda-terms

Danvy has described how the same effect as lambda-mix style specialization can be obtained using "type-directed partial evaluation" [2] (also see the article by Danvy in this volume). Type-directed partial evaluation is in essence a normalization procedure that works by systematically eta-expanding terms as directed by their type.

Also emphasizing types, Hughes [10] has shown how specialization of functional programs can be carried out using type inference. His approach was motivated by the desire to avoid producing the unnecessary type tag manipulation in residual programs that often appears when specializing an interpreter written in a strongly typed language. Lambda-mix is untyped and so does not suffer from this problem, but like any untyped language involves substantial run-time type tag checking.

11   Exercises

Some of the exercises involve finding a minimal completion. The formal algorithm to do this is targeted for an efficient implementation and is not suited to be executed by hand (for other than very small examples). So if not otherwise stated just use good sense for finding minimal completions.

Exercise 1. Find a minimal completion for the lambda expression listed below given the binding-time assumptions $\tau = [\text{m0} \mapsto S, \text{n0} \mapsto D]$. Specialize the program with respect to m0 = 42.

$\quad (\lambda \text{m}.\lambda \text{n}.+ \text{ m n}) \text{ m0 n0}$

Exercise 2. Find a minimal completion for the lambda expression listed below given the binding-time assumptions $\tau = [\text{x0} \mapsto S, \text{xs0} \mapsto S, \text{vs0} \mapsto D]$. Specialize the program with respect to x0 = c and xs0 = (a b c d).

```
(fix
λlookup.λx.λxs.λvs.
if (null? xs)
   then 'error
   else if (equal? x (car xs))
        then (car vs)
        else (lookup x (cdr xs) (cdr vs))) x0 xs0 vs0
```

Exercise 3. In the previous book chapters, a self-interpreter sint has been defined by

$$[\![\text{sint}]\!]_L \ p \ d = [\![p]\!]_L \ d$$

Define sint, basing it on $\mathcal{E}$ for instance, such that this equation holds for the lambda calculus.

Exercise 4.

1. Write a self-interpreter sint for the lambda calculus by transforming the function $\mathcal{E}$ into a lambda expression fix $\lambda\mathcal{E}.\lambda e.\lambda\rho.\text{if} \dots e'$ ρ' with free variables e' and ρ'.
2. Find a minimal completion for sint given binding-time assumptions $\tau = [\text{env}' \mapsto S, \rho' \mapsto D]$.
3. Find a minimal completion for sint given binding-time assumptions $\tau = [\text{env}' \mapsto S, \rho' \mapsto (S \rightarrow D)]$.
4. Specialize sint with respect to the power program in Section 2. The free variables e' and ρ' of sint shall have the following static values: e' = ((fix $\lambda p.\lambda n'.\lambda x'. \dots$) n x) and $\rho' = [n \mapsto n, x \mapsto x]$.

Exercise 5. Implement the partial evaluator from Figure 3 in a programming language of your own choice.

Exercise 6. * Implement the partial evaluator from Figure 3 in the lambda calculus. It might be a good idea to implement the self-interpreter first and then extend it to handle the two-level expressions. Use the partial evaluator to specialize sint with respect to various lambda expressions. Is the partial evaluator optimal? Try self-application of the partial evaluator.

Exercise 7.

1. At the end of Section 2 is listed how the lambda calculus interpreter in [12, Section 3.1] has been revised to obtain that in Figure 1. How do these revisions affect the residual programs produced by partial evaluation of these interpreters?
2. What further revisions would be necessary to achieve optimality?

Exercise 8. Prove that residual programs are identical for completions te₁ and te₂ if te₁ $\sqsubseteq$ te₂ and te₂ $\sqsubseteq$ te₁. Discuss the impact of different choices on efficiency of the partial evaluation process itself.

References

1. Anders Bondorf and Dirk Dussart. Improving cps-based partial evaluation: Writing cogen by hand. In *ACM SIGPLAN Workshop on Partial Evaluation and Semantics-Based Program Manipulation*, volume 94/9 of *Technical Report*, pages 1–9. University of Melbourne, Australia, 1994.
2. Olivier Danvy. Pragmatics of type-directed partial evaluation. In Olivier Danvy, Robert Glück, and Peter Thiemann, editors, *Partial Evaluation*, volume 1110 of *Lecture Notes in Computer Science*, pages 73–94. Springer-Verlag, 1996.
3. Olivier Danvy, Karoline Malmkjær, and Jens Palsberg. The essence of eta-expansion in partial evaluation. *Lisp and Symbolic Computation*, 8(3):209–227, 1995.
4. C.K. Gomard. Partial type inference for untyped functional programs. In *1990 ACM Conference on Lisp and Functional Programming, Nice, France*, pages 282–287. ACM, 1990.
5. C.K. Gomard and N.D. Jones. A partial evaluator for the untyped lambda-calculus. *Journal of Functional Programming*, 1(1):21–69, January 1991.
6. John Hatcliff. Mechanically verifying the correctness of an offline partial evaluator. In Manuel Hermenegildo and S. Doaitse Swierstra, editors, *Proceedings of the Seventh International Symposium on Programming Languages, Implementations, Logics and Programs*, number 982 in Lecture Notes in Computer Science, pages 279–298, Utrecht, The Netherlands, September 1995.
7. John Hatcliff. Foundations of partial evaluation of functional programs with computational effects. *ACM Computing Surveys*, 1998. (in press).
8. John Hatcliff and Olivier Danvy. A computational formalization for partial evaluation. *Mathematical Structures in Computer Science*, 7:507–541, 1997. Special issue devoted to selected papers from the *Workshop on Logic, Domains, and Programming Languages*. Darmstadt, Germany. May, 1995.
9. Fritz Henglein. Efficient type inference for higher-order binding-time analysis. In J. Hughes, editor, *FPCA*, pages 448–472. 5th ACM Conference, Cambridge, MA, USA, Berlin: Springer-Verlag, August 1991. Lecture Notes in Computer Science, Vol. 523.
10. John Hughes. Type specialisation for the λ-calculus; or a new paradigm for partial evaluation based on type inference. In Olivier Danvy, Robert Glück, and Peter Thiemann, editors, *Partial Evaluation*, volume 1110 of *Lecture Notes in Computer Science*, pages 183–215. Springer-Verlag, 1996.
11. J. Hatcliff. An introduction to partial evaluation using a simple flowchart language. *This volume*, 1998.
12. N.D. Jones, C. Gomard, P. Sestoft. *Partial Evaluation and Automatic Program Generation*. Prentice Hall, 1993.
13. Julia L. Lawall and Olivier Danvy. Continuation-based partial evaluation. *LFP*, pages 227–238, 1994.
14. Julia L. Lawall and Peter Thiemann. Sound specialization in the presence of computational effects. In *Proceedings of Theoretical Aspects of Computer Software*, Lecture Notes in Computer Science, September 1997. (to appear).
15. R. Milner. A theory of type polymorphism in programming. *Journal of Computer and System Sciences*, 17:348–375, 1978.
16. R. Milner, M. Tofte, and R. Harper. *The Definition of Standard ML*. Cambridge, MA: MIT Press, 1990.

17. T. Mogensen. Self-applicable partial evaluation for pure lambda calculus. In *Partial Evaluation and Semantics-Based Program Manipulation, San Francisco, California, June 1992. (Technical Report YALEU/DCS/RR-909, Yale University)*, pages 116–121, 1992.

18. T. Æ. Mogensen. Self-applicable online partial evaluation of the pure lambda calculus. In William L. Scherlis, editor, *Proceedings of PEPM '95*, pages 39–44. ACM, ACM Press, 1995.

19. Eugenio Moggi. Computational lambda-calculus and monads. In *Proceedings of the Fourth Annual IEEE Symposium on Logic in Computer Science*, pages 14–23, Pacific Grove, California, June 1989. IEEE Computer Society Press.

20. Eugenio Moggi. Notions of computation and monads. *Information and Computation*, 93:55–92, 1991.

21. Eugenio Moggi. A categorical account of two-level languages. In *Mathematical Foundations of Programming Semantics*, Technical Report, pages 199–212. Electronic Notes in Theoretical Computer Science, 1997.

22. H.R. Nielson and F. Nielson. Automatic binding time analysis for a typed λ-calculus. *Science of Computer Programming*, 10:139–176, 1988.

23. H.R. Nielson and F. Nielson. Two-Level Functional Languages. *Cambridge University Press*, 1992. Cambridge Tracts in Theoretical Computer Science **vol. 34**.

24. Jens Palsberg. Correctness of binding-time analysis. *Journal of Functional Programming*, 3(3):347–363, 1993.

25. Frank Pfenning. Logic programming in the LF logical framework. In Gérard Huet and Gordon Plotkin, editors, *Logical Frameworks*, pages 149–181. Cambridge University Press, 1991.

26. M. Wand. Specifying the correctness of binding-time analysis. In *Twentieth ACM Symposium on Principles on Programming Languages, Charleston, South Carolina*, pages 137–143. New York: ACM, 1993.

Partial Evaluation of Hardware

Satnam Singh[1] and Nicholas McKay[2]

[1] Xilinx Inc., San Jose, California 95124-3450, U.S.A.
Satnam.Singh@xilinx.com

[2] Dept. Computing Science, The University of Glasgow, G12 8QQ, U.K.
nicholas@dcs.gla.ac.uk

Abstract. The preliminary results of dynamically specialising Xilinx XC6200 FPGA circuits using partial evaluation are presented. This method provides a systematic way to manage to complexity of dynamic reconfiguration in the special case where a general circuit is specialised with respect to one input which changes more slowly than the other inputs.

1   Introduction

Imagine a decryption circuit with two inputs: the key and the data to be decrypted. The key (typically a few bytes) changes infrequently with respect to the data (megabytes). Imagine at run-time being able to specialise this circuit every time the key changes, *calculating* a circuit that decrypts only for the given key. This would incur a run-time cost i.e. the calculation needed to specialise the circuit description and then reconfigure the device. But in return it computes a circuit with a shorter critical path, allowing data to be decrypted faster. This paper describes a project which is developing technology to achieve exactly this kind of fine grain dynamic circuit specialisation.

Rather than solving the general problem of how to perform dynamic synthesis, we first select a special case of dynamic reconfiguration which is an easier problem to solve. In particular, we are researching how to specialise circuits systematically by taking a general circuit and some data known at run-time and then using this to *transform* the general circuit into a specialised circuit. By trying to solve this simpler problem which has useful structure and properties, we hope to get insight into how to solve more general problems in the area of dynamic reconfiguration.

Instead of devising a totally new methodology for dynamic circuit specialisation, we have borrowed from existing ideas in the areas of off-line constant propagation from HDL compiler technology and from partial evaluation techniques developed for the run-time specialisation of software.

We describe all the stages that make up our dynamic specialisation process, from high level language descriptions down to the level of programming data bits and multiplexor reconfigurations, allowing others to reproduce our experiments.

We also describe how we verify circuits that are modified at run-time, which is an issue which is often overlooked when one is typically struggling just to effect dynamic reconfiguration at all.

2   FPGAs

Field Programmable Gate Arrays are chips that typically comprise of a grid of cells
that can be programmed to assume a given logic function, and an interconnection network for connecting cells together to form large digital systems.

The XC6200™ FPGA chips being used in our project can have their configuration state mapped onto the address space of the host system, so that reconfiguration
under software control is as simple as assigning to variables in a program. This allows
the dynamic reprogramming of subsections of the FPGA, even while the remainder of
the chip is running. Circuits may be swapped into and out of the FPGA at will and at
high speed. An analogy with virtual memory is appealing, and we call this technique
virtual hardware.

However in addition to swapping in static, pre-compiled circuits, one could imagine synthesising circuits *dynamically*, on a need to use basis, before downloading them
to the FPGA at run-time. For example, consider the example from the introduction of
a device designed to decrypt a data stream with a given key. For each new session key,
a specialised circuit can be dynamically synthesised which decrypts the associated
stream with the relevant key. This circuit will be smaller and faster than a general circuit which stores the key in a register.

How we exploit this novel idea is illustrated by the following example. Here is a
simple 5 by 6 bit parallel multiplier circuit shown as a stylised XC6200 design:

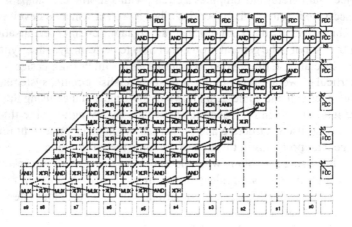

Figure 1   A stylised description of a shift-add multiplier

Assume we know at run-time that input b is going to be 6 for many subsequent
iterations. It might therefore pay off to specialise this circuit at that time to:

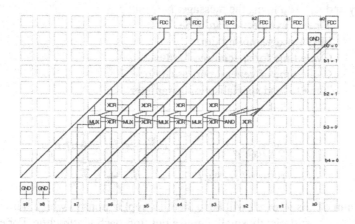

Figure 2 A shift-add multiplier specialised to multiply by 6

The circuit has been reduced to simply one addition operation and several long wires; the b register has disappeared. The critical path is now much shorter than the general parallel multiplier. No attempt has been made to compact cells; the specialised circuit still occupies the same area but it goes much faster.

In an experiment we used a partial evaluator proto-type developed at Glasgow University that can take a general shift-add 8-bit multiplier and specialise by performing run-time constant propagation. Th general 8-bit multiplier has a critical path of 123ns. By propagating the constant 20 as the multiplicand through the general circuit and then modifying the programming information for the affected cells, yiels a design with a critical path of 53ns. The extreme case of propagating the multiplicand of 2 yields a circuit with a critical path of 11ns i.e. about ten times faster than the general circuit. It is exactly these kind of optimisations that we hope to achieve in an economical manner at run-time.

In this approach, the important question is when the cost of calculating new configurations are amortised over sufficient time to make the approach worthwhile. Consider a data stream consisting of a specialisation parameter followed by n data items:

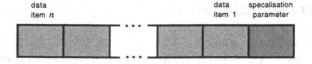

In the encryption example mentioned above the specialisation parameter would be the key and the data items the message. Now suppose:

Ts   Time to synthesise hardware
Tp   FPGA programming time
Tc   Cycle time for specialised hardware
Tg   Cycle time of general purpose device
Tk   Time to load specialisation parameter

We are concerned with the ratio:

$$\frac{dynamic}{conventional} = \frac{(T_s + T_p) + nT_c}{T_k + nT_g}$$

One aim of this research will be to identify applications in which n is sufficiently large and Tc=Tg sufficiently small to make our approach worthwhile. For example, a circuit realising the DES ('Data Encryption Standard') [3] algorithm has the very useful property that under specialisation the combinatorial logic associated with the generation of the key schedule and transposition stages can be converted to a sequence of inverters, which them-selves can then be absorbed into a modified S-box. In this case 768 gates will have been replaced by wires and (in a design without pipelining) 16 gates delays removed from the critical path; Tc will be substantially smaller than Tg.

3   Low-Level Partial Evaluation

In the first stage of this project we have been implementing a very simple form of partial evaluation that corresponds to run-time constant propagation. By propagating known values at run-time, we can transform cells implementing logic functions like AND and OR into cells that just route wires, avoiding the delay incurred by going through the interior of the function block.

By turning cells into wires we get worthwhile time saving, but further savings are possible when we can spot that four cells in a 4x4 block are all converted into wires. This allows us to concatenate these 4 single cell wires into one length 4 flyover wire. This kind of optimisation brings to greatest time savings since a single length 4 wires has a very small delay.

4   A Simple Partial Evaluator

This section describes the implementation of a partial evaluator using the Xilinx XC6216 chip on the VCC Hotworks XC6200 board. This is a PCI board which contains an XC6200 FPGA and some static RAM. The RAM can be accessed over the bus or via the XC6216 chip.

Downloading the general design to the board is done via a CAL file. This file contains a series of address data pairs. The 16-bit address points to one of the XC6216 configuration registers. These registers control the function unit logic and the routing multiplexers on the chip.

In order to have access to the routing information we developed a program which partially evaluated the design at the CAL file level.

The C++ program sets up a structure which stores information on a net.

```
struct Net
{ unsigned short x, y ;
  unsigned short inv ;
} ;
```

The x and y variables store the co-ordinate of the nets source or destination cell. The inv variable contains how many inversions the net has gone through. In the XC6200 architecture many of the routing multiplexors perform an inversion on their output signal. This is important when we come to perform the partial evaluation.

A NetListNode structure is also defined. This enables us to build up a linked list of nets using the AddNetListNode function.

```
struct NetListNode ;
typedef NetListNode *NetList ;
struct NetListNode
{ Net net ;
  NetList next ;
} ;
void AddNetListNode (NetList &nl, Net net)
{ NetList NewNodeRef ;
  NewNodeRef = new NetListNode ;
  NewNodeRef->next = nl ;
  NewNodeRef->net = net ;
  nl = NewNodeRef ;
} ;
```

The **Cell** class is used to store information on the inputs to each cell on the FPGA, the logic function that the cell implements and to what cells its outputs are routed to. It contains the following data members.

```
CellFunction f ;
CellFunction old_f ;
NetList OutputList ;
Net x1, x2, x3 ;
Net old_x1, old_x2, old_x3 ;
unsigned short y2, y3 ;
unsigned short old_y2, old_y3 ;
void AddOutput (Net n) ;
  { AddNetListNode (OutputList, n) ; }
NetList GetOutputList () ;
  { return OutputList ; }
```

The OutputList is a linked list of nets, built up using the AddNetListN-ode function. This contains information on all the locations that the output of a cell is routed to.

The variables x1, x2, x3, y2 and y3 hold information on the inputs to the FPGA cell. Figure 3 shows a schematic of the cell structure. The x1, x2 and x3 variables hold the nets that are routed to the cell's X1, X2 and X3 inputs. The y2 and y3 variables hold information on the inversions applied to the inputs by the multiplexors on the left of the figure.

From knowledge of the x and y inputs the cell function can be deduced. This is stored in the variable f. The cell function can be any of the values listed in Table 1.

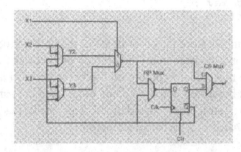

Figure 3 The architecture of an XC6200 FPGA cell

During the partial evaluation stage a list of the cells that have been changed is built up. To re-program the general circuit onto the chip the program needs to hold a copy of each cells non-partially evaluated function and inputs. This data is held in the old_f, old_x1, old_x2, old_x3, old_y2 and old_y3 variables. When the general circuit is to be re-loaded the program looks through the list of changed cells and re-programs them according to the data held in these variables.

The class also contains an AddOutput function to add nodes to a cells output list and a GetOutputList function to enable the program to access the cells outputs.

4.1   Class Initialisation

The partial evaluation program sets up a NxN array of **Cell** objects, where NxN is the number of cells on the chip. To obtain the data to write into the class members the program first connects to the VCC board and initializes the XC6216 chip. It then asks the user for a CAL file to download. The information in the **Cell** class is built up from the data that is sent to each of the configuration registers on the chip.

4.2   Constant Propagation

Once a picture of the general circuit has been constructed the program can use constant propagation to optimize the circuit. This technique is described below.

Firstly, a net is labelled as being constant. The program then examines the data in all the **Cell** objects that the net is input to. For each net destination the program calls a function which performs the following steps:
•   Finds out the value of the constant at the input to the cell. This depends on two

things: The constant that the net was set to and the number of inversions that it goes through between it's source and destination.

* Retrieves the function of the cell from the **Cell** object.

The function then uses the above information to optimize the cell.

Figure 3 shows an example where the cell performs an AND function on the inputs a and b. If the constant input, a, is 0 at the input then the cell is reconfigured to output a zero. If the input is 1 then the cell is reprogrammed to be a buffer. The input to the buffer is provided by the other, non-constant input, b.

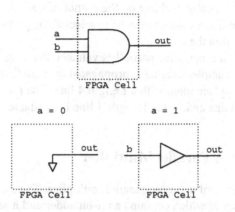

Figure 4 Optimisation of AND Cell.

The code shown below performs the optimisation. `value_a` is the constant input, while fn holds a local copy of the `cell_function` variable. `cell[i][j]` is the cell object at co-ordinates (i,j).

```
if (fn == AND2) {
    if (value_a == ZERO) {
        cell[i][j].cell_function = ZERO;
        setFunction(i,j,ZERO, cell[i][j].input_a);
        return ZERO;
    }
    else if (value_a == ONE) {
        cell[i][j].cell_function = BUF;
        setFunction(i, j, BUF, cell[i][j].input_b);
        return BUF;
    }
}
```

The cell is reprogrammed by setFunction. This takes as its arguments the co-ordinates of the cell, the new function and, in the case of a buffer, the non-constant input

input_b. The function reprograms the x1, x2, x3, y2 and y3 inputs to the cell's function unit, altering it's operation.

In the case of a buffer the setFunction function also tries to bypass the function unit completely. This is possible if the non-constant input arrives at the cell via one of the nearest neighbour routes. These routes (north, south, east and west) can be switched directly to the cell's output. This results in a bigger speed improvement.

If the result of the optimisation is a cell with a constant output the destinations of the cell are optimised. This process continues until no more reductions are possible.

4.3   Program Operation

The user can chose to partially evaluate on the output of a single cell or on the output of a column of cells. When a column of cells is selected the partial evaluation process is repeated for each cell in the column.

After all the constant inputs are partially evaluated the program looks for further optimisations. If, for example, a signal is propagated through four inverters or buffers it may be possible to replace them with a Length 4 line. The program checks through the circuit for such chains and, if the Length 4 line is available, reprograms the chip accordingly.

5   Case Study: A Parallel Multiplier

Figure 3 gives the layout of a simple parallel multiplier. The multiplier consists of a series of columns, each of which contains an n-bit adder and n AND gates. A N-bit by M-bit multiplier contains M columns each containing an N-bit adder. In the first column each bit of N is ANDed with the LSB of M and the result input into the adder. The other input of the adder is set to zero. The LSB of the adder output is routed to the LSB of the final output. In the next column each bit of N is ANDed with the next bit of M and input to the adder. The other input is given by bits 1 to N of the previous adders result and the final carry. This process is repeated M times.

If we partially evaluate on the M input then when a bit of M is zero the adder and the AND gates in the Mth column disappear. When M is equal to one then the AND gates are reduced to buffers.

A test circuit consisting of a multiplier fed from two input registers has been designed. The output from the multiplier is fed to an output register. All the registers are clocked by two pulses. The first pulse writes the input values to the registers, the second samples the multipliers output.

Table 2: gives the speed-up results for an 8-bit by 8-bit multiplier with the M input partially evaluated to a selection of constant values. The non-p.e. (non partially evaluated) row gives the maximum clock speed for the general multiplier circuit. The p.e. row gives the maximum clock speed after partial evaluation. Figure 5 displays the information in bar graph format.

Table 1. Multiplier Specialisation

	times 1	times 2	times 8	times 85
p.e.	23.5 MHz	23.5 MHz	23 MHz	16 MHz
non-p.e.	14 MHz	16.5 MHz	16 MHz	15 MHz
	times 126	times 128	times 170	times 255
p.e.	13.5 MHz	20 MHz	16 MHz	11 MHz
non-p.e.	11 MHz	14.5 MHz	13.5 MHz	11 MHz

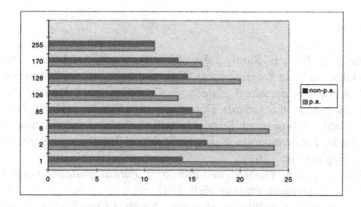

Figure 5 Data from Table 2: in bar graph form.

6   Summary and Future Work

We have developed a proto-type partial evaluator which actually performs run-time constant propagation with the XC6200 devices. However, the first proto-type takes too long to calculate circuit specialisations. Now that we have the technology to actually perform dynamic reconfiguration, we are investigating new algorithms and data structures which speed up partial evaluation.

So far we have achieved only modest speed improvements using localised partial evaluation and performing just one pass over the circuit. However, we are confident of achieving far better speed improvements by concatenating single wires into longer wires e.g. by using length 4 fly-overs. The implementation of a scheme for performing on-line partial evaluation is in itself a significant research result.

We are currently formalising and verifying the partial evaluation algorithm. Then we can use traditional verification techniques (formal or otherwise) on the general circuit and be reasonable confident of dynamically synthesising correct circuits.

Another barrier to immediately deploying this work in real systems is that we currently have no accurate way of knowing how fast a specialised circuit executes. To perform traditional timing analysis at run-time would take too long. We are investigating techniques for combining partial timing information quickly at run-time to get a safe estimate for the circuit delay. Once we have refined our run-time specialiser to operate quickly enough, we shall then concentrate further on the timing problem. Another alternative is to produce asynchronous circuits, perhaps realised on a special asynchronous FPGA.

All the circuits in this project have been described in the Lava language, which is a variant of the Ruby [6] algebraic hardware description language. This allows us to control circuit layout in a convenient manner [8]. In the future, we may consider porting our partial evaluation technology to VHDL descriptions.

This work is part of a project funded by EPSRC and the United Kingdom Ministry of Defence (MoD), managed by Satnam Singh (Xilinx Inc.), Tom Melham (University of Glasgow) and Derek McAuley (Microsoft Research Labs, Cambridge). "XC6200" is a trademark of Xilinx Inc.

References

1. T. Kean, B. New, B. Slous. *A Multiplier for the XC6200*. Sixth International Workshop on Field Programmable Logic and Applications. Darmstadt, 1996.
2. H. T. Kung. *Why Systolic Architectures*. IEEE Computer. January 1982.
3. National Bureau of Standards. *Data Encryption Standard* (DES), Technical Report, National Bureau of Standards (USA), Federal Information Processing Standards, Publication 46, National Technical Information Services, Springfield, Virginia, April 1997.
4. N. D. Jones, C. K. Gomard, and P. Sestoft, *Partial Evaluation and Automatic Program Generation*, Prentice-Hall, 1993.
5. Jason Leonard and William H. Mangione-Smith. *A Case Study of Partially Evaluated Hardware Circuits: Key-Specific DES*. FPL'97. 1997.
6. M. Sheeran, G. Jones. *Circuit Design in Ruby*. Formal Methods for VLSI Design, J. Stanstrup, North Holland, 1992.
7. Satnam Singh and Pierre Bellec. *Virtual Hardware for Graphics Applications using FPGAs*. FCCM'94. IEEE Computer Society, 1994.
8. Satnam Singh. Architectural Descriptions for FPGA Circuits. FCCM'95. IEEE Computer Society. 1995.
9. Michael J. Wirthlin and Brad L. Hutchings. *Improving Functional Density Through Run-Time Constant Propagation*. FPGA'97. 1997.
10. Xilinx. *XC6200 FPGA Family Data Sheet*. Xilinx Inc. 1995.

Partial Evaluation in Aircraft Crew Planning*

Lennart Augustsson

Carlstedt Research & Technology
Stora badhusgatan 18-20
S-411 21 Göteborg, Sweden
Email: augustss@carlstedt.se
WWW: http://www.carlstedt.se/ augustss
and
Department of Computing Sciences
Chalmers University of Technology
S-412 96 Göteborg, Sweden
Email: augustss@cs.chalmers.se
WWW: http://www.cs.chalmers.se/ augustss

1 Introduction

Next to fuel costs, crew costs are the largest direct operating cost of airlines. In 1991 American Airlines reported spending $1.3 billion on crew [AGPT91]. Other major airlines have similar costs. Therefore much work has been devoted to the planning and scheduling of crews over the last thirty years.

The planning of aircrafts and crews in large airlines is a very complex problem, see [AHKW97] for a good overview. To make the problem tractable it is normally divided into four parts.

Construct timetable First, the time table is produced with the objective to match the expectations of the marketing department with the available fleets and other constraints. The output of this process is a number of legs (non-stop flights) which the airline decides to operate.

Fleet assignment Second, aircrafts are allocated to the legs. Again there must be a match between expected number of passengers and goods and the available aircraft fleets. The output of this problem is the timetable augmented with aircraft information.

Crew pairing Third, pairings are constructed. A pairing is a sequence of flight legs for an unspecified crew member starting and ending at the same crew base. Such a sequence is often called a CRew Rotation (CRR). The crew member will normally be working on these legs, but a pairing may also contain

---

* First appeared in *Proceedings of ACM SIGPLAN Symposium on Partial Evaluation and Semantics-Based Program Manipulation, PEPM '97*, pages 127–136 [Aug97].
© 1997 ACM, Inc., New York. Reprinted by permission.

legs where the crew member is just transported. Such a leg is called a deadhead. Legs are naturally grouped into duty periods (working days) called RoTation Days (RTD). Each rotation day is separated by a lay-over (an overnight stop). Legal pairings must satisfy a large number of governmental regulations and collective agreements which vary from airline to airline. The output of this phase is a set of pairings covering the legs in the timetable.

Crew assignment   The fourth planning problem is to assign pairings to named individuals. This is the crew assignment or rostering problem. The objective is to cover the pairings from the previous stage as well as training requirements, vacations, etc. while satisfying work rules and regulations.

Carmen Systems AB markets a system that handles the last two parts of the planning problem. The system is in use in most of the major European airlines. The optimiser runs in stages, first it generates a large number of possible pairings (using some clever heuristics [HE96], second it selects a subset of these that covers all the legs that should be scheduled, and does it to a minimal cost. The second part is a huge set covering problem, [Wed95]. Each covering (potential solution) needs to be checkedso that if fulfils all the rules mentioned above. A run of the optimizer is a computationally heavy job; a run may take from a few minutes to a few days of computer time. It is important to make this a fast as possible, since this enables more tries to find a good solution to be made (finding good solution usually requires some manual "tweaking" and rerunning the optimizer). Testing of rule validity usually takes up the largest part of the computation time so any improvement of it will be beneficial.

The rules in the Carmen system are expressed in a special language (described below). A complete rule set is usually rather large, containing thousands of lines, because it covers all fleets, long haul, short haul, all crew categories, different union agreements, scheduling standards, etc. However, when a particular problem is to be solved, only a subset of the rules are really needed, because the problem may only be for a particular crew category, on a specific aircraft type etc.

So we have a large program (the rule set) where some of the input data is known (such as the crew category etc), this spells: *partial evaluation*.

2   The rule language

To express the rules that affect the legality and costs of different solutions to the planning problem, Carmen Systems has developed a proprietary language, the Carmen Rule Language (CRL), [Boh90]. CRL can be said to be a pure, "zeroth order", strongly types, functional language. "Zeroth order" because the language does not have any functions, except a few built in ones. The evaluation of the rules also uses a form of lazy evaluation, but that is of no consequence for us.

A leg has a number of attributes. Some of these attributes, e.g., *aircraft type*, *arrival time*, and *departure time*, are given for each leg. Other attributes, e.g., *length of flight*, are computed from the given ones. It is these calculations that the rule language describes.

The input to a rule evaluation is a set of pairings, i.e., a number CRRs where each CRR contains of a number of RTDs. Each RTD contains a number of legs. The task of a rule evaluation is to find out if the given set of CRRs is legal or not. (If it is legal, a cost is also computed, but that is less important here.) In each of the legs, RTDs, and CRRs some attributes are given, but most of them are computed from other attributes.

In our examples we will use a different syntax than the real language uses to (hopefully) make things clearer. To define externally given attributes we will write "`level.attribute :: type;`" where the level is leg, RTD, or CRR. Attributes defined in the language will be written "`level.attribute :: type = expression;`". Both the level and the type of the definitions are not really necessary since they can be deduced, but they are given for clarity. Such a definition means that for each item on the given level (leg, RTD, or CRR) an attributed will be computed according to the formula.

A rule set, or program, defines a number of attributes and rules. The rules are boolean expressions preceeded by the keyword `rule`. Checking if a solution (i.e., a grouping of legs into RTDs and CRRs) is legal amounts to checking that all the rules evaluate to true.

The types and operators of the language are fairly limited and mostly self-explanatory, so we will give no formal description of them except for the simplified grammar in Fig. 1. Two unfamiliar types are probably `AbsTime` and `RelTime`. They represent absolute times and time differences respectively.

The aggregate functions evaluate an expression a lower level and aggregate them. A where clause acts as a guard and makes it possible to only aggregate those expressions on the lower level where the guard is true. E.g., "`sum(leg, x) where(y)`" will compute (for an RTD) the sum of all the x attributes of the legs where the y attributes are true.

The language has been carefully designed so that it is impossible to write non-terminating computations and there is no way a program can fail.[1] These properties make the rule language very amenable to program transformations since ⊥ cannot occur.

2.1 Rule example

Figure 2 shows a simple rule set that expects the departure, arrival, and aircraft type to be supplied externally for each leg, whereas the blocktime[2] is computed for each leg. There is also a rule which states that the blocktime should be

---

[1] A program can in principle divide by 0, but we were told to ignore this. Divisions are very rare in "real life."

[2] Blocktime is the time from when the wheel blocks are removed at departure until they are replaced at arrival; it is considered the total time of the flight.

```
program           ::= {definition}
definition        ::= constant-definition
                   |  level-definition
                   |  rule-definition
constant-definition ::= name :: type = expression ;
level-definition  ::= level . name :: type = expression ;
rule-definition   ::= rule level . name = expression ;
type              ::= Int | Bool | String | AbsTime | RelTime
level             ::= leg | RTD | CRR
expression        ::= literal
                   |  name
                   |  expression binop expression
                   |  if expression then expression else expression
                   |  aggregate(level , expression) [where(expression)]
                   |  built-in-function(expressions)
                   |  case expressions of
                          {case-block otherwise} case-block endcase
                   |  case expressions external string-literal endcase
case-block        ::= {pattern , } pattern -> expression ;
pattern           ::= literal
                   |  literal .. literal
binop             ::= + | − | * | / | div | and | or
expressions       ::= {expression , } expression
aggregate         ::= sum | any | all | count
                   |  next | prev | first | last
```

Fig. 1. Simplified grammar for CRL.

```
leg.departure :: AbsTime;      -- The time the plane departs.
leg.arrival :: AbsTime;        -- The time the plane arrives.
leg.aircraft_type :: String;   -- Type of plane, e.g. "747"
leg.deadhead :: Bool;          -- Deadhead leg

leg.blocktime :: RelTime = arrival - departure;

rule leg.short_legs =
    blocktime < 4:00;          -- No more than 4 hours per flight
```

Fig. 2. A simple example.

```
leg.briefing :: RelTime =
    if aircraft_type = "747" then 1:00 else 0:30;
leg.debriefing :: RelTime = 0:15;


leg.worktime :: RelTime = briefing + blocktime + debriefing;

RTD.total_worktime :: RelTime = sum(leg, worktime);

max_total_worktime :: RelTime = 9:00;

rule RTD.short_days =
    total_worktime < max_total_worktime;

rule leg.even_legs =          -- No leg may be longer than half
    worktime < total_worktime / 2;      -- the work in a day.

RTD.deadheads_per_rtd :: Int = count(leg) where(deadhead);

CRR.deadheads_per_crr :: Int = sum(RTD, deadheads_per_rtd);

rule CRR.few_deadheads =     -- At most 2 deadheads in a pairing
    deadheads_per_crr < 3;
```

Fig. 3. Extension of the simple example.

---

less than 4 hours for each leg. There is no need to quantify the rule expression because is it automatically tested wherever it applies.

The extended example (Fig. 3) defines other leg attributes and, on the RTD level, total_worktime. It is defined as the sum of worktime for each leg belonging to the RTD. Sum is one of a few built in functions that aggregate data on a lower level in the hierarchy. Remember that the hierarchy is wired into the problem, and thus into the language. Therefore there are no ambiguities as to which legs to sum over for any given RTD. Note how the second rule refers to both an attribute at the leg level and at the RTD level. Since each leg belongs to exactly one RTD, there is again no ambiguity as to what RTD to use in the computation of the rule.

2.2 Tables

A lot of rule computations can be simply expressed as table lookups. CRL has a fairly powerful case construct to express this. In the case construct several values (keys) are matched simultaneously against a set of patterns. Each pattern can be a literal or a range. The patterns are only allowed to overlap if marked so explicitly. Figure 4 shows some simple examples of these table constructs. The first one determines a briefing time depending on the time of the day of the

```
leg.briefing :: RelTime =
    case time_of_day(departure) of
        00:00 .. 06:00  -> 0:15;
        06:01 .. 18:00  -> 0:30;
        18:01 .. 23:59  -> 0:20;
    endcase;

leg.minimum_ground_stop :: RelTime =
    case arrival_airport_name, deadhead, day_of_week(arrival) of
        "FRA", False, 1 .. 5  -> 1:00;
    otherwise
        _,       False, 1 .. 5  -> 0:45;
    otherwise
        _,        _,     _      -> 0:30;
    endcase;
```

Fig. 4. Some table/case expressions.

---

arrival (arrival is a AbsTime, but the time_of_day function drops the date part
of it). The second table states that the minimum ground stop is one hour if the
arrival is in Frankfurt (FRA) on a non-deadhead leg on a Monday thru Friday,
etc.

External tables To avoid repeated recompilations of a rule set, and to make it
more flexible, there is a concept of external tables. An external table is like the
case construct just described, but the case arms are not given in the rule file.
Instead they are loaded dynamically from a file at run time. Because the case
arms are not available to the compiler, this construct is less efficient.

2.3   Void

Although CRL is defined in such a way that everything terminates and there
are no failures, there is a small complication. To handle some functions (and
sometimes given attributes) that can fail there is a concept of exception, called
void. A typical expression that could give rise to *void* is "next(leg, x)" which
is supposed to give the value of the x attribute of the next leg (relative to the leg
where it is computed) within an RTD. But for the final leg in an RTD it does
not exist, so it gives the "value" *void*. If a *void* occurs in an expression it will be
propageted to the result. *Void* propagates until caught with a special language
construct.

3   Program transformations

The transformations done to the program really fall into three categories. First, the transformations that can be performed given just the program. These transformations are like constant propagation and constant folding. Second, there are the transformations that can be made given the static data from the problem. The static are most what are called *parameters*. A parameter is like a global rule constant, but it is not given at compile time, but instead at run time. External tables are also considered to be static data. The third category is those transformations that can be performed because all the legs are known.

3.1   Constant propagation and folding

A typical rule set contains many definitions that are merely constants. These constants can, of course, be substituted into the code and constant folding can be applied. This step can do much more work than one might imagine at first.

The constant folding does not only handle built in functions, but it also includes matching in case expressions. If one of the keys turns out to be a constant that means that a column of the case expression can be removed together with all the rows that did not match the key.

External tables External tables are turned into internal tables by the partial evaluator, because internal tables are more efficient. The semantics of external tables is unfortunately somewhat different from the internal tables. In an internal table no overlap is allowed between entries unless explicitly stated, however for external tables the entries are matched from top to bottom. This means that when an external table is converted to an internal one it cannot be used as is. The overlap annotation could be inserted between each entry in the resulting table, but in doing so much efficiency would be lost since the rule compiler handles non-overlapping entries much more efficiently.

Therefore the external table needs to be transformed to remove overlaps when it is converted to an internal table. This processing is complicated by the fact that in each column of a table there can be a range as well as a literal. In fact if we have a table with n columns each table entry can be thought of as defining an n-dimensional box, i.e., a rectangular parallelopiped, that defines what it matches in the n-dimensional space defined by the columns. This is the key insight in the transformation of the external tables.

As each new table entry is processed (top-down) its box is computed and from that all the boxes from the preceding entries are subtracted. The result of subtracting one box from another can always be expressed as a sum of boxes. After subtracting all preceding boxes we are left with a (possibly empty) set of boxes that correspond to non-overlapping entries with the same right-hand-side. These boxes are converted to entries which are added to the internal table.

```
leg.debriefing :: RelTime = expr;
```

Before deadhead cloning.

```
leg.debriefing :: RelTime =
    if deadhead then debriefing__dh else debriefing__ndh;
leg.debriefing__dh  :: RelTime = expr;
leg.debriefing__ndh :: RelTime = expr;
```

After deadhead cloning.

Fig. 5. A simple example.

3.2 Cloning

One of the features of partial evaluation is that it generates a different special-isation of the same function for each distinct argument. In CRL there are no functions, so the same kind of function specialisation does not carry over di-rectly. The CRL partial evaluator also does some specialisation, but it is very ad hoc.

Deadhead flights are not really part of the normal flight you want to plan, since they are only used as transport. This means that many attributes are computed in a very different way for deadhead legs compared to ordinary legs. Furthermore, the leg set contains much more precise information if the deadheads are not considered. The reason being that even if the problem at hand is to plan for a particular aircraft fleet, deadheads may happen on completely different fleets, or even on different airlines.

To handle deadheads in a good way they are treated specially during the transformation. Each definition on the leg level is split into two part, one where it assumed that **deadhead** is true and one where it is assumed that **deadhead** is false. See Fig. 5 for an example. The definition of the original attribute (**debriefing**) is inlined everywhere it occurs. The two new definitions will op-timized under the assumtion that **deadhead** is true (resp. false). The inlined **if** expressions will very often reduce to one of the branches because the value of **deadhead** is known in the local context.

3.3 Set based evaluation

In any given planning situation there is a set of legs that should be arranged into RTDs and CRRs. This means that we actually have a lot of information about the values of the externally supplied leg attributes. These leg attributes can only take on the values of the leg attributes as they appear in the flight plan.

This is really valuable information, considering many of the attributes only take on one or two different values. The reason for this is that a flight plan normally covers only a week or two of time, a limited geographical area, and a few aircraft types.

$$\begin{aligned}
\mathcal{S}[\![x]\!]\rho &= \rho x \\
\mathcal{S}[\![l]\!]\rho &= \{\mathcal{L}[\![l]\!]\} && \text{a literal} \\
\mathcal{S}[\![e_1 + e_2]\!]\rho &= \{x + y \mid x \in \mathcal{S}[\![e_1]\!], y \in \mathcal{S}[\![e_2]\!]\} \\
\mathcal{S}[\![e_1 = e_2]\!]\rho &= \{x = y \mid x \in \mathcal{S}[\![e_1]\!], y \in \mathcal{S}[\![e_2]\!]\} \\
\mathcal{S}[\![e_1 < e_2]\!]\rho &= \{x < y \mid x \in \mathcal{S}[\![e_1]\!], y \in \mathcal{S}[\![e_2]\!]\} \\
\mathcal{S}[\![e_1 \text{ and } e_2]\!]\rho &= \mathcal{S}[\![\text{if } e_1 \text{ then } e_2 \text{ else false}]\!] \\
\mathcal{S}[\![e_1 \text{ or } e_2]\!]\rho &= \mathcal{S}[\![\text{if } e_1 \text{ then true else } e_2]\!]
\end{aligned}$$

$$\mathcal{S}[\![\text{if } c \text{ then } t \text{ else } e]\!] = \begin{cases} \mathcal{S}[\![t]\!]\rho_t & \text{if } v_c = \{true\} \\ \mathcal{S}[\![e]\!]\rho_e & \text{if } v_c = \{false\} \\ \mathcal{S}[\![t]\!]\rho_t \cup \mathcal{S}[\![e]\!]\rho_e & \text{otherwise} \end{cases}$$

$$\begin{aligned}
&\text{where } v_c = \mathcal{S}[\![c]\!]\rho \\
& \rho_t = \mathcal{T}[\![c]\!]\rho \\
& \rho_e = \mathcal{F}[\![c]\!]\rho
\end{aligned}$$

$$\mathcal{S}[\![\texttt{sum}(l, e)]\!] = U_{Int}$$

$$\begin{aligned}
\mathcal{T}[\![\text{not } e]\!]\rho &= \mathcal{F}[\![e]\!]\rho \\
\mathcal{T}[\![e_1 \text{ and } e_2]\!]\rho &= \mathcal{T}[\![e_2]\!](\mathcal{T}[\![e_1]\!]\rho) \\
\mathcal{T}[\![x = l]\!]\rho &= \rho[x \mapsto \{\mathcal{L}[\![l]\!]\}] && \text{a literal} \\
\mathcal{T}[\![x < l]\!]\rho &= \rho[x \mapsto \{v \mid v \in \rho x, v < \mathcal{L}[\![l]\!]\}] && \text{a literal} \\
\mathcal{T}[\![\_]\!]\rho &= \rho && \text{otherwise} \\
\mathcal{F}[\![\text{not } e]\!]\rho &= \mathcal{T}[\![e]\!]\rho \\
\mathcal{F}[\![e_1 \text{ or } e_2]\!]\rho &= \mathcal{F}[\![e_2]\!](\mathcal{F}[\![e_1]\!]\rho) \\
\mathcal{F}[\![x = l]\!]\rho &= \rho[x \mapsto \rho x \setminus \{\mathcal{L}[\![l]\!]\}] && \text{a literal} \\
\mathcal{F}[\![x < l]\!]\rho &= \rho[x \mapsto \{v \mid v \in \rho x, v \geq \mathcal{L}[\![l]\!]\}] && \text{a literal} \\
\mathcal{F}[\![\_]\!]\rho &= \rho && \text{otherwise} \\
\mathcal{L}[\![\text{true}]\!] &= true
\end{aligned}$$

$$\vdots$$

Fig. 6. A set based evaluator.

The practical consequence of this that an expression like "if aircraft_type = "747" then x else y" can be simplified to "y" if the flight plan contains no 747 aircrafts.

These transformations are quite frequent because a rule set typically covers all of the airline's operation, so it has information about sort haul and long haul, cockpit and cabin personnel, all times of the year, etc. But a given flight plan will only use a subset of the rules because it is only about e.g., short haul cabin personnel during one week in August.

The set based transformations are based on a set evaluator. The set evaluator is like an ordinary evaluator for expressions in the language, except that the environment contains sets of values for the variables instead of single values, and that the result of evaluation is again a set. A fragment of the set evaluator is shown Fig. 6. The sets computed by the set evaluator are always as large or larger than the real set of values an expression can have.

The only interesting part of the set evaluator is the handling of if. The most naïve way would be to just take the union of the sets from the two branches. Slightly more sophisticated is to check if the condition is a singleton true or false and pick the corresponding branch if it is a singleton and otherwise take the union. However, in this case, there is actually additional information within each of the branches; the condition is known to hold or not to hold.

This means that when evaluating "if x=5 then e1 else e2" within the then branch, x is known to be 5, and within the else branch it is known not to be 5. The use of these facts account for the change of environment in the evaluation of the branches. The environment modification function looks for relational operations on variables to modify the environment. You can imagine a much more much sophisticated analysis which keeps track of the condition and then uses it as a premise for a theorem prover within each branch. We currently do not implement this since it looks like it would have little practical impact.

The set evaluator in Fig. 6 does not handle *void*. *Void* could be seen as an ordinary value in the set, but it can, of course, not take part of any arithmetic or other operations. *Void* also needs to be handled specially since even if we need to use the worst possible approximation (like for sum), i.e., the universal set, we still want to know if *void* can be part of it or not.

Using the set evaluator as a tool, it is possible to transform the program. For each subexpression the set evaluator is invoked. If it yields a singleton value, this value replaces the subexpression. If it does not yield a single value, the parts of the subexpressions are examined and transformed in the same way. After such a pass over the whole program, the constant propagation and constant folding can be rerun to take advantage of the new constants.

It might seem like a lot of work to repeatedly run the set evaluator like this. Some form of caching could be used, but practice shows that this is not essential.

Implementation of the value sets The operations that the value sets must support are the usual for set operations (union, membership test, etc.). These are used in set based evaluation for handling the different language constructs.

To handle arithmetic, different operations are needed. E.g., the possible values of the expression "x+y" is the set $\{x + y \mid x \in v_x, y \in v_y\}$. So the operations on sets must include these cross-product like arithmetic operations.

The cardinality of the sets of values as obtained from the input data could, in the worst case, be as large as the number of legs in the flight plan. This number can range from a few hundred to 10000, but the cardinality is usually much lower than this; normally being less than 15. Unfortunately the arithmetic operations on sets cause the cardinality of the resulting sets to explode. After a few arithmetic operations the size of the set could easily exceed the memory of the computer. To be able to handle those large sets efficiently, they need to be approximated. The approximation used here is to switch from an exact set representation to an interval representation. The interval retains the smallest and largest of the elements in the original set. Arithmetic on these sets then becomes ordinary interval arithmetic.

The implementation does, in fact, switch between four representations: singleton set, exact list of elements, interval, and the universal set. The first of these are only present to improve space and time efficiency. Each of these representations also keeps track of if the set contains *void* or not.

3.4   Ad hoc transformation rules

By studying the output of the partial evaluator you can easily find a number of expressions which can be simplified. The transformations that are needed cannot be done by the constant folding, nor the set based evaluation since these only deal with actual values. The transformations of interest here are symbolic in nature.

The needed transformations range from the trivial, e.g., "0 * x" should be replaced by "0", to the not so trivial, e.g., "count(level) where(p) > 0" should be replaced by "any(level, p)".

Many of the transformation rules have side conditions that relate to *void*. E.g., "x * 0" can only be replaced by 0, if x cannot have the value *void*, since CRL hs left-to-right evaluation so the expression is *void* if x is. During the transformation, these side conditions can be checked by using the set evaluator to examine the possible values of subexpressions.

Figure 7 contains a partial list of the transformations utilised. All of these have been derived ad-hoc by studying the output of the partial evaluator, but they can be verified to be correct using the semantics of the language The set of transformations could be extended, of course, but it handles many of the cases that occur in practice.

3.5   Other transformations

Some other transformations are also performed:

- Simple (e.g. a literal or a variable) definitions and definitions used only once are inlined.
- Identical definitions are coalesced.
- Unused definitions are removed.
- Simple theorem proving is used to removed rules that are covered by other rules. E.g. "rule 1.r1 = x < 5" can be removed if there is also a rule "rule 1.r1 = x < 0".

4   Implementation

The partial evaluator reads a dump of the abstract syntax tree of the input program and generates a new rule set in concrete syntax. The dump of the abstract syntax tree is generated by the ordinary CRL compiler. The output of the partial evaluator is a quite readable program (this was one of the requirements of it), some of the comments are even preserved.

The way the system is used without partial evaluation follows these steps:

if true then t else e	$\Rightarrow t$
if false then t else e	$\Rightarrow e$
if c then true else false	$\Rightarrow c$
if c then false else true	$\Rightarrow$ not c
if not c then t else e	$\Rightarrow$ if c then e else t
if c then t else if c then t' else e	$\Rightarrow$ if c then t else e
(if c then t else e)$+x$	$\Rightarrow$ if c then $t+x$ else $e+x$ x variable
$x+$(if c then t else e)	$\Rightarrow$ if c then $x+t$ else $x+e$ x variable

$$\vdots$$

$e=$true	$\Rightarrow e$
$e=$false	$\Rightarrow$ not e
$e+0$	$\Rightarrow e$
$0+e$	$\Rightarrow e$
$e*1$	$\Rightarrow e$
$1*e$	$\Rightarrow e$
$e*0$	$\Rightarrow 0$ if $void \notin \mathcal{S}[\,e\,]\rho$
$0*e$	$\Rightarrow 0$
$e-e$	$\Rightarrow 0$ if $void \notin \mathcal{S}[\,e\,]\rho$

$$\vdots$$

e and e	$\Rightarrow e$
e or e	$\Rightarrow e$
not (not e)	$\Rightarrow e$
not (e_1 and e_2)	$\Rightarrow$ not e_1 or not e_2
not (e_1 or e_2)	$\Rightarrow$ not e_1 and not e_2
not all(l,e)	$\Rightarrow$ any$(l,$ not $e)$
not any(l,e)	$\Rightarrow$ all$(l,$ not $e)$
sum$(l,0)$	$\Rightarrow 0$
all$(l,$ true$)$	$\Rightarrow$ true
any$(l,$ false$)$	$\Rightarrow$ false
any(l,e_1) and any(l,e_2)	$\Rightarrow$ any$(l,e_1$ and $e_2)$
count$(l)$where$(e)> 0$	$\Rightarrow$ any(l,e)

Fig. 7. A few of the symbolic transformation rules.

- Compile rule set using the CRL compiler. The CRL compiler translates the rule language to C which is then compiled with a standard C compiler. For the user this step looks like one operation.
- Use the compiled rule set to solve different problems. Different problems may have different parameters, different external table, and different leg sets as input. The compiled rule set is dynamically linked with the runtime system for each run.

It is important to have the system look exactly the same when the partial evaluator is in use. The steps looks the same to the user, but they are different internally.

- Compilation of the rule set will invoke just the CRL compiler which will collect the used modules together and produce a dump of the abstract syntax tree.
- To use a "compiled" rule set the following happens:
  - The partial evaluator is run with the dumped rule set, the current parameters, the external tables, and the leg set as input. These are the same values as would be used by the runtime system had the partial evaluator not been used.
  - The resulting rule set is then compiled with the CRL compiler (which uses the C compiler), and then used by the runtime system just as above.

The partial evaluator consists of about 7000 lines of Haskell, [Hud92], code. Early in the development the Hugs system, [Jon96a,Jon96b], was used, but after an initial period the HBC compiler, [Aug93], was used exclusively. Heap profiling [RW93] and time profiling was used to improve the performance of the program.

5 Practical evaluation and conclusions

The partial evaluator has been used on most of the rule sets written in CRL. Table 1 presented the figures for a Lufthansa problem. Lufthansa has the biggest rule set of all the airlines.

As can be seen from the table the running time decreases to about half. When tested on a larger variety of problems the running time varies between 30% and 65 % of the original time, with 50% being a typical figure. When you consider that these runs most often takes several hours this is a quite a gain. The total time for processing (rule compilation + partial evaluation + C compilation) the rule set has also decreased. The rule compiler generates a huge C program, which takes very long to compile.[3] The number of definitions is reduced because unused definitions are removed (a few) simple definitions are inlined (many). Many definitions becomes simple after the transformations. The reason the number of rules has increased is the cloning of leg level definitions

---

[3] Actually, it has to be broken into smaller pieces since most C compiler cannot compile files that are several megabytes.

	Before PE	After PE
Rules	88	90
Leg definitions	209	68
RTD definitions	391	106
CRR definitions	192	22
Total rule size	461 kbyte	176 kbyte
C code generated	2.17 Mbyte	0.99 Mbyte
Time for PE	-	3 min
Time for C compilation	30 min	10 min
Running time	55 min	25 min

Table 1. Summary of partial evaluation results for a Lufthansa rule set partially evaluated for the Lufthansa Express (a few aircraft types flying within Europe) problem for a captain. The run time is for solving a small subset of a weeks scheduling.

to handle deadheads. Without this cloning the number of rules would also have been reduced.

The running time of the partial evaluator has not been a problem and is not remarkably long when one considers that, in the example in the table, the in input program is almost five hundred kbytes, the external tables another hundred kbytes, and the given attributes for the legs in the flight plan is about five hundred kbytes.

Even if the running time of the transformed program decreased by a fair amount this is, surprisingly, not always where the biggest gain in speed was made. For a particularly difficult planning problem the output from the partial evaluator, which is human readable, was inspected by an expert planner/rule-writer. Since the rule set had decreased so much in size he was able to grasp what the rules meant and make some manual adjustments to them. These adjustments made the program run an order of magnitude faster. These changes could, of course, have been made in the original program, but studying and comprehending it would have been a daunting task.

The partial evaluator is now part of the Carmen system and is delivered to several customers that use it in their daily work.

6 Acknowledgements

I would like to thank the people at Carmen Systems, especially Tommy Bohlin, who answered my naïve questions about airline scheduling problems. I would also like to thank Jessica Twitchell for proof reading and improving the English of this paper.

References

[AGPT91] R. Anbil, E. Gelman, B. Patty, and R. Tanga. Recent Advances in Crew-Pairing Optimization at American Airlines. *Interfaces*, 21(1):62–74, 1991.

[AHKW97] E. Andersson, E. Housos, N. Kohl, and D. Wedelin. Crew Pairing Optimization. In *OR in Airline Industry*. Kluwer Academic Press, 1997.

[Aug93] L. Augustsson. *HBC User's Manual.* Programming Methodology Group, Department of Computer Sciences, Chalmers, S–412 96 Göteborg, Sweden, 1993. Distributed with the HBC compiler. See `http://www.cs.chalmers.se/~augustss/hbc/hbc.html`

[Aug97] L. Augustsson. Partial evaluation in aircraft crew planning. In *Proc. ACM SIGPLAN Symposium on Partial Evaluation and Semantics-Based Program Manipulation PEPM '97*, pages 127–136, Amsterdam, The Netherlands, June 1997. ACM Press.

[Boh90] T. Bohlin. The Carmen Rule Language. Technical report, Carmen Systems AB, 1990.

[HE96] E. Housos and T. Elmroth. Automatic Subproblem Optimisation for Airline Crew Scheduling. *Interfaces (to appear)*, 1996.

[Hud92] P. Hudak et al. *Report on the Programming Language Haskell: A Non-Strict, Purely Functional Language*, March 1992. Version 1.2. Also in Sigplan Notices, May 1992.

[Jon96a] M. P. Jones. Hugs 1.3 user manual. Technical Report NOTTCS-TR-96-2, Department of Computer Science, University of Nottingham, August 1996.

[Jon96b] M. P. Jones. The Hugs distribution. Currently available from `http://www.cs.nott.ac.uk/Department/Staff/mpj/hugs.html`, 1996.

[RW93] C. Runciman and D. Wakeling. Heap profiling of lazy functional programs. *Journal of Functional Programming*, 3(2):217–245, April 1993.

[Wed95] D. Wedelin. An algorithm for large scale 0–1 integer programming with application to airline crew scheduling. *Annals of Operations Research*, 57:283–301, 1995.

Introduction to Supercompilation

Morten Heine B. Sørensen and Robert Glück

Department of Computer Science, University of Copenhagen (DIKU)
Universitetsparken 1, DK-2100 Copenhagen Ø, Denmark
rambo@diku.dk, glueck@diku.dk

Abstract. This paper gives an introduction to Turchin's *supercompiler*, a program transformer for functional programs which performs optimizations beyond *partial evaluation* and *deforestation*. More precisely, the paper presents *positive supercompilation*.

1 Introduction

The *Refal project*—or the *supercompiler project* as we shall call it—was conceived in the mid 1960's by Valentin F. Turchin and co-workers in Russia.

A central idea in the supercompiler project is that of a *metasystem transition* [25]: a jump from a system S to a metasystem S' that integrates, modifies, and controls a number of S-systems as its subsystems. Turchin considers metasystem transition as a key to creative, human thinking—others are *computation* (or *deduction*) and *generalization* (or *abstraction* or *induction*).

As an illustration of these ideas, consider how we might solve some scientific problem. We observe phenomena, generalize observations, and try to construct a self-sufficient model of the reality we observe in terms of these generalizations. If we fail to obtain a solution, we start to analyze why we failed, and for this purpose we examine the process of applying our methods for solving the problem; we perform a metasystem transition with respect to the ground-level set of rules. This may give us new, more elaborate methods to solve the problem. If we fail once more, we make another metasystem transition and analyze our means of finding new rules. These transitions may proceed infinitely.

The supercompiler project [26, 27, 29] is a product of this cybernetic thinking. A program is seen as a machine and to make sense of it, one must control and observe (*super*vise) its operations. A supercompiler is a program transformer that creates a graph of configurations and transitions between possible configurations of the computing system. This process, called *driving*, will usually go on infinitely. To make it finite and self-sufficient (*closed*) a supercompiler performs *generalization* on the systems configurations. Application of the supercompiler to a program can be seen as a metasystem transition, and repeated metasystem transition can be expressed by self-application of the supercompiler.

One of the motivations [27] for the project comes from artificial intelligence. If metasystem transition is taken to be one of the main sources for creative thinking, an implementation on a computer of the concept would indeed seem an interesting approach to artificial intelligence.

Another motivation [26] for the supercompiler project is related to a particular instance of metasystem transition. The appearance of numerous programming languages, some for application specific purposes, motivated the idea of a programming environment that facilitates the introduction of new languages and hierarchies of languages. The language *Refal* [27], developed by Turchin, can be viewed as a meta-algorithmic language: the specification of a new language L is an L-interpreter written in Refal. In such a setting one needs a means of turning programs written in application specific languages into efficient programs, preferably in the ground-level language. This task is undertaken by the supercompiler written for Refal programs, and implemented in Refal—Turchin independently realized all three *Futamura projections* stated in terms of metasystem transition.

A number of other applications of metasystem transition in the computer have emerged, e.g., [7, 11, 17, 28]. The most widely appreciated application of supercompilation is as a *program optimizer* performing *program specialization* and *elimination of intermediate data structures* as well as more dramatic optimizations. This is the only application of supercompilation we shall be concerned with in this paper.

From its very inception, Turchin's supercompiler was formulated for the language Refal. The authors have since reconsidered the theory of supercompilation—the part dealing with program optimizations—in the context of a more familiar functional language [6, 21]. A variant of supercompilation, called *positive supercompilation,* was developed in an attempt to understand the essence of supercompilation, how it achieves its effects, and its correspondence to related transformers [8, 9, 18, 22, 23]. For this variant, results were developed dealing with the problems of preserving semantics, evaluating efficiency of transformed programs, and ensuring termination [21, 24].

Turchin developed the philosophy underlying the supercompiler project in [25]. His recent account [29] contains historical information and an introduction to several aspects of supercompilation—as seen by Turchin. Experiments with Turchin's supercompilation have been reported [30, 27, 17], see also [29]. Other experimental systems for supercompilation have been developed, e.g. [6, 31, 13], including earlier systems by the Refal group (most unpublished). The first non-Refal supercompiler was [6]. A comprehensive bibliography can be found in [9].

This paper presents positive supercompilation following [6, 8, 9, 21–24]. We first present examples of driving and generalization (Section 2). After some preliminaries (Section 3) we introduce driving (Section 4), illustrated by a classical application (Section 5). We then present generalization (Section 6), which can be viewed as a technique to ensure termination of driving. After some more examples (Section 7), the paper ends with some remarks about correctness and the relation to other program transformers (Section 8).

2 Examples of Driving and Generalization

This section illustrates driving and generalization by means of examples. The first example primarily illustrates driving, the second example generalization.

Example 1. Consider a functional program appending two lists.

$$a([], vs) = vs$$
$$a(u{:}us, vs) = u{:}a(us, vs)$$

A simple and elegant way to append *three* lists is to use the expression $a(a(xs, ys), zs)$. However, this expression is inefficient since it traverses xs twice. We now illustrate a standard transformation obtaining a more efficient method.

We begin with a tree whose single node is labeled with $a(a(xs, ys), zs)$:

$$\boxed{a(a(xs, ys), zs)}$$

Whenever the reduction step has different possible outcomes, new children are added to account for all possibilities. By a *driving step* which replaces the inner call to append according to the different patterns in the definition of a, two new expressions are added as labels on children:

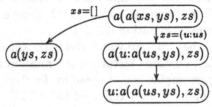

In the rightmost child we can perform a driving step which replaces the outer call to append:

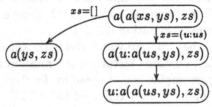

The label of the new child contains an outermost constructor. For transformation to propagate to the subexpression of the constructor we again add children:

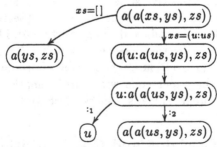

The expression in the rightmost child is a renaming of the expression in the root; that is, the two expressions are identical up to choice of variable names. As we shall see below, no further processing of such a node is required. Driving the child with label $a(ys, zs)$ two steps leads to:

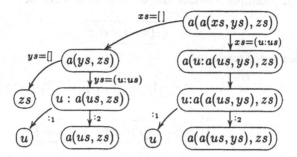

The tree is now *closed* in the sense that each leaf expression either is a renaming of an ancestor's expression, or contains a variable or a 0-ary constructor. Informally, a closed tree is a representation of all possible computations with the expression e in the root, where branchings in the tree correspond to different runtime values for the variables of e. The nodes can be perceived as states, and the edges correspond to transitions.

In the above tree, computation starts in the root, and then branches to one of the successor states depending on the shape of xs. Assuming xs has form $(u:us)$, the constructor ":" is then emitted and control is passed to the two states corresponding to nodes labeled u and $a(a(us, ys), zs)$, etc.

To construct a new program from the closed tree, we introduce, roughly, for each node α with child β a definition where the left and right hand side of the definition are derived from α and β, respectively. More specifically, we rename expressions of form $a(a(xs, ys), zs)$ and $a(ys, zs)$ as $aa(xs, ys, zs)$ and $a'(ys, zs)$, respectively, and derive from the tree the following new program:

$$
\begin{aligned}
aa([], ys, zs) &= a'(ys, zs) \\
aa(u{:}us, ys, zs) &= u : aa(us, ys, zs)
\end{aligned}
$$

$$
\begin{aligned}
a'([], zs) &= zs \\
a'(u{:}us, zs) &= u{:}a'(us, zs)
\end{aligned}
$$

The expression $aa(xs, ys, zs)$ in this program is more efficient than the expression $a(a(xs, ys), zs)$ in the original program, since the new expression traverses xs only once.

The transformation in Example 1 proceeded in three phases the first two of which were interleaved. In the first phase we performed driving steps that added children to the tree. In the second phase we made sure that no node with an expression which was a renaming of an ancestor's expression was driven, and we continued the overall process until the tree was closed. In the third phase we recovered from the resulting finite, closed tree a new expression and program.

In the above transformation we ended up with a finite closed tree. Often, special measures must be taken to ensure that this situation is eventually encountered, as in the next example.

Example 2. Suppose we want to transform the expression $a(a(xs, ys), xs)$, where a is defined as in Example 1—note the double occurrence of xs. As above we start out with:

$$a(a(xs, ys), xs)$$

After the first few steps we have:

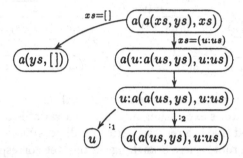

Unlike the situation in Example 1, the label of the rightmost node is not a renaming of the expression at the root. In fact, repeated driving will *never* lead to that situation; special measures must be taken.

One solution is to ignore the information that the argument xs to the inner call and the argument xs to the outer call are the same. This is achieved by a *generalization step* that replaces the whole tree by a single new node:

$$\textbf{let } zs{=}xs \textbf{ in } a(a(xs, ys), zs)$$

When dealing with nodes of the new form **let** $zs{=}e$ **in** e' we then transform e and e' independently. Thus we arrive at:

$$\textbf{let } zs{=}xs \textbf{ in } a(a(xs, ys), zs)$$
$$\text{let } zs{=} \swarrow \qquad \downarrow \text{in}$$
$$xs \qquad\qquad a(a(xs, ys), zs)$$

Driving of the node labeled $a(a(xs, ys), zs)$ leads to the last tree in Example 1.

When generating a new term and program from such a tree, we can eliminate all let-expressions; in particular, in the above example, we generate the expression $aa(xs, ys, xs)$ and the same program as in Example 1. In some cases such let-expression elimination may be undesirable for reasons pertaining to efficiency of the generated program—but such issues are ignored in the present paper.

Again transformation proceeds in three phases, but the second phase is now more sophisticated, sometimes replacing a subtree by a new node in a generalization step.

The positive supercompiler is an algorithm that repeatedly applies driving and generalization steps until a closed tree is encountered from which a new program can then be recovered. In Section 4 we rigorously define driving steps and in Section 6 we similarly define generalization steps along with the positive supercompilation algorithm.

3   Preliminaries

This section introduces preliminaries on trees, programs, and substitutions.

3.1   Trees

We introduce trees in a rigorous manner, following Courcelle [1].

Definition 1. A *tree* over a set E is a partial map[1] $t : \mathbf{N}_1^* \to E$ such that

1. $\mathrm{dom}(t) \neq \emptyset$ (t is *non-empty*);
2. if $\alpha\beta \in \mathrm{dom}(t)$ then $\alpha \in \mathrm{dom}(t)$ ($\mathrm{dom}(t)$ is *prefix-closed*);
3. if $\alpha \in \mathrm{dom}(t)$ then $\{i \mid \alpha i \in \mathrm{dom}(t)\}$ is finite (t is *finitely branching*);
4. if $\alpha j \in \mathrm{dom}(t)$ then $\alpha i \in \mathrm{dom}(t)$ for all $1 \leq i \leq j$ (t is *ordered*).

Let t be a tree over E. The elements of $\mathrm{dom}(t)$ are called *nodes* of t; the empty string ϵ is the *root*, and for any node α in t, the nodes αi of t (if any) are the *children* of α, and we also say that α is the *parent* of these nodes. A node α in t is *to the left* of another node β in t if there is a node γ in t such that $\alpha = \gamma i \gamma'$ and $\beta = \gamma j \gamma''$, where $i < j$. A *branch* in t is a finite or infinite sequence $\alpha_0, \alpha_1, \ldots \in \mathrm{dom}(t)$ where, for all i, α_{i+1} is a child of α_i. A node with no children is a *leaf*. We denote by $\mathrm{leaf}(t)$ the set of all leaves in t. For any node α of t, $t(\alpha) \in E$ is the *label* of α. Also, t is *finite*, if $\mathrm{dom}(t)$ is finite. Finally, t is *singleton* if $\mathrm{dom}(t) = \{\epsilon\}$, i.e., if $\mathrm{dom}(t)$ is singleton. $T(E)$ is the set of all finite trees over E.

Example 3. Let $\mathcal{E}_H(V)$ be the set of expressions over symbols H and variables V. Let $x, xs, \ldots \in V$ and $a, cons, nil \in H$, denoting $(x\!:\!xs)$ by $cons(x, xs)$ and $[]$ by nil. The trees in Example 1 (ignoring labels on edges) are a diagrammatic presentation of trees over $\mathcal{E}_H(V)$.

The following notions pertaining to trees will be used in the remainder.

Definition 2. Let E be a set, and $t, t' \in T(E)$.

1. For $\alpha \in \mathrm{dom}(t)$, $t\{\alpha := t'\}$ denotes the tree t'' defined by:

$$\mathrm{dom}(t'') = (\mathrm{dom}(t) \setminus \{\alpha\beta \mid \alpha\beta \in \mathrm{dom}(t)\}) \cup \{\alpha\beta \mid \beta \in \mathrm{dom}(t')\}$$
$$t''(\gamma) \quad = \begin{cases} t'(\beta) & \text{if } \gamma = \alpha\beta \text{ for some } \beta \\ t(\gamma) & \text{otherwise} \end{cases}$$

2. We write $t = t'$, if $\mathrm{dom}(t) = \mathrm{dom}(t')$ and $t(\alpha) = t'(\alpha)$ for all $\alpha \in \mathrm{dom}(t)$.
3. Let $\alpha \in \mathrm{dom}(t)$. The *ancestors of* α *in* t is the set

$$\mathrm{anc}(t, \alpha) = \{\beta \in \mathrm{dom}(t) \mid \exists \gamma : \alpha = \beta\gamma\}$$

---

[1] We let $\mathbf{N}_1 = \mathbf{N} \setminus \{0\}$. S^* is the set of finite strings over S, and $\mathrm{dom}(f)$ is the domain of a partial function f. We use α, β to denote elements of $\mathbf{N}_1^*$ and i, j to denote elements of $\mathbf{N}_1$.

4. We denote by $e \to e_1, \ldots, e_n$ the tree $t \in T(E)$ with

$$
\begin{aligned}
\text{dom}(t) &= \{\epsilon\} \cup \{1, \ldots, n\} \\
t(\epsilon) &= e \\
t(i) &= e_i
\end{aligned}
$$

As a special case, $e \to$ denotes the $t \in T(E)$ with $\text{dom}(t) = \{\epsilon\}$ and $t(\epsilon) = e$.

The tree $t\{\alpha := t'\}$ is the tree obtained by replacing the subtree with root α in t by the tree t'. The ancestors of a node are the nodes on the path from the root to the node (including the node itself). Finally, the tree $e \to e_1, \ldots, e_n$ is the tree with root labeled e and n children labeled $e_1, \ldots, e_n$, respectively.

3.2   Programs

We consider the following first-order functional language; the intended operational semantics is normal-order graph reduction to weak head normal form.

Definition 3. We assume a denumerable set of symbols for variables $x \in X$ and finite sets of symbols for constructors $c \in C$, and functions $f \in F$ and $g \in G$, where X, C, F, and G are pairwise disjoint. All symbols have fixed arity. The sets Q of programs, D of definitions, E of expressions, and P of patterns are defined by:

$$
\begin{array}{lll}
Q \ni q & ::= \; d_1 \ldots d_m & \\
D \ni d & ::= \; f(x_1, \ldots, x_n) = e & \text{(f-function)} \\
& \; | \;\; g(p_1, x_1, \ldots, x_n) = e_1 & \\
& \quad\quad\quad\vdots & \text{(g-function)} \\
& \;\;\;\; g(p_m, x_1, \ldots, x_n) = e_m & \\
E \ni e & ::= \; x & \text{(variable)} \\
& \; | \;\; c(e_1, \ldots, e_n) & \text{(constructor)} \\
& \; | \;\; f(e_1, \ldots, e_n) & \text{(f-function call)} \\
& \; | \;\; g(e_0, e_1, \ldots, e_n) & \text{(g-function call)} \\
& \; | \;\; \textbf{if } e_1 {=} e_2 \textbf{ then } e_3 \textbf{ else } e_4 & \text{(conditional with equality test)} \\
P \ni p & ::= \; c(x_1, \ldots, x_n) & \\
\end{array}
$$

where $m > 0, n \geq 0$. We require that no two patterns p_i and p_j in a g-function definition contain the same constructor c, that no variable occur more than once in a left side of a definition, and that all variables in the right side of a definition be present in its left side. By $\text{vars}(e)$ we denote the set of variables occurring in the expression e.

Example 4. The append program in Example 1 is a program in this language using the short notation $[]$ and $(x : xs)$ for the list constructors *nil* and *cons*(x, xs).

Remark 1. In some accounts of positive supercompilation the language contains case-expressions instead of g-functions (pattern-matching definitions). The difference between *deforestation* [32] and positive supercompilation is clearest in presentations with case-expressions, but the formulation of generalization steps is simplest in presentations with pattern-matching definitions.

Remark 2. There is a close relationship between the set $\mathcal{E}$ of expressions introduced in Definition 3 and the set $\mathcal{E}_H(V)$ introduced in Example 3. In fact, $\mathcal{E} = \mathcal{E}_{C \cup F \cup G \cup \{if\}}(X)$, where we view if as a 4-ary operator symbol. Therefore, we can make use of well-known facts about $\mathcal{E}_H(V)$ in reasoning about $\mathcal{E}$.

3.3 Substitutions

Finally we introduce substitutions and some related operations.

Definition 4.

1. A *substitution* on $\mathcal{E}_H(V)$ is a total map from V to $\mathcal{E}_H(V)$. Substitutions are lifted to expressions as usual. Application of substitutions is written postfix.
2. A substitution θ is a *renaming* if it is a bijection from V to $V \subseteq \mathcal{E}_H(V)$.
3. If θ is a renaming and $\theta_2 = \theta \circ \theta_1$ then θ_2 is a renaming of θ_1; if $e_2 = e_1 \theta$ then e_2 is a renaming of e_1.
4. We denote by $\{x_1 := e_1, \ldots, x_n := e_n\}$ the substitution that maps x_i to e_i and all other variables to themselves.

Definition 5.

1. Two expressions e_1, e_2 are *unifiable* if there exists a substitution θ such that $e_1 \theta = e_2 \theta$. Such a θ is a *unifier*. Moreover, θ is a *most general unifier* (mgu) if, for any other unifier θ', there is a substitution σ such that $\theta' = \sigma \circ \theta$.
2. Two expressions e_1, e_2 are *disunifiable* if there exists a substitution θ such that $e_1 \theta \neq e_2 \theta$.

Proposition 1. *Let H, V be some sets. If $e_1, e_2 \in \mathcal{E}_H(V)$ are unifiable, then they have exactly one mgu modulo renaming (of substitutions).*

Proof. See [14]. □

Definition 6. By $e_1 \sqcup e_2$ we denote some mgu of e_1 and e_2.

Definition 7. Let $e_1, e_2 \in \mathcal{E}_H(V)$, for some H, V.

1. The expression e_2 is an *instance* of e_1, $e_1 \leq e_2$, if $e_1 \theta = e_2$ for a substitution θ.
2. A *generalization* of e_1, e_2 is an expression e_g such that $e_g \leq e_1$ and $e_g \leq e_2$.
3. A *most specific* generalization (msg) of e_1 and e_2 is a generalization e_g such that, for every generalization e'_g of e_1 and e_2, it holds that $e'_g \leq e_g$.

Proposition 2. *Let H, V be some sets. Any two $e_1, e_2 \in \mathcal{E}_H(V)$ have exactly one msg modulo renaming (of expressions).*

Proof. See [14]. □

Definition 8. By $e_1 \sqcap e_2$ we denote some msg of e_1 and e_2.[2] Two expressions e_1 and e_2 are *incommensurable*, $e_1 \leftrightarrow e_2$, if $e_1 \sqcap e_2$ is a variable.

---

[2] As a matter of technicality, we shall require that if $e_1 \leq e_2$ then $e_1 \sqcap e_2 = e_1$. In other words, whenever e_2 is an instance of e_1, the variable names of $e_1 \sqcap e_2$ will be chosen so that the resulting term is identical to e_1.

Generalization can be viewed as a dual to unification. Whereas a unifier of e_1 and e_2 is a *substitution* θ that maps both e_1 and e_2 to some e_u, a generalization of e_1 and e_2 is an *expression* e_g such that both e_1 and e_2 are instances of e_g:

$$
\begin{array}{ccc}
 & e_u & \\
{}^{\theta}\nearrow & & \nwarrow^{\theta} \\
e_1 & & e_2 \\
{}_{\theta_1}\searrow & & \nearrow_{\theta_2} \\
 & e_g &
\end{array}
$$

Remark 3. Note that we now use the term *generalization* in two distinct senses: to denote certain operations on trees performed by supercompilation (cf. Example 2), and to denote the above operation on expressions. The two senses are related: generalization in the former sense will make use of generalization in the latter sense.

Example 5. The following illustrates most specific generalizations $e_1 \sqcap e_2$ of $e_1, e_2 \in \mathcal{E}_H(V)$ where $(e_1 \sqcap e_2)\theta_i = e_i$ and $x, y \in V$, $b, c, d, f \in H$.

e_1	e_2	$e_1 \sqcap e_2$	θ_1	θ_2
b	$f(b)$	x	$\{x := b\}$	$\{x := f(b)\}$
$c(b)$	$c(f(b))$	$c(x)$	$\{x := b\}$	$\{x := f(b)\}$
$c(y)$	$c(f(y))$	$c(y)$	$\{\}$	$\{y := f(y)\}$
$d(b,b)$	$d(f(b), f(b))$	$d(x,x)$	$\{x := b\}$	$\{x := f(b)\}$

Remark 4. An msg of $e, e' \in \mathcal{E}_H(V)$ and the corresponding substitutions can be obtained by exhaustively applying the following rewrite rules to the initial triple $(x, \{x := e\}, \{x := e'\})$:

$$
\begin{pmatrix} e_g \\ \{x := h(e_1, \ldots, e_n)\} \cup \theta_1 \\ \{x := h(e_1', \ldots, e_n')\} \cup \theta_2 \end{pmatrix} \rightarrow \begin{pmatrix} e_g\{x := h(y_1, \ldots, y_n)\} \\ \{y_1 := e_1, \ldots, y_n := e_n\} \cup \theta_1 \\ \{y_1 := e_1', \ldots, y_n := e_n'\} \cup \theta_2 \end{pmatrix}
$$

$$
\begin{pmatrix} e_g \\ \{x := e, y := e\} \cup \theta_1 \\ \{x := e', y := e'\} \cup \theta_2 \end{pmatrix} \rightarrow \begin{pmatrix} e_g\{x := y\} \\ \{y := e\} \cup \theta_1 \\ \{y := e'\} \cup \theta_2 \end{pmatrix}
$$

4 Driving

We now present the driving steps mentioned in Section 2, as used in positive supercompilation.

4.1 Driving Step

When we perform driving steps, we instantiate variables to patterns, e.g., xs to $(u:us)$. To avoid confusion of variables, we must choose the variables in the pattern with some care. The following definition introduces useful terminology to deal with that problem.

Definition 9. A substitution θ is *free for* an expression $e \in \mathcal{E}_H(V)$ if for all $x \in V$: $(\text{vars}(x\theta)\backslash\{x\}) \cap \text{vars}(e) = \emptyset$.

The crucial property of a substitution θ which is free for an expression e is, roughly, that the variables in the range of θ (at least those variables that are not simply mapped to themselves) do not occur already in e.

When we drive conditionals we distinguish the case where no transformations are possible for the two expressions in the equality test. The following class of terms is useful for that purpose.

Definition 10. The sets $\mathcal{B}$ of basic values where $n \geq 0$, is defined by:

$$\mathcal{B} \ni b \quad ::= \quad x \mid c(b_1, \dots, b_n)$$

The following relation $\Rightarrow$ is similar to the small-step semantics for normal-order reduction to weak head normal form (the outermost reducible subexpression is reduced). However, $\Rightarrow$ also propagates to the arguments of constructors and works on expressions with variables; the latter is done by *unification-based information propagation* [6, 9] (the assumed outcome of an equality test and constructor test is propagated by a substitution—notice, e.g., the substitution $\{y := p\}$ in the third rule).

Definition 11. For a program q, the relations $e \Rightarrow e'$, $e \rightarrow_\theta e'$, and $e \twoheadrightarrow_\theta e'$ where $e, e' \in \mathcal{E}$ and θ is a substitution on $\mathcal{E}$, are defined in Figure 1.

Example 6. The rules (1)-(5) are the base cases. For instance,

$$a(xs, ys) \rightarrow_{\{xs:=(u:us)\}} u : a(us, ys) \qquad \text{Rule (3)}$$

The rules (6), (9), and (10) allow reduction in contexts, i.e., inside the first argument of a g-function and inside the test in a conditional. For instance,

$$a(a(xs, ys), xs) \rightarrow_{\{xs:=(u:us)\}} a(u : a(us, ys), xs) \quad \text{Rule (6)}$$

The rules (9) and (10) are more complicated than (6). The reason is that in the former rules we are allowed to reduce under constructors, because the expressions in the test must be reduced to basic values; for the first argument in a g-function we only need an expression with an outermost constructor.

Finally, the rules (11) and (12) are the main rules. For instance,

$$a(a(xs, ys), xs) \qquad \Rightarrow a(u : a(us, ys), u : us) \qquad \text{Rule (11)}$$
$$u : a(a(us, ys), u : us) \Rightarrow a(a(us, ys), u : us) \qquad \text{Rule (12)}$$

Remark 5. In some accounts of positive supercompilation we use so-called *contexts* and *redexes* instead of the above inference rules to define the relation $\Rightarrow$. The choice between contexts and redexes on the one hand and inference rules on the other hand is mostly a matter of taste.

Definition 12. Let $t \in T(\mathcal{E})$ and $\beta \in \text{leaf}(t)$. Then

$$\text{drive}(t, \beta) = t\{\beta := t(\beta) \rightarrow e_1, \dots, e_n\}$$

where $\{e_1, \dots, e_n\} = \{e \mid t(\beta) \Rightarrow e\}$.

Example 7. All the steps in Example 1 are, in fact, driving steps in this sense.

Base Cases:

$$\frac{f(x_1,\ldots,x_n) = e \;\in\; q}{f(e_1,\ldots,e_n) \to_{\{\}} e\{x_1 := e_1,\ldots,x_n := e_n\}} \tag{1}$$

$$\frac{g(c(x_1,\ldots,x_m),x_{m+1},\ldots,x_n) = e \;\in\; q}{g(c(e_1,\ldots,e_m),e_{m+1},\ldots,e_n) \to_{\{\}} e\{x_1 := e_1,\ldots,x_n := e_n\}} \tag{2}$$

$$\frac{g(p,x_1\ldots,x_n) = e \;\in\; q}{g(y,e_1,\ldots e_n) \to_{\{y:=p\}} e\{x_1 := e_1,\ldots,x_n := e_n\}} \tag{3}$$

$$\frac{b_1 \text{ unifiable with } b_2}{\text{if } b_1 {=} b_2 \text{ then } e_3 \text{ else } e_4 \to_{b_1 \sqcup b_2} e_3} \tag{4}$$

$$\frac{b_1 \text{ disunifiable with } b_2}{\text{if } b_1 {=} b_2 \text{ then } e_3 \text{ else } e_4 \to_{\{\}} e_4} \tag{5}$$

Reduction in Context:

$$\frac{e \to_\theta e'}{g(e,e_1,\ldots,e_n) \to_\theta g(e',e_1,\ldots,e_n)} \tag{6}$$

$$\frac{e \to_\theta e'}{e \twoheadrightarrow_\theta e'} \tag{7}$$

$$\frac{e \twoheadrightarrow_\theta e'}{c(b_1,\ldots,b_i,e,e_{i+1},\ldots,e_n) \twoheadrightarrow_\theta c(b_1,\ldots,b_i,e',e_{i+1},\ldots,e_n)} \tag{8}$$

$$\frac{e_1 \twoheadrightarrow_\theta e_1'}{\text{if } e_1 {=} e_2 \text{ then } e_3 \text{ else } e_4 \to_\theta \text{ if } e_1' {=} e_2 \text{ then } e_3 \text{ else } e_4} \tag{9}$$

$$\frac{e_2 \twoheadrightarrow_\theta e_2'}{\text{if } b_1 {=} e_2 \text{ then } e_3 \text{ else } e_4 \to_\theta \text{ if } b_1 {=} e_2' \text{ then } e_3 \text{ else } e_4} \tag{10}$$

Driving Step:

$$\frac{e \to_\theta e' \;\&\; \theta \text{ is free for } e'}{e \Rightarrow e'\theta} \tag{11}$$

$$\frac{i \in \{1,\ldots,n\}}{c(e_1,\ldots,e_n) \Rightarrow e_i} \tag{12}$$

Fig. 1. Driving step

4.2   Driving with Folding

The positive supercompiler is an algorithm which applies driving steps interleaved with generalization steps in the style of Example 2. It will be considered in Section 6. However, the driving step is powerful enough on its own to achieve fascinating effects. We therefore consider next an algorithm which only performs driving steps and looks for recurring nodes as in Example 1. This strategy is known as *α-identical folding* [23] (the same approach is taken in deforestation [32]). The following algorithm will be called *driving with identical folding*.

Definition 13. Let $t \in T(\mathcal{E})$. A $\beta \in \text{leaf}(t)$ is *processed* if one of the following conditions are satisfied:

1. $t(\beta) = c()$ for some $c \in C$;
2. $t(\beta) = x$ for some $x \in X$;
3. there is an $\alpha \in \text{anc}(t, \beta) \backslash \{\beta\}$ such that $t(\alpha)$ is a renaming of $t(\beta)$.

Also, t is *closed* if all leaves in t are processed.

The driving algorithm can then be defined as follows.[3]

Definition 14. Let q be a program, and define $M_d : \mathcal{E} \rightarrow T(\mathcal{E})$ by:

> **input** $e \in \mathcal{E}$;
> **let** $t = e \rightarrow$;
> **while** t is not closed
>   **let** $\beta \in \text{leaf}(t)$ be an unprocessed node;
>   **let** $t = \text{drive}(t, \beta)$;
> **return** t;

Example 8. The sequence of steps in Example 1 could be computed by M_d.

5   The Knuth-Morris-Pratt Example

In this section we review one of the classical examples of supercompilation: to generate from a general pattern matcher and a fixed pattern, a specialized pattern matcher of efficiency similar to the one generated by the Knuth-Morris-Pratt algorithm [12]. We will do this with the driving algorithm of Definition 13.

Consider the following *general matcher* which takes a pattern and a string as input and returns *True* iff the pattern occurs as a substring in the string.[4]

$$
\begin{aligned}
match(p, s) &= m(p, s, p, s) \\
m([], ss, op, os) &= True \\
m(p{:}pp, ss, op, os) &= x(p, pp, ss, op, os) \\
x(p, pp, [], op, os) &= False \\
x(p, pp, s{:}ss, op, os) &= \textbf{if } p{=}s \textbf{ then } m(pp, ss, op, os) \textbf{ else } n(op, os) \\
n(op, []) &= False \\
n(op, s{:}ss) &= m(op, ss, op, ss)
\end{aligned}
$$

Now consider the following *naively specialized matcher* $match_{AAB}$ which matches the fixed pattern $[A,A,B]$ with a string u by calling *match*:

$$
match_{AAB}(u) \quad = \quad match([A,A,B], u)
$$

---

[3] A number of choices are left open in the algorithm, e.g., how one chooses among the unprocessed leaf nodes. Such details are beyond the scope of the present paper. Also, as we shall see, M_d is actually a partial map. Finally, we omit the definition of code generation.

[4] By a small abuse, we permit x to be defined by patterns on the third argument instead of the first argument.

Evaluation proceeds by comparing A to the first component of u, A to the second, B to the third. If at some point the comparison failed, the process is restarted with the tail of u.

This strategy is not optimal. If the string u begins, e.g., with three A's, then the steps of the naively specialized matcher can be depicted as follows:

ss: $\boxed{AAA\,?\cdots}$ $\rightarrow$ $\boxed{AA\,?\cdots}$ $\rightarrow$ $\boxed{A\,?\cdots}$ $\rightarrow$ $\boxed{AA\,?\cdots}$

pp: $\boxed{AAB}$ $\boxed{AB}$ $\boxed{B}$ $\boxed{AAB}$

After matching the two A's in the pattern with the first two A's in the string, the B in the pattern fails to match the A in the string. Then the process is restarted with the string's tail, even though it is known that the first two comparisons will succeed. Rather than performing these tests whose outcome is already known, we should *skip* the three first A's in the original string and proceed directly to compare the B in the pattern with the fourth element of the original string. This is done in the *KMP specialized matcher*.

$$match_{AAB}(u) = m_{AAB}(u)$$
$$m_{AAB}([]) \quad = \textit{False}$$
$$m_{AAB}(s{:}ss) \quad = \textbf{if } A{=}s \textbf{ then } m_{AB}(ss) \textbf{ else } m_{AAB}(ss)$$
$$m_{AB}([]) \quad = \textit{False}$$
$$m_{AB}(s{:}ss) \quad = \textbf{if } A{=}s \textbf{ then } m_{B}(ss) \textbf{ else } m_{AAB}(ss)$$
$$m_{B}([]) \quad = \textit{False}$$
$$m_{B}(s{:}ss) \quad = \textbf{if } B{=}s \textbf{ then } \textit{True} \textbf{ else if } A{=}s \textbf{ then } m_{B}(ss) \textbf{ else } m_{AAB}(ss)$$

After finding two A's and a third symbol which is not a B in the string, this program checks (in m_B) whether the third symbol of the string is an A. If so, it continues immediately by comparing the next symbol of the string with the B in the pattern (by calling m_B), thereby avoiding repeated comparisons.

We will now see how the driving algorithm of the previous section can be used to derive matchers similar to the above one. Figure 2 shows the closed tree that arises by application of M_d to $match([A,A,B], u)$, the body of the naively specialized matcher.

From this tree we can generate the following almost optimal specialized matcher.

$$m_{AAB}([]) \quad = \textit{False}$$
$$m_{AAB}(s : ss) = \textbf{if } A{=}s \textbf{ then } m_{AB}(ss) \textbf{ else } n_{AAB}(ss, s)$$
$$m_{AB}([]) \quad = \textit{False}$$
$$m_{AB}(s : ss) \quad = \textbf{if } A{=}s \textbf{ then } m_{B}(ss) \textbf{ else } n_{AB}(ss, s)$$
$$m_{B}([]) \quad = \textit{False}$$
$$m_{B}(s : ss) \quad = \textbf{if } B{=}s \textbf{ then } \textit{True} \textbf{ else } n_{B}(ss, s)$$
$$n_{AAB}(ss, s) \quad = m_{AAB}(ss)$$
$$n_{AB}(ss, s) \quad = \textbf{if } A{=}s \textbf{ then } m_{AB}(ss) \textbf{ else } n_{AAB}(ss, s)$$
$$n_{B}(ss, s) \quad = \textbf{if } A{=}s \textbf{ then } m_{B}(ss) \textbf{ else } n_{AB}(ss, s)$$

The term $m_{AAB}(u)$ in this program is more efficient than $match([A,A,B], u)$ in the original program. In fact, this is the desired KMP specialized matcher, disregarding the redundant test $A = s$ in n_{AB}. But these redundant tests do not affect run-time seriously: there is a constant c such that the total number of redundant tests in the entire evaluation of $m_\mathrm{p}(ss)$ for any pattern p and subject string ss is bound by $c \cdot |ss|$, as shown in [21].

The reason for the redundant test $A = s$ is that driving—as defined in this paper—ignores *negative* information: when driving proceeds to the false branch of a conditional, the information that the equality does not hold is forgotten. Driving maintains only *positive* information: in the true-branch of a conditional a substitution is performed representing the information that the equality test is assumed to come out true. This explains the terminology *positive* supercompilation! Representing negative information, i.e. the information that an equality does not hold, requires a more sophisticated representation than positive information. A transformer that has the capacity to eliminate all unreachable branches in a program has *perfect* information propagation [6].

6   Generalization

Example 2 showed that the driving algorithm does not always terminate. In this section we add generalization steps in such a way that the resulting positive supercompilation algorithm always terminates.

6.1   Driving Step

As we saw in Example 2, although the input and output programs of the transformer are expressed in the language of Definition 3, the trees considered during transformation might have nodes containing let-expressions. Therefore, the positive supercompiler will work on trees over $\mathcal{L}$, defined as follows.

Definition 15. The set $\mathcal{L}$ of let-expressions is defined by:

$$\mathcal{L} \ni \ell \quad ::= \quad \mathbf{let}\ x_1 {=} e_1, \dots, x_n {=} e_n\ \mathbf{in}\ e$$

where $n \geq 0$. If $n > 0$ then we say that $\mathcal{L}$ is a *proper* let-expression and require that $x_1, \dots, x_n \in \mathrm{vars}(e)$, that $e \notin X$, and that $e\{x_1 := e_1, \dots, x_n := e_n\}$ is not a renaming of e. If $n = 0$ we identify the expression $\mathbf{let}\ x_1 {=} e_1, \dots, x_n {=} e_n\ \mathbf{in}\ e$ with e. Thus, $\mathcal{E}$ is a subset of $\mathcal{L}$.

Example 9. The trees in Example 2 (ignoring labels on edges) are a diagrammatic presentation of trees over $\mathcal{L}$.

In order to formulate positive supercompilation we must adapt Definition 11 of *driving step* to deal with the new set of expressions. This is done as follows.

Definition 16.

1. For a program q, the relations $\ell \Rightarrow e'$, $e \rightarrow_\theta e'$, and $e \twoheadrightarrow_\theta e'$ where $e, e' \in \mathcal{E}$, $\ell \in \mathcal{L}$, and θ is a substitution on $\mathcal{E}$, are defined as in Figure 1 with the addition of the rule

$$\frac{i \in \{1, \dots, n+1\}}{\mathbf{let}\ x_1 {=} e_1, \dots, x_n {=} e_n\ \mathbf{in}\ e_{n+1} \Rightarrow e_i}$$

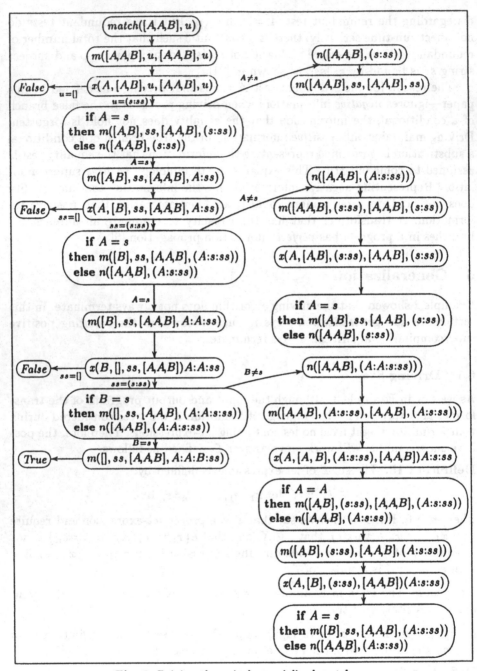

Fig. 2. Driving the naively specialized matcher

2. Let $t \in T(\mathcal{L})$ and $\beta \in \text{leaf}(t)$. Then drive(t, β) is defined as in Definition 12.

Remark 6. The reason that only the relation $\Rightarrow$ is affected, not $\rightarrow_\theta$ and $\twoheadrightarrow_\theta$, is that let-expressions are allowed at the top-level of an expression only.

The new rule for $\Rightarrow$ expresses the semantics of generalizations: that we are trying to keep subexpressions apart.

Example 10. let $zs = xs$ in $a(a(xs, ys), zs) \Rightarrow a(a(xs, ys), zs)$.

Example 11. The driving steps in Example 2 are driving steps in the above sense.

6.2   Generalization Step

There are two types of generalization step in positive supercompilation: *abstract* and *split*. Both types of step are invoked when the expression of a leaf node is similar, in a certain sense, to an ancestor's expression.

The generalization step in Example 2 is an example of an abstract step. In this type of step we replace the tree whose root is the *ancestor* by a single new node labeled with a new expression which captures the common structure of the leaf and ancestor expressions. This common structure is computed by the most specific generalization operation. More precisely, this kind of step is an *upwards abstract* step.

In case the expression is an instance of the ancestor expression, we can replace the *leaf* node by a new node with an expression capturing the common structure. This type of step is called a *downwards abstract* step. For instance, if the leaf expression is $f([])$ and the ancestor expression is $f(xs)$, we can replace the leaf node by a node with expression let $xs = []$ in $f(xs)$. By driving, this node will receive two children labeled $[]$ and $f(xs)$; since the latter node is now a renaming of the ancestor's expression, no further processing of it is required.

In some cases, the expression of a leaf node may be similar to an ancestor's expression, and yet the two expressions have no common structure in the sense of msg's, i.e., the expressions are incommensurable (their msg is a variable). In this case, performing an abstract step would not make any progress towards termination of the supercompilation process. For instance, we might have a leaf with expression $f(g(x))$ and an ancestor with expression $g(x)$. We shall see later that these expressions will be counted as similar, but their msg is a variable. Therefore, applying an abstract step (upwards or downwards) would replace a node labeled e with a new node labeled let $z = e$ in z which, by driving, would receive a child labeled e. Thus, no progress has been made. Instead, a split step is therefore performed. The idea behind a split step is that if the ancestor expression is similar to the leaf expression, then there is a subterm of the leaf expression which has non-trivial structure in common with the ancestor. Hence, the split step digs out this structure.

The following, then, are the generalization steps used in positive supercompilation; they are inspired by similar operations in [16]. The driving and generalization steps are illustrated in Figure 3.

Definition 17. Let $t \in T(\mathcal{L})$.

1. For $\beta \in \text{leaf}(t)$ with $t(\beta) = h(e_1, \ldots, e_n)$, $h \in C \cup F \cup G \cup \{\text{if}\}$, and $e_i \notin X$ for some $i \in \{1, \ldots, n\}$, define

$$\text{split}(t, \beta) = t\{\beta := \text{let } x_1 = e_1, \ldots, x_n = e_n \text{ in } h(x_1, \ldots, x_n) \rightarrow\}$$

2. For $\alpha, \beta \in \text{dom}(t)$, $t(\alpha), t(\beta) \in \mathcal{E}$ with $e_g = t(\alpha) \sqcap t(\beta)$ where $e_g \notin X$, $x_1, \ldots, x_n \in \text{vars}(e_g)$, $t(\alpha) = e_g\{x_1 := e_1, \ldots, x_n := e_n\}$, and $t(\alpha)$ not a renaming of e_g, define

$$\text{abstract}(t, \alpha, \beta) = t\{\alpha := \text{let } x_1 = e_1, \ldots, x_n = e_n \text{ in } e_g \rightarrow\}$$

Remark 7. Note that the above operations are allowed only under circumstances that guarantee that the constructed let-expression is well-formed according to the conditions of Definition 15.

Example 12. The generalization step in Example 2 is an abstract step.

6.3 When to Stop?

Above we described *how* to generalize in positive supercompilation. It remains to decide *when* to generalize, i.e., to decide when expressions are similar. The following relation $\trianglelefteq$ is used for that end.

Definition 18. The *homeomorphic embedding* $\trianglelefteq$ is the smallest relation on $\mathcal{E}_H(V)$ such that, for all $h \in H$, $x, y \in V$, and $e_i, e_i' \in \mathcal{E}_H(V)$:

$$x \trianglelefteq y \qquad \frac{\exists i \in \{1, \ldots, n\} : e \trianglelefteq e_i'}{e \trianglelefteq h(e_1', \ldots, e_n')} \qquad \frac{\forall i \in \{1, \ldots, n\} : e_i \trianglelefteq e_i'}{h(e_1, \ldots, e_n) \trianglelefteq h(e_1', \ldots, e_n')}$$

Example 13. The following expressions from $\mathcal{E}_H(V)$ give examples and non-examples of embedding, where $x, y \in V$, and $b, c, d, f \in H$.

$$\begin{array}{ll}
b \trianglelefteq f(b) & f(c(b)) \ntrianglelefteq c(b) \\
c(b) \trianglelefteq c(f(b)) & f(c(b)) \ntrianglelefteq c(f(b)) \\
d(b, b) \trianglelefteq d(f(b), f(b)) & f(c(b)) \ntrianglelefteq f(f(f(b)))
\end{array}$$

The rationale behind using the homeomorphic embedding relation in program transformers is that in any infinite sequence $e_0, e_1, \ldots$ of expressions, there *definitely* are $i < j$ with $e_i \trianglelefteq e_j$ (this property holds regardless of how the sequence $e_0, e_1, \ldots$ was produced and is known as *Kruskal's Theorem*—see e.g. [3]). Thus, if driving is stopped at any node with an expression in which an ancestor's expression is embedded, driving cannot construct an infinite branch. Conversely, if $e_i \trianglelefteq e_j$ then all the subexpressions of e_i are present in e_j embedded in extra subexpressions. This suggests that e_j *might* arise from e_i by some infinitely continuing system, so driving is stopped for a good reason.

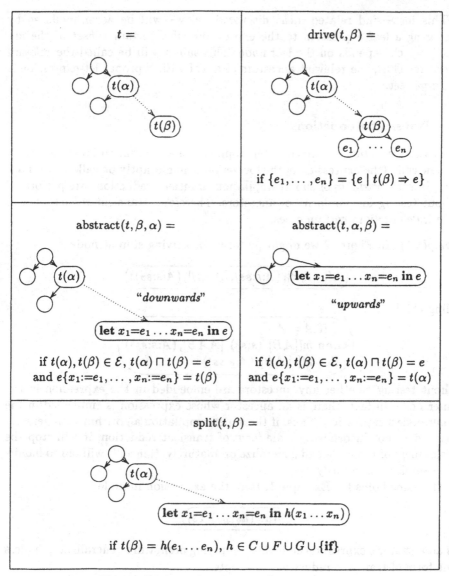

Fig. 3. Steps used in Positive Supercompilation

The homeomorphic embedding relation and the most specific generalization operation are defined on elements of $\mathcal{E}$, not on elements $\mathcal{L}$. Therefore, in order to compare nodes and compute new nodes in trees over $\mathcal{L}$, we have to either extend these operations to $\mathcal{L}$ or make sure that they are not applied to elements of $\mathcal{L}$. We choose the latter by always driving a node with a proper let-expression without comparing to ancestors. Also, when a node is compared to ancestors we do not compare it to those with proper let-expressions.

This idea—and related ideas discussed below—will be accommodated by comparing a leaf expression to the expressions of a certain *subset* of the ancestors which depends on the leaf node. This subset will be called the *relevant* ancestors. Thus, the relevant ancestors of a leaf with a proper let-expression is the empty set.

6.4 Transient Reductions

A *transient reduction* is a driving step applied to a node that will receive exactly one new child (the expression in the former node might aptly be called *deterministic.*) In some variants of supercompilation, transient reductions are performed without testing for similarity of ancestors. Therefore, transient reductions can go on indefinitely in certain cases.

Example 14. In Figure 2 we might perform the driving step at node

$$m([A,A,B], (A{:}s{:}ss), [A,A,B], (A{:}s{:}ss))$$

adding child

$$\begin{aligned} &\textbf{if } A = A\\ &\textbf{then } m([A,B], (s{:}ss), [A,A,B], (A{:}s{:}ss))\\ &\textbf{else } n([A,A,B], (A{:}s{:}ss)) \end{aligned}$$

without testing whether any ancestors are embedded in the expression in the former node. In fact, there is an ancestor whose expression is embedded in the former node's expression. Thus, if the supercompilation algorithm with generalization does not incorporate some form of transient reduction, it will stop the development of the node and generalize prematurely. Hence, it will fail to handle the example satisfactorily.

The same holds for Example 1. Here the expression in node

$$a(u{:}a(us, ys), zs)$$

has an ancestor's expression embedded implying premature generalization unless some form of transient reductions is adopted.

We shall adopt a form of transient reductions that does not endanger termination of positive supercompilation and which is similar to *local unfolding* as adopted in partial deduction—see e.g. [15]. We will divide all nodes with non-proper let-expressions into two categories: global ones and local ones. The *global* nodes are those that give rise to instantiation of variables in driving steps. In other words, their reduction is non-transient. For instance, in Example 1, the nodes labeled $a(a(xs, ys), zs)$ and $a(ys, zs)$ are global. Conversely, the *local* nodes are the non-global ones. Local nodes give rise to transient reductions.

When considering a global leaf node we will compare it only to its global ancestors. When considering a local node, we will compare it only to its immediate local ancestors up to (but *not* including) the nearest global ancestor.

Definition 19. Let $t \in T(\mathcal{L})$ and $\beta \in \text{dom}(t)$.

1. β is *proper* if $t(\beta)$ is a proper let-expression.
2. β is *global* if β is non-proper and $t(\beta) \rightarrow_\theta e$ for some $\theta \neq \{\}$. Also β is *local* if β is non-proper and not global.
3. The set of *immediate local ancestors* of β in t, $\text{locanc}(t, \beta)$, is the set of local nodes in the longest branch $\alpha_1, \ldots, \alpha_n, \beta$ in t $(n \geq 0)$ such that $t(\alpha_1), \ldots, t(\alpha_n)$ are all local or proper.
4. The set of *global ancestors* of β in t, $\text{globanc}(t, \beta)$, is the set of global nodes in $\text{anc}(t, \beta)$.

In conclusion, a leaf node is driven when no relevant ancestor's expression is embedded in the leaf's expression. It remains to define the set of relevant ancestors.

Definition 20. Let $t \in T(\mathcal{L})$ and $\beta \in \text{dom}(t)$. The set of *relevant ancestors* of β in t, $\text{relanc}(t, \beta)$, is defined by:

$$\text{relanc}(t, \beta) = \begin{cases} \{\} & \text{if } t(\beta) \text{ is proper} \\ \text{locanc}(t, \beta) & \text{if } t(\beta) \text{ is local} \\ \text{globanc}(t, \beta) & \text{if } t(\beta) \text{ is global} \end{cases}$$

6.5   Positive Supercompilation

First we adapt the notions of *processed node* and *closed tree* to trees over $\mathcal{L}$, then we define positive supercompilation $M_{ps} : \mathcal{E} \rightarrow T(\mathcal{L})$.

Definition 21. Let $t \in T(\mathcal{L})$. A $\beta \in \text{leaf}(t)$ is *processed* if $t(\beta)$ is non-proper and one of the conditions in Definition 13 hold. Also, t is *closed* if all leaves in t are processed.

Definition 22. Let q be a program, and define $M_{ps} : \mathcal{E} \rightarrow T(\mathcal{L})$ by:

> **input** $e \in \mathcal{E}$;
> **let** $t = e \rightarrow$;
> **while** t is not closed
>   **let** $\beta \in \text{leaf}(t)$ be an unprocessed node;
>   **if** $\forall \alpha \in \text{relanc}(t, \beta) \backslash \{\beta\} : t(\alpha) \not\trianglelefteq t(\beta)$ **then** $t = \text{drive}(t, \beta)$
>   **else begin**
>   **let** $\alpha \in \text{relanc}(t, \beta)$ and $t(\alpha) \trianglelefteq t(\beta)$.
>   **if** $t(\alpha) \leq t(\beta)$ **then** $t = \text{abstract}(t, \beta, \alpha)$
>   **else if** $t(\alpha) \leftrightarrow t(\beta)$ **then** $t = \text{split}(t, \beta)$
>   **else** $t = \text{abstract}(t, \alpha, \beta)$.
>   **end**
> **return** t;

Example 15. The algorithm computes exactly the trees in Examples 1 and 2, and the tree in Figure 2.

Remark 8. The algorithm calls abstract and split only in cases where these operations are well-defined.

As for termination, it is proven [24] that (a variant of) this positive supercompiler always terminates, i.e., the algorithm actually defines a total map.

7   More Examples

This section illustrates how positive supercompilation works on a number of examples. Positive supercompilation makes no improvement on the programs; the interesting point is how termination is ensured. The first example covers accumulating parameters, the second example obstructing function calls.

Example 16 (The accumulating parameter). Consider the following functional program reversing a list by means of an accumulating parameter:

$$
\begin{aligned}
rev(xs) &= r(xs, []) \\
r([], vs) &= vs \\
r(u{:}us, vs) &= r(us, u{:}vs)
\end{aligned}
$$

What happens if we apply M_{ps} to $rev(xs)$? After two driving steps we have:

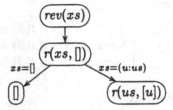

Then a generalization step yields:

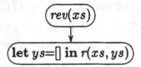

A few more driving steps yield:

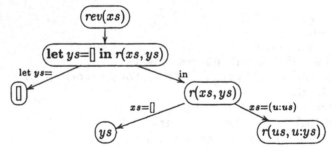

Another generalization step yields:

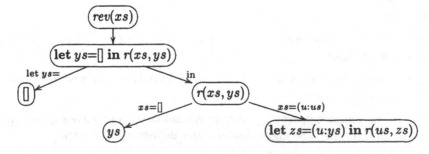

Driving finally leads to the following closed tree:

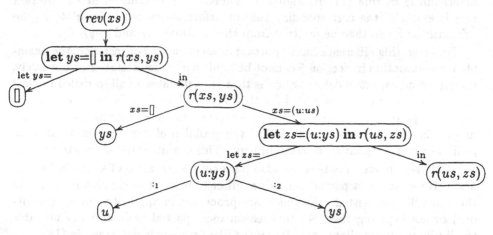

From this tree one can construct a new term and program which turn out to be identical to the original term and program.

Example 17 (The obstructing function call). Consider another functional program reversing a list:

$$rev([]) \quad = []$$
$$rev(u{:}us) \quad = a'(rev(us), u)$$
$$a'([], v) \quad = [v]$$
$$a'(u{:}us, v) = u{:}a'(us, v)$$

What happens if we apply M_{ps} to $rev(xs)$?

Example 18 (The accumulating side effect). Finally, consider the following functional program.

$$f([], ys) \quad = ys$$
$$f(x{:}xs, ys) = f(xs, ys)$$

Here f is not intended to be an interesting function, merely to provide a simple illustration of a problem that occurs in more complicated contexts.

What happens if we apply M_{ps} to $f(v, v)$?

8   Discussion

We end the paper by briefly discussing correctness of the positive supercompiler and comparing it to other program transformers.

First of all, the driving algorithm in Section 4 is very similar to Wadler's *deforestation* [32]. This is perhaps not so surprising since we saw in Example 1 that positive supercompilation can eliminate intermediate data structures, which is the purpose of deforestation. The common features of the two transformers that facilitate elimination of intermediate data structures are that nested calls are kept together and that these are processed in normal order (outside-in).

In fact, the only essential difference between deforestation and the driving algorithm is in rule (11) in Figure 1: whereas the conclusion in the present rule is $e \Rightarrow e'\theta$, the corresponding rule in deforestation would be $e \Rightarrow e'$ (the substitution θ can then be omitted from the relations $\rightarrow_\theta$ and $\twoheadrightarrow_\theta$).

However, this difference has important consequences. For instance, the example transformation in Section 5 cannot be achieved by deforestation. Conversely, an important aspect of deforestation is that it terminates on all so-called *treeless* programs, and this does not hold for the driving algorithm. In other words, the increased power of driving comes at the expense of rarer termination, and this in turn is responsible for the fact that the problem of ensuring termination of positive supercompilation is quite difficult. This is elaborated at length in [23].

Positive supercompilation can also perform specialization like *partial evaluation*. However, most partial evaluators differ from positive supercompilation in their handling of nested calls which are processed in applicative order (inside-out) or not kept together. For this reason most partial evaluators are not able to eliminate intermediate data structures like lists—as is explained in [18].

Also, most partial evaluators do not perform *unification-based information propagation* [6, 9]; that is, there is the same difference between partial evaluators and positive supercompilation as there is between deforestation and positive supercompilation—the difference in rule (11) of driving. For this reason, partial evaluators typically cannot achieve the transformation in Section 5 without changes in the original matcher. On the other hand, the implementation aspects of partial evaluators are far more well-developed than those for supercompilers. An abstract framework for describing constant-based partial evaluation and driving is provided in [10].

In positive supercompilation, negative information (restrictions) are ignored when entering an else-branch of a conditional. *Perfect driving* [6] is a variant of supercompilation that propagates positive and negative information. Hence, the loss of information in supercompilation can be restricted to one phase in the transformer, namely generalization. However, generalization is not considered in [6].

Finally, positive supercompilation is related to *partial deduction*, e.g., [15, 16] and, more closely, to *conjunctive partial deduction* [5], as is developed at length in [8]. *Generalized partial computation* [4] has a similar effect and power as supercompilation, but requires the use of a theorem prover. A taxonomy of related transformers can be found in [9].

What does it mean that positive supercompilation is correct? There are three issues: preservation of semantics, non-degradation of efficiency, and termination.

As for *preservation of semantics*, the new program recovered from the tree produced by M_{ps} (if any) should be semantically equivalent to the original program. The main point is that the new program terminates neither more nor less than the original one. A general technique due to Sands [20] can be used to prove this for positive supercompilation [19].

As for *non-degradation in efficiency*, the output of M_{ps} should be at least as efficient as the input. There are several aspects of this problem.

First, there is the problem of avoiding *duplication of computation*. Since driving can cause function call duplication, a polynomial time program can be changed into an exponential time program. In deforestation this is avoided by considering only *linear* terms. This issue is beyond the scope of this paper.

Second, there is the problem of *code duplication*. Unrestrained unfolding may increase the size of a program dramatically. In principle, the size of a program does not degrade its efficiency. Again, this issue is beyond the scope of this paper.

As for *termination*, it is proven [24] that (a variant of) M_{ps} always terminates.

References

1. B. Courcelle. Fundamental properties of infinite trees. *Theoretical Computer Science*, 25:95–169, 1983.
2. O. Danvy, R. Glück, and P. Thiemann, editors. *Partial Evaluation*, volume 1110 of *Lecture Notes in Computer Science*. Springer-Verlag, 1996.
3. N. Dershowitz. Termination of rewriting. *Journal of Symbolic Computation*, 3, 1987.
4. Y. Futamura, K. Nogi, and A. Takano. Essence of generalized partial computation. *Theoretical Computer Science*, 90(1):61–79, 1991.
5. R. Glück, J. Jørgensen, B. Martens, and M.H. Sørensen. Controlling conjunctive partial deduction. In H. Kuchen and D.S. Swierstra, editors, *Programming Languages: Implementations, Logics and Programs*, volume 1140 of *Lecture Notes in Computer Science*, pages 137–151. Springer-Verlag, 1996.
6. R. Glück and A.V. Klimov. Occam's razor in metacomputation: the notion of a perfect process tree. In P. Cousot, M. Falaschi, G. Filè, and G. Rauzy, editors, *Workshop on Static Analysis*, volume 724 of *Lecture Notes in Computer Science*, pages 112–123. Springer-Verlag, 1993.
7. R. Glück and A.V. Klimov. A regeneration scheme for generating extensions. *Information Processing Letters*, 62(3):127–134, 1997.
8. R. Glück and M.H. Sørensen. Partial deduction and driving are equivalent. In M. Hermenegildo and J. Penjam, editors, *Programming Languages: Implementations, Logics and Programs*, volume 844 of *Lecture Notes in Computer Science*, pages 165–181. Springer-Verlag, 1994.
9. R. Glück and M.H. Sørensen. A roadmap to metacomputation by supercompilation. In Danvy et al. [2], pages 137–160.
10. N.D. Jones. The essence of program transformation by partial evaluation and driving. In N.D. Jones, M. Hagiya, and M. Sato, editors, *Logic, Language, and Computation*, volume 792 of *Lecture Notes in Computer Science*, pages 206–224. Springer-Verlag, 1994. Festschrift in honor of S.Takasu.
11. A.V. Klimov and S.A. Romanenko. Metavychislitel' dlja jazyka Refal. Osnovnye ponjatija i primery. (A metaevaluator for the language Refal. Basic concepts and examples). Preprint 71, Keldysh Institute of Applied Mathematics, Academy of Sciences of the USSR, Moscow, 1987. (in Russian).
12. D.E. Knuth, J.H. Morris, and V.R. Pratt. Fast pattern matching in strings. *SIAM Journal on Computing*, 6(2):323–350, 1977.
13. M. Krog and P. Rasmussen. Positive supercompilation. Manuscript, 1998.
14. J.-L. Lassez, M.J. Maher, and K. Marriott. Unification revisited. In J. Minker, editor, *Foundations of Deductive Databases and Logic Programming*, pages 587–625. Morgan Kaufmann, Los Altos, Ca., 1988.

15. M. Leuschel and B. Martens. Global control for partial deduction through characteristic atoms and global trees. In Danvy et al. [2], pages 263–283.
16. B. Martens and J. Gallagher. Ensuring global termination of partial deduction while allowing flexible polyvariance. In L. Sterling, editor, *International Conference on Logic Programming*, pages 597–613. MIT Press, 1995.
17. A.P. Nemytykh, V.A. Pinchuk, and V.F. Turchin. A self-applicable supercompiler. In Danvy et al. [2], pages 322–337.
18. K. Nielsen and M.H. Sørensen. Call-by-name CPS-translation as a binding-time improvement. In A. Mycroft, editor, *Static Analysis Symposium*, volume 983 of *Lecture Notes in Computer Science*, pages 296–313. Springer-Verlag, 1995.
19. D. Sands. Proving the correctness of recursion-based automatic program transformation. In P. Mosses, M. Nielsen, and M.I. Schwartzbach, editors, *Theory and Practice of Software Development*, volume 915 of *Lecture Notes in Computer Science*, pages 681–695. Springer-Verlag, 1995.
20. D. Sands. Total correctness by local improvement in program transformation. In *Conference Record of the Annual ACM SIGPLAN-SIGACT Symposium on Principles of Programming Languages*, pages 221–232. ACM Press, 1995.
21. M.H. Sørensen. Turchin's supercompiler revisited. Master's thesis, Department of Computer Science, University of Copenhagen, 1994. DIKU-rapport 94/17.
22. M.H. Sørensen and R. Glück. An algorithm of generalization in positive supercompilation. In J.W. Lloyd, editor, *Logic Programming: Proceedings of the 1995 International Symposium*, pages 465–479. MIT Press, 1995.
23. M.H. Sørensen, R. Glück, and N.D. Jones. A positive supercompiler. *Journal of Functional Programming*, 6(6):811–838, 1996.
24. M.H.B. Sørensen. Convergence of program transformers in the metric space of trees. In J. Jeuring, editor, *Mathematics of Program Construction*, volume 1422 of *Lecture Notes in Computer Science*, pages 315–337. Springer-Verlag, 1998.
25. V.F. Turchin. *The Phenomenon of Science*. Columbia University Press, New York, 1977.
26. V.F. Turchin. A supercompiler system based on the language Refal. *SIGPLAN Notices*, 14(2):46–54, 1979.
27. V.F. Turchin. The concept of a supercompiler. *ACM Transactions on Programming Languages and Systems*, 8(3):292–325, 1986.
28. V.F. Turchin. Program transformation with metasystem transitions. *Journal of Functional Programming*, 3(3):283–313, 1993.
29. V.F. Turchin. Metacomputation: Metasystem transition plus Supercompilation. In Danvy et al. [2], pages 481–510.
30. V.F. Turchin, R. Nirenberg, and D. Turchin. Experiments with a supercompiler. In *ACM Conference on Lisp and Functional Programming*, pages 47–55. ACM Press, 1982.
31. W. Vanhoof. Implementatie van een supercompilator voor een functionele taal (in dutch). Master's thesis, University of Leuven, 1996.
32. P.L. Wadler. Deforestation: Transforming programs to eliminate intermediate trees. *Theoretical Computer Science*, 73:231–248, 1990.

Advanced Logic Program Specialisation

Michael Leuschel

Department of Electronics and Computer Science
University of Southampton
Highfield, Southampton, SO17 1BJ, UK
mal@ecs.soton.ac.uk
www: http://www.ecs.soton.ac.uk/~mal

1 Introduction

In first part of this course [28] we have laid the theoretical foundations for logic program specialisation, notably introducing the technique of *partial deduction* along with some basic techniques to automatically control it. In this part of the course we first present in Section 2 an advanced way of controlling polyvariance based upon *characteristic trees*. We then show in Section 3 how partial deduction can be extended into *conjunctive partial deduction*, incorporating much of the power of unfold/fold program transformation techniques, such as tupling and deforestation, while keeping the automatic control of partial deduction. Finally, in Section 4 we elaborate on combining *abstract interpretation* with conjunctive partial deduction, showing how together they are more powerful than either method alone.

2 Characteristic Trees for Global Control

2.1 Structure and abstraction

In the first part of the course [28] we have presented the generic partial deduction Algorithm 3.1. This algorithm is parametrised by an unfolding rule for the local control and by an abstraction operator for the control of polyvariance. The abstraction operator examines a set of atoms and then decides which of the atoms should be abstracted and which ones should be left unmodified.

An abstraction operator like the *msg* is just based on the *syntactic structure* of the atoms to be specialised. However, two atoms can be specialised in a very similar way in the context of one program P_1, and in a very dissimilar fashion in the context of another program P_2. The syntactic structure of the two atoms being unaffected by the particular context, an operator like the *msg* will perform exactly the same abstraction within P_1 and P_2, even though very different generalisations might be called for. A much better idea might therefore be to examine the SLDNF-trees generated for these atoms. These trees capture (to some depth) how the atoms behave computationally in the context of the respective programs. They also capture (part of) the specialisation that has been performed on these atoms. An abstraction operator which takes these trees into account will notice their similarity in the context of P_1 and their dissimilarity in P_2, and can therefore take appropriate actions in the form of different generalisations. The following example illustrates these points.

Example 1. Let P be the *append* program:

    (1) $append([], Z, Z) \leftarrow$
    (2) $append([H|X], Y, [H|Z]) \leftarrow append(X, Y, Z)$

Note that we have added clause numbers, which we will henceforth take the liberty to incorporate into illustrations of SLD-trees in order to clarify which clauses have been resolved with.

Let $\mathcal{A} = \{B, C\}$ be a set of atoms, where $B = append([a], X, Y)$ and $C = append(X, [a], Y)$. Typically a partial deducer will unfold the two atoms of $\mathcal{A}$ in the way depicted in Fig. 1, returning the finite SLD-trees τ_B and τ_C. These two trees, as well as the associated resultants, have a very different structure. The atom $append([a], X, Y)$ has been fully unfolded and we obtain as only resultant the fact:

    $append([a], X, [a|X]) \leftarrow$

while for $append(X, [a], Y)$ we obtain the following resultants:

    $append([], [a], [a]) \leftarrow$
    $append([H|X], [a], [H|Z]) \leftarrow append(X, [a], Z)$

In this case, it is thus vital to keep separate specialised versions for B and C. However, it is very easy to come up with another context in which the specialisation behaviour of B and C are almost indiscernible. Take for instance the following program P^* in which $append^*$ no longer appends two lists but finds common elements at common positions:

    (1*) $append^*([X|T_X], [X|T_Y], [X]) \leftarrow$
    (2*) $append^*([X|T_X], [Y|T_Y], E) \leftarrow append^*(T_X, T_Y, E)$

The associated finite SLD-trees τ_B^* and τ_C^*, depicted in Fig. 2, are now almost fully identical. In that case, it is not useful to keep different specialised versions for B and C because the following single set of specialised clauses could be used for B and C without specialisation loss:

    $append^*([a|T_1], [a|T_2], [a]) \leftarrow$

This illustrates that the syntactic structures of B and C alone provide insufficient information for a satisfactory control of polyvariance.

2.2   Characteristic trees

The above illustrates the interest of (also) examining the "essential structure" of the SLDNF-trees generated for the atoms to be partially deduced. This leads to the definition of *characteristic trees*, initially presented in [13, 12] and later exploited in [31, 33], which abstracts SLDNF-trees by only remembering, for the non-failing branches[1]:

---

[1] The failing branches do not materialise within the residual code and it is not interesting to know how a certain branch has failed; see [31, 33].

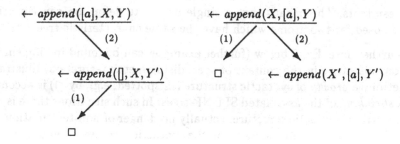

Fig. 1. SLD-trees τ_B and τ_C for Example 1

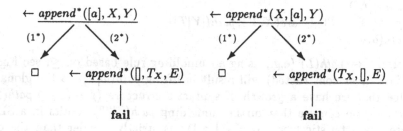

Fig. 2. SLD-trees τ_B^* and τ_C^* for Example 1

1. the position of the selected literals and
2. the (number of the) clauses that have been resolved with.

We will now use *pos ∘ cl* to denote a selection of a literal at position *pos* within a goal which is resolved with the clause numbered *cl*. We will represent trees by the set of their branches. For example, the characteristic trees of the finite SLD-trees τ_B and τ_C in Fig. 1 are then $\{\langle 1 \circ 2, 1 \circ 1\rangle\}$ and $\{\langle 1 \circ 1\rangle, \langle 1 \circ 2\rangle\}$ respectively. The characteristic trees of the finite SLD-trees τ_B^* and τ_C^* in Fig. 2 are both $\{\langle 1 \circ 1^*\rangle\}$.

The characteristic tree of an atom A explicitly or implicitly captures the following important aspects of specialisation:

- the branches that have been pruned through the unfolding process (namely those that are absent from the characteristic tree). For instance, by inspecting the characteristic trees of τ_B and τ_C from Ex. 1, we can see that two branches have been pruned for the atom B (thereby removing recursion) whereas no pruning could be performed for C.
- how deep $\leftarrow A$ has been unfolded and which literals and clauses have been resolved with each other in that process. This captures the computation steps that have already been performed at partial deduction time.
- the number of clauses in the resultants of A (namely one per characteristic path) and also (implicitly) which predicates are called in the bodies of the

resultants. This means that a single predicate definition can (in principle) be used for two atoms which have the same characteristic tree.

Furthermore, Ex. 2 below (further examples can be found in [33]; similar situations also arise in the context of specialising metainterpreters) illustrate that sometimes a *growth* of syntactic structure (as spotted, e.g., by ⊴) is accompanied by a *shrinking* of the associated SLDNF-trees. In such situations there is, despite the growth of syntactic structure, actually no danger of non-termination. An abstraction operator solely focussing on the syntactic structure would unnecessarily force generalisation, thus often resulting in sub-optimal specialisation.

Example 2. Let P be the following definite program:

(1) $path([N]) \leftarrow$
(2) $path([X,Y|T]) \leftarrow arc(X,Y), path([Y|T])$
(3) $arc(a,b) \leftarrow$

Unfolding $\leftarrow path(L)$ (e.g., using an unfolding rule based on ⊴; see Fig. 3 for the SLD-trees constructed) will result in lifting $path([b|T])$ to the global level. Notice that we have a growth of syntactic structure ($path(L) \trianglelefteq path([b|T])$). However, one can see that further unfolding $path([b|T])$ results in a SLD-tree whose characteristic tree $\tau_B = \{\langle 1 \circ 1 \rangle\}$ is strictly smaller than the one for $path(L)$ (which is $\tau_A = \{\langle 1 \circ 1 \rangle, \langle 1 \circ 2, 1 \circ 3 \rangle\}$).

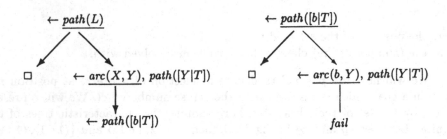

Fig. 3. SLD-trees for Example 2

In summary, characteristic trees seem to be an almost ideal vehicle for a refined control of polyvariance, a fact we will try to exploit in the following section.

2.3   An abstraction operator using characteristic trees

A first attempt at using characteristic might be as follows: classify atoms at the global control level by their associated characteristic tree and apply generalisation (msg) only on those atoms which have the same characteristic tree. The following example illustrates this approach.

Example 3. Let P be the program reversing a list using an accumulating parameter:

(1) $rev([], Acc, Acc) \leftarrow$
(2) $rev([H|T], Acc, Res) \leftarrow rev(T, [H|Acc], Res)$

We will use an unfolding rule U based on $\trianglelefteq$ inside the generic Algorithm 3.1 in [28].

When starting out with $\mathcal{A}_0 = \{rev([a|B], [], R)\}$ the following steps are performed by Algorithm 3.1:

- the only atom in $\mathcal{A}_0$ is unfolded (see Fig. 4) and the atoms in the leaves are added, yielding: $\mathcal{A}'_0 = \{rev([a|B], [], R), rev(B, [a], R)\}$.
- the atoms in $\mathcal{A}'_0$ all have different characteristic trees, and we obtain $\mathcal{A}_1 = \mathcal{A}'_0$.
- the atoms in $\mathcal{A}_1$ are unfolded (see Fig. 4) and the atoms in the leaves are added, yielding:
  $\mathcal{A}'_1 = \{rev([a|B], [], R), rev(B, [a], R), rev(T, [H, a], R)\}$.
- the atoms $rev(B, [a], R)$ and $rev(T, [H, a], R)$ have the same characteristic tree (see Fig. 4) and we thus apply the *msg* and obtain:
  $\mathcal{A}_2 = \{rev([a|B], [], R), rev(T, [A|B], R)\}$.
- the atoms in $\mathcal{A}_2$ are unfolded and the leaf atoms added:
  $\mathcal{A}'_2 = \{rev([a|B], [], R), rev(T, [A|B], R), rev(T', [H', A|B], R)\}$.
- the atoms $rev(T, [A|B], R)$ and $rev(T', [H', A|B], R)$ have the same characteristic tree and we thus apply the *msg* and obtain: $\mathcal{A}_3 = \mathcal{A}_2$. We have reached a fixpoint and thus obtain the following partial deduction satisfying the closedness condition (and which is also independent without renaming):
  $rev([a|B], [], R) \leftarrow rev(B, [a], R)$
  $rev([], [A|B], [A|B]) \leftarrow$
  $rev([H|T], [A|B], Res) \leftarrow rev(T, [H, A|B], Res)$

Because of the selective application of the *msg*, no loss of precision has been incurred, e.g., the pruning and pre-computation for $rev([a|B], [], R)$ has been preserved. An abstraction operator allowing just one version per predicate would have lost this local specialisation, while a method with unlimited polyvariance (called dynamic renaming, in [1]) does not terminate.

For this example, our approach provides a terminating and fine grained control of polyvariance, conferring just as many polyvariant versions as necessary.

The above example is thus very encouraging and one might hope that characteristic trees are always preserved upon generalisation and that we already have a refined solution to the control of polyvariance problem. Unfortunately, the approach still has two major problems:

1. it does not always preserve the characteristic trees, entailing a loss of precision and specialisation, and
2. it is not guaranteed to terminate (even if the number of distinct characteristic trees is finite).

We illustrate these problems and show how they can be overcame in the Sections 2.4 and 2.5 below.

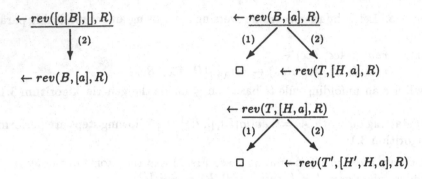

Fig. 4. SLD-trees for Example 3

2.4 Preserving characteristic trees upon generalisation

Let us show why the approach described in Section 2.3 does not preserve characteristic trees:

Example 4. Let P be the program:

   (1) $p(X) \leftarrow q(X)$
   (2) $p(c) \leftarrow$

Let $\mathcal{A} = \{p(a), p(b)\}$. Supposing that we do not unfold $q(X)$, $p(a)$ and $p(b)$ have the same characteristic tree $\tau = \{\langle 1 \circ 1 \rangle\}$. We thus calculate $msg(p(a), p(b)) = p(X)$ which has unfortunately the characteristic tree $\tau' = \{\langle 1 \circ 1 \rangle, \langle 1 \circ 2 \rangle\} \neq \tau$ and the pruning that was possible for the atoms $p(a)$ and $p(b)$ has been lost. More importantly, there exists *no* atom, more general than $p(a)$ and $p(b)$, which has τ as its characteristic tree.

The problem in the above example is that, through generalisation, a new non-failing derivation has been added, thereby modifying the characteristic tree. Another problem can occur when negative literals are selected by the unfolding rule. More involved and realistic examples can be found in [33, 31].

These losses of precision can have some regrettable consequences in practice:

- opportunities for specialisation can be lost and
- termination of Algorithm 3.1 in [28] can be undermined (even assuming a finite number of characteristic trees).

Two different solutions to this problem:

1. *Ecological Partial Deduction* [25, 33]
   The basic idea is to simply *impose* characteristic trees on the generalised atoms. To solve Ex. 4 one would produce the generalisation $p(X)$ on which we impose $\tau = \{\langle 1 \circ 1 \rangle\}$ (this is denoted by $(p(X), \tau)$ in [25, 33], also called a *characteristic atom*). The residual code generated for $(p(X), \tau)$ is:

       $p(X) \leftarrow q(X)$

In other words the pruning possible for $p(a)$ and $p(b)$ has now been preserved. However, the above residual code is not valid for all instances of $p(X)$; it is only valid for those instances (called concretisations) for which τ is a "proper" characteristic tree. For example, the code is valid for $p(a)$, $p(b)$, $p(d)$, but *not* for $p(c)$. The full details, along with correctness results, of this approach can be found in [25, 33].

2. *Constrained Partial Deduction* [31]

The basic idea of constrained partial deductions is to, instead of producing a partial deduction for a set of atoms, to produce it for a set of *constrained atoms*. A constrained atom is a formula of the form $C \,\square\, A$, where A is an ordinary atom and C a constraint over some domain $\mathcal{D}$ (see also [21]). The set of "proper" instances (called concretisations) of a constrained atom $C \,\square\, A$ are then all the atoms $A\theta$ such that $C\theta$ holds in $\mathcal{D}$.

[31] then achieves the preservation of characteristic trees by using *disequality constraints*, designed in such a way as to prune the possible computations into the right shape. To solve Ex. 4 one would produce the generalisation of $X \neq c \,\square\, p(X)$. The residual code generated for this generalisation is the same as for ecological partial deduction, and again the pruning possible for $p(a)$ and $p(b)$ has been preserved:

$$p(X) \leftarrow q(X)$$

The approach in [31] is more general and constraints are also propagated globally (i.e., in the terminology of supercompilation [44, 19, 43, 42], one can "drive negative information"). On the other hand, the method in [33] is conceptually simpler and can handle *any* unfolding rule as well as *normal* logic programs, while the concrete algorithm in [31] is currently limited to determinate unfoldings without a lookahead and definite programs.

2.5 Ensuring termination without depth-bounds

It turns out that for a fairly *large class of realistic programs* (and unfolding rules), the characteristic tree based approaches described above only terminate when imposing a depth bound on characteristic trees. [33] presents some natural examples which show that this leads to undesired results in cases where the depth bound is actually required. (These examples can also be adapted to prove a similar point about neighbourhoods in the context of supercompilation of functional programs.)

We illustrate the problem through a slightly artificial, but very simple example.

Example 5. The following is the reverse with accumulating parameter of Ex. 3 where a list type check (in the style of [14]) on the accumulator has been added.

(1) $rev([], Acc, Acc) \leftarrow$
(2) $rev([H|T], Acc, Res) \leftarrow ls(Acc), rev(T, [H|Acc], Res)$
(3) $ls([]) \leftarrow$
(4) $ls([H|T]) \leftarrow ls(T)$

As can be noticed in Fig. 5, unfolding (determinate, $\unlhd$-based, and well-founded, among others) produces an infinite number of different atoms, all with a different characteristic tree. Imposing a depth bound of say 100, we obtain termination; however, 100 different characteristic trees (and instantiations of the accumulator) arise, and 100 different versions of *rev* are generated: one for each characteristic tree. The specialised program thus looks like:

(1') $rev([], [], []) \leftarrow$

(2') $rev([H|T], [], Res) \leftarrow rev_2(T, [H], Res)$

(3') $rev_2([], [A], [A]) \leftarrow$

(4') $rev_2([H|T], [A], Res) \leftarrow rev_3(T, [H, A], Res)$

$\vdots$

(197') $rev_{99}([], [A_1, \ldots, A_{98}], [A_1, \ldots, A_{98}]) \leftarrow$

(198') $rev_{99}([H|T], [A_1, \ldots, A_{98}], Res) \leftarrow$
$$rev_{100}(T, [H, A_1, \ldots, A_{98}], Res)$$

(199') $rev_{100}([], [A_1, \ldots, A_{99}|AT], [A_1, \ldots, A_{99}|AT]) \leftarrow$

(200') $rev_{100}([H|T], [A_1, \ldots, A_{99}|AT], Res) \leftarrow$
$$ls(AT), rev_{100}(T, [H, A_1, \ldots, A_{99}|AT], Res)$$

(201') $ls([]) \leftarrow$

(202') $ls([H|T]) \leftarrow ls(T)$

This program is certainly far from optimal and clearly exhibits the ad hoc nature of the depth bound.

Situations like the above typically arise when an accumulating parameter influences the computation, because then the growing of the accumulator causes a corresponding growing of the characteristic trees. With most simple programs, this is not the case. For instance, in the standard reverse with accumulating parameter, the accumulator is only copied in the end, but never influences the computation. For this reason it was generally felt that natural logic programs would give rise to only finitely many characteristic trees.

However, among larger and more sophisticated programs, cases like the above become more and more frequent, even in the absence of type-checking. For instance, in an explicit unification algorithm, one accumulating parameter is the substitution built so far. It heavily influences the computation because new bindings have to be added and checked for compatibility with the current substitution.

A solution to this problem is developed in [33], whose basic ingredients are as follows:

1. Register descendency relationships among atoms at the global level by putting them into a *global tree* (instead of a global set).
2. To watch over the evolution of the characteristic trees associated with atoms along the branches of the global tree in order to detect dangerous growths. Obviously, just measuring the depth of characteristic trees would be far too crude. As can be seen in Fig. 5, we need a more refined measure which would

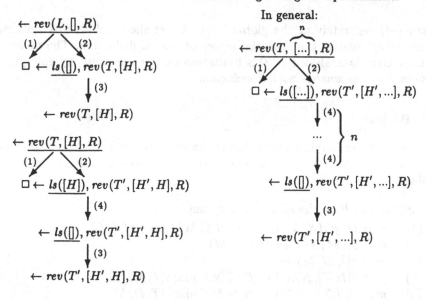

Fig. 5. SLD-trees for Example 5.

somehow spot when a characteristic tree (piecemeal) "contains" characteristic trees appearing earlier in the same branch of the global tree. If such
a situation arises—as it indeed does in Ex. 5—it seems reasonable to stop
expanding the global tree, generalise the offending atoms, and produce a
specialised procedure for the generalisation instead. As shown in [33], this
can be accomplished by extending the homeomorphic embedding relation ⊴
to work on characteristic trees.

The techniques formally elaborated in [33] have led to the implementation
of the ECCE partial deduction system which is publicly available [26]. Extensive
experiments are reported on in [33, 27]. The ECCE system also handles a lot of
Prolog built-ins, like for instance =, is, <, =<, <, >=, *number*, *atomic*, *call*,
\==, \=. All built-ins are supposed to be declarative and their selection delayed
until they are sufficiently instantiated. These built-ins are then also registered
within the characteristic trees (see [27]).

3   Conjunctive Partial Deduction

Partial deduction, based upon the Lloyd-Shepherdson framework [35], specialises
a *set of atoms*. Even though conjunctions may appear within the SLDNF-trees
constructed for these atoms, only atoms are allowed at the global level. In other
words, when we stop unfolding, every conjunction at the leaf is automatically
split into its atomic constituents which are then specialised (and possibly further

abstracted) separately at the global level. As we show below, this restriction considerably restricts the potential power of partial deduction. The main goal of this section is to show how this limitation can be overcome, by going to the framework of *conjunctive partial deduction*.

3.1   Basics

Let us start by examining a very simple example. In the following, we introduce the connective $\wedge$ to avoid confusion between conjunction and the set punctuation symbol ",".

Example 6. Let P be the following program.

(1) $max\_length(X, M, L) \leftarrow max(X, M) \wedge length(X, L)$
(2) $max(X, M) \leftarrow max\_1(X, 0, M)$
(3) $max1([\,], M, M) \leftarrow$
(4) $max1([H|T], N, M) \leftarrow H \leq N \wedge max1(T, N, M)$
(5) $max1([H|T], N, M) \leftarrow H > N \wedge max1(T, H, M)$
(6) $length([\,], 0) \leftarrow$
(7) $length([H|T], L) \leftarrow length(T, K) \wedge L \text{ is } K + 1$

Let us try to specialise this program for calls to $max\_length(x, m, l)$, which calculate the length and maximum element of a list. One can see that the original program above is needlessly inefficient at this: it traverses the list x twice, once to calculate the maximum and then again to compute the length. One might hope that by specialisation this inefficiency can be removed, i.e., that these two computations can be "tupled" together. Unfortunately this optimisation is out of the reach of partial deduction, due to its inability to handle conjunctions at the global level. For instance, assume that we construct the finite SLD-tree for $max\_length(x, m, l)$ depicted at the left in Fig. 6. Now the atoms $max\_1(x, 0, m)$ and $length(X, l)$ have to be specialised separately and the specialised program will contain two predicates each traversing x on its own. The situations remains the same, no matter how deeply we unfold $max\_length(x, m, l)$. In other words, partial deduction is incapable of translating multiple visits of the same data structure into a single visit (called *tupling*); something which can be achieved using unfold/fold program transformation methods [39].

To overcome this limitation, [32, 17, 27] present a minimal extension to partial deduction, called *conjunctive partial deduction*. This technique extends the standard partial deduction approach by simply considering a set $S = \{C_1, \ldots, C_n\}$ of *conjunctions of atoms* instead of just atoms.

Now, as the SLDNF-trees constructed for each C_i are no longer restricted to having *atomic* top-level goals, resultants (cf. Definition 25 in the first part of the course [28]) are not necessarily Horn clauses anymore: their left-hand side may contain a conjunction of atoms. To transform such resultants back into standard clauses, conjunctive partial deduction requires a *renaming* transformation, from conjunctions to atoms, in a post-processing step. We illustrate this below; the formal details are in [32, 17, 27].

Let us return to Ex. 6 to illustrate the basic workings of conjunctive partial deduction. Let $S = \{max\_length(x, m, l), max\_1(x, n, m) \land length(x, l)\}$ be the set of conjunctions we specialise. Assume that we construct the SLD-trees depicted in Fig. 6. The associated resultants are $\{R_{1,1}\}$ and $\{R_{2,1}, R_{2,2}, R_{2,3}\}$ with:

$(R_{1,1})$ $max\_length(X, M, L) \leftarrow max1(X, 0, M) \land length(X, L)$

$(R_{2,1})$ $max1([\,], N, N) \land length([\,], 0) \leftarrow$

$(R_{2,2})$ $max1([H|T], N, M) \land length([H|T], L) \leftarrow$
$\qquad H \leq N \land max1(T, N, M) \land length(T, K) \land L \text{ is } K + 1$

$(R_{2,3})$ $max1([H|T], N, M) \land length([H|T], L) \leftarrow$
$\qquad H > N \land max1(T, H, M) \land length(T, K) \land L \text{ is } K + 1$

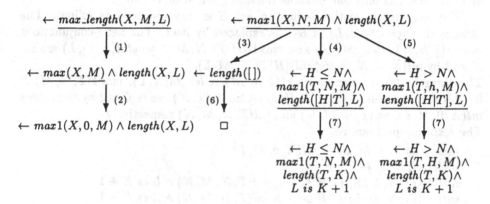

Fig. 6. SLD-trees τ_1 and τ_2 for Example 6

Clearly $R_{2,1}, R_{2,2}, R_{2,3}$ are not program clauses. Apart from that, with the exception that the redundant variable still has multiple occurrences, the above set of resultants has the desired tupling structure. The two functionalities ($max/3$ and $length/2$) in the original program have been merged into single traversals. In order to convert the above into a standard logic program, we will rename conjunctions of atoms into atoms. Such renamings require some care. For one thing, there may be ambiguity concerning which conjunctions in the bodies to rename. For instance, if we have the resultant $p(x, y) \leftarrow r(x) \land q(y) \land r(z)$ and S contains $r(u) \land q(v)$, then either the first two, or the last two atoms in the body of this resultant are candidates for renaming. To formally fix such choices, we introduce the notion of a *partitioning function* p. Second, a particular conjunction in the body might be an instance of several elements in S (unless S is independent). Finally, we have to fix a mapping α (called an *atomic renaming* in [32]) from each element C_i of S to an atom A_i, having exactly the same variables as C_i, and such that each A_i uses a distinct predicate symbol.

For the *max_length* example, we simply use a partitioning function p which splits the conjunctions

$$H \leq N \wedge max1(T, N, M) \wedge length(T, K) \wedge L \text{ is } K + 1$$
$$H > N \wedge max1(T, H, M) \wedge length(T, K) \wedge L \text{ is } K + 1$$

into

$$\{H \leq N, \quad max1(T, N, M) \wedge length(T, K), \quad L \text{ is } K + 1\}$$
$$\{H > N, \quad max1(T, H, M) \wedge length(T, K), \quad L \text{ is } K + 1\}$$

respectively. Let us now map each element of S to an atom:
- $\alpha(max\_length(X, M, L)) = max\_length(X, M, L)$ and
- $\alpha(max1(X, N, M) \wedge length(X, L)) = ml(X, N, M, L)$.

S does not contain elements with common instances and for the resultants at hand there exists only one possible renaming based on α and p.

The conjunctive partial deduction wrt S is now obtained as follows. The head $max\_length(X, M, L)$ in $R_{1,1}$ is replaced by itself. The head-conjunctions $max1([], N, N) \wedge length([], 0)$ and $max1([H|T], N, M) \wedge length([H|T], L)$ are replaced by $ml([], N, N, 0)$ and $ml([H|T], N, M, L)$.
The three body occurrences $max1(X, 0, M) \wedge length(X, L)$, $max1(T, N, M) \wedge length(T, K)$ as well as $max1(T, H, M) \wedge length(T, K)$ are replaced by the atoms $ml(X, 0, M, L)$, $ml(T, N, M, K)$ and $ml(T, H, M, K)$ respectively.
The resulting program is:

$$max\_length(X, M, L) \leftarrow ml(X, 0, M, L)$$
$$ml([], N, N, 0) \leftarrow$$
$$ml([H|T], N, M, L) \leftarrow H \leq N \wedge ml(T, N, M, K) \wedge L \text{ is } K + 1$$
$$ml([H|T], N, M, L) \leftarrow H > N \wedge ml(T, H, M, K) \wedge L \text{ is } K + 1$$

We were thus able to produce an ordinary logic program in which the two functionalities of *max* and *length* are accomplished in a single traversal.

3.2   Deforestation

In this section we show how conjunctive partial deduction can be used to get rid of intermediate data structures, something which is called *deforestation* [49].

Example 7. Let P be the *append* program from Ex. 1. One way to append *three* lists is to use the goal $append(Xs, Ys, I) \wedge append(I, Zs, R)$, which is simple and elegant, but inefficient to execute. Given Xs, Ys, Zs and assuming left-to-right execution, $append(Xs, Ys, I)$ constructs from Xs and Ys an intermediate list I which is then traversed to append Zs to it. We now show how conjunctive partial deduction offers salvation.

Let $S = \{append(X, Y, I) \wedge append(I, Z, R), append(X, Y, Z)\}$ and assume that we construct the finite SLD-tree τ_1 depicted in Fig. 7 for the query $\leftarrow append(X, Y, I) \wedge append(I, Z, R)$ as well as a simple tree τ_2 with a single unfolding step for $\leftarrow append(X, Y, Z)$, whose resultants are simply the original program P. For τ_1 we get the following resultants:

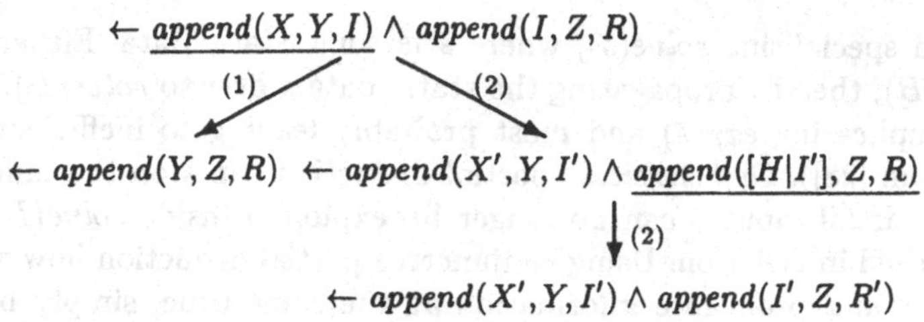

$$\leftarrow \underline{append(X,Y,I)} \wedge append(I,Z,R)$$

$$(1) \qquad \qquad (2)$$

$$\leftarrow append(Y,Z,R) \quad \leftarrow append(X',Y,I') \wedge \underline{append([H|I'],Z,R)}$$

$$\downarrow (2)$$

$$\leftarrow append(X',Y,I') \wedge append(I',Z,R')$$

Fig. 7. SLD-tree for Example 7

$(R_1) \quad append([\,],Y,Y) \wedge append(Y,Z,R) \leftarrow append(Y,Z,R)$

$(R_2) \quad append([H|X'],Y,[H|I']) \wedge append([H|I'],Z,[H|R']) \leftarrow$
$\qquad \qquad append(X',Y,I') \wedge append(I',Z,R')$

Suppose that we use a partitioning function p which performs no partitioning, i.e., $p(B) = \{B\}$ for all conjunctions B. If we now take an atomic renaming α for S such that $\alpha(append(X,Y,I) \wedge append(I,Z,R)) = da(X,Y,I,Z,R)$ and $\alpha(append(X,Y,Z)) = append(X,Y,Z)$ (i.e. the distinct variables have been collected and have been ordered according to their first appearance), then the conjunctive partial deduction wrt S will contain, in addition to the original program P (re-created from the resultants of τ_2), the following:

$(3) \quad da([\,],Y,Y,Z,R) \leftarrow append(Y,Z,R)$

$(4) \quad da([H|X'],Y,[H|I'],Z,[H|R']) \leftarrow da(X',Y,I',Z,R')$

Executing $G = \leftarrow append(X,Y,I) \wedge append(I,Z,R)$ in the original program leads to the construction of an intermediate list I by $append(X,Y,I)$, which is then traversed again (consumed) by $append(I,Z,R)$. In the conjunctive partial deduction, the inefficiency caused by the unnecessary traversal of I is avoided as the elements encountered while traversing X and Y are stored directly in R. However, the intermediate list I is still constructed, and if we are not interested in its value, then this is an unnecessary overhead. This can be remedied through a post-processing phase called *redundant argument filtering* (RAF) presented in [34, 27]. The resulting specialised program then contains the original append program P as well as:

$(3') \quad da([\,],Y,Z,R) \leftarrow append(Y,Z,R)$

$(4') \quad da([H|X'],Y,Z,[H|R']) \leftarrow da(X',Y,Z,R')$

The unnecessary variable I, as well as the inefficiencies caused by it, have now been completely removed; i.e., we have achieved *deforestation*.

3.3 Diminished Need for Aggressive Local Control

In addition to enabling tupling- and deforestation-like optimisations, conjunctive partial deduction also solves a problem already raised in [38]. Take for example a metainterpreter containing the clause $solve(X) \leftarrow exp(X) \wedge clause(X,B) \wedge solve(B)$, where $exp(X)$ is an expensive test which for some reason cannot be (fully) unfolded. Here "classical" partial deduction faces an unsolvable dilemma, e.g., when specialising $solve(\bar{s})$, where $\bar{s}$ is some static data. Either it unfolds $clause(\bar{s}, B)$, thereby propagating the static data $\bar{s}$ over to $solve(B)$, but at the cost of duplicating $exp(\bar{s})$ and most probably leading to inefficient programs (cf. Ex. 6 in [28]). Or "classical" partial deduction can stop the unfolding, but then the partial input $\bar{s}$ can no longer be exploited inside $solve(B)$ as it will be specialised in isolation. Using conjunctive partial deduction however, we can be efficient *and* propagate information at the same time, simply by stopping unfolding and specialising the conjunction $clause(\bar{s}, B) \wedge solve(B)$.

In other words, the local control no longer has to be clever about propagating partial input ($\bar{s}$) from one atom ($clause(\bar{s}, B)$) to the other ($solve(B)$); it can concentrate solely on efficiency concerns (not duplicating the expensive $exp(\bar{s})$). Conjunctive partial deduction therefore diminishes the need for aggressive unfolding rules (a claim empirically verified in [24, 27]) and allows to reconcile precision and efficiency.

3.4   Global Control and Implementation

A termination problem specific to conjunctive partial deduction lies in the possible appearance of ever growing conjunctions at the global level. To cope with this, abstraction in the context of conjunctive partial deduction must include the ability to *split* a conjunction into several parts, thus producing *subconjunctions* of the original one (cf. Ex. 6). A method to deal with this problem has been developed in [17, 9].

Apart from this aspect, the conventional control notions described earlier also apply in a conjunctive setting. Notably, the concept of characteristic trees can be generalised to handle conjunctions. The ECCE system [26], discussed earlier, has been extended to handle conjunctive partial deduction and the extensive experiments conducted in [24, 27] suggest that it was possible to consolidate partial deduction and unfold/fold program transformation, incorporating most of the power of the latter while keeping the automatic control and efficiency of the former. There are, however, still some practical limitations of the ECCE system concerning tupling and deforestation (getting rid of these limitations is a topic of further research, see [24, 27]).

3.5   Conjunctive Partial Deduction and Supercompilation

Partial deduction and related techniques in functional programming are often very similar [18] (and cross-fertilisation has taken place). Actually, conjunctive partial deduction has in part been inspired by supercompilation of functional programming (and by unfold/fold transformation techniques [39]) and the techniques have a lot in common. However, there are still some subtle differences. Notably, while conjunctive partial deduction can perform deforestation *and* tupling, supercompilation [19, 43] is incapable of achieving tupling. On the other hand, the techniques developed for tupling of functional programs [5, 6] are incapable of performing deforestation.

The reason for this extra power conferred by conjunctive partial deduction, is that conjunctions with shared variables can be used both to elegantly represent *nested function calls*

$$f(g(X)) \quad \mapsto \quad g(X, \underline{ResG}) \wedge f(\underline{ResG}, Res)$$

as well as *tuples*

$$\langle f(X), g(X) \rangle \quad \mapsto \quad g(\underline{X}, ResG) \wedge f(\underline{X}, ResF)$$

or any mixture thereof. The former enables deforestation while the latter is vital for tupling, explaining why conjunctive partial deduction can achieve both.

Let us, however, also note that actually achieving the tupling or deforestation in a logic programming context can be harder. For instance, in functional programming we know that for the same function call we always get the same, unique output. This is often important to achieve tupling, as it allows one to replace multiple function calls by a single call. For example we can safely transform $fib(N) + fib(N)$ into $\mathtt{let}\ X = fib(N)\ \mathtt{in}\ X + X$. In the context of logic programming it is, however, generally unsafe to transform the corresponding conjunction $fib(N, R1) \wedge fib(N, R2) \wedge Res\ is\ R1 + R2$ into $fib(N, R) \wedge Res\ is\ R + R$. If, e.g., *fib* is defined by the facts $fib(N, 1)$ and $fib(N, 2)$ then the first conjunction allows for three results $Res = 2, 3, 4$ while the second conjunction only allows $Res = 2, 4$. The above transformation is thus generally unsafe, unless we are certain that *fib* behaves like a function. Tupling in logic programming thus often requires one to establish *functionality* of the involved predicates. This can for instance be done via the approach presented in the next section or via (correct) user declarations (e.g., "$\mathtt{:-\ mode\ fib(i,o)\ is\ determinate.}$").

Furthermore, in functional programming function calls cannot *fail* while predicate calls in logic programming can. This means that *reordering* calls in logic programming can induce a change in the termination behaviour; something which is not a problem in (pure) functional programming. For instance reordering the conjunction $fail \wedge loop$ (where *loop* is a predicate that does not terminate) into $loop \wedge fail$ will change the Prolog termination behaviour: the former conjunction fails finitely while the latter does not terminate. Unfortunately, reordering is often required to achieve deforestation or tupling (although it was not required for the examples treated earlier). Let for example r and p be two predicates taking a binary tree as input and producing a modified tree as output. If we apply conjunctive partial deduction to $r(In, T) \wedge p(T, Out)$ we will typically get in the leaf of one of the branches of the SLD-tree the conjunction $r(InL, TL) \wedge r(InR, TR) \wedge p(TL, OutL) \wedge p(TR, OutR)$ where $InL, TL, OutL$ ($InR, TR, OutR$ respectively) are the left (right respectively) subtrees of L, T and Out. To achieve deforestation we need to reorder this conjunction into $r(InL, TL) \wedge p(TL, OutL) \wedge r(InR, TR) \wedge p(TR, OutR)$ so as to be able to eventually produce a residual conjunction such as $rp(InL, OutL) \wedge rp(InR, OutR)$. This means that to actually achieve deforestation or tupling in logic programming one often needs an additional analysis to ensure that termination is preserved [3, 2].

4   Incorporating Abstract Interpretation

The main idea of *abstract interpretation* [8, 4, 20] is to analyse programs by executing them over some *abstract domain*. This is done in such a way as to ensure termination of the abstract interpretation and to ensure that the so derived results are a *safe approximation* of the programs concrete runtime behaviour(s).

Abstract interpretation has already been used successfully as a post-processing optimisation [10, 14, 11] and it is often felt that there is a close relationship between abstract interpretation and program specialisation. Recently, there has been a lot of interest in the integration of these two techniques [30, 23, 41, 40, 47, 29, 48]. In this section we illustrate, on a simple example in the context of logic programming, why this integration is a worthwhile goal.

Example 8. Take the following simple program:

$app\_last(L, X) \leftarrow append(L, [a], R) \land last(R, X)$
$append([], L, L) \leftarrow$
$append([H|X], Y, [H|Z]) \leftarrow append(X, Y, Z)$
$last([X], X) \leftarrow$
$last([H|T], X) \leftarrow last(T, X)$

One would hope that some of the specialisation techniques we have seen so far are sufficiently strong to infer that a query $\leftarrow app\_last(L, X)$ only produces answers where $X = a$. Unfortunately, this is not the case. Even more surprisingly, most abstract interpretation techniques proposed in the literature, such as [22, 15, 37], on their own are incapable of deriving this result.

This is a very simple example where a statically known value (a) is stored (using *append*) in an unknown datastructure (L) and then later consulted (using *last*). More involved and realistic examples occur in, e.g., interpreters for imperative languages (where variable bindings are stored in some environment and then later consulted again) or explicit unification algorithms. Not being able to solve Ex. 8 means that any value stored in some (partially) unknown datastructure is lost for successive specialisation. This limitation is thus very regrettable for a lot of practical applications.

The reason why most abstract interpretation techniques are incapable of solving Ex. 8 is that they analyse atoms *separately*. In this program (and many, much more relevant others), we are interested in analysing the conjunction $append(L, [a], R) \land last(R, X)$ with a linking intermediate variable (whose structure is too complex for the particular abstract domain). If we could consider this conjunction as a *basic unit*, and therefore not perform abstraction on the separate atoms, but only on conjunctions of the involved atoms, we would retain a precise side-ways information passing analysis. This is exactly what can be achieved by combining the abstract interpretation with conjunctive partial deduction (the latter can also propagate goal dependent information).

Let us illustrate how conjunctive partial deduction combined with a simple abstract interpretation technique from [36] *does* solve Ex. 8. Starting from the

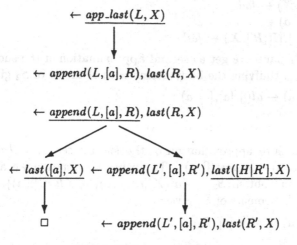

Fig. 8. SLD-trees for Ex. 8

atom $app\_last(X)$ and using straightforward control for conjunctive partial deduction [24], we can obtain $S = \{\ app\_last(X),\ append(L, [a], R) \land last(R, X)\ \}$ and the corresponding SLD-trees in Fig. 8.

Using a renaming transformation based on $\alpha(append(x, y, z) \land last(z, u)) = al(x, y, z, u)$ the resulting transformed program is:

$app\_last(L, X) \leftarrow al(L, [a], R, X)$
$al([], [a], [a], a) \leftarrow$
$al([H|L'], [a], [H|R'], X) \leftarrow al(L', [a], R', X)$

Notice that conjunctive partial deduction *alone* does not yet produce the desired result (X is not instantiated to a in the first clause). This is due to a lack of inference of global success information, i.e., being unable to extract information from an infinite number of different computation paths. If the length of the list L were given, then (conjunctive) partial deduction could obtain the desired result simply by unfolding. Here, however, the length of L is unknown, and an infinite number of unfoldings would be required. It is here that abstract interpretation comes to the rescue, as it can infer information about an infinite number of different computation paths. One way [36] this can be done, is by examining the above program bottom-up:

1. Start by assuming that every call fails: we approximate the *success set* (i.e., those atoms that succeed) by $S_1 = \emptyset$ and set $i = 1$.
2. Unify every atom in the body of a clause with an element of S_i and instantiate the head accordingly. Put the so obtained heads into S_{i+1}.
3. Apply the *msg* predicatewise to S_{i+1} and stop if $S_{i+1} = S_i$; otherwise increment i and goto step 2.

Performing these steps on our residual program, we obtain the following scenario. First we unify the body atoms with elements of $S_1 = \emptyset$:

$app\_last(L, X) \leftarrow fail$
$al([], [a], [a], a) \leftarrow$
$al([H|L'], [a], [H|R'], X) \leftarrow fail$

Examining each clause we get as second approximation of the success set $S_2 = \{al([], [a], [a], a)\}$. Unifying the body atoms with elements of S_2 gives:

$app\_last([], a) \leftarrow al([], [a], [a], a)$
$al([], [a], [a], a) \leftarrow$
$al([H], [a], [H, a], a) \leftarrow al([], [a], [a], a)$

We thus get as third approximation of the success set $S_3 = \{al([], [a], [a], a), al([H], [a], [H, a], a), app\_last([], a)\}$. To ensure termination we apply the *msg* predicate-wise and obtain $S_3 = \{al(X, [a], Y, a), app\_last([], a)\}$. Unifying the body atoms with elements of S_3 gives:

$app\_last([], a) \leftarrow al([], [a], R, a)$
$al([], [a], [a], a) \leftarrow$
$al([H|L'], [a], [H|R'], a) \leftarrow al(L', [a], R', a)$

At the next step we obtain $S_4 = \{al(X, [a], Y, a), app\_last(L, a)\}$ as well as the instantiated program P_4:

$app\_last(L, a) \leftarrow al(L, [a], R, a)$
$al([], [a], [a], a) \leftarrow$
$al([H|L'], [a], [H|R'], a) \leftarrow al(L', [a], R', a)$

We now obtain $S_5 = S_4$ and our abstract interpretation is complete. This residual program P_4 now explicitly contains the information that $X = a$ in $app\_last(L, X)$. According to the results in [36] we can actually use this program in place of the original residual program delivered by conjunctive partial deduction (computed answers and finite failure is preserved; however, infinite failure might be replaced by finite one).

Note, that the above technique *fails* to deliver this information when applied to the original program, even after a magic-set transformation (see [30, 27]). Via filtering and redundant argument filtering (cf. Section 3.2) we can even further simplify this into the "optimal"[2] program:

$app\_last(L, a) \leftarrow al(L)$
$al([]) \leftarrow$
$al([H|L']) \leftarrow al(L')$

In addition to the already stated applications, the combination of conjunctive partial deduction and abstract interpretation is an elegant way to infer functionality of predicates [30, 27], perform some basic inductive theorem proving tasks[3] [30, 27], sophisticated program inversion tasks, as well as software verification tasks such as model checking. For further details, comprising algorithms and technical results, we refer to [30, 27, 29].

---

[2] In the absence of type information we have to keep the call to $al(L)$, ensuring that we deliver $X = a$ only if L is actually a list (see also [29]).

[3] The relation between program specialisation and *(inductive) theorem proving* has already been raised several times in the literature [45, 16, 46].

5 Conclusion and Outlook

In Section 2 we have investigated the problematic question of when is it sensible to generate different specialised versions for a particular predicate and when is it sensible to perform abstraction instead. For this recurring, difficult problem, termed the control of polyvariance problem, we presented the advantages of characteristic trees over a purely syntactic approach. We thereafter illustrated some of the technical difficulties of using characteristic trees in practice, related to precision and termination, and have shown how they can be overcome.

The control of polyvariance problem occurs in different disguises in many areas of program analysis, manipulation and optimisation. We therefore believe that the presented techniques can be adapted for other (declarative) programming paradigms and that they might prove equally useful in the context of, e.g., abstract interpretation systems or optimising compilers.

Section 3 was aimed at augmenting the power of partial deduction. Indeed, partial deduction was heretofore incapable of performing certain useful unfold/fold transformations, like tupling or deforestation. We presented the framework of conjunctive partial deduction which, by specialising conjunctions instead of individual atoms, is able to accommodate these optimisations. Deforestation and tupling like transformation are useful even in the absence of partial input. This warrants the integration of the presented techniques into a compiler, as their systematic use might prove to be highly beneficial and allow users to more easily decompose and combine procedures and programs without having to worry about the ensuing inefficiencies.

In Section 4 we illustrated that abstract interpretation and (conjunctive) partial deduction have limitations on their own and that a combination of these techniques might therefore be extremely useful in practice. We have illustrated how this can be accomplished on a simple example and have hinted at the benefits of such an integration for practical applications.

Acknowledgements

The author greatly benefited from discussions and joint work with Maurice Bruynooghe, Danny De Schreye, Robert Glück, Jesper Jørgensen, Neil Jones, Bern Martens, and Morten Heine Sørensen.

References

1. K. Benkerimi and P. M. Hill. Supporting transformations for the partial evaluation of logic programs. *Journal of Logic and Computation*, 3(5):469–486, October 1993.
2. A. Bossi and N. Cocco. Replacement can Preserve Termination. In J. Gallagher, editor, Logic Program Synthesis and Transformation. *Proceedings of LOPSTR'96*, LNCS 1207, pages 104–129, Stockholm, Sweden, August 1996. Springer-Verlag.
3. A. Bossi, N. Cocco and S. Etalle. Transformation of Left Terminating Programs: The Reordering Problem. In M. Proietti, editor, Logic Program Synthesis and Transformation. *Proceedings of LOPSTR'95*, LNCS 1048, pages 33–45, Utrecht, Netherlands, September 1995. Springer-Verlag.

4. M. Bruynooghe. A practical framework for the abstract interpretation of logic programs. *The Journal of Logic Programming*, 10:91–124, 1991.
5. W.-N. Chin. Towards an automated tupling strategy. In *Proceedings of PEPM'93, the ACM Sigplan Symposium on Partial Evaluation and Semantics-Based Program Manipulation*, pages 119–132. ACM Press, 1993.
6. W.-N. Chin and S.-C. Khoo. Tupling functions with multiple recursion parameters. In *Proceedings of the Third International Workshop on Static Analysis*, number 724 in LNCS 724, pages 124–140, Padova, Italy, Sept. 1993. Springer-Verlag.
7. C. Consel and S. C. Khoo. Parameterized partial evaluation. *ACM Transactions on Programming Languages and Systems*, 15(3):463–493, 1993.
8. P. Cousot and R. Cousot. Abstract interpretation and application to logic programs. *The Journal of Logic Programming*, 13(2 & 3):103–179, 1992.
9. D. De Schreye, R. Glück, J. Jørgensen, M. Leuschel, B. Martens, and M. H. Sørensen. Conjunctive partial deduction: Foundations, control, algorithms and experiments. *The Journal of Logic Programming*, 1999. To appear.
10. D. A. de Waal and J. Gallagher. Specialisation of a unification algorithm. In T. Clement and K.-K. Lau, editors, Logic Program Synthesis and Transformation. *Proceedings of LOPSTR'91*, pages 205–220, Manchester, UK, 1991.
11. D. A. de Waal and J. Gallagher. The applicability of logic program analysis and transformation to theorem proving. In A. Bundy, editor, *Automated Deduction—CADE-12*, pages 207–221. Springer-Verlag, 1994.
12. J. Gallagher. A system for specialising logic programs. Technical Report TR-91-32, University of Bristol, November 1991.
13. J. Gallagher and M. Bruynooghe. The derivation of an algorithm for program specialisation. *New Generation Computing*, 9(3 & 4):305–333, 1991.
14. J. Gallagher and D. A. de Waal. Deletion of redundant unary type predicates from logic programs. In K.-K. Lau and T. Clement, editors, Logic Program Synthesis and Transformation. *Proceedings of LOPSTR'92*, pages 151–167, Manchester, UK, 1992.
15. J. Gallagher and D. A. de Waal. Fast and precise regular approximations of logic programs. In P. Van Hentenryck, editor, *Proceedings of the Eleventh International Conference on Logic Programming*, pages 599–613. The MIT Press, 1994.
16. R. Glück and J. Jørgensen. Generating transformers for deforestation and supercompilation. In B. Le Charlier, editor, *Proceedings of SAS'94*, LNCS 864, pages 432–448, Namur, Belgium, September 1994. Springer-Verlag.
17. R. Glück, J. Jørgensen, B. Martens, and M. H. Sørensen. Controlling conjunctive partial deduction of definite logic programs. In H. Kuchen and S. Swierstra, editors, *Proceedings of the International Symposium on Programming Languages, Implementations, Logics and Programs (PLILP'96)*, LNCS 1140, pages 152–166, Aachen, Germany, September 1996. Springer-Verlag.
18. R. Glück and M. H. Sørensen. Partial deduction and driving are equivalent. In M. Hermenegildo and J. Penjam, editors, *Programming Language Implementation and Logic Programming. Proceedings, Proceedings of PLILP'94*, LNCS 844, pages 165–181, Madrid, Spain, 1994. Springer-Verlag.
19. R. Glück and M. H. Sørensen. A roadmap to supercompilation. In O. Danvy, R. Glück, and P. Thiemann, editors, *Proceedings of the 1996 Dagstuhl Seminar on Partial Evaluation*, LNCS 1110, pages 137–160, Schloß Dagstuhl, 1996. Springer-Verlag.
20. M. Hermenegildo, R. Warren, and S. K. Debray. Global flow analysis as a practical compilation tool. *The Journal of Logic Programming*, 13(4):349–366, 1992.

21. J. Jaffar and M. J. Maher. Constraint logic programming: A survey. *The Journal of Logic Programming*, 19 & 20:503–581, 1994.
22. G. Janssens and M. Bruynooghe. Deriving descriptions of possible values of program variables by means of abstract interpretation. *The Journal of Logic Programming*, 13(2 & 3):205–258, 1992.
23. N. D. Jones. Combining abstract interpretation and partial evaluation. In P. Van Hentenryck, editor, *Static Analysis, Proceedings of SAS'97*, LNCS 1302, pages 396–405, Paris, 1997. Springer-Verlag.
24. J. Jørgensen, M. Leuschel, and B. Martens. Conjunctive partial deduction in practice. In J. Gallagher, editor, *Proceedings of the International Workshop on Logic Program Synthesis and Transformation (LOPSTR'96)*, LNCS 1207, pages 59–82, Stockholm, Sweden, August 1996. Springer-Verlag.
25. M. Leuschel. Ecological partial deduction: Preserving characteristic trees without constraints. In M. Proietti, editor, Logic Program Synthesis and Transformation. *Proceedings of LOPSTR'95*, LNCS 1048, pages 1–16, Utrecht, The Netherlands, September 1995. Springer-Verlag.
26. M. Leuschel. The ECCE partial deduction system and the DPPD library of benchmarks. Obtainable via http://www.cs.kuleuven.ac.be/~dtai, 1996.
27. M. Leuschel. *Advanced Techniques for Logic Program Specialisation*. PhD thesis, K.U. Leuven, May 1997.
     Accessible via http://www.cs.kuleuven.ac.be/~michael.
28. M. Leuschel. *Logic Program Specialisation*. In J. Hatcliff, T. Mogensen, and P. Thiemann, editors, *DIKU 1998 International Summerschool on Partial Evaluation*, LNCS 1706, pages 155–188, Copenhagen, Denmark, July 1998. Springer-Verlag. In *this volume*.
29. M. Leuschel. Program specialisation and abstract interpretation reconciled. In J. Jaffar, editor, *Proceedings of the Joint International Conference and Symposium on Logic Programming JICSLP'98*, pages 220–234, Manchester, UK, June 1998. MIT Press.
30. M. Leuschel and D. De Schreye. Logic program specialisation: How to be more specific. In H. Kuchen and S. Swierstra, editors, *Proceedings of the International Symposium on Programming Languages, Implementations, Logics and Programs (PLILP'96)*, LNCS 1140, pages 137–151, Aachen, Germany, September 1996. Springer-Verlag.
31. M. Leuschel and D. De Schreye. Constrained partial deduction and the preservation of characteristic trees. *New Generation Computing*, 16(3):283–342, 1998.
32. M. Leuschel, D. De Schreye, and A. de Waal. A conceptual embedding of folding into partial deduction: Towards a maximal integration. In M. Maher, editor, *Proceedings of the Joint International Conference and Symposium on Logic Programming JICSLP'96*, pages 319–332, Bonn, Germany, September 1996. MIT Press.
33. M. Leuschel, B. Martens, and D. De Schreye. Controlling generalisation and polyvariance in partial deduction of normal logic programs. *ACM Transactions on Programming Languages and Systems*, 20(1):208–258, January 1998.
34. M. Leuschel and M. H. Sørensen. Redundant argument filtering of logic programs. In J. Gallagher, editor, *Proceedings of the International Workshop on Logic Program Synthesis and Transformation (LOPSTR'96)*, LNCS 1207, pages 83–103, Stockholm, Sweden, August 1996. Springer-Verlag.
35. J. W. Lloyd and J. C. Shepherdson. Partial evaluation in logic programming. *The Journal of Logic Programming*, 11(3& 4):217–242, 1991.

36. K. Marriott, L. Naish, and J.-L. Lassez. Most specific logic programs. *Annals of Mathematics and Artificial Intelligence*, 1:303–338, 1990.
37. A. Mulkers, W. Winsborough, and M. Bruynooghe. Live-structure data-flow analysis for prolog. *ACM Transactions on Programming Languages and Systems*, 16(2):205–258, 1994.
38. S. Owen. Issues in the partial evaluation of meta-interpreters. In H. Abramson and M. Rogers, editors, *Meta-Programming in Logic Programming, Proceedings of the Meta88 Workshop, June 1988*, pages 319–339. MIT Press, 1989.
39. A. Pettorossi and M. Proietti. Transformation of logic programs: Foundations and techniques. *The Journal of Logic Programming*, 19& 20:261–320, May 1994.
40. G. Puebla, J. Gallagher, and M. Hermenegildo. Towards integrating partial evaluation in a specialization framework based on generic abstract interpretation. In M. Leuschel, editor, *Proceedings of the ILPS'97 Workshop on Specialisation of Declarative Programs and its Application*, K.U. Leuven, Tech. Rep. CW 255, pages 29–38, Port Jefferson, USA, October 1997.
41. G. Puebla and M. Hermenegildo. Abstract specialization and its application to program parallelization. In J. Gallagher, editor, *Proceedings of the International Workshop on Logic Program Synthesis and Transformation (LOPSTR'96)*, LNCS 1207, pages 169–186, Stockholm, Sweden, August 1996.
42. M. H. Sørensen and R. Glück. *Introduction to Supercompilation*. In J. Hatcliff, T. Mogensen, and P. Thiemann, editors, *DIKU 1998 International Summerschool on Partial Evaluation*, LNCS 1706, pages 246–270, Copenhagen, Denmark, July 1998. Springer-Verlag. In *this volume*.
43. M. H. Sørensen, R. Glück, and N. D. Jones. A positive supercompiler. *Journal of Functional Programming*, 6(6):811–838, 1996.
44. V. F. Turchin. The concept of a supercompiler. *ACM Transactions on Programming Languages and Systems*, 8(3):292–325, 1986.
45. V. F. Turchin. Program transformation with metasystem transitions. *Journal of Functional Programming*, 3(3):283–313, 1993.
46. V. F. Turchin. Metacomputation: Metasystem transitions plus supercompilation. In O. Danvy, R. Glück, and P. Thiemann, editors, *Proceedings of the 1996 Dagstuhl Seminar on Partial Evaluation*, LNCS 1110, pages 482–509, Schloß Dagstuhl, 1996. Springer-Verlag.
47. W. Vanhoof. Bottom-up information propagation for partial deduction. In M. Leuschel, editor, *Proceedings of the ILPS'97 Workshop on Specialisation of Declarative Programs and its Application*, K.U. Leuven, Tech. Rep. CW 255, pages 73–82, Port Jefferson, USA, October 1997.
48. W. Vanhoof, B. Martens, D. De Schreye, and K. De Vlaminck. Specialising the other way around. In J. Jaffar, editor, *Proceedings of the Joint International Conference and Symposium on Logic Programming JICSLP'98*, Manchester, UK, June 1998. MIT Press.
49. P. Wadler. Deforestation: Transforming programs to eliminate intermediate trees. *Theoretical Computer Science*, 73:231–248, 1990. Preliminary version in ESOP'88, LNCS 300.

A Type Specialisation Tutorial

John Hughes

Department of Computing Science, Chalmers University of Technology, S-41296
Göteborg, SWEDEN. `rjmh@cs.chalmers.se`

1 Introduction

The essence of partial evaluation is beautifully simple: we just take a program, together with values of some of its inputs; we perform the operations that depend only on known inputs, build a new program from the other operations, and finally obtain a residual program which solves the same problem as the original for a subclass of the cases. Work by Neil Jones and his group over the past decade and a half has demonstrated just how powerful this simple idea really is.

But unfortunately, partial evaluation suffers from a serious problem: it fits badly with types. Since most real programming languages are typed, this is a major drawback. The problem is that the basic partial evaluation mechanism, evaluation and simplification of expressions, does not take types into account. As a result, simple partial evaluators cannot specialise types; residual programs operate on just the same types as the original program. But in principle, we might expect to gain just as much by specialising the data structures used in a program, as by specialising its code. While various forms of type specialisation have been added to partial evaluators in the past, the techniques needed are complicated, and the results not as far reaching as one might wish.

Type specialisation [3, 2, 1, 4] is a new approach to program specialisation which integrates types into the basic specialiser mechanisms, so that specialisation of data-structures can be achieved just as simply as specialisation of code. In this chapter we give a tutorial introduction to the subject via examples in a simple functional language.

How to use this tutorial. Much of the material in this chapter is contained in exercises, which encourage you to use the type specialiser in ways which syntax-directed partial evaluators cannot emulate. The intention is that readers solve the exercises on a machine while reading this chapter, and in our examples we therefore use the concrete ASCII syntax which the implemented specialiser accepts. The specialiser is written in Haskell 1.4, and the source code is available on the World Wide Web; for greatest convenience, download and compile the specialiser to use on your own machine. Readers without access to a Haskell 1.4 compiler may instead solve the exercises by running the specialiser on the Chalmers University web server. The URL is

`http://www.cs.chalmers.se/~rjmh/TypeSpec2`

2   Type Specialisation Basics

A partial evaluator specialises an expression to produce a residual expression, for example 2 + 2 specialises to 4. As in this example, if the original expression is static, then the residual expression will be a constant.

In contrast, the type specialiser specialises an expression *and type* to a residual expression *and residual type*. Thus both source and residual programs are typed. But while source types look much like the types in any other functional language, except that static and dynamic types are distinguished, the residual types carry very precise information. In this example, 2 +@ 2 (using the type specialiser's syntax) specialises to

Residual type: 4

Residual code:
void

Here the residual type, 4, is a 'singleton type' which tells us the value of the expression precisely. And since the value is explicit in the residual type, it need not appear at all in the residual code, which is just a dummy expression void.

This example illustrates one of the basic principles of type specialisation: static information is always carried in *residual types*, and consequently it need never appear in *residual terms*. We will see later how this property enables us to achieve stronger specialisations than partial evaluation can.

The example also illustrates another property of type specialisation: source programs are explicitly annotated to distinguish static from dynamic operations. Static operations are indicated with an '@' symbol; in this case +@ is the static addition operator. Unlike most partial evaluators, there is no binding-time analyser to insert such annotations automatically; we will discuss the reason for this later.

Let us consider a very simple example, to show how types can be used to propagate static information during specialisation. Consider the annotated expression

(\f. lift (f 3)) (\x. x +@ 1)

Here \x.e is our notation for a λ-expression, and juxtaposition is function application. In this example, the λs and the applications are dynamic, and so will not be reduced by the specialiser. The lift operator just modifies binding-times; it converts a static integer into a dynamic one.

Given this input, the type specialiser specialises 3 (which is static) to void with residual type 3; the static information is carried by the type. Since f is applied to this expression, it must have residual type 3 -> a for some type a. But since the λ-expression \x... is bound to f, it must have the same residual type 3 -> a. It follows that x has residual type 3. Given this information, x +@ 1 can be specialised to void with residual type 4 (once again, the static information is carried in the type). So now we know that \x..., and consequently also f, has

residual type 3 -> 4. As a result f 3 can be specialised to f void with residual
type 4, and then the lift ... can be specialised to 4, with residual type int.
The *type* of lift's argument tells us what residual *code* we should generate for
it. Since the result of lift is dynamic, the only static information expressed in
its residual type is that it is an integer. The final result is

(\f. 4) (\x. void)

with residual type int.

Type specialisation often produces programs containing 'dummy' void expressions, as in this case; indeed, every static expression specialises to one. The
implementation therefore includes a post-processor called the *arity raiser*, which
deletes every expression and every variable binding with a void type. (Actually,
as we will see, arity raising is a little more general than this). In this example, it
deletes the binding of f and the corresponding actual parameter, producing the
final result 4.

The interesting thing about this example is that the λ-expression \x. ...
can be specialised, and can produce a static result, even though it is a dynamic
function passed as a parameter to another dynamic function. When static information is propagated via types, there is no need to unfold a function application
in order to produce a static result. Consequently the type specialiser can propagate more static information than a partial evaluator can, and thus achieve
stronger specialisation.

Indeed, this example *as annotated* could not be specialised by an offline partial evaluator. Binding-time analysis imposes constraints on the ways in which
binding-times are used, for example, that dynamic functions must return dynamic results. That constraint is broken in this example, and so this annotation
could never be produced by binding-time analysis. In contrast, the type specialiser allows any binding-time to be used anywhere (provided, of course, they
are used consistently; this is enforced by assigning static and dynamic values
different types in the source language). In particular, dynamic functions may
very well have static or partly static results.

In this particular example, there is no reason to make the λ-expressions
dynamic; by annotating them static instead, then the same final result could be
achieved by partial evaluation. But in general, a specialiser cannot unfold *every*
function call, and the ability of the type specialiser to return static information
even from the calls which are not unfolded gives significant extra power.

3   Polyvariance

Let us consider a slight variation on the example above:

(\f. f 3 + f 4) (\x. lift (x +@ 1))

When we try to specialise this term, we obtain the slightly surprising error
message

Error: Cannot unify 4 with 3

The problem is that the arguments of f in the two calls have *different* residual types, namely 3 and 4, and f cannot be assigned both 3 -> ... and 4 -> ... as its type. Of course, our intention is to specialise f twice, but the type specialiser will not do so without further annotations.

Duplication by Unfolding. One possibility is to make the λs and applications static, so that they are unfolded. Our notation is to add @ to both λs and applications:

(\@f. f@3 + f@4)@(\@x. lift (x +@ 1))

Since unfolding duplicates the body of \@x... at two places, it can be specialised twice with different residual types for the bound variable x. The result is

4 + 5

But this is hardly satisfactory in general: we would not wish to have to unfold *every* function which is applied to several different static arguments. Instead, we would like to specialise f *polyvariantly*, to produce several residual functions rather than just one.

Polyvariant Specialisation. Polyvariance is introduced via an explicit annotation: the expression poly e specialises to a *tuple* (e1,...,en) of specialisations of e, with a residual type (t1,...,tn) which is a product of the residual types of the individual specialisations. In the source language, poly e has the type poly t, where t is the type of e. Consequently, a value created by poly cannot be used directly as a value of type t; to recover such a value we use the operator spec. When e is polyvariant, and so specialises to a tuple, then spec e specialises to an appropriate selection from the tuple. Using poly and spec we can annotate our example as

(\f. spec f 3 + spec f 4) (poly \x. lift (x +@ 1))

which specialises to

(\f. (fst f) void + (snd f) void) (\x.4, \x.5)

in which f has the residual type (3 -> int, 4 -> int).

The tuples introduced by polyvariance quickly make residual programs unreadably messy; we therefore let the arity raiser eliminate not only void values, but also all tuples. In this case, the result of arity raising is

(\f_1.\f_2.f_1 + f_2) 4 5

where the void values bound to x have been removed, and the residual pair that f specialised to has been replaced by two separate parameters. The relationship to traditional arity raising in partial evaluation is clear[1].

---

[1] We shall return to arity raising later: we use an aggressive variant which can lead to code duplication. However, this occurs in predictable circumstances which the programmer can avoid when writing the program to be specialised. See section 8.

Constructor Specialisation. There is actually a third way to specialise this example. Instead of generating two residual versions of f with different argument types, we may generate a single version whose argument type is a *sum* of the two types. We introduce such polyvariant sums using the special constructor In; just as **poly** e specialises to a residual expression with a product type, so In e specialises to an expression with a sum type, with one summand for each residual type of value which flows together. (Of course, all these values must have the same *source* type, otherwise the source program would be ill-typed). Values are extracted from sum types by pattern matching; a **case** over a polyvariant sum specialises to a **case** with one branch for each residual summand. This is just a version of Mogensen's constructor specialisation [6].

In our example, we tag the two different arguments to f with In, so that they specialise to elements of a common sum type, and we strip off the tag by pattern matching in the body of f:

```
(\f. f (In 3) + f (In 4))
  (\z. case z of In x: lift (x +@ 1) esac)
```

In the residual program, the two occurrences of In specialise to different constructors, and the **case** specialises to a **case** with two branches:

```
(\f.f (In1 void) + f (In0 void))
  (\z.case z of In0 x : 5, In1 x : 4 esac)
```

The type of z in this case is In0 4 | In1 3, which as usual carries all the static information: it records the two values passed to f, and their association with the specialised constructors.

Finally, the arity raiser deletes the void components, and the corresponding bound variable x, to produce

```
(\f.f In1 + f In0)
  (\z.case z of In0 : 5, In1 : 4 esac)
```

4   Syntactic Sugar

Now it is time to put these techniques into practice. As a first example, we shall employ them to specialise the ubiquitous **power** function. But first, we must introduce a little more syntax: the minimal language we have introduced so far cannot even express **power** palatably!

It is tedious to bind names with λs the whole time, so we introduce a form of **let** definitions. The example in the previous section can then be written more readably as

```
let f = \x. lift (x +@ 1) in
  f 3 + f 4
```

or, with the usual syntactic sugar for λ, as

```
let f x = lift (x +@ 1) in
 f 3 + f 4
```

This defines f as a dynamic, or non-unfoldable function. To make f unfoldable, we write

```
let f@x = lift (x +@ 1) in
 f@3 + f@4
```

which is just syntactic sugar for a let definition binding f to a static λ-expression \@x....

We can also make the let itself unfoldable, causing the specialiser to substitute the specialised first expression into the second, rather than build a residual let expression. For example,

```
let@ f x = lift (x +@ 1) in
 f 3 + f 4
```

But note that making a let expression unfoldable *has no effect* on the static information available during specialisation; the residual type of the bound variable is the same regardless of whether or not its specialised code is substituted into the body. In this example, even though the let is unfolded, f is still bound to a dynamic λ-expression, and so only *one* specialisation of f is generated to be substituted for each occurrence. Of course, as a result we encounter the 'cannot unify 3 and 4' error.

The syntactic sugar extends to polyvariant function definitions: the polyvariant version of our example can be written

```
let poly f x = lift (x +@ 1) in
 spec f 3 + spec f 4
```

which is sugar for

```
let f = poly \x. ... in ...
```

Finally, recursive functions can be defined with letrec; to make a recursive function unfoldable, label both the letrec and the corresponding λs static[2].

5   *Exercise*: Specialising the power function

Now we can set our first exercise: the power function (with a static first parameter) can be defined and tested by[3]

---

[2] There is a trap for the unwary here. As far as the specialiser is concerned, it makes perfect sense to define an unfoldable recursive function using a dynamic letrec. The effect is to unfold calls, but generate a recursive definition of the residual part of the function value. Although this is unproblematic for the specialiser, such recursive definitions would usually cause the arity raiser to construct a type with an infinite representation, and this is reported as an error. To avoid these rather obscure errors, see to it that you always define recursive unfoldable functions with letrec@ rather than letrec.

[3] We test for n=@1 rather than n=@0 here to avoid generating residual terms of the form x*1. We ignore the case n=@0 for simplicity.

```
letrec power n x = if@ n=@ 1 then x else x*power (n-@1) x
in \x. power 3 x
```

But this program cannot be specialised as it stands, because n would need to be assigned several different residual types.

1. Solve the problem by making the **power** function polyvariant. Notice the effect of arity raising.
2. Alternatively, make the **power** function unfoldable instead.
3. Find a third solution, by using constructor specialisation to pass several different static arguments to **power**.

6   Datatypes in the Type Specialiser

The type specialiser supports datatypes with constructors, with pattern matching over them in **case** expressions, much as in Haskell [5] (although nested patterns are not allowed). Any name beginning with a capital letter is a constructor. However, datatypes are not declared: instead, appropriate type definitions (recursive if need be) are inferred automatically by the type specialiser. Moreover, the same constructor can appear in more than one inferred datatype. The same holds true of residual types.

For example,

- **Pair (lift 1) (lift 2)**
  specialises to **Pair 1 2** with residual type **Pair int int**. We reuse the constructor name to express the type it constructs.
- **\b. if b then Left (lift 1) else Right (lift 2)**
  specialises to **\b.if b then Left 1 else Right 2** with residual type

  bool->Left int | Right int

  which illustrates how we write types with more than one constructor.
- **Cons (lift 1) (Cons (lift 2) Nil)**
  specialises to **Cons 1 (Cons 2 Nil)**. Here the two occurrences of **Cons** and the occurrence of **Nil** are quite independent; nothing forces them to belong to the same type, and so the specialiser infers the residual type of this term to be **Cons int (Cons int Nil)**.
- **letrec x = Cons (lift 1) x in x**
  specialises to **letrec x = Cons 1 x in x**, with a recursive residual type which can be expressed as

  _5 where _5 = Cons int _5

  (Here _5 is a type variable).

The reason for this slightly odd language design is that the specialiser *must* be able to infer new specialised type definitions in residual programs, since the programmer obviously cannot write them, and it is convenient then to allow constructors to appear in many types, so that the specialiser is not forced to invent new constructor names. Given that we infer appropriate data types in residual programs, it then seems natural to do the same in the source language.

Dynamic data structures may very well have static components: recall once again that the type specialiser does *not* restrict where static values may appear. For example, `Pair 1 (lift 2)` specialises to `Pair void 2` with residual type `Pair 1 int`. Arity raising then erases the void component, so that the final term is just `Pair 2`.

As usual, the static information is carried by the residual type. Of course, for residual types to match, this means that *every* `Pair` that an expression might evaluate to must have the same static component. For example,

```
\b. if b then Pair 1 (lift 2) else Pair 2 (lift 3)
```

cannot be specialised: if we try, we get a 'cannot unify 1 with 2' error.

However, if the two arms of the conditional use *different* constructors, then the program becomes specialisable. For example,

```
\b. if b then Left 2 else Right 3
```

specialises (after arity raising) to

```
\b.if b then Left else Right
```

with residual type `bool->Left 2 | Right 3`. Such a type carries just the right information to specialise a `case` expression over the result; we specialise the `Left` branch giving the variable bound in the `Left` pattern residual type 2, and the `Right` branch giving the variable in the `Right` pattern residual type 3.

So why not allow residual types such as `Pair 1 int | Pair 2 int`, so that the previous example could also be specialised? The problem with such types is that the constructor name is no longer sufficient to identify the residual types of the components. A `case` over this type would need *two* specialised `Pair` branches, and of course we cannot allow two branches with the same constructor. To make this idea work, we would need to generate two specialised versions of the `Pair` constructor. But constructor specialisation is already provided via the special constructor `In`, as we have already seen. There is no need to provide it in the context of ordinary datatypes also.

Data types may also have static constructors. In this case, the constructors appear in residual types, not in residual terms. So for example, `Left@ (lift 1)` specialises to just 1, in which no constructor appears. But the residual type is `Left@ int`, recording the fact that the value represents an application of `Left@`. Since the residual type of a static data type tells us exactly which constructor was applied, then `case@` expressions over such types can always be specialised to one of their branches. For example,

```
let p = Pair@ (lift 1) (lift 2) in
let first x = case@ x of Pair y z: y esac in
first p
```

specialises to

```
let p_1 = 1
    p_2 = 2
in let first x_1 x_2 = x_1
   in first p_1 p_2
```

from which both the Pair0 constructor, and the case0 over it, have been removed. Removing the constructor exposes the tuple of its components, which the arity raiser then removes.

7   *Exercise*: Specialising the append function

The append function can be defined and tested as follows:

```
letrec append xs ys =
  case xs of
    Nil: ys,
    Cons x xs: Cons x (append xs ys)
  esac
in
append (Cons (lift 1) (Cons (lift 2) Nil)) (Cons (lift 3) Nil)
```

This program can be supplied to the specialiser as it stands, but no interesting specialisation occurs since all the constructors are dynamic.

1. Make the constructors of the *first* argument static, to create a specialised version of append for lists of length two. You will need to do more than simply change the binding times.
2. Now make the constructors of the second argument and of the result static also. Can you explain the result you obtain?

8   *Exercise*: Experiments with Arity Raising

We can explore the behaviour of the arity raiser by giving the specialiser purely dynamic terms with pairs in different contexts, and examining the output. For terms with no static parts, the type specialisation phase is the identity function, and so we know that the term we write is the input to the arity raiser. Thus we can explore its behaviour in isolation.

1. For example, try specialising

   ```
   let f x = x in f (lift 1, lift 2)
   ```

   and

   ```
   let proj x = case x of Inj y: y esac
   in proj (Inj (lift 1, lift 2))
   ```

You will observe duplication of code in the output. Can you find a simple modification to the examples which avoids it? *Hint: insert a dynamic constructor somewhere.*

2. To see a larger example of arity raising at work, try defining function composition as a higher order function, and a function **swap** which swaps the components of a pair, and then try composing **swap** with itself.

9   *Exercise*: Simulating Constructor Specialisation: An Exercise in First-Class Polyvariance

Polyvariance in the type specialiser is more general than in most partial evaluators, in that *any* expression can be specialised polyvariantly, not just top-level definitions. In this exercise we will show that such first-class polyvariance can actually simulate constructor specialisation. To do so, we shall model the specialisable constructor In, and **case** over it, by λ-terms which are specialised polyvariantly.

One way to model data-structures in the pure lambda-calculus is as follows. Model data values by functions from the branches of a **case** over the datatype to the result of the **case**. Model **case** branches by functions from the components to the result of the branch. Model constructors by functions which select the appropriate branch, and apply it to the components. For example, lists can be modelled as follows:

```
nil c n = n
cons x xs c n = c x xs
listcase xs c n = xs c n
```

If we apply this idea to a datatype with one unary constructor, we obtain

```
inj x k = k x
caseinj xi k = xi k
```

Now we want to model the behaviour of the *specialisable* constructor In. By representing **case** branches as a *polyvariant* function, show how **poly** and **spec** can model constructor specialisation.

10   *Exercise*: Optimal Specialisation

A self-interpreter for the specialiser's metalanguage can be specialised optimally if, for any program p,

$$mix\ int\ p = p$$

(up to trivialities such as renaming of variables). Intuitively, the specialiser can remove a complete layer of interpretation. If the meta-language is typed, then an optimal specialiser must specialise types, since otherwise this equation cannot hold for any p containing a type not found in *int*. In particular, the 'universal' type used to represent values in the interpreter must be specialised to the types of those values. The type specialiser was the first to be able to do so for the lambda-calculus. In this exercise, you will repeat this experiment.

Take the following typed interpreter for the lambda-calculus plus constants:

```
letrec eval env e =
  case e of
    Cn n: Num n,
    Vr x: env x,
    Lm x e: Fun (\v.
                let env y = if x=y then v else env y
                in eval env e),
    Ap e1 e2:case eval env e1 of
                 Fun f: f (eval env e2)
               esac
  esac
in

eval (\i.Wrong)

(Ap (Ap (Lm (lift "x") (Lm (lift "f")
        (Ap (Vr (lift "f")) (Vr (lift "x"))))) (Cn (lift 3)))
    (Lm (lift "z") (Vr (lift "z"))))
```

For your convenience, it is applied to a small example program.

The interpreter can be specialised as it stands, but since everything is dynamic then no specialisation occurs. Make the following changes to the binding-times in the interpreter, along with any other necessary changes to make specialisation possible, and see how the results change.

1. Make the constructors Cn, Vr, Lm and Ap static.
2. Make the constants and variable names in the program static.
3. Unfold calls of eval, if you have not already done so.
4. Make the constructors Num, Fun and Wrong static.
5. Have you achieved optimal specialisation? (If not: keep trying.) What happens if you specialise this interpreter to an ill-typed lambda-term, such as

    (Ap@ (Cn@ 3) (Cn@ 4))

Is this the behaviour you would expect?

11 *Exercise*: Transforming Polymorphism to Monomorphism

The type specialiser is not optimal for the polymorphic λ-calculus, because both source and residual programs are simply typed (*i.e.* monomorphic). However, we can write an *interpreter* for a polymorphic language in the type specialiser's meta-language. Specialising such an interpreter to a polymorphic program will translate it into a monomorphic one.

Begin by adding a case to your optimal interpreter from the previous exercise so that it also interprets a **let** construct:

```
Let x e1 e2
```

represents let $x = e_1$ in e_2. Test your interpreter by specialising it to

```
(Let@ "id" (Lm@ "x" (Vr@ "x")) (Ap@ (Vr@ "id") (Cn@ 3)))
```

Make sure that specialisation is still optimal — that is, you obtain a corresponding **let** in the residual program.

What happens if you specialise your interpreter to a program which requires polymorphism to be well-typed? For example,

```
(Let@ "id" (Lm@ "x" (Vr@ "x"))
    (Ap@ (Ap@ (Vr@ "id") (Vr@ "id")) (Cn@ 3)))
```

Modify your interpreter so that it can be specialised to this term. You will need to generate *two* versions of id in the residual program, with two different monotypes — could polyvariance be useful perhaps? Following the Hindley-Milner type system, you may wish to distinguish between λ-bound and let-bound variables, where only the latter may be polymorphic.

12 *Exercise*: Transforming Higher-Order to First-Order

Higher-order programs can be transformed to first-order ones by representing function values as data-structures called closures, consisting of a tag identifying the function, and the values of its free variables. Function calls are interpreted by calling a dispatch function which inspects the tag, and then behaves like the function that the tag identifies. The transformation to first-order form is called *closure conversion* or *firstification*, and is a little tricky in a typed language. The object of this exercise is to develop an interpreter for the λ-calculus, which when specialised to a λ-term produces the result of firstifying it.

Start from the optimal interpreter you developed above. Can you change the representation of functions in the interpreter in such a way that *residual* functions will be represented by tagged tuples of their free variables? Don't forget to introduce a dispatching function, which can be specialised to produce the dispatch function in the firstified code!

A suitable lambda-expression to test your firstifier on is

```
(Ap@ (Lm@ "ap" (Ap@ (Ap@ (Vr@ "ap") (Lm@ "z" (Vr@ "z")))
                     (Ap@ (Ap@ (Vr@ "ap") (Lm@ "w" (Cn@ 3)))
                          (Cn@ 4))))
     (Lm@ "f" (Lm@ "x" (Ap@ (Vr@ "f") (Vr@ "x")))))
```

which represents

$$(\lambda ap.ap\ (\lambda z.z)\ (ap\ (\lambda w.3)\ 4))\ (\lambda f.\lambda x.f\ x)$$

13   *Exercise*: Interpreting Imperative Programs

Below is an interpreter for a simple imperative language, supporting assignments, conditional statements, and sequencing. Variables in the interpreted language need not be declared: a variable is given a value simply by assigning to it. The interpreter given below is purely dynamic; your job is to modify it so that the program to be interpreted, and the names in the environment, are static.

```
let look env x = env x in
let assign env x v =
   \i. if i=x then v else env i
in

letrec eval env e =
  case e of
    Con n: n,
    Var s: look env s,
    Add e1 e2: eval env e1 + eval env e2
  esac
in

letrec exec env p =
  case p of
    Skip: env,
    Assign x e: assign env x (eval env e),
    Seq p1 p2: let env=exec env p1 in exec env p2,
    If e p1 p2: if eval env e=lift 0 then exec env p2
                else exec env p1
  esac
in

let run p e = let env = exec (\i.lift 0) p in
              eval env e
in

run
(Seq (Assign (lift "x") (Con (lift 3)))
    (Seq (If (Var (lift "x"))
             (Assign (lift "y")
                 (Add (Var (lift "x")) (Con (lift 1))))
             Skip)
         (Assign (lift "z") (Var (lift "y")))))

(Add (Var (lift "x")) (Var (lift "y")))
```

This interpreter would be difficult to specialise with a partial evaluator, because of the dynamic conditional in the function **exec**, which forces the result of exec to be dynamic. But exec returns the environment, which should of course be partially static. Luckily the type specialiser allows dynamic conditionals to have partially static results, so the problem will not arise. One solution using a partial evaluator would be to use CPS specialisation, which specialises the context of a dynamic conditional with partially static branches twice, once in each branch. In the example above, the statement following the If statement would need to be 'compiled' twice (that is, two different specialisations of exec to this statement would need to be generated), since one branch of the If introduces the variable y into the environment, while the other branch does not. Thus the partially static environment would have a different shape, depending on which branch of the conditional statement was chosen, and the reference to y in

```
(Assign (lift "z") (Var (lift "y")))
```

would need to be compiled differently in each case. The type specialiser on the other hand 'compiles' this last statement once only. Inspect the residual code: how is the problem of different variables in the environment after each branch of an If resolved?

In the interpreter given above, uninitialised variables have the value zero. Modify the interpreter to distinguish between initialised and uninitialised variables in the environment. What is the effect of making this distinction static, in the example above?

(The answer to this exercise is not included in the appendix).

References

[1] D. Dussart, J. Hughes, and P. Thiemann. Type Specialisation for Imperative Languages. In *International Conference on Functional Programming*, pages 204–216, Amsterdam, June 1997. ACM.

[2] J. Hughes. An Introduction to Program Specialisation by Type Inference. In *Functional Programming*. Glasgow University, July 1996. published electronically.

[3] J. Hughes. Type Specialisation for the Lambda-calculus; or, A New Paradigm for Partial Evaluation based on Type Inference. In O. Danvy, R. Glück, and P. Thiemann, editors, *Partial Evaluation*, volume 1110 of *LNCS*, pages 183–215. Springer-Verlag, February 1996.

[4] J. Hughes. Type Specialisation. In O. Danvy, R. Glück, and P. Thiemann, editors, *1998 Symposium on Partial Evaluation*, volume 30 of *Computing Surveys*, Sept. 1998.

[5] S. P. Jones, J. Hughes, (editors), L. Augustsson, D. Barton, B. Boutel, W. Burton, J. Fasel, K. Hammond, R. Hinze, P. Hudak, T. Johnsson, M. Jones, J. Launchbury, E. Meijer, J. Peterson, A. Reid, C. Runciman, and P. Wadler. Report on the Programming Language Haskell 98, a Non-strict, Purely Functional Language. available from http://haskell.org, February 1999.

[6] T. Æ. Mogensen. Constructor specialization. In D. Schmidt, editor, *ACM Symposium on Partial Evaluation and Semantics-Based Program Manipulation*, pages 22–32, June 1993.

A   Answers to the Exercises

A.1   Specialising the power function.

Part 1. *To make* power *polyvariant:*

```
letrec poly power n x = if@ n=@ 1 then x else x*spec power (n-@1) x
in \x. spec power 3 x
```

producing residual code

```
letrec power_1 x' = x' * power_2 x'
       power_2 x' = x' * power_3 x'
       power_3 x' = x'
in \x.power_1 x
```

In this example, the *specialiser* produces a single recursive definition of a 3-tuple from the recursive definition of power, and it is the *arity raiser* which splits this into three separate function definitions.

Part 2. *To unfold the* power *function:*

```
letrec@ power@n@x = if@ n=@ 1 then x else x*power@(n-@1)@x
in \x. power@3@x
```

producing residual code

```
\x.x * (x * x)
```

Part 3. *To use constructor specialisation:*

```
letrec power m x =
  case m of In n:
    if@ n=@ 1 then x else x*power (In (n-@1)) x
  esac
in \x. power (In 3) x
```

producing residual code

```
letrec power m x =
        case m of
            In0 : x,
            In1 : x * power In0 x,
            In2 : x * power In1 x
        esac
in \x.power In2 x
```

In this code the specialised constructors In0, In1 and In2 are *nullary* — since the argument of In in the source code is completely static, it is removed altogether by the arity raiser. The specialised constructors are just tags telling the residual power function which power to compute.

A.2 Specialising the append function.

Part 1. *Making the first argument partially static:* To change the binding times
of the constructors in the first argument, we annotate the case@ in append static,
and similarly for the constructors in the actual parameter.

```
letrec append xs ys =
  case@ xs of
    Nil: ys,
    Cons x xs: Cons x (append xs ys)
  esac
in
append (Cons@ (lift 1) (Cons@ (lift 2) Nil@)) (Cons (lift 3) Nil)
```

But this program cannot be specialised as it stands: we obtain the error message
'Cannot unify Nil@ with Cons@ int (Nil@)'. The problem is that a specialisation of append to lists of length two needs to call a specialisation to lists of
length one, and so on. Thus we must specialise the body of append several times.

This is the same problem that we encountered in the previous example, and
we can use the same solutions. Using polyvariance, we rewrite the program as

```
letrec poly append xs ys =
  case@ xs of
    Nil: ys,
    Cons x xs: Cons x (spec append xs ys)
  esac
in
spec append (Cons@ (lift 1) (Cons@ (lift 2) Nil@))
            (Cons (lift 3) Nil)
```

which specialises to

```
letrec append_1 xs_1 xs_2 ys = Cons xs_1 (append_2 xs_2 ys)
       append_2 xs ys = Cons xs (append_3 ys)
       append_3 ys = ys
in append_1 1 2 (Cons 3 Nil)
```

Once the static constructors of append's first argument are removed, then the
arity raiser can replace it by several arguments, one for each component.

Alternatively, we might use constructor specialisation, and tag append's first
argument with the specialisable constructor In:

```
letrec append t ys =
  case t of
    In xs:
      case@ xs of
        Nil: ys,
        Cons x xs: Cons x (append (In xs) ys)
      esac
```

```
        esac
in
append (In (Cons@ (lift 1) (Cons@ (lift 2) Nil@)))
       (Cons (lift 3) Nil)
```

In this case, the residual program is

```
letrec append t ys =
          case t of
            In0 : ys,
            In1 xs: Cons xs (append In0 ys),
            In2 xs_1 xs_2: Cons xs_1 (append (In1 xs_2) ys)
          esac
in append (In2 1 2) (Cons 3 Nil)
```

Here the specialised constructors provide efficient representations for lists of length zero, one and two, and the append function contains a case dispatch that enables it to append any one of these to another list.

Part 2. *Making the second argument partially static also:* Taking the polyvariant solution as a starting point, we can make the other constructors static also just by annotating them with a @; no other changes are required.

```
letrec poly append xs ys =
  case@ xs of
    Nil: ys,
    Cons x xs: Cons@ x (spec append xs ys)
  esac
in
spec append (Cons@ (lift 1) (Cons@ (lift 2) Nil@))
            (Cons@ (lift 3) Nil@)
```

But the residual program we obtain is surprisingly large; it is:

```
(letrec append_1 xs_1 xs_2 ys = xs_1
        append_2 xs_1 xs_2 ys = append_4 xs_2 ys
        append_3 xs_1 xs_2 ys = append_5 xs_2 ys
        append_4 xs ys = xs
        append_5 xs ys = append_6 ys
        append_6 ys = ys
 in append_1 1 2 3,
 (letrec append_1 xs_1 xs_2 ys = xs_1
        append_2 xs_1 xs_2 ys = append_4 xs_2 ys
        append_3 xs_1 xs_2 ys = append_5 xs_2 ys
        append_4 xs ys = xs
        append_5 xs ys = append_6 ys
        append_6 ys = ys
  in append_2 1 2 3,
```

```
letrec append_1 xs_1 xs_2 ys = xs_1
       append_2 xs_1 xs_2 ys = append_4 xs_2 ys
       append_3 xs_1 xs_2 ys = append_5 xs_2 ys
       append_4 xs ys = xs
       append_5 xs ys = append_6 ys
       append_6 ys = ys
 in append_3 1 2 3))
```

with residual type Cons@ int (Cons@ int (Cons@ int (Nil@))).

This large term is the result of arity raising. After just the type specialisation phase, the residual term is more recognisable:

```
letrec append = (\xs.\ys. (fst xs, pi2 append (snd xs) ys),
                 \xs.\ys. (fst xs, pi3 append (snd xs) ys),
                 \xs.\ys. ys)
in pi1 append (1,(2,void)) (3,void)
```

Here the append function has been replaced by a triple of specialisations, while the static list constructors have been removed. The residual lists are just represented by nested pairs of their dynamic components.

Arity raising eliminates the triple that append is bound to by transforming it into separate function definitions instead. It eliminates the tuples passed to append by passing the components as separate parameters instead. But it also eliminates the tuples in the *result* of append, by splitting each function that returns a tuple into several functions, one returning each component. Since the first specialisation of append returns nested pairs with a total of three components, then it is split into three separate functions, append_1, append_2, and append_3 (one for each list element in the result of the original call). The second specialisation of append returns a structure with two integer components, and is split into append_4 and append_5. Finally, the last specialisation corresponds to append_6.

This process results in an expression of the form letrec...in (a,(b,c)). In order to eliminate the last pairs, the arity raiser moves the letrec definitions into each component, thus transforming the entire expression into a triple of independent expressions, within which no tuples appear. It is this last step which creates multiple copies of the residual function definitions.

We will explore the arity raiser's behaviour further in the next exercise.

A.3   Experiments with Arity Raising.

Part 1. *Preventing code duplication:* Specialising the first example yields

```
(let f_1 x_1 x_2 = x_1
     f_2 x_1 x_2 = x_2
 in f_1 1 2,
 let f_1 x_1 x_2 = x_1
     f_2 x_1 x_2 = x_2
 in f_2 1 2)
```

Just as in the previous exercise, the residual let definition is floated inside the pair, in order to express the entire term in the form (a,b). To prevent this, we must modify the body of the let expression, so that it no longer has a product type. A simple way to do so is to wrap a dynamic constructor around the body:

```
let f x = x in Wrap (f (lift 1, lift 2))
```

Specialising this expression produces

```
let f_1 x_1 x_2 = x_1
    f_2 x_1 x_2 = x_2
in Wrap (f_1 1 2) (f_2 1 2)
```

Now the arity raiser eliminates the pair in the body of the let just by giving the Wrap constructor extra components; the definitions of f_1 and f_2 need no longer be duplicated.

The code duplication in the proj example, and indeed in the append example in the previous exercise, can be avoided in the same way.

Part 2. *Arity raising higher-order functions:* We can define and test compose and swap as follows:

```
let compose f g x = f (g x) in
let swap x = case@ x of Pair y z: Pair@ z y esac in
let h = compose swap swap in
Wrap (h (Pair@ (lift 1) (lift 2)))
```

Here values constructed by Pair@ specialise to pairs, which the arity raiser then removes; we use these values rather than the explicit pair notation because the implemented type specialiser does not support pattern matching on the latter.

The result of specialising this example is

```
let compose_1 f_1 f_2 g_1 g_2 x_1 x_2 =
      f_1 (g_1 x_1 x_2) (g_2 x_1 x_2)
    compose_2 f_1 f_2 g_1 g_2 x_1 x_2 =
      f_2 (g_1 x_1 x_2) (g_2 x_1 x_2)
in let swap_1 x_1 x_2 = x_2
       swap_2 x_1 x_2 = x_1
   in let h_1 = compose_1 swap_1 swap_2 swap_1 swap_2
          h_2 = compose_2 swap_1 swap_2 swap_1 swap_2
      in Wrap (h_1 1 2) (h_2 1 2)
```

Here swap is a function from pairs to pairs, and so is arity raised into two functions, each with two arguments. Thus compose, which takes two such functions and a pair as arguments, becomes a function of six parameters after arity raising – or rather two functions of six parameters, since it also returns a pair.

A.4 Simulating Constructor Specialisation: An Exercise in First-Class Polyvariance

Recall our first example of constructor specialisation:

```
(\f. f (In 3) + f (In 4))
  (\z. case z of In x: lift (x +@ 1) esac)
```

Let us use this example to test our simulation using polyvariance. To begin with, let us replace In and the case by the functions given in the statement of the exercise, that simulate a single unary constructor:

```
let inj x k = k x in
let caseinj xi k = xi k in
(\f. f (inj 3) + f (inj 4))
  (\z. caseinj z (\x. lift (x +@ 1)))
```

This cannot be specialised as it stands, of course, because inj is applied to both 3 and 4, which causes a unification failure. We have to make inj *polyvariant*, so that it can specialise to many different 'constructors':

```
let poly inj x k = k x in
let caseinj xi k = xi k in
(\f. f (spec inj 3) + f (spec inj 4))
  (\z. caseinj z (\x. lift (x +@ 1)))
```

However, attempting to specialise this program still produces an error message, 'cannot unify 3 with 4'. The problem is caused by the λ-expression passed to caseinj, the 'body of the case', which must also be specialised to 3 and 4. We therefore make this λ-expression polyvariant where it is passed to caseinj, and insert a corresponding spec in the body of inj, where the 'body of the case' is finally invoked. The result is

```
let poly inj x k = spec k x in
let caseinj xi k = xi k in
(\f. f (spec inj 3) + f (spec inj 4))
  (\z. caseinj z (poly \x. lift (x +@ 1)))
```

Specialisation now succeeds, and produces

```
let inj_1 k_1 k_2 = k_2
    inj_2 k_1 k_2 = k_1
in let caseinj xi k_1 k_2 = xi k_1 k_2
    in (\f.f inj_1 + f inj_2) (\z.caseinj z 5 4)
```

We can see that the two functions inj_1 and inj_2 model the constructors of a type with two nullary constructors, and caseinj models a case over such a type. At the call of caseinj, two specialised 'case branches' are passed as parameters. This program is exactly the λ-calculus model of the program we obtain by specialising the original code which uses built-in constructor specialisation:

```
(\f.f In1 + f In0) (\z.case z of In0 : 5, In1 : 4 esac)
```

Of course, if there were more than one call of `caseinj` then we might wish to generate several residual versions of it; we ought to make `caseinj` polyvariant also to allow for this. But even so, we cannot hope to model *every* use of constructor specialisation by this technique. The problem is that the simple type system of our source language constrains us too sharply: because it does not support polymorphism, every use of the `inj` function must be applied to arguments of the same (source) type. Using the polyvariant constructor In we could for example construct both In 3 (with source type In Int@) and In true (with source type In Bool@) in the same program (although since these have different source types we could not inspect both in the same `case` expression). But in our simulation, we must choose whether `inj` should have source type

```
poly (Int@ -> poly (Int@ -> t) -> t)
```

for some t, or

```
poly (Bool@ -> poly (Bool@ -> t) -> t)
```

Whichever choice we make, only one of `spec inj 3` and `spec inj true` can be well-typed.

Indeed, to model datatypes fully in a typed λ-calculus requires first-class polymorphism. What this exercise shows is that, if the type specialiser could be extended to handle a language with first-class polymorphism, then constructor specialisation could be reduced to polyvariance. In the meantime it must be provided as a separate feature.

A.5 Optimal Specialisation

Specialising the interpreter as it is given produces a residual program identical up to renaming:

```
letrec eval env e =
        case e of
           Cn n: Num n,
           Vr x: env x,
           Lm xe_1 xe_2: Fun (\v.let env' y =
                                     if xe_1 = y then v else env y
                                 in eval env' xe_2),
           Ap e1e2_1 e1e2_2: case eval env e1e2_1 of
                                Fun f: f (eval env e1e2_2)
                             esac
        esac
in eval (\i.Wrong)
     (Ap (Ap (Lm "x" (Lm "f" (Ap (Vr "f") (Vr "x")))) (Cn 3))
         (Lm "z" (Vr "z")))
```

The main difference from the source program is the names of case-bound variables: as you see, the type specialiser fails to preserve their names properly. Of course, this is just a deficiency of the implementation, and nothing fundamental.

The residual type reported may look a little surprising at first sight:

```
Residual type: Num _12 | _13
where
_13 = Fun ((Num _12 | _13)->Num _12 | _13) | Wrong
_12 = int
```

but it is isomorphic to

```
Univ
where
Univ = Num int | Fun (Univ->Univ) | Wrong
```

which is the type we would expect. The type specialiser represents types as graphs, and does not distinguish types which have the same infinite unfolding. Types are printed as *some* graph with the right infinite unfolding, but not always the one we would expect!

Part 1. *Making the abstract syntax static:* To make the constructors of the program syntax static, we annotate the case in eval as static, and likewise each occurrence of a constructor. But if we do no more than this, then we encounter a specialisation time error:

```
Error: Cannot unify:
Lm@ string (Lm@ string (Ap@ (Vr@ string) (Vr@ string)))

with
Ap@ (Lm@ string (Lm@ string (Ap@ (Vr@ string) (Vr@ string))))
    (Cn@ int)
```

These are the residual types of the arguments to the top-level and first recursive call of eval. Since the arguments of eval are now partially static, we must make it polyvariant. Doing so, we obtain

```
letrec poly eval env e =
  case@ e of
    ...
    Lm x e: Fun (\v.
              let env y = if x=y then v else env y
              in spec eval env e),
    Ap e1 e2:case spec eval env e1 of
                Fun f: f (spec eval env e2)
              esac
  esac
in

spec eval (\i.Wrong) ...
```

which specialises to

```
letrec eval_1 env e_1 e_2 e_3 e_4 e_5 e_6 e_7 =
        case eval_2 env e_1 e_2 e_3 e_4 e_5 of
          Fun f: f (eval_3 env e_6 e_7)
        esac
      eval_2 env e_1 e_2 e_3 e_4 e_5 =
        case eval_4 env e_1 e_2 e_3 e_4 of
          Fun f: f (eval_5 env e_5)
        esac
      eval_3 env e_1 e_2 =
        Fun (\v.let env' y = if e_1 = y then v else env y
                in eval_6 env' e_2)
      eval_4 env e_1 e_2 e_3 e_4 =
        Fun (\v.let env' y = if e_1 = y then v else env y
                in eval_7 env' e_2 e_3 e_4)
      eval_5 env e = Num e
      eval_6 env e = env e
      eval_7 env e_1 e_2 e_3 =
        Fun (\v.let env' y = if e_1 = y then v else env y
                in eval_8 env' e_2 e_3)
      eval_8 env e_1 e_2 =
        case eval_6 env e_1 of Fun f: f (eval_6 env e_2) esac
in eval_1 (\i.Wrong) "x" "f" "f" "x" 3 "z" "z"
```

Part 2. *Making variable names and constants static:* Look again at the specialised code above. Notice all the arguments to the residual versions of **eval**! Inspection of the final call reveals that they are the identifiers and constants in the interpreted program; of course, we must make these static also. The easiest way to do so is to remove the uses of **lift** from the term to interpret, and instead **lift** the constants and variables when they are used in **eval**. We obtain

```
letrec poly eval env e =
  case@ e of
    Cn n: Num (lift n),
    Vr x: env (lift x),
    Lm x e: Fun (\v.
              let env y = if lift x=y then v else env y
              in spec eval env e),
    ...
  esac
in

spec eval (\i.Wrong)

(Ap@ (Ap@ (Lm@ "x" (Lm@ "f"
          (Ap@ (Vr@ "f") (Vr@ "x")))) (Cn@ 3))
```

```
        (Lm@ "z" (Vr@ "z")))
```

Specialising this program, we obtain

```
letrec eval_1 env =
          case eval_2 env of Fun f: f (eval_3 env) esac
        eval_2 env = case eval_4 env of Fun f: f (eval_5 env) esac
        eval_3 env =
          Fun (\v.let env' y = if "z" = y then v else env y
                   in eval_6 env')
        eval_4 env =
          Fun (\v.let env' y = if "x" = y then v else env y
                   in eval_7 env')
        eval_5 env = Num 3
        eval_6 env = env "z"
        eval_7 env =
          Fun (\v.let env' y = if "f" = y then v else env y
                   in eval_8 env')
        eval_8 env = case eval_9 env of Fun f: f (eval_10 env) esac
        eval_9 env = env "f"
        eval_10 env = env "x"
in eval_1 (\i.Wrong)
```

However, in this version the environment lookup is still done dynamically. Of course, now that we have made the identifiers static, we would like to perform environment lookups statically also. The environment is a function from dynamic strings to values; we must change the type of its argument to static strings. Moreover, since one environment may very well be applied to several different static identifiers, the environment must be a *polyvariant* function. We therefore reannotate the source program as follows:

```
letrec poly eval env e =
  case@ e of
    ...
    Vr x: spec env x,
    Lm x e: Fun (\v.
              let poly env y = if@ x=@y then v else spec env y
              in spec eval env e),
    ...
  esac
in

spec eval (poly \i.Wrong) ...
```

and now obtain

```
letrec eval_1 = case eval_2 of Fun f: f eval_3 esac
        eval_2 = case eval_4 of Fun f: f eval_5 esac
```

```
      eval_3 = Fun (\v.let env' = v in eval_6 env')
      eval_4 = Fun (\v.let env' = v in eval_7 env')
      eval_5 = Num 3
      eval_6 env = env
      eval_7 env =
        Fun (\v.let env'_1 = v
                    env'_2 = env
                 in eval_8 env'_1 env'_2)
      eval_8 env_1 env_2 =
        case eval_9 env_1 env_2 of
          Fun f: f (eval_10 env_1 env_2)
        esac
      eval_9 env_1 env_2 = env_1
      eval_10 env_1 env_2 = env_2
in eval_1
```

as the result of specialisation.

Looking at this code, we see that the residual environment has been replaced by multiple parameters, one for each name in the environment. How has this happened? Firstly, since the environment is now a polyvariant object, its residual value is a tuple of specialisations, which the arity raiser then splits into individual parameters. There will be one specialisation (= one parameter) for each name *which is looked up* in the environment, not for each name which is bound in it. Although this example doesn't show it, polyvariance gives us 'dead variable elimination' for free.

Each component of the tuple is the specialisation of the environment to look up one particular identifier, and has residual type x->Value, where x is the identifier it looks up. Since identifiers are completely static, the arity raiser converts such functions just to values.

Thus the environment is replaced in residual programs by individual parameters, each of which is the value of a name in the interpreted program.

Part 3. *Unfolding* eval: Up to this point, it is useful *not* to unfold calls of eval, because that enables us to see residual environments clearly. But of course, we cannot obtain optimal specialisation without unfolding eval, so let us do so now. We convert eval into a static function (and define it therefore with a static letrec), and since the body is now specialised at each call, it need no longer be polyvariant. The reannotated program is

```
letrec@ eval@ env@ e =
  case@ e of
    ...
    Lm x e: Fun (\v.
              let poly env y = if@ x=@y then v else spec env y
              in eval@ env@ e),
    Ap e1 e2:case eval@ env@ e1 of
                Fun f: f (eval@ env@ e2)
```

```
            esac
   esac
in

eval@ (poly \i.Wrong)@ ...
```

and the residual code is

```
case case Fun (\v.let env = v
                in Fun (\v'.let env'_1 = v'
                              env'_2 = env
                          in case env'_1 of
                                Fun f: f env'_2
                             esac))
      of
        Fun f: f (Num 3)
      esac
of
   Fun f: f (Fun (\v.let env = v in env))
esac
```

Part 4. *Eliminating run-time type tags:* Now it is clear that the major remaining overhead is the tagging and tag checking of the constructors of the value type: Fun, Num and Wrong. Since we intend the *type* of interpreted values to be a compile-time property, we can make these constructors static also. By doing so, we exploit the extra power of the type specialiser: since function values in the interpreted language map values to values, and since such function values are necessarily dynamic, then most partial evaluators would insist that the value type itself must be completely dynamic. This is a consequence of the rule that a dynamic function may not have static arguments or results. But since the type specialiser places no such restrictions, we are free to reannotate the interpreter as

```
letrec@ eval@ env@ e =
  case@ e of
    Cn n: Num@ (lift n),
    Vr x: spec env x,
    Lm x e: Fun@ (\v.
              let poly env y = if@ x=@y then v else spec env y
              in eval@ env@ e),
    Ap e1 e2:case@ eval@ env@ e1 of
               Fun f: f (eval@ env@ e2)
             esac
  esac
in

eval@ (poly \i.Wrong@)@ ...
```

and obtain

```
(\v.let env = v
    in \v'.let env'_1 = v'
             env'_2 = env
         in env'_1 env'_2)
  3
  (\v.let env = v in env)
```

as the residual code. This is not quite isomorphic to the interpreted program, because the variables in the environment are rebound in every λ-expression. The residual let expressions in this code arise from the let in the interpreter in the case for Lm x e; replacing this let with let@ we obtain instead

```
(\v.\v'.v' v) 3 (\v.v)
```

as the residual code, and we have attained optimal specialisation at last.

Part 5. *'Compiling' ill-typed programs:* The residual type of our example is now Num@ int; that is, we know statically that the result is an integer, representing a value tagged Num@. Specialising this interpreter to a λ-expression both 'compiles' it into the meta-language, and infers its type. If we try to specialise the interpreter to an ill-typed term, such as (Ap@ (Cn@ 3) (Cn@ 4)), then residual type inference fails:

```
Error: Cannot unify: Fun@ _20 with Num@ _26
```

We could hardly expect anything else: by making the constructors of the value type static, we 'compile' programs to code without run-time type checks; compilers for statically typed languages are able to do that precisely *because* they reject ill-typed programs altogether.

Another way to look at it is like this: an optimal specialiser must satisfy

$$mix\ int\ p = p$$

by definition; specialising a suitable interpreter to a program p must yield an identical program as the result (up to renaming, etc). But if the input program p is ill-typed, then the result of specialisation must also be ill-typed, by this equation. An optimal specialiser which generates well-typed residual programs in a typed language *must* therefore reject such inputs, because its defining equation cannot be satisfied at all.

A.6 Transforming Polymorphism to Monomorphism

Let us begin by adding a new case to the interpreter to handle let expressions:

```
letrec@ eval@ env@ e =
  case@ e of
    ...
```

```
    Let x e1 e2: let v = eval@ env@ e1 in
                 let@ poly newenv y =
                          if@ x=@y then v else spec env y
                 in eval@ newenv@ e2
   esac
in
```

```
eval@ (poly \i.Wrong@)@
```

```
(Let@ "id" (Lm@ "x" (Vr@ "x")) (Ap@ (Vr@ "id") (Cn@ 3)))
```

The interpreter binds v to the result of evaluating e1 with a *dynamic* let; this
generates a let expression in the residual program corresponding to the Let in
the interpreted program, and so we obtain optimal specialisation. In this case,
the residual program is

```
let v v = v in v 3
```

which is isomorphic to the interpreted one. (The choice of names is a little
confusing here, since the specialiser renames variables only when necessary to
avoid a name clash. There *are* two different variables in this residual term, but
they are both called v).

If we try to specialise this interpreter to the second example term, we encounter an error:

```
Cannot unify Num@ int with Fun@ _46 where ...
```

The residual let-bound variable corresponding to id cannot be given a *monomorphic* residual type which matches both occurrences.

The solution to this problem is to give that variable a polyvariant type, and
specialise it at each occurrence. Thus we modify the new environment created
by interpreting a Let to bind the new variable to a polyvariant object. But now
we encounter a typing problem in the source language: the environment must be
well-typed in the source program, it cannot map some variables to polyvariant
values and others to monovariant ones.

Our solution is to tag the result of looking up a name in the environment as
either monovariant or polyvariant; that is, we give the environment the source
type

```
poly (String@ -> Mono@ Univ | Poly@ (poly Univ))
```

Of course these tags are static: we know at compile-time which variables are
Let-bound. We modify the interpreter accordingly, adding tags where variables
are bound, and checking them where variables are interpreted:

```
letrec@ eval@ env@ e =
  case@ e of
    ...
    Vr x: case@ spec env x of
```

```
            Mono v: v,
            Poly v: spec v
        esac,
    Lm x e: Fun@ (\v.
            let@ poly env y = if@ x=@y then Mono@ v else spec env y
            in eval@ env@ e),
    ...
    Let x e1 e2: let poly v = eval@ env@ e1 in
                 let@ poly newenv y =
                    if@ x=@y then Poly@ v else spec env y
                 in eval@ newenv@ e2
    esac
in

eval@ (poly \i.Mono@ Wrong@)@

(Let@ "id" (Lm@ "x" (Vr@ "x"))
  (Ap@ (Ap@ (Vr@ "id") (Vr@ "id")) (Cn@ 3)))
```

Residual environments now contain a tuple of specialisations for each Let-bound variable, one for each residual (mono) type at which the variable is used. The residual type of an environment records, for each variable, whether it is mono- or poly-morphic, and for the polymorphic ones, which instances it is used at. After arity raising, polymorphic variables are replaced by a collection of variables, one for each instance. Our example specialises to

```
let v_1 v' = v'
    v_2 v' = v'
in v_1 v_2 3
```

Thus we obtain the well-known transformation of Hindley-Milner polymorphic programs to simply typed ones as the specialisation of an interpreter.

A.7 Transforming Higher-Order to First-Order

In the optimal interpreter we have already developed, functions in the interpreted language are represented as *dynamic* functions from values to values, and therefore specialise to functions in residual programs. To obtain first-order residual programs, we must change this representation. The obvious choice is to represent function values by *static* functions instead. In residual programs, static functions are replaced by tuples of their free variables, which is close to the representation of closures that we are aiming for.

However, if we simply change the interpretation of Lm to construct a static function, and change the interpretation of Ap to use static application, then the effect of specialising the interpreter will be to unfold all function applications at the point of call. Ineed, the whole point of static applications is that they are unfolded! Since our little interpreted language is non-recursive this would actually work, but is of course not the solution we are looking for.

To avoid unfolding function calls at the point of application, we introduce a dispatch function to 'apply' a function value; the intention is that each function in the interpreted program will be unfolded only once, inside the body of the residual dispatch function. Intuitively we 'compile' interpreted programs to one dispatch function which can apply any function value that the interpreted program can generate. With these modifications, the interpreter becomes:

```
let dispatch f x = f@x in
letrec@ eval@ env@ e =
  case@ e of
    ...
    Lm x e: Fun@ (\@v.
              let@ poly env y = if@ x=@y then v else spec env y
              in eval@ env@ e),
    Ap e1 e2:case@ eval@ env@ e1 of
              Fun f: dispatch f (eval@ env@ e2)
              esac
  esac
in ...
```

However, specialising this interpreter to our example produces a unification failure, which in retrospect is easy to understand: by making function values static, we make the definition of a function a part of its residual type, with the result that each function-valued variable can only ever be bound to one function. In particular, dispatch may only be applied to one function. But of course, dispatch is used to invoke *every* function, and since our example contains more than one, a unification failure results.

To avoid it, we tag function representations with the specialisable constructor In. As a result, a function-valued variable can now be bound to different functions, but in the residual program they will be tagged with different specialised constructors. That is, the representation of a function value in residual programs will be a tag identifying the particular function, and a tuple of its free variables – exactly the conventional representation of closures. The residual dispatch function will contain a case with a branch for every possible function tag, as we would expect. The modifications read:

```
let dispatch f x = case f of In g: g@x esac in
letrec@ eval@ env@ e =
  case@ e of
    ...
    Lm x e: Fun@ (In (\@v.
              let@ poly env y = if@ x=@y then v else spec env y
              in eval@ env@ e)),
    ...
  esac
```

in ...

However, although we have now chosen the right representation for functions, we *still* get a unification failure when we try to specialise the interpreter! The problem is that the residual dispatch function must not only be able to apply different functions, it must be able to apply functions *with different residual types*. One residual dispatch function cannot apply both functions of type Int->Int and functions of type Bool->Bool. We must therefore make dispatch polyvariant, so that a different residual dispatch function can be generated for each *type* of function in the interpreted program. The modifications read:

```
let poly dispatch f x = case f of In g: g@x esac in
letrec@ eval@ env@ e =
  case@ e of
    ...
    Ap e1 e2:case@ eval@ env@ e1 of
              Fun f: spec dispatch f (eval@ env@ e2)
            esac
  esac
in ...
```

and at last specialisation succeeds, producing

```
let dispatch_1 f x =
      case f of
        In0 g_1 g_2 g_3: g_3 (g_2 x (In1 x g_1 g_2 g_3))
                           (g_3 (g_2 x (In0 x g_1 g_2 g_3)) 4)
      esac
    dispatch_2 f x =
      case f of In0 g_1 g_2 g_3: In2 x g_1 g_2 g_3 esac
    dispatch_3 f x =
      case f of
        In0 g_1 g_2 g_3 g_4: 3,
        In1 g_1 g_2 g_3 g_4: x,
        In2 g_1 g_2 g_3 g_4: g_4 g_1 x
      esac
in dispatch_1 (In0 dispatch_1 dispatch_2 dispatch_3)
    (In0 dispatch_1 dispatch_2 dispatch_3)
```

Just as we would expect, the residual program contains three residual dispatch functions, which interpret functions of type Int->Int, (Int->Int)->(Int->Int), and ((Int->Int)->(Int->Int))->Int from bottom to top. There are three different functions of type Int->Int, while there is only one of each of the other two types.

As an exercise, try to predict what would have happened if we had *begun* by making dispatch polyvariant, without first tagging function representations with the specialisable constructor In[4].

However, we observe that the function closures have bewilderingly many free variables. Moreover, the residual program is *not* first-order: some of these free variables are themselves function values! Indeed, they are specialised versions of the dispatch function itself!

What is going on here is that the static functions representing function values contain calls to dispatch, which is therefore a free variable, and appears in the function's residual representation. To avoid this, we must represent function values by static functions which *do not* depend on dispatch. We can do so simply, by passing the dispatch function as an extra parameter when a function value is invoked; thus the static function itself need not contain any reference to it. Since dispatch is actually called from eval, we need to make dispatch a parameter of eval also. The modifications to the interpreter read:

```
letrec poly dispatch f x = case f of In g: g@ dispatch@ x esac in
letrec@ eval@ dispatch@ env@ e =
  case@ e of
    ...
    Lm x e: Fun@ (In (\@dispatch1. \@v.
               let@ poly env y = if@ x=@y then v else spec env y
               in eval@ dispatch1@ env@ e)),
    Ap e1 e2:case@ eval@ dispatch@ env@ e1 of
                Fun f: spec dispatch f (eval@ dispatch@ env@ e2)
              esac
  esac
in

eval@ dispatch@ (poly \i.Wrong@)@ ...
```

Now dispatch itself is recursive, so that it can pass its own value to closures being invoked. Of course, we would expect the residual dispatcher functions to be recursive if the program to be firstified is; this recursion in residual programs arises from the letrec we have just introduced.

Notice also that in the case for interpreting a Lm-expression there are *two* versions of dispatch in scope. We are careful to use dispatch1 rather than dispatch, so as to avoid referring to a free variable of the static function we are constructing.

The result of specialising this program is now

```
letrec dispatch_1 f x =
```

---

[4] We would obtain a residual version of dispatch for each *function* in the interpreted program, rather than for each *type* of function. This is not what we want: when two different function values can both reach the same dispatch then we would still suffer a unification error, since it would quite simply be impossible to decide which residual dispatch function to call.

```
          case f of
            In0 : dispatch_3 (dispatch_2 x (In1 x))
                    (dispatch_3 (dispatch_2 x (In0 x)) 4)
          esac
          dispatch_2 f x = case f of In0 : In2 x esac
          dispatch_3 f x =
            case f of In0 g: 3, In1 g: x, In2 g: dispatch_3 g x esac
in dispatch_1 In0 In0
```

which we can at last see is a firstified version of the original term,

$$(\lambda ap.ap\ (\lambda z.z)\ (ap\ (\lambda w.3)\ 4))\ (\lambda f.\lambda x.f\ x)$$

- At type `Int->Int` (in function `dispatch_3`),
  - `In0 ap` represents $\lambda w.3$,
  - `In1 ap` represents $\lambda z.z$,
  - `In2 f` represents $\lambda x.fx$.

  (Closure representations contain all variables in scope, whether they are actually used or not: there is room for a little further improvement here).
- At type `(Int->Int)->(Int->Int)` (in function `dispatch_2`), In0 represents $\lambda f.\lambda x.f\ x$.
- At type `((Int->Int)->(Int->Int))->Int` (in `dispatch_1`), In0 represents $\lambda ap.ap\ (\lambda z.z)\ (ap\ (\lambda w.3)\ 4)$.

Multi-Level Specialization
(Extended Abstract)

Robert Glück[1] and Jesper Jørgensen[2]

[1] DIKU, Department of Computer Science, University of Copenhagen,
Universitetsparken 1, DK-2100 Copenhagen, Denmark.
Email: glueck@diku.dk
[2] Department of Mathematics and Physics, Royal Veterinary and Agricultural
University, Thorvaldsensvej 40, DK-1871 Frederiksberg C, Denmark.
Email: jesper@dina.kvl.dk

Abstract. Program specialization can divide a computation into several computation stages. The program generator which we designed and implemented for a higher-order functional language converts programs into very compact multi-level generating extensions that guarantee fast successive specialization. Experimental results show a remarkable reduction of generation time and generator size compared to previous attempts of multiple self-application.

1 Introduction

The division of programs into *two stages* has been studied intensively in partial evaluation and mixed computation to separate those program expressions that can be safely evaluated at specialization time from those that cannot. The main problem with the binding-time analysis of standard *partial evaluation, e.g.* as presented in [13], is the need to specify the availability of data in terms of 'early' (*static*) and 'late' (*dynamic*). This two-point domain does not allow to specify multi-level transition points (*e.g.* "dynamic until stage n"). This has limited the operation of partial evaluators to a conservative two-level approximation. Our goal is more general: *multi-level specialization*.

This paper presents the key ingredients of our approach to multi-level specialization. We introduce a general binding-time domain that expresses different 'shades' of static input. This means that a given program can be optimized with respect to some inputs at an earlier stage, and others at later stages. This modification requires several non-obvious extensions of standard partial evaluation techniques, such as *multi-level generating extensions* [10], a generalization of Ershov's (two-level) generating extension [8]. The main payoff of this novel approach becomes apparent in multiple self-application: experimental results show an impressive reduction of generation time and code size compared to previous attempts of multiple self-application.

Our approach to multi-level specialization, which we call *multi-cogen approach*, shares the advantages of the traditional cogen approach [3]: the generator and the generating extensions can use all features of the implementation language (no restrictions due to self-application); the generator manipulates only syntax trees (no need to implement a self-interpreter); values in generating extensions are represented directly (no encoding overhead); and it becomes easier to demonstrate correctness for non-trivial languages (due to the simplicity of the transformation). Multi-level generating extensions are portable, stand-alone programs that can be run independently of the multi-level generator.

Our multi-level binding-time analysis [11] has the same accuracy as and is slightly faster than the two-level analysis in Similix [5] (when compared on two levels), a state-of-the-art partial evaluator, which is notable because we did not optimize our implementation for speed. The results are also significant because they clearly demonstrate that multi-level specialization scales up to advanced languages without performance penalties. The methods developed for converting programs into fast and compact multi-level generating extensions can also be taken advantage of in conventional (two-level) compiler generators.

Recently our approach was extended to continuation-based partial evaluation [20] and used in a program generator system for Standard Scheme [21]. Closely related work has been initiated by several researchers including a language for hand-writing program generators [19] and an algebraic description of multi-level lambda-calculi [16, 17].

We assume familiarity with the basic notions of partial evaluation, for example as presented in [14] or [13, Part II]. Additional details about multi-level specialization can be found in [11, 12] on which this presentation is based.

2   Generating Extensions

We summarize the concept of multi-level generating extensions [10]. The notation is adapted from [13]: for any program text, p, written in language L we let $[\![p]\!]_L$ in denote the application of the L-program p to its input in. For notational convenience we assume that all program transformers are L-to-L-transformers written in L.

Ershov's Generating Extensions. A program generator cogen, which we call a *compiler generator* for historical reasons, is a program that takes a program p and its binding-time classification (bt-classification) as input and generates a program generator p-gen, called a *generating extension* [8], as output. The task of p-gen is to generate a residual program p-res, given static data in_0 for p's first input. We call p-gen a *two-level* generating extension of p because it realizes a two-staged computation of p. A generating extension p-gen runs potentially much faster than a program specializer because it is a program generator devoted to the generation of residual programs for p.

$$\begin{aligned}
\text{p-gen} &= [\![\text{cogen}]\!]_L \ \text{p 'SD'} \\
\text{p-res} &= [\![\text{p-gen}]\!]_L \ in_0 \\
\text{out} &= [\![\text{p-res}]\!]_L \ in_1
\end{aligned} \right\} \ \textit{two stages}$$

Multi-Level Generating Extensions. Program specialization can do more than stage a computation into two stages. Suppose p is a source program with n inputs. Assume the input is supplied in the order $in_0 \ldots in_{n-1}$. Given the first input in_0 a multi-level generating extension produces a new specialized multi-level generating extension p-mgen_0 and so on, until the final output out is produced given the last input in_{n-1}. Multi-level specialization using multi-level generating extensions is described by

$$
\left.
\begin{aligned}
\text{p-mgen}_0 &= [\![\text{mcogen}]\!]_L \ \text{p} \ `0 \ldots n-1\text{'} \\
\text{p-mgen}_1 &= [\![\text{p-mgen}_0]\!]_L \ in_0 \\
&\ \ \vdots \\
\text{p-mgen}_{n-2} &= [\![\text{p-mgen}_{n-3}]\!]_L \ in_{n-3} \\
\text{p-res}'_{n-1} &= [\![\text{p-mgen}_{n-2}]\!]_L \ in_{n-2} \\
\text{out} &= [\![\text{p-res}'_{n-1}]\!]_L \ in_{n-1}
\end{aligned}
\right\} n \ stages
$$

Our approach to multi-level specialization is *purely off-line*. A program generator mcogen, which we call a multi-level compiler generator, or short multi-level generator, is a program that takes a program p and a bt-classification $t_0 \ldots t_{n-1}$ of p's input parameters and generates a *multi-level generating-extension* p-mgen_0. The order in which input is supplied is specified by the bt-classification. The smaller the bt-value t_i, the earlier the input becomes available.

It is easy to see that a standard (two-level) generating extension is a special case of a multi-level generating extension: it returns only an 'ordinary' program and never a generating extension. Programs p-gen and p-mgen_{n-2} are examples of two-level generating extensions.

3   Construction Principles

We now turn to the basic methods for constructing multi-level generating extensions. Our aim is to develop a program generator well-suited for multi-level specialization. Efficiency of the multi-level generating extensions, as well as their compactness are our main goals. We will use Scheme, an untyped, strict functional programming language, as presentation language.

Construction Principles Our approach is based on the observation that the standard static/dynamic annotation of a program is a special case of a more general multi-level annotation and on the observation that annotated programs can be considered as generating extensions given an appropriate interpretation for their annotated operations. From these two observations, we draw the following conclusions for the design of our multi-level program generator and the corresponding generating extensions.

- A non-standard, *multi-level binding-time analysis* together with a phase converting annotations into executable multi-level generating extensions forms the core of a multi-level generator mcogen.
- Multi-level generating extensions p-mgen_i can be represented using a *multi-level language* providing support for code generation etc.

Multi-Level Language. The multi-level language, called MetaScheme, is an annotated, higher-order subset of Scheme where every construct has a bt-value $t \geq 0$ as additional argument (Fig. 1). The underlining of an operator, e.g. $\underline{\text{if}}_t$, together with the bt-value t attached to it, is its *annotation*. The language provides a lift operator $\underline{\text{lift}}_t^s$ to coerce a value with bt-value t to a value with a later bt-time $t + s$. It is clear that not all multi-level programs have a consistent annotation. The typing rules given in the next section define *well-annotated* multi-level programs.

$p \in Program;\ d \in Definition;\ e \in Expression;\ c \in Constant;$
$x \in Variable;\ f \in FctName;\ op \in Operator;\ s,t \in BindingTimeValue$

$p ::= d_1...d_m$
$d ::= (\text{define } (f\ x_1...x_n)\ e)$

$e ::= c$	$\mid\ x$	$\mid\ (\underline{\text{if}}_t\ e_1\ e_2\ e_3)$
$\mid\ (\underline{\text{lambda}}_t\ (x_1...x_n)\ e)$	$\mid\ (e_0\ \underline{@}_t\ e_1...e_n)$	$\mid\ (\underline{\text{let}}_t\ ((x\ e_1))\ e_2)$
$\mid\ (f\ e_1...e_n)$	$\mid\ (\underline{op}_t\ e_1...e_n)$	$\mid\ (\underline{\text{lift}}_t^s\ e)$

Fig. 1. Abstract syntax of MetaScheme $(0 \leq n, 0 < m)$.

Representing Multi-Level Generating Extensions Programs annotated with multiple binding-times need to be represented as executable programs and supplied with an appropriate interpretation for their annotated operations.

We follow the approach suggested by the observation that multi-level programs can be considered as programs provided a suitable interpretation for their annotated operations. Static expressions $(t = 0)$ can be evaluated by the underlying implementation, while dynamic expressions $(t > 0)$ are calls to code generating functions. A generating extension then consists of two parts:

1. *Multi-level program.* Representation of an annotated program as executable program.
2. *Library.* Functions for code generation and specialization.

Example 1. Consider as example the three-input program iprod which computes the inner product v·w of two vectors v, w of dimension n (Figure 2). Depending on the availability of the input, the computation of the inner product can be performed in one, two, and three stages. The residual program obtained by specializing iprod *wrt* two inputs n=3 and v=[7 8 9] is shown in Figure 3. A call of the form (ref i v) returns the i'th element of vector v.

Figure 4 shows a three-level version of the inner product where the arguments of iprod have the following binding-times: n:0, v:1, and w:2. The program is annotated using a *concrete multi-level syntax* of MetaScheme where all dynamic operations have a binding-time value as additional argument. Binding-time annotations can be represented conveniently by marking every dynamic operation with an underscore (_). The general format of dynamic operations is

```
(define (iprod n v w)          (define (iprod-nv w)
  (if (> n 0)                    (+ (* 9 (ref 3 w))
     (+                            (+ (* 8 (ref 2 w))
        (* (ref n v)                 (+ (* 7 (ref 1 w)) 0))))
           (ref n w))
        (iprod (- n 1) v w))
     0))
```

Fig. 2. Source program.   **Fig. 3.** Residual program (n=3, v=[7 8 9]).

```
(define (iprod3 n v w)          (define (_ op t . es)
  (if (> n 0)                    (if (= t 1)
     (_ '+ 2                       '(,op . ,es)
        (_ '* 2                    '(_ (QUOTE ,op) ,(- t 1) . ,es)))
           (_ 'lift 1 1
              (_ 'ref 1 (lift 1 n) v))   (define (lift s e)
              (_ 'ref 2 (lift 2 n) w))    (if (= s 1)
        (iprod3 (- n 1) v w))             '(QUOTE ,e)
     (lift 2 0)))                         '(LIFT ,(- s 1) (QUOTE ,e))))
```

Fig. 4. A multi-level program.   **Fig. 5.** Multi-level code generation.

$(\_ \ 'op \ t \ e_1 \ ... \ e_n)$ where t is the binding-time value and e_i are annotated argument expressions (the underscore _ is a legal identifier in Scheme). If $t = 0$, then we simply write $(op \ e_1 \ ... \ e_n)$. For example, for $(if_0 \ e_1 \ e_2 \ e_3)$ we write $(if \ e_1 \ e_2 \ e_3)$, and for $(lift_0^s \ e)$ we write $(lift \ s \ e)$.

Multi-Level Code Generation Figure 5 shows an excerpt of the library. The functions are the same for all generating extensions.

Function _ has three arguments: an operator op, a binding-time value t, and the arguments es of the operator op (code fragments). If t equals 1 then the function produces an expression for op that can be evaluated directly by the underlying implementation. Otherwise, it reproduces a call to itself where t is decreased by 1. Argument t is decremented until t reaches 1 which means that op expects its arguments in the next stage.

Function lift 'freezes' its argument e (a value). It counts the binding-time value s down to 1 before releasing s as literal constant. An expression of the form $(\_ \ 'lift \ t \ s \ e)$ is used when it takes t specializations before the value of e is known and $t + s$ specializations before it can be consumed by the enclosing expression $(s > 0)$. Since lift is just an ordinary function, it can be delayed using function _ (necessary as long as the value of e is not available).

Running a Multi-Level Program The body of the two-level generating extension in Figure 6 is obtained by evaluating the three-level generating extension

```
(define (iprod3-n v w)
  (_ '+ 1 (_ '* 1 (lift 1 (ref 3 v))
               (_ 'ref 1 (lift 1 3) w))
       (_ '+ 1 (_ '* 1 (lift 1 (ref 2 v))
                  (_ 'ref 1 (lift 1 2) w))
            (_ '+ 1 (_ '* 1 (lift 1 (ref 1 v))
                       (_ 'ref 1 (lift 1 1) w))
                 (lift 1 0))))))
```

Fig. 6. A generated generating extension (n=3).

in Figure 4 together with the definitions for multi-level code generation in Figure 5 where n = 3. Bound checks are eliminated, binding time arguments are decremented, e.g. (_ 'ref 1 ... w). Evaluating iprod-n with v=[7 8 9] returns the same program as shown in Figure 3.

The example illustrates the main advantages of this approach: fast and compact generating extensions. No extra interpretive overhead is introduced since library functions are linked with the multi-level program at loading/compile-time. The library adds only a constant size of code to a multi-level program. Static operations can be executed by the underlying implementation. One could provide an interpreter for multi-level programs, but this would be less efficient.

Programs can be generated very elegantly in Scheme because its abstract and concrete syntax coincide. Other programming languages may need more effort to obtain syntactically correct multi-level programs. Generating extensions for languages with side-effects, such as C, require an additional management of the static store to restore previous computation states [1]. The paper [12] extends the above methods into a full implementation with higher-order, polyvariant specialization.

4 Multi-Level Binding-Time Analysis

We specify a *multi-level binding-time analysis* (MBTA) for the multi-level generator mcogen in the remainder of this paper. The task of the MBTA is briefly stated: given a source program p, the binding-time values (bt-values) t_i of its input parameters together with a maximal bt-value ν, find a consistent multi-level annotation of p which is, in some sense, the 'best'. We give typing rules that define well-annotated multi-level programs and specify the analysis.

The typing rules formalize the intuition that early values may not depend on late values. They define *well-annotated* multi-level programs. Before we give the set of rules, we formalize bt-values and bt-types.

Definition 1 (binding-time value). *A binding-time value (bt-value) is a natural number $t \in \{0, 1, \ldots, \nu\}$ where ν is the maximal bt-value for the given problem.*

A *binding-time type* τ contains information about the type of a value, as well as the bt-value of the type. The bt-value of an expression e in a multi-level program is equal to the bt-value $\|\tau\|$ of its bt-type τ. In case an expression is well-typed (*wrt* a monomorphic type system with recursive types and one common base type), the type component of its bt-type τ is the same as the standard type.

Definition 2 (binding-time type). *A type τ is a (well-formed) binding-time type wrt ν, if $\vdash\tau{:}t$ is derivable from the rules below. If $\vdash\tau{:}t$ then the type τ represents a bt-value t, and we define a mapping $\|\cdot\|$ from bt-types to bt-values:* $\|\tau\| = t$ *iff* $\vdash\tau{:}t$.

$$\{Base\}\ \frac{t \leq \nu}{\Delta\vdash B^t{:}t} \qquad\qquad \{Fct\}\ \frac{\Delta\vdash\tau_i{:}s_i \quad \Delta\vdash\tau{:}s \quad s_i \geq t \quad s \geq t}{\Delta\vdash\tau_1...\tau_n \rightarrow^t \tau{:}t}$$

$$\{Btv\}\ \frac{\alpha{:}t \text{ in } \Delta \quad t \leq \nu}{\Delta\vdash\alpha{:}t} \qquad\qquad \{Rec\}\ \frac{\Delta \oplus \{\alpha{:}t\}\vdash\tau{:}t}{\Delta\vdash\mu\alpha.\tau{:}t}$$

Base bt-types, shown in Rule $\{Base\}$, are denoted by B^t where t is the bt-value. We do not distinguish between different base types, *e.g.* integer, boolean, *etc.*, since we are only interested in the distinction between base values and functions. Rule $\{Fct\}$ for function types requires that the bt-values of the argument types $\tau_1...\tau_n$ and the result type τ are *not* smaller than the bt-value t of the function itself because neither the arguments are available to the function's body nor can the result be computed *before* the function is applied. Rule $\{Btv\}$ ensures that the bt-value t assigned to a type variable α is never greater than ν. Rule $\{Rec\}$ for recursive types $\mu\alpha.\tau$ states that τ has the same bt-value t as the recursive type $\mu\alpha.\tau$ under the assumption that the type variable α has the bt-value t. The notation $\Delta \oplus \{\alpha : t\}$ denotes that the bt-environment Δ is extended with $\{\alpha : t\}$ while any other assignment $\alpha : t'$ is removed from Δ. This is in accordance with the equality $\mu\alpha.\tau = \tau[\mu\alpha.\tau/\alpha]$ which holds for recursive types.

An *equivalence relation* on bt-types allows us to type *all* expressions in our source language even though the language is dynamically typed. In particular, we can type expressions where the standard types cannot be unified because of potential type errors (function values used as base values, base values used as function values). By using this equivalence relation we can defer such errors to the latest possible binding time.

Definition 3 (equivalence of bt-types). *Let ν be a maximal bt-value and let U be the following axiom:*

$$\vdash B^\nu ... B^\nu \rightarrow^\nu B^\nu \doteq B^\nu$$

Given two bt-types τ and τ' well-formed wrt ν, we say that τ and τ' are equivalent, denoted by $\vdash\tau \doteq \tau'$, if $\vdash\tau \doteq \tau'$ is derivable from

1. *Axiom U*
2. *the equivalence of recursive types (based on types having the same regular type)*
3. *symmetry, reflexivity, transitivity, and compatibility of $=$ with arbitrary contexts*

Typing Rules. The typing rules for well-annotated multi-level programs are defined in Fig. 7. Most of the typing rules are generalizations of the corresponding rules used for two-level programs in partial evaluation, e.g. [13]. For instance, rule $\{If\}$ for if-expressions annotates the construct if with the bt-value t of the test-expression e_1 (the if-expression is reducible when the result of the test-expression becomes known at time t). The rule also requires that the test expression has a first-order type.

Rule $\{Lift\}$ shows the multi-level operator $\mathtt{lift}_t^s$: the value of its argument e has bt-value t, but its results is not available until $t + s$ ($s > 0, t \geq 0$). The bt-value of an expression ($\mathtt{lift}_t^s \ e$) is the sum of the bt-values s and t. In other words, the operator delays a value to a later binding time. As is customary in partial evaluation, the rule allows lifting of first-order values only.

Rule $\{Op\}$ requires that all higher-order arguments of primitive operators have bt-value ν because this is the only way to equate them with the required base type B^t (see Definition 3). This is a necessary and safe approximation since we assume nothing about the type of a primitive operator.

$$\{Con\} \ \Gamma \vdash c : B^0 \qquad\qquad \{Var\} \ \frac{x : \tau \text{ in } \Gamma}{\Gamma \vdash x : \tau}$$

$$\{If\} \ \frac{\Gamma \vdash e_1 : B^t \quad \Gamma \vdash e_2 : \tau \quad \Gamma \vdash e_3 : \tau \quad |\tau| \geq t}{\Gamma \vdash (\mathtt{if}_t \ e_1 \ e_2 \ e_3) : \tau} \qquad \{Call\} \ \frac{\Gamma \vdash e_i : \tau_i \quad f : \tau_1 \dots \tau_n \to^t \tau \text{ in } \Gamma}{\Gamma \vdash (f \ e_1 \dots e_n) : \tau}$$

$$\{Let\} \ \frac{\Gamma \vdash e : \tau \quad \Gamma\{x : \tau\} \vdash e' : \tau' \quad |\tau'| \geq |\tau|}{\Gamma \vdash (\mathtt{let}_{\|\tau\|} \ ((x \ e)) \ e') : \tau'} \qquad \{Op\} \ \frac{\Gamma \vdash e_i : B^t}{\Gamma \vdash (\underline{op}_t \ e_1 \dots e_n) : B^t}$$

$$\{Abs\} \ \frac{\Gamma\{x_i : \tau_i\} \vdash e : \tau'}{\Gamma \vdash (\underline{\lambda}_t \ x_1 \dots x_n . e) : \tau_1 \dots \tau_n \to^t \tau'} \qquad \{App\} \ \frac{\Gamma \vdash e_0 : \tau_1 \dots \tau_n \to^t \tau' \quad \Gamma \vdash e_i : \tau_i}{\Gamma \vdash (e_0 \ \underline{@}_t \ e_1 \dots e_n) : \tau'}$$

$$\{Lift\} \ \frac{\Gamma \vdash e : B^t \quad s > 0}{\Gamma \vdash (\mathtt{lift}_t^s \ e) : B^{t+s}} \qquad \{Equ\} \ \frac{\Gamma \vdash e : \tau \quad \vdash \tau \doteq \tau'}{\Gamma \vdash e : \tau'}$$

Fig. 7. Typing rules for well-annotated multi-level programs (i ranges over $0 \leq i \leq n$).

Definition 4 (well-annotated completion, minimal completion). *Given a program p, a maximal bt-value ν, and a bt-pattern $t_1 \dots t_k$ of p's goal function f_0, a* well-annotated completion *of p is a multi-level program p' with $|p'| = p$ iff the following judgment can be derived:*

$$\vdash p' : \{f_0 : B^{t_1} \dots B^{t_k} \to B^\nu, f_1 : \tau_{11} \dots \tau_{1n_1} \to^{t_1} \tau_1, \dots, f_n : \tau_{n1} \dots \tau_{nn_n} \to^{t_n} \tau_n\}$$

A well-annotated completion is minimal *if the bt-value of every subexpression e in p is less than or equal to the bt-value of e in any other well-annotated completion of p.*

Every program p has at least one well-annotated completion p' since the operations of a program can always be annotated with ν, which corresponds to all subexpressions in the completion having the bt-type B^ν. A program p can have have more than one well-annotated completion. The goal of the MBTA is to determine a well-annotated completion p' which is, preferably, 'minimal', *i.e.* all operations in a program shall be performed as early as possible.

Certain programming styles can unnecessarily dynamize operations, while others make it easier to perform operations earlier. Binding-time improvements are semantics-preserving transformations of a program that make it easier for the binding-time analysis to make more operations static [13]. Fortunately, the problem of binding-time improving programs for multi-level specialization can be reduced to the two-level case where all known techniques apply.

Example 2. Let us illustrates the use of recursive types in the MBTA. Without recursive types the expression

```
(lambda (x) (x x))
```

is only typable with type B^ν (or an equivalent type) with *maximal* bt-value ν, because the expression is not typable in the simply typed λ-calculus. The following typing with *minimal* bt-value 0 makes use of recursive type $\tau \to^0 B^0$ where τ denotes $\mu\alpha.(\alpha \to^0 B^0)$:

$$
\cfrac{\cfrac{\cfrac{}{\{x{:}\tau\} \vdash x{:}\tau}{\scriptstyle\{Var\}} \quad \vdash \tau \doteq \tau \to^0 B^0}{\{x{:}\tau\} \vdash x{:}\tau \to^0 B^0}{\scriptstyle\{Equ\}} \quad \cfrac{}{\{x{:}\tau\} \vdash x{:}\tau}{\scriptstyle\{Var\}}}{\cfrac{\{x{:}\tau\} \vdash x \; @_0 \; x{:}B^0}{\vdash \underline{\lambda}_0 x.x \; @_0 \; x{:}\tau \to^0 B^0}{\scriptstyle\{Abs\}}}{\scriptstyle\{App\}}
$$

Here we use equivalence $\doteq$ of bt-types $\mu\alpha.\alpha \to^0 B^0$ and $\mu\alpha.(\alpha \to^0 B^0) \to^0 B^0$. The two types are equivalent because their regular types (infinite unfolded types) are equal (Definition 3). In our case unfolding $\mu\alpha.\alpha \to^0 B^0$ once gives $\mu\alpha.(\alpha \to^0 B^0) \to^0 B^0$ which proves the equality. In conclusion, recursive types enable the MBTA to give earlier binding times.

5   Results

Multiple Self-Application The payoff of the multi-cogen approach becomes apparent when compared to multiple self-application. The main problem of multiple self-application is the exponential growth of generation time and code size (in the number of self-applications). While this problem has not limited self-applicable specializers up to two self-applications, it becomes critical in applications that beyond the third Futamura projection.

An experiment with multiple self-application was first carried out in [9]: staging a program for matrix transposition into $2 - 5$ levels. To compare both approaches, we repeated the experiment using the multi-level generator. We generate a two-level and a five-level generating extension, gen2 and gen5, respectively.

Table 1. Performance of program generators.

out	run	time/s	mem/kcells	size/cells
mint-gen = [mcogen] mint '012'		10.0	529	1525
comp = [mint-gen] def		.63	34	840
tar = [comp₂] pgm		.083	5.18	109

Table 2. Performance of programs.

out	run	speedup	time/ms	mem/kcells
out = [mint] def pgm dat		1	630	44.3
out = [tar] dat		72	8.7	1.93
out = [fac] dat		708	.89	.037

The results [12] show an impressive reduction of generation time and code size compared to the result reported for multiple self-application [9]. The ratio between the code size of gen2 and gen5 is reduced from 1:100 when using multiple self-application to 1:2 when using the multi-level generator. The ratio between the time needed to generate gen2 and gen5 is reduced from 1:9000 when using multiple self-application to 1:1.8 when using the multi-level generator.

Meta-Interpreter As another example consider a meta-interpreter mint, a three-input program, that takes a language definition def, a program pgm, and its data dat as input. Let def be written in some definition language D, let pgm be written in programming language P (defined by def), and let mint be written in programming language L. The equational definition of mint is

$$[\text{mint}]_L \text{ def pgm dat} = [\text{def}]_D \text{ pgm dat} = [\text{pgm}]_P \text{ dat} = \text{out}$$

While this approach has many theoretical advantages, there are substantial efficiency problems in practice: considerable time may be spent on interpreting the language definition def rather than on computing the operations specified by the P-program pgm. What we look for is a three-level generating extension mint-gen of the meta-interpreter mint to perform the computation in three stages.

$$\left.\begin{array}{l} \text{comp} = [\text{mint-gen}]_L \text{ def} \\ \text{tar} = [\text{comp}]_L \text{ pgm} \\ \text{out} = [\text{tar}]_L \text{ dat} \end{array}\right\} \textit{three stages}$$

The three-level generating extension mint-gen is a compiler generator which, when applied to def, yields comp. The two-level generating extension comp is a compiler which, when given a P-program pgm, returns a target program tar.

In our experiment [12], the meta-interpreter mint interprets a denotational-style definition language. The definition def describes a small functional language (the applied lambda calculus extended with constants, conditionals, and a fix-operator). The program pgm is the factorial function and the input dat is the number 10.

Table 1 shows the generation times, the memory allocated during the generation and the sizes of the program generators (number of cons cells). Table 2 shows the run times of the example program using the meta-interpreter and the generated target program. For comparison, we also list the run time of fac, the standard implementation of the factorial in Scheme. All run times were measured on a SPARC station 1 using SCM version 4e1.

We notice that the generation of the compiler comp is fast (0.63s), as well as the generation of the target program tar (0.083s). The conversion of the meta-interpreter mint into a compiler generator mint-gen is quite reasonable (10s).

The results in Table 2 demonstrate that specialization yields substantial speedups by reducing mint's interpretive overhead: they improve the performance by a factor 72. The target program tar produced by comp is 'only' around 10 times slower than the factorial fac written directly in Scheme. Finally, interpreting pgm with mint is 700 times slower than running the Scheme version of the factorial fac.

One of the main reasons why the target program tar is slower than the standard version fac is that primitive operations are still interpreted in the target programs. This accounts for a factor of around 4. Post unfolding of function calls improves the runtime of these programs further by a factor 1.3.

6   Related Work

The first hand-written compiler generator based on partial evaluation techniques was, in all probability, the system *RedCompile* for a dialect of Lisp [2]. Romanenko [18] gave transformation rules that convert annotated first-order programs into two-level generating extensions. Holst [15] was the first to observe that the annotated version of a program is already a generating extension. What Holst called "syntactic currying" is now known as the "cogen approach" [3]. The multi-cogen approach presented here is based on earlier work [10–12]. Thiemann [20] extended our approach to continuation-based specialization and implemented a multi-cogen for Standard Scheme [21].

Multi-level languages have become an issue for several reasons. They are, among others, a key ingredient in the design and implementation of generative software, e.g. [7]. Taha and Sheard [19] introduce MetaML, a statically typed multi-level language for hand-writing multi-level generating extensions. Although MetaScheme was not designed for a human programmer – we were interested in automatically generating program generators – it can be seen, together with the multi-level typing-rules, as a statically typed multi-level programming language (specialization points can be inserted manually or automatically based on the annotations).

References

1. L.O. Andersen. *Program Analysis and Specialization for the C Programming Language*. PhD thesis, DIKU Report 94/19, Dept. of Computer Science, University of Copenhagen, 1994.

2. L. Beckman, A. Haraldson, Ö. Oskarsson, E. Sandewall. A partial evaluator and its use as a programming tool. *Artificial Intelligence*, 7:319–357, 1976.
3. L. Birkedal, M. Welinder. Hand-writing program generator generators. In M. Hermenegildo, J. Penjam (eds.), *Programming Language Implementation and Logic Programming*. LNCS 844, 198–214, Springer-Verlag 1994.
4. D. Bjørner, A.P. Ershov, N.D. Jones (eds.). *Partial Evaluation and Mixed Computation*. North-Holland 1988.
5. A. Bondorf, J. Jørgensen. Efficient analyses for realistic off-line partial evaluation. *Journal of Functional Programming*, 3(3):315–346, 1993.
6. O. Danvy, R. Glück, P. Thiemann (eds.). *Partial Evaluation*. LNCS 1110, Springer-Verlag 1996.
7. U. Eisenecker. Generative programming with C++. In H. Mössenböck (ed.), *Modular Programming Languages, LNCS* 1204, 351–365, Springer-Verlag 1997.
8. A.P. Ershov. On the essence of compilation. In E.J. Neuhold (ed.), *Formal Description of Programming Concepts*, 391–420. North-Holland 1978.
9. R. Glück. Towards multiple self-application. In *Proceedings of the Symposium on Partial Evaluation and Semantics-Based Program Manipulation*, 309–320, ACM Press 1991.
10. R. Glück, J. Jørgensen. Efficient multi-level generating extensions for program specialization. In M. Hermenegildo, S.D. Swierstra (eds.) *Programming Languages, Implementations, Logics and Programs*, LNCS 982, 259–278, Springer-Verlag 1995.
11. R. Glück, J. Jørgensen. Fast binding-time analysis for multi-level specialization. In D. Bjørner, M. Broy, I.V. Pottosin (eds.) *Perspectives of System Informatics*, LNCS 1181, 261–272, Springer-Verlag 1996.
12. R. Glück, J. Jørgensen. An automatic program generator for multi-level specialization. *Lisp and Symbolic Computation*, 10(2): 113–158, 1997.
13. N.D. Jones, C.K. Gomard, and P. Sestoft. *Partial Evaluation and Automatic Program Generation*. Prentice-Hall 1993.
14. N.D. Jones, P. Sestoft, and H. Søndergaard. Mix: a self-applicable partial evaluator for experiments in compiler generation. *LISP and Symbolic Computation*, 2(1):9–50, 1989.
15. C.K. Holst. Syntactic currying: yet another approach to partial evaluation. Student report, DIKU, Dept. of Computer Science, University of Copenhagen, 1989.
16. F. Nielson, H.R. Nielson. Multi-level lambda-calculus: an algebraic description. In [6], 338–354, 1996.
17. F. Nielson, H.R. Nielson. Prescriptive frameworks for multi-level lambda-calculi. In *ACM SIGPLAN Symposium on Partial Evaluation and Semantics-Based Program Manipulation*, 193–202, ACM Press 1997.
18. S.A. Romanenko. A compiler generator produced by a self-applicable specializer can have a surprisingly natural and understandable structure. In [4], 445–463, 1988.
19. W. Taha, T. Sheard. Multi-stage programming with explicit annotations. In *ACM SIGPLAN Symposium on Partial Evaluation and Semantics-Based Program Manipulation*, 203–217, ACM Press 1997.
20. P. Thiemann. Cogen in six lines. In *International Conference on Functional Programming*, 180–189, ACM Press 1996.
21. P. Thiemann. The PGG system – user manual. Dept. of Computer Science, University of Nottingham, 1998.

Faster Fourier Transforms via Automatic Program Specialization

Julia L. Lawall

IRISA – Compose group
Campus Universitaire de Beaulieu
35042 Rennes Cedex, France
e-mail: jll@irisa.fr

Abstract. Because of its wide applicability, many efficient implementations of the Fast Fourier Transform have been developed. We propose that an efficient implementation can be produced automatically and reliably by partial evaluation. Partial evaluation of an unoptimized implementation produces a speedup of over 9 times. The automatically generated result of partial evaluation has performance comparable to or exceeding that produced by a variety of hand optimizations. We analyze the benefits of partial evaluation at both compile time and run time, focusing on compiler issues that affect the performance of the specialized program.

1 Introduction

The Fourier transform and its inverse are widely used in a variety of scientific applications, such as audio and image processing [21], integration [21], and calculation using very large numbers [3,22]. The transform converts a function defined in terms of time to a function defined in terms of frequency. When a function is defined over the frequency domain, some expensive calculations are more tractable. This technique was made practical by the development of the Fast Fourier Transform (FFT) [7], which uses a divide-and-conquer algorithm to calculate the Fourier transform of a function represented as a discrete set of evenly-spaced data points. The divide-and-conquer algorithm reduces the complexity from $O(n^2)$ to $O(n \log n)$, where n is the number of data points.

Despite the significantly improved performance, the FFT remains an expensive operation. Many computations spend a substantial amount of time performing FFT's. For example, the 125.turb3d program of the SPEC95 Benchmark suite [8] spends about 40% of the time performing FFT's of 32 or 64 elements, using a hand-optimized implementation. Much effort has gone into hand-optimizing implementations of the algorithm. These optimizations include using recurrences to limit the number of calls to sine and cosine, eliminating the calls to these math library routines completely by reimplementing them more efficiently or using tables, reducing the number of real multiplications, and unrolling loops.

In this paper, we investigate whether partial evaluation is a suitable tool for generating an efficient FFT implementation. One measure of success is how many expressions are eliminated or simplified by partial evaluation. In this paper, we take a lower-level approach, and analyze the performance obtained on a particular architecture (the Sun Ultrasparc). We find that partial evaluation improves the unoptimized implementation over 9 times when the input contains 16 elements and over 3 times when the input contains 512 elements. In an expanded version of this paper [16], we demonstrate that these results are competitive with the performance of hand optimization techniques, as illustrated by a variety of existing, publicly-available implementations.

The rest of this paper is organized as follows: Section 2 presents an overview of partial evaluation. Section 3 assesses the opportunities for specialization presented by the FFT algorithm, and estimates the speedup that can be obtained. Section 4 carries out the specialization of a simple implementation of the FFT. In Sections 5 and 6, we slightly rewrite the source program to get better results from specialization at compile-time and run-time, respectively. Finally, Section 7 describes other related work and Section 8 concludes.

2   Overview of partial evaluation

Partial evaluation is an automatic program transformation that specializes a program with respect to part of its input. Expressions that depend only on the known input and on program constants are said to be *static*. These expressions can be evaluated during specialization. Other expressions are said to be *dynamic*. These expressions are reconstructed to form the residual program. An *offline* partial evaluator begins with a *binding-time analysis* phase that determines which constructs are static and which are dynamic. Constructs are annotated to be evaluated or reconstructed accordingly. Binding-time analysis is followed by *specialization*, which builds the specialized program following these annotations.

We use the *Tempo* partial evaluator [5, 13] for the C programming language. Tempo is the only partial evaluator for C that provides specialization at both compile time and run time, based on a single, compile-time, binding-time analysis. This structure is illustrated in Figure 1.

Compile-time specialization maps source code into specialized source code, based on invariants supplied at compile time. The specialized program may subsequently be compiled by any C compiler. Thus, this approach is not tied to a particular compiler or architecture.

Run-time specialization specializes a program based on invariants that are not available until run time. Run-time specialization directly produces object code for a particular architecture. To limit the run-time overhead, Tempo constructs the specialized code out of code fragments, known as *templates*, that are compiled at compile time [6], *i.e.*, before run time. These templates contain *holes* to represent static subexpressions, whose values are not available until specialization. Specialization at run time consists of evaluating the static expressions, copying the compiled templates, and filling the holes. Experiments have shown that the overhead for specialization at run time following this approach is small [18].

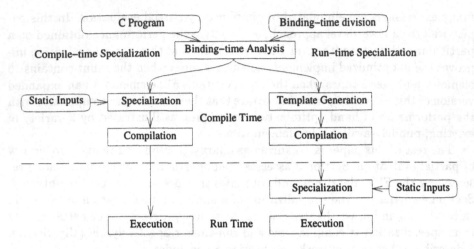

Fig. 1. Overview of Tempo

3   Why specialize the FFT?

We first consider why an implementation of the FFT is a good candidate for optimization via partial evaluation. The FFT is generally a module in another program. The benefit accrued from specializing a module depends on two factors: how often it is invoked with the inputs to which it is specialized, and what proportion of the computation of the module depends only on those inputs. The former requires examination of typical calling contexts, while the latter requires that we analyze the FFT implementation itself.

Using the analysis of the implementation, we then approximate the speedup obtainable from this approach. This approximation will be used to evaluate the success of our subsequent specializations of the FFT.

3.1   Typical calling contexts

We consider the FFT of a function represented as a one-dimensional array of complex numbers. In many applications, such an FFT is repeatedly applied to a stream of functions of fixed size. Furthermore, a multi-dimensional FFT can be implemented as a one-dimensional FFT iterated over all the rows and columns of the array. Thus, in a typical application, a one-dimensional FFT is applied many times to data sets of the same size. These observations suggest that it may be useful to specialize an implementation of the FFT to the number of elements in one dimension and the direction of the transformation.

3.2   Analysis of the implementation

An unoptimized implementation, adapted from Arndt [2], of the FFT is shown in Figure 2. The program consists of two procedures: fft and scramble. The arguments to the main procedure, fft, are two one-dimensional arrays (representing the real and complex components of the function respectively), the size of each array, and an integer representing the direction of the transformation. Because of the divide-and-conquer strategy, each of the pair of arrays representing the function to transform has a size that is a power of two. The procedure fft first calls scramble to reorder the array elements, and then carries out the transform. The implementation follows the structure of the mathematical algorithm. This structure is typical of more optimized implementations.

The fonts used in Figure 2 represent the result of binding-time analysis with the array size and the direction of the transformation static. Static constructs are italicized, while dynamic constructs are in bold face.

The most computationally intensive part of the program consists of the three nested loops in the fft procedure. As indicated by the result of the binding-time analysis, this portion of the program contains the following opportunities for improvement by specialization:

- All loop tests are static. Thus loops can be unfolded, leading to straight-line code.
- The second of the three nested loops contains a static call to the sine function and a static call to the cosine function on each iteration. Eliminating these expensive function calls should lead to a significant performance improvement.
- In the innermost loop, there are numerous references to static variables within dynamic expressions. When specialization is performed at compile time, the compiler of the specialized code can exploit the resulting constant values. For example, the compiler can eliminate multiplications by 0 and 1.

Overall, both the opportunities for shifting significant computation to specialization time, and, in the case of compile-time specialization, the prospect of more effective compilation of the specialized program, make implementations of the FFT attractive candidates for partial evaluation.

3.3 Speedup estimation

While partial evaluation would seem intuitively to improve performance by eliminating expensive computations, it can also degrade performance by producing code that is too large to fit in the instruction cache, or to be compiled well. To assess the speedup obtained by partial evaluation, we characterize the expected speedup based on an analysis of the implementation. The expected speedup depends on two factors: the amount of code that is eliminated by specialization and the execution time of this code. We estimate the former using a complexity analysis of the implementation, described in terms of the number of elements n and the costs of the static and dynamic parts of the fft and scramble procedures.[1] We estimate the latter using the speedup obtained by specialization to

---

[1] N.B. For the fft and scramble procedures, the number of iterations of the inner loop(s) depends on the current value of the loop index of the outermost loop. To

```
#define M_PI 3.14159265358979323846
#define REAL double
#define SWAP(x, y) {REAL tmp = x; x = y; y = tmp; }
```

```
void                                    void
fft(REAL *fr, REAL *fi, int ldn, int is) scramble(REAL *fr, REAL *fi, int n)
{                                       {
   int n2,ldm,m,mh,j,r,t1,t2;             int m,j;
   REAL pi,phi,c,s;                       for (m=1,j=0; m<n-1; m++) {
   REAL ur,vr, ui,vi;                       int k;
                                            for (k=n>>1; !((j^=k)&k); k>>=1);
   n2=1<<ldn;
   pi=is*M_PI;                             if (j>m) {
   scramble(fr,fi,n2);                       SWAP(fr[m],fr[j]);
                                             SWAP(fi[m],fi[j]);
   for (ldm=1; ldm<=ldn; ldm++) {         }
      m=(1<<ldm);                         }
      mh=(m>>1);                       }
      phi=pi/(REAL)(mh);

      for (j=0; j<mh; j++) {
         REAL w=phi*(REAL)j;
         c=cos(w);
         s=sin(w);

         for (r=0; r<n2; r+=m) {
            t1=r+j;
            t2=t1+mh;

            vr=fr[t2]*c-fi[t2]*s;
            vi=fr[t2]*s+fi[t2]*c;

            ur=fr[t1];
            fr[t1]+=vr;
            fr[t2]=ur-vr;

            ui=fi[t1];
            fi[t1]+=vi;
            fi[t2]=ui-vi;
         }
      }
   }
}
```

Fig. 2. Binding-time analysis of `fft` and `scramble`. Static expressions are in italics and dynamic expressions are in boldface.

16 elements (the smallest number of elements considered in our tests). Special-ization for 16 elements produces a relatively small program, which we assume does not cause cache problems and can be compiled effectively. We then combine this information to estimate the speedup expected for more values.

The `scramble` procedure consists of two nested loops. Both loops are unrolled by specialization. The outer loop contains the completely static inner loop and some dynamic code. This dynamic code has complexity $\frac{n}{2}$. The static inner loop has complexity n. Let s_s represent the cost of one iteration of the static inner loop, and s_d represent the cost of one iteration of the dynamic part of the outer loop. Then, the complexity S_{un} of the unspecialized `scramble` procedure is:

$$S_{un} = ns_s + \frac{n}{2}s_d$$

The specialized procedure consists of just the dynamic code of the outer loop. Thus, its complexity S_{sp} is:

$$S_{sp} = \frac{n}{2}s_d$$

The `fft` procedure consists of three nested loops. All loops are unrolled by specialization. The complexity of the outermost loop is $\log n$. The complexity of the second loop is n. The complexity of the innermost loop is $\frac{n\log n}{2}$. The outer two loops consist of static code and the nested loop. Thus, only code from the body of the innermost loop appears in the residual program. The cost of the static code in the outermost loop should be negligible, and the complexity of the loop is comparatively small as well, so we omit the outermost loop from our complexity estimate. Let f_s represent the cost of the static code in the second loop, and f_d represent the cost of the dynamic code in the innermost loop. Then, the complexity F_{un} of the unspecialized `fft` procedure is:

$$F_{un} = nf_s + \frac{n\log n}{2}f_d$$

The complexity F_{sp} of the specialized procedure is:

$$F_{sp} = \frac{n\log n}{2}f_d$$

Solving the above equations for s_s, s_d, f_s, and f_d in terms of S_{un}, S_{sp}, F_{un}, and F_{sp} gives the following equations:

---

simplify the presentation, we describe the complexity of a loop as the number of times its body is executed per invocation of the enclosing procedure, rather than per invocation of the enclosing block of code.

$$s_s = \frac{S_{un} - S_{sp}}{n} \quad f_s = \frac{F_{un} - F_{sp}}{n}$$

$$s_d = \frac{2}{n}S_{sp} \qquad f_d = \frac{2}{n\log n}F_{sp}$$

Substituting the actual execution times of the specialized and unspecialized procedures for 16 elements gives an estimate of the costs of the static and dynamic blocks of code.

The speedup obtained by specialization of the complete program is:

$$\frac{S_{un} + F_{un}}{S_{sp} + F_{sp}} = \frac{\frac{n}{2}s_d + ns_s + nf_s + \frac{n\log n}{2}f_d}{\frac{n}{2}s_d + \frac{n\log n}{2}f_d}$$

The expression on the right, instantiated with the estimated values of s_s, s_d, f_s, and f_d, calculates the expected speedup for any number of elements.

4   Specialization of a simple FFT implementation

We now assess the performance of the result of specializing the FFT implementation, shown in Figure 2, to the number of elements and the direction of the transformation static. We carry out specialization at both compile time and run time.

4.1   Methodology

The experimental results were obtained on a 200MHz Sun ultrasparc running Solaris (SunOS 5.5). The machine has 256MB of main memory, a 16KB primary data cache, a 16KB primary instruction cache, and a 512KB secondary cache. Programs were compiled with gcc version 2.8.1 using the options -O2 -mcpu=ultrasparc -ffast-math and Sun's cc compiler version 4.2 using the options -fast -xO5 -xinline=[]. These are the maximum optimization levels for these compilers, omitting inlining, which is not interesting for this program. For run-time specialization, templates were compiled with gcc with the additional option -fno-schedule-insns to prevent unwanted scheduling optimizations within templates. This option was not used in compiling the unspecialized reference program. Run times were calculated using getrusage and include only the user time.

4.2   Compile-time specialization

The specialized program consists of the specialized fft procedure, which calls the specialized scramble procedure. The specialized fft procedure is straight-line code, built from the dynamic code in the innermost loop. The calls to sin and `cos` have been eliminated, and the uses of their values have been replaced by explicit constants. Array indices are constant as well. The specialized `scramble` procedure is similar.

Figure 3 shows the performance of the specializations for 16 to 512 elements. The expected speedups are shown in parentheses after the actual speedups, and are based on applying the formula derived in Section 3.3 to the speedup obtained for 16 elements. For 32 and 64 elements, the actual speedup achieved when using gcc is slightly lower than the expected speedup, while the actual speedup achieved when using cc is slightly higher than the expected speedup. In both cases there is a significant drop off in performance at 128 elements. We examine some reasons for this behavior in Section 5.

	gcc			cc		
	Source	Compile-time specialization		Source	Compile-time specialization	
Size	Time	Time	**Speedup**	Time	Time	**Speedup**
16	40.89	4.54	**9.00**	34.94	4.66	**7.50**
32	89.63	11.53	**7.77** (8.09)	76.27	10.21	**7.47** (6.90)
64	193.07	27.73	**6.96** (7.37)	160.74	23.41	**6.87** (6.40)
128	402.10	73.46	**5.47** (6.78)	331.45	71.95	**4.61** (5.98)
256	818.38	199.50	**4.10** (6.29)	678.74	143.65	**4.72** (5.62)
512	1682.42	518.32	**3.25** (5.87)	1398.50	337.74	**4.14** (5.31)

Fig. 3. Performance of the source program and compile-time specializations (times in microseconds).

4.3 Run-time specialization

The structure of the code produced by run-time specialization is the same as the structure of the code produced by compile-time specialization. The speedups obtained by run-time specialization are shown in Figure 4. Again, the expected speedups, shown in parentheses after the actual speedups, are based on applying the formula derived in Section 3.3 to the speedup obtained for 16 elements. Figure 4 also shows the cost of specialization, itself. Because specialization is performed at run time, the specialized code must be run several times to pay for the cost of specialization. The number of runs required to amortize this cost is shown in the column labeled "=". (Where specialization slows down the program, this value is ∞.)

The speedups obtained by run-time specialization are quite low, when compared to the speedups obtained by compile-time specialization. Furthermore, for more than 16 elements, the speedup is consistently lower than the expected speedup. For 512 elements, the specialized program is actually substantially slower than the original program. The time required to generate the specialized program is also substantial. We examine some solutions to these problems in Section 6.

	Source		Run-time specialization		
Size	Time	Generate	Time	Speedup	=
16	40.74	366.59	12.07	**3.38**	13
32	89.19	893.12	34.40	**2.59** (2.96)	17
64	188.53	2130.64	88.01	**2.14** (2.67)	22
128	390.71	4923.36	203.10	**1.92** (2.45)	27
256	812.21	11089.39	476.79	**1.70** (2.29)	34
512	1669.31	25691.15	2584.33	**0.65** (2.15)	∞

Fig. 4. Performance of the source program and run-time specializations (gcc only, times in microseconds).

5 Improving the result of compile-time specialization

Compile-time specialization of the FFT implementation produces two quite large procedures containing many integer and floating-point constants. These features are atypical of handwritten C code, and thus hardware and compilers may not be optimized for such programs. We now examine the effects of cache behavior and compiler optimizations on the performance of specialized programs.

5.1 Hardware considerations

The ultrasparc has a 16KB primary instruction, a 16KB data cache, and a 512KB secondary cache. Figure 5 presents the size of the assembly code for the specialized programs and the size of the dynamic arrays. In all of our experiments the data fits within the primary data cache. For more than 64 elements, the specialized code does not fit within the primary instruction cache. Nevertheless, both the data cache and the instruction cache affect the performance of the specialized program.

	Array	Specialized code size	
Size	size	cc	gcc
16	0.256	2.036	2.052
32	0.512	5.168	5.188
64	1.024	12.860	12.868
128	2.048	30.228	32.612
256	4.096	70.132	82.852
512	8.192	158.948	164.004

Fig. 5. Data and code sizes (KB)

The behavior of the data cache has a significant effect on the performance of the specialized programs. In our experiments, we iterate the fft procedure many times on the same pair of arrays. In the best case, all of the array elements remain in the cache between each iteration. Thus there are few data cache misses during the execution of the fft procedure. In the worst case, all the array elements are overwritten with values in other locations between each iteration. Figure 6 compares the performance at these two extremes. For readability, we normalize the runtime by the complexity of the implementation, following the strategy of Frigo and Johnson [10]. For both gcc and cc, the specialized program is significantly faster when the data cache is preserved between iterations. Overwriting the data cache between iterations of the fft procedure slows down the unspecialized program only 3-5%, however. We have thus omitted this case from the figure.

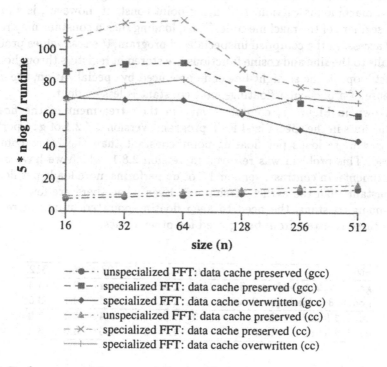

Fig. 6. Performance of the unspecialized and specialized implementations, comparing data cache behavior.

As shown in Figure 5, for more than 64 elements, the size of the specialized program exceeds the size of the instruction cache. Figure 6 shows that in all cases there is a drop off in performance at this point. The drop off is more significant when the data cache remains intact between iterations. When the specialized program is compiled with gcc the performance declines steadily, whereas when the specialized program is compiled with cc the performance levels off. Thus, we now turn to the difference between the behavior of cc and gcc on the specialized

FFT implementation. We only consider the case where the data cache is overwritten between iterations, since a real application would likely apply the FFT to a different pair of arrays each time, or perform other calculations between successive calls to the FFT that would modify the data cache.

5.2   Compiler considerations

We now examine the effect of compiling the specialized FFT programs, focusing on the treatment of floating-point constants and the effect of very large procedures on register allocation.

Floating-point constants A reference to a small integer constant can be inlined in a machine instruction. A floating-point constant, however, is stored in the data segment of the machine code. Thus, loading such a constant may require memory access. In the compiled unspecialized program, the real values produced by the calls to the sine and cosine functions are stored in registers throughout the innermost loop. In the straight-line code produced by specialization, the extent of the reuse of a particular floating-point constant is less evident.

As shown in Figure 7, compilers vary in their treatment of the floating-point constants in the specialized FFT program. Version 2.7.2.1 of gcc performs significantly more loads per floating-point constant than the other compilers considered. This problem was resolved in version 2.8.1, which we have used in our experiments. In contrast, version 4.2 of cc performs more loads per floating-point constant than the earlier version 4.0. Even when there are few loads per floating-point constant, the need to keep floating-point constants in registers prevents these registers from being used for other values.

Size	16	32	64	128	256	512
gcc 2.7.2.1 loads per float	1.0	1.0	3.5	6.4	9.7	13.4
gcc 2.8.1 loads per float	1.0	1.0	1.4	2.3	3.1	3.5
cc 4.0 loads per float	1.0	1.0	1.0	1.4	2.1	3.0
cc 4.2 loads per float	1.0	1.2	2.2	2.6	3.2	3.5

Fig. 7. Average loads per distinct floating-point constant.

Register allocation within very large procedures Procedure size affects the compiler's ability to allocate registers. For the source program, both cc and gcc generate assembly code that stores all intermediate values in registers. Ignoring for the moment the need to store floating-point constants in registers, it should be possible to compile the specialized program to use only registers as well.

When a compiler is unable to allocate registers to all the temporary values, it moves values from registers onto the stack. This operation is relatively expensive. In compiling the FFT program specialized for 128 or 256 elements, gcc generates many stack operations, including storing values on the stack that are never read again. No stack operations are generated by cc. These extra memory references account for some of the drop off in performance of the specialized program when compiled by gcc.

5.3 Obtaining better performance from the specialized code

The useless stack operations generated by gcc suggest that the complex operations performed at optimization level -O2 perform badly on the large blocks of simple straight-line code. Compiling instead with optimization level -O1, using the additional option -fschedule-insns to perform some instruction scheduling, both eliminates all the stack operations and produces faster code, as shown in Figure 8. Nevertheless, because of exceeding the instruction cache, we still do not obtain the expected speedup for large numbers of elements.

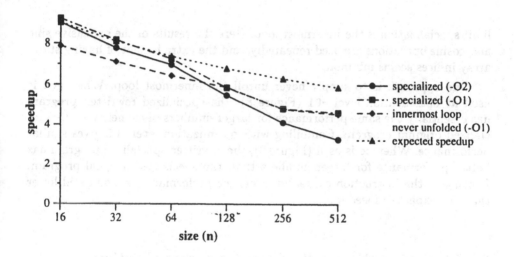

Fig. 8. Performance of variants of the specialized program (compiled with gcc).

At optimization level -O1, gcc performs slightly more loads per floating-point constant than at optimization level -O2. By avoiding optimizations that are harmful, we have also eliminated some optimizations that could be beneficial. Thus, particularly because specialized programs do not have the form of typical C programs, there are some trade-offs involved in obtaining the best performance.

Overall, the problems with compiling and running large procedures suggest that we may recover some of the expected speedup by performing less specialization, thus generating smaller procedures. A particularly appealing place to

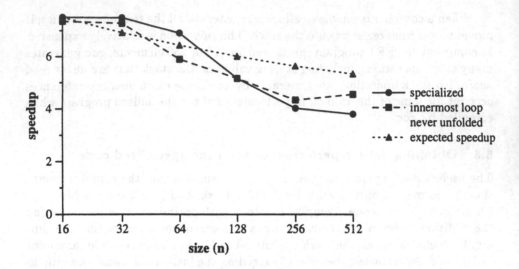

Fig. 9. Performance of variants of the specialized program (compiled with cc).

limit specialization is the innermost loop. Here the results of the expensive sine and cosine operations are used repeatedly, and the extra benefit of having static array indices seems minimal.

One approach is to simply never unroll the innermost loop. When gcc is used at optimization level -O1 (Figure 8), the specialized rewritten program has essentially the same performance for larger numbers of elements as the specialized original program. Compiling with optimization level -O2 gives similar performance. When cc is used (Figure 9), the rewritten specialized program has better performance for larger numbers than the specialized original program. Because of the instruction cache, however, the performance is again still lower than the expected speedup.

6   Improving the result of run-time specialization

Run-time specialization introduces different performance considerations. Because compilation is performed at compile time on a set of templates whose total size is bounded by the size of the source program, the duplication of templates at specialization time does not affect the quality of the compiled code. On the other hand, because the templates are compiled before the static constants become available, the compiler cannot take advantage of their values. By rewriting the program slightly, we can improve on the performance shown in Figure 4, and indeed achieve much of the speedup obtained by compile-time specialization. These transformations are described below.

6.1   The problem of a static value in a dynamic context

A static value in a dynamic context results in a *hole* within a template. Holes are represented such that each hole is considered by the compiler to be a unique, unknown constant [18]. The run-time specializer modifies the assembly code of the template by writing a load of the static value on top of the assembly code generated for the hole. This approach can harm the quality of the specialized code by preventing compile-time simplifications and by reducing opportunities for reuse of values loaded from memory.

To resolve these problems, we shift some specialization-time values to compile time (by explicitly enumerating the possible values), and shift others to execution time (by making them dynamic). Both approaches reduce the number of holes, which shortens specialization time and produces more efficient specialized code.

6.2   Compile-time optimizations based on explicit constants

Because static values are not available at compile time, run-time specialization does not introduce opportunities for compile-time optimizations based on explicit constants, such as eliminating multiplications by 0 or 1. To achieve this effect during run-time specialization, we introduce conditionals that test for these values and hand specialize the code accordingly. These extra conditionals are reduced during specialization, and thus only affect the specialization time. This rewriting is a variant of what is widely known within the partial evaluation community as "The Trick" [14].

For 16 elements the result of specialization after this optimization achieves a speedup of 4.25, which is significantly better than the speedup of 3.38 obtained by specialization of the original program. For more than 64 elements there is less improvement, reflecting the smaller percentage of computations affected by the optimization.

6.3   Sharing

The array indices of the innermost loop are also static values occurring in dynamic contexts. These values do not trigger any optimizations, so we simply instruct the binding-time analysis to consider these values as dynamic. This annotation strategy dramatically increases the amount of sharing in the specialized program.

In the innermost loop of the source program, several array elements are referenced repeatedly, without intervening writes. Thus the compiler can detect that the value stored in a register after the first load of such an array element can be used in the second occurrence, avoiding a second memory access. Run-time specialization, however, obscures this property completely. Each hole is encoded as a unique, unknown constant. Thus the compiler generates a separate memory access for each array reference. Making the array index dynamic reintroduces the possibility of sharing these values. The values of the calls to cosine and sine that are not eliminated by the test for 0 and 1 are also shared after this optimization.

With this optimization, the speedup obtained ranges from 6.25 for 16 elements to 3.60 for 512 elements, in contrast to the speedups of between 3.38 and 0.65 obtained by the specialized original program.

6.4   Combining the optimizations

As shown in Figure 10, with both optimizations, the speedups range from 7.81 for 16 elements to 3.79 for 512 elements. Beginning with 64 elements, the actual speedup is significantly lower than the expected speedup. In every case, the run-time specialized code is larger than the compile-time specialized code. Thus, the run-time specialized code exceeds the size of the instruction cache starting at 64, rather than 128, elements (*c.f.* Figure 5). Combining the two optimizations also reduces the generation time by a factor of two. The cost of specialization is amortized after at most 9 invocations.

The final column of Figure 10 compares the execution time of the run-time specialized code with the execution time of the result of compile-time specialization, compiled at optimization level -O1. With both optimizations, run-time specialization achieves up to 76% of the performance of compile-time specialization. This figure is comparable to the results of other experiments with Tempo's run-time specialization [18].

Size	Source Time	Run-time specialization Generate	Time	Speedup	=	CT/RT Time
16	40.66	205.22	5.20	**7.81**	6	76%
32	89.90	451.71	12.90	**6.97** (6.86)	6	76%
64	192.06	1020.68	35.76	**5.37** (6.14)	7	66%
128	393.78	2279.70	94.32	**4.17** (5.58)	8	64%
256	819.32	5045.29	204.78	**4.00** (5.13)	9	74%
512	1678.38	10937.41	442.27	**3.79** (4.76)	9	73%

Fig. 10. Performance of the result of run-time specialization after all optimizations to the source program (gcc only, times in microseconds).

7   Related work

Because we are investigating the application of partial evaluation to scientific code, we focus on partial evaluators for Fortran and C.

Glück *et al.* have specialized the FFT using their partial evaluator for Fortran [11]. They achieve speedups ranging from 5.05 for 16 elements to 1.83 for 512 elements. Their good results on this example motivated our investigation.

C-Mix is a partial evaluator for C developed by Andersen [1]. Using C-Mix, it should be possible to achieve similar results similar to our results for compile-time specialization. C-Mix does not provide run-time specialization. Furthermore, to achieve good results from run-time specialization, we require a binding-time analysis that can consider a variable to be both static and dynamic. C-Mix does not provide this facility.

Grant *et al.* have also developed a run-time specializer for C [12]. Like Tempo, their approach is based on templates. Their system allows the user to annotate particular program points as static or dynamic, rather than only allowing entry point annotations. This facility could be useful in our experiments to specify that a loop should not be unrolled or that a static variable in a dynamic context should be treated as dynamic. Their system, however, provides fewer automatic analyses than Tempo, and thus relies more heavily on user annotations. Unlike Tempo, their system performs optimizations on the code produced by run-time specialization. These optimizations require extra run-time overhead. As shown by Figure 10, even without optimization at run-time, we obtain between 64% and 76% of the performance obtained by compile-time specialization, which can be viewed as specialization with maximal optimization of the specialized code. Their system does not provide compile-time specialization.

Tick C is a C-like language for describing code to be generated at run time, using Lisp-like backquote and comma operators [9]. Tick C is not a partial evaluator. Thus the code to generate the specialized program must be written by hand.

In this paper, we have assessed our experimental results by comparison with an expected speedup based on the complexity of the static and dynamic parts of the program. Jones *et al.* have also considered the problem of estimating the speedup achieved by partial evaluation [14]. Their analysis, however, considers only the limit of the speedup as the size of the input increases. In the case of the FFT, the limit is 1, indicating no speedup, because the dynamic code of the innermost loop of the fft procedure has a greater complexity than the static parts of the program.

8 Conclusion

In this paper, we have investigated the problem of generating an efficient FFT implementation by using automatic program specialization. We obtained significant performance improvement from both compile-time specialization (up to over 9 times faster) and run-time specialization (up to over 7 times faster). We carefully assessed compiler characteristics that affect the performance of specialized programs, and proposed simple rewritings of the source program to generate specialized programs that have better performance. Elsewhere, we have shown that this specialized FFT implementation, generated automatically and thus reliably, has performance comparable to hand optimized implementations [16].

While the partial evaluation techniques we have focused on, compile-time and run-time specialization, are not practical for FFT's of very large sequences, there are realistic applications, such as the 125.turb3d simulation program in the SPEC95 Benchmark suite [8], that repetitively perform FFT's of data sets of the sizes used in our experiments. Furthermore, data specialization [4, 15, 17] shows promise for extending automatic optimization within the partial-evaluation framework to much larger data sets.

A focus of this work has been to analyze the benefits of compile-time and run-time specialization given particular compilers and program rewritings before specialization. Two observations stand out. For compile-time specialization, the benefits of loop unrolling are offset by the possibility of exceeding the size of the instruction cache and the problems of compiling large procedures. Thus, specialization with respect to loop indices is not always beneficial. For run-time specialization, we have seen a significant performance decline when there are many trivial holes. Considering a static variable in a dynamic context to be dynamic more than doubles the speedup obtained by run-time specialization of the FFT. These observations suggest that while compile-time and run-time specialization can share the same preprocessing framework, as illustrated in Figure 1, at the low level, different annotation strategies are appropriate. Further work is required to fully assess this approach. It is hoped that the analysis presented in this paper will prove useful in guiding the application of specialization, and in particular of Tempo, to other programs, and will motivate similar detailed analyses of the benefits of specialization.

Acknowledgements

The author would like to thank Gilles Muller, Olivier Danvy, Renaud Marlet, and Ulrik Schultz for helpful comments on the organization of the paper, André Seznec and Pascal Rigaux for help in understanding the Sparc architecture, and Charles Consel and the entire Compose group for support and encouragement during this work.

References

1. L.O. Andersen. *Program Analysis and Specialization for the C Programming Language*. PhD thesis, Computer Science Department, University of Copenhagen, May 1994. DIKU Technical Report 94/19.
2. J. Arndt.
   URL: http://www.jjj.de/fxt/fxt970929.tgz
   in the file hfloat/src/fxt/simplfft/fft.c.
3. E. Bach and J. Shallit. *Algorithmic Number Theory*. The MIT Press, 1996.
4. G. J. Barzdins and M. A. Bulyonkov. Mixed computation and translation: Linearisation and decomposition of compilers. Preprint 791, Computing Centre of Siberian division of USSR Academy of Sciences, Novosibirsk, 1988.
5. C. Consel, L. Hornof, F. Noël, J. Noyé, and E.N. Volanschi. A uniform approach for compile-time and run-time specialization. In O. Danvy, R. Glück, and P. Thiemann, editors, *Partial Evaluation, International Seminar, Dagstuhl Castle*, number 1110 in Lecture Notes in Computer Science, pages 54–72, February 1996.
6. C. Consel and F. Noël. A general approach for run-time specialization and its application to C. In POPL96 [20], pages 145–156.

7. J. W. Cooley and J. W. Tukey. An algorithm for the machine calculation of complex Fourier series. *Mathematics of Computation*, 19(90):297–301, April 1965.
8. Standard Performance Evaluation Corporation. SPEC95.
   URL: http://www.specbench.org.
9. D.R. Engler, W.C. Hsieh, and M.F. Kaashoek. 'C: A language for high-level, efficient, and machine-independent dynamic code generation. In POPL96 [20], pages 131–144.
10. M. Frigo and S. Johnson. FFTW user's manual, 1997.
    URL: http://theory.lcs.mit.edu/~fftw/.
11. R. Glück, R. Nakashige, and R. Zöchling. Binding-time analysis applied to mathematical algorithms. In J. Doležal and J. Fidler, editors, *System Modelling and Optimization*, pages 137–146. Chapman & Hall, 1995.
12. B. Grant, M. Mock, M. Philipose, C. Chambers, and S.J. Eggers. Annotation-directed run-time specialization in C. In PEPM'97 [19], pages 163–178.
13. L. Hornof and J. Noyé. Accurate binding-time analysis for imperative languages: Flow, context, and return sensitivity. In PEPM'97 [19], pages 63–73.
14. N.D. Jones, C. Gomard, and P. Sestoft. *Partial Evaluation and Automatic Program Generation*. International Series in Computer Science. Prentice-Hall, June 1993.
15. T.B. Knoblock and E. Ruf. Data specialization. In *Proceedings of the ACM SIGPLAN '96 Conference on Programming Language Design and Implementation*, pages 215–225, Philadelphia, PA, May 1996. ACM SIGPLAN Notices, 31(5). Also TR MSR-TR-96-04, Microsoft Research, February 1996.
16. J.L. Lawall. Faster Fourier transforms via automatic program specialization. Publication interne 1192, IRISA, Rennes, France, May 1998.
17. K. Malmkjær. Program and data specialization: Principles, applications, and self-application. Master's thesis, DIKU, University of Copenhagen, Denmark, August 1989.
18. F. Noël, L. Hornof, C. Consel, and J. Lawall. Automatic, template-based run-time specialization : Implementation and experimental study. In *International Conference on Computer Languages*, pages 132–142, Chicago, IL, May 1998. IEEE Computer Society Press. Also available as IRISA report PI-1065.
19. *ACM SIGPLAN Symposium on Partial Evaluation and Semantics-Based Program Manipulation*, Amsterdam, The Netherlands, June 1997. ACM Press.
20. *Conference Record of the 23rd Annual ACM SIGPLAN-SIGACT Symposium on Principles Of Programming Languages*, St. Petersburg Beach, FL, USA, January 1996. ACM Press.
21. W.H. Press, S.A. Teukolsky, W.T. Vetterling, and B.P. Flannery. *Numerical Recipes in C The Art of Scientific Computing*. Cambridge University Press, Cambridge, 2nd edition, 1995.
22. A. Schönhage, A.F.W. Grotefeld, and E. Vetter. *Fast Algorithms: A Multitape Turing Machine Implementation*. BI-Wissenschaftsverlag, 1994.

Eta-Redexes in Partial Evaluation

Jens Palsberg

Purdue University, Dept of Computer Science
W Lafayette, IN 47907, palsberg@cs.purdue.edu

Abstract. Source-program modifications can make a partial evaluator yield dramatically better results. For example, eta-redexes can preserve static data flow by acting as an interface between values and contexts. This note presents a type-based explanation of what eta-expansion achieves, why it works, and how it can be automated. This leads to a unified view of various source-code improvements, including a popular transformation called "The Trick."

1 Introduction

This note presents ideas from papers by Danvy, Malmkjær, and Palsberg [9, 10].

1.1 Background

Partial evaluation is a program-transformation technique for specializing programs [6, 14]. As such, it contributes to solving the tension between program generality (to ease portability and maintenance) and program specificity (to have them attuned to the situation at hand). An offline partial evaluator is divided into two stages:

1. a *binding-time analysis* determining which parts of the source program are known (the "static" parts) and which parts may not be known (the "dynamic" parts);
2. a *program specializer* reducing the static parts and reconstructing the dynamic parts, thus producing the residual program.

The two stages must fit together such that (1) no static computation depends on the result of a dynamic computation, and (2) no static parts are left in the residual program [13, 19, 20, 25]. As a rule, binding-time analyses lean toward safety in the sense that in case of doubt a dynamic classification is safer than a static one. In an offline partial evaluator, the precision of the binding-time analysis determines the effectiveness of the program specializer [6, 14]. Informally, the more parts of a source program are classified to be static by the binding-time analysis, the more parts are processed away by the specializer.

Recall that a context is an expression with one hole [1]. A static (resp. dynamic) context is an expression with one hole where the expression fitting this hole is static (resp. dynamic).

To obtain consistency, Mix-style partial evaluators [14] coerce static values and contexts to be respectively dynamic values and dynamic contexts, when they encounter a clash. This is acceptable if source programs are first-order and values are either fully static or fully dynamic. However these coercions are excessive for programs with partially static values and contexts.

Practical experience with partial evaluation shows that users need to massage their source programs to make binding-time analysis classify more program parts as static, and thus to make specialization yield better results. Jones, Gomard, and Sestoft's textbook [14, Ch. 12] documents three such "binding-time improvements": continuation-passing style, eta-expansion, and "The Trick." In this note we present the basic idea which in [9, 10] is fully developed into a unified view of these binding-time improvements.

1.2   Eta-expansion

Eta-expanding a higher-order expression e of type $\tau_1 \to \tau_2$ yields the expression

$$\lambda v.e@v$$

where v does not occur free in e [1]. By analogy, "eta-expanding" a product expression e of type $\tau_1 \times \tau_2$ yields the expression

$$Pair(Fst\, e, Snd\, e) \,,$$

and "eta-expanding" a disjoint-sum expression e of type $\tau_1 + \tau_2$ yields the expression

$$\text{case } e \text{ of inleft}(x_1) \Rightarrow \text{inleft}(x_1) \;[\!]\; \text{inright}(x_2) \Rightarrow \text{inright}(x_2) \text{ end.}$$

In the following section we will show how eta-expansion *prevents* a binding-time analysis from

- dynamizing static values in dynamic contexts, and
- dynamizing static contexts around dynamic values

when the values are of function, product, or disjoint-sum type. (We use "dynamize" to mean "make dynamic.) Preventing static values and contexts from being dynamized improves the annotation in cases where the static values are used elsewhere or in cases where other static values may also occur in the same context. Thus, eta-expansion serves as a binding-time coercion for static values in dynamic contexts and for dynamic values in potentially static contexts. We can view an eta-redex as providing a syntactic representation of a binding-time coercion, either from static to dynamic, or from dynamic to static. Eta-expansion can also help ensure termination of a partial evaluator [5, 17, 18].

In the case of using eta-expansion where the value is of disjoint-sum type, the binding-time improvement enables "The Trick." Intuitively, "The Trick" is used to process dynamic choices of static values, *i.e.*, when finitely many static values may occur in a dynamic context. Enumerating these values makes it possible to plug each of them into the context, thereby turning it into a static context and enabling more static computation.

The Trick can also be used on any finite type, such as booleans or characters, by enumerating its elements. Alternatively, one may wish to reduce the number of static possibilities that can be encountered at a program point — for example, only finitely many characters (instead of the whole alphabet) may occur in a regular-expression interpreter [14, Sec. 12.2]. The Trick is usually carried out explicitly by the programmer (see the while loop in Jones and Gomard's Imperative Mix [14, Sec. 4.8.3]).

This enumeration of static values could also be obtained by program analysis, for example using Heintze's set-based analysis [12]. Exploiting the results of such a program analysis would make it possible to automate The Trick. In fact, a program analysis determining finite ranges of values that may occur at a program point does enable The Trick. For example, control-flow analysis [24] (also known as closure analysis [23]) determines a conservative approximation of which λ-abstractions can give rise to a closure that may occur at an application site. The application site can be transformed into a case-expression listing all the possible λ-abstractions and performing a first-order call to the corresponding λ-abstraction in each branch. This defunctionalization technique was proposed by Reynolds in the early seventies [22] and recently cast in a typed setting [16]. Since the end of the eighties, it is used by such partial evaluators as Similix to handle higher-order programs [3]. The conclusion of this is that Jones, Gomard, and Sestoft actually do use an automated version of The Trick [14, Sec. 10.1.4, Item (1)], even if they do not present it as such.

In this note we concentrate on eta-expansion of expressions of function type. In the following section we give several examples of what eta-expansion achieves and why it works. In Section 3 we present a binding-time analysis that inserts eta-redexes automatically using two coercion rules, and we show that it transforms Plotkin's CPS-transformation into the improved form studied by Danvy and Filinski [8].

2   The essence of eta-expansion

We show three examples, where

- a number occurs both in a static and in a dynamic context,
- a *higher-order* value occurs both in a static and in a dynamic context, and
- a function is applied to both a static and a dynamic *higher-order* argument.

After the examples, we summarize why eta-expansion improves binding times, given a monovariant binding-time analysis. We use "@" (pronounced "apply") to denote applications, and we abbreviate $(e_0@e_1)@e_2$ by $e_0@e_1@e_2$.

2.1   First-order static values in dynamic contexts

The following expression is partially evaluated in a context with y dynamic.

$$(\lambda x.(x + y) \times (x - 1))@42$$

Assume that this β-redex will be reduced. The addition depends on the dynamic operand y, so it should be reconstructed (in other words, x occurs in a dynamic context, $[\cdot] + y$). Both subtraction operands are static, so the subtraction can be performed (in other words, x occurs in a static context, $[\cdot] - 1$). The multiplication should be reconstructed since its first operand is dynamic. Overall, binding-time analysis yields the following two-level term.

$$(\overline{\lambda}x.(x \underline{+} y) \underline{\times} (x \overline{-} 1)) \overline{@} 42$$

(Consistently with Nielson and Nielson [19], overlined means static and underlined means dynamic.)

We can summarize some of the binding-time information by giving the binding-time types of variables, as in Lambda-Mix [11, 14]. Here, x has type s (static) and y has type d (dynamic). After specialization (*i.e.*, two-level reduction), the residual term reads as follows.

$$(42 + y) \times 41$$

Lambda-Mix's binding-time analysis is able to give an appropriate annotation of the above program because the argument to $\lambda x.(x + y) \times (x - 1)$ is a *first-order* value. Inserting the static value in the dynamic context ($[\cdot] + y$) poses no problem. We now move on to the case where the inserted value is higher-order.

2.2   Higher-order static values in dynamic contexts

The following expression is partially evaluated in a context with g dynamic.

$$(\lambda f.f @ g @ f) @ (\lambda a.a)$$

Again, assume that this β-redex is to be reduced. f occurs twice: once as the function part of an application (which here is a static context), and once as the argument of $f @ g$ (which here is a dynamic context). The latter occurrence forces the binding-time analysis to classify f, and thus the rightmost λ-abstraction, to be dynamic. Overall, binding-time analysis yields the following two-level term.

$$(\overline{\lambda}f.f \underline{@} g \underline{@} f) \overline{@} (\underline{\lambda} a.a)$$

Here, f has type d, and g has also type d. After specialization, the residual term reads as follows.

$$(\lambda a.a) @ g @ (\lambda a.a)$$

So unlike the first-order case, the fact that f, the static value, occurs in the dynamic context $f @ g @ [\cdot]$ "pollutes" its occurrence in the static context $[\cdot] @ g @ f$, so that neither is reduced statically.

NB: Since f is dynamic and occurs twice, a cautious binding-time analysis would reclassify the outer application to be dynamic: there is usually no point in duplicating residual code. In that case, the expression is totally dynamic and so is not simplified at all.

In this situation, a binding-time improvement is possible since $\lambda a.a$ will occur in a dynamic context. We can coerce this occurrence by eta-expanding the occurrence of f in the dynamic context (the eta-redex is boxed).

$$(\lambda f.f@g@\boxed{\lambda y.f@y}\,)@(\lambda a.a)$$

Binding-time analysis now yields the following two-level term.

$$(\overline{\lambda}f.f\overline{@}g\underline{@}(\underline{\lambda}y.f\overline{@}y))\overline{@}(\overline{\lambda}a.a)$$

Here, f has type $d \to d$, and both g and y have type d. Specialization yields the residual term

$$g@(\lambda y.y)$$

which is more reduced statically.

In this case, the eta-redex effectively protects the static higher-order expression $\lambda a.a$ from being dynamized in the remainder of the computation. Instead, only the occurrence in the dynamic context is affected.

2.3   Higher-order dynamic values in static contexts

The following expression is partially evaluated in a context with d_0 and d_1 dynamic.

$$(\lambda f.f@d_0@(f@(\lambda x_1.x_1)@d_1))@(\lambda a.a)$$

f is applied twice: once to d_0, and once to $\lambda x_1.x_1$. In a monovariant higher-order binding-time analysis, d_0 dynamizes $\lambda x_1.x_1$, since the first parameter of f can only have one binding time. Overall, binding-time analysis yields the following two-level term.

$$(\overline{\lambda}f.f\overline{@}d_0\underline{@}(f\overline{@}(\underline{\lambda}x_1.x_1)\underline{@}d_1))\overline{@}(\overline{\lambda}a.a)$$

Here, f has type $d \to d$, x_1 has type d, and a has type d (corresponding to the type of d_0). Specialization yields the following residual term.

$$d_0@((\lambda x_1.x_1)@d_1)$$

The context $f@[\cdot]$ occurs twice in the source term. The dynamic value d_0 appears in the first occurrence, and the static value $\lambda x_1.x_1$ appears in the second occurrence. Since the context can only have one binding time (since it is the same f), d_0 pollutes $f@[\cdot]$, which in turn pollutes $\lambda x_1.x_1$. Since f is in fact $\lambda a.a$, the result of the application becomes dynamic. So the two potentially static applications of this result, respectively $[\cdot]@(f@(\lambda x_1.x_1)@d_1)$ and $[\cdot]@d_1$, become dynamic.

In this situation, a binding-time improvement is possible since both d_0 and $\lambda x_1.x_1$ occur (as results) in a potentially static context. We coerce d_0 by eta-expanding it (the eta-redex is boxed).

$$(\lambda f.f@\boxed{(\lambda x_0.d_0@x_0)}@(f@(\lambda x_1.x_1)@d_1))@(\lambda a.a)$$

Binding-time analysis now yields the following two-level term.

$$(\overline{\lambda}f.f\overline{@}(\overline{\lambda}x_0.d_0\underline{@}x_0)\overline{@}(f\overline{@}(\overline{\lambda}x_1.x_1)\overline{@}d_1))\overline{@}(\overline{\lambda}a.a)$$

Here, f has type $(d \to d) \to (d \to d)$, corresponding to statically applying f to both arguments. x_0 and x_1 both have type d, and a has type $d \to d$ (corresponding to the type of $\lambda x_1.x_1$). Specialization yields the residual term

$$d_0 @ d_1$$

which is more reduced statically.

In this case, the eta-redex effectively prevents the dynamic expression d_0 from being propagated to f and dynamizing $\lambda x_1.x_1$ in the remainder of the computation. Instead, only the occurrence in the static context is affected.

2.4 Summary

In a monovariant binding-time analysis, each time a higher-order static value occurs both in a potentially static context and in a dynamic context, the dynamic context dynamizes the higher-order value, which in turn dynamizes the potentially static context. Conversely, each time a higher-order static value and a dynamic value occur in the same potentially static context, the dynamic value dynamizes the context, which in turn dynamizes the higher-order value. Both problems can be circumvented by inserting eta-redexes in source programs. The eta-redex serves as "padding" around a value and inside a context, keeping one from dynamizing or from being dynamized by the other.

Eta-expanding a higher-order static expression f (when it occurs in a dynamic context) into

$$\underline{\lambda}v.f\overline{@}v$$

creates a value that can be used for replacement. This prevents the original expression from being dynamized by a dynamic context. Instead, the new abstraction is dynamized.

Eta-expanding a higher-order dynamic expression g (when it occurs in a potentially static context) into

$$\overline{\lambda}v.g\underline{@}v$$

creates a value that can be used for replacement. This prevents a potentially static context from being dynamized by g. Instead, the new application is dynamized.

Informally, eta-expansion changes the *two-level type* [19] of a term as follows. Assume that f and g have type $t_1 \to t_2$, where t_1 and t_2 are ground types. The first eta-expansion coerces the type $t_1 \overline{\Rightarrow} t_2$ to be $t_1 \underline{\to} t_2$. The second eta-expansion coerces the type $t_1 \underline{\to} t_2$ to be $t_1 \overline{\Rightarrow} t_2$. Note that *inside* the redexes, the type of f is still $t_1 \overline{\Rightarrow} t_2$ and the type of g is still $t_1 \underline{\to} t_2$.

Further eta-expansion is necessary if t_1 or t_2 are not ground types. In fact, both kinds of eta-redex synergize. For example, if a higher-order static expression h has type $(t_1 \overline{\Rightarrow} t_2) \overline{\Rightarrow} t_3$ then its associated eta-redex reads

$$\underline{\lambda}v.h\overline{@}(\overline{\lambda}w.v\underline{@}w) \ .$$

In this example, the outer eta-expansion (of a static value in a dynamic context) creates the occurrence of a dynamic expression in a static context — hence the inner eta-redex.

To make our approach applicable to untyped languages, we will in the rest of the paper give dynamic entities the ground type d, as in Lambda-Mix [11, 14], rather than a two-level type such as $t_1 \underline{\to} t_2$.

Information to guide the insertion of eta-redexes can *not* be obtained directly from the output of a binding-time analysis: at that point all conflicts have been resolved. Moreover, it would be naïve to insert, say, one eta-redex around every subterm: sometimes more than one is needed for good results, as in the last example and in the CPS-transformation example in Section 3.2. Alternatively, programs could be required to be simply typed. Then the type of each subterm determines the maximal number of eta-redexes that might be necessary for that subterm. Such type-driven eta-redex insertion is closely related to Danvy's type-directed partial evaluation [7].

In the following section we demonstrate how to insert a small and appropriate number of eta-redexes automatically. Our approach does not require programs to be typed and both for the example in Section 2.2 and for Plotkin's CPS transformation we show that it gives a good result.

3   Automatic insertion of eta-redexes

3.1   The binding-time analysis

Our binding-time analysis is specified in Figure 1. It can easily be extended to handle products and sums. Details of this together with a correctness proof are given in [10].

The definition in Figure 1 has three parts. The first part is the binding-time analysis of Gomard [11], restricted to the pure λ-calculus. Types are finite and generated from the following grammar.

$$t ::= d \mid t_1 \to t_2$$

The type d denotes the type of dynamic entities. The judgment $A \vdash e : t \triangleright w$ means that under hypothesis A, the λ-term e can be assigned type t with annotated term w.

The second part of our analysis is two rules for binding-time coercion. Intuitively, the two rules can be understood as being able (1) to coerce the binding-time type d to any type τ and (2) to coerce any type τ to the type d. The combination of the two rules allows us to coerce the type of any λ-term to any other type.

Eta-expansion itself is defined in the third part of our analysis. It is type-directed, and thus it can insert several embedded eta-redexes in a way that is reminiscent of Berger and Schwichtenberg's normalization of λ-terms [2, 7].

Consider the first binding-time coercion rule in Figure 1. Intuitively, it works as follows. We are given a λ-term e that we would like to assign the type τ. In

Gomard's binding-time analysis:

$$A \vdash x : A(x) \triangleright x$$

$$\frac{A[x \mapsto t_1] \vdash e : t_2 \triangleright w}{A \vdash \lambda x.e : t_1 \rightarrow t_2 \triangleright \underline{\lambda} x.w} \qquad \frac{A[x \mapsto d] \vdash e : d \triangleright w}{A \vdash \lambda x.e : d \triangleright \underline{\lambda} x.w}$$

$$\frac{A \vdash e_0 : t_1 \rightarrow t_2 \triangleright w_0 \qquad A \vdash e_1 : t_1 \triangleright w_1}{A \vdash e_0 @ e_1 : t_2 \triangleright w_0 \underline{@} w_1}$$

$$\frac{A \vdash e_0 : d \triangleright w_0 \qquad A \vdash e_1 : d \triangleright w_1}{A \vdash e_0 @ e_1 : d \triangleright w_0 \underline{@} w_1}$$

Rules for binding-time coercion:

$$\frac{A \vdash e : d \triangleright w \qquad \tau \vdash z \Rightarrow m \qquad \emptyset[z \mapsto d] \vdash m : \tau \triangleright w'}{A \vdash e : \tau \triangleright w'[w/z]}$$

$$\frac{A \vdash e : \tau \triangleright w \qquad \tau \vdash z \Rightarrow m \qquad \emptyset[z \mapsto \tau] \vdash m : d \triangleright w'}{A \vdash e : d \triangleright w'[w/z]}$$

Rules for eta-expansion:

$$d \vdash e \Rightarrow e \qquad\qquad \frac{t_1 \vdash x \Rightarrow x' \qquad t_2 \vdash e @ x' \Rightarrow e'}{t_1 \rightarrow t_2 \vdash e \Rightarrow \lambda x.e'}$$

Fig. 1. The binding-time analysis.

case we can only assign it type d, and $\tau \neq d$, we can use the rule to coerce the type to be τ. The first hypothesis of the rule is that e has type d and annotated term w. The second hypothesis of the rule takes a fresh variable z and eta-expands it according to the type τ. This creates a λ-term m with type τ. Notice that z is the only free variable in m. The third hypothesis of the rule annotates m under the assumption that z has type d. The result is an annotated term w' with the type τ and with a hole of type d (the free variable z) where we can insert the previously constructed w. Thus, w' makes the coercion happen. The second binding-time coercion rule in Figure 1 works in a similar way.

Our binding-time analysis inserts the expected eta-redex in the example program $(\lambda f.f @ g @ f) @ (\lambda a.a)$ from Section 2.2:

$$\frac{\dfrac{A \vdash f @ g : d \triangleright f \underline{@} g \qquad A \vdash f : d \triangleright \underline{\lambda} y.f \underline{@} y}{A \vdash f @ g @ f : d \triangleright f \underline{@} g \underline{@} (\underline{\lambda} y.f \underline{@} y)} \qquad \emptyset[g \mapsto d][x \mapsto d] \vdash x : d \triangleright x}{\dfrac{\emptyset[g \mapsto d] \vdash \lambda f.f @ g @ f : t \rightarrow d \triangleright \underline{\lambda} f.f \underline{@} g \underline{@} (\underline{\lambda} y.f \underline{@} y) \qquad \emptyset[g \mapsto d] \vdash \lambda a.a : t \triangleright \underline{\lambda} a.a}{\emptyset[g \mapsto d] \vdash (\lambda f.f @ g @ f) @ (\lambda a.a) : d \triangleright (\underline{\lambda} f.f \underline{@} g \underline{@} (\underline{\lambda} y.f \underline{@} y)) \underline{@} (\underline{\lambda} a.a)}}$$

where t abbreviates $d \rightarrow d$ and A abbreviates $\emptyset[g \mapsto d][f \mapsto t]$.

Here follows part of the derivation of $A \vdash f : d \vartriangleright \underline{\lambda}y.f\overline{@}y$.

$$\frac{A \vdash f : t \vartriangleright f \qquad t \vdash z \Rightarrow \lambda y.z@y \qquad \emptyset[z \mapsto t] \vdash \lambda y.z@y : d \vartriangleright \underline{\lambda}y.z\overline{@}y}{A \vdash f : d \vartriangleright \underline{\lambda}y.f\overline{@}y}$$

Notice that $\underline{\lambda}y.f\overline{@}y$ is dynamic while f remain static.

3.2   Example: the CPS transformation

Let us now turn to the transformation of λ-terms into continuation-passing style (CPS). This example is significant because historically, the virtue of eta-redexes became apparent in connection with partial evaluation of CPS interpreters and with CPS transformers [3, 8]. It also has practical interest since the pattern of construction and use of higher-order values in the CPS transform is prototypical. The first part of Figure 2 displays Plotkin's original CPS transformation for the call-by-value lambda-calculus [21], written as a two-level term.

Before eta-expansion, where $[e]$ is the CPS-version of the expression e:

$$[.] : \text{syntax} \Rightarrow \text{CPSsyntax} \rightarrow \text{CPSsyntax}$$
$$[x] = \underline{\lambda}k.k\underline{@}x$$
$$[\lambda x.e] = \underline{\lambda}k.k\underline{@}(\underline{\lambda}x.[e])$$
$$[e_0@e_1] = \underline{\lambda}k.[e_0]\underline{@}(\underline{\lambda}v_0.[e_1]\underline{@}(\underline{\lambda}v_1.(v_0\underline{@}v_1)\underline{@}k))$$

After eta-expansion, where $\underline{\lambda}k.[e]\overline{@}\underline{\lambda}v.k\underline{@}v$ is the CPS-version of the expression e:

$$[.] : \text{syntax} \Rightarrow (\text{CPSsyntax} \Rightarrow \text{CPSsyntax}) \Rightarrow \text{CPSsyntax}$$
$$[x] = \overline{\lambda}k.k\overline{@}x$$

$$[\lambda x.e] = \overline{\lambda}k.k\overline{@}(\underline{\lambda}x.\boxed{\underline{\lambda}k.[e]\overline{@}\,\boxed{(\overline{\lambda}v.k\underline{@}v)}})$$

$$[e_0@e_1] = \overline{\lambda}k.[e_0]\overline{@}(\overline{\lambda}v_0.[e_1]\overline{@}(\overline{\lambda}v_1.(v_0\underline{@}v_1)\underline{@}\,\boxed{(\underline{\lambda}v_2.k\overline{@}v_2)}))$$

Fig. 2. Two-level formulation of Plotkin's CPS transformation.

Since the transformation is a syntax constructor, *all* occurrences of @ and λ are dynamic. And in fact, Gomard's binding-time analysis does classify all occurrences to be dynamic.

But CPS terms resulting from this transformation contain redundant "administrative" beta-redexes, which have to be post-reduced [15]. These beta-redexes can be avoided by inserting eta-redexes in the CPS transformation, allowing some beta-redexes in the transformation to become static.

The second part of Figure 2 shows the revised transformation containing three extra eta-redexes: one for the CPS transformation of applications, and two for the CPS transformation of abstractions (the eta-redexes are boxed.)

As analyzed by Danvy and Filinski [8], the eta-redex $\lambda k.[\![e]\!]@k$ prevents the outer $\lambda k....$ from being dynamized. The two other eta-redexes $\lambda v.k@v$ and $\lambda v_2.k@v_2$ enable k to be kept static. The types of the transformations (shown in the figures) summarize the binding-time improvement.

Our new analysis inserts exactly these three eta-redexes, given Plotkin's original specification. Here follows part of the derivation for the case of abstraction. We use the abbreviations $t = (d \to d) \to d$ and $A = \emptyset[\![e]\!] \mapsto t][k \mapsto d \to d]$.

$$\cfrac{A \vdash k : d \to d \rhd k \qquad A \vdash \lambda x.[\![e]\!] : d \rhd \underline{\lambda x.\lambda k.[\![e]\!]\overline{@}(\overline{\lambda}v.k\underline{@}v)}}{\cfrac{A \vdash k@(\lambda x.[\![e]\!]) : d \rhd k\overline{@}(\underline{\lambda x.\lambda k.[\![e]\!]\overline{@}(\overline{\lambda}v.k\underline{@}v)})}{\emptyset[\![e]\!] \mapsto t] \vdash \lambda k.k@(\lambda x.[\![e]\!]) : t \rhd \overline{\lambda}k.k\overline{@}(\underline{\lambda x.\lambda k.[\![e]\!]\overline{@}(\overline{\lambda}v.k\underline{@}v)})}}$$

We need to derive $A \vdash \lambda x.[\![e]\!] : d \rhd \underline{\lambda x.\lambda k.[\![e]\!]\overline{@}(\overline{\lambda}v.k\underline{@}v)}$. We use the abbreviation $E = \lambda k.z@(\lambda v.k@v)$. Here follows the last two steps of the derivation.

$$\cfrac{\cfrac{A[x \mapsto d] \vdash [\![e]\!] : t \rhd [\![e]\!] \qquad t \vdash z \Rightarrow E \qquad \emptyset[z \mapsto t] \vdash E : d \rhd \underline{\lambda k.z\overline{@}(\overline{\lambda}v.k\underline{@}v)}}{A[x \mapsto d] \vdash [\![e]\!] : d \rhd \underline{\lambda k.[\![e]\!]\overline{@}(\overline{\lambda}v.k\underline{@}v)}}}{A \vdash \lambda x.[\![e]\!] : d \rhd \underline{\lambda x.\lambda k.[\![e]\!]\overline{@}(\overline{\lambda}v.k\underline{@}v)}}$$

Bondorf and Dussart's work [4] relies on two key eta-expansions that are analogous to those studied in this section.

References

1. Henk P. Barendregt. *The Lambda Calculus: Its Syntax and Semantics*. North-Holland, 1984.
2. U. Berger and H. Schwichtenberg. An inverse of the evaluation functional for typed λ-calculus. In *LICS'91, Sixth Annual Symposium on Logic in Computer Science*, pages 203–211, 1991.
3. Anders Bondorf. Automatic autoprojection of higher order recursive equations. *Science of Computer Programming*, 17(1–3):3–34, December 1991.
4. Anders Bondorf and Dirk Dussart. Improving CPS-based partial evaluation: Writing cogen by hand. In *Proc. ACM SIGPLAN Workshop on Partial Evaluation and Semantics-Based Program Manipulation*, pages 1–10, 1994.
5. Anders Bondorf and Jens Palsberg. Generating action compilers by partial evaluation. *Journal of Functional Programming*, 6(2):269–298, 1996. Preliminary version in Proc. FPCA'93, Sixth ACM Conference on Functional Programming Languages and Computer Architecture, pages 308–317, Copenhagen, Denmark, June 1993.
6. Charles Consel and Olivier Danvy. Tutorial notes on partial evaluation. In *Proc. POPL'93, Twentieth Annual SIGPLAN-SIGACT Symposium on Principles of Programming Languages*, pages 493–501, 1993.
7. Olivier Danvy. Type-directed partial evaluation. In *Proc. POPL'96, 23nd Annual SIGPLAN-SIGACT Symposium on Principles of Programming Languages*, pages 242–257, 1996.

8. Olivier Danvy and Andrzej Filinski. Representing control, a study of the CPS transformation. *Mathematical Structures in Computer Science*, 2(4):361–391, 1992.
9. Olivier Danvy, Karoline Malmkjær, and Jens Palsberg. The essence of eta-expansion in partial evaluation. *Lisp and Symbolic Computation*, 8(3):209–227, 1995. Preliminary version in Proc. PEPM'94, ACM SIGPLAN Workshop on Partial Evaluation and Semantics-Based Program Manipulation, pages 11–20, Orlando, Florida, June 1994.
10. Olivier Danvy, Karoline Malmkjær, and Jens Palsberg. Eta-expansion does the trick. *ACM Transactions on Programming Languages and Systems*, 18(6):730–751, November 1996.
11. Carsten K. Gomard. *Program Analysis Matters*. PhD thesis, DIKU, University of Copenhagen, November 1991. DIKU Report 91–17.
12. Nevin Heintze. *Set Based Program Analysis*. PhD thesis, Carnegie Mellon University, October 1992. CMU–CS–92–201.
13. Neil D. Jones. Automatic program specialization: A re-examination from basic principles. In *Proc. Partial Evaluation and Mixed Computation*, pages 225–282, 1988.
14. Neil D. Jones, Carsten K. Gomard, and Peter Sestoft. *Partial Evaluation and Automatic Program Generation*. Prentice-Hall International, 1993.
15. Guy L. Steele Jr. Rabbit: A compiler for Scheme. Technical Report AI-TR-474, Artificial Intelligence Laboratory, Massachusetts Institute of Technology, Cambridge, Massachusetts, May 1978.
16. Y. Minamide, G. Morrisett, and R. Harper. Typed closure conversion. In *Proc. POPL'96, 23nd Annual SIGPLAN-SIGACT Symposium on Principles of Programming Languages*, pages 271–283, 1996.
17. Torben Æ Mogensen. Constructor specialization. In *Proc. PEPM'93, Second ACM SIGPLAN Symposium on Partial Evaluation and Semantics-Based Program Manipulation*, pages 22–32, 1993.
18. Christian Mossin. Partial evaluation of general parsers. In *Proc. PEPM'93, Second ACM SIGPLAN Symposium on Partial Evaluation and Semantics-Based Program Manipulation*, pages 13–21, 1993.
19. Flemming Nielson and Hanne Riis Nielson. *Two-Level Functional Languages*. Cambridge University Press, 1992.
20. Jens Palsberg. Correctness of binding-time analysis. *Journal of Functional Programming*, 3(3):347–363, 1993.
21. Gordon D. Plotkin. Call-by-name, call-by-value and the λ-calculus. *Theoretical Computer Science*, 1:125–159, 1975.
22. John C. Reynolds. Definitional interpreters for higher-order programming languages. In *Proc. 25th ACM National Conference*, pages 717–740. ACM Press, 1972.
23. Peter Sestoft. Replacing function parameters by global variables. In *Proc. Conference on Functional Programming Languages and Computer Architecture*, pages 39–53, 1989.
24. Olin Shivers. *Control-Flow Analysis of Higher-Order Languages*. PhD thesis, CMU, May 1991. CMU–CS–91–145.
25. Mitchell Wand. Specifying the correctness of binding-time analysis. *Journal of Functional Programming*, 3(3):365–387, 1993.

Type-Directed Partial Evaluation

Olivier Danvy

BRICS *
Department of Computer Science
University of Aarhus
Building 540, Ny Munkegade, DK-8000 Aarhus C, Denmark
E-mail: {danvy,tdpe}@brics.dk
Home pages: http://www.brics.dk/~{danvy,tdpe}

Abstract. Type-directed partial evaluation uses a normalization function to achieve partial evaluation. These lecture notes review its background, foundations, practice, and applications. Of specific interest is the modular technique of offline and online type-directed partial evaluation in Standard ML of New Jersey.

1 Background and introduction

1.1 Partial evaluation by normalization

Partial evaluation is traditionally presented as follows [11, 40]. Given a program processor 'run', and a source program p with some input $\langle s, d \rangle$ such that running p on this input yields some output a,

$$\text{run } p \ \langle s, d \rangle = a$$

specializing p with respect to $\langle s, \_ \rangle$ with a partial evaluator 'PE' yields a residual program $p_{\langle s, \_ \rangle}$ such that running $p_{\langle s, \_ \rangle}$ on the remaining input $\langle \_, d \rangle$ yields the same output a, provided that the source program, the partial evaluator, and the specialized program all terminate. Equationally:

$$\begin{cases} \text{run PE } \langle p, \langle s, \_ \rangle \rangle = p_{\langle s, \_ \rangle} \\ \text{run } p_{\langle s, \_ \rangle} \ \langle \_, d \rangle = a \end{cases}$$

The challenge of partial evaluation lies in writing a non-trivial partial evaluator, i.e., one performing the operations in p that depend on s and yielding the corresponding simplified residual program.

---

* Basic Research in Computer Science (http://www.brics.dk),
  Centre of the Danish National Research Foundation.

This requirement reminds one of the concept of normalization in the lambda-calculus [4] and in rewriting systems [26]. Given three terms $e_0 : t_1 \to t_2 \to t_3$, $e_1 : t_1$, and $e_2 : t_2$ such that applying e_0 to e_1 and e_2 yields some result a,

$$e_0\ e_1\ e_2 = a$$

normalizing the result of applying e_0 to e_1 yields a residual term $r : t_2 \to t_3$, such that by construction, applying r to e_2 yields the same result a, provided that applying e_0, normalization, and applying r all converge. Equationally:

$$\begin{cases} e_0\ e_1 = r \\ \quad r\ e_2 = a \end{cases}$$

In these lecture notes, we show how to achieve partial evaluation using normalization in the lambda-calculus. More precisely, we use a *normalization function*, as developed in Section 2.

1.2   Prerequisites and notation

We assume a basic familiarity with partial evaluation, such as that which can be gathered in the present volume. More specifically, we assume that the reader knows that an offline partial evaluator is a two-stage processor with

1. a binding-time analysis that decorates a source program with static and dynamic annotations, and
2. a static reducer that reduces all the static constructs away, yielding a residual program.

We also assume that it is clear to the reader that a binding-time analysis should produce a well-annotated "two-level" term, and that a two-level term is well-annotated if static reduction "does not go wrong" and yields a completely dynamic term.

The canonical example of the power function: The power function, of type

$$\text{int} * \text{int} \rightarrow \text{int}$$

maps a integer x (the base parameter) and a natural number n (the exponent parameter) into x^n. It can be programmed in various ways. The version we consider throughout these notes is written in ML [44] as follows.

```
fun power (x, 0) = 1
  | power (x, n) = x * (power (x, n-1))
```

If we want to specialize it with respect to a static value for n, the recursive calls, the conditional expression, and the decrement are classified as static, and the multiplication is classified as dynamic. As a result, the power function is completely unfolded at specialization time. (The multiplication by 1 may or may not be simplified away.) Specializing the power function with respect to $n = 3$, for example, yields the following residual program:

```
fun power_d3 x = x * x * x
```

where the multiplication by 1 was simplified away.

If we want to specialize the power function with respect to a static value for x, the recursive calls, the conditional expression, the decrement, and the multiplication all are classified as dynamic. As a result, the power function is essentially reconstructed at specialization time. (The static value is inlined.) Specializing the power function with respect to x = 8, for example, yields the following residual program:

```
fun power_8d 0 = 1
  | power_8d n = 8 * (power_8d (n-1))
```

Lambda-calculus, two-level lambda-calculus: The rest of Section 1 assumes the following grammar for the pure simply typed lambda-calculus:

$$t ::= \alpha \mid t_1 \to t_2 \mid t_1 \times t_2$$
$$e ::= x \mid \lambda x.e \mid e_0 @ e_1 \mid \text{pair}(e_1, e_2) \mid \pi_1 \, e \mid \pi_2 \, e$$

Applications are noted with an infix "@", pairs are constructed with a prefix operator "pair" and projections are noted "π". As for α, it stands for an unspecified atomic type.

The corresponding two-level lambda-calculus is obtained by overlining static syntax constructors and underlining dynamic syntax constructors:

$$e ::= x \mid \overline{\lambda} x.e \mid e_0 \overline{@} e_1 \mid \overline{\text{pair}}(e_1, e_2) \mid \overline{\pi_1} \, e \mid \overline{\pi_2} \, e$$
$$\mid \underline{\lambda} x.e \mid e_0 \underline{@} e_1 \mid \underline{\text{pair}}(e_1, e_2) \mid \underline{\pi_1} \, e \mid \underline{\pi_2} \, e$$

A "completely static expression" (resp. "completely dynamic expression") is a two-level lambda-term where all syntax constructors are overlined (resp. underlined).

1.3 Two-level programming in ML

We consider the two-level lambda-calculus implemented in ML by representing overlines with ordinary syntax constructs and underlines with constructors of a data type representing residual terms. Let us illustrate this implementation in ML using the data type Exp.exp of Figure 1.

For example, the ML expressions

```
fn x => x
Exp.LAM ("x", Exp.VAR "x")
```

respectively represent the completely static expression $\overline{\lambda} x.x$ and the completely dynamic expression $\underline{\lambda} x.x$.

```
structure Exp
= struct
    datatype exp = VAR of string
                 | LAM of string * exp | APP of exp * exp
                 | PAIR of exp * exp | FST of exp | SND of exp
  end
```

Fig. 1. Abstract syntax of residual expressions

Run time: Static reduction is achieved by ML evaluation. For example, the two-level expression $\underline{\lambda}x.(\overline{\lambda}v.v)\overline{@}x$ is represented as

```
Exp.LAM ("x", (fn v => v) (Exp.VAR "x"))
```

This ML expression evaluates to

```
Exp.LAM ("x", Exp.VAR "x")
```

which represents the completely dynamic expression $\underline{\lambda}x.x$.

Compile time: What it means for a two-level expression to be "well-annotated" can be non-trivial [40, 46, 48, 57]. These considerations reduce to the ML typing discipline here. As already mentioned, well-annotatedness boils down to two points:

1. static reduction should not go wrong, and
2. the result should be completely dynamic.

Each of these points is trivially satisfied here:

1. the ML type system ensures that evaluation will not go wrong, and
2. the result is completely dynamic if it has type Exp.exp.

Assessment: Implementing the two-level lambda-calculus in ML simplifies it radically. Conceptually, well-annotatedness is reduced to ML typeability and static reduction to ML evaluation. And practically, this implementation directly benefits from existing programming-language technology rather than requiring one to duplicate this technology with a two-level-language processor. It provides, however, no guarantees that the residual program is well typed in any sense.

1.4   Binding-time coercions

The topic of binding-time coercions is already documented in Jens Palsberg's contribution to this volume [47]. Briefly put, a binding-time coercion maps an expression into a new expression to ensure well-annotatedness between expressions and their contexts during static reduction. In that, binding-time coercions fulfill the same task as, e.g., subtype coercions [37].

$$\downarrow^{\alpha} e = e$$

$$\downarrow^{t_1 \to t_2} e = \underline{\lambda} x_1 . \downarrow^{t_2} (e \underline{\overline{@}} (\uparrow_{t_1} x_1)) \qquad \text{where } x_1 \text{ is fresh.}$$

$$\downarrow^{t_1 \times t_2} e = \underline{\text{pair}} (\downarrow^{t_1} (\overline{\pi_1} e), \downarrow^{t_2} (\overline{\pi_2} e))$$

$$\uparrow_{\alpha} e = e$$

$$\uparrow_{t_1 \to t_2} e = \overline{\lambda} x_1 . \uparrow_{t_2} (e \underline{\overline{@}} (\downarrow^{t_1} x_1)) \qquad \text{where } x_1 \text{ is fresh.}$$

$$\uparrow_{t_1 \times t_2} e = \overline{\text{pair}} (\uparrow_{t_1} (\underline{\pi_1} e), \uparrow_{t_2} (\underline{\pi_2} e))$$

Fig. 2. Type-directed binding-time coercions

We are only interested in one thing here: how to coerce a closed, completely static expression into the corresponding dynamic expression. This coercion is achieved using the type-directed translation displayed in Figure 2, which can be seen to operate by "two-level eta expansion" [22, 23]. Given a closed, completely static expression e of type t,

$$\downarrow^t e$$

coerces it into its dynamic counterpart. Notationally, the down arrow converts overlines into underlines. We refer to it as "reification."

To process the left-hand side of an arrow, reification uses an auxiliary type-directed translation, which we refer to as "reflection." We write it with an up arrow, to express the fact that it converts underlines into overlines.

In turn, to process the left-hand side of an arrow, reflection uses reification. Reification and reflection are thus mutually recursive. They operate in a type-directed way, independently of their argument.

Examples (of reifying a static expression):

$$\downarrow^{\alpha \to \alpha} e = \underline{\lambda} x_1 . e \overline{@} x_1$$

$$\downarrow^{((\alpha \times \alpha \to \alpha) \to \alpha) \to \alpha} e = \underline{\lambda} x_1 . e \overline{@} (\overline{\lambda} x_2 . x_1 \underline{@} (\underline{\lambda} x_3 . x_2 \overline{@} \overline{\text{pair}} (\underline{\pi_1} x_3, \underline{\pi_2} x_3)))$$

In ML, using the data type of Figure 1, these two type-indexed down arrows are respectively expressed as follows:

```
fn e => LAM ("x1",e (VAR "x1"))
(* (Exp.exp -> Exp.exp) -> Exp.exp *)

fn e => LAM ("x1",
             e (fn x2 => APP (VAR "x1",
                              LAM ("x3",
                                   x2 (FST (VAR "x3"),
                                       SND (VAR "x3"))))))
(* (((Exp.exp * Exp.exp -> Exp.exp) -> Exp.exp) -> Exp.exp) -> Exp.exp *)
```

Examples (of reflecting upon a dynamic expression):

$$\uparrow_{\alpha\to\alpha} e = \overline{\lambda}x_1.e@x_1$$

$$\uparrow_{((\alpha\times\alpha\to\alpha)\to\alpha)\to\alpha} e = \overline{\lambda}x_1.e@(\underline{\lambda}x_2.x_1@(\overline{\lambda}x_3.x_2@\underline{pair}(\overline{\pi_1}\,x_3,\overline{\pi_2}\,x_3)))$$

In ML, these two type-indexed up arrows are respectively expressed as follows:

```
fn e => fn x1 => APP (e,x1)
(* Exp.exp -> Exp.exp -> Exp.exp *)

fn e => fn x1 => APP (e,
                      LAM ("x2",
                           x1 (fn (x3_1, x3_2)
                               => APP (VAR "x2", PAIR (x3_1, x3_2)))))
(* Exp.exp -> ((Exp.exp * Exp.exp -> Exp.exp) -> Exp.exp) -> Exp.exp *)
```

1.5 Summary and conclusion

We have reviewed the basic ideas of partial evaluation and more specifically of Neil Jones's offline partial evaluation. We have settled on the particular brand of two-level language that arises when one implements "dynamic" with an ML data type representing the abstract syntax of residual programs and "static" with the corresponding ML language constructs. And we have reviewed binding-time coercions and how they are implemented in ML.

The type of each binding-time coercion matches the type of its input. Therefore, a polymorphic value corresponding to a pure lambda-term is reified into a residual expression by (1) instantiating all its type variables with Exp.exp and (2) plugging it in a two-level, code-generating context manufactured in a type-directed way.

2 Normalization by evaluation

In one way or another, the translation displayed in Figure 2 is a familiar sight in the offline-partial-evaluation community [8, 22, 23, 40]. It is, however, also known in other areas of computer science, and we review how in Section 2.1. In Section 2.2, we describe how reification can "decompile" ML values corresponding to pure lambda-terms in normal form. In Section 2.3, we illustrate normalization by evaluation, i.e., how reification can decompile values corresponding to pure lambda-terms into the representation of their normal form. In Section 2.4, we then turn to the implementation of reification and reflection in ML, which is not obvious, since they are type-indexed. Thus equipped, we then consider how to use normalization by evaluation to achieve partial evaluation, as outlined in Section 1.1. However, as analyzed in Section 2.5, normalization by evaluation needs to be adjusted to ML, which we do in Section 2.6. The result is type-directed partial evaluation.

2.1   A normalization function

In logic, proof theory, and category theory, the contents of Figure 2 has been discovered and studied as a *normalization function* [19]. There, the dynamic parts of the two-level lambda-calculus live in a term model, and the static parts live in a lambda-model with term constructors. The normalization function is type-indexed and maps a closed, completely static lambda-term into a closed, completely dynamic lambda-term in normal form:

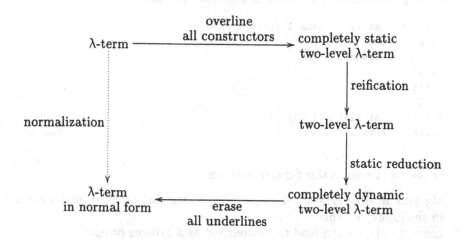

Ulrich Berger and Helmut Schwichtenberg, for example, discovered this normalization function in the area of proof theory [5]. They also observed that this function provides an efficient way to normalize lambda-terms if the overlines are implemented with ordinary syntax constructs and the underlines are implemented with constructors of residual terms, similarly to what is described in Section 1.3, but in Scheme [42]. In effect, the Scheme evaluator carries out both the normalization steps and the construction of the residual program.

Berger and Schwichtenberg present the normalization function as a left inverse of the evaluation function for the simply typed lambda-calculus; the idea is that an evaluator maps a dynamic lambda-term (an abstract-syntax tree) into its static counterpart (its value), while the normalizer has the inverse functionality. The interested reader is kindly directed to the proceedings of the workshop on "Normalization by Evaluation" for further independent discoveries of this normalization function [1, 12, 13, 19].

In summary, if one implements the two-level lambda-calculus as in Section 1.3, then reifying a simply typed, closed, and completely static higher-order function into a dynamic expression automatically yields a representation of its normal form. In the rest of this section, we illustrate this phenomenon with decompilation, before turning to the implementation of a normalization function in ML.

2.2   Application to decompilation

Reification lets us "decompile" values into the text of a corresponding expression – an observation due to Mayer Goldberg [31, 32].

Analogy with a first-year Scheme exercise: To build an appreciation of programs as data, beginners in Scheme are often asked to write a function constructing a list that represents a Scheme program. One such function is `reify-int-list` that maps a list of numbers into the Scheme list that, when evaluated, will yield that list of numbers. Here is the transcript of an interactive Scheme session illustrating the exercise (">" is the interactive prompt):

```
> (reify-int-list (cons 1 (cons 2 '())))
(cons 1 (cons 2 '()))
> (cons 1 (cons 2 '()))
(1 2)
> '(1 2)
(1 2)
> (reify-int-list '(1 2))
(cons 1 (cons 2 '()))
>
```

There are two issues in this Scheme exercise:

1. algorithmically, `reify-int-list` performs a straightforward recursive descent in the input list; and
2. conceptually, we can read the output list as a Scheme program.

In ML and in Haskell, it is more natural to output an abstract-syntax tree (represented with an inductive data type) and then to unparse it into concrete syntax (represented with a string) and possibly to pretty-print it.

Let us illustrate decompilation in ML without any unparser and pretty-printer, using the data type of Figure 1. We consider several examples in turn, reproducing transcripts of an interactive ML session ("-" is the interactive prompt).

The identity combinator I *at type* $\alpha \to \alpha$
   The associated reifier reads $\overline{\lambda}v.\underline{\lambda}x.v\overline{@}x$.

```
- val I = fn x => x;                    (* the identity combinator *)
val I = fn : 'a -> 'a
- val reify_a2a                         (* the associated reifier *)
    = fn v => Exp.LAM ("x",v (Exp.VAR "x"));
val reify_a2a = fn : (Exp.exp -> Exp.exp) -> Exp.exp
- reify_a2a I;                          (* decompilation *)
val it = LAM ("x",VAR "x") : Exp.exp
-
```

Compared to `reify-int-list` above, the striking thing here is that we do not decompile first-order values, but higher-order ones, i.e., functions.

The cancellation combinator K *at type* $\alpha \to \beta \to \alpha$
The associated reifier reads $\overline{\lambda}v.\underline{\lambda}x.\underline{\lambda}y.(v\overline{@}x)\overline{@}y$.

```
- fun K x y = x;                              (* the K combinator *)
val K = fn : 'a -> 'b -> 'a
- local open Exp
  in val reify_a2b2a                    (* the associated reifier *)
        = fn v => LAM ("x",LAM ("y",v (VAR "x") (VAR "y")))
  end;
val reify_a2b2a = fn : (Exp.exp -> Exp.exp -> Exp.exp) -> Exp.exp
- reify_a2b2a K;                              (* decompilation *)
val it = LAM ("x",LAM ("y",VAR "x")) : Exp.exp
-
```

A random higher-order function at type $((\alpha \to \alpha) \to \beta) \to \beta$
The associated reifier reads $\overline{\lambda}v.\underline{\lambda}f.v\overline{@}(\overline{\lambda}v_1.f\underline{@}(\underline{\lambda}x.v_1\overline{@}x))$.

```
- val foo = fn f => f (fn x => x);
val foo = fn : (('a -> 'a) -> 'b) -> 'b
- local open Exp
  in val reify_foo                      (* the associated reifier *)
        = fn v => LAM ("f",
                    v (fn v1 => APP (VAR "f",
                                  LAM ("x",
                                    v1 (VAR "x")))))
  end;
val reify_foo
    = fn : (((Exp.exp -> Exp.exp) -> Exp.exp) -> Exp.exp) -> Exp.exp
- reify_foo foo;                              (* decompilation *)
val it = LAM ("f",APP (VAR "f",LAM ("x",VAR "x"))) : Exp.exp
-
```

In each case we have decompiled a higher-order function corresponding to a pure lambda-term by reifying it according to its type.

As these examples have just illustrated, decompilation is the inverse of the evaluation function for normal forms [5, 14, 27].

2.3   Normalization by evaluation

Let us now illustrate normalization by evaluation. We consider two source terms that are not in normal form, and how they are reified into a representation of their normal form. The two input values have the same type and thus we normalize them with the same reifier.

In the next interaction, we consider a source term with a beta-redex in the body of a lambda-abstraction. Because of ML's evaluation strategy, the corresponding beta-reduction takes place each time this source term is applied. This reduction, however, can be performed "at normalization time."

```
- reify_a2a (fn x => (fn y => y) x);                    (* a beta-redex *)
val it = LAM ("x",VAR "x") : Exp.exp
-
```

In the next interaction, we revisit the standard definition of the identity combinator I in terms of the Hilbert combinators S and K.

```
- fun S f g x = f x (g x);                              (* the S combinator *)
val S = fn : ('a -> 'b -> 'c) -> ('a -> 'b) -> 'a -> 'c
- reify_a2a (S K K);                    (* reification of S K K into I *)
val it = LAM ("x",VAR "x") : Exp.exp
-
```

2.4   Naive normalization by evaluation in ML

In Sections 1.4, 2.2, and and 2.3, we have written one reifier per type. Let us now turn to implementing a type-indexed normalization function nbe, i.e., to writing the contents of Figure 2 in ML. But how does one write a type-indexed function in ML? In Figure 2, reification and reflection very obviously are dependently typed – and ML does not provide any support for dependent types. Fortunately, Andrzej Filinski and Zhe Yang have recently devised the technique of defining reification and reflection pairwise, in a polymorphically typed way [17, 59].

Figure 3 displays an implementation of normalization by evaluation in Standard ML using the Filinski-Yang programming technique. The data type rr embodies each reify/reflect pair:

- rra denotes the "type constructor" corresponding to the atomic type α (noted a' in Figure 4);
- rrf denotes the "type constructor" corresponding to functions (infix and noted --> in Figure 4); and
- rrp denotes the "type constructor" corresponding to products (infix and noted ** in Figure 4).

Overall, given the representation of a type and a polymorphic value of the corresponding type, normalization by evaluation boils down to reifying the value. For readability, the generator of fresh variables is also initialized in passing.

Examples: Thus equipped, we now revisit the reifiers of Section 2.2.

```
- val reify_a2a = nbe (a' --> a');
val reify_a2a = fn : (Exp.exp -> Exp.exp) -> Exp.exp
- val reify_a2b2a = nbe (a' --> a' --> a');
val reify_a2b2a = fn : (Exp.exp -> Exp.exp -> Exp.exp) -> Exp.exp
- val reify_foo = nbe (((a' --> a') --> a') --> a');
val reify_foo
    = fn : (((Exp.exp -> Exp.exp) -> Exp.exp) -> Exp.exp) -> Exp.exp
-
```

As can be noticed, we only use one atomic type: to repeat the last paragraph of Section 1, all type variables are instantiated with Exp.exp.

```
structure Naive_nbe
= struct
    local open Exp
    in datatype 'a rr = RR of ('a -> exp) * (exp -> 'a)

        val rra
            = RR (fn e => e, fn e => e)

        fun rrf (RR (reify1, reflect1), RR (reify2, reflect2))
            = RR (fn f => let val x = Gensym.new "x"
                          in LAM (x, reify2 (f (reflect1 (VAR x))))
                          end,
                    fn e => fn v => reflect2 (APP (e, reify1 v)))

        fun rrp (RR (reify1, reflect1), RR (reify2, reflect2))
            = RR (fn (v1, v2) => PAIR (reify1 v1, reify2 v2),
                    fn e => (reflect1 (FST e), reflect2 (SND e)))

        fun nbe (RR (reify, reflect)) v
            = (Gensym.init (); reify v)
    end
end
```

Fig. 3. Naive normalization by evaluation in Standard ML (definition)

```
val a' = Naive_nbe.rra

infixr 5 -->
val op --> = Naive_nbe.rrf

infixr 6 **
val op ** = Naive_nbe.rrp

val nbe = Naive_nbe.nbe
```

Fig. 4. Naive normalization by evaluation in Standard ML (interface)

Refinement: We can also decompile a single polymorphic value with respect to more refined types:

```
- nbe ((a' --> a') --> a' --> a') (fn x => x);
val it = LAM ("x1",LAM ("x2",APP (VAR "x1",VAR "x2"))) : Exp.exp
- nbe (a' ** a' --> a' ** a') (fn x => x);
val it = LAM ("x1",PAIR (FST (VAR "x1"),SND (VAR "x1"))) : Exp.exp
-
```

As Guy Steele and Gerry Sussman once said about the Y combinator, "That this manages to work is truly remarkable." [55, page 70].

2.5   Towards type-directed partial evaluation

Now that we have coded normalization by evaluation in ML, we can go back to our initial goal, as stated in Section 1.1: to achieve partial evaluation by partially applying a source function to a static argument and normalizing the result. To this end, we proceed with the following swift generalizations [14]:

1. We use more of ML in our source programs than what corresponds to the pure lambda-calculus. For example, residualizing the open function

   ```
   fn x => (fn i => if i >= 0 then x else x) 42
   ```

   with reify_a2a also yields the residual (closed) identity function.
   Our extension, however, must stay reasonable in some sense. For example, residualizing the open function

   ```
   fn x => (print "hello world"; x)
   ```

   with reify_a2a also yields the residual identity function, but the string "hello world" is output during residualization, which may or may not be what we want.

2. Correspondingly, we can extend the residual syntax of Figure 1 with literals. The reification function at the type of each literal is then simply defined as the corresponding syntax constructor. The reflection function, however, is undefined in general. Indeed, we could only determine an integer-expecting context, for example, by feeding it with an infinite number of integers. As a consequence, we cannot residualize a function such as

   ```
   fn x => x+1
   ```

   This is in contrast with the pure simply typed lambda-calculus where a term can be totally determined by observing the result of plugging it into finitely many contexts – a property which is at the root of normalization by evaluation for the pure simply typed lambda-calculus [3, 19].

3. It is also tempting to use ML's recursion in a source program, even though this introduces the risk of non-termination at partial-evaluation time.

4. Correspondingly, we can code residual recursive functions using fixed-point operators.

5. Finally, ML follows call-by-value, whereas naive normalization by evaluation assumes call-by-name. For example, the possibly non-terminating function

```
fn f => fn x => (fn y => x) (f x)
```

is residualized into the term

```
fn f => fn x => x
```

which denotes a terminating function.

This phenomenon requires us to extend normalization by evaluation with the partial-evaluation technique of dynamic let insertion [7, 35, 43], so that the residual term reads as follows.

```
fn f => fn x => let val _ = f x
                in x
                end
```

Let insertion also solves the problem of computation duplication, which is significant in the presence of residual functions with computational effects [35]. For example, a function such as

```
fn (f, g, h, x) => (fn y => g (y, h x, y)) (f x)
```

is naively residualized into the term

```
fn (f, g, h, x) => g (f x, h x, f x)
```

where the function denoted by f is applied twice and out of order with respect to the function denoted by h. Let insertion maintains the proper sequencing in the residual program:

```
fn (f, g, h, x) => let val y = f x
                       val z = h x
                   in g (y, z, y)
                   end
```

In his study of normalization by evaluation [29, 30], Andrzej Filinski scrutinizes the generalizations above:

- Normalization by evaluation is defined in a fairly restricted setting – the pure simply typed lambda-calculus. This formal setting needs to be extended to account for base types and for the corresponding operations.
- As soon as we introduce recursion, arguments based on strong normalization cease to apply. The overall picture of partial evaluation by partial application and normalization thus needs to be adjusted.
- Normalization by evaluation is formally defined in a normal-order setting. It needs to be adjusted to work in a call-by-value language, especially in the presence of computational effects such as divergence.

In summary, normalization by evaluation was originally defined for the pure lambda-calculus. It is not immediately clear whether it can be directly transcribed in a richer functional language and still be claimed to work in some sense. Filinski, however, has proven that it can be transcribed in call-by-name PCF [29, 30].

Treating a full-fledged call-by-value functional language such as Scheme and ML thus requires one to adapt normalization by evaluation. This is the goal of Section 2.6.

```
    structure Exp
    = struct
        datatype exp = VAR of string
                     | LAM of string * exp
                     | APP of exp * exp
                     | PAIR of exp * exp
                     | FST of exp
                     | SND of exp
                     | LET of string * exp * exp
                     | INT of int
                     | BOOL of bool
                     | COND of exp * exp * exp

        fun pp e = ...  (* a pretty-printer *)
    end
```

Fig. 5. Abstract syntax of residual expressions (extended)

2.6 Normalization by evaluation in ML

Because of call-by-value, the standard technique of dynamic let insertion has
to be adapted to avoid the computation mismatch illustrated in Item 5 of Section 2.5; this extension makes it possible to handle observationally effectful functions, as well as booleans and more generally disjoint sums [14, 15]. In the rest
of these lecture notes, we consider this version of normalization by evaluation,
displayed in Figure 6.

Figure 6 requires the extended residual syntax of Figure 5, i.e., let expressions because of call-by-value, integer and boolean literals, and conditional expressions. The overall structure of reification and reflection is the same as in
Figure 3. Integers, in particular, are implemented as described in Item 2 of
Section 2.5, page 378: the integer reification function is defined as the abstract-
syntax constructor for integers, and the integer reflection function raises an un-
caught exception. In the rest of the figure, the new parts involve the control
operators shift and reset [21].

Shift and reset are respectively used to abstract (delimited) control and to
delimit control. They are most tellingly used for booleans (rrb in Figure 6): the
challenge there is to implement the reflection function, which must have the type
exp -> bool. Since there are only two booleans, we successively provide them to
the context, yielding two residual expressions that form the two branches of
a residual conditional expression. We lay our hands on the context using the
control operator shift, which provides us with a functional abstraction of the
current context. Supplying a value to this context then reduces to applying the
functional abstraction to this value, which we successively do with true and
false. This programming technique is illustrated in Figure 8 and also in the
literature [14, 15, 20, 21, 43].

```
structure Nbe =
struct
  local open Exp
  in structure Ctrl = Control (type ans = exp)
    datatype 'a rr = RR of ('a -> exp) * (exp -> 'a)

    val rra = RR (fn e => e, fn e => e)

    fun rrf (RR (reify1, reflect1), RR (reify2, reflect2))
        = RR (fn f => let val x = Gensym.new "x"
                      in LAM (x, Ctrl.reset
                                   (fn ()
                                    => reify2 (f (reflect1 (VAR x)))))
                      end,
             fn e => fn v => let val r = Gensym.new "r"
                             in Ctrl.shift
                                  (fn k
                                   => LET (r,
                                           APP (e, reify1 v),
                                           Ctrl.reset
                                            (fn ()
                                             => k (reflect2 (VAR r)))))
                             end)

    fun rrp (RR (reify1, reflect1), RR (reify2, reflect2))
        = RR (fn (v1, v2) => PAIR (reify1 v1, reify2 v2),
             fn e => (reflect1 (FST e), reflect2 (SND e)))

    exception NoWay
    val rri = (INT,
                 fn _ => raise NoWay)

    val rrb
      = RR (BOOL,
            fn e => Ctrl.shift
                      (fn k => COND (e,
                                     Ctrl.reset (fn () => k true),
                                     Ctrl.reset (fn () => k false))))

    fun nbe (RR (reify, reflect)) v
        = (Gensym.init (); reify v)
    fun nbe' (RR (reify, reflect)) e
        = reflect e
  end
end
```

Fig. 6. Normalization by evaluation in Standard ML (definition)

```
val a' = Nbe.rra
val int' = Nbe.rra
val bool' = Nbe.rra

infixr 5 -->; val op --> = Nbe.rrf

infixr 6 **; val op ** = Nbe.rrp

val int = Nbe.rri

val bool = Nbe.rrb

val nbe = Nbe.nbe
val nbe' = Nbe.nbe'
```

Fig. 7. Normalization by evaluation in Standard ML (interface)

```
structure Example
= struct
    structure Ctrl = Control (type ans = int)

    val x1 = 10 + (Ctrl.reset
                    (fn () => 500 + Ctrl.shift
                                (fn k => (k 0) + (k 100))))
    val x2 = 10 + let fun k v = 500 + v
                    in (k 0) + (k 100)
                    end
  end
```

The two computations above declare an outer context 10 + [ ]. They also declare a delimited context [500 + [̄]], which is abstracted as a function denoted by k. This function is successively applied to 0, yielding 500, and to 100, yielding 600. The two results are added, yielding 1100 which is then plugged in the outer context. The overall result is 1110.

In the first computation, the context is delimited by reset and the delimited context is abstracted into a function with shift. The second computation is the continuation-passing counterpart of the first one [21].

It should be noted that shift yields a control abstraction that behaves as a function, i.e., that returns a result to the context of its invocation and thus can be composed. In contrast, the Scheme control operator call/cc yields a control abstraction that behaves as a goto, in the sense that invoking it does not return any result to the context of its invocation.

Shift and reset are documented further in the literature [20, 21, 28].

Fig. 8. An example of using shift and reset

```
signature ESCAPE
= sig
    type void
    val coerce : void -> 'a
    val escape : (('a -> void) -> 'a) -> 'a
  end

structure Escape : ESCAPE
= struct
    datatype void = VOID of void
    fun coerce (VOID v) = coerce v
    fun escape f
        = SMLofNJ.Cont.callcc (fn k => f (fn x => SMLofNJ.Cont.throw k x))
  end

signature CONTROL
= sig
    type ans
    val shift : (('a -> ans) -> ans) -> 'a
    val reset : (unit -> ans) -> ans
  end

functor Control (type ans) : CONTROL =
struct
  open Escape
  exception MissingReset
  val mk : (ans -> void) ref = ref (fn _ => raise MissingReset)
  fun abort x = coerce (!mk x)
  type ans = ans
  fun reset t
      = escape (fn k => let val m = !mk
                        in mk := (fn r => (mk := m; k r));
                           abort (t ())
                        end)
  fun shift h
      = escape (fn k => abort (h (fn v => reset (fn () => coerce (k v)))))
end
```

Fig. 9. Shift and reset in Standard ML of New Jersey [28]

We reproduce Filinski's implementation of shift and reset in Figure 9. This implementation relies on the Scheme-like control operator callcc available in Standard ML of New Jersey [28].

Let insertion: Let us consider the following simple program, where two functions are intertwined, and one is specified to be the identity function:

```
structure Let_example
= struct
    fun main f g x = g (f (g (f (g (f (g x))))))
    fun spec f x = main f (fn a => a) x
  end
```

We residualize `Let_example.spec` according to its most general type as follows:

```
nbe ((a' --> a') --> a' --> a') Let_example.spec
```

The raw result is of type `Exp.exp` and reads as follows.

```
LAM ("x1", LAM ("x2", LET ("r3",
                        APP (VAR "x1",VAR "x2"),
                        LET ("r4",
                            APP (VAR "x1",VAR "r3"),
                            LET ("r5",
                                APP (VAR "x1",VAR "r4"),
                                VAR "r5")))))
```

The static function has been eliminated statically and let expressions have been inserted to name each intermediate result.

Once unparsed and pretty-printed, the residual program reads as follows.

```
fn x1 => fn x2 => let val r3 = x1 x2
                      val r4 = x1 r3
                  in x1 r4
                  end
```

The attentive reader will have noticed that the output of the pretty-printer is properly tail-recursive, i.e., it does not name the last call.

Booleans: Let us consider function composition:

```
structure Boolean_example
= struct
    fun main f g x = f (g x)
    fun spec f x g = main f g x
  end
```

Residualizing `Boolean_example.spec` with respect to the type

```
(bool' --> bool) --> bool' --> (bool' --> bool') --> bool
```

yields the following residual program:

```
fn x1 => fn x2 => fn x3 => let val r4 = x3 x2
                               val r5 = x1 r4
                           in if r5
                              then true
                              else false
                           end
```

As above, residual let expressions have been inserted. In addition, the boolean variable r5 has been "eta-expanded" into a conditional expression. This insertion of conditional expressions also has the effect of duplicating boolean contexts, as illustrated next.

Residualizing Boolean_example.spec with respect to the type

```
(bool --> bool') --> bool' --> (bool' --> bool) --> bool'
```

yields the following residual program, where the application of x1 is duplicated in the conditional branches.

```
fn x1 => fn x2 => fn x3 => let val r4 = x3 x2
                           in if r4
                              then x1 true
                              else x1 false
                           end
```

Similarly, residualizing Boolean_example.spec with respect to the type

```
(bool' --> bool') --> bool --> (bool --> bool') --> bool'
```

yields the following residual program, where a function definition is cloned in the conditional branches.

```
fn x1 => fn x2 => if x2
                  then fn x3 => let val r4 = x3 true
                                in x1 r4
                                end
                  else fn x6 => let val r7 = x6 false
                                in x1 r7
                                end
```

As an exercise, the reader might want to residualize Boolean_example.spec with respect to the type

```
(bool --> bool) --> bool --> (bool --> bool) --> bool.
```

Duplicating boolean contexts is usually justified because of the static computations it may enable. If these are neglectable, one can avoid code duplication by generalizing the static type bool into the dynamic type bool' defined in Figure 7.

2.7   An alternative approach

Suppose one proscribes booleans and disjoint sums in residual programs. Could one then implement let insertion in a simpler way than with shift and reset? In June 1998, Eijiro Sumii answered positively to this question.[1]

And indeed what is the goal of shift and reset in the definition of rrf in Figure 6? Essentially to name each intermediate result and to sequentialize its computation. Let us capture this goal with the alternative data type for residual expressions displayed in Figure 10. This data type accounts for lambda-calculus terms, plus a sequential let expression.

Thus equipped, let us observe that each shift in rrf adds a let binding. But we can obtain the same effect with state instead of with control, by keeping a list of let bindings in a global hook and making the reflect component of rrf extend this list:

```
fn e => fn v => let val r = Gensym.new "r"
                in hook := (r, APP (e, reify1 v)) :: !hook;
                   reflect2 (VAR r)
                end
```

Conversely, in the reify component of rrf, we can initialize the global list when creating a residual lambda-abstraction and package the list of bindings when completing its residual body:

```
fn f => let val x = Gensym.new "x"
            val previous_hook = !hook
            val _ = hook := []
            val body = reify2 (f (reflect1 (VAR x)))
            val header = rev (!hook)
            val _ = hook := previous_hook
        in LAM (x, LET (header, body))
        end
```

The complete specification is displayed in Figure 11. In practice, it enables one to implement type-directed partial evaluation in a call-by-value functional language without control facilities such as Caml. Sumii's state-based technique also applies for let insertion in traditional syntax-directed partial evaluation, which, according to Peter Thiemann, is folklore.

2.8   Summary and conclusion

In this section, we have presented "normalization by evaluation" and we have adapted it to the call-by-value setting corresponding to our encoding of the two-level lambda-calculus in ML. Similarly, the proof techniques can be (non-trivially) adapted from call-by-name to call-by-value with monadic effects to show the correctness of this variant. Also, in the spring of 1999, Andrzej Filinski has formalized the relation between control-based and state-based let insertion.

We are now ready to use normalization to perform partial evaluation.

---

[1] Personal communication, Aarhus, Denmark, September 1998.

```
    structure Exp_alt
    = struct
        datatype exp = VAR of string
                     | LAM of string * exp
                     | APP of exp * exp
                     | LET of (string * exp) list * exp
        end
```

Fig. 10. Alternative abstract syntax of residual expressions

```
structure Nbe_alt =
struct
  local open Exp_alt
  in val hook = ref [] : (string * Exp_alt.exp) list ref
     datatype 'a rr = RR of ('a -> exp) * (exp -> 'a)

     val rra = RR (fn e => e, fn e => e)

     fun rrf (RR (reify1, reflect1), RR (reify2, reflect2))
         = RR (fn f => let val x = Gensym.new "x"
                           val previous_hook = !hook
                           val _ = hook := []
                           val body = reify2 (f (reflect1 (VAR x)))
                           val header = rev (!hook)
                           val _ = hook := previous_hook
                       in LAM (x, LET (header, body))
                       end,
               fn e => fn v => let val r = Gensym.new "r"
                               in hook := (r, APP (e, reify1 v)) :: !hook;
                                  reflect2 (VAR r)
                               end)

     fun nbe (RR (reify, reflect)) v
         = (Gensym.init (); reify v)
     fun nbe' (RR (reify, reflect)) e
         = reflect e
  end
end
```

Fig. 11. Alternative normalization by evaluation in ML

3   Offline type-directed partial evaluation

We define type-directed partial evaluation as normalization by evaluation over ML values, as defined in Figures 6 and 7, pages 381 and 382. Since normalization by evaluation operates over closed terms, we close our source programs by abstracting all their dynamic variables.

In practice, it is a simple matter to close source programs by abstracting all their dynamic free variables. This is naturally achieved by lambda-abstraction in Scheme [14, 25]. In ML, however, it is more natural to use parameterized modules, i.e., functors [44], to abstract the dynamic primitive operators from a source program.

Functors make it possible not only to parameterize a source program with its primitive operators but also with their type, while ensuring a proper binding-time division through the ML typing system.

- Running a source program is achieved by instantiating the corresponding functor with a "standard" interpretation of the domains and the operators to perform evaluation.
- Specializing a source program is achieved by instantiating the corresponding functor with a "non-standard" interpretation to perform partial evaluation.

A residual program contains free variables, namely the primitive operators. We thus unparse it and pretty-print it as a functor parameterized with these operators. We can then instantiate residual programs with the standard interpretation to run them and with the non-standard interpretation to specialize them further, incrementally.

The rest of this session illustrates the practice of offline type-directed partial evaluation. We consider the traditional example of the power function, and we proceed in two steps.

3.1   The power function, part 1/2

In this section, we specialize the power function with respect to its exponent parameter. Therefore its multiplication is dynamic and we abstract it. Figure 12 displays the signature of the abstracted types and primitive operators: integers and multiplication. For typing purposes, we also use a "quote" function to map an actual integer into an abstracted integer. Figure 13 displays the standard interpretation of this signature: it is the obvious one, and thus integers are ML's integers, quoting is the identity function, and multiplication is ML's native multiplication. Figure 14 displays a non-standard interpretation: integers are residual expressions, quoting is the integer constructor of expressions, and multiplication constructs a (named) residual application of the identifier "mul" to its two actual parameters, using reflection. Figure 15 displays the actual power function, which is declared in a functor parameterized with the interpretation of integers and of multiplication.

```
signature PRIMITIVE_power_ds
= sig
    type int_

    val qint : int -> int_
    val mul : int_ * int_ -> int_
  end
```

Fig. 12. Signature for abstracted components

```
structure Primitive_power_ds_e : PRIMITIVE_power_ds
= struct
    type int_ = int

    fun qint i = i
    val mul = op *
  end
```

Fig. 13. Standard interpretation: evaluation

```
structure Primitive_power_ds_pe : PRIMITIVE_power_ds
= struct
    local open Exp
    in type int_ = exp

      val qint = INT
      fun mul (e1, e2)
          = nbe' (int' ** int' --> int') (VAR "mul") (e1, e2)
    end
  end
```

Fig. 14. Non-standard interpretation: partial evaluation

```
functor mkPower_ds (structure P : PRIMITIVE_power_ds)
= struct
    local open P
    in fun power (x, n)
          = let fun loop 0 = qint 1
                  | loop n = mul (x, loop (n-1))
              in loop n
              end
    end
  end
```

Fig. 15. Source program

```
structure Power_ds_e
= mkPower_ds (structure P = Primitive_power_ds_e)
```
Fig. 16. Standard instantiation: evaluation

```
structure Power_ds_pe
= mkPower_ds (structure P = Primitive_power_ds_pe)
```
Fig. 17. Non-standard instantiation: partial evaluation

Evaluation: In Figure 16, we instantiate mkPower_ds with the standard interpretation of Figure 13. The result is a structure that we call Power_ds_e, and in which the identifier power denotes the usual power function.

Partial evaluation: In Figure 17, we instantiate mkPower_ds with the non-standard interpretation of Figure 14. The result is a structure that we call Power_ds_pe.

We specialize the power function with respect to the exponent 3 by partially applying its non-standard version and residualizing the result:

```
nbe (int' --> int') (fn d => Power_ds_pe.power (d, 3))
```

The residual code has the type Exp.exp and reads as follows.

```
LAM ("x1",
      LET ("r2",
           APP (VAR "mul",PAIR (VAR "x1",INT 1)),
           LET ("r3",
                APP (VAR "mul",PAIR (VAR "x1",VAR "r2")),
                LET ("r4",
                     APP (VAR "mul",PAIR (VAR "x1",VAR "r3")),
                     VAR "r4"))))
```

This residual code contains free variables. Pretty-printing it (providing the parameters "mkPower_d3", "PRIMITIVE_power_ds", "power", "qint", and "mul") yields a residual program that is closed, more readable, and also directly usable:

```
functor mkPower_d3 (structure P : PRIMITIVE_power_ds)
= struct
    local open P
    in fun power x1
           = let val r2 = mul (x1, qint 1)
                 val r3 = mul (x1, r2)
             in mul (x1, r3)
             end
    end
  end
```

This residual program is ready to be instantiated with `Primitive_power_ds_e` for evaluation or (hypothetically here) with `Primitive_power_ds_pe` for further partial evaluation. Compared to the source program, the recursive function `loop` has been unfolded, as could be expected.

3.2   The power function, part 2/2

In this section, we specialize the power function with respect to its base parameter. All the components of the definition are dynamic and thus we abstract them. Figure 18 displays the signature of the abstracted types and primitive operators: integers, booleans, and the corresponding operations. For typing purposes, we still use a quote function for integers; we also use an "unquote" function for booleans, in order to use ML's conditional expression. Besides the usual arithmetic operators, we also use a call-by-value fixed-point operator to account for the recursive definition of the power function. Figure 19 displays the standard interpretation of this signature: it is the obvious one. Figure 20 displays a nonstandard interpretation: integers and booleans are residual expressions, quoting is the integer constructor of expressions, and unquoting a boolean expression reflects upon it at boolean type. As for the primitive operators, they construct residual applications of the corresponding identifier to their actual parameters. Figure 21 displays the actual power function, which is declared in a parameterized functor.

Evaluation: In Figure 22, page 393, we instantiate `mkPower_sd` with the standard interpretation of Figure 19. The result is a structure that we call `Power_sd_e`, and in which the identifier `power` denotes the usual power function.

Partial evaluation: In Figure 23, page 393, we instantiate `mkPower_sd` with the non-standard interpretation of Figure 20. The result is a structure that we call `Power_sd_pe`.

   We specialize the power function with respect to the base 8 by partially applying its non-standard version and residualizing the result:

```
nbe (int' --> int') (fn d => Power_sd_pe.power (8, d))
```

Pretty-printing the residual code yields the following residual program, which is similar to the source program of Figure 21 except that the base parameter has disappeared, 8 has been inlined in the induction case, and let expressions have been inserted.

```
signature PRIMITIVE_power_sd
= sig
    type int_
    type bool_

    val qint : int -> int_
    val ubool : bool_ -> bool
    val dec : int_ -> int_
    val mul : int_ * int_ -> int_
    val eqi : int_ * int_ -> bool_
    val fix : ((int_ -> int_) -> int_ -> int_) -> int_ -> int_
  end
```

Fig. 18. Signature for abstracted components

```
structure Primitive_power_sd_e : PRIMITIVE_power_sd
= struct
    type int_ = int
    type bool_ = bool

    fun qint i = i
    fun ubool b = b
    fun dec i = i-1
    val mul = op *
    val eqi = op =
    fun fix f x = f (fix f) x (* fix is a CBV fixed-point operator *)
  end
```

Fig. 19. Standard interpretation: evaluation

```
structure Primitive_power_sd_pe : PRIMITIVE_power_sd
= struct
    local open Exp
    in type int_ = exp
       type bool_ = exp

       val qint = INT
       val ubool = nbe' bool
       val dec = nbe' (int' --> int') (VAR "dec")
       val mul = nbe' (int' ** int' --> int') (VAR "mul")
       val eqi = nbe' (int' ** int' --> int') (VAR "eqi")
       val fix = nbe' (((int' --> int') --> int' --> int')
                       --> int' --> int')
                      (VAR "fix")
    end
  end
```

Fig. 20. Non-standard interpretation: partial evaluation

```
functor mkPower_sd (structure P : PRIMITIVE_power_sd)
= struct
    local open P
    in fun power (x, n)
            = fix (fn loop => fn n => if ubool (eqi (n, qint 0))
                                      then qint 1
                                      else mul (qint x, loop (dec n)))
                n
    end
end
```

Fig. 21. Source program

```
structure Power_sd_e
= mkPower_sd (structure P = Primitive_power_sd_e)
```

Fig. 22. Standard instantiation: evaluation

```
structure Power_sd_pe
= mkPower_sd (structure P = Primitive_power_sd_pe)
```

Fig. 23. Non-standard instantiation: partial evaluation

```
functor mkPower_8d (structure P : POWER)
= struct
    local open P
    in fun power x1
            = let val r2 = fix (fn x3
                    => fn x4
                        => let val r5 = eqi (x4, qint 0)
                           in if ubool r5
                              then qint 1
                              else let val r6 = dec x4
                                       val r7 = x3 r6
                                   in mul (qint 8, r7)
                                   end)
                in r2 x1
                end
    end
end
```

As in Section 3.1, this residual program is as could be expected.

3.3   Summary and conclusion

To use offline type-directed partial evaluation, one thus

1. specifies a signature for dynamic primitive operators and the corresponding types;
2. specifies their evaluation and their partial evaluation;
3. parameterizes a source program with these primitive operators and types;
4. instantiates the source program with the partial-evaluation operators and types, and residualizes a value at an appropriate type; and
5. pretty-prints the result into a parameterized residual program.

The first results of offline type-directed partial evaluation have been very encouraging: it handles the standard examples of the trade (i.e., mostly, the first and the second Futamura projections) with an impressive efficiency. Its functionality is otherwise essentially the same as Lambda-Mix's: higher-order monovariant specialization over closed programs [39]. Its use, however, is considerably more convenient since the binding-time separation of each source program is guided and ensured by the ML type system. There is therefore no need for expert binding-time improvements [40, Chapter 12]. In fact, we believe that this disarming ease of use is probably the main factor that has let offline type-directed partial evaluation scale up, as illustrated in the work of Vestergaard and the author [25] and of Harrison and Kamin [34].

In practice, however, offline type-directed partial evaluation imposes a restriction on its user: the binding-time signatures of primitive operators must be monovariant. This restriction forces the user to distinguish between "static" and "dynamic" occurrences of primitive operators in each source program. Against this backdrop, we have turned to the "online" flavor of partial evaluation, where one abstracts the source program completely and makes each primitive operator probe its operands for possible simplifications. This is the topic of Section 4.

4   Online type-directed partial evaluation

A partial evaluator is online if its operators probe their operands dynamically to decide whether to perform an operation at partial-evaluation time or to residualize it until run time [58]. In his PhD thesis [52], Erik Ruf described how to obtain the best of both offline and online worlds:

- on the one hand, one can trust the static information of the binding-time analysis since it is safe; and
- on the other hand, one should make dynamic operators online because a binding-time analysis is conservative.

The idea applies directly here: in Figure 14, page 14, if we define multiplication to probe its operands, we can naturally look for obvious simplifications, as in Figure 24. (NB: the simplifications by zero are safe because of let insertion.)

Specializing Power_ds_pe.power (in Figure 15, page 389 and in Figure 17, page 390) with respect to 3 then yields the following simpler residual program.

```
structure Primitive_power_ds_pe : PRIMITIVE_power_ds
= struct
    local open Exp
    in type int_ = exp
       val qint = INT
       fun mul (INT i1, INT i2) = INT (i1 * i2)
         | mul (INT 0, _) = INT 0
         | mul (_, INT 0) = INT 0
         | mul (INT 1, e2) = e2
         | mul (e1, INT 1) = e1
         | mul e = nbe' (int' ** int' --> int') (VAR "mul") e
    end
end
```
Fig. 24. Online version of Figure 14, page 389

```
functor mkPower_d3 (structure P : POWER)
= struct
    local open P
    in fun power x1 = let val r2 = mul (x1, x1)
                      in mul (x1, r2)
                      end
    end
end
```

Compared with the earlier definition of mkPower_d3, page 391, the vacuous multiplication of x1 by 1 has been simplified away.

In the rest of this section, we illustrate online type-directed partial evaluation with two case studies. In Section 4.1, we consider a very simple example where the uses of a primitive operator need not be split into static and dynamic occurrences, which is more practical. And in Section 4.2, we revisit the power function: this time, we abstract all of its operators and we make them online. This makes it possible to specialize the *same* source program with respect to either the base parameter or the exponent parameter. On the way, we come across the familiar tension between unfolding and residualizing recursive function calls, as epitomized by Schism's filters [10].

4.1 Online simplification for integers

Figure 25 displays the signature of a minimal implementation of integers: a type int_, a quote function for integer literals, and an addition function.

Figure 26 displays the obvious standard interpretation of integers: int_ is instantiated to be the type of integers, qint is defined as the identity function, and add is defined as addition.

Figure 27 displays a non-standard interpretation of integers where int_ is instantiated to be the type of residual expressions, qint is defined as the integer

```
signature PRIMITIVE1
= sig
    type int_

    val qint : int -> int_
    val add : int_ * int_ -> int_
  end
```

Fig. 25. Signature for integers

```
structure Primitive1_e : PRIMITIVE1
= struct
    type int_ = int

    fun qint x = x
    val add = op +
  end
```

Fig. 26. Standard interpretation for integers: evaluation

```
structure Primitive1_pe : PRIMITIVE1
= struct
    local open Exp
    in type int_ = exp

      val qint = INT
    fun add (INT i1, INT i2)
        = INT (i1+i2)
      | add (INT 0, e2)
        = e2
      | add (e1, INT 0)
        = e1
      | add e
        = nbe' (int' ** int' --> int') (VAR "add") e
    end
  end
```

Fig. 27. Non-standard interpretation for integers: partial evaluation

```
functor mkEx1 (structure P : PRIMITIVE1)
= struct
    local open P
    in fun main x y = add (add (x, qint 10), y)
       val spec = main (qint 100)
    end
  end
```

Fig. 28. Sample source program

constructor, and add is defined as a mapping of two integer-typed expressions into a simplified integer-typed expression. If there is nothing to simplify, then the variable "add" is reflected upon at type int' ** int' --> int' and the result is applied to the argument of add, which is a pair of expressions. The result is an expression.

Thus equipped, let us consider the source program of Figure 28. It is parameterized by the implementation of integers specified in Figure 25. It involves two literals, 10 and 100, both of which are quoted. Our goal is to residualize the value of spec. It thus should appear clearly that the inner occurrence of add is applied to two static integers and that the outer occurrence is applied to a static integer and a dynamic one.

Evaluation: Instantiating mkEx1 with Prim1_e for P yields a structure that we call Ex1_e. Applying Ex1_e.spec to 1000 yields 1110, which has the type Prim1_e.int_.

Partial evaluation: Instantiating mkEx1 with Prim1_pe for P yields a structure that we call Ex1_pe. Residualizing Ex1_pe.spec at type int' --> int' yields

```
LAM ("x1", APP (VAR "add", PAIR (INT 110,VAR "x1")))
```

which has the type Exp.exp.

Pretty-printing this residual code (providing "mkEx1'", "PRIMITIVE1", "spec", and "qint") yields the following more readable residual program:

```
functor mkEx1' (structure P : PRIMITIVE1)
= struct
    local open P
    in fun spec x1
            = add (qint 110, x1)
    end
  end
```

Compared to the source program, the inner addition has been simplified.

4.2   The power function, revisited

We now reconsider the canonical example of the power function. To this end, we need integers, booleans, decrement, multiplication, integer equality, and a recursion facility. Again, we use a quote function for integers, an unquote function for booleans, and a call-by-value fixed-point operator over functions of type int_ -> int_ for recursion. This paraphernalia is summarized in the signature of Figure 29.

The standard interpretation for evaluation is the obvious one and thus we omit it.

Figure 30 displays the non-standard interpretation for partial evaluation. The only remarkable point is the definition of fix, which embodies our unfolding strategy: if the exponent is known, then the call to fix should be unfolded; otherwise, it should be residualized.

The (parameterized) source program is displayed in Figure 31.

```
signature POWER
= sig
    type int_
    type bool_

    val qint : int -> int_
    val ubool : bool_ -> bool

    val dec : int_ -> int_
    val mul : int_ * int_ -> int_
    val eqi : int_ * int_ -> bool_
    val fix : ((int_ -> int_) -> int_ -> int_) -> int_ -> int_
end
```

Fig. 29. Signature of primitive operations for the power function

```
structure Primitive_power_pe : POWER
= struct
    local open Exp
    in type int_ = exp
       type bool_ = exp

       val qint = INT
       fun ubool (BOOL true) = true
         | ubool (BOOL false) = false
         | ubool e = nbe' bool e

       fun dec (INT i) = INT (i-1)
         | dec e = nbe' (int' --> int') (VAR "dec") e
       fun mul (INT i1, INT i2) = INT (i1 * i2)
         | mul (INT 0, _) = INT 0
         | mul (_, INT 0) = INT 0
         | mul (INT 1, e) = e
         | mul (e, INT 1) = e
         | mul e = nbe' (int' ** int' --> int') (VAR "mul") e
       fun eqi (INT i1, INT i2) = BOOL (i1=i2)
         | eqi e = nbe' (int' ** int' --> bool') (VAR "eqi") e
       fun fix f (x as (INT _))
             = Fix.fix f x   (* Fix.fix is a CBV fixed-point operator *)
         | fix f x
             = nbe' (((int' --> int') --> int' --> int')
                     --> int' --> int')
                    (VAR "fix") f x
    end
end
```

Fig. 30. Non-standard interpretation for the power function: partial evaluation

```
functor mkPower (structure P : POWER)
= struct
    local open P
    in fun power (x, n)
            = fix (fn loop => fn n => if ubool (eqi (n, qint 0))
                                      then qint 1
                                      else mul (x, loop (dec n))) n
    end
end
```

Fig. 31. Source program

Evaluation: Instantiating mkPower with a standard interpretation for P yields the usual power function.

Partial evaluation: Instantiating mkPower with Primitive_power_pe for P yields a structure that we call Power_pe.

```
structure Power_pe
= mkPower (structure P = Primitive_power_pe)
```

Let us specialize Power_pe.power with respect to its second parameter:

```
val power_d3 = let val power = Power_pe.power
                   val qint = Primitive_power_pe.qint
               in nbe (int' --> int') (fn x => power (x, qint 3))
               end
```

The exponent is static and thus all the calls to loop are unfolded. Also, to account for call-by-value, let expressions are inserted to name all intermediate function calls. Finally, in the base case, the primitive operator mul is given the opportunity to simplify a multiplication by 1. The result is identical to that obtained in the introduction to Section 4, page 395.

Let us specialize Power_pe.power with respect to its first parameter:

```
val power_8d = let val power = Power_pe.power
                   val qint = Primitive_power_pe.qint
               in nbe (int' --> int') (fn n => power (qint 8, n))
               end
```

The exponent is dynamic and thus the calls to loop are residualized. The residual code is thus essentially the same as the source code, modulo the facts that (1) let expressions are inserted to name all intermediate function calls, and (2) the literal 8 is inlined. The result is identical to that obtained in Section 3.2, page 393.

From the same source program, we thus have obtained the same results as in Section 3, where we considered two distinct binding-time annotated versions of power.

4.3   Summary and conclusion

Online type-directed partial evaluation extends offline type-directed partial evaluation by making the abstracted operators probe their operands for possible simplifications. As we pointed out elsewhere [16], this probing idea is partial-evaluation folklore.

In this section, we have pushed the online idea to its natural limit by making source programs completely closed: all variables are either local to the source program or they are declared through its parameters. Declaring recursive functions through fixed points has forced us to address their unfolding policy by guarding the call to each fixed-point operator, in a manner reminiscent of Schism's filters. (Of course, the same could be said of all the primitive operators that pattern match their operands.) More stylistically, specifying a programming-language interpreter as a functor parameterized by structures nicely matches the format of denotational semantics, i.e., domains, semantic algebras, and valuation functions [53], making type-directed partial evaluation a convenient and effective "semantic back-end."

In practice, divergence and code duplication are the main problems one must address when using type-directed partial evaluation:

- divergence is dealt with by guarding each fixed-point operator and possibly by using several distinct instances; and
- code duplication arises from conditional expressions and is dealt with by generalizing boolean types into the dynamic type bool'.

Turning to performance, one might wonder how much the online overhead penalizes type-directed partial evaluation. The answer is: less than one might think, since in our experience, an online type-directed partial evaluator is noticeably more efficient than an offline syntax-directed partial evaluator such as Similix [24].

5   Incremental type-directed partial evaluation

The goal of this section is to spell out the mechanics of incremental type-directed partial evaluation. We consider the following function super_power.

```
fun super_power (s3, s2, s1)
    = power (s3, power (s2, s1))
```

We specialize super_power with respect to s1 = 3. Then we specialize the result with respect to s2 = 2, obtaining the same result as if we had directly specialized super_power with respect to s1 = 3 and s2 = 2.

The source program: The source program is displayed in Figure 32. It uses the functor mkPower of Figure 31, page 399.

```
functor mkSuperPower_ddd (structure P : POWER)
= struct
    local structure Power = mkPower (structure P = P)
    in fun main (s3, s2, s1)
           = Power.power (s3, Power.power (s2, s1))
    end
  end
```

Fig. 32. Source program: mkSuperPower_ddd

```
structure SuperPower_ddd_pe
= mkSuperPower_ddd (structure P = Primitive_power_pe)
```

Fig. 33. Instantiation of mkSuperPower_ddd

```
functor mkSuperPower_dd3 (structure P : POWER)
= struct
    local open P
    in fun main (x0, x1)
           = let val r2 = mul (x1, x1)
                 val r3 = mul (x1, r2)
                 val r4 = fix (fn x5
                          => fn x6
                          => let val r7 = eqi (x6, qint 0)
                             in if ubool r7
                                then qint 1
                                else let val r8 = dec x6
                                         val r9 = x5 r8
                                     in mul (x0, r9)
                                     end
                             end)
             in r4 r3
             end
    end
  end
```

Fig. 34. Residual program: mkSuperPower_dd3

```
structure SuperPower_dd3_pe
= mkSuperPower_dd3 (structure P = Primitive_power_pe)
```

Fig. 35. Instantiation of mkSuperPower_dd3

```
functor mkSuperPower_d23 (structure P : POWER)
= struct
    local open P
    in fun main x1
            = let val r2 = mul (x1, x1)
                  val r3 = mul (x1, r2)
                  val r4 = mul (x1, r3)
                  val r5 = mul (x1, r4)
                  val r6 = mul (x1, r5)
                  val r7 = mul (x1, r6)
              in mul (x1, r7)
              end
    end
end
```

Fig. 36. Residual program: mkSuperPower_d23

First degree of specialization: In Figure 33, we instantiate mkSuperPower_ddd for partial evaluation. We then specialize the main function with respect to its third argument:

```
let val main = SuperPower_ddd_pe.main
    val qint = Primitive_power_pe.qint
in nbe (int' ** int' --> int') (fn (x, y) => main (x, y, qint 3))
end
```

The residual program is displayed in Figure 34. The inner occurrence of power has been specialized away, and the outer occurrence has been inlined in the residual program.

Second degree of specialization: In Figure 35, we instantiate mkSuperPower_dd3 for further partial evaluation. We then specialize the main function with respect to its second argument:

```
let val main = SuperPower_dd3_pe.main
    val qint = Primitive_power_pe.qint
in nbe (int' --> int') (fn x => main (x, qint 2))
end
```

The residual program is displayed in Figure 36. The remaining occurrence of power has been specialized away.

Both degrees of specialization at once: We would have obtained textually the same residual program as in Figure 36 by specializing the original main function with respect to both its static arguments:

```
let val main = SuperPower_ddd_pe.main
    val qint = Primitive_power_pe.qint
in nbe (int' --> int') (fn x => main (x, qint 2, qint 3))
end
```

6 Type-directed partial evaluation and the cogen approach

The question often arises how type-directed partial evaluation and the cogen approach compare. In this section, we situate type-directed partial evaluation within the cogen approach.

6.1 On normalization by evaluation

At the core of type-directed partial evaluation, the notion of static reduction matches the notion of evaluation in a functional language. This match also holds in a simply typed system, making it possible for it to ensure that static reduction will not go wrong.

Such a correspondence, however, does not hold in general. For example, it does not in the two-level functional languages Flemming and Hanne Nielson consider in their book [46]. These two-level languages have their own notions of binding times and of static reduction. For each of them, a dedicated binding-time analysis and the corresponding static reducer need to be studied [45, 48, 57].

In contrast, type-directed partial evaluation results from a deliberate effort to make static reduction and evaluation coincide. In a type-directed partial evaluator, static expressions are thus represented as native code (see Section 1.3). Therefore, static reduction takes place at native speed, and specialization using a type-directed partial evaluator can be quite efficient.

6.2 On type-directed partial evaluation

Type-directed partial evaluation builds on normalization by evaluation by introducing primitive operations, thus staging source programs into user-defined functions and primitive operators, as in Schism and Similix. Primitive operations are then instantiated either for evaluation or for partial evaluation. Specialization is still carried out by evaluation, with a binding-time discipline that still corresponds to the simply typed λ-calculus: static or dynamic base types, and static (but no dynamic) compound type constructors.

6.3 From traditional partial evaluation to the cogen approach

In a traditional partial evaluator, static values are represented symbolically and static reduction is carried out by symbolic evaluation. Therefore, specialization takes place with a certain interpretive overhead. Against this backdrop, the "cogen approach" was developed to represent static values natively.

Let us reconsider the partial-evaluation equation of Section 1.1.

$$\text{run PE } \langle p, \langle s, \_ \rangle \rangle = p_{\langle s, \_ \rangle}$$

Traditionally [40], a partial evaluator operates as an interpreter. However, both for expressiveness and for efficiency, modern partial evaluators such as ML-Mix [6], pgg [56], and Tempo [9] specialize any program p by first constructing a dedicated partial evaluator $PE_{\langle p, \_ \rangle}$ and then running $PE_{\langle p, \_ \rangle}$ on the static input.

$$\text{run } PE_{\langle p, \_ \rangle} \langle s, \_ \rangle = p_{\langle s, \_ \rangle}$$

Such dedicated partial evaluators are called "generating extensions." Generating extensions are constructed by a program traditionally named "cogen," and the overall approach is thus called "the cogen approach."

The cogen approach was developed for offline partial evaluators, and thus cogen usually operates on binding-time analyzed (i.e., two-level) source programs.

Let us assume a binding-time analysis that makes it possible to implement two-level terms as we have done in Section 1.3:

- static expressions are translated into syntactic constructs ($\overline{\lambda}$ into fn, etc.), giving rise to native values; and
- dynamic expressions are translated into constructors of residual syntax ($\underline{\lambda}$ into LAM, etc.).

The resulting two-level programs can then be compiled and run at native speed, just as with type-directed partial evaluation. Furthermore, if the binding-time analysis inserts binding-time coercions [36, 47], generating extensions have the same performance and produce the same residual programs as type-directed partial evaluation. This property has been verified in practice by Morten Rhiger and the author for Action Semantics [24] and also, independently, by Simon Helsen and Peter Thiemann [36].

6.4 A first example

Let us compare the cogen approach and type-directed partial evaluation on an example that does not require any binding-time coercion. Applying the cogen approach to the (static) identity function $\overline{\lambda}x.x$ yields the following generating extension.

```
let val x = Gensym.new "x"
in Exp.LAM (x, Exp.VAR x)
end
```

In comparison, residualizing the identity function at type $\alpha \rightarrow \alpha$ amounts to plugging it into a context induced by its type, i.e., passing it to the following function (that implements $\downarrow^{\alpha \rightarrow \alpha}$).

```
fn f => let val x = Gensym.new "x"
        in Exp.LAM (x, f (Exp.VAR x))
        end
```

Modulo some administrative reductions, the two approaches work identically here.

6.5   A second example

Let us compare the cogen approach and type-directed partial evaluation on an example that does require a binding-time coercion:

$$(\lambda f.\lambda g.f@(g@f))@(\lambda a.a)$$

g is dynamic, and therefore the context g@[·] has to be dynamic. $\lambda a.a$ flows both to the evaluation context [·]@(g@f) where it can be considered static, and to the context g@[·], where it must be considered dynamic. As illustrated in Jens Palsberg's chapter [47], the binding-time analysis can either classify $\lambda a.a$ as dynamic, since it will flow into a dynamic context, or classify it as static and coerce the dynamic context into a static one with the two-level eta-redex $\underline{\lambda}x.[·]\overline{@}x$.

Below, we can see that binding-time coercion by two-level eta-expansion is immaterial in type-directed partial evaluation, whereas it is an issue in the cogen approach.

Type-directed partial evaluation: Residualizing the term above at type $((\alpha \to \alpha) \to \alpha) \to \alpha$ yields the following optimal residual term.

$$\lambda g.g\underline{@}(\lambda x.x)$$

Cogen without binding-time improvement: Binding-time analysis without any coercion yields the following two-level term, where $\lambda a.a$ is dynamic.

$$(\overline{\lambda}f.\underline{\lambda}g.f\underline{@}(g@f))\overline{@}(\overline{\lambda}a.a)$$

And static reduction yields the following sub-optimal residual term.

$$\lambda g.(\underline{\lambda}a.a)\underline{@}(g\underline{@}(\underline{\lambda}a.a))$$

Cogen with binding-time improvement: Binding-time analysis with a coercion yields the following two-level term, where $\lambda a.a$ is static. (The coercion is put in a box, as an aid to the eye.)

$$(\overline{\lambda}f.\underline{\lambda}g.f\overline{@}(g\underline{@}(\boxed{\underline{\lambda}x.f\overline{@}x})))\overline{@}(\overline{\lambda}a.a)$$

And static reduction yields the same optimal result as type-directed partial evaluation:

$$\lambda g.g\underline{@}(\lambda x.x)$$

Modulo binding-time coercions, the two approaches thus work identically here.

6.6   Summary and conclusion

In their independent comparison between type-directed partial evaluation and the cogen approach [36], Simon Helsen and Peter Thiemann observe that both specializers yield equivalent results in comparable time in the presence of binding-time coercions. Now unlike in the cogen approach, type-directed partial evaluation does not involve creating a textual two-level program and compiling it. Nevertheless we believe that type-directed partial evaluation can be viewed as an instance of the cogen approach, where static reduction is carried out by evaluation. This instance is very simple, using a binding-time discipline that corresponds to the simply typed λ-calculus and does not necessitate explicit binding-time coercions.

This relationship between type-directed partial evaluation and the cogen approach is not accidental, as type-directed partial evaluation grew out of binding-time improvements [22, 23]. And indeed, as the reader can see, the equations defining binding-time coercions are the same ones as the equations defining type-directed partial evaluation (see Figure 2). These coercions can serve as an independent specialization mechanism because they implement a normalization function.

7   Conclusion and issues

Type-directed partial evaluation is still largely a topic under exploration. It stems from a normalization function operating on values instead of on symbolic expressions (i.e., annotated abstract-syntax trees), as is usual in traditional, syntax-directed partial evaluation. This normalization function in effect propagates constants and unfolds function calls. The user is left with deciding the policy of unfolding recursive function calls through the corresponding fixed-point operators. Otherwise, a type-directed partial evaluator provides essentially the same functionality as Lambda-Mix [39], though in a statically typed setting which makes much for its ease of use.

Type-directed partial evaluation was first developed in Scheme, and amounted to achieving specialization by Scheme evaluation [14–16]. Andrzej Filinski, and then Zhe Yang [59] and Morten Rhiger [49, 50] found how to express it in a Hindley-Milner type setting, i.e., in ML and in Haskell, thus achieving specialization by ML and Haskell evaluation. In addition, the Hindley-Milner typing system ensures that specialization will not go wrong. Then Kristoffer Rose expressed type-directed partial evaluation in Haskell using type classes [51] and Belmina Dzafic formalized it in Elf [27]. Andrzej Filinski, Zhe Yang, and Morten Rhiger also noticed that type-directed partial evaluation in ML could be made online by pattern matching over the residual abstract syntax. A more comprehensive review of related work is available elsewhere [16]. There, we distinguish between native and meta-level type-directed partial evaluation: a native implementation, such as the one presented here, uses an underlying evaluator, whereas a meta-level implementation uses an interpreter [1, 54]. This choice entails the usual tradeoff between flexibility and efficiency.

The most sizeable applications of type-directed partial evaluation so far involve the Futamura projections, type specialization, and run-time code generation [2, 17, 24, 25, 33, 34]. Having made type-directed partial evaluation online has improved its usability, but it is still limited because it only provides monovariant program-point specialization (as opposed to polyvariant program-point specialization as in Similix [41]) and does not handle inductive types very naturally.

An extended version of this chapter is available in the BRICS series [18].

Acknowledgements

Thanks to the organizers and to the participants of the summer school for a pleasant event, to Neil Jones, for his encouragement, and to the editors of this volume, especially Peter Thiemann, for their patience.

I am also grateful to Andrzej Filinski for several substantial rounds of critical comments; alas time was too short to address them all.

Finally, thanks are due to several participants of the BRICS Programming-Language Café (http://www.brics.dk/~danvy/PLC/): Belmina Dzafic, Daniel Damian, Niels O. Jensen, Lasse R. Nielsen, and Morten Rhiger, and also to Lars R. Clausen, Julia L. Lawall, Karoline Malmkjær, Eijiro Sumii, and Zhe Yang for their timely feedback.

References

1. Thorsten Altenkirch, Martin Hofmann, and Thomas Streicher. Categorical reconstruction of a reduction-free normalization proof. In David H. Pitt and David E. Rydeheard, editors, *Category Theory and Computer Science*, number 953 in LNCS, pages 182–199. Springer-Verlag, 1995.
2. Vincent Balat and Olivier Danvy. Strong normalization by type-directed partial evaluation and run-time code generation. In Xavier Leroy and Atsushi Ohori, editors, *Proceedings of the Second International Workshop on Types in Compilation*, number 1473 in LNCS, pages 240–252. Springer-Verlag, 1998.
3. Henk Barendregt. *The Lambda Calculus — Its Syntax and Semantics*. North-Holland, 1984.
4. Henk P. Barendregt. *Functional Programming and Lambda Calculus*, chapter 7, pages 321–364. Volume B of van Leeuwen [38], 1990.
5. Ulrich Berger and Helmut Schwichtenberg. An inverse of the evaluation functional for typed λ-calculus. In *Proceedings of the Sixth Annual IEEE Symposium on Logic in Computer Science*, pages 203–211. IEEE Computer Society Press, 1991.
6. Lars Birkedal and Morten Welinder. Partial evaluation of Standard ML. Master's thesis, DIKU, Computer Science Department, University of Copenhagen, August 1993. DIKU Rapport 93/22.
7. Anders Bondorf and Olivier Danvy. Automatic autoprojection of recursive equations with global variables and abstract data types. *Science of Computer Programming*, 16:151–195, 1991.
8. Anders Bondorf and Jens Palsberg. Generating action compilers by partial evaluation. *Journal of Functional Programming*, 6(2):269–298, 1996.

9. The COMPOSE Project. Effective partial evaluation: Principles and applications. Technical report, IRISA (www.irisa.fr), Campus Universitaire de Beaulieu, Rennes, France, January 1996 – May 1998. A selection of representative publications.

10. Charles Consel. New insights into partial evaluation: the Schism experiment. In Harald Ganzinger, editor, *Proceedings of the Second European Symposium on Programming*, number 300 in LNCS, pages 236–246. Springer-Verlag, 1988.

11. Charles Consel and Olivier Danvy. Tutorial notes on partial evaluation. In Susan L. Graham, editor, *Proceedings of the Twentieth Annual ACM Symposium on Principles of Programming Languages*, pages 493–501. ACM Press, 1993.

12. Thierry Coquand and Peter Dybjer. Intuitionistic model constructions and normalization proofs. *Mathematical Structures in Computer Science*, 7:75–94, 1997.

13. Djordje Čubrić, Peter Dybjer, and Philip Scott. Normalization and the Yoneda embedding. *Mathematical Structures in Computer Science*, 8:153–192, 1998.

14. Olivier Danvy. Type-directed partial evaluation. In Guy L. Steele Jr., editor, *Proceedings of the Twenty-Third Annual ACM Symposium on Principles of Programming Languages*, pages 242–257. ACM Press, 1996.

15. Olivier Danvy. Pragmatics of type-directed partial evaluation. In Olivier Danvy, Robert Glück, and Peter Thiemann, editors, *Partial Evaluation*, number 1110 in LNCS, pages 73–94. Springer-Verlag, 1996. Extended version available as the technical report BRICS RS-96-15.

16. Olivier Danvy. Online type-directed partial evaluation. In Masahiko Sato and Yoshihito Toyama, editors, *Proceedings of the Third Fuji International Symposium on Functional and Logic Programming*, pages 271–295. World Scientific, 1998. Extended version available as the technical report BRICS RS-97-53.

17. Olivier Danvy. A simple solution to type specialization. In Kim G. Larsen, Sven Skyum, and Glynn Winskel, editors, *Proceedings of the 25th International Colloquium on Automata, Languages, and Programming*, number 1443 in LNCS, pages 908–917. Springer-Verlag, 1998.

18. Olivier Danvy. Type-directed partial evaluation. Lecture Notes BRICS LN-98-3, Department of Computer Science, University of Aarhus, Aarhus, Denmark, December 1998. Extended version of the present lecture notes.

19. Olivier Danvy and Peter Dybjer, editors. *Preliminary Proceedings of the 1998 APPSEM Workshop on Normalization by Evaluation, NBE '98,* (Chalmers, Sweden, May 8–9, 1998), number NS-98-1 in BRICS Note Series, Department of Computer Science, University of Aarhus, May 1998.

20. Olivier Danvy and Andrzej Filinski. Abstracting control. In Mitchell Wand, editor, *Proceedings of the 1990 ACM Conference on Lisp and Functional Programming*, pages 151–160. ACM Press, 1990.

21. Olivier Danvy and Andrzej Filinski. Representing control, a study of the CPS transformation. *Mathematical Structures in Computer Science*, 2(4):361–391, December 1992.

22. Olivier Danvy, Karoline Malmkjær, and Jens Palsberg. The essence of eta-expansion in partial evaluation. *Lisp and Symbolic Computation*, 8(3):209–227, 1995.

23. Olivier Danvy, Karoline Malmkjær, and Jens Palsberg. Eta-expansion does The Trick. *ACM Transactions on Programming Languages and Systems*, 8(6):730–751, 1996.

24. Olivier Danvy and Morten Rhiger. Compiling actions by partial evaluation, revisited. Technical Report BRICS RS-98-13, Department of Computer Science, University of Aarhus, Aarhus, Denmark, June 1998.

25. Olivier Danvy and René Vestergaard. Semantics-based compiling: A case study in type-directed partial evaluation. In Herbert Kuchen and Doaitse Swierstra, editors, *Eighth International Symposium on Programming Language Implementation and Logic Programming*, number 1140 in LNCS, pages 182–197. Springer-Verlag, 1996. Extended version available as the technical report BRICS-RS-96-13.
26. Nachum Dershowitz and Jean-Pierre Jouannaud. *Rewrite Systems*, chapter 6, pages 243–320. Volume B of van Leeuwen [38], 1990.
27. Belmina Dzafic. Formalizing program transformations. Master's thesis, DAIMI, Department of Computer Science, University of Aarhus, Aarhus, Denmark, December 1998.
28. Andrzej Filinski. Representing monads. In Hans-J. Boehm, editor, *Proceedings of the Twenty-First Annual ACM Symposium on Principles of Programming Languages*, pages 446–457. ACM Press, 1994.
29. Andrzej Filinski. From normalization-by-evaluation to type-directed partial evaluation. In Danvy and Dybjer [19].
30. Andrzej Filinski. A semantic account of type-directed partial evaluation. In Gopalan Nadathur, editor, *International Conference on Principles and Practice of Declarative Programming*, LNCS. Springer-Verlag, 1999. To appear. Extended version available as the technical report BRICS RS-99-17.
31. Mayer Goldberg. Gödelization in the λ-calculus. Technical Report BRICS RS-95-38, Computer Science Department, Aarhus University, Aarhus, Denmark, July 1995.
32. Mayer Goldberg. *Recursive Application Survival in the λ-Calculus*. PhD thesis, Computer Science Department, Indiana University, Bloomington, Indiana, May 1996.
33. Bernd Grobauer. Types for proofs and programs. Progress report, BRICS PhD School, University of Aarhus. Available at http://www.brics.dk/~grobauer, June 1999.
34. William L. Harrison and Samuel N. Kamin. Modular compilers based on monads transformers. In Purush Iyer and Young il Choo, editors, *Proceedings of the IEEE International Conference on Computer Languages*, pages 122–131. IEEE Computer Society, 1998.
35. John Hatcliff and Olivier Danvy. A computational formalization for partial evaluation. *Mathematical Structures in Computer Science*, pages 507–541, 1997. Extended version available as the technical report BRICS RS-96-34.
36. Simon Helsen and Peter Thiemann. Two flavors of offline partial evaluation. In Jieh Hsiang and Atsushi Ohori, editors, *Advances in Computing Science - ASIAN'98*, number 1538 in LNCS, pages 188–205. Springer-Verlag, 1998.
37. Fritz Henglein. Dynamic typing: Syntax and proof theory. *Science of Computer Programming*, 22(3):197–230, 1993.
38. Jan van Leeuwen, managing editor. *Handbook of Theoretical Computer Science*. The MIT Press, 1990.
39. Neil D. Jones, Carsten K. Gomard, and Peter Sestoft. Partial evaluation for the lambda calculus. In John Hatcliff, Torben Mogensen and Peter Thiemann, editors, *DIKU 1998 International Summerschool on Partial Evaluation*, number 1706 in LNCS, pages 203–220. Springer-Verlag, 1999. This volume.
40. Neil D. Jones, Carsten K. Gomard, and Peter Sestoft. *Partial Evaluation and Automatic Program Generation*. Prentice Hall International Series in Computer Science. Prentice-Hall, 1993.

41. Jesper Jørgensen. Similix: A self-applicable partial evaluator for Scheme. In John Hatcliff, Torben Mogensen and Peter Thiemann, editors, *DIKU 1998 International Summerschool on Partial Evaluation*, number 1706 in LNCS, pages 83–107. Springer-Verlag, 1999. This volume.

42. Richard Kelsey, William Clinger, and Jonathan Rees, editors. Revised[5] report on the algorithmic language Scheme. *Higher-Order and Symbolic Computation*, 11(3):7–105, 1998. Also appears in ACM SIGPLAN Notices 33(9), September 1998.

43. Julia L. Lawall and Olivier Danvy. Continuation-based partial evaluation. In Carolyn L. Talcott, editor, *Proceedings of the 1994 ACM Conference on Lisp and Functional Programming*, LISP Pointers, Vol. VII, No. 3. ACM Press, 1994.

44. Robin Milner, Mads Tofte, Robert Harper, and David MacQueen. *The Definition of Standard ML (Revised)*. The MIT Press, 1997.

45. Eugenio Moggi. A categorical account of two-level languages. In Stephen Brookes and Michael Mislove, editors, *Proceedings of the 13th Annual Conference on Mathematical Foundations of Programming Semantics*, volume 6 of *Electronic Notes in Theoretical Computer Science*. Elsevier Science, 1997.

46. Flemming Nielson and Hanne Riis Nielson. *Two-Level Functional Languages*, volume 34 of *Cambridge Tracts in Theoretical Computer Science*. Cambridge University Press, 1992.

47. Jens Palsberg. Eta-redexes in partial evaluation. In John Hatcliff, Torben Mogensen and Peter Thiemann, editors, *DIKU 1998 International Summerschool on Partial Evaluation*, number 1706 in LNCS, pages 256–366. Springer-Verlag, 1999. This volume.

48. Jens Palsberg. Correctness of binding-time analysis. *Journal of Functional Programming*, 3(3):347–363, 1993.

49. Morten Rhiger. A study in higher-order programming languages. Master's thesis, DAIMI, Department of Computer Science, University of Aarhus, Aarhus, Denmark, December 1997.

50. Morten Rhiger. Deriving a statically typed type-directed partial evaluator. In Olivier Danvy, editor, *Proceedings of the ACM SIGPLAN Workshop on Partial Evaluation and Semantics-Based Program Manipulation*, pages 84-88, Technical report BRICS-NS-99-1, University of Aarhus, 1999.

51. Kristoffer Rose. Type-directed partial evaluation using type classes. In Danvy and Dybjer [19].

52. Erik Ruf. *Topics in Online Partial Evaluation*. PhD thesis, Stanford University, Stanford, California, February 1993. Technical report CSL-TR-93-563.

53. David A. Schmidt. *Denotational Semantics: A Methodology for Language Development*. Allyn and Bacon, Inc., 1986.

54. Tim Sheard. A type-directed, on-line, partial evaluator for a polymorphic language. In Charles Consel, editor, *Proceedings of the ACM SIGPLAN Symposium on Partial Evaluation and Semantics-Based Program Manipulation*, pages 22–35. ACM Press, 1997.

55. Guy L. Steele Jr. and Gerald J. Sussman. The art of the interpreter or, the modularity complex (parts zero, one, and two). AI Memo 453, Artificial Intelligence Laboratory, Massachusetts Institute of Technology, Cambridge, Massachusetts, May 1978.

56. Peter Thiemann. Aspects of the PGG system: Specialization for standard Scheme. In John Hatcliff, Torben Mogensen and Peter Thiemann, editors, *DIKU 1998 International Summerschool on Partial Evaluation*, number 1706 in LNCS, pages 411–431. Springer-Verlag, 1999. This volume.

57. Mitchell Wand. Specifying the correctness of binding-time analysis. *Journal of Functional Programming*, 3(32):365–387, 1993.
58. Daniel Weise, Roland Conybeare, Erik Ruf, and Scott Seligman. Automatic online partial evaluation. In John Hughes, editor, *Proceedings of the Fifth ACM Conference on Functional Programming and Computer Architecture*, number 523 in LNCS, pages 165–191. Springer-Verlag, 1991.
59. Zhe Yang. Encoding types in ML-like languages. In Paul Hudak and Christian Queinnec, editors, *Proceedings of the 1998 ACM SIGPLAN International Conference on Functional Programming*, pages 289–300. ACM Press, 1998. Extended version available as the technical report BRICS RS-98-9.

Aspects of the PGG System:
Specialization for Standard Scheme

Peter Thiemann

Institut für Informatik
Universität Freiburg, Germany
Email: thiemann@informatik.uni-freiburg.de

Abstract. PGG is an offline partial evaluation system for the full Scheme language, conforming to the current R5RS standard [12]. This exposition concentrates on two aspects of the system:
- specialization of higher-order primitives;
- specialization of operations that involve state.

The machinery for higher-order primitives enables the specialization of operations like `eval`, `call-with-current-continuation`, etc; specialization with state overcomes one of the major restrictions of traditional offline partial evaluators for functional languages. Both aspects require significant additions to the standard binding-time analysis for the lambda calculus, as well as to the specialization algorithm itself. We present an informal outline of the principles underlying the respective analyses and their associated specializers including motivating examples (parser generation and programming with message passing).

1 Introduction

Many specializers for higher-order programming languages suffer from severe restrictions. For example, primitive operations are often restricted to handle only first-order data and side-effects at specialization time are usually forbidden. We argue that these restrictions are arbitrary and show how to remove them.

In particular, we show how an augmented binding-time analysis in concert with a representation analysis not only removes the restriction of primitive operations to first-order types, but it also improves the efficiency of the specializer and it allows to specialize programs using `eval` without having to implement `eval`.

Furthermore, we show that a region and effect analysis provides the foundation of a binding-time analysis for a specializer that performs operations on a mutable state at specialization time.

In both instances, we simplify the presentation with respect to the actual implementation by using a simply-typed lambda calculus as the starting point for defining binding-time analyses and specializers. The appropriate starting point for Scheme would be a calculus with a partial type discipline (as in the implementation) [8], although soft typing [6] or dynamic typing [9] could provide a foundation for alternative designs.

The material presented in these notes is based on results from publications of the author, some in collaboration with Julia Lawall and Dirk Dussart [14, 20, 21, 24].

2 Primitive operations

All specializers permit using external functions or defined primitives. The idea of these primitives is that the specializer is not aware of their implementation, so it simply calls them or generates calls to them when needed. This is of course much more efficient than having the specializer interpret the primitives and it also supports a clean and modular style of programming: for example, in an interpreter the underlying semantic algebra may be defined using primitives of a specific signature or in a ray-tracer the primitive graphics functions may be defined in this manner.

Primitive operations also enjoy nice binding-time properties: even in systems using a monovariant binding-time analysis, primitives can be used in static as well as dynamic contexts, whereas a defined function can only be used in one binding-time context.

However, many specializers for functional languages restrict primitive operations to have first-order types. If an argument or the result has a higher-order type, the binding-time analysis classifies the whole operation as dynamic. This approach works well with arithmetic functions like +, *, ... and also with primitive graphics functions, but it fails with typical examples of higher-order functions like members of list processing libraries like `fold`, `map`, and `filter`, with function composition, control operators, and with semantic algebras in continuation-passing style.

We present an extension of a binding-time analysis for Scheme that permits the use of higher-order polymorphic primitive operations and constants. These operations have the same good binding-time properties as the traditional first-order primitive operations. The same extension enables to conservatively specialize programs containing operators like `call-with-current-continuation`, `call-with-values`[1], as well as reflective operators like `eval`.

2.1 Why the restriction?

The first question that we have to ask ourselves is: Why does the restriction to first-order primitive operations exist? To answer this question, we consider a denotational semantics for a two-level lambda calculus (or a specializer in a functional programming language) in Fig. 1. In a two-level lambda calculus, every construct (except a variable has a static variant (indicated by the superscript S) which is to be executed at specialization time and a dynamic variant (indicated by D) which generates code.

The domain of semantic values is a separated and lifted sum of the discrete CPO Int of integers, the continuous functions from values to values, the domain

---

[1] `call-with-values` calls a functions that returns multiple values

variables	Var	infinite set
two-level expressions	TLE	$::=$ Var $\mid c^S \mid \lambda^S x.\text{TLE} \mid \text{TLE}@^S\text{TLE} \mid$
		$c^D \mid \lambda^D x.\text{TLE} \mid \text{TLE}@^D\text{TLE}$
semantic values	Val	$= \text{Int} + (\text{Val} \to \text{Val}) + \text{RExpr} + \{\text{wrong}\}$
environments	Env	$= \text{Var} \to \text{Val}$
	$\mathcal{S}$	$: \text{TLE} \to \text{Env} \to \text{Val}$

$$\mathcal{S}[\![c^S]\!] = \lambda\rho.\text{In}_1(c)$$

$$\mathcal{S}[\![x]\!] = \lambda\rho.\rho(x)$$

$$\mathcal{S}[\![\lambda^S x.e]\!] = \lambda\rho.\text{In}_2(\lambda y.\mathcal{S}[\![e]\!]\rho[x \mapsto y])$$

$$\mathcal{S}[\![e_1@^S e_2]\!] = \lambda\rho.\ let\ y_1 = \mathcal{S}[\![e_1]\!]\rho\ in$$
$$let\ y_2 = \mathcal{S}[\![e_2]\!]\rho\ in$$
$$if\ y_1 = \bot \lor y_2 = \bot\ then\ \bot\ else$$
$$if\ y_1 \in \text{Val} \to \text{Val} \land y_2 \notin \{\text{wrong}\}$$
$$then\ (\downarrow_2(y_1))y_2$$
$$else\ \text{In}_4(\text{wrong})$$

$$\mathcal{S}[\![e_1 +^S e_2]\!] = \lambda\rho.\ let\ y_1 = \mathcal{S}[\![e_1]\!]\rho\ in$$
$$let\ y_2 = \mathcal{S}[\![e_2]\!]\rho\ in$$
$$if\ y_1 = \bot \lor y_2 = \bot\ then\ \bot\ else$$
$$if\ y_1 \in \text{Int} \land y_2 \in \text{Int}$$
$$then\ \text{In}_1(\downarrow_1(y_1) + \downarrow_1(y_2))$$
$$else\ \text{In}_4(\text{wrong})$$

$$\mathcal{S}[\![c^D]\!] = \lambda\rho.\text{In}_3(c)$$

$$\mathcal{S}[\![\lambda^D x.e]\!] = \lambda\rho.\text{In}_3(\underline{\text{lam}}\ \lambda z.\ let\ y = \mathcal{S}[\![e]\!]\rho[x \mapsto z]\ in$$
$$if\ y = \bot\ then\ \bot\ else$$
$$if\ y \in \text{RExpr}$$
$$then\ \downarrow_3(y)$$
$$else\ \text{In}_4(\text{wrong}))$$

$$\mathcal{S}[\![e_1@^D e_2]\!] = \lambda\rho.\ let\ y_1 = \mathcal{S}[\![e_1]\!]\rho\ in$$
$$let\ y_2 = \mathcal{S}[\![e_2]\!]\rho\ in$$
$$if\ y_1 = \bot \lor y_2 = \bot\ then\ \bot\ else$$
$$if\ y_1 \in \text{RExpr} \land y_2 \in \text{RExpr}$$
$$then\ \text{In}_3(\downarrow_3(y_1)\underline{@}\downarrow_3(y_2))$$
$$else\ \text{In}_4(\text{wrong})$$

$$\mathcal{S}[\![e_1 +^D e_2]\!] = \lambda\rho.\ let\ y_1 = \mathcal{S}[\![e_1]\!]\rho\ in$$
$$let\ y_2 = \mathcal{S}[\![e_2]\!]\rho\ in$$
$$if\ y_1 = \bot \lor y_2 = \bot\ then\ \bot\ else$$
$$if\ y_1 \in \text{RExpr} \land y_2 \in \text{RExpr}$$
$$then\ \text{In}_3(\downarrow_3(y_1)\underline{+}\downarrow_3(y_2))$$
$$else\ \text{In}_4(\text{wrong})$$

Fig. 1. Semantics of two-level lambda calculus

REExpr of residual expressions, and a one-element error domain. We are completely explicit in the use of the injection and projection operations into and out of the domain of semantic values. In_i is the injection into summand i (later on we use a symbolic name instead of the number i) and $\downarrow_i(x)$ is the corresponding projection. We write, for example, $x \in \text{REExpr}$ to test the membership of $x \in \text{Val}$ in the REExpr summand.

The domain REExpr of residual expressions is left unspecified. The reason is that the generation of residual binding expressions, such as lambda expressions and let expressions, requires a mechanism for name generation to create fresh identifiers for bound variables. Unfortunately, a satisfactory specification of name generation using elementary domain theoretic methods seems to be hard [16].

To evade this problem, we specify residual code generation using an abstract datatype REExpr with an interface inspired by higher-order abstract syntax [17]. This approach leads to a well-defined semantics and it simplifies the specification by moving the issue of name generation out of the specializer.

We assume the following interface for the REExpr datatype:

- <u>lam</u> : $(\text{Var} \rightarrow \text{REExpr}) \rightarrow \text{REExpr}$ builds a residual lambda expression. Due to the functional argument, the necessary generation of fresh variables is hidden in REExpr: one possible implementation simply applies the argument function to a freshly generated identifier.
- @,$\underline{+}$: $\text{REExpr} \times \text{REExpr} \rightarrow \text{REExpr}$, which we write infix, build an application expression or an addition expression.

Figure 2 defines a well-formedness criterion for two-level expressions in the form of a type system (a monomorphic version of the system considered by Dussart and others [7]). In the figure, $\leq$ refers to the standard ordering on binding times, $S < D$, and $\text{Top}(\tau)$ extracts the top-level binding-time annotation from τ, for example, $\text{Top}(\text{int}^D \rightarrow^S \text{int}^D) = S$. The intention of the typing rules is that the specialization of well-formed two-level expressions does not lead to a specialization-time error due to—for example—confusing int with $(\text{Val} \rightarrow \text{Val})$ or with REExpr.

Without delving into too many details we consider the case for the primitive operation $e_1 + e_2$. Binding-time-wise, the typing rule determines that the binding times of the arguments and of the result are equal and that this is also the execution time of the operation. Type-wise, the type system informs us that the arguments are either members of the summand int of Val (if $\beta = S$) or that they belong to summand REExpr (if $\beta = D$).

In the case of a first-order primitive operation, the top-level annotation β of the type int^β of an argument provides sufficient information to decide whether the argument is a number or a piece of code. However, if an argument g to a primitive operation had type $\text{int}^D \rightarrow^S \text{int}^D$ then the knowledge that g is a static function is not sufficient to conclude that its semantic value does not involve dealing with code. In fact, for an application of g in the implementation of the primitive, the result would be either a runtime error or a piece of code of type int^D. Sure enough, the implementation of the primitive does not know how to process a piece of code. This is in contrast to a dynamic argument where the

$$\begin{array}{ll}
\text{binding times} & \beta ::= S \mid D \qquad \text{with } S < D \\
\text{types} & \tau ::= \text{int}^\beta \mid \tau \to^\beta \tau
\end{array}$$

$$\text{int}^\beta \text{ wft}$$

$$\frac{\tau_2 \text{ wft} \qquad \tau_1 \text{ wft} \qquad \beta \le \text{Top}(\tau_2) \qquad \beta \le \text{Top}(\tau_1)}{\tau_2 \to^\beta \tau_1 \text{ wft}}$$

$$\text{(s-cst)} \qquad A \vdash c : \text{int}^\beta$$

$$\text{(s-var)} \qquad A\{x : \tau\} \vdash x : \tau$$

$$\text{(s-abs)} \quad \frac{A\{x : \tau_2\} \vdash e : \tau_1 \qquad \tau_2 \to^\beta \tau_1 \text{ wft}}{A \vdash \lambda^\beta x.e : \tau_2 \to^\beta \tau_1}$$

$$\text{(s-app)} \quad \frac{A \vdash e_1 : \tau_2 \to^\beta \tau_1 \qquad A \vdash e_2 : \tau_2}{A \vdash e_1 @^\beta e_2 : \tau_1}$$

$$\text{(s-add)} \quad \frac{A \vdash e_1 : \text{int}^\beta \qquad A \vdash e_2 : \text{int}^\beta}{A \vdash e_1 +^\beta e_2 : \text{int}^\beta}$$

Fig. 2. Type system for simple well-formedness

well-formedness enforces that it is pure code and the specializer only combines pieces of code.

For example, consider taking the function $\texttt{twice} : (\text{int} \to \text{int}) \to (\text{int} \to \text{int})$ as a primitive with two arguments. Suppose its definition

$$\texttt{twice} = \lambda f.\lambda x.f@(f@x)$$

has been compiled separately. Taking the function

$$g = \lambda^S x.x +^D y$$

for some dynamic variable y, we see that g has type $\text{int}^D \to^S \text{int}^D$. Now it is obvious that the two-level term $\texttt{twice}^S g \, 5$ does not make sense even though the top-level annotations of g's type and 5's type are ^{S}. Indeed, a short reduction sequence reveals that residual code and numbers would be confused:

$$\begin{aligned}
& \texttt{twice}^S g \, 5 \\
={} & (\lambda f.\lambda x.f@(f@x)) \, (\lambda^S x.x +^D y) \, 5 \\
\to{} & (\lambda^S x.x +^D y)@((\lambda^S x.x +^D y)@5) \\
\to{} & (\lambda^S x.x +^D y)@(5 +^D y)
\end{aligned}$$

Specializing $5 +^D y$ leads to an error.

$$\text{types}\quad \tau ::= \text{int}^{\beta\gamma} \mid \tau \to^{\beta\gamma} \tau$$

$$\frac{\beta = \gamma}{\text{int}^{\beta\gamma}\ \text{wft}}$$

$$\frac{\tau_2\ \text{wft}\quad \tau_1\ \text{wft}\quad \beta \leq \text{Top}(\tau_2)\quad \beta \leq \text{Top}(\tau_1)}{\text{TopG}(\tau_2) \leq \gamma \qquad \text{TopG}(\tau_1) \leq \gamma}{\tau_2 \to^{\beta\gamma} \tau_1\ \text{wft}}$$

(b-cst)
$$\frac{\text{int}^{\beta\gamma}\ \text{wft}}{A \vdash c : \text{int}^{\beta\gamma}}$$

(b-var)
$$A\{x : \tau\} \vdash x : \tau$$

(b-abs)
$$\frac{A\{x : \tau_2\} \vdash e : \tau_1 \quad \tau_2 \to^{\beta\gamma} \tau_1\ \text{wft}}{A \vdash \lambda^\beta x.e : \tau_2 \to^{\beta\gamma} \tau_1}$$

(b-app)
$$\frac{A \vdash e_1 : \tau_2 \to^{\beta\gamma} \tau_1 \quad A \vdash e_2 : \tau_2}{A \vdash e_1 @^\beta e_2 : \tau_1}$$

(b-prim)
$$\frac{A \vdash e_1 : \tau_1 \quad \ldots \quad A \vdash e_n : \tau_n}{\beta = \text{Top}(\tau_0) = \text{TopG}(\tau_0) = \ldots = \text{Top}(\tau_n) = \text{TopG}(\tau_n)}{A \vdash p^\beta(e_1 \ldots e_n) : \tau_0}$$

Fig. 3. Type system for homogeneous well-formedness

2.2 How to overcome it

Therefore, we need a way to express that the argument to a primitive is either a pure value that neither contains nor manipulates code or it is pure code. In the first case, the primitive can be applied safely, whereas in the other case code must be generated for its call and the arguments must be classified as dynamic. No other cases are admissible.

If any part of a value's type is dynamic then the construction of its semantic value involves In_3 and $\downarrow_3(x)$ operations and vice versa. We call a semantic value of the form $\text{In}_3(x)$ *completely dynamic*, and a semantic value is *completely static* if it is an element of the ideal $I \cong \text{Int} + I \to I \leq \text{Val}$ (where $I \leq \text{Val}$ means that there is an embedding-projection pair $I \to \text{Val}$). A value is *homogeneous* if it is either completely static or completely dynamic. Whereas completely dynamic is the same as dynamic, completely static is different from just static, as witnessed by the function type $\text{int}^D \to^S \text{int}^D$ which is static but not completely static.

To discover that part of a value's type is dynamic, we introduce a second annotation γ on two-level types that indicates the minimum binding time at which an expression of this type may be homogeneous. $\text{TopG}(\tau)$ extracts the top-level γ annotation from τ. Figure 3 shows the corresponding extension of the type semantic values $\text{Val} = \ldots + (\text{Var} \times \text{TLE} \times \text{Var}^* \times \text{Val}^*)$

$$S[\![\lambda^{SM} x.e]\!] = \lambda\rho.\text{In}_5(x, e, x_1 \ldots x_f, \rho(x_1) \ldots \rho(x_f))$$
$$\text{where } \{x_1, \ldots, x_f\} = \text{FV}(\lambda^{SM} x.e)$$
$$S[\![e_1 @^{SM} e_2]\!] = \lambda\rho.\text{let } y_1 = S[\![e_1]\!]\rho \text{ in}$$
$$\text{let } y_2 = S[\![e_2]\!]\rho \text{ in}$$
$$\text{if } y_1 = \bot \vee y_2 = \bot \text{ then } \bot \text{ else}$$
$$\text{if } y_1 \in \text{Var} \times \text{TLE} \times \text{Var}^* \times \text{Val}^* \wedge y_2 \notin \{\text{wrong}\}$$
$$\text{then } \text{let } (x, e, x_1 \ldots x_f, z_1 \ldots z_f) = \downarrow_5 (y_1) \text{ in}$$
$$S[\![e]\!][x_1 \mapsto z_1, \ldots, x_f \mapsto z_f, x \mapsto y_2]$$
$$\text{else } \text{In}_4(\text{wrong})$$

Fig. 4. Closure-passing semantics for two-level lambda calculus

system for well-formedness. It is easy to show that if $A \vdash e : \tau$ with $\text{Top}(\tau) = \beta$ and $\text{TopG}(\tau) = \gamma$ then $\beta \leq \gamma$. For higher-order primitives, it is sufficient to require that $\beta = \gamma$ for their argument and result types. This constraint forces all binding-time annotations in the type to be equal thus ensuring homogeneity. This approach works for higher-order primitives without requiring the programmer to declare their types.

For example, applying the primitive twice to the function $g : \text{int}^D \to^S \text{int}^D$ is not acceptable since g's type is not homogeneous. In forcing the type of g to be homogeneous, the type of g would become $\text{int}^D \to^D \text{int}^D$ and the application of twice would also become dynamic.

2.3   Representation analysis

The semantic issue is not the only problem that stops us from using primitives with higher-order types. Another issue is that many specializers [10] do not represent functions by functions internally (as suggested in Fig. 1), but instead they represent functions explicitly by closures. Figure 4 shows an excerpt of such a specializer. A static lambda abstraction constructs a closure that contains the abstracted variable, the body of the lambda, the list of free variables, and the list of their values. A static application constructs an environment from the contents of the closure and the argument and runs the body of the lambda.

Unfortunately, the specializer has to do so to perform *memoization*. Memoization enables folding by comparing different specialized program points for equality. Since the static data part of a program point may contain functions, functions must be represented so that they can be tested for intensional equality (which is the best approximation available, since extensional equality is undecidable). A simple representation for this purpose is a flat closure, which implements a lambda expression by a code pointer paired with a vector of free variables.

Apparently, this wreaks havoc on the business with higher-order primitives, because these expect their arguments to be functions, not closures. Fortunately, this is not the whole truth. First, only static functions require a representation as closures, this is not necessary for dynamic functions. Second, not every function is actually subject to a comparison during memoization. A simple closure analysis suffices to determine the set of functions that may be compared for equality and only those must assume a representation by closures. It is straightforward to express this analysis by another annotation on the types.

The annotation μ can be either M, for a memoized type, or N (not memoized) with $N < M$ and a program may contain *both* styles of lambda and application intermixed, those from Fig. 1 and those from Fig. 4. In addition, another mark ν recursively collects the memoization attributes. For integers, the representation is the same no matter whether they are memoized or not. Therefore, ν is always N for the integer type. The memoized representation of a function is clearly different from the standard one, so for a function type, we must have $\mu \leq \nu$. In addition, the ν annotation must be greater than or equal to the ν annotation on the argument and result types of the function. Figure 5 shows the revised well-formedness rules and the typing rules, with $\mathrm{TopM}(\tau)$ extracting the top-level μ annotation from τ and $\mathrm{TopN}(\tau)$ extracting the top-level ν annotation.

The first interesting rule in Fig. 5 is the (bsm-lam) rule: if the function is memoized then it must be represented by a closure. But in order to compare two closures the specializer must compare the values of their free variables, too. Therefore, if the function is memoized then so are all of its free variables, and so on, recursively. The M annotation on their types propagates to the definition and to all uses, changing representations as appropriate.

The next rule (bsm-app) uses the μ annotation on the function type to determine its representation and to choose the appropriate implementation of function application.

The rule (bsm-prim) states that if some argument or the result contains a memoized representation then the primitive operation must be dynamic. This constraint avoids any contact of a primitive operation with a memoized representation.

The (bsm-memo) rule type-checks a memoization point memo e. It ensures that the result of a memoization point is dynamic and that all free variables of e are in memoized representation.

2.4   Circles

Most specializers insert memoization points automatically on top of dynamic conditionals and dynamic lambdas [2, 5]. However, the introduction of M constraints due to rule (bsm-memo) might lead to changes in the binding-time assignment due to rule (bsm-prim). The last change may then lead to a reclassification of a conditional or a lambda from static to dynamic. This may lead to the introduction of new memoization points, which leads to more M constraints, and so on until every expression is annotated as dynamic.

While this unfortunate behavior is possible in theory, we have never encountered it in practice, not even the initial change of the binding time of a primitive.

$$\begin{array}{ll}
\text{memoization marks} & \mu, \nu ::= M \mid N \qquad N < M \\
\text{types} & \tau \quad ::= \text{int}^{\beta\gamma\mu\nu} \mid \tau \to^{\beta\gamma\mu\nu} \tau
\end{array}$$

$$\frac{\beta = \gamma \qquad \nu = N}{\text{int}^{\beta\gamma\mu\nu} \text{ wft}}$$

$$\frac{\tau_2 \text{ wft} \quad \tau_1 \text{ wft} \quad \beta \leq \text{Top}(\tau_2) \quad \beta \leq \text{Top}(\tau_1) \quad \mu \leq \nu}{\text{TopG}(\tau_2) \leq \gamma \quad \text{TopG}(\tau_1) \leq \gamma \quad \text{TopN}(\tau_2) \leq \nu \quad \text{TopN}(\tau_1) \leq \nu}{\tau_2 \to^{\beta\gamma\mu\nu} \tau_1 \text{ wft}}$$

(bsm-const)
$$\frac{\text{int}^{\beta\gamma\mu\nu} \text{ wft}}{A \vdash c : \text{int}^{\beta\gamma\mu\nu}}$$

(bsm-var)
$$A\{x : \tau\} \vdash x : \tau$$

(bsm-lam)
$$\frac{A\{x : \tau_2\} \vdash e : \tau_1 \qquad \tau_2 \to^{\beta\gamma\mu\nu} \tau_1 \text{ wft}}{\forall y \in \text{FV}(\lambda^{\beta\mu}x.e).\mu \leq \text{TopM}(A(y))}{A \vdash \lambda^{\beta\mu}x.e : \tau_2 \to^{\beta\gamma\mu\nu} \tau_1}$$

(bsm-app)
$$\frac{A \vdash e_1 : \tau_2 \to^{\beta\gamma\mu\nu} \tau_1 \qquad A \vdash e_2 : \tau_2}{A \vdash e_1 @^{\beta\mu} e_2 : \tau_1}$$

(bsm-prim)
$$\frac{\begin{array}{c} A \vdash e_1 : \tau_1 \quad \ldots \quad A \vdash e_n : \tau_n \\ \beta = \text{Top}(\tau_1) = \ldots = \text{Top}(\tau_n) = \text{Top}(\tau) \\ \beta = \text{TopG}(\tau_1) = \ldots = \text{TopG}(\tau_n) = \text{TopG}(\tau) \\ \exists i \in \{0, \ldots, n\}.\text{TopN}(\tau_i) = M \Rightarrow \beta = D \end{array}}{A \vdash p^\beta(e_1 \ldots e_n) : \tau_0}$$

(bsm-memo)
$$\frac{\begin{array}{c} A \vdash e : \tau \\ \text{Top}(\tau) = D \\ \forall y \in \text{FV}(e).\text{TopM}(A(y)) = M \end{array}}{A \vdash \text{memo } e : \tau}$$

Fig. 5. Representation typing

2.5   Extras

Homogeneous well-formedness and representation analysis give us exactly the information that we need to specialize the function `eval`. In Scheme [12], `eval` takes two arguments, an expression `e` and an environment that contains the bindings of the free variables in `e`. A typical argument is `(interaction-environment)`, the top-level environment which contains the bindings that are due to interactively loaded or typed-in definitions. For example,

```
(eval '(lambda (x) (foo x)) (interaction-environment))
```

returns a function that applies `foo` to its argument, drawing the binding of `foo` from `(interaction-environment)`.

Integrating `eval` into a programming language either requires the implementation of a full-blown interpreter which may be called recursively if the argument `e` contains `eval`. Or it must be possible to compile the expression `e` on-the-fly and execute it directly, like in runtime code generation.

Interestingly, specializing `(eval e env)` can be simpler than evaluating it, especially if the binding time of `e` is static and the binding time of the context is dynamic. In this case, the specializer computes the value of `e` statically. The value itself is another expression `e1` which `eval` should now evaluate. Since the binding time of the context is dynamic—which means that the value of `e1` is not needed at specialization time—it is not necessary to evaluate `e1` directly. Instead, the specializer defers the evaluation of `e1` to runtime simply by inserting `e1` in place of the `eval` expression in the specialized program. For this to work, `e1` must not refer to definitions in the program submitted to the specializer but only to bindings int he standard environment. This is left to the programmer since the set of free variables in the value of `e1` is undecidable.

If the binding times of the context and `e` are equal then the specializer either performs an `eval` operation at specialization time (if all binding times are static) or it generates an `eval` expression.

2.6   Example: parsers

As a typical example for using `eval` to advantage in specialization, we consider the generation of parsers from simple attribute grammars. An attribute grammar is determined by a set of productions where each production `production` has an associated semantic action (`action production`). This action is (the text of) a function that maps the attribute values of the symbols on the right side of the production to the attribute value of the left side of the production, i.e.,

```
(define (ll-parse symbol input)
  ...
  (let ((right-side-values
          ... (ll-parse symbol input) ...
          ... (right-side production)) ...)
    (values (apply (eval (action production)
```

```
                        (interaction-environment))
            right-side-values)
        input))
```

With static `left-symbol` and dynamic `input` we expect that `right-side-values` is a list with dynamic elements obtained by "mapping" `ll-parse` over the (static) right side of the selected production. Hence we have the above-mentioned situation that the argument of `eval` is the static (`action production`) and the context is dynamic.

Suppose now that the grammar contains

```
(E (F + E) '(lambda (x1 x2 x3) (+ x1 x3))
```

that is, a production $E \rightarrow F+E$ where the semantic action adds the values of F and E on the right side. The result is the value of E on the left side.

We expect the specializer to generate the following code:

```
(values (apply (lambda (x1 x2 x3) (+ x1 x3))
                (cons y1 (cons y2 (cons y3 '()))))
        input)
```

In fact, it generates slightly better code due to clever handling of `apply` [20]:

```
(values ((lambda (x1 x2 x3) (+ x1 x3))
            y1 y2 y3)
        input)
```

leaving the remaining reduction step to the compiler.

2.7   More operations

The specializer treats occurrences of `values` and `call-with-values` as primitive operations, too, the latter one with a higher-order type. Our typing rule provides for their correct specialization.

Similarly, `call-with-current-continuation` and other control operators specialize correctly when considered as higher-order primitives. Of course, they will only be executed if their arguments are completely static. There may be less conservative approaches to specialize control operators, but this is a topic for further research.

3   Specialization with state

A few specializers guarantee the correct handling of side effects. The common approach to do so is to classify all potentially side-effecting operations as dynamic. This way, the specializer only has to worry about keeping these operations in order and neither to discard nor to duplicate them [2, 5]. While this approach is safe and sound, and is even satisfactory for a lot of applications, it rules out some common programming styles for the static part of a computation. The subsequent subsections give some motivation followed by a brief account of the binding-time analysis and the specialization techniques involved in achieving specialization with higher-order functions and state.

```
;;; source program
(define-data object (object set get add))
;; record type with constructor "object"
;; and selectors "set", "get", "add"
(define (main)
  (let ((counter-class
          (lambda ()
            (let* ((slot 0)
                   (mset (lambda (x) (set! slot x) x))
                   (mget (lambda () slot))
                   (madd (lambda (x) (set! slot (+ slot x)) x)))
              (object mset mget madd )))))
    (let ((cnt (counter-class)))
      ((set cnt) 21)
      ((add cnt) ((get cnt)))
      ((get cnt)))))
```

Fig. 6. Specializing counter objects

3.1 Objects and message-passing

The first example is message-passing style in Scheme [1]: A typical representation for a class is a function that maps the initial values of the instance variables to a tuple of closures, the representation of an object. The closures represent the possible messages and they share the current values of the instance variables among them. These values are not accessible otherwise, they are local to the object. Sending a message to the object is implemented by calling one of the closures with appropriate arguments. Thus, we have an instance of a programming technique that employs higher-order functions with shared local state.

Figure 6 shows an example for this programming style. A conservative specializer like Similix [4] removes the message dispatch, but it does not perform any computation. In contrast, the methods presented in this article enable the specializer to perform all operations in this example.

3.2 Compilation of modular languages

For another example, suppose we want to compile an imperative language with modules in the style of Modula-2 by partial evaluation. Each module M has private variables, it imports a number of modules, and it has an initialization section and a body. Another module which imports M can call the body of M as a procedure with one parameter. Figure 7 shows some syntax.

Writing the interpreter is straightforward and we only consider the interpretation of module initialization. Obviously, each module should be initialized exactly once and all imported modules of M must be initialized before M because M's initialization code may call any of the imported modules. The typical

```
⟨module⟩ ::=
  (module ((⟨mod-ident⟩ ⟨var-ident⟩))
    (import ⟨mod-ident⟩*)
    (vars  ⟨var-ident⟩*)
    (init  ⟨cmd⟩)
    (body  ⟨cmd⟩ ⟨exp⟩)))

⟨cmd⟩ ::=
  (skip) |
  (assign ⟨var-ident⟩ ⟨exp⟩) |
  (seq    ⟨cmd⟩ ⟨cmd⟩) |
  (if     ⟨exp⟩ ⟨cmd⟩ ⟨cmd⟩) |
  (while  ⟨exp⟩ ⟨cmd⟩)

⟨exp⟩ ::=
  ⟨var-ident⟩ |
  ⟨constant⟩ |
  (plus   ⟨cmd⟩ ⟨cmd⟩) |
  (minus  ⟨cmd⟩ ⟨cmd⟩) |
  (=      ⟨cmd⟩ ⟨cmd⟩) |
  (call   ⟨mod-ident⟩ ⟨exp⟩)
```

Fig. 7. Syntax of a tiny modular language

implementation is to equip the code of each module with a flag which indicates whether or not the module has been initialized. The initialization procedure first tests the flag. If it is set then the module is already initialized and the procedure returns. Otherwise, it sets the flag, the initialization proceeds with the imported modules, and finally, it calls the initialization part of module M. This corresponds to a depth-first traversal of the module dependency graph. Of course, we would like the compiler to do the traversal for us and just generate the initialization code as indicated, so that there is no flag manipulation in the compiled code.

Here is an illustrative sample of the initialization section of the code following the informal outline above.

```
(define (initialize module)
  (let ((done (mod->flag module)))
    (if (not (cell-ref done))
        (begin
          (cell-set! done #t)
          (let loop ((mods (mod->dependencies module)))
            (if (null? mods)
                (exec-cmd (mod->init module) (mod->store module))
                (begin
                  (initialize (car mods))
```

```
(loop (cdr mods)))))))))
```

If we use one of the conservative specializers mentioned above, the compiled code performs the traversal of the module graph at runtime. Our specializer with state performs the traversal at specialization time.

3.3   Binding-time aspects

We consider the following slightly extended language of two-level expressions.

$$\text{TLE} ::= \text{Var} \mid \lambda^S \text{Var}.\text{TLE} \mid \text{TLE@}^S\text{TLE} \mid \text{ref}^S \text{ TLE} \mid \,!^S\text{TLE} \mid \text{TLE} :=^S \text{TLE} \mid$$
$$\lambda^D \text{Var}.\text{TLE} \mid \text{TLE@}^D\text{TLE} \mid \text{ref}^D \text{ TLE} \mid \,!^D\text{TLE} \mid \text{TLE} :=^D \text{TLE}$$

The constructs ref, !, and := have the usual ML-style interpretation.

The binding-time analysis is based on an effect system [11, 15, 18, 25]. An effect system infers not just the type of an expression it also infers which parts (regions) of the store may be read from or written to during evaluation of the expression. Therefore, the type of a mutable memory cell—a reference—includes a *region annotation* which determines the part of the store that the reference lives in. In addition, every function type carries an *effect annotation* which determines the latent effect that occurs when the function is eventually called. Formally, we have

- region variables ρ drawn from an infinite set RegVar;
- effects ϵ which are subsets of $\{\text{init}(\rho), \text{read}(\rho), \text{write}(\rho) \mid \rho \in \text{RegVar}\}$; and
- region-annotated types generated by the grammar

$$\theta ::= \text{int} \mid \text{ref}_\rho \, \theta \mid \theta \xrightarrow{\epsilon} \theta$$

Here, int is a representative base type, $\text{ref}_\rho \, \theta$ is the type of references to values of type θ allocated in region ρ, and $\theta_2 \xrightarrow{\epsilon} \theta_1$ is the type of functions that map values of type θ_2 to values of type θ_1 with latent effect ϵ. An effect can contain $\text{init}(\rho)$ for allocating in region ρ, $\text{read}(\rho)$ for reading from region ρ, and $\text{write}(\rho)$ for writing into region ρ. The function frv extracts the set of free region variables out of effects, types, and type assumptions.

On top of this type language we add binding-time annotations. Each region ρ has a particular binding time $B(\rho)$ given by the binding-time assumption $B : \text{RegVar} \rightarrow \{S, D\}$. This binding time indicates when a particular region is allocated: if it is S then the region exists only at specialization time, otherwise it exists only at runtime of the specialized program. Reference types and function types must be well-formed, that is, a dynamic reference cannot point to a static value and the binding time of a reference must be identical to the binding time of the region of the reference. The first constraint on the annotation of a function type is standard: the binding times of the argument and of the result must be greater than or equal to the binding time of the function. In addition, well-formedness ensures that a dynamic function never has an effect on a static region. This leads to the following definition of well-formed binding-time annotated types:

$$B \vdash \text{int}^\beta \text{ wft}$$

$$\frac{B \vdash \theta \text{ wft} \quad \beta \leq \text{Top}(\theta) \quad B(\rho) = \beta}{B \vdash \text{ref}_\rho^\beta \ \theta \text{ wft}}$$

$$\frac{B \vdash \theta_1 \text{ wft} \quad B \vdash \theta_2 \text{ wft} \quad \beta \leq \text{Top}(\theta_1) \quad \beta \leq \text{Top}(\theta_2) \quad \forall \rho \in \text{frv}(\epsilon).\beta \leq B(\rho)}{B \vdash \theta_1 \overset{\epsilon}{\to}^\beta \theta_2 \text{ wft}}$$

Fig. 8. Well-formedness rules for binding-time annotated types

Definition 1. θ *is a well-formed binding-time annotated type with respect to binding-time assumption B if $B \vdash \theta$ wft can be derived using the rules in Fig. 8.*

With the definition of well-formedness in the back, the typing rules for a binding-time annotated language are straightforward (see Fig. 9). They derive the judgement $A, B \vdash e : \theta, \epsilon$ where A is the type assumption, B the binding-time assumption, e a two-level expression, θ a binding-time annotated type, and ϵ an effect.

The rule (br-var) is standard. The rule (br-abs) is also standard except for the statement of the well-formedness constraint on the newly formed function type. The rule (br-app) is again standard, it only collects the effects of the evaluation of the subexpressions, adds the latent effect of the function, and matches the binding time of the function with the binding-time annotation on the application. The rules (br-ref), (br-deref), and (br-assn) deal with the actual operations on references. They also collect the effects of the evaluation of the subexpressions, add their own effect, and make sure that their binding-time annotation is identical to that on the reference type. The creation of a reference enforces the well-formedness condition on the newly formed reference type and hence that the binding time of its region matches the binding time of the operation.

The subeffecting rule (br-esub) is important in effect systems. It ensures that different functions that may flow together can have the same type, including the latent effect.

The rule (br-mask) performs effect masking. Whenever a region is mentioned in the effect of an expression, but neither occurs in the environment nor in the return type, then this region is local to the evaluation of the expression. In consequence, it can be masked out of the expression's effect. This rule is important for the binding-time analysis because it avoids to classify regions that are local to a dynamic lambda as dynamic. The idea is that as much as possible of the effect of a lambda's body is masked away using the (br-mask) rule because any region that ends up in the latent effect of a function type that becomes dynamic in the end, becomes dynamic, too.

The rules as shown constitute a logical specification of a binding-time analysis. To obtain an algorithm, roughly, we construct a syntactic specification by combining every rule with a use of the (br-esub) rule and by restricting the (br-mask) rule to the body of every lambda, as explained above. The syntactic

$$\text{(br-var)} \quad \frac{B \vdash A \text{ wft} \quad x : \theta \text{ in } A}{A, B \vdash x : \theta, \emptyset}$$

$$\text{(br-abs)} \quad \frac{A[x \mapsto \theta_1], B \vdash e : \theta_2, \epsilon \quad B \vdash \theta_1 \xrightarrow{\epsilon^\beta} \theta_2 \text{ wft}}{A, B \vdash \lambda^\beta x.e : \theta_1 \xrightarrow{\epsilon^\beta} \theta_2, \emptyset}$$

$$\text{(br-app)} \quad \frac{A, B \vdash e_1 : \theta_2 \xrightarrow{\epsilon^\beta} \theta_1, \epsilon_1 \quad A, B \vdash e_2 : \theta_2, \epsilon_2}{A, B \vdash e_1 @^\beta e_2 : \theta_1, \epsilon \cup \epsilon_1 \cup \epsilon_2}$$

$$\text{(br-ref)} \quad \frac{A, B \vdash e : \theta, \epsilon \quad B \vdash \text{ref}_\rho^\beta \theta \text{ wft}}{A, B \vdash \text{ref}^\beta e : \text{ref}_\rho^\beta \theta, \epsilon \cup \{\text{init}(\rho)\}}$$

$$\text{(br-deref)} \quad \frac{A, B \vdash e : \text{ref}_\rho^\beta \theta, \epsilon}{A, B \vdash \,!^\beta e : \theta, \epsilon \cup \{\text{read}(\rho)\}}$$

$$\text{(br-assn)} \quad \frac{A, B \vdash e_1 : \text{ref}_\rho^\beta \theta, \epsilon_1 \quad A, B \vdash e_2 : \theta, \epsilon_2}{A, B \vdash e_1 :=^\beta e_2 : \theta, \epsilon_1 \cup \epsilon_2 \cup \{\text{write}(\rho)\}}$$

$$\text{(br-esub)} \quad \frac{A, B \vdash e : \theta, \epsilon}{A, B \vdash e : \theta, \epsilon'} \, \epsilon \subseteq \epsilon'$$

$$\text{(br-mask)} \quad \frac{A, B[\rho \mapsto \beta] \vdash e : \theta, \epsilon \qquad \rho \in \text{frv}(\epsilon) \quad \rho \notin \text{frv}(A) \cup \text{frv}(\theta) \quad \epsilon' = \epsilon \setminus \{\rho\}}{A, B \vdash e : \theta, \epsilon'}$$

Fig. 9. Decorated region inference

specification gives rise to an inference algorithm for monomorphic region and effect information that runs in polynomial time ($O(n^4)$ where n is the size of the input program). A second pass computes the values of the binding-time annotations. This pass runs in time linear in the size of the program. In practice, the overall behavior is linear in n. Elsewhere [24], we give a detailed description of this algorithm.

Example Consider the expression

$$\lambda z.(\lambda f. \,!f@z)@(\text{ref } \lambda y.y)$$

The binding-time analysis of a specializer like Similix [4] would classify the operations on references as dynamic. Hence the contents of the reference must be dynamic, too. In the resulting two-level expression everything except the redex $(\lambda f....)@...$ is annotated as dynamic:

$$\lambda^D z.(\lambda^S f. \,!^D f@^D z)@^S(\text{ref}^D \lambda^D y.y)$$

Running the specializer on this two-level expression yields

$$\lambda z.\text{let } f = \text{ref } \lambda y.y \text{ in } !f@z$$

which desugars to the original expression.

In contrast, the analysis presented in this section determines that the reference ref $\lambda y.y$ is local to the outermost lambda abstraction. Consequently, it classifies the reference as static. Therefore it can assign a static binding time to the contents of the reference, too. The result is:

$$\lambda^D z.(\lambda^S f. \, !^S f @^S z) @^S (\mathrm{ref}^S \, \lambda^S y.y)$$

Running the specializer on this two-level expression yields

$$\lambda z.z$$

which is clearly an optimized version of the original expression.

3.4 Specialization

The specializer is based on a continuation-passing and store-passing style semantics. This semantics determines the interpretation of the static constructs. The interpretation of the dynamic constructs specifies the generation of residual code. The design of this part of the interpretation implies the definition of the well-formedness criterion given above.

The following domains are used in the specializer.

$$
\begin{array}{rl}
\mathrm{Comp} & = \mathrm{Cont} \to \mathrm{Store} \to \mathrm{Val} \\
k \in \mathrm{Cont} & = \mathrm{Val} \to \mathrm{Store} \to \mathrm{Val} \\
\rho \in \mathrm{Env} & = \mathrm{Var} \to \mathrm{Val} \\
y \in \mathrm{Val} & = \mathrm{Int} + \mathrm{Loc} + \mathrm{RExpr} + (\mathrm{Val} \to \mathrm{Comp}) + \{\mathrm{wrong}\} \\
\sigma \in \mathrm{Store} & = \mathrm{Loc} \to (\mathrm{Val} \oplus \{\mathrm{unused}\}_\perp) \\
\mathrm{Int} & = \text{set of integers} \\
\mathrm{Loc} & = \text{unspecified infinite set of store locations} \\
\mathrm{RExpr} & = \text{unspecified domain of residual expressions}
\end{array}
$$

As standard in continuation semantics with store, a *computation* of type Comp is a function that maps a continuation and a store to a semantic value, the type of final answers. A *continuation* $k \in \mathrm{Cont}$ maps a value and a store to a final answer. A *semantic value* has type Val and it is either a number, a store location (a heap address), a residual expression, a function that maps a value to a computation, or an error. An *environment* ρ is a finite mapping from variables to semantic values and a *store* σ is a finite mapping from store locations to semantic values.

Of course, we have to extend the interface to RExpr to cover the new syntactic constructs.

- <u>let</u> : RExpr × (Var → RExpr) → RExpr builds a residual let-expression. Roughly, <u>let</u> $(e_1, \lambda x.e_2)$ can be thought of as building "let $x = e_1$ in e_2".
- := : RExpr × RExpr → RExpr, which we write infix, creates an assignment expression and <u>ref</u>, ! : RExpr → RExpr create a reference and a dereference expression.

$$\mathcal{S} : \text{Expr} \to \text{Env} \to \text{Comp}$$

$$\mathcal{S}[\![\lambda x.e]\!] = \lambda\rho.\lambda k.\lambda\sigma.(\lambda y.\mathcal{S}[\![e]\!]\rho[y/x])\sigma$$

$$\mathcal{S}[\![e_1@e_2]\!] = \lambda\rho.\lambda k.\lambda\sigma.\mathcal{S}[\![e_1]\!]\rho(\lambda f.\lambda\sigma.\mathcal{S}[\![e_2]\!]\rho(\lambda a.\lambda\sigma.fak\sigma)\sigma)\sigma$$

$$\mathcal{S}[\![\text{ref } e]\!] = \lambda\rho.\lambda k.\lambda\sigma.\mathcal{S}[\![e]\!]\rho(\lambda y.\lambda\sigma'.k\alpha(\sigma'[\alpha \mapsto y]))\sigma$$
$$\text{where } \sigma'\alpha = \text{unused}$$

$$\mathcal{S}[\![\ !e]\!] = \lambda\rho.\lambda k.\lambda\sigma.\mathcal{S}[\![e]\!]\rho(\lambda\alpha.\lambda\sigma'.k(\sigma'\alpha)\sigma)\sigma$$

$$\mathcal{S}[\![e_1 := e_2]\!] = \lambda\rho.\lambda k.\lambda\sigma.\mathcal{S}[\![e_1]\!]\rho(\lambda\alpha.\lambda\sigma.\mathcal{S}[\![e_2]\!]\rho(\lambda y.\lambda\sigma'.ky(\sigma'[\alpha \mapsto y]))\sigma)\sigma$$

$$\mathcal{S}[\![\lambda^D x.e]\!] = \lambda\rho.\lambda k.\lambda\sigma'.\underline{\text{let}}\ (\underline{\text{lam}}\ \lambda y.\mathcal{S}[\![e]\!]\rho[n/y](\lambda y.\lambda\sigma'.y)\sigma_{\text{empty}}, \lambda n.kn\sigma')$$

$$\mathcal{S}[\![e_1@^D e_2]\!] = \lambda\rho.\lambda k.\lambda\sigma.\,\mathcal{S}[\![e_1]\!]\rho(\lambda y_1.\lambda\sigma.$$
$$\mathcal{S}[\![e_2]\!]\rho(\lambda y_2.\lambda\sigma'.\underline{\text{let}}\ (y_1@y_2, \lambda n.kn\sigma'))\sigma)\sigma$$

$$\mathcal{S}[\![\text{ref}^D\ e]\!] = \lambda\rho.\lambda k.\lambda\sigma.\mathcal{S}[\![e]\!]\rho(\lambda y.\lambda\sigma'.\underline{\text{let}}\ (\underline{\text{ref}}\ y, \lambda n.kn\sigma'))\sigma$$

$$\mathcal{S}[\![\ !^D e]\!] = \lambda\rho.\lambda k.\lambda\sigma.\mathcal{S}[\![e]\!]\rho(\lambda y.\lambda\sigma'.\underline{\text{let}}\ (!y, \lambda n.kn\sigma'))\sigma$$

$$\mathcal{S}[\![e_1 :=^D e_2]\!] = \lambda\rho.\lambda k.\lambda\sigma.\,\mathcal{S}[\![e_1]\!]\rho(\lambda y_1.\lambda\sigma.$$
$$\mathcal{S}[\![e_2]\!]\rho(\lambda y_2.\lambda\sigma'.\underline{\text{let}}\ (y_1 := y_2, \lambda n.kn\sigma'))\sigma)\sigma$$

Fig. 10. Specializer using continuation-passing and store-passing

Figure 10 shows the specification of the specializer. We look at some of the defining equations in more detail. This time, we are omitting the injections and projections to avoid clutter and to save some space.

The specialization of $\lambda^D x.e$ proceeds as follows: after taking the environment, the continuation, and the store as parameters, the specializer generates code for the lambda by specializing the body with respect to an empty continuation $(\lambda y.\lambda\sigma'.y)$ and an empty store σ_{empty}. The specializer binds the resulting lambda expression to a new identifier and passes this identifier as the specialized value of the lambda to the continuation k.

Why is it correct to specialize the body with respect to the empty store? First, recall that the store passed by the specializer is the specialization-time part of the store, the *static store*. The remaining *dynamic store* is not modeled at specialization time. The specializer only guarantees that not to discard, duplicate, or reorder operations that potentially depend on the dynamic store—or modify it. Second, what static store should we use to specialize the body of a dynamic lambda? At least one call-site for this specialized lambda must be unknown: otherwise the binding-time analysis would have classified it as static. But if one call-site is unknown we cannot determine the static store at the call-site, hence it is impossible to conjure up a non-empty static store for the body of the lambda. Third, this restriction corresponds to the specification of the binding-time analysis. The latter states that a dynamic lambda should not have an effect on a static region. Since our effect system enforces this restriction, the dynamic lambda can only affect the dynamic store. Therefore, the specialization of the body neither depends on nor modifies data in the static store, which may be empty in consequence. At the end of the specialization of the body, the empty continuation $(\lambda y.\lambda\sigma'.y)$ discards the final static store. This is again correct, since the (br-mask) rule of the effect system guarantees that the context does not depend on the static results computed in the body of the lambda.

Abstracting the newly generated lambda in a let merely avoids the duplication of generated code. It is not required for the correctness of the specializer because the evaluation of a lambda expression does not have an observable effect for the context. So it actually does not matter whether it is duplicated or discarded.

The specialization of a dynamic application $e_1 @^D e_2$ is a little bit more delicate, because the function e_1 might have a latent effect. In that case it is vital that the application appears in the generated code exactly once. Here is how: The specializer first processes the function part e_1, then the argument part e_2, and finally it generates the residual application. By wrapping the application in a let expression the specializer guarantees that the application appears in the residual code exactly once and that it is evaluated before any computation from the context of the application takes place. Inserting the let on-the-fly makes sure that the generated application appears directly at the correct place.

The same let insertion method applies to the definitively side-effecting constructs $ref^D e$, $!^D e$, and $e_1 :=^D e_2$. Each of them specializes their arguments and then inserts a let to name the dynamic result of the operation. The rationale for so doing is identical to that for the application.

3.5 Discussion

The above style of writing a specializer is strongly reminiscent of continuation-based partial evaluation [3]. However, its treatment of let expressions and the actual strategy of inserting them are subtly different. Lawall and Thiemann [14] explain and prove correct the method outlined above.

Another point worth mentioning is the connection to continuation-based partial evaluation in direct style [13]. In that work, Lawall and Danvy propose to write the specializer in direct style and to perform context manipulations using control operators. It turns out that we can also rephrase specialization with continuations and store in direct style with control operators (in fact, the PGG system is implemented in this way). However, it is vital to choose the correct extension of the control operators with respect to the store handling. Simple-minded use of the operators is incorrect in the presence of a store [22].

4 Conclusion

We have discussed two aspects of the PGG system that overcome traditional limitations of offline partial evaluation. We have explained the origin of the restriction to first-order primitives and have shown a notion of homogeneity that replaces the first-order requirement. The resulting system is very natural in practice. Despite the apparent complexity, the implemented analysis is not significantly slower than just the binding-time analysis. The original motivation for implementing the extended analysis was the desire to handle specialization of `eval` correctly.

The other aspect is specialization of higher-order languages with state. We have found that—again despite the apparent complexity of the analysis—the system is well-behaved in practice and produces the expected results. One might argue that a region and effect analysis must be polymorphic to yield reasonable results, but in the examples that we have investigated so far the monomorphic analysis turned out to be sufficient to achieve satisfactory results.

These two extension are orthogonal as witnessed by our implementation in the system. The only tricky point is to come up with a suitable memoized representation for references, which is implemented in a similar way as outlined elsewhere for functions and algebraic datatypes [19].

The PGG system [23] is available for anonymous ftp at ftp://ftp.informatik.uni-tuebingen.de/pub/PU/thiemann/software/pgg/. The distribution contains the examples mentioned in Sections 2.6, 3.1, and 3.2.

References

1. Harold Abelson, Gerald Jay Sussman, and Julie Sussman. *Structure and Interpretation of Computer Programs*. MIT Press, Cambridge, Mass., second edition, 1996.
2. Anders Bondorf. Automatic autoprojection of higher order recursive equations. *Science of Computer Programming*, 17:3–34, 1991.
3. Anders Bondorf. Improving binding times without explicit CPS-conversion. In *Proc. 1992 ACM Conference on Lisp and Functional Programming*, pages 1–10, San Francisco, California, USA, June 1992.
4. Anders Bondorf. *Similix 5.0 Manual*. DIKU, University of Copenhagen, May 1993.
5. Anders Bondorf and Olivier Danvy. Automatic autoprojection of recursive equations with global variables and abstract data types. *Science of Computer Programming*, 16(2):151–195, 1991.
6. Robert Cartwright and Mike Fagan. Soft typing. In *Proc. Conference on Programming Language Design and Implementation '91*, pages 278–, Toronto, June 1991. ACM.
7. Dirk Dussart, Fritz Henglein, and Christian Mossin. Polymorphic recursion and subtype qualifications: Polymorphic binding-time analysis in polynomial time. In Alan Mycroft, editor, *Proc. International Static Analysis Symposium, SAS'95*, volume 983 of *Lecture Notes in Computer Science*, pages 118–136, Glasgow, Scotland, September 1995. Springer-Verlag.
8. Carsten K. Gomard. Partial type inference for untyped functional programs. In *Proc. 1990 ACM Conference on Lisp and Functional Programming*, pages 282–287, Nice, France, 1990. ACM Press.
9. Fritz Henglein. Dynamic typing: Syntax and proof theory. *Science of Computer Programming*, 22:197–230, 1994.
10. Neil D. Jones, Carsten K. Gomard, and Peter Sestoft. *Partial Evaluation and Automatic Program Generation*. Prentice-Hall, 1993.
11. Pierre Jouvelot and David K. Gifford. Algebraic reconstruction of types and effects. In *Proc. 18th Annual ACM Symposium on Principles of Programming Languages*, pages 303–310, Orlando, Florida, January 1991. ACM Press.

12. Richard Kelsey, William Clinger, and Jonathan Rees. Revised[5] report on the algorithmic language scheme. Technical report, 1998.
13. Julia L. Lawall and Olivier Danvy. Continuation-based partial evaluation. In *Proc. 1994 ACM Conference on Lisp and Functional Programming*, pages 227–238, Orlando, Florida, USA, June 1994. ACM Press.
14. Julia L. Lawall and Peter Thiemann. Sound specialization in the presence of computational effects. In *Proc. Theoretical Aspects of Computer Software*, volume 1281 of *Lecture Notes in Computer Science*, pages 165–190, Sendai, Japan, September 1997. Springer-Verlag.
15. John M. Lucassen and David K. Gifford. Polymorphic effect systems. In *Proc. 15th Annual ACM Symposium on Principles of Programming Languages*, pages 47–57, San Diego, California, January 1988. ACM Press.
16. Eugenio Moggi. Functor categories and two-level languages. In M. Nivat and A. Arnold, editors, *Foundations of Software Science and Computation Structures, FoSSaCS'98*, Lecture Notes in Computer Science, Lisbon, Portugal, April 1998.
17. Frank Pfenning and Conal Elliott. Higher-order abstract syntax. In *Proc. Conference on Programming Language Design and Implementation '88*, pages 199–208, Atlanta, July 1988. ACM.
18. Jean-Pierre Talpin and Pierre Jouvelot. Polymorphic type, region and effect inference. *Journal of Functional Programming*, 2(3):245–272, July 1992.
19. Peter Thiemann. Implementing memoization for partial evaluation. In Herbert Kuchen and Doaitse Swierstra, editors, *International Symposium on Programming Languages, Implementations, Logics and Programs (PLILP '96)*, volume 1140 of *Lecture Notes in Computer Science*, pages 198–212, Aachen, Germany, September 1996. Springer-Verlag.
20. Peter Thiemann. Towards partial evaluation of full Scheme. In Gregor Kiczales, editor, *Reflection'96*, pages 95–106, San Francisco, CA, USA, April 1996.
21. Peter Thiemann. Correctness of a region-based binding-time analysis. In *Proc. Mathematical Foundations of Programming Semantics, Thirteenth Annual Conference*, volume 6 of *Electronic Notes in Theoretical Computer Science*, page 26, Pittsburgh, PA, March 1997. Carnegie Mellon University, Elsevier Science BV. URL: http://www.elsevier.nl/locate/entcs/volume6.html.
22. Peter Thiemann. A generic framework for specialization. In Chris Hankin, editor, *Proc. 7th European Symposium on Programming*, volume 1381 of *Lecture Notes in Computer Science*, pages 267–281, Lissabon, Portugal, April 1998. Springer-Verlag.
23. Peter Thiemann. *The PGG System—User Manual*. University of Nottingham, Nottingham, England, June 1998. Available from ftp://ftp.informatik.uni-tuebingen.de/pub/PU/thiemann/software/pgg/.
24. Peter Thiemann and Dirk Dussart. Partial evaluation for higher-order languages with state. Berichte des Wilhelm-Schickard-Instituts WSI-97-XX, Universität Tübingen, April 1997.
25. Mads Tofte and Jean-Pierre Talpin. Implementation of the typed call-by-value λ-calculus using a stack of regions. In *Proc. 21st Annual ACM Symposium on Principles of Programming Languages*, pages 188–201, Portland, OG, January 1994. ACM Press.

Author Index

Lecture Notes in Computer Science

For information about Vols. 1–1659
please contact your bookseller or Springer-Verlag

Vol. 1695: P. Barahona, J.J. Alferes (Eds.), Progress in Artificial Intelligence. Proceedings, 1999. XI, 385 pages. 1999. (Subseries LNAI).

Vol. 1696: S. Abiteboul, A.-M. Vercoustre (Eds.), Research and Advanced Technology for Digital Libraries. Proceedings, 1999. XII, 497 pages. 1999.

Vol. 1697: J. Dongarra, E. Luque, T. Margalef (Eds.), Recent Advances in Parallel Virtual Machine and Message Passing Interface. Proceedings, 1999. XVII, 551 pages. 1999.

Vol. 1698: M. Felici, K. Kanoun, A. Pasquini (Eds.), Computer Safety, Reliability and Security. Proceedings, 1999. XVIII, 482 pages. 1999.

Vol. 1699: S. Albayrak (Ed.), Intelligent Agents for Telecommunication Applications. Proceedings, 1999. IX, 191 pages. 1999. (Subseries LNAI).

Vol. 1700: R. Stadler, B. Stiller (Eds.), Active Technologies for Network and Service Management. Proceedings, 1999. XII, 299 pages. 1999.

Vol. 1701: W. Burgard, T. Christaller, A.B. Cremers (Eds.), KI-99: Advances in Artificial Intelligence. Proceedings, 1999. XI, 311 pages. 1999. (Subseries LNAI).

Vol. 1702: G. Nadathur (Ed.), Principles and Practice of Declarative Programming. Proceedings, 1999. X, 434 pages. 1999.

Vol. 1703: L. Pierre, T. Kropf (Eds.), Correct Hardware Design and Verification Methods. Proceedings, 1999. XI, 366 pages. 1999.

Vol. 1704: Jan M. Żytkow, J. Rauch (Eds.), Principles of Data Mining and Knowledge Discovery. Proceedings, 1999. XIV, 593 pages. 1999. (Subseries LNAI).

Vol. 1705: H. Ganzinger, D. McAllester, A. Voronkov (Eds.), Logic for Programming and Automated Reasoning. Proceedings, 1999. XII, 397 pages. 1999. (Subseries LNAI).

Vol. 1706: J. Hatcliff, T. Æ. Mogensen, P. Thiemann (Eds.), Partial Evaluation – Practice and Theory. 1998. IX, 433 pages. 1999.

Vol. 1707: H.-W. Gellersen (Ed.), Handheld and Ubiquitous Computing. Proceedings, 1999. XII, 390 pages. 1999.

Vol. 1708: J.M. Wing, J. Woodcock, J. Davies (Eds.), FM'99 – Formal Methods. Proceedings Vol. I, 1999. XVIII, 937 pages. 1999.

Vol. 1709: J.M. Wing, J. Woodcock, J. Davies (Eds.), FM'99 – Formal Methods. Proceedings Vol. II, 1999. XVIII, 937 pages. 1999.

Vol. 1710: E.-R. Olderog, B. Steffen (Eds.), Correct System Design. XIV, 417 pages. 1999.

Vol. 1711: N. Zhong, A. Skowron, S. Ohsuga (Eds.), New Directions in Rough Sets, Data Mining, and Granular-Soft Computing. Proceedings, 1999. XIV, 558 pages. 1999. (Subseries LNAI).

Vol. 1712: H. Boley, A Tight, Practical Integration of Relations and Functions. XI, 169 pages. 1999. (Subseries LNAI).

Vol. 1713: J. Jaffar (Ed.), Principles and Practice of Constraint Programming – CP'99. Proceedings, 1999. XII, 493 pages. 1999.

Vol. 1714: M.T. Pazienza (Eds.), Information Extraction. IX, 165 pages. 1999. (Subseries LNAI).

Vol. 1715: P. Perner, M. Petrou (Eds.), Machine Learning and Data Mining in Pattern Recognition. Proceedings, 1999. VIII, 217 pages. 1999. (Subseries LNAI).

Vol. 1716: K.Y. Lam, E. Okamoto, C. Xing (Eds.), Advances in Cryptology – ASIACRYPT'99. Proceedings, 1999. XI, 414 pages. 1999.

Vol. 1717: Ç. K. Koç, C. Paar (Eds.), Cryptographic Hardware and Embedded Systems. Proceedings, 1999. XI, 353 pages. 1999.

Vol. 1718: M. Diaz, P. Owezarski, P. Sénac (Eds.), Interactive Distributed Multimedia Systems and Telecommunication Services. Proceedings, 1999. XI, 386 pages. 1999.

Vol. 1719: M. Fossorier, H. Imai, S. Lin, A. Poli (Eds.), Applied Algebra, Algebraic Algorithms and Error-Correcting Codes. Proceedings, 1999. XIII, 510 pages. 1999.

Vol. 1720: O. Watanabe, T. Yokomori (Eds.), Algorithmic Learning Theory. Proceedings, 1999. XI, 365 pages. 1999. (Subseries LNAI).

Vol. 1721: S. Arikawa, K. Furukawa (Eds.), Discovery Science. Proceedings, 1999. XI, 374 pages. 1999. (Subseries LNAI).

Vol. 1722: A. Middeldorp, T. Sato (Eds.), Functional and Logic Programming. Proceedings, 1999. X, 369 pages. 1999.

Vol. 1723: R. France, B. Rumpe (Eds.), UML'99 – The Unified Modeling Language. XVII, 724 pages. 1999.

Vol. 1725: J. Pavelka, G. Tel, M. Bartošek (Eds.), SOFSEM'99: Theory and Practice of Informatics. Proceedings, 1999. XIII, 498 pages. 1999.

Vol. 1726: V. Varadharajan, Y. Mu (Eds.), Information and Communication Security. Proceedings, 1999. XI, 325 pages. 1999.

Vol. 1727: P.P. Chen, D.W. Embley, J. Kouloumdjian, S.W. Liddle, J.F. Roddick (Eds.), Advances in Conceptual Modeling. Proceedings, 1999. XI, 389 pages. 1999.

Vol. 1728: J. Akoka, M. Bouzeghoub, I. Comyn-Wattiau, E. Métais (Eds.), Conceptual Modeling – ER '99. Proceedings, 1999. XIV, 540 pages. 1999.

Vol. 1729: M. Mambo, Y. Zheng (Eds.), Information Security. Proceedings, 1999. IX, 277 pages. 1999.

Vol. 1730: M. Gelfond, N. Leone, G. Pfeifer (Eds.), Logic Programming and Nonmonotonic Reasoning. Proceedings. 1999. XI, 391 pages. 1999. (Subseries LNAI).

Vol. 1734: H. Hellwagner, A. Reinefeld (Eds.), SCI: Scalable Coherent Interface. XXI, 490 pages. 1999.

Vol. 1564: M. Vazirgiannis, Interactive Multimedia Documents. XIII, 161 pages. 1999.

Vol. 1591: D.J. Duke, I. Herman, M.S. Marshall, PREMO: A Framework for Multimedia Middleware. XII, 254 pages. 1999.

Vol. 1735: J.W. Amtrup, Incremental Speech Translation. XV, 200 pages. 1999. (Subseries LNAI).

Vol. 1736: L. Rizzo, S. Fdida (Eds.): Networked Group Communication. Proceedings, 1999. XIII, 339 pages. 1999.

Vol. 1740: R. Baumgart (Ed.): Secure Networking – CQRE [Secure] '99. Proceedings, 1999. IX, 261 pages. 1999.